The
Practice of
Public
Relations

The
Practice of
Public
Relations

TENTH EDITION

Fraser P. Seitel

Managing Partner, Emerald Partners

Senior Counselor, Burson-Marsteller

Adjunct Assistant Professor, New York University

Visiting Professor, Florida International University

Foreword by David Rockefeller

PEARSON

Prentice
Hall

Upper Saddle River, New Jersey 07458

Library of Congress Cataloging-in-Publication Data

Seitel, Fraser P.
    The practice of public relations / Fraser P. Seitel.—10th ed.
      p. cm.
    Includes bibliographical references and index.
    ISBN 0-13-230451-1
    1. Public relations—United States. I. Title.
    HM1221.S45 2007
    659.2—dc22

                                      2006017757

Editorial Director: Leah Jewell
Executive Editor: Deirdre Anderson
Assistant Editor: Melissa Casciano
Editorial Assistant: Christina Volpe
Marketing Director: Brandy Dawson
Marketing Manager: Kate Mitchell
VP/Director of Production and Manufacturing:
  Barbara Kittle
Production Editor: Bruce Hobart, Pine Tree
  Composition
Senior Production Liaison: Shelly Kupperman
Prepress & Manufacturing Assistant Manager:
  Mary Ann Gloriande
Manufacturing Buyer: Christina Amato
Creative Design Director: Leslie Osher
Art Director: Amy Rosen
Interior and Cover Designer: Wanda España/
  Wee Design Group

Director, Image Resource Center: Melinda Patelli
Manager, Rights and Permissions: Zina Arabia
Manager: Visual Research: Beth Brenzel
Manager, Cover Visual Research & Permissions:
  Karen Sanatar
Image Permission Coordinator: Elaine Soares
Image Researcher: Craig A. Jones
Composition/Full-Service Project Management:
  Pine Tree Composition
Printer/Binder: Courier Companies, Inc.
Cover Printer: Phoenix Color Corp.
Typeface: 11/12 Apollo MT
Cover Photos (by order of appearance):
  Stockbyte/Getty Images—Creative Express;
  Hill Street Studios/Getty Images—Creative
  Express; Vincent Hazat/Getty Images—
  PhotoAlto/Royalty Free; Getty Images/Digital
  Vision; Chabruken/Taxi/Getty Images

Credits and acknowledgments borrowed from other sources and reproduced, with permission, in this textbook appear on appropriate page within text (or on page 429).

Pearson Prentice Hall™ is a trademark of Pearson Education, Inc.
Pearson® is a registered trademark of Pearson plc
Prentice Hall® is a registered trademark of Pearson Education, Inc.

Pearson Education LTD.
Pearson Education Singapore, Pte. Ltd
Pearson Education, Canada, Ltd
Pearson Education–Japan
Pearson Education Australia PTY, Limited

Pearson Education North Asia Ltd
Pearson Educación de Mexico, S.A. de C.V.
Pearson Education Malaysia, Pte. Ltd
Pearson Education, Upper Saddle River, NJ 07458

10 9 8 7 6 5 4 3
ISBN 0-13-230451-1

Dedicated to my two finest students

Raina Gittlin, producer, "Good Morning America," *ABC*
David Seitel, global media licensing, *NBA*

Brief Contents

Contents

Part II   Preparation/Process

Chapter 3   Communication   45

Chapter 4   Public Opinion   64

Foreword

The need for clear, simple, and effective communications—the essence of public relations—has never been more apparent, or more necessary. The corporate scandals of the first years of this century, the devastating impact of the September 11th terrorist attacks, and the halting manner in which our country's political leadership has reacted to crises both foreign and domestic has placed all of our institutions under unprecedented stress. As Fraser P. Seitel points out in the tenth edition of his text, our well-being as stockholders, customers, employers, and most importantly, citizens, depends directly on the dissemination of principled policies by professionals who understand that basic integrity must take priority over rosy quarterly reports, and short-term political advantage.

Regaining and maintaining public confidence is an absolute essential as we move forward. But saying it and doing it are two very different things. For students and even for professionals who have worked in the field for some time, *The Practice of Public Relations* is an excellent place to start. Seitel bridges the gap between theory and practice in a compelling and vivid way. His use of case studies, interviews, news photos, and other techniques, as well as his humorous and lucid text, brings the process brilliantly to life. His latest edition also includes case studies about individuals such as Martha Stewart, Donald Trump, and George W. Bush, who have had to deal with the media and the court of public opinion, and have sometimes done it unsuccessfully.

Leaders in the public, private, and not-for-profit sectors have learned from painful experience that they should rely on their public relations counselors for cogent advice on strategy and policy as well as communications. I learned to trust Mr. Seitel's instincts and abilities long ago when I was the chairman and chief executive officer of The Chase Manhattan Bank. I continue to rely on his advice to this day.

For those who are working to restore and enhance the capacity of our institutions and their leaders to deal honestly and effectively with the public, this book will provide useful and essential guidance.

—*David Rockefeller*

David Rockefeller is one of the most influential figures in the history of U.S. business, finance, and philanthropy, considered by many, "America's last great business statesman." Through four decades, Mr. Rockefeller served as an executive with The Chase Manhattan Bank, joining as assistant manager in the foreign department in 1946 and retiring in 1981, after 11 years as chairman and CEO. Over his 90+ years, Mr. Rockefeller has met hundreds of world leaders and traveled around the globe many times. Since his retirement, Mr. Rockefeller has continued to stay active, with wide-ranging interests and involvement in the fields of international relations and civic affairs. He is the last remaining child of John D. Rockefeller, Jr., who hired Ivy Lee in 1914 as the first modern-day public relations counselor.

Preface

First, thank you for buying the book. (Whatever you do, don't sell it back to the book store!)

Second, permit me a less-than-modest observation: I really *like* this tenth edition of *The Practice of Public Relations*. It was a hoot to write. I mean any work of scholarship that can combine the public relations lessons learned from the likes of Michael Jackson, Martha Stewart, George W. Bush, Britney Spears, Donald Trump, and Buckethead can't be all bad!

This book is shorter than previous editions and, as a consequence, moves more briskly through the important theoretical and practical elements that underpin the practice of public relations. The book discusses these principles exclusively in the context of twenty-first-century events and communications technologies.

Public relations has never been a more potent force in society or a more valuable factor in an organization's reputation. In the twenty-first century, public relations crises and opportunities are front page news on a daily basis.

The field remains, at heart, a personal, relationship-oriented practice, demanding experienced judgment and finely honed interpersonal communications skills. And so, this tenth edition of *The Practice of Public Relations* places its emphasis on the principles, processes, and practices that lead to building positive relationships in a 24/7 communications environment.

Among the highlights of the tenth edition:

Refortified Theoretical Framework

Proper public relations practice must be underpinned by a strong sense of ethics. This edition focuses on the ethical base that provides the theoretical foundation of effective communications and public relations.

The book's introductory chapters place significant attention on how an understanding of and facility with communications research, theory, and public opinion can be applied to strategic public relations planning and creation of believable and persuasive messages.

The process of communication to achieve specific goals—informing, motivating, persuading, building mutual understanding—is explored in the context of acting ethically. "*Speaking of Ethics*" features in each chapter complement introductory theoretical material and bring to life the daily dilemmas that confront professional public relations practitioners.

New Contemporary Cases

Public relations practice confronts an ever-changing landscape of problems and opportunities. It is imperative, therefore, that a textbook in the field keep current with the most contemporary examples of the good, the bad, and the ugly in public relations work.

This tenth edition does so by chronicling the most important contemporary public relations cases—from Martha Stewart's disastrous handling of insider trading charges to Wal-Mart's public relations offensive to improve its image; from the NBA's valiant attempt to recover from an ugly on-court brawl to the Bush administration's fumbling attempts to change the image of America in the Muslim world. These contemporary cases are complemented by the field's most historic conundrums—from Tylenol's poisoned pills to Exxon's Gulf of Valdez disaster—as well as hypothetical student cases on issues from sex discrimination to organizational positioning to Internet sabotage and surveillance.

Every case is designed to test student application of the theories discussed in solving real-world challenges.

Bolstered Internet Chapter

As in so many other lines of work, the Internet has become a key tool for public relations practitioners. This edition, therefore, offers an extensive discussion of evolving Internet technologies such as blogs, webcasts, podcasts, Wikis, RSS feeds, and the other applications that are becoming public relations staples.

The tenth edition also discusses how a concentrated communications campaign on the Web can assist the delivery of one message—as in the case of Michael Jackson—or torpedo another—as in the case of Dan Rather. The importance of monitoring the Web is also explored.

Additional New Elements

The strength of this book rests in its application of theory to real-life practice.

In addition to the new, contemporary cases and the expanded Internet discussion, unique elements added in the tenth edition include:

- **NEW! Voice of Authority** interviews with distinguished communicators from the worlds of management, media, and academe, including two of the most legendary public relations counselors, Harold Burson and Howard Rubenstein; cable TV talk show star Rita Cosby; Wal-Mart public relations chief Mona Williams; Internet communications guru Shel Holtz; and even the public relations industry's most notorious critic, John Stauber. There's also a "non-interview" with befuddled former White House Press Secretary Scott McClellan that is revealing in what it doesn't say.
- **NEW! Speaking of Ethics** features, which highlight the ethical challenges that public relations professionals face on a daily basis—from the Catholic Church's summer of shame to Sony's spray painting publicity campaign to a lapse in judgment by an *American Idol* judge.
- **NEW! Talking Points** features that expose off-line curiosities that make the practice of public relations such a fascinating art form.
- **NEW! Suggested Readings,** encompassing the most comprehensive, post-2000 bibliography in public relations literature.
- **NEW! Associated Press photos,** taken straight from the news wire, add a real-life feel to this edition that isn't found in any other textbook.

All of these elements add to the excitement of this book. So, too, does the full-color format that underscores the liveliness, vitality, and relevance of the field.

Teaching and Learning Resources

Faculty Resources

The following resources are available to faculty who adopt the tenth edition of *The Practice of Public Relations* for use in their classroom.

Instructor's Manual (ISBN 0-13-230452-X)
Prepared by the author, the Instructor's Manual includes brief chapter outlines, suggested teaching devices to enhance topics discussed, suggested answers for the case studies, the "Speaking of Ethics" mini-case studies and the "Discussion Starters." Review Quizzes are provided for each chapter as are one suggested midterm and one final exam.

Test Item File (ISBN 0-13-230453-8).
Revised and updated for the tenth edition by industry professional and visiting lecturer at SUNY College at Geneseo, Jerry M. Engel, APR, the Test Item File includes nearly 50 or more test questions per chapter, including multiple choice, true/false, and short essay. Each question is rated high, medium, or low in level of difficulty, and includes a reference to the text page where correct answers can be found.

TestGen (ISBN 0-13-230457-0)
This computerized package allows instructors to customize, save, and generate classroom tests. The test program permits instructors to edit, add, or delete questions from the test banks, create questions with graphics, analyze test results, and organize a database of tests and student results. This software allows for extensive flexibility and ease of use. It provides many options for organizing and displaying tests, along with search and sort features. The software and the test banks can be downloaded from the Instructor's Resource Center (www.prenhall.com/seitel).

PowerPoint (Online at www.prenhall.com/seitel)
Completely revised and updated for the tenth edition by Dr. Leslie Turner of Youngstown University, the PowerPoint files include 20–30 slides per text chapter. The slides complement the text as well as class lecture by outlining all major concepts. The PowerPoint slides can be downloaded from the Instructor's Resource Center (www.prenhall.com/seitel).

Student Resources

Companion Website (www.prenhall.com/seitel)
Significantly expanded for the tenth edition, the Companion Website for *The Practice of Public Relations* is a great study tool with chapter objectives, applicable links, and a review quiz for each chapter.

Unique Perspective

Clearly, *The Practice of Public Relations,* Tenth Edition, isn't your mother's PR textbook.

This book is a lot different from other introductory texts in the field. Its premise is that public relations is a thoroughly-engaging and constantly-changing field. Although other texts may steer clear of the up-to-date cases, the ethical challenges, the "how to" counsel, and the public relations conundrums that force students to think, this book confronts them all.

It is, if you'll forgive the vernacular, an in-your-face textbook for an in-your-face profession.

Most important, *The Practice of Public Relations,* Tenth Edition, is built around the technical knowledge of theory, history, process and practice, judgmental skills, and personal relationships that underlie public relations practice and will be so essential in building the trust and respect of diverse communities in the twenty-first century.

Happy reading, and thanks again for buying the book.

ACKNOWLEDGMENTS

The tenth edition of *The Practice of Public Relations* owes much to a multitude of professors and others, who have helped immeasurably in the evolution of this work.

First and foremost, my friend and client David Rockefeller, was most kind to agree to write the Foreword. David Rockefeller is a legendary world business statesman and a unique figure in modern history. It is an honor to include his words in these pages.

I am also most grateful to the busy people who agreed to be newly-interviewed for this text. Public relations leaders Harold Burson, Mona Williams, Kathleen Hessert, Howard Rubenstein, John Kramer, Mike Paul, Amy Binder, Marina Maher, Shel Holtz, and Bill Heyman are the top of the industry. When they speak, as they do here, students and professionals ought to listen.

I am equally indebted to three extraordinary public-relations professors—Jim Fahey, Shaunee Wallace, and Bonnie Grossman—whose interviews here are highlights. And finally, candid interviews with the lovely Rita Cosby, television talk show star, and the equally lovely John Stauber, public relations critic, make this edition special.

Why, I'm even grateful that President Bush's former White House Press Secretary Scott McClellan reneged on an interview request, so that I could use his off again/on again indecisiveness as an example of "what not to do" as a public relations professional.

Thank you, all.

The distinguished citizens at Prentice Hall, recognizing the author's ineptitude in a multitude of areas, assigned the first team to this effort, led by our captain, the ever-radiant Executive Editor, Deirdre Cavanaugh Anderson. Deirdre was supported by the eminently talented cadre of: Editorial Assistant, Christina Volpe; Assistant Editor, Melissa Beth Casciano; Marketing Manager, Kate Mitchell; Senior Production Liaison, Shelly Kupperman; Art Director, Amy Rosen; and the always reliable Production Editor, Bruce Hobart at Pine Tree Composition Production Services. Truly, the New York Yankees of publishing.

I am also most grateful to the very kind professors whose critiques were invaluable in preparation for this edition: Johnny Mac Allen, Oral Roberts University; Thomas Boyle, Millersville University; Christopher J. Fenner, Florida Southern College; Jan W. Kelly, University of Scranton; Bruce L. Smith, Texas State University—San Marcos; Erin E. Wilgenbusch, Iowa State University; and Beth Wood, Indiana University.

Other professors who have reviewed past editions include: Carolina Acosta-Alzuru at the University of Georgia; Bill Brewer at Miami University; Meta G. Carstarphen at University of North Texas; Jerry M. Engel at Ithaca College; Lisa Ferree at Eastern Kentucky University; Susan Gonders at Southeast Missouri State University; Carole Gorney at Lehigh University; Kirk Hallahan at Colorado State University; Christine R. Helsel at Eastern Illinois University; Liese L. Hutchison at Saint Louis University; Ken McMillen at University of Oklahoma; Robert J. O'Gara at Point Park College; E. Jerald Ogg at the University of Tennessee at Martin; Michael G. Parkinson at Texas Tech University; Betty J. Pritchard at Grand Valley State University; Robert S. Pritchard at Ball State University; William E. Sledzik at Kent State University; and Don W. Stacks at the University of Miami.

Also, Thomas Bivins at the University of Oregon, Charles Lubbers at Kansas State University, and Nancy Wolfe at Elon College all were quite helpful. They join in the Hall of Thanks those other distinguished professors who have reviewed past editions: Nickieann Fleener, Department of Communication, University of Utah; Mort Kaplan, Department of Marketing Communication, Columbia College (Chicago); Jack Mauch,

Department of Communication, University of Idaho; Donnalyn Pompper, Department of Communication, Cabrini College; Cornelius B. Pratt, Department of Communications, Michigan State University; J. D. Rayburn II, Department of Communication, Florida State University; Nancy Roth, Department of Communication, Rutgers, The State University (New Jersey); William C. Adams, School of Journalism and Mass Communications, Florida International University; John Q. Butler; Rachel L. Holloway, Department of Communications Studies, Virginia Tech; Diana Harney, Department of Communication and Theater, Pacific Lutheran University; Cornelius Pratt, Department of Advertising, Communications, and Public Relations, Michigan State University; Robert Cole, Pace University; Janice Sherline Jenny, College of Business, Herkimer County Community College; Craig Kelly, School of Business, California State University, Sacramento; Lyle J. Barker, Ohio State University; William G. Briggs, San Jose State University; E. Brody, Memphis State University; John S. Detweiler, University of Florida; Jim Eiseman, University of Louisville; Sandy Grossbart, University of Nebraska; Marjorie Nadler, Miami University; Sharon Smith, Middle Tennessee State University; Robert Wilson, Franklin University; Jack Mandel, Nassau Community College; Carol L. Hills, Boston University; George Laposky, Miami-Dade Community College; Mack Palmer, University of Oklahoma; Judy VanSlyke Turk, Louisiana State University; Roger B. Wadsworth, Miami-Dade Community College; James E. Grunig, University of Maryland; Robert T. Reilly, University of Nebraska at Omaha; Kenneth Rowe, Arizona State University; Dennis L. Wilcox, San Jose State University; Albert Walker, Northern Illinois University; Stanley E. Smith, Arizona State University; Jan Quarles, University of Georgia; Pamela J. Creedon, Ohio State University; Joel P. Bowman, Western Michigan University; Thomas H. Bivins, University of Oregon; Joseph T. Nolan, University of North Florida; Frankie A. Hammond, University of Florida; Bruce Joffe, George Mason University; Larissa Grunig, University of Maryland; Maria P. Russell, Syracuse University; and Melvin L. Sharpe, Ball State University.

Thank you, all.

Finally, as ever, the top management team of Chief Executive Officer, Rosemary Seitel; Chief Operating Officers, Raina and Adam Gittlin; and Treasurer, David Seitel, merit special commendation; as does office manager Theo Gittlin, despite his skittishness.

Again, thank you, one and all.

—Fraser P. Seitel

About the Author

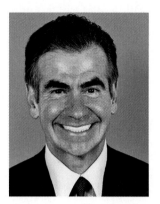

Fraser P. Seitel is a veteran of more than three decades in the practice of public relations. In 2000, *PR Week* magazine named Mr. Seitel one of the "100 Most Distinguished Public Relations Professionals of the 20th Century."

In 1992, after serving for a decade as senior vice president and director of public affairs for The Chase Manhattan Bank, Mr. Seitel formed Emerald Partners, a management and communications consultancy, and also became senior counselor at the world's largest public affairs firm, Burson-Marsteller.

Mr. Seitel is a frequent contributor to television. Among other programs, he has appeared on ABC's *Good Morning America*; Fox News Channel's *The O'Reilly Factor, Fox and Friends, Rivera Live, Fox Weekend,* and *On the Record with Greta Van Susteren;* MSNBC's *The News with Brian Williams and Nachman;* CNBC's *Wall Street Journal Report;* and CNN's *Connie Chung Tonight, Inside Politics, Paula Zahn Now,* and *Larry King Live.*

Mr. Seitel has counseled hundreds of corporations, nonprofits, associations, and individuals in the area for which he had responsibility at Chase—media relations, speech writing, consumer relations, employee communications, financial communications, philanthropic activities, and strategic management consulting.

Mr. Seitel is an Internet columnist at odwyerpr.com and a frequent lecturer and seminar leader on communications topics. Over the course of his career, Mr. Seitel has taught thousands of public relations professionals and students.

After studying and examining many texts in public relations, he concluded that not one of them "was exactly right." Therefore, in 1980, he wrote the first edition of *The Practice of Public Relations* "to give students a feel for how exciting this field really is." In more than two decades of use at hundreds of colleges and universities, Mr. Seitel's book has introduced generations of students to the excitement, challenge, and uniqueness of the practice of public relations.

The
Practice of
Public
Relations

1 What Is Public Relations, Anyway?

That is the question asked even by many of the 150,000 plus people in the United States and the thousands of others overseas who practice public relations.

In order to begin to understand what exactly "public relations" means today, let's begin with this man:

Michael Jackson faced a precarious challenge in the winter of 2005. Jury selection was about to begin in a case in which the quirky, bordering on otherworldly, pop icon was charged with molesting a child with whom he shared his California Neverland bed. The lurid accusations unfortunately seemed all too believable for the aging, eccentric pop star with the pretend face, peculiar mannerisms, and outlandish outfits. Jackson's challenge, in the face of jury selection and a judge's order not to speak publicly about the case, was to convince people that he "wasn't all that odd after all."

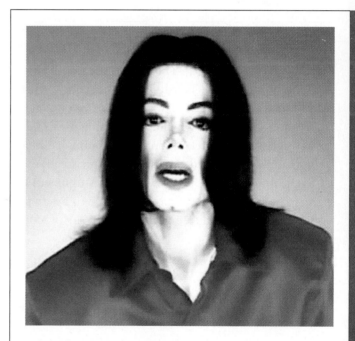

FIGURE 1-1 Seizing the agenda. Michael Jackson in his on-target 2005 Web site video. (Reuters Limited)

Few gave the gloved one much chance of achieving such a formidable objective. But achieve it he did—through a master stroke of inspired public relations.

What Jackson did was go directly to the public with a video on his Web site in which he appeared normal—or at least "normal" relative to his usual appearance—and spoke succinctly, logically, and sincerely to all who viewed the video. Using the Internet to communicate "person-to-person" with fans, critics, and the public-at-large—including, most important, *potential jurors*—Jackson came across as a man who had been wrongly accused, was concerned about his family, but felt confident that the American legal system would render him a fair trial.

FIGURE 1-2 The verdict. The fans revealed the outcome after Michael Jackson used skillful public relations techniques to help escape prison in 2005. (AP Wide World Photos)

Dressed simply in a plain blue shirt, Jackson looked directly at the camera and delivered a brief, carefully worded statement that said, in part

> I allowed this family into my home because they told me their son was ill with cancer and needed my help. . . . These events have caused a nightmare for my family, my children, and me. I never intend to place myself in so vulnerable a position again. . . . Please keep an open mind and let me have my day in court. I deserve a fair trial like every other American citizen. I will be acquitted and vindicated when the truth is told.[1]

Six months later, in a surprising verdict heard round the world, Michael Jackson was acquitted of all charges (Figure 1-2). There was little doubt that his opening Internet video—understated, direct, frank but heartfelt—helped set the stage for the ultimate acquittal.

Such is the impact in the 21st century of effective public relations.

In a society overwhelmed by communications—from traditional newspapers and magazines, to 24/7 talk radio and television, to nontraditional blogs, pod casts, and assorted other Internet exotica—the public is bombarded with nonstop messages of every variety. The challenge for a communicator is to cut through this clutter to deliver an argument that is persuasive, believable, and actionable.

The answer, more often than not today, lies in public relations. Stated another way, in the 21st century, the power, value, and influence of the practice of public relations have never been greater.

Prominence of Public Relations

In the initial decade of the 21st century, public relations as a field has grown immeasurably both in numbers and in respect. Today, the practice of public relations is clearly a growth industry.

- In the United States alone, public relations is a multibillion-dollar business practiced by 158,000 professionals, according to the U.S. Bureau of Labor Statistics. Furthermore, the Bureau says that "employment of public relations specialists is expected to increase faster than the average for all occupations through 2012. The need for good public relations in an increasingly competitive business environment should spur demand for public relations specialists in organizations of all types and sizes."[2]

- Around the world, the practice of public relations has grown enormously. The International Public Relations Association boasts a strong membership, and the practice flourishes from Latin America to Africa and from Europe to Russia to China.

- In a 2005 study by the Council of the Public Relations Society of America and Harris Interactive to assess the views of Fortune 1000 company executives on public relations, 84 percent felt the practice helped "raise awareness about important issues that the public might not know about," and 81 percent felt public relations helped "get the media to address issues that would otherwise fail to receive the attention they deserve."[3]

- Approximately 250 colleges and universities in the United States and many more overseas offer a public relations sequence or degree program. Many more offer public relations courses. Undergraduate enrollments in public relations programs at U.S. four-year colleges and universities are conservatively estimated to be well in excess of 20,000 majors.[4] In the vast majority of college journalism programs, public relations sequences rank first or second in enrollment.

- The U.S. government has thousands of communications professionals—although none, as we will learn, are labeled *public relations specialists*—who keep the public informed about the activities of government agencies and officials. The Department of Defense alone has 7,000 professional communicators spread out among the Army, Navy, and Air Force.

- The world's largest public relations firms are all owned by media conglomerates—among them Omnicom, The Interpublic Group, and WPP Group—which refuse to divulge public relations revenues. Nonetheless, in 2001, revenues of the 20 largest public relations agencies were in excess of $2 billion, and the rest of the industry generated another $1 billion.[5]

- The field's primary trade associations have strong membership, with the Public Relations Society of America encompassing nearly 20,000 members in 116 chapters and the International Association of Business Communicators including 13,000 members in more than 60 countries.

In the 21st century, as all elements of society—companies, nonprofits, governments, religious institutions, sports teams and leagues, arts organizations, and all others—wrestle with constant shifts in economic conditions and competition, security concerns, and popular opinion, the public relations profession is expected to thrive because increasing numbers of organizations are interested in communicating their stories.

Indeed, public relations people have already attained positions of prominence in every aspect of society. Karen Hughes, a public relations advisor to George W. Bush since his earliest days in politics, moved from a Special Assistant to the President in the White House to become, in 2005, Undersecretary of State for Public Diplomacy (see Case Study, Chapter 15) responsible primarily for changing attitudes internationally about the United States. That same year, the UPS Company appointed communications professional Christine Owens to its management committee. Said CEO Mike Eskew, "Communications is just too important not to be represented on the management committee of this company."[6]

Perhaps the most flattering aspect of the field's heightened stature is that competition from other fields has become more intense. Today the profession finds itself vulnerable to encroachment by people with non–public relations backgrounds, such as lawyers, marketers, and general managers of every type, all eager to gain the management access and persuasive clout of the public relations professional.

The field's strength stems from its roots: "a democratic society where people have freedom to debate and to make decisions—in the community, the marketplace, the home, the workplace, and the voting booth. Private and public organizations depend on good relations with groups and individuals whose opinions, decisions, and actions affect their vitality and survival."[7]

What Is Public Relations?

Public relations is a *planned process to influence public opinion, through sound character and proper performance, based on mutually satisfactory two-way communication.*

At least that's what your author believes it is.

The fact is that there are many different definitions of public relations. American historian Robert Heilbroner once described the field as "a brotherhood of some 100,000, whose common bond is its profession and whose common woe is that no two of them can ever quite agree on what that profession is."[8]

In 1923, the late Edward Bernays described the function of his fledgling public relations counseling business as one of providing

> *information given to the public, persuasion directed at the public to modify attitudes and actions, and efforts to integrate attitudes and actions of an institution with its publics and of publics with those of that institution.*[9]

Today, although a generally accepted definition of public relations still eludes practitioners, there is a clearer understanding of the field. One of the most ambitious searches for a universal definition was commissioned in 1975 by the Foundation for Public Relations Research and Education. Sixty-five public relations leaders participated in the study, which analyzed 472 different definitions and offered the following 88-word sentence:

> *Public relations is a distinctive management function which helps establish and maintain mutual lines of communications, understanding, acceptance, and cooperation between an organization and its publics; involves the management of problems or issues; helps management to keep informed on and responsive to public opinion; defines and emphasizes the responsibility of management to serve the public interest; helps management keep abreast of and effectively utilize change, serving as an early warning system to help anticipate trends; and uses research and sound and ethical communication techniques as its principal tools.*[10]

In 1988, the Public Relations Society of America formally adopted the following definition of public relations:

> *Public relations helps an organization and its publics adapt mutually to each other.*

The Public Relations Society noted that its definition implied the functions of research, planning, communications dialogue, and evaluation, all essential in the practice of public relations.[11]

No matter which formal definition one settles on to describe the practice, in order to be successful, public relations professionals must always engage in a planned process to influence the attitudes and actions of their targets.

Planned Process to Influence Public Opinion

What is the process through which public relations might influence public opinion? Communications professor John Marston suggested a four-step model based on specific functions: (1) research, (2) action, (3) communication, and (4) evaluation.[12] Whenever a public relations professional is faced with an assignment—whether promoting a client's product or defending a client's reputation—he or she should apply Marston's *R-A-C-E* approach:

1. **Research.** Research attitudes about the issue at hand.
2. **Action.** Identify action of the client in the public interest.
3. **Communication.** Communicate that action to gain understanding, acceptance, and support.
4. **Evaluation.** Evaluate the communication to see if opinion has been influenced.

The key to the process is the second step—action. You can't have effective communication or positive publicity without proper action. Stated another way, performance must precede publicity. Act first and communicate later. Indeed, some might say that public relations—PR—really should stand for *performance recognition*. In other words, positive action communicated straightforwardly will yield positive results.

This is the essence of the R-A-C-E process of public relations.

Public relations professor Sheila Clough Crifasi has proposed extending the R-A-C-E formula into the five-part R-O-S-I-E to encompass a more managerial approach to the field. R-O-S-I-E prescribes sandwiching the functions of objectives, strategies, and implementation between research and evaluation. Indeed, setting clear objectives, working from set strategies, and implementing a predetermined plan is a key to sound public relations practice.

Still others suggest a process called R-P-I-E for research, planning, implementation, and evaluation, which emphasizes the element of planning as a necessary step preceding the activation of a communications initiative.

All three approaches, R-A-C-E, R-O-S-I-E, and R-P-I-E, echo one of the most widely repeated definitions of public relations, developed by the late Denny Griswold, who founded a public relations newsletter.

> *Public relations is the management function which evaluates public attitudes, identifies the policies and procedures of an individual or an organization with the public interest, and plans and executes a program of action to earn public understanding and acceptance.*[13]

The key words in this definition are *management* and *action*. Public relations, if it is to serve the organization properly, must report to top management. Public relations must serve as an honest broker to management, unimpeded by any other group. For public relations to work, its advice to management must be unfiltered, uncensored, and unexpurgated. This is often easier said than done because many public relations departments report through marketing, advertising, or even legal departments.

Nor can public relations take place without appropriate action. As noted, no amount of communications—regardless of its persuasive content—can save an organization whose performance is substandard. In other words, if the action is flawed or the performance rotten, no amount of communicating will change the reality. (Don't believe me? Check out the Martha Stewart Case Study at the end of this chapter!) Stated another way, it is axiomatic in public relations that "You can't pour perfume on a skunk."

The process of public relations, then, as Professor Melvin Sharpe has put it, "harmonizes long-term relationships among individuals and organizations in society."[14] To "harmonize," Professor Sharpe applies five principles to the public relations process:

- Honest communication for credibility
- Openness and consistency of actions for confidence
- Fairness of actions for reciprocity and goodwill

- Continuous two-way communication to prevent alienation and to build relationships
- Environmental research and evaluation to determine the actions or adjustments needed for social harmony

And if that doesn't yet give you a feel for what precisely the practice of public relations is, then consider public relations Professor Janice Sherline Jenny's description as "the management of communications between an organization and all entities that have a direct or indirect relationship with the organization, i.e., its publics."

No matter what definition one may choose to explain the practice, few would argue that the goal of effective public relations is to harmonize internal and external relationships so that an organization can enjoy not only the goodwill of all of its publics but also stability and long life.

Public Relations as Management Interpreter

The late Leon Hess, who ran one of the nation's largest oil companies and the New York Jets football team, used to pride himself on *not* having a public relations department. Mr. Hess, a very private individual, abhorred the limelight for himself and for his company.

But times have changed.

Today, the CEO who thunders, "I don't need public relations!" is a fool. He or she doesn't have a choice. Every organization *has* public relations whether it wants it or not. The trick is to establish *good* public relations. That's what this book is all about—professional public relations, the kind you must work at.

Public relations affects almost everyone who has contact with other human beings. All of us, in one way or another, practice public relations daily. For an organization, every phone call, every letter, every face-to-face encounter, is a public relations event.

Public relations professionals, then, are really the organization's interpreters.

- On the one hand, they must interpret the philosophies, policies, programs, and practices of their management to the public.
- On the other hand, they must convey the attitudes of the public to their management.

Let's consider management first.

Before public relations professionals can gain attention, understanding, acceptance, and ultimately action from target publics, they have to know what management is thinking.

Good public relations can't be practiced in a vacuum. No matter what the size of the organization, a public relations department is only as good as its access to management. For example, it's useless for a senator's press secretary to explain the reasoning behind an important decision without first knowing what the senator had in mind. So, too, an organization's public relations staff is impotent without firsthand knowledge of the reasons for management's decisions and the rationale for organizational policy.

The public relations department in any organization can counsel management. It can advise management. It can even exhort management to take action. But it is management who must call the shots on organizational policy.

It is the role of the public relations practitioner, once policy is established by management, to communicate these ideas accurately and candidly to the public. Anything less can lead to major problems.

Public Relations as Public Interpreter

Now let's consider the flip side of the coin—the public.

Interpreting the public to management means finding out what the public really thinks about the firm and letting management know. Regrettably, recent history is filled with examples of powerful institutions—and their public relations departments—failing to anticipate the true sentiments of the public.

■ In the 1960s, General Motors paid little attention to an unknown consumer activist named Ralph Nader, who spread the message that General Motors' Corvair was "unsafe at any speed." When Nader's assault began to be believed, the automaker assigned professional detectives to trail him. In short order, General Motors was forced to acknowledge its act of paranoia, and the Corvair was eventually sacked at great expense to the company.

■ In the 1970s, as both gasoline prices and oil company profits rose rapidly, the oil companies were besieged by an irate gas-consuming public. When, at the height of the criticism, Mobil Oil spent millions in excess cash to purchase the parent of the Montgomery Ward department store chain, the company was publicly battered for failing to cut its prices.

■ In the 1980s, President Ronald Reagan rode to power on the strength of his ability to interpret what was on the minds of the electorate. But his successor in the early 1990s, George H. W. Bush, a lesser communicator than Reagan, failed to "read" the nation's economic concerns. After leading America to a victory over Iraq in the Gulf War, President Bush failed to heed the admonition, "It's the economy, stupid," and lost the election to upstart Arkansas Governor Bill Clinton.

■ As the 20th century ended, President Clinton forgot the candid communication skills that earned him the White House and lied to the American public about his affair with an intern. The subsequent scandal, ending in impeachment hearings before the U.S. Congress, tarnished Clinton's administration and ruined his legacy.

■ In the first decade of the 21st century, Clinton's successor, George W. Bush, earned great credit for strong actions and communications following the September 11, 2001, attacks on the nation. The Bush administration's public relations then suffered when the ostensible reason for attacking Iraq—weapons of mass destruction—failed to materialize, and failures to act promptly and communicate frankly in subsequent crises, such as Hurricane Katrina, hurt Bush's credibility.

■ At the same time, CEOs of some of the nation's mightiest corporations—among them Enron, Arthur Andersen, Tyco, Sotheby's, and WorldCom—were dragged into court, and many imprisoned, for a variety of ethical violations that misled the public and in many cases ruined their companies (Figure 1-3). As a consequence, tough new laws were passed to deal with corporate criminals.[15]

FIGURE 1-3 Police escort. The initial years of the 21st century saw companies and careers, such as that of former Tyco International CEO Dennis Kozlowski, ruined because of ethical transgressions that torpedoed reputations. (AP Wide World Photos)

Speaking of Ethics

CommunicatingTerror—in English

The attacks on America in September 2001 changed the rules of war forever. The new enemy represented no nation and wore no uniform. Al-Qaeda terrorists, led by Osama bin Laden, the son of a wealthy Saudi Arabian businessman, sought to eradicate everything represented by Western society.

One weapon bin Laden used skillfully was public relations—to entice his followers and terrorize his enemies. Four years after 9/11, bin Laden introduced a new weapon to his communications arsenal: English-language videos.

In 2005, four years after its attacks on America, al-Qaeda's periodic Arabic-language videos, featuring bin Laden and his deputy, received scant attention on Western media. What to do?

Al-Qaeda's answer was to have an English-speaking terrorist deliver the blood-curdling threats. In September, ABC-TV aired an al-Qaeda video featuring a hooded man carrying an AK-47 (Figure 1-4). The spokesman, who delivered his threats in stilted English, was believed to be a former Californian who attended an al-Qaeda training camp and became a terrorist translator.

By introducing its hate tapes in English, al-Qaeda hoped that English-speaking media would be its unwitting accomplice in spreading the terrorist public relations gospel throughout the West.

FIGURE 1-4 English hate speech. Al-Qaeda's use of 21st-century public relations techniques, including English-language videos, made the war on terror that much more difficult. (AP Wide World Photos)

For further information, see Mark Hosenball, "Bloodcurdling Qaeda Threats—In English," *Newsweek* (September 26, 2005): 6.

Despite being individuals of incalculable wealth, these men and women failed to understand one simple public relations principle. The savviest institutions—be they government, corporate, or nonprofit—understand the importance of effectively interpreting their management and organizational philosophies, policies, and practices to the public and, even more important, interpreting how the public views their organization back to management.

The Publics of Public Relations

The term *public relations* is really a misnomer. *Publics* relations, or relations with the publics, would be more to the point. Practitioners must communicate with many different publics—not just the general public—each having its own special needs and requiring different types of communication. Often the lines that divide these publics are thin, and the potential overlap is significant. Therefore, priorities, according to organizational needs, must always be reconciled (Figure 1-5).

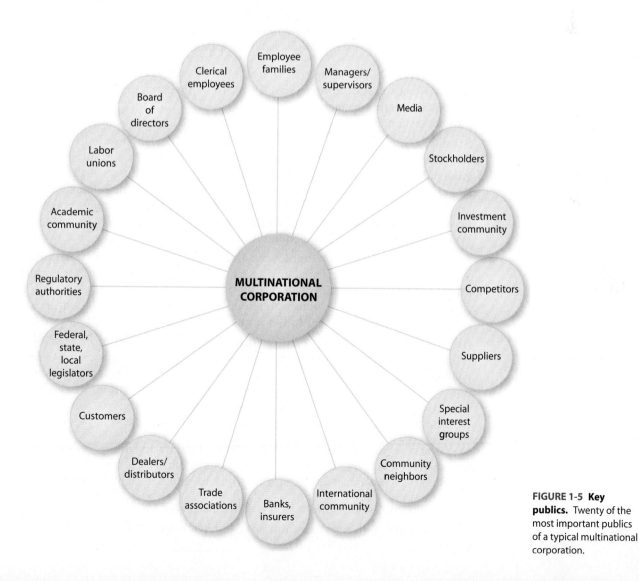

FIGURE 1-5 **Key publics.** Twenty of the most important publics of a typical multinational corporation.

Technological change—particularly weblogs, the Internet, satellite links for television, and the computer in general—has brought greater interdependence to people and organizations, and there is growing concern in organizations today about managing extensive webs of interrelationships. Indeed, managers have become interrelationship conscious.

Internally, managers must deal directly with various levels of subordinates as well as with cross-relationships that arise when subordinates interact with one another.

Externally, managers must deal with a system that includes government regulatory agencies, labor unions, subcontractors, consumer groups, and many other independent—but often related—organizations. The public relations challenge in all of this is to manage effectively the communications between managers and the various publics, which often pull organizations in different directions. Stated another way, public relations professionals are very much mediators between client (management) and public (all those key constituent groups on whom an organization depends).

Definitions differ on precisely what constitutes a public. One time-honored definition states that a public arises when a group of people (1) faces a similar indeterminate situation, (2) recognizes what is indeterminate and problematic in that situation, and (3) organizes to do something about the problem.[16] In public relations, more specifically, a public is a group of people with a stake in an issue, organization, or idea.

Publics can also be classified into several overlapping categories:

- **Internal and external.** Internal publics are inside the organization: supervisors, clerks, managers, stockholders, and the board of directors. External publics are those not directly connected with the organization: the press, government, educators, customers, suppliers, and the community.

- **Primary, secondary, and marginal.** Primary publics can most help—or hinder—the organization's efforts. Secondary publics are less important, and marginal publics are the least important of all. For example, members of the Federal Reserve Board of Governors, who regulate banks, would be the primary public for a bank awaiting a regulatory ruling, whereas legislators and the general public would be secondary. On the other hand, to the investing public, interest rate pronouncements of the same Federal Reserve Board are of primary importance.

- **Traditional and future.** Employees and current customers are traditional publics; students and potential customers are future ones. No organization can afford to become complacent in dealing with its changing publics. Today, a firm's publics range from women to minorities to senior citizens to homosexuals. Each might be important to the future success of the organization.

- **Proponents, opponents, and the uncommitted.** An institution must deal differently with those who support it and those who oppose it. For supporters, communications that reinforce beliefs may be in order. But changing the opinions of skeptics calls for strong, persuasive communications. Often, particularly in politics, the uncommitted public is crucial. Many a campaign has been decided because the swing vote was won over by one of the candidates.

Another way of segmenting publics is on the basis of values and lifestyles. Such segmentation is used regularly by marketers to focus product and service appeals on particular socioeconomic levels. Segmentation separates consumers into eight distinct categories:

1. Actualizers are those with the most wealth and power.

2. Fulfilleds have high resources and are principle-oriented professionals or retirees.

3. Believers are Fulfilleds without the resources.

4. Achievers have high resources and are status oriented.

5. Strivers lack the resources of Achievers but are equally status oriented.

6. Experiencers have high resources, are action oriented, and are disposed toward taking risks.

7. Makers also are action oriented but have low resources.

8. Strugglers have the lowest resources.[17]

Applying such lifestyle characterizations to publics can help companies make marketing and public relations decisions to effectively target key audiences.

The typical organization is faced with a myriad of critical publics with which it must communicate on a frequent and direct basis. It must be sensitive to the self-interests, desires, and concerns of each public. It must understand that self-interest groups today are themselves more complex. Therefore, the harmonizing actions necessary to win and maintain support among such groups should be arrived at in terms of public relations consequences.[18]

Whereas management must always speak with one voice, its communications inflection, delivery, and emphasis should be sensitive to all constituent publics.

The Functions of Public Relations

There is a fundamental difference between the functions of public relations and the functions of marketing and advertising. Marketing and advertising promote a product or a service. Public relations promotes an entire organization.

The functions associated with public relations work are numerous. Among them are the following:

- **Writing**—*the* fundamental public relations skill, with written vehicles from news releases to speeches and from brochures to advertisements falling within the field's purview.

- **Media relations**—dealing with the press is another frontline public relations function.

- **Planning**—of special events, media events, management functions, and the like.

- **Counseling**—in dealing with management and its interactions with key publics.

- **Researching**—of attitudes and opinions that influence behavior and beliefs.

- **Publicity**—the marketing-related function, most commonly misunderstood as the "only" function of public relations, generating positive publicity for a client or employer.

- **Marketing communications**—other marketing-related functions, such as creating brochures, sales literature, meeting displays, and promotions.

- **Community relations**—positively putting forth the organization's messages and image within the community.

- **Consumer relations**—interfacing with consumers through written and verbal communications.

- **Employee relations**—communicating with the all-important internal publics of the organization, those managers and employees who work for the firm.

- **Government affairs**—dealing with legislators, regulators, and local, state, and federal officials—all of those who have governmental interface with the organization.

- **Investor relations**—for public companies, communicating with stockholders and those who advise them.

- **Special publics relations**—dealing with those publics uniquely critical to particular organizations, from African Americans to women to Asians to senior citizens.

- **Public affairs and issues management**—dealing with public policy and its impact on the organization, as well as identifying and addressing issues of consequence that affect the firm.

- **Web site development and Web interface**—creating what often is the organization's principle interface with the public: its Web site. Also important is monitoring the World Wide Web and responding, when appropriate, to organizational challenge.

This is but a partial list of what public relations practitioners do. In sum, the public relations practitioner is manager/orchestrator/producer/director/writer/arranger and all-around general communications counsel to management. It is for this reason, then, that the process works best when the public relations director reports directly to the CEO.

The Curse of "Spin"

So pervasive has the influence of public relations become in our society that some even fear it as a pernicious force; they worry about the power of public relations to exercise a kind of thought control over the American public.

Which brings us to *spin*.

In its most benign form, spin signifies the distinctive interpretation of an issue or action to sway public opinion, as in putting a positive slant on a negative story. In its most virulent form, spin means confusing an issue or distorting or obfuscating it or even lying.

The propensity in recent years for presumably respected public figures to lie in an attempt to deceive the public has led to the notion that "spinning the facts" is synonymous with public relations practice.

It isn't.

Spinning an answer to hide what really happened—that is, lying, confusing, distorting, obfuscating, whatever you call it—is antithetical to the proper practice of public relations. In public relations, if you lie once, you will never be trusted again—particularly by the media.

Nonetheless, public relations spin has come to mean the twisting of messages and statements of half-truths to create the appearance of performance, which may or may not be true.

This association with spin has hurt the field. *The New York Times* headlined a critical article on public relations practice, "Spinning Frenzy: P.R.'s Bad Press."[19] Other critics admonish the field as "a huge, powerful, hidden medium available only to wealthy individuals, big corporations, governments, and government agencies because of its high cost."[20]

In recent years, the most high-profile government public relations operatives have often fallen guilty to blantant spin techniques. In the Clinton administration, communications counselors, such as James Carville, Paul Begala, and Lanny Davis, eagerly spun the tale that intern Monica Lewinsky was, in effect, delusional about an Oval Office affair with the President. *(She wasn't!)* In the Bush administration, high-level advisors Karl Rove and Lewis Libby were implicated in a spinning campaign against former Ambassador Joseph Wilson, who questioned the motives of the war in Iraq. In 2005, Libby, Vice President Dick Cheney's top aide, was indicted for "obstruction of justice, false statement, and perjury" in the Wilson case.[21]

Faced with this era of spin and unrelenting questioning by the media and the public about the ethics of public relations, practitioners must always be sensitive to and considerate of how their actions and their words will influence the public.

Above all—in defiance of charges of spinning—public relations practitioners must consider as their cardinal rule: to never, ever lie.

What Manner of Man or Woman?

What kind of individual does it take to become a competent public relations professional?

A 2004 study of agency, corporate, and nonprofit public relations leaders, sponsored by search firm Heyman Associates, reported seven areas in particular that characterize a successful public relations career:

Talking Points

The Scanlon Scandal and the Problem with Public Relations

Try as it might, the practice of public relations can't get a break.

While public relations professionals proclaim the imperative of "always telling the truth," there always seems to be a practitioner or agency somewhere found guilty of conning the public.

Typical, alas, was the 2005 case against Michael Scanlon (Figure 1-6), a hot shot Washington public relations man with expensive tastes—very expensive, as it turned out.

Scanlon, a former aide to former House Speaker Tom DeLay of Texas and partner to crooked lobbyist Jack Abramoff, pleaded guilty to a conspiracy to bribe public officials and defraud his Indian tribal clients of $19 million—a sum Scanlon agreed to pay back in return for a reduced sentence in the slammer.

The Scanlon scandal was but the latest blemish on the terminally misunderstood practice of public relations.

FIGURE 1-6 Rain on his parade. Lawyers and the media accompany disgraced public relations executive Michael Scanlon into federal court, where he pleaded guilty to conspiring to bribe public officials. (AP Wide World Photos)

1. Diversity of experience
2. Performance
3. Communications skills
4. Relationship building
5. Proactivity and passion
6. Teamliness
7. Intangibles, such as personality, likeability, and chemistry[22]

Beyond these success-building areas, in order to make it, a public relations professional ought to possess a set of specific technical skills as well as an appreciation of the proper attitudinal approach to the job. On the technical side, the following six skills are important:

1. **Knowledge of the field.** The underpinnings of public relations—what it is, what it does, and what it ought to stand for.
2. **Communications knowledge.** The media and the ways in which they work; communications research; and, most important, how to write.
3. **Technological knowledge.** Familiarity with computers and associated technologies, as well as with the World Wide Web, are imperative.
4. **Current events knowledge.** Knowledge of what's going on around you—daily factors that influence society: history, literature, language, politics, economics, and all the rest—from the Ming Dynasty to Yao Ming; from Ben Stein to bin Laden; from Dr. Phil to Dr. Dre; from Three Penny Opera to 50 Cent; from Fat Joe to J Lo to Big Mo and the Mau-Mau. A public relations professional must be, in the truest sense, a Renaissance man or woman.
5. **Business knowledge.** How business works, a bottom-line orientation, and a knowledge of your company and industry.
6. **Management knowledge.** How senior managers make decisions, how public policy is shaped, and what pressures and responsibilities fall on managers.

In terms of the "attitude" that effective public relations practitioners must possess, the following six requisites are imperative:

1. **Pro communications.** A bias toward disclosing rather than withholding information. Public relations professionals should want to communicate with the public, not shy away from communicating. They should practice the belief that the public has a right to know.
2. **Advocacy.** Public relations people must *believe in* their employers. They must be advocates for their employers. They must stand up for what their employers represent. Although they should never distort, lie, or hide facts, occasionally it may be in an organization's best interest to avoid comment on certain issues. If practitioners don't believe in the integrity and credibility of their employers, their most honorable course is to go to "Plan B,"—find work elsewhere.
3. **Counseling orientation.** A compelling desire to advise senior managers. Top executives are used to dealing in tangibles, such as balance sheets, costs per thousand, and cash flows. Public relations practitioners deal in intangibles, such as public opinion, media influence, and communications messages. Practitioners must be willing to support their beliefs—often in opposition to lawyers or personnel executives. They must even be willing to disagree with management at times. Far from being compliant, public relations practitioners must have the gumption to say *no*.

4. **Ethics.** The counsel that public relations professionals deliver must always be ethical. The mantra of the public relations practitioner must be to *do the right thing.*

5. **Willingness to take risks.** Public relations is one of those pursuits that many people—even those for whom you work—don't understand. Consequently, it's easy to be overlooked as a public relations staff member. You therefore must be willing to stick your neck out, to stand up for what you believe in, to take risks. Public relations professionals must have the courage of their convictions and the personal confidence to proudly represent their curious—yet critical—role in any organization.

6. **Positive outlook.** Public relations work occasionally is frustrating work. Management doesn't always listen to your good counsel, preferring instead to follow attorneys and others into safer positions. No matter. A public relations professional, if he or she is to perform at optimum effectiveness, can't afford to be a "sad sack." You win some. You lose some. But in public relations, at least, the most important thing is to keep on swinging and smiling.

Last Word

Spin, cover-up, distortion, and subterfuge are the antitheses of good public relations.

Ethics, truth, credibility—these values are what good public relations is all about.

To be sure, public relations is not yet a profession like law, accounting, or medicine, in which all practitioners are trained, licensed, and supervised. Nothing prevents someone with little or no formal training from hanging out a shingle as a public relations specialist. Such frauds embarrass professionals in the field and, thankfully, are becoming harder to find.

Indeed, both the Public Relations Society of America and the International Association of Business Communicators have strong codes of ethics that serve as the basis of their membership philosophies (Appendix A).

Meanwhile, the importance of the practice of public relations in a less certain, more chaotic, overcommunicated, and competitive world cannot be denied.

Despite its considerable problems—in attaining leadership status, finding its proper role in society, disavowing spin, and earning enduring respect—the practice of public relations has never been more prominent. Approaching its first 100 years as a formal, integrated, strategic-thinking process, public relations has become part of the fabric of modern society.

Here's why.

Much more than customers for their products, managers today desperately need constituents for their beliefs and values. In the 21st century, the role of public relations is vital in helping guide management in framing its ideas and making its commitments. The counsel that management needs must come from advisers who understand public attitudes, public moods, public needs, and public aspirations.

Contrary to what misinformed critics may charge, "More often than not, public relations strategies and tactics are the most effective and valuable arrows in the quiver of the disaffected and the powerless."[23] Civil rights leaders, labor leaders, public advocates, and grassroots movements of every stripe have been boosted by proven communications techniques to win attention and build support and goodwill.

Winning this elusive goodwill takes time and effort. Credibility can't be won overnight, nor can it be bought. If management policies aren't in the public's best interest, no amount of public relations effort can obscure that reality. Public relations is not effective as a temporary defensive measure to compensate for management misjudgment. If management errs seriously, the best—and only—public relations advice must be to get the story out immediately. Indeed, working properly, the public relations department of an organization often serves as the firm's "conscience."

This is why the relationship between public relations and other parts of the organization—

advertising and marketing, for example—is occasionally a strained one. The function of the public relations department is distinctive from that of any other internal area. Few others share the access to management that public relations enjoys. Few others share the potential for power that public relations may exercise.

No less an authority than Abraham Lincoln once said: "Public sentiment is everything . . . with public sentiment, nothing can fail. Without it, nothing can succeed. He who molds public sentiment goes deeper than he who executes statutes or pronounces decisions. He makes statutes or decisions possible or impossible to execute."[24]

Stated another way, no matter how you define it, the practice of public relations has become an essential element in the conduct of relationships for a vast variety of organizations in the 21st century.

Discussion Starters

1. How prominent is the practice of public relations around the world in the 21st century?
2. How would you define the practice of public relations?
3. Why is the practice of public relations generally misunderstood by the public?
4. How would you describe the significance of the planning aspect in public relations?
5. Within the R-A-C-E process of public relations, what would you say is the most critical element?
6. In what ways does public relations differ from advertising or marketing?
7. If you were the public relations director of the local United Way, whom would you consider your most important "publics" to be?
8. What are seven functions of public relations practice?
9. How do professional public relations people regard the aspect of "spin" as part of what they do?
10. What are the technical and attitudinal requisites most important for public relations success?

Top of the Shelf

Public Relations: The Complete Guide

Joe Marconi, Mason, OH: Thompson South-Western, 2004.

This comprehensive book traces public relations from its earliest antecedents—the time of Edward Bernays (see Chapter 2) in the 1930s to the present day. It covers, in depth, most aspects of the field, including the role of the public relations practitioner today.

The guide focuses on the power of public relations and how it remains more important than ever and manages to hold its own despite the large amounts of money spent by companies on advertising and marketing.

To his credit, marketing consultant Joe Marconi delves into the importance of acting ethically at all times, especially during a crisis and when dealing with a potentially unethical company. "For all its popular identification with hype," the author acknowledges, "PR is serious business, effective, and highly cost efficient when compared to other marketing functions." Amen.

CASE STUDY

The Rise and Fall and Rise of Queen Martha

In the winter of 2001, few Americans could dispute that Martha Stewart was "Queen of the Kitchen."

The tough-willed, hot-tempered, blunt-speaking perfectionist had morphed from a modest upbringing to become the undisputed, multimillionaire-closing-in-on-billionaire, domestic doyenne—the homemaker's homemaker, arbiter of all things tasteful in the home, numero uno in all matters of domesticity.

Her parents, Martha and Edward Kostyra, were Polish Americans, her mother a school teacher and her father a pharmaceutical sales-man, who raised their five children in Nutley, New Jersey. Her mother taught young Martha cooking and baking and sewing, and her fa-ther taught her how to garden. That was just the start the serious-minded model student needed. After a brief fling in the stock brokerage business and a failed marriage, Stewart began to build an empire that would become the stuff of legends.

- She co-authored a book called *Entertaining*, which became an instant best seller.
- She followed that with lucrative publishing ventures, pro-ducing video tapes, dinner-music CDs, television specials, and dozens of books on matters of domesticity—from hors d'oeuvres to pies, from weddings to Christmas, from gar-dening to restoring old houses.

- She appeared regularly on NBC's *Today Show,* becoming a household name.
- She became a board member of the New York Stock Exchange.
- She delivered lectures for $10,000 a pop and charged eager attendees $900 a head to attend seminars at her farm.
- She signed an advertising/consulting contract with depart-ment chain Kmart for $5 million.
- She presided over a long-running syndicated television show, *Martha Stewart Living*.
- She parlayed the program into the creation of multimillion dollar company Martha Stewart Living Omnimedia (MSO), with branches in publishing, merchandising, and Internet/direct commerce, selling products in eight discrete categories.

Without exaggeration, Stewart was Queen of the Kitchen (Figure 1-7) until one day when it all came tumbling down.

Selling in the nick of time

In December 2001, Stewart sold nearly 4,000 shares of biotech company ImClone Systems stock under mysterious circum-stances. The company was run by Stewart's pal Samuel Waksal, who had presided over a rapid stock price ascension, due princi-pally to the company's promising cancer-fighting drug, Erbitux, which had been submitted for approval to the Federal Drug Administration (FDA).

So with everything looking good for the company, it was surprising on Decem-ber 27 that Stewart decided suddenly to unload all her shares at a $60 price. The next day, the case got even curiouser: On December 28, the FDA rejected Im-Clone's application for Erbitux. The stock cratered. But Stewart, having presciently decided to sell the day before, avoided a $51,000 loss.

Serendipity perhaps?

The government didn't think so.

FIGURE 1-7 Before ... her fall from grace, a jubilant Martha Stewart cooked up a deal with Kmart CEO Chuck Conaway to sell her products at Kmart stores. (AP Wide World Photos)

Charges of insider trading

Stewart may have been smart, but according to the U.S. attorney for the Southern District of New York, she was not smart enough to know about the FDA's timing in rejecting Erbitux. Rather, argued the government, Stewart had learned about the FDA's intention from her stockbroker. The stockbroker had received an urgent call from Waksal, then relayed the information to Stewart, who immediately decided to sell.

If true, Stewart had acted on classic insider information, a federal crime, which gives privileged investors an unfair advantage over all other shareholders. Indeed, prosecutors argued that this was precisely what had happened and that Stewart and her stockbroker were both guilty of illegally acting on insider information. Accordingly, in June 2003, the U.S. Attorney formally indicted both of them.

Stewart's attorneys argued that this was not the case at all. Stewart, they said, had always had a "plan" to sell her stock when it reached the $60 level.

After Waksal was sentenced to seven years in prison and family members he had tipped off were fined, attention turned to Stewart. The question was: Would she come forward and acknowledge "mistakes," or would she hold firm and deny any impropriety?

Silence of the diva

The answer, painfully revealed over the next excruciating two years, was that Stewart became the "silent diva." She said little to elaborate on the case, preferring instead to allow her attorneys to speak for her. In one celebrated appearance on the *CBS Morning Show,* Stewart defiantly cut cabbage while an exasperated host tried to get her to react to the charges against her.

Soon thereafter, Stewart's guest appearances on television became fewer and fewer. She stopped lecturing. Her ubiquitous Kmart ads ceased to appear. She resigned as chairwoman and CEO of MSO. Indeed, the woman who had seemed to be everywhere was now virtually out of sight.

In her place, a battery of lawyers negotiated with the Feds and argued with the judge to have her charges reduced. U.S. District Judge Miriam Cedarbaum, taking a page from the domestic doyenne herself, adamantly refused to throw out the charges.

Those who expected the typically feisty Stewart to come out fighting were sadly disappointed. In June 2003, Stewart unveiled a personal Web site on which she proclaimed her innocence and insisted she would fight to clear her name. But beyond those Web site notations, she remained tight-lipped. Meanwhile, in the vacuum of Stewart's silence, the Internet, cable television, and the public press were flooded with "experts" surmising on just what poor Martha Stewart had done to herself.

An excruciating trial

Stewart's trial began January 27, 2004, two full years after the alleged insider trading violation.

The trial was excruciating for Martha. For two months, she was forced to endure a phalanx of cameras greeting her in the morning for her arrival at the lower Manhattan courthouse and waiting for her each evening when the day's session was over (Figure 1–8). She said nothing, again relying on attorneys to explain to the media exactly what went on that day in court. As her lawyers spoke each night, a stone-faced Stewart would stare straight ahead. Meanwhile, the share price of her company's stock plummeted, and her reputation wasn't far behind.

On March 5, 2004, with the world waiting breathlessly for the verdict, Stewart was found guilty on all four counts of obstructing justice and lying to federal investigators. Her broker was also found guilty, and both faced prison time.

About an hour after the verdict was read, Stewart—radiant as ever with a fur around her neck, a black overcoat, and a tasteful, brown leather bag at her side—strode poker-faced down the stairs of the courthouse, accompanied by her lawyers. She did not respond to questions shouted at her by reporters. Instead, the following statement was posted on her Web site:

Dear Friends,
I am obviously distressed by the jury's verdict but I take comfort in knowing that I have done nothing wrong and that I have the enduring support of my family and friends.

Her lawyers vowed to appeal.

Four months later, after losing her job, her company, close to $500,000 in stock market

FIGURE 1-8 During . . . her trial ordeal, a harried Martha Stewart was forced to endure daily bombardment both within and outside the courthouse. (AP Wide World Photos)

wealth, and her reputation, Martha Stewart lost her freedom. She was sentenced to five months in prison and two years' probation.

Still, Stewart was defiant, telling a television interviewer that "many, many good people have gone to prison" and comparing herself to Nelson Mandela, South Africa's persecuted anti-Apartheid hero. And outside the courthouse, after her sentencing, an unrepentant Stewart vowed, "I'll be back."

Winter at Camp Cupcake

Stewart's attorneys, taking the lead from their defiant client, appealed her conviction and vowed to spare her hard time. But, suddenly, in mid-September 2004, Stewart had a change of heart.

Shocking her supporters, the domestic doyenne announced that she would not wait for the verdict on her appeal and rather wished to begin serving her five-month prison sentence early "to put this nightmare behind me, both personally and professionally."

And so on October 8, 2004, Stewart, 63 and a multimillionaire, slipped into women's federal prison in Alderson, West Virginia, to join petty thieves and embezzlers and drug offenders, all performing day labor at rates between 12 and 40 cents an hour.

And wonder of wonder, Stewart was an ideal prisoner. Reports from "Camp Cupcake," as it was labeled, were glowing in their praise of Stewart.

- She praised her guards, the warden, and fellow prisoners.
- She wrote passionately about the unfairness of federal sentencing guidelines, which shackled many of those whom she met behind the walls.
- She even participated in prison events—failing to win the "prison bakeoff."

Thursday, March 3, 2004, when Stewart was sprung from the slammer to return to her 153-acre Westchester Estate, she was met with cameras, microphones, and a hero's welcome, (Figure 1-9).

Comeback Kid

It was a new Martha Stewart who emerged from prison. She was more relaxed, more open, and more available to questioners. She also was very much back in business.

- She signed deals to begin two new television shows—one a daytime lifestyles show, the other a spinoff of Donald Trump's, *The Apprentice.*
- She signed a $30 million deal for a Sirius satellite radio program.
- She signed a lucrative book deal to produce a Martha memoir, discussing her time in prison.

By the winter of 2005, Stewart was back with a vengeance. She still hadn't acknowledged—even after her conviction and subsequent

FIGURE 1-9 **After . . .** her return from five months in prison, a beaming Martha Stewart received a hero's welcome from her company's employees in New York City. (AP Wide World Photos)

jail time—that she had done anything "wrong." But there would be ample opportunity for an admission, as Martha momentum—"Martha Mo"—began to build and the "queen" set out to retake her throne.

Postscript: On January 6, 2006, the United States Court of Appeals for the Second Circuit rejected the arguments of Stewart's lawyers and upheld her conviction.

Questions

1. How would you characterize Martha Stewart's initial public relations response to the charges against her?

2. What key public relations principle did Martha Stewart violate?

3. Had you been advising her, what public relations strategy and tactics would you have recommended? How "vocal" should she have been?

4. How important, from a public relations perspective, was her decision to go to jail early?

5. What public relations strategy should Stewart adopt now?

6. Should she acknowledge that she made mistakes?

For further information, see Michael Barbaro, "Court Rejects Appeal by Martha Stewart," *New York Times,* January 7, 2006, C3; Krysten Crawford, "Martha: I Cheated No One," *CNN Money,* July 20, 2004; Krysten Crawford, "Martha, Out and About," March 4, 2005; Gene Healy, "Lessons of Martha Stewart Case," *Cato Institute,* July 16, 2004; "Martha Stewart Wants to Enter Prison Early," *CBC News,* September 16, 2004; Brooke A. Masters, "Stewart Begins Prison Term," *Washington Post,* October 9, 2004, EO1; Fraser P. Seitel, "Martha's Final PR Hurdle," http://www.odwyerpr.com, March 6, 2005; Fraser P. Seitel, "Martha Finally Gets PR Religion," August 26, 2005; "Stewart Convicted on All Charges," *CNN Money,* March 5, 2004; "Timeline of Martha Stewart Scandal," *Associated Press,* Copyright 2005.

Voice of Authority

An Interview with Harold Burson

Harold Burson is the world's most influential public relations practitioner. He has spent more than 50 years serving as counselor to and confidante of corporate CEOs, government leaders, and heads of public sector institutions. As founder and chairman of Burson-Marsteller, he was the architect of the largest public relations agency in the world. Mr. Burson, widely cited as the standard bearer of public relations ethics, has received virtually every major honor awarded by the profession, including the Harold Burson Chair in Public Relations at Boston University's College of Communication, established in 2003.

How would you define public relations?

One of the shortest—and most precise—definitions of public relations I know is "doing good and getting credit for it." I like this definition because it makes clear that public relations embodies two principal elements. One is behavior, which includes policy and attitude; the other is communications—the dissemination of information. The first tends to be strategic, the second tactical—although strategy plays a major role in many, if not most, media relations programs.

How has the business of public relations changed over time?

Public relations has, over time, become more relevant as a management function for all manner of institutions—public and private sector, profit and not-for-profit. CEOs increasingly recognize the need to communicate to achieve their organizational objectives. Similarly, they have come to recognize public relations as a necessary component in the decision-making process. This has enhanced the role of public relations both internally and for independent consultants.

How do ethics apply to the public relations function?

In a single word, pervasively. Ethical behavior is at the root of what we do as public relations professionals. We approach our calling with a commitment to serve the public interest, knowing full well that the public interest lacks a universal definition and knowing that one person's view of the public interest differs markedly from that of another. We must therefore be consistent in our personal definition of the public interest and be prepared to speak up for those actions we take.

At the same time, we must recognize our roles as advocates for our clients or employers. It is our job to reconcile client and employer objectives with the public interest. And we must remember that while clients and employers are entitled to have access to professional public relations counsel, you and I individually are in no way obligated to provide such counsel when we feel that doing so would compromise us in any way.

What are the qualities that make up the ideal public relations man or woman?

It is difficult to establish a set of specifications for all the kinds of people wearing the public relations mantle. Generally, I feel five primary characteristics apply to just about every successful public relations person I know.

- They're smart—bright, intelligent people; quick studies. They ask the right questions. They have that unique ability to establish credibility almost on sight.

- They know how to get along with people. They work well with their bosses, their peers, their subordinates. They work well with their clients and with third parties like the press and suppliers.

- They are emotionally stable—even (especially) under pressure. They use the pronoun "we" more than "I."

- They are motivated, and part of that motivation involves an ability to develop creative solutions. No one needs to tell them what to do next; instinctively, they know.

- They don't fear starting with a blank sheet of paper. To them, the blank sheet of paper equates with challenge and opportunity. They can write; they can articulate their thoughts in a persuasive manner.

What is the future of public relations?

More so than ever before, those responsible for large institutions whose existence depends on public acceptance and support recognize the need for sound public relations input. At all levels of society, public opinion has been brought to bear in the conduct of affairs both in the public and private sectors. Numerous CEOs of major corporations have been deposed following initiatives undertaken by the media, by public interest groups, by institutional stockholders—all representing failures that stemmed from a lack of sensitivity to public opinion. Accordingly, my view is that public relations is playing and will continue to play a more pivotal role in the decision-making process than ever before. The sources of public relations counsel may well become less structured and more diverse, simply because of the growing pervasive understanding that public tolerance has become so important in the achievement of any goals that have a recognizable impact on society.

Suggested Readings

Center, Allen H., and Patrick Jackson, *Public Relations Practices: Managerial Case Studies and Problems,* 5th ed. Upper Saddle River, NJ: Prentice Hall, 2000.

Cutlip, Scott M., Allen H. Center, and Glen M. Broom, *Effective Public Relations,* 8th ed. Upper Saddle River, NJ: Prentice Hall, 2000. Without question, the first and still most comprehensive textbook in the field.

Dozier, David M., Larissa A. Grunig, and James E. Grunig, et al., *Manager's Guide to Excellence in Public Relations and Communication Management.* Hillsdale, NJ: Lawrence Erlbaum Associates, 1995.

Ewen, Stuart, *PR! A Social History of Spin.* New York: Basic Books, 1996.

Guth, David, and Charles Marsh, *Public Relations: A Values Driven Approach,* 2nd ed., Boston: Allyn & Bacon, 2002.

Heath, Robert L., *Handbook of Public Relations.* Thousand Oaks, CA: Sage Publications, 2004.

Henslowe, Philip, *Public Relations: A Practical Guide to the Basics.* Sterling, VA: Kogan Page, 2003. A British approach to the practice, endorsed by the London-based Institute of Public Relations.

Johnston, Jane, and Clara Zawawi, *Public Relations Theory and Practice.* Crow's Nest, NSW, Australia: Allen & Unwin, 2000.

Lattimore, Dan (Ed.), *Public Relations: The Practice and the Profession.* New York: McGraw-Hill College, 2003.

Ledingham, John, and Stephen Brunig, *Public Relations as Relationship Management, A Relational Approach to the Study and Practice of Public Relations.* Mahwah, NJ: Lawrence Erlbaum Associates, 2001.

Newsom, Doug, Judy Vanslyke Turk, and Dean Kruckeberg, *This Is PR: The Realities of Public Relations,* 7th ed. Stamford, CT: Thomson Advantage Books, 2003.

Pohl, Gayle M. *No Mulligans Allowed: Strategically Plotting Your Public Relations Course.* Dubuque, IA: Kendall Hunt Publishers, 2005. A fresh, creative, and useful perspective on charting a public relations career, authored by one of the nation's foremost public relations professors.

Rampton, Sheldon, and John Stauber, *Trust Us, We're Experts: How Industry Manipulates Science and Gambles with Your Future* New York: J.P. Tarcher/Putnam, 2002. A super-cynical look at what public relations people do for a living, authored by two of the industry's most ardent—yet lovable—critics.

Ries, Al, and Laura Ries, *The Fall of Advertising and the Rise of PR.* New York: Harperbusiness, 2004. An old ad hand and his daughter blow the lid off the advertising profession.

Slater, Robert, *No Such Thing as Over-Exposure: Inside the Life and Celebrity of Donald Trump.* Upper Saddle River, NJ: Financial Times/Prentice-Hall, 2005. The story, if you can bear it, of Donald Trump, in which the promotion-craving megalomaniac sat for 100 hours of private conversations.

Wilcox, Dennis (Ed.), *Public Relations: Strategies and Tactics,* 7th ed. Boston: Allyn & Bacon, 2005.

Yaverbaum, Eric, *Public Relations Kit for Dummies.* Foster City, CA: IDG Books Worldwide, 2001. A tongue-in-cheek, but useful, primer.

Notes

1. "January 30, 2005, Michael's Video Statement," Michael Jackson World Network Web site www.mjworld.net.
2. Bureau of Labor Statistics, U.S. Department of Labor, *Occupational Outlook Handbook, 2004–05 Edition,* Public Relations Specialists, http://www.bls.gov/oco/ocos086.htm.
3. "Executive, Congressional and Consumer Attitudes Toward the Media, Marketing and Public Relations Profession," sponsored by the Public Relations Society of America and Harris Interactive, November 10, 2005.
4. Kirk Hallahan, "Challenges Confronting PR Education," Public Relations Society of America Web site, www.prsa.org, November 2005.
5. "2002 Industry Documentation & Rankings," Council of Public Relations Firms, New York.
6. "Company Expands Its Management Committee to Include Communicator," Ragan Report (September 19, 2005): 2.
7. "The Design for Undergraduate Public Relations Education," a study cosponsored by the public relations division of the Association for Education in Journalism and Mass Communication, the Public Relations Society of America, and the educators' section of PRSA, 1987, 1.
8. Cited in Scott M. Cutlip and Allen H. Center, *Effective Public Relations,* 6th ed. (Upper Saddle River, NJ: Prentice Hall, 1985): 5.
9. Edward L. Bernays, *Crystallizing Public Opinion* (New York: Liveright, 1961).
10. Rex F. Harlow, "Building a Public Relations Definition," *Public Relations Review 2,* no. 4 (Winter 1976): 36.
11. "About Public Relations," Public Relations Society of America Web site, www.prsa.org, November 2005.
12. John E. Marston, *The Nature of Public Relations* (New York: McGraw-Hill, 1963): 161.

13. "Denny Griswold, PRN Founder and Industry Luminary, Dies at 92," *Public Relations News* (March 12, 2001): 1.
14. Dr. Melvin L. Sharpe, professor and coordinator of the Public Relations Sequence, Department of Journalism, Ball State University, Muncie, IN 47306.
15. Sandra Sobieraj, "Senate Bans Company Loans to Officials," Associated Press (July 13, 2002).
16. John Dewey, *The Public and Its Problems* (Chicago: Swallow Press, 1927).
17. Linda P. Morton, "Segmenting Publics by Lifestyles," *Public Relations Quarterly* (Fall 1999): 46–47.
18. Dr. Melvin L. Sharpe.
19. Timothy L. O'Brien, "Spinning Frenzy: P.R.'s Bad Press," *New York Times* (February 13, 2005): B1.
20. Derrick Jensen, "The War on Truth: The Secret Battle for the American Mind," interview with John Stauber, http://www.mediachannel.org (June 7, 2000).
21. "White House Official I. Lewis Libby Indicted on Obstruction of Justice, False Statement and Perjury Charges Relating to Leak of Classified Information Revealing CIA Officer's Identity," news release of Office of Special Counsel, (October 28, 2005), http://www.usdoj.gov/usao/iln/osc.
22. "Heyman Associates Study Finds Critical Patterns for Public Relations Success," news release of Heyman Associates, (June 28, 2004), http://www.heymanassociates.com.
23. Fraser P. Seitel, "Relax Mr. Stauber, Public Relations Ain't That Dangerous," http://www.mediachannel.org, (June 7, 2000).
24. Abraham Lincoln, Lincoln–Douglas Debates, Ottawa, IL, August 21, 1858.

2 The Growth of Public Relations

FIGURE 2-1 Pondering a crisis. John D. Rockefeller (right) needed public relations help in 1914, when the Colorado coal company he owned was the scene of a massacre of women and children. (Rockefeller Archive Center)

Unlike accounting, economics, medicine, and law, public relations is still a young field, not even 100 years old.

Modern-day public relations is clearly a 20th century phenomenon. The impetus for its growth might, in fact, be traced back to this man:

John D. Rockefeller Jr. was widely attacked in 1914, when the coal company he owned in Ludlow, Colorado, was the scene of a bloody massacre staged by Colorado militiamen and company guards against evicted miners and their families. When a dozen women and small children were killed at the Ludlow massacre, one of those Rockefeller called in to help him deal with the crisis was a journalist named Ivy Ledbetter Lee.

Lee, whom we discuss later in this chapter, would go on to become "the father of public relations." His employer, John D. Rockefeller Jr., whose own legendary father had always adhered to a strict policy of silence, would bear responsibility for the birth of a profession built on open communications.[1]

The relative youthfulness of the practice of public relations means that the field is still evolving. It is also *improving* every day. The professionals entering the practice today are by and large superior in intellect, training, and even experience to their counterparts of decades ago.

The strength of the practice of public relations today is based on the enduring commitment of the public to participate in a free and open democratic society. At least five trends are related to the evolution of public relations:

1. **Growth of big institutions.** The days of the mom-and-pop grocery store, the tiny community college, and the small local bank are rapidly disappearing. In their place have emerged Wal-Marts, Home Depots, and Citigroups, statewide community college systems, and nationwide banking networks. The public relations profession has evolved to interpret these large institutions to the publics they serve.

2. **Heightened public awareness and media sophistication.** First came the invention of the printing press. Then came mass communications: the print media, radio, and television. Later it was the development of cable, satellite, videotape, videodisks, video typewriters, portable cameras, word processors, fax machines, cell phones, the Internet, blogs, podcasts, vlogs, and all the other communications technologies that have helped fragment audiences. In the 1960s, McGill University Professor Marshall McLuhan predicted the world would become a "global village," where people everywhere could witness events—no matter where they occurred—in real time. In the 21st century, McLuhan's prophesy has become a reality.

3. **Increasing incidence of societal change, conflict, and confrontation.** Minority rights, women's rights, senior citizens' rights, gay rights, animal rights, consumerism, environmental awareness, downsizings, layoffs, and resultant unhappiness with large institutions all have become part of day-to-day society. With the growth of the Web, activists have become increasingly more daring, visible, and effective.

4. **Growing power of global media, public opinion, and democracy.** The outbreak of democracy in Latin America, Eastern Europe, the former Soviet Union, South Africa, and, in the 21st century, Afghanistan and Iraq, has heightened the power of public opinion in the world. The process has been energized by print and electronic media that span the globe. Public opinion is a powerful force not only in democracies like the United States but also for oppressed peoples around the world. Accordingly, the practice of public relations as a facilitator for understanding has increased in prominence.

5. **Dominance of the Internet.** Nearly one billion of the world's people today use the Internet.[2] The extraordinary growth of the Internet and the World Wide Web has made millions of people around the world instant consumers of unlimited communication. The profound change this continues to bring to society is monumental.

Ancient Beginnings

Although modern public relations is a 20th-century phenomenon, its roots are ancient. Leaders in virtually every great society throughout history understood the importance of influencing public opinion through persuasion. For example, archeologists have found bulletins in Iraq, dating from as early as 1800 B.C., that told farmers of the latest techniques of harvesting, sowing, and irrigating.[3] The more food the farmers grew, the better the citizenry ate and the wealthier the country became—a good example of planned persuasion to reach a specific public for a particular purpose—in other words, public relations.

The ancient Greeks also put a high premium on communication skills. The best speakers, in fact, were generally elected to leadership positions. Occasionally, aspiring Greek politicians enlisted the aid of sophists (individuals renowned for both their reasoning and their rhetoric) to help fight verbal battles. Sophists gathered in the amphitheaters of the day to extol the virtues of particular political candidates. Thus, the sophists set the stage for today's lobbyists, who attempt to influence legislation through effective communications techniques. From the time of the sophists, the practice of public relations has been a battleground for questions of ethics. Should a sophist or a lobbyist—or a public relations professional, for that matter—"sell" his or her talents to the highest bidder, regardless of personal beliefs, values, and ideologies? When modern-day public relations professionals agree to represent repressive governments, such as Cuba or North Korea, or to defend the questionable actions of troubled celebrities, from Ron Artest and Terrell Owens to Robert Blake and O. J. Simpson, these ethical questions remain very much a focus of modern public relations.

The Romans, particularly Julius Caesar, were also masters of persuasive techniques. When faced with an upcoming battle, Caesar would rally public support through published pamphlets and staged events. Similarly, during World War I, a special U.S. public information committee, the Creel Committee, was formed to channel the patriotic sentiments of Americans in support of the U.S. role in the war. Stealing a page from Caesar, the committee's massive verbal and written communications effort was successful in marshaling national pride behind the war effort. According to a young member of the Creel Committee, Edward L. Bernays (later considered by many to be the father of public relations), "This was the first time in U.S. history that information was used as a weapon of war."[4]

Even the Catholic Church had a hand in the creation of public relations. In the 1600s, under the leadership of Pope Gregory XV, the church established a College of Propaganda to "help propagate the faith." In those days, the term *propaganda* did not have a negative connotation; the church simply wanted to inform the public about the advantages of Catholicism. Today, the pope and other religious leaders maintain communications staffs to assist in relations with the public. Indeed, the chief communications official in the Vatican maintains the rank of Archbishop of the Church. It was largely his role to deal with perhaps the most horrific scandal ever to face the Catholic Church— the priest pedophile issue of 2002.[5]

Early American Experience

The American public relations experience dates back to the founding of the republic. Influencing public opinion, managing communications, and persuading individuals at the highest levels were at the core of the American Revolution. The colonists tried to persuade King George III that they should be accorded the same rights as Englishmen. *Taxation without representation is tyranny* became their public relations slogan to galvanize fellow countrymen.

When King George refused to accede to the colonists' demands, they combined the weaponry of sword and pen. Samuel Adams, for one, organized Committees of Correspondence as a kind of revolutionary Associated Press to disseminate anti-British

Speaking of Ethics

The Church's Spring of Shame

The Spring of 2002 was a bitter and shameful period for the Catholic Church. In January, the American Catholic Church was rocked by a series of articles in the *Boston Globe,* exposing how known pedophile priests had been protected by the Boston Archdiocese and its archbishop, 70-year-old Cardinal Bernard Law, who oversaw 362 parishes serving 2.1 million members (Figure 2-2).

By Spring, the criminal trial of Father John Geoghan, a former Boston priest named as a defendant in more than 80 civil lawsuits, became front-page news around the nation. The Geoghan trial shed light on the complicity of Catholic bishops in paying off complainants, sealing records, and moving offending priests from parish to parish to avoid their problems becoming public. Geoghan was defrocked and sentenced to 10 years in prison.

Another former Boston priest, Father Paul Shanley, was arrested in California and convicted of even worse and more pervasive offenses. Documents showed that Shanley was moved around various Boston parishes until he was transferred to California. Church officials there were never told of his past problems.

The scandal was, inarguably, the most profound public relations problem in the history of the Roman Catholic Church. While the floodgates opened and similar cases of pedophilia were reported involving clergy throughout the nation, Cardinal Law remained in his post. Indeed, he was defended by fellow priests, some of whom argued that the U.S. media was "obviously and openly anti-Catholic."

Although Cardinal Law acknowledged, "We were too focused on the individual components of each case, when we should have been more focused on the protection of children," he adamantly refused to resign.

After a summer emergency meeting at the Vatican with Pope John Paul II, the Church adopted strict rules to deal with transgressing priests. Nonetheless, many wondered why the Archbishop of Boston, who acknowledged mishandling the cases of numerous pedophile priests in his jurisdiction—and, in fact, paid $10 million to settle the case in the fall of 2002—hadn't felt it was his ethical duty to resign.

Finally, nearly a full year after the revelation of the Catholic Church's worst scandal in history, Cardinal Law stepped down.

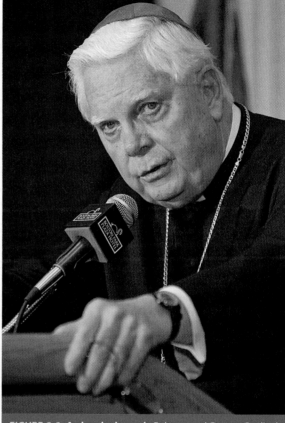

FIGURE 2-2 A church shamed. Beleaguered Boston Cardinal Bernard Law. (AP Wide World Photos)

For further information, see Eric J. Lyman, "Cardinal Blasts U.S. Media for Sex Coverage," *United Press International,* June 8, 2002; Cathy Lynn Grossman, "Church Expected to Settle for $10M," *USA Today,* September 19, 2002; Robert Paul Reyes, "Pope's Response to Sex Scandal Is Inadequate," Aboutpolitics.com, April 1, 2002; and Allyson Smith, "Catholic Organization Grateful to See Boston Pedophile Scandal Exposed," *Culture & Family Report,* March 1, 2002.

information throughout the colonies. He also staged events to build up revolutionary fervor, such as the Boston Tea Party, in which colonists, masquerading as Indians, boarded British ships in Boston Harbor and pitched chests of imported tea overboard—as impressive a media event as has ever been recorded sans television.

Thomas Paine, another early practitioner of public relations, wrote periodic pamphlets and essays that urged the colonists to band together. In one essay contained in his *Crisis* papers, Paine wrote poetically: "These are the times that try men's souls. The summer soldier and the sunshine patriot will, in this crisis, shrink from the service of their country." The people listened, were persuaded, and took action—testifying to the power of early American communicators.

Later American Experience

The creation of the most important document in our nation's history, the Constitution, also owed much to public relations. Federalists, who supported the Constitution, fought tooth and nail with anti-Federalists, who opposed it. Their battle was waged in newspaper articles, pamphlets, and other organs of persuasion in an attempt to influence public opinion. To advocate ratification of the Constitution, political leaders such as Alexander Hamilton, James Madison, and John Jay banded together, under the pseudonym Publius, to write letters to leading newspapers. Today those letters are bound in a document called *The Federalist Papers* and are still used in the interpretation of the Constitution.

After its ratification, the constitutional debate continued, particularly over the document's apparent failure to protect individual liberties against government encroachment. Hailed as the father of the Constitution, Madison framed the Bill of Rights in 1791, which ultimately became the first 10 amendments to the Constitution. Fittingly, the first of those amendments safeguarded, among other things, the practice of public relations:

> *Congress shall make no law respecting an establishment of religion, or prohibiting the free exercise thereof; or abridging the freedom of speech, or of the press, or the rights of the people peaceably to assemble, and to petition the government for a redress of grievances.*

In other words, people were given the right to speak up for what they believed in and the freedom to try to influence the opinions of others. Thus was the practice of public relations ratified.[6]

Into the 1800s

The practice of public relations continued to percolate in the 19th century. Among the more prominent, yet negative, antecedents of modern public relations that took hold in the 1800s was press agentry. Two of the better-known—some would say notorious—practitioners of this art were Amos Kendall and Phineas T. Barnum.

In 1829, President Andrew Jackson selected Kendall, a Kentucky writer and editor, to serve in his administration. Within weeks, Kendall became a member of Old Hickory's "kitchen cabinet" and eventually became one of Jackson's most influential assistants.

Kendall performed just about every White House public relations task. He wrote speeches, state papers, and messages, and turned out press releases. He even conducted basic opinion polls and is considered one of the earliest users of the "news leak." Although Kendall is generally credited with being the first authentic presidential press secretary, his functions and role went far beyond that position.

Among Kendall's most successful ventures in Jackson's behalf was the development of the administration's own newspaper, the *Globe*. Although it was not uncommon for the governing administration to publish its own national house organ, Kendall's deft editorial touch refined the process to increase its effectiveness. Kendall would pen a Jackson news release, distribute it for publication to a local newspaper, and then reprint the press clipping in the *Globe* to underscore Jackson's nationwide popularity. Indeed, that popularity continued unabated throughout Jackson's years in office, with much of the credit going to the president's public relations adviser.*

Most public relations professionals would rather not talk about P. T. Barnum as an industry pioneer. Barnum, some say, was a huckster whose motto might well have been "The public be fooled." Barnum's defenders suggest that although the impresario may have had his faults, he nonetheless was respected in his time as a user of written and verbal public relations techniques to further his museum and circus.

Like him or not, Barnum was a master publicist. In the 1800s, as owner of a major circus, Barnum generated article after article for his traveling show. He purposely gave his star performers short names—for instance, Tom Thumb, the midget, and Jenny Lind, the singer—so that they could easily fit into the headlines of narrow newspaper columns. Barnum also staged bizarre events, such as the legal marriage of the fat lady to the thin man, to drum up free newspaper exposure. And although today's practitioners scoff at Barnum's methods, some press agents still practice his techniques. Nonetheless, when today's public relations professionals bemoan the specter of shysters and hucksters that still overhangs their field, they inevitably place the blame squarely on the fertile mind and silver tongue of P. T. Barnum.

Emergence of the Robber Barons

The American Industrial Revolution ushered in many things at the turn of the century, not the least of which was the growth of public relations. The 20th century began with small mills and shops, which served as the hub of the frontier economy, eventually giving way to massive factories. Country hamlets, which had been the centers of commerce and trade, were replaced by sprawling cities. Limited transportation and communications facilities became nationwide railroad lines and communications wires. Big business took over, and the businessman was king.

The men who ran America's industries seemed more concerned with making a profit than with improving the lot of their fellow citizens. Railroad owners led by William Vanderbilt, bankers led by J. P. Morgan, oil magnates led by John D. Rockefeller, and steel impresarios led by Henry Clay Frick ruled the fortunes of thousands of others. Typical of the reputation acquired by this group of industrialists was the famous—and perhaps apocryphal—response of Vanderbilt when questioned about the public's reaction to his closing of the New York Central Railroad: "The public be damned!"

Little wonder that Americans cursed Vanderbilt and his ilk as "robber barons," who cared little for the rest of society. Although most who depended on these industrialists for their livelihood felt powerless to rebel, the seeds of discontent were being sown liberally throughout society.

---

*Kendall was decidedly not cut from the same cloth as today's neat, trim, buttoned-down press secretaries. On the contrary, Jackson's man was described as "a puny, sickly looking man with a weak voice, a wheezing cough, narrow and stooping shoulders, a sallow complexion, silvery hair in his prime, slovenly dress, and a seedy appearance." (Fred F. Endres, "Public Relations in the Jackson White House," *Public Relations Review* 2, no. 3 [Fall 1976]: 5–12.)

Talking Points

P. T. Barnum Lives

Self-respecting public relations professionals despise the legacy of P. T. Barnum, who created publicity through questionable methods. They lament, as noted in Chapter 1, that public relations communication should always reflect "performance" and "truth."

Ah, were it so.

Alas, Barnum's bogus methods are just as effective with 21st-century media as they were with 19th-century media.

Doubt it?

Then consider two 21st-century public relations creations, the Reverend Al Sharpton and the real estate mogul Donald Trump (see Figure 2-3).

Sharpton, a minor aide in the days of Martin Luther King, first gained notoriety in the 1980s by vigorously defending a Newburgh, New York, woman who claimed she had been abducted and raped in a racially motivated crime. The woman's story turned out to be a lie, and Sharpton lost a lawsuit for his role in the ruse.

No matter. Despite a series of ethical lapses, the loquacious Reverend Al was "good copy." And when the Reverend called, the media listened. By 2004, Al Sharpton was a bona fide candidate for the Democratic Presidential nomination.

Similarly, Trump, son of a wealthy New York real estate landlord, was a master wheeler-dealer, more heralded for his bravado and arrogance than for his acumen. Indeed, in the 1980s, Trump, despite outrageous claims to the contrary, narrowly escaped real estate bankruptcy and was forced to trade part of his empire to restructure debts. In 2004, Trump's Atlantic City casino did go bankrupt, again despite The Donald's continuous claims that "things are going great." And then in 2005, *The New York Times* had the audacity to question Trump's claims that he was "a billionaire."*

No matter. Trump continued to thrive with his television show *The Apprentice* and endorsement deals for a variety of products from Trump Perfume to Trump University. The media, meanwhile, continued to quote his every word. Some even called him "the P. T. Barnum of Finance."

Amen.

FIGURE 2-3 P. T. Barnum's legacy. The Reverend Al and The Donald. (AP Wide World Photos)

* Timothy L. O'Brien, "What's He Really Worth?" *New York Times,* October 23, 2005, Section 3, 1.

Enter the Muckrakers

When the axe fell on the robber barons, it came in the form of criticism from a feisty group of journalists dubbed *muckrakers*. The "muck" that these reporters and editors "raked" was dredged from the supposedly scandalous operations of America's business enterprises. Upton Sinclair's novel *The Jungle* attacked the deplorable conditions of the meatpacking industry. Ida Tarbell's *History of the Standard Oil Company* stripped away the public facade of the nation's leading petroleum firm. Her accusations against Standard Oil Chairman Rockefeller, many of which were unproven, nonetheless stirred up public attention.

Magazines such as *McClure's* struck out systematically at one industry after another. The captains of industry, used to getting their own way and having to answer to no one, were wrenched from their peaceful passivity and rolled out on the public carpet to answer for their sins. Journalistic shock stories soon led to a wave of sentiment for legislative reform.

As journalists and the public became more anxious, the government got more involved. Congress began passing laws telling business leaders what they could and couldn't do. Trust-busting became the order of the day. Conflicts between employers and employees began to break out, and newly organized labor unions came to the fore. The Socialist and Communist movements began to take off. Ironically, it was "a period when free enterprise reached a peak in American history, and yet at that very climax, the tide of public opinion was swelling up against business freedom, primarily because of the breakdown in communications between the businessman and the public."[7]

For a time, these men of inordinate wealth and power found themselves limited in their ability to defend themselves and their activities against the tidal wave of public condemnation. They simply did not know how to get through to the public. To tell their side of the story, the business barons first tried using the lure of advertising to silence journalistic critics; they tried to buy off critics by paying for ads in their papers. It didn't work. Next, they paid publicity people, or press agents, to present their companies' positions. Often these hired guns painted over the real problems of their client companies. The public saw through this approach.

Clearly, another method had to be discovered to get the public to at least consider the business point of view. Business leaders were discovering that a corporation might have capital, labor, and natural resources, yet be doomed to fail if it couldn't influence public opinion. The best way to influence public opinion, as it turned out, was through honesty and candor. This simple truth was the key to the accomplishments of American history's first great public relations counselor.

Ivy Lee: The Real Father of Modern Public Relations

Ivy Ledbetter Lee was a former Wall Street reporter, the son of a Methodist minister, who plunged into publicity work in 1903 (Figure 2-4). Lee believed neither in Barnum's public-be-fooled approach nor Vanderbilt's public-be-damned philosophy. For Lee, the key to business acceptance and understanding was that the public be informed.

Lee disdained the press agents of the time, who used any influence or trick to get a story on their clients printed, regardless of the truth or merits. By contrast, Lee firmly believed that the only way business could answer its critics convincingly was to present

FIGURE 2-4 Father of public relations. Ivy Lee. (Courtesy of Seely G. Mudd Manuscript Library, Princeton University Library, Ivy Lee Papers, Public Policy Papers, Department of Rare Books and Special Collections)

its side honestly, accurately, and forcefully. Instead of merely appeasing the public, Lee thought a company should strive to earn public confidence and goodwill.

In 1914, John D. Rockefeller Jr., son of one of the nation's most maligned and misunderstood men, hired Lee to assist with the fallout from the Ludlow massacre, affecting his Colorado Fuel and Iron Company. Lee's advice to Rockefeller was simple:

> *Tell the truth, because sooner or later the public will find it out anyway. And if the public doesn't like what you are doing, change your policies and bring them into line with what the people want.*[8]

Despite the tragedy of Ludlow, Lee encouraged Rockefeller to create a joint labor–management board to mediate all workers' grievances on wages, hours, and working conditions. It was a great success. The mine workers—and the public—began to see John D. Rockefeller Jr. in a different light. Most important, he began to see them in a new light as well. As Rockefeller's youngest son, David, recalled nearly a century later, "My father was changed profoundly by his meetings with the workers. It was a lesson that stayed with him throughout the rest of his life and one of the most important things that ever happened to our family."[9]

In working for the Rockefellers, Lee tried to "humanize" them, to feature them in real-life situations such as playing golf, attending church, and celebrating birthdays. Simply, Lee's goal was to present the Rockefellers in terms that every individual could understand and appreciate.

Ironically, even Ivy Lee could not escape the glare of public criticism. In the late 1920s, Lee was asked to serve as adviser to the parent company of the German Dye Trust, which, as it turned out, was an agent for the policies of Adolf Hitler. For his involvement with the Dye Trust, Lee was branded a traitor and dubbed "Poison Ivy" by members of Congress investigating un-American activities. Ironically, the smears against him in the press rivaled the most vicious ones against any of the robber barons.[10]

Despite his unfortunate involvement with the Dye Trust, Ivy Lee is recognized as the individual who began to distinguish "publicity" and "press agentry" from "public relations" based on honesty and candor. For his seminal contributions to the field, Ivy Lee should be considered the real father of public relations.

The Growth of Modern Public Relations

Ivy Lee helped to open the gates for modern public relations. After he established the idea that high-powered companies and individuals have a responsibility to inform their publics, the practice began to grow in every sector of American society.

Government

During World War I, President Woodrow Wilson established the Creel Committee under the leadership of journalist George Creel. Creel's group, composed of the nation's leading journalists, scholars, and public relations leaders, mounted an impressive effort to mobilize public opinion in support of the war effort and to stimulate the sale of war bonds through Liberty Loan publicity drives. Not only did the war effort get a boost, but so did the field of public relations. The nation was mightily impressed with the potential power of publicity as a weapon to encourage national sentiment and support.

During World War II, the public relations field received an even bigger boost. The Office of War Information (OWI) was established to convey the message of the United States at home and abroad. Under the directorship of Elmer Davis, a veteran journalist, the OWI laid the foundations for the U.S. Information Agency as America's voice around the world.

World War II also saw a flurry of activity to sell war bonds, boost the morale of those at home, spur production in the nation's factories and offices, and, in general, support America's war effort as intensively as possible. By virtually every measure, this full-court public relations offensive was an unquestioned success.

The proliferation of public relations officers in World War II led to a growth in the number of practitioners during the peace that followed. One reason companies saw the need to have public relations professionals to "speak up" for them was the more combative attitude of President Harry Truman toward many of the country's largest institutions. For example, Truman's seizure of the steel mills touched off a massive public relations campaign, the likes of which had rarely been seen outside the government.

Later in the century, the communications problems of President Richard Nixon, surrounding the "cover up" of the Watergate political scandal, brought new criticism of public relations. But the subsequent administration of the "great communicator" Ronald Reagan reaffirmed the value of public relations.

Counseling

The nation's first public relations firm, the Publicity Bureau, was founded in Boston in 1900 and specialized in general press agentry. The first Washington, D.C., agency was begun in 1902 by William Wolff Smith, a former correspondent for the *New York Sun* and the *Cincinnati Inquirer*. Two years later, Ivy Lee joined with a partner to begin his own counseling firm.

The most significant counselor this side of Ivy Lee was Edward L. Bernays, who began as a publicist in 1913. He was the nephew of Sigmund Freud and author of the landmark book *Crystallizing Public Opinion* (see interview at the end of this chapter).

Bernays was a giant in the public relations field for nearly the entire century. In addition to contributing as much to the field as any other professional in its history, Bernays was a true public relations scholar. He taught the first course in public relations in 1923 and was also responsible for "recruiting" the field's first distinguished female practitioner, his wife Doris E. Fleischman.

Fleischman, former editor of the *New York Tribune,* was a skilled writer, and her husband was a skilled strategist and promoter. Together they built Edward L. Bernays, Counsel on Public Relations into a top agency. In many ways, Fleischman was the "mother" of public relations, paving the way for a field that is today dominated by talented women (Figure 2-5).

Bernays's seminal writings in the field underscored the importance of strategic communications advice for clients. For example, Bernays wrote:

> *At first we called our activity "publicity direction." We intended to give advice to clients on how to direct their actions to get public visibility for them. But within a year we changed the service and its name to "counsel on public relations." We recognized that all actions of a client that impinged on the public needed counsel. Public visibility of a client for one action might be vitiated by another action not in the public interest.*[11]

After Bernays's pioneering counseling efforts, a number of public relations firms, most headquartered in New York, began to take root, most notably among them Hill & Knowlton, Carl Byoir & Associates, Newsom & Company, and Burson-Marsteller. One of the earliest African American counselors was D. Parke Gibson, who authored two books on African American consumerism and advised companies on multicultural relations.

FIGURE 2-5 Dynamic duo. Edward L. Bernays and his wife, Doris Fleischman, formed the 20th century's greatest public relations tandem. (Courtesy of the Museum of Public Relations, http://www.prmuseum.com)

For many years, Hill & Knowlton and Burson-Marsteller jockeyed for leadership in the counseling industry. One early counselor, Harold Burson (see interview in Chapter 1), emphasized marketing-oriented public relations "to help clients sell their goods and services, maintain a favorable market for their stock, and foster harmonious relations with employees." In 2000, Burson was named the most influential PR person of the 20th century.[12]

In the 1990s, the counseling business saw the emergence of international super-agencies, many of which were merged into advertising agencies. Indeed, both Hill & Knowlton and Burson-Marsteller were eventually merged under one corporation, WPP, which also includes the J. Walter Thompson and Young & Rubicam advertising agencies. Another mega-communications firm, Omnicom Group, owned seven major public relations firms, including Fleishman-Hillard, Porter Novelli, and Ketchum. Despite these communications conglomerates, most public relations agencies still operate as independent entities.

In the 21st century then, the public relations counseling business boasts a diverse mix of huge national agencies, medium-sized regional firms, and one-person local operations. Public relations agencies may be general in nature or specialists in everything from consumer products to entertainment to health care to technology.

Corporations

As the 20th century rolled on, the perceptual problems of corporations and their leaders diminished. Opinion polls after World War II ranked business as high in public esteem. People were back at work, and business was back in style.

Smart companies—General Electric, General Motors, and American Telephone & Telegraph (AT&T), for example—worked hard to preserve their good names through both words and actions. Arthur W. Page became AT&T's first public relations vice president in 1927. Page was a legendary public relations figure, helping to maintain AT&T's reputation as a prudent and proper corporate citizen. Page also was one of the few public relations executives to serve on prestigious corporate boards of directors, including Chase Manhattan Bank, Kennecott Copper, Prudential Insurance, and Westinghouse Electric.[13]

Page's five principles of successful corporate public relations are as relevant now as they were in the 1930s:

1. To make sure management thoughtfully analyzes its overall relation to the public
2. To create a system for informing all employees about the firm's general policies and practices
3. To create a system giving contact employees (those having direct dealings with the public) the knowledge needed to be reasonable and polite to the public
4. To create a system drawing employee and public questions and criticism back up through the organization to management
5. To ensure frankness in telling the public about the company's actions[14]

Another early corporate public relations luminary was Paul Garrett. A former news reporter, he became the first director of public relations for mighty General Motors in 1931, working directly for GM's legendary CEO Alfred Sloan. Garrett once reportedly explained that the essence of his job was to convince the public that the powerful auto company deserved trust, that is, "to make a billion-dollar company seem small."

Ironically, as good as Garrett was, he nevertheless reflected the universal public relations complaint, still common today, of "never feeling like an insider" within his organization.[15]

One would think that companies today all recognize the importance of proper public relations in the conduct of their business. Most do. But, as the corporate scandals of the last years of the 20th century—from Enron to WorldCom to Tyco to Adelphia—indicate, smart corporate leaders will still seek out the counsel of trained public relations professionals in dealing with their key constituent publics.

Public Relations Comes of Age

As noted, public relations came of age largely as a result of the confluence of five general factors in our society:

1. The growth of large institutions
2. Heightened public awareness and media sophistication
3. Increasing incidence of societal change, conflict, and confrontation
4. Growing power of global media, public opinion, and democracy
5. Dominance of the Internet

Growth of Large Institutions

Ironically, the public relations profession received perhaps its most important thrust when business confidence suffered its most severe setback. The economic and social upheaval caused by the Great Depression of the 1930s provided the impetus for corporations to seek public support by telling their stories. Public relations departments sprang up in scores of major companies, among them Bendix, Borden, Eastman Kodak, Eli Lilly, Ford, General Motors, Standard Oil, and U.S. Steel. The role that public relations played in regaining post-Depression public trust in big business helped project the field into the relatively strong position it has enjoyed since World War II.

Today, businesses of every size recognize that aggressively communicating corporate products and positions can help win public receptivity and support and ward off government intrusion.

Heightened Public Awareness and Media Sophistication

In the 1970s and 1980s, companies were obligated to consider minority rights, consumer rights, environmental implications, and myriad other social issues. Business began to contribute to charities. Managers began to consider community relations a first-line responsibility. The general policy of corporations confronting their adversaries was abandoned. In its place, most large companies adopted a policy of conciliation and compromise.

This new policy of social responsibility continued into the 1990s. Corporations came to realize that their reputations are a valuable asset to be protected, conserved, defended, nurtured, and enhanced at all times. In truth, institutions in the 1990s had little choice but to get along with their publics. The general prosperity of the 1990s, fueled by enormous stock market gains, helped convey goodwill between organizations and their publics.

By the 21st century, the vast majority of American homes had television, with millions wired for cable and another 185 million with online access. Where once three television networks dominated, now a plethora of channels and cable networks, catering to every persuasion, enable media consumers to choose what they want to view.

As a result of all this communication, publics have become much more segmented, specialized, and sophisticated.

Societal Change, Conflict, and Confrontation

Disenchantment with big institutions peaked in the 1960s, coincident with an unpopular war. The social and political upheavals of the 1960s dramatically affected many areas, including the practice of public relations. The Vietnam War fractured society. Movements were formed by various interest groups. An obscure consumer advocate named Ralph Nader began to look pointedly at the inadequacies of the automobile industry. Women, long denied equal rights in the workplace and elsewhere, began to mobilize into activist groups such as the National Organization for Women (NOW). Environmentalists, worried about threats to the land and water by business expansion, began to support groups such as the Sierra Club. Minorities, particularly African Americans and Hispanics, began to petition and protest for their rights. Homosexuals, AIDS activists, senior citizens, birth control advocates, and social activists of every kind began to challenge the legitimacy of large institutions. Not since the days of the robber barons had large institutions so desperately needed professional communications help.

By the 21st century, such movements had morphed into established, well-organized, and powerful interest groups.

Growing Power of Global Media, Public Opinion, and Democracy

In the 21st century, democracy, as someone once said, "has broken out everywhere." At the end of 2002, there were 121 democracies governing more than 60 percent of the world's population.[16]

In recent years, significant events to spur democracy—all conveyed in real time by pervasive global media—have been breathtaking.

- In 1989, the Berlin Wall's destruction was transmitted live around the world. So was the dissolution of the Union of Soviet Socialist Republics.

- In 1993, two long-time archenemies, Nelson Mandela and Frederik Willem De-Klerck, stood together to share the Nobel Peace Prize as free elections were held in South Africa and a black former prisoner of the state became president.

- By the year 2000, the defeat and imprisonment of Slobodan Milosevic in the Balkans allowed the people of Yugoslavia to experience freedom.

- In 2002, the vanquishing in Afghanistan of the repressive Taliban regime, supported by the terrorist al-Qaeda network, allowed that poor country, too, to begin to experience democratic institutions.

- In 2005, after the defeat of Saddam Hussein signaled the potential for a democratic Iraq, an astounding 10 million citizens—70 percent of eligible voters—went to the polls to elect new leaders (Figure 2-6).

Today, with the world near-completely "wired," the power of communications and public relations to bring down tyrants and build up democracy is profound.

FIGURE 2-6 Televised war. In 2003, as U.S. solidiers in Baghdad draped a Saddam Hussein statue with old glory, the world watched in real time. (AP Wide World Photos)

Dominance of the Internet

In the 21st century, true two-way communication has arrived largely as a result of the growth of online access. Cable, satellite, mobile phones, pagers, faxes, bar code scanners, voice mail systems, videodisk technologies, and a multitude of other developments have revolutionized the information transmission and receiving process. The emergence of the Internet and the World Wide Web has radically intensified the spread of communications even further.

Beginning during the cold war in 1969 as a U.S. Department of Defense system, the annual global Internet economy today accounts for more than $80 billion in revenue.[17] More important, with 75 percent of homes in the United States with access to the Internet and 185 million U.S. online users, the Net as a communications medium dwarfs all others.[18]

The impact of the Internet on public relations practice has been phenomenal. E-mail dominates internal communications. Journalists, like many other Americans, regard the Internet as their primary choice of most organizational communications. In the 21st century, knowledge of and facility with the Internet has become a front-burner necessity for public relations practitioners.

Public Relations Education

As the practice of public relations has developed, so too has the growth of public relations education. In 1951, 12 schools offered major programs in public relations. Today, well in excess of 200 journalism or communication programs offer concentrated study in public relations, with nearly 300 others offering at least one course dealing with the profession.

One of the most comprehensive studies of public relations education was done in 1999 by the Commission on Public Relations Education, chartered by the Public Relations Society of America. This commission recommended a public relations curriculum imparting knowledge in such nontraditional but pivotal areas as relationship building, societal trends, and multicultural and global issues.[19]

While public relations education isn't incorporated into most business schools, it should be. As noted, the practice has become an integral part in the daily workings and ongoing relationships of most organizations—from companies to churches, from governments to schools. Therefore, business students should be exposed to the discipline's underpinnings and practical aspects before they enter the corporate world.

Likewise, in journalism, with more than 70 percent of daily newspaper copy emanating from public relations–generated releases, journalists, too, should know what public relations is all about before they graduate. As the debate continues about where public relations education should appropriately be housed—either in business or journalism schools—the best answer is that both should offer public relations courses.[20]

Wherever the function is located on the university level, it is clear that the field's enhanced educational dimension has contributed to the respect and acceptance accorded public relations in modern society.

Last Word

From humble beginnings less than 100 years ago, the practice of public relations today is big business around the world.

- The Public Relations Society of America, organized in 1947, boasts a growing membership of 20,000 in 116 chapters nationwide.

- The Public Relations Student Society of America, formed in 1968 to facilitate communications between students interested in the field and public relations professionals, has 8,500 student members at 270 college chapters.

- The International Association of Business Communicators boasts 13,000 members in more than 60 countries.

- More than 5,300 U.S. companies, 2,100 trade associations, 187 foreign embassies, and 130 federal government departments, bureaus, agencies, and commissions have public relations departments.[21]

- More than 3,000 public relations agencies exist in the United States, with more than 700 public relations firms residing in 80 foreign countries.[22]

- Top communications executives at major companies and agencies draw six-figure salaries.

The scope of modern public relations practice is vast. Press relations, government relations, Web relations, employee communications, public relations counseling and research, local community relations, audiovisual communications, contributions, interactive public relations, and numerous other diverse activities fall under the public relations umbrella. This may be one reason public relations is variously labeled *external affairs, corporate communications, public affairs, corporate relations,* and a variety of other confusing euphemisms.

Just as the name of the field generates confusion, so too does its purpose. Specifically, public relations professionals lament that the practice is still often accused of being a haven for snake oil salesman peddling cosmetics, subterfuge, and spin. When the *New York Times* talks about disgraced Enron CEO Ken Lay, it blames him most for practicing what it terms "public relations." To wit:

> *Mr. Lay's belief in the power of public relations is the reason he gave a news conference the day after he was indicted. And it's the reason he made that speech in Houston this week. He seems to believe that if he says something often enough and loudly enough, it will become true.*[23]

What the *Times* and many others still fail to understand is that proper public relations—the kind that builds credibility—must begin and end with one important commodity: *truth*.

Indeed, there is no more important characteristic for public relations people to emulate than the candor that comes from high ethical character. The field's finest ethical moment, in fact, occurred when the Johnson & Johnson Company, in the wake of unspeakable tragedy brought about by its lead product Tylenol, didn't hesitate to choose the ethical course.

As the case study at the conclusion of this chapter suggests, the handling of the Tylenol tragedy was public relations' most shining hour.

Despite the stereotypes that still overhang the field, the fact remains that with 200,000 men and women in its practice in the United States and thousands more overseas, public relations has become solidly entrenched as an important, influential, and professional component of 21st-century society.

Discussion Starters

1. What societal factors have influenced the spread of public relations?
2. Why do public relations professionals think of P. T. Barnum as a mixed blessing?
3. What is the significance to the practice of public relations of American revolutionary hero Samuel Adams?
4. What did the robber barons and muckrakers have to do with the development of public relations?
5. Why are Ivy Lee and Edward Bernays considered two of the fathers of public relations?
6. What impact did the Creel Committee and the Office of War Information have on the development of public relations?
7. What was the significance of Arthur Page to the development of corporate public relations?
8. What did the legacy of Watergate mean to the practice of public relations?
9. What are some of the yardsticks that indicated that public relations had "arrived" in the latter part of the 20th century?
10. What are some of the issues that confront public relations in the 21st century?

Top of the Shelf

The Father of Spin: Edward L. Bernays and the Birth of Public Relations

Larry Tye, New York: Henry Holt, 2001.

The author's background as a *Boston Globe* journalist, not a public relations practitioner or professor, both limits the depth of this biography and offers the refreshing viewpoint of an "outsider."

Tye uses Bernays's life "as a prism to understand the evolution of the craft of public relations and how it came to play such a critical—and sometimes insidious—role in American life." Granted a Nieman Fellowship at Harvard University to write this book, Tye waded into 800 boxes of personal and professional papers Bernays left the Library of Congress, papers that detail cases he worked on and tactics and strategies he employed over a career that spanned eight decades.

This is an enjoyable, enlightening read, bolstered by a seven-page bibliography. Serious students of public relations may frown on the word *spin* to describe one of the field's patron saints, but no harm, no foul. This is worth the read.

CASE STUDY

The Tylenol Murders

Arguably, the two most important cases in the history of the practice of public relations occurred within four years of each other to the same company and product.

For close to 100 years, Johnson & Johnson Company of New Brunswick, New Jersey, was the epitome of a well-managed, highly profitable, and tight-lipped consumer products manufacturer.

Round I

That image changed on the morning of September 30, 1982, when Johnson & Johnson faced as devastating a public relations problem as had confronted any company in history.

That morning, Johnson & Johnson's management learned that its premier product, extra-strength Tylenol, had been used as a murder weapon to kill three people. In the days that followed, another three people died from swallowing Tylenol capsules loaded with cyanide. Although all the cyanide deaths occurred in Chicago, reports from other parts of the country also implicated extra-strength Tylenol capsules in illnesses of various sorts. These latter reports were later proved to be unfounded, but Johnson & Johnson and its Tylenol-producing subsidiary, McNeil Consumer Products Company, found themselves at the center of a public relations trauma the likes of which few companies had ever experienced.

Tylenol had been an astoundingly profitable product for Johnson & Johnson. At the time of the Tylenol murders, the product held 35 percent of the $1 billion analgesic market. It contributed an estimated 7 percent to the company's worldwide sales and almost 20 percent to its profits. Throughout the years, Johnson & Johnson had not been—and hadn't needed to be—a particularly high-profile company. Its chairman, James E. Burke, who had been with the company for almost 30 years, had never appeared on television and had rarely participated in print interviews.

Johnson & Johnson's management was caught totally by surprise when the news hit. The company recognized that it needed the media to get out as much information to the public as quickly as possible to prevent a panic. Therefore, almost immediately, Johnson & Johnson made a key decision: to open its doors to the media.

On the second day of the crisis, Johnson & Johnson discovered that an earlier statement that no cyanide was used on its premises was wrong. The company didn't hesitate. Its public relations department quickly announced that the earlier information had been false. Even though the reversal embarrassed the company briefly,

Johnson & Johnson's openness was hailed and made up for any damage to its credibility.

Early on in the crisis, the company was largely convinced that the poisonings had not occurred at any of its plants. Nonetheless, Johnson & Johnson recalled an entire lot of 93,000 bottles of extra-strength Tylenol associated with the reported Chicago murders. In the process, it telegrammed warnings to doctors, hospitals, and distributors, at a cost of half a million dollars. McNeil also suspended all Tylenol advertising to reduce attention to the product.

But what about all those other millions of dollars worth of Tylenol capsules on the nation's shelves?

The company was convinced such a massive recall wasn't warranted by the facts. It was convinced that the tampering had taken

FIGURE 2-7 New packaging. The triple-safety-sealed, tamper-resistant package for Tylenol capsules had (1) glued flaps on the outer box, (2) a tight plastic neck seal, and (3) a strong inner foil seal over the mouth of the bottle. A bright yellow label on the bottle was imprinted with a red warning: "Do not use if safety seals are broken." As it turned out, all these precautions didn't work. (Courtesy of Johnson & Johnson)

place during the product's Chicago distribution and not in the manufacturing process. Further, the FBI was worried that a precipitous recall would encourage copycat poisoning attempts. Nonetheless, five days later, when a copycat strychnine poisoning occurred in California, Johnson & Johnson did recall all extra-strength Tylenol capsules—31 million bottles—at a cost of more than $100 million.

Although the company believed it had done nothing wrong, Johnson & Johnson acted to assuage public concerns. It also posted a $100,000 reward for the killer or killers. Through advertisements promising to exchange capsules for tablets, through thousands of letters to the trade, and through statements to the media, the company hoped to put the incident into proper perspective.

At the same time, Johnson & Johnson commissioned a nationwide opinion survey to assess the consumer implications of the Tylenol poisonings. The good news was that 87 percent of Tylenol users surveyed said they realized that the maker of Tylenol was "not responsible" for the deaths. The bad news was that 61 percent still said they were "not likely to buy" extra-strength Tylenol capsules in the future. In other words, even though most consumers knew the deaths weren't Tylenol's fault, they still feared using the product.

But Chairman Burke and Johnson & Johnson weren't about to knuckle under to the deranged saboteur or saboteurs who had poisoned their product. Despite predictions of the imminent demise of extra-strength Tylenol, Johnson & Johnson decided to relaunch the product in a new triple-safety-sealed, tamper-resistant package (Figure 2-7). Many on Wall Street and in the marketing community were stunned by Johnson & Johnson's bold decision.

So confident was Johnson & Johnson's management that it launched an all-out media blitz to make sure that people understood its commitment. Chairman Burke appeared on television shows and in newspaper interviews.

The company even invited the investigative news program *60 Minutes*—the scourge of corporate America—to film its executive strategy sessions to prepare for the new launch. When the program was aired, reporter Mike Wallace concluded that although Wall Street had been ready at first to write off the company, it was now "hedging its bets because of Johnson & Johnson's stunning campaign of facts, money, the media, and truth."

Finally, on November 11, 1982, less than two months after the murders, Johnson & Johnson's management held an elaborate video news conference in New York City, beamed to additional locations around the country, to introduce the new extra-strength Tylenol package.

In the months that followed Burke's news conference, it became clear that Tylenol would not become a scapegoat. In fact, by the beginning of 1983, Tylenol had recaptured an astounding 95 percent

---

OUR CREDO

We believe our first responsibility is to the doctors, nurses and patients,
to mothers and fathers and all others who use our products and services.
In meeting their needs everything we do must be of high quality.
We must constantly strive to reduce our costs
in order to maintain reasonable prices.
Customers' orders must be serviced promptly and accurately.
Our suppliers and distributors must have an opportunity
to make a fair profit.

We are responsible to our employees,
the men and women who work with us throughout the world.
Everyone must be considered as an individual.
We must respect their dignity and recognize their merit.
They must have a sense of security in their jobs.
Compensation must be fair and adequate,
and working conditions clean, orderly and safe.
We must be mindful of ways to help our employees fulfill
their family responsibilities.
Employees must feel free to make suggestions and complaints.
There must be equal opportunity for employment, development
and advancement for those qualified.
We must provide competent management,
and their actions must be just and ethical.

We are responsible to the communities in which we live and work
and to the world community as well.
We must be good citizens — support good works and charities
and bear our fair share of taxes.
We must encourage civic improvements and better health and education.
We must maintain in good order
the property we are privileged to use,
protecting the environment and natural resources.

Our final responsibility is to our stockholders.
Business must make a sound profit.
We must experiment with new ideas.
Research must be carried on, innovative programs developed
and mistakes paid for.
New equipment must be purchased, new facilities provided
and new products launched.
Reserves must be created to provide for adverse times.
When we operate according to these principles,
the stockholders should realize a fair return.

Johnson & Johnson

FIGURE 2-8 **The Johnson & Johnson credo.** (Courtesy of Johnson & Johnson)

A special message from the makers of TYLENOL® products.

If you have TYLENOL capsules, we'll replace them with TYLENOL caplets.

And we'll do it at our expense.

As you know, there has been a tragic event. A small number of Extra-Strength TYLENOL® Capsules in one isolated area in New York have been criminally tampered with.

This was an outrageous act which damages all of us.

Both federal and local authorities have established that it was only capsules that were tampered with.

In order to prevent any further capsule tampering, we have removed all our capsules from your retailers' shelves. This includes Regular and Extra-Strength TYLENOL capsules, CO-TYLENOL® capsules, Maximum-Strength TYLENOL® Sinus Medication capsules, Extra-Strength SINE-AID® capsules, and DIMENSYN® Menstrual Relief capsules.

And Johnson & Johnson's McNeil Consumer Products Company has decided to cease the manufacture, sale, and distribution of **all** capsule forms of over-the-counter medicines.

If you're a regular capsule user, you may be wondering what to use instead. That's why we'd like you to try TYLENOL caplets.

The caplet is a solid form of TYLENOL pain reliever, which research has proven is the form most preferred by consumers. Unlike tablets, it is specially shaped and coated for easy, comfortable swallowing.

And the caplet delivers a full extra-strength dose quickly and effectively.

So, if you have any TYLENOL Capsules in your home, do one of the following:

1. Return the bottles with the unused portion to us, together with your name and address on the form below. And we'll replace your TYLENOL Capsules with TYLENOL Caplets (or tablets, if you prefer). We'll also refund your postage. Or. . .

2. If you prefer, you can receive a cash refund for the unused capsules by sending the bottle to us along with a letter requesting the refund.

We are taking this step because, for the past 25 years, over 100 million Americans have made TYLENOL products a trusted part of their health care.

We're continuing to do everything we can to keep your trust.

Send to
TYLENOL® Capsule Exchange
P.O. Box 2000
Maple Plain, MN 55348

Please send my coupon for free replacement caplets or tablets to:

Please print

Name _____

Address _____

City _____

State _____ Zip _____

Offer expires May 1, 1986

(Courtesy of Johnson & Johnson)

FIGURE 2-9 A special message. (Courtesy of Johnson & Johnson)

of its prior market share. Morale at the company, according to its chairman, was "higher than in years." It had acted true to the "Credo," which spelled out the company's beliefs (Figure 2-8). The euphoria lasted until February 1986 when, unbelievably, tragedy struck again.

Round II

Late in the evening of February 10, 1986, news reports began to circulate that a woman had died in Yonkers, New York, after taking poisoned capsules of extra-strength Tylenol.

The nightmare for Johnson & Johnson began anew.

Once again, the company sprang into action. Chairman Burke addressed reporters at a news conference a day after the incident. A phone survey found that the public didn't blame the company. However, with the discovery of other poisoned Tylenol capsules two days later, the nightmare intensified. The company recorded 15,000 toll-free calls at its Tylenol hot line. Once again, production of Tylenol capsules was halted. "I'm heartsick," Burke told the press. "We didn't believe it could happen again, and nobody else did either."

This time, although Tylenol earned some 13 percent of the company's net profits, the firm decided once and for all to cease production of its over-the-counter medications in capsule form. It offered to replace all unused Tylenol capsules with new Tylenol caplets, a solid form of medication that was less tamper-prone (Figure 2-9). This time the withdrawal of its capsules cost Johnson & Johnson more than $150 million after taxes.

Once again, in the face of tragedy, the company and its chairman received high marks. As President Reagan said at a White House reception two weeks after the crisis hit, "Jim Burke of Johnson & Johnson, you have our deepest appreciation for living up to the highest ideals of corporate responsibility and grace under pressure."

Questions

1. What might have been the consequences if Johnson & Johnson had decided to "tough out" the first reports of Tylenol-related deaths and not recall the product?

2. What other public relations options did Johnson & Johnson have in responding to the first round of Tylenol murders?

3. Do you think the company made a wise decision by reintroducing extra-strength Tylenol?

4. In light of the response of other companies not to move precipitously when faced with a crisis, do you think Johnson & Johnson should have acted so quickly to remove the Tylenol product when the second round of Tylenol murders occurred in 1986?

5. What specific lessons can be derived from the way in which Johnson & Johnson handled the public relations aspects of these tragedies?

6. What was the media environment when the Tylenol crises occurred? How might the results have differed if the crises occurred today?

7. See what information Johnson & Johnson offers for its customers on the Tylenol Web site (www.tylenol.com). Follow the links to the Care Cards, House Calls, and FAQ sections. How do these sections demonstrate Johnson & Johnson's concern for customers? How do you think Johnson & Johnson would use this Web site to communicate with the public if new health scares surfaced?

For further information on the first round of Tylenol murders, see Jerry Knight, "Tylenol's Maker Shows How to Respond to Crisis," *Washington Post* (October 11, 1982): 1; Thomas Moore, "The Fight to Save Tylenol," *Fortune* (November 29, 1982): 48; Michael Waldholz, "Tylenol Regains Most of No. 1 Market Share, Amazing Doomsayers," *Wall Street Journal* (December 24, 1982): 1, 19; and *60 Minutes,* CBS-TV (December 19, 1982).

For further information on the second round of Tylenol murders, see Irvin Molotsky, "Tylenol Maker Hopeful on Solving Poisoning Case," *New York Times* (February 20, 1986); Steven Prokesch, "A Leader in a Crisis," *New York Times* (February 19, 1986): B4; Michael Waldholz, "For Tylenol's Manufacturer, the Dilemma Is to Be Aggressive—But Not Appear Pushy," *Wall Street Journal* (February 20, 1986): 27; and "Tylenol II: How a Company Responds to a Calamity," *U.S. News & World Report* (February 24, 1986): 49.

For an overall view of Johnson & Johnson and Tylenol, see Lawrence G. Foster, *Robert Wood Johnson: The Gentleman Rebel.* State College, PA: Lillian Press, 1999.

Voice of Authority

An Interview with Edward L. Bernays

Edward L. Bernays, who died in 1995 at the age of 103, was a public relations patriarch. A nephew of Sigmund Freud, Bernays pioneered the application of the social sciences to public relations. In partnership with his late wife, he advised presidents of the United States, industrial leaders, and legendary figures from Enrico Caruso to Eleanor Roosevelt. This interview was conducted with the legendary counselor in his 98th year.

When you taught the first public relations class, did you ever envision the field growing to its present stature?
I gave the first course in public relations after *Crystallizing Public Opinion* was published in 1923. I decided that one way to give the term "counsel on public relations" status was to lecture at a university on the principles, practices, and ethics of the new vocation. New York University was willing to accept my offer to do so. But I never envisioned at that time that the vocation would spread throughout the United States and then throughout the free world.

What were the objectives of that first public relations course?
The objectives were to give status to the new vocation. Many people still believed the term "counsel on public relations" was a euphemism for publicity man, press agent, flack. Even H. L. Mencken, in his book on the American language, ranked it as such. But in his *Supplement to the American Language,* published some years later, he changed his viewpoint and used my definition of the term.

What are the most significant factors that have led to the rise in public relations practice?
The most significant factor is the rise in people power and its recognition by leaders. Theodore Roosevelt helped bring this about with his Square Deal. Woodrow Wilson helped with his New Freedom, and so did Franklin Delano Roosevelt with his New Deal. And this tradition was continued as time went on.

Do you have any gripes with the way public relations is practiced today?

I certainly do. The meanings of words in the United States have the stability of soap bubbles. Unless words are defined as to their meaning by law, as in the case of professions—for instance, law, medicine, architecture—they are in the public domain. Anyone can use them. Today, any plumber or car salesman or unethical character can call himself or herself a public relations practitioner. Many who call themselves public relations practitioners have no education, training, or knowledge of what the field is. And the public equally has little understanding of the meaning of the two words. Until licensing and registration are introduced, this will continue to be the situation.

What pleases you most about current public relations practice?

What pleases me most is that there are, indeed, practitioners who regard their activity as a profession, an art applied to a science, in which the public interest, and not pecuniary motivation, is the primary consideration; and also that outstanding leaders in society are grasping the meaning and significance of the activity.

How would you compare the caliber of today's public relations practitioner with that of the practitioner of the past?

The practitioner today has more education in his subject. But, unfortunately, education for public relations varies with the institution where it is being conducted. This is due to the lack of a standard definition. Public relations activity is applied social science to the social attitudes or actions of employers or clients.

Where do you think public relations will be 20 years from now?

It is difficult to appraise where public relations will be 20 years from now. I don't like the tendency of advertising agencies gobbling up large public relations organizations. That is like surgical instrument manufacturers gobbling up surgical medical colleges or law book publishers gobbling up law colleges. However, if licensing and registration take place, then the vocation is assured a long lifetime, as long as democracy's.

Suggested Readings

Alsop, Ron J., *The 18 Immutable Laws of Corporate Reputation: Creating, Protecting, and Repairing Your Most Valuable Asset.* New York: Free Press, 2004. Written by a *Wall Street Journal* news editor, this book shows the benefits of a good reputation, the consequences of a bad one, and how to measure and nurture reputation.

Baskin, Otis. *The Profession and the Practice of Public Relations,* 4th ed. New York: McGraw-Hill, 1996.

Bernays, Edward L. *Crystallizing Public Opinion.* New York: Liveright, 1961. The original 1923 version was the first significant book in the field. It deserves to be read for its historical value as well as for the amazingly progressive ideas that its author forwarded about the modern practice for which he was so responsible.

Bernays, Edward L. *Public Relations.* Norman: University of Oklahoma Press, 1963. This book offers an informative history of public relations, from Ancient Sumeria through the 1940s, and includes Bernays's view of what public relations ought to stand for.

Bernays, Edward L. *The Later Years: Public Relations Insights, 1956–1986.* Rhinebeck, NY: H & M, 1987. Essentially, this is a series of columns that Edward Bernays authored for the late *Public Relations Quarterly.*

Boorstin, Daniel J. *The Image: A Guide to Pseudo Events in America.* New York: Harper & Row, 1964. A not-very-flattering account of America's emphasis on image over reality, written 40 years ago by one of the nation's most eminent 20th-century thinkers.

Burson, Harold. "A Decent Respect to the Opinion of Mankind." Speech delivered at the Raymond Simon Institute for Public Relations (Burson-Marsteller, 866 Third Avenue, New York, NY 10022), March 5, 1987. This speech highlights public relations activities that have influenced the United States from colonial times to the present day.

Chomsky, Noam. *Necessary Illusions: Thought Control in Democratic Societies.* Boston: South End Press, 1989. A contrary view to Bernays's concept of public relations, this book, written by a well-known social critic, expresses all "that is wrong" about the media and attempts to persuade the public.

Cutlip, Scott M. *Public Relations History from the 17th to the 20th Century.* Hillsdale, NJ: Lawrence Erlbaum Associates, 1995.

Cutlip, Scott M. *The Unseen Power—Public Relations, A History.* Hillsdale, NJ: Lawrence Erlbaum Associates, 1994. This 800-page book is perhaps the definitive history of public relations in the 20th century. And it's not always "positive" either.

Key, V. O., Jr. *Public Opinion and American Democracy.* New York: Alfred A. Knopf, 1964. A pragmatic look at the role of public opinion and political activists in 20th-century democracies.

Marchand, Roland. *Creating the Corporate Soul: The Rise of Public Relations and Corporate Imagery in American Big Business.* Berkeley and Los Angeles: University of California Press, 2001.

Mitroff, Ian I., and Warren Bennis. *The Unreality Industry: The Deliberate Manufacturing of Falsehood and What It Is Doing to Our Lives.* London, England: Oxford University Press, 1993.

Nevins, Allan. "The Constitution Makers and the Public, 1785–1790." An address before the Conference of the Public Relations Society of America, November 13, 1962. Reprinted as "At the Beginning . . . A Series of Lecture-Essays." Gainesville, FL: The Institute for Public Relations Research and Education, 1997.

Ni, Chen, and Hugh Culbertson. *International Public Relations, A Comparative Analysis.* Hillsdale, NJ: Lawrence Erlbaum Associates, 1996.

Olasky, Marvin N. "Roots of Modern Public Relations: The Bernays Doctrine." *Public Relations Quarterly,* Winter 1984. Olasky wages a spirited defense of Bernays as a more pragmatic and effective public relations representative than Ivy Lee.

Ries, Al, and Laura Ries. *The Fall of Advertising and the Rise of PR.* New York: HarperBusiness, 2002. A well-known advertising professional and his daughter take on the common wisdom that advertising is more effective than public relations.

Schramm, Wilbur. *The Story of Communication: Cave Painting to Microchip.* New York: Harper & Row, 1988. One of the nation's foremost communications historians traces the sweep and scope of communications evolution.

Tedlow, Richard S. *Keeping the Corporate Image: Public Relations and Business, 1900–1950.* Greenwich, CT: JAI Press, 1979. An analytical and comprehensive history of corporate public relations in the first half of the 20th century.

Notes

1. John E. Harr and Peter J. Johnson, *The Rockefeller Century: Three Generations of America's Greatest Family* (New York: Simon & Schuster, 1988): 129.
2. "World Internet Usage and Population Statistics," Internet World Stats—Web Site Directory, Miniwatts International, Ltd., 2005.
3. Scott M. Cutlip, Allen H. Center, and Glen M. Broom, *Effective Public Relations,* 8th ed. (Upper Saddle River, NJ: Prentice Hall, 2000): 102.
4. Fraser P. Seitel, "The Company You Keep," http://www.odwyerpr.com (July 22, 2002).
5. "Boston's Cardinal Law Resists Calls for His Resignation," CNN.com (April 12, 2002).
6. Harold Burson, speech at Utica College of Syracuse University, Utica, NY (March 5, 1987).
7. Ray Eldon Hiebert, *Courtier to the Crowd: The Story of Ivy L. Lee and the Development of Public Relations* (Ames: Iowa State University Press, 1966).
8. Harr and Johnson, p. 130.
9. Interview with David Rockefeller, November 30, 2005.
10. Cited in Alvin Moscow, *The Rockefeller Inheritance* (Garden City, NY: Doubleday, 1977): 23.
11. Edward L. Bernays, "Bernays: 62 Years in Public Relations," *Public Relations Quarterly* (Fall 1981): 8.
12. "Burson Hailed as PR's No. 1 Influential Figure," *PR Week* (October 18, 1999): 1.
13. Cited in Noel L. Griese, "The Employee Communications Philosophy of Arthur W. Page," *Public Relations Quarterly* (Winter 1977): 8–12.
14. Noel L. Griese, *Arthur W. Page: Publisher, Public Relations Pioneer, Patriot* (Tucker, GA: Anvil Publishers, 2001).
15. "An Afternoon with Peter Drucker," *The Public Relations Strategist* (Fall 1998): 10.
16. Charles J. Hanley, "War Making Headlines But Peace Breaks Out," Associated Press (August 30, 2004).
17. Enid Burns, "Online Shopping's Holiday Surge," ClickZ Stats, www.clickZ.com/stats (December 16, 2005).
18. "Population Explosion," ClickZ Stats www.clickZ.com/stats, (November 3, 2005).
19. John L. Paluszek, "Public Relations Students: Today Good, Tomorrow Better," *The Public Relations Strategist* (Winter 2000): 27.
20. J. David Pincus, "Changing How Future Managers View Us," *The Public Relations Strategist* (Spring 1997).
21. Jack O'Dwyer (Ed.), *O'Dwyer's Directory of Corporate Communications* (New York: J. R. O'Dwyer Co., 2004).
22. Jack O'Dywer (Ed.), *O'Dwyer's Directory of Public Relations Firms* (New York: J. R. O'Dwyer Co., 2005).
23. Joseph Nocera, "Living in the Enron Dream World," *New York Times* (December 17, 2005): C1–12.

3 Communication

In the 21st century, the whole world is truly "wired." The power of communication, through the oral and written word and the images that flash around the world to millions of people in real time, is more awesome than any individual or group or even nation.

What happens at a market in Baghdad is witnessed in a manner of seconds in Berlin and Bangkok and Boise. The world has become, as a 20th century communications professor once put it, "a global village."

And perhaps no individual is more responsible for this global phenomenon than this man:

Sir Arthur Clarke was a British science fiction novelist who, in 1945, wrote a short article that talked about combining the technologies of rocketry, wireless communications, and radar to envision an extraterrestrial system that relied on orbiting space stations to relay radio signals around the world.

Today, more than 60 years later, Sir Arthur's vision has morphed into the global system of two dozen geo-synchronous satellites that orbit 22,300 miles above the earth, transmitting words and images around the world at the speed of light. Thanks to the "Clarke Orbit" and the uplink technology that continues to be developed, events from wars to coronations to courtroom trials are now broadcast globally at 186,000 miles per second (Figure 3-2).[1]

FIGURE 3-1 Father of the communications satellite. Sir Arthur C. Clarke, science fiction novelist, in 1945 invented the concept that today beams images around the world in real time. (Photo by Rohan De Silva, Courtesy Arthur C. Clarke Foundation)

FIGURE 3-2 **Show trial.** The murder and torture trial of Saddam Hussein, his half-brother Barzan Ibrahim al-Tikriti, and six co-defendants was broadcast for all the world to see in real time in 2005 and 2006. (AP Wide World Photos)

As a consequence, communication has never been a more potent tool, and communications must be handled with great care.

Which brings us back to public relations.

First and foremost, the public relations practitioner is a professional communicator. More than anyone else in an organization, the practitioner must know how to communicate.

Fundamentally, communication is a process of exchanging information, imparting ideas, and making oneself understood by others. It also includes understanding others in return. Indeed, *understanding* is critical to the communications process. If one person sends a message to another, who disregards or misunderstands it, then communication hasn't taken place. But if the idea received is the one intended, then communication has occurred. Thus, a boss who sends subordinates dozens of e-mails isn't necessarily communicating with them. If the idea received is not the one intended, then the sender has done little more than convert personal thoughts to words—and there they lie.

Although all of us are endowed with some capacity for communicating, the public relations practitioner must be better at it than most. Before public relations practitioners can earn the respect of management and become trusted advisers, they must demonstrate a mastery of many communications skills—writing, speaking, listening, promoting, and counseling. Just as the comptroller is expected to be an adept accountant, and the legal counsel is expected to be an accomplished lawyer, the public relations professional must be the best communicator in the organization. Period.

Goals of Communication

When communication is planned, as it should be in public relations, every communication must have a goal, an objective, a purpose. If not, why communicate in the first place? What are typical communications goals?

1. **To inform.** Often the communications goal of an organization is to inform or educate a particular public. For example, before holidays, the Automobile Association of America (AAA) will release information providing advice on safe driving habits for long trips. In so doing, the AAA is performing a valuable information service to the public.

2. **To persuade.** A regular goal of public relations communicators is to persuade people to take certain actions. Such persuasion needn't be overly aggressive; it can be subtle. For example, a mutual fund annual report that talks about the fund's long history of financial strength and security may provide a subtle persuasive appeal for potential investors.

3. **To motivate.** Motivation of employees to "pull for the team" is a regular organizational communications goal. For example, the hospital CEO who outlines to her managers the institution's overriding objectives in the year ahead is communicating to motivate these key employees to action.

4. **To build mutual understanding.** Often communicators have as their goal the mere attainment of understanding of a group in opposition. For example, a community group that meets with a local plant manager to express its concern about potential pollution of the neighborhood is seeking understanding of the group's rationale and concern.

The point is that whether written release, annual report, speech, or meeting—all are valid public relations communications vehicles designed to achieve communications goals with key constituent publics. Again, the best way to achieve one's goals is through an integrated and strategically planned approach.

Traditional Theories of Communication

Books have been written on the subject of communications theory. This book is *not* one of them. Consequently, we won't attempt to provide an all-encompassing discussion on how people ensure that their messages get through to others. But in its most basic sense, communication commences with a source, who sends a message through a medium to reach a receiver who, we hope, responds in the manner we intended.

Many theories exist—from the traditional to the contemporary—about the most effective ways for a source to send a message through a medium to elicit a positive response. Here are but a few.

- One early theory of communication, the *two-step flow theory,* stated that an organization would beam a message first to the mass media, which would then deliver that message to the great mass of readers, listeners, and viewers for their response. This theory may have given the mass media too much credit. People today are influenced by a variety of factors, of which the media may be one but is not necessarily the dominant one.

- Another theory, the *concentric-circle theory,* developed by pollster Elmo Roper, assumed that ideas evolve gradually to the public at large, moving in concentric circles from great thinkers to great disciples to great disseminators to lesser disseminators to the politically active to the politically inert. This theory suggests that people pick up and accept ideas from leaders, whose impact on public opinion may be greater than that of the mass media. The overall study of how communication is used for direction and control is called *cybernetics.*

- The communications theories of the late Pat Jackson have earned considerable respect in the public relations field. Jackson's public relations communications models, too, emphasized "systematic investigation—setting clear strategic goals and identifying key stakeholders."[2] One Jackson communications approach to stimulate behavioral change encompassed a five-step process:

1. **Building awareness.** Build awareness through all the standard communications mechanisms that we discuss in this book, from publicity to advertising to public speaking to word of mouth.

2. **Developing a latent readiness.** This is the stage at which people begin to form an opinion based on such factors as knowledge, emotion, intuition, memory, and relationships.

3. **Triggering event.** A triggering event is something—either natural or planned—that makes you want to change your behavior. Slimming down in time for beach season is an example of a natural triggering event. Staged functions, rallies, campaigns, and appearances are examples of planned triggering events.

4. **Intermediate behavior.** This is what Jackson called the "investigative" period, when an individual is determining how best to apply a desired behavior. In this stage, information about process and substance is sought.

5. **Behavioral change.** The final step is the adoption of new behavior.

■ Another traditional public relations theory of communications is the basic *S-E-M-D-R communications process.* This model suggests that the communication process begins with the source (S), who issues a message (M) to a receiver (R), who then decides what action to take, if any, relative to the communication. Two additional steps, an encoding stage (E), in which the source's original message is translated and conveyed to the receiver, and a decoding stage (D), in which the receiver interprets the encoded message and takes action, complete the model. It is in these latter two stages, encoding and decoding, that the public relations function most comes into play.

■ There are even those who focus on the growing import of the "silent" theories of communication. The most well known of these, Elisabeth Noelle-Neumann's *spiral of silence,* suggests that communications that work well depend on the silence and nonparticipation of a huge majority. This so-called "silent majority" fears becoming isolated from and therefore ostracized by most of their colleagues. Thus, they invariably choose to "vote with the majority."[3]

All of these theories and many others have great bearing on how public relations professionals perform their key role as organizational communicators.

Contemporary Theories of Communication

Many other communications theories abound today as Internet communication changes the ways and speed at which many of us receive our messages. Professor Everett Rogers talks about the unprecedented "diffusion" of the Internet as a communications vehicle that spans cultures and geographies. Others point to the new reality of "convergence" of video, data and voice, mobile and fixed, traditional and new age communications mechanisms with which public relations professionals must be familiar.

The complexity of communications in contemporary society—particularly in terms of understanding one's audience—has led scholars to author additional "audience-centric" theories of how best to communicate.

- *Constructivism* suggests that knowledge is *constructed,* not transmitted. Constructivism, therefore, is concerned with the cognitive process that proceeds the actual communication within a given situation rather than with the communication itself.

  This theory suggests that in communicating, it is important to have some knowledge of the receiver and his or her beliefs, predilections, and background. Simply dispensing information and expecting receivers to believe in or act on it, according to this theory, is a fool's errand. The task of the communicator, rather, is to understand and identify how receivers think about the issues in question and then work to challenge these preconceived notions and, hopefully, convert audience members into altering their views.[4]

- *Coordinated management of meaning* is a theory of communications based on social interaction. Basically, this theory posits that when we communicate—primarily through conversation—we construct our own social realities of what is going on and what kind of action is appropriate. We each have our own "stories" of life experience, which we share with others in conversation. When we interact, say the creators of this theory, we attempt to "coordinate" our own beliefs, morals, and ideas of "good" and "bad" with those of others so that a mutual outcome might occur.

  The point, again, is that communication, rather than being the simple "transmission" of ideas, is rather a complex, interconnected series of events, with each participant affected by the other.[5]

- Another widely discussed theoretical model of public relations communications are the *Grunig-Hunt public relations models,* formulated by Professors James E. Grunig and Todd Hunt. Grunig and Hunt proposed four models that define public relations communications.

    1. **Press agentry/publicity.** This early form of communication, say the authors, is essentially one-way communication that beams messages from a source to a receiver with the express intention of winning favorable media attention.

    2. **Public information.** This is another early form of one-way communication designed not necessarily to persuade but rather to inform. Both this and the press agentry model have been linked to the common notion of "public relations as propaganda."

    3. **Two-way asymmetric.** This is a more sophisticated two-way communication approach that allows an organization to put out its information and to receive feedback from its publics about that information. Under this model, an organization wouldn't necessarily change decisions as a result of feedback but rather would alter its responses to more effectively persuade publics to accept its position.

    4. **Two-way symmetric.** This preferred way of communicating advocates free and equal information flow between an organization and its publics, based on mutual understanding. This approach is more "balanced"—*symmetrical*—with the public relations communicator serving as a mediator between the organization and the publics.[6]

These are but a few of the prominent theories of communications—all revolving around "feedback"—of which public relations practitioners must be aware. In Chapter 4, we review relevant theories in forming public opinion.

The Word

Communication begins with words. Words are among our most personal and potent weapons. Words can soothe us, bother us, or infuriate us. They can bring us together or drive us apart. They can even cause us to kill or be killed. Words mean different things to different people, depending on their backgrounds, occupations, education, and geographic locations. What one word means to you might be dramatically different from what that same word means to your neighbor. The study of what words really mean is called *semantics,* and the science of semantics is a peculiar one indeed.

Words are perpetually changing in our language. What a word denotes according to the dictionary may be thoroughly dissimilar to what it connotes in its more emotional or visceral sense. Even the simplest words—*liberal, conservative, profits, consumer activists*—can spark semantic skyrockets.

Particularly sensitive today is so-called "discriminatory language"—words that connote offensive meanings—in areas such as gender, race, ethnicity, and physical impairment. Words such as *firemen, manpower, housewife, cripple, midget, Negro,* may be considered offensive. While "political correctness" can go too far, it is nonetheless incumbent on public relations communicators to carefully assess words before using them.

Many times, without knowledge of the territory, the semantics of words may make no sense. Take the word *fat.* In our American culture and vernacular, a person who is fat is generally not associated with the apex of attractiveness. A person who is thin, on the other hand, may indeed be considered highly attractive. But along came 50 Cent and Kanye West and Jay-Z and hip-hop, and pretty soon *phat*—albeit with a new spelling—became the baddest of the bad, the coolest of the cool, the height of fetching pulchritudinousness (if you smell what I'm cookin').

Words have a significant influence on the message conveyed to the ultimate receiver. Thus the responsibility of a public relations professional, entrusted with *encoding* a client's message, is significant. Public relations encoders must understand, for example, that in today's technologically changing world, words and phrases change meaning and drop out of favor with blinding speed (see Talking Points). During the past century, the English language has added an average of 900 new words every year.[7] For an intended message to get through, then, a public relations "interpreter" must accurately understand and effectively translate the true meaning—with all its semantic complications—to the receiver.

The Message

The real importance of words, in a public relations sense, is using them to build the messages that move publics to action. Framing "key messages" lies at the top of every public relations to-do list.

Messages may be transmitted in a myriad of communications media: speeches, newspapers, radio, television, news releases, press conferences, broadcast reports, and face-to-face meetings. Communications theorists differ on what exactly constitutes the message, but here are three of the more popular explanations.

1. **The content is the message.** According to this theory, which is far and away the most popular, the content of a communication—what it says—constitutes its message. According to this view, the real importance of a communication— the message—lies in the meaning of an article or in the intent of a speech. Neither the medium through which the message is being communicated nor the individual doing the communicating is as important as the content. This is why

Talking Points

Profizzle of Lexicizzle

The 21st century lexicon of current words and phrases is ever-changing. What's *in* today is *out* tomorrow.

Doubt it?

Then translate the following phrases that your parents considered colloquial.

- *I'll be a monkey's uncle*
- *This is a fine kettle of fish*
- *Knee high to a grasshopper*
- *Going like 60*
- *Iron Curtain*
- *Domino theory*

Or explain what they meant by the following items.

- *Boob tube*
- *L.D.*
- *Segregation*
- *Mailman*
- *Stewardess*

Or reconcile what you mean with what they mean by the following terms.

- *Gay*
- *Menu*
- *Virus*
- *Crack, smack, snow,* and, of course, *blow*

Words change so quickly these days that we even have new instant languages being created before our eyes. Among them, the *gangsta* lexicon of one, Snoop Dogg (Figure 3-3), affectionately known as *izzle speak,* is designed primarily to confuse anyone who isn't an urban Black rapper. To wit:

FIGURE 3-3 Rapper Snoop Dogg. The Profizzle of Lexicizzle himself. (AP Wide World Photos)

- *Valentizzle*
- *Tonizzle*
- *Televizzle*
- *Secretary of State Condoleezza Rizzle*

All of which means that for public relations professionals in the 21st century, properly interpreting messages to key publics has become a complicated proposition.

Fo shizzle.

professional public relations people insist on accurate and truthful content in the messages they prepare.

2. **The medium is the message.** Other communications theorists argue that the content of a communication may be less important than the medium in which the message is carried. This theory was originally proffered by the late Canadian communications professor Marshall McLuhan. This theory is relevant in today's hyper-media society, where the reputation and integrity of a particular media source may vary wildly. For example, a story carried on an Internet blog would generally carry considerably less weight than one reported in *The New York Times.* That is not to say that for some receivers, a particular blog's credibility might surpass that of the *Times.* Personal bias, as we will discuss, is always

brought to bear in assessing the power and believability of communications messages. In other words, to some, conservative Fox News is the "last word" in credibility; to others, it's the liberal *Los Angeles Times*.

3. ***The man*—or, to avoid political incorrectness, the *person*—is the message.** Still other theorists argue that it is neither the content nor the medium that is the message, but rather the speaker. For example, the evil Adolf Hitler was a master of persuasion. His minister of propaganda, Josef Goebbels, used to say, "Any man who thinks he can persuade, can persuade." Hitler practiced this self-fulfilling communications prophecy to the hilt. Feeding on the perceived desires of the German people, Hitler was concerned much less with the content of his remarks than with their delivery. His maniacal rantings and frantic gestures seized public sentiment and sent friendly crowds into a frenzy. In every way, Hitler himself was the primary message of his communications.

Today, in a similar vein, we often refer to a leader's charisma. Frequently, the charismatic appeal of a political leader may be more important than what that individual says. Such has been the historic appeal of Fidel Castro, for example. Political orators in particular, such as former President Bill Clinton, the Reverend Jesse Jackson, and former Governor Mario Cuomo, for example, can move an audience by the very inflection of their words. Experienced speakers, from James Carville on the left to Rush Limbaugh on the right, to retired military leaders like Colin Powell and Norman Schwarzkopf, to sports coaches like Pat Riley and Phil Jackson, can also rally listeners with their personal charismatic demeanor.

Speaking of Ethics

Messing with the Medium

When does the medium become an "instrument of torture"?

According to Human Rights Watch, when it takes the form of forced listening to the rapturous rap music of Dr. Dre and Eminem (Figure 3-4).

In 2005, the human rights watchdog group accused the United States of operating a secret prison in Afghanistan and "torturing" prisoners by keeping them chained to walls in pitch black conditions while listening to loud, round-the-clock warbling from Eminem and Dr. Dre.

One detainee said he was forced to endure the rapping for 20 straight days before the music was replaced by "horrible ghost laughter and Halloween sounds."

Human Rights Watch alleged that such communication amounted to "cruel and unusual punishment" and called for an official investigation of the communications methods of the United States.

FIGURE 3-4 Will the real Slim Shady please shut up! Alleged communications perpetrator, Eminem. (AP and Wide World Photos)

The point is that a speaker's words, face, body, eyes, attitude, timing, wit, presence—all form a composite that, as a whole, influences the listener. In such cases, the source of the communication becomes every bit as important as the message itself.

Receiver's Bias

Communicating a message is futile unless it helps achieve the desired goal of the communicator. As the bulk of the communications theories cited in this chapter suggest, the element of feedback is critical. And important to feedback is understanding the precognitions and predilections that receivers bring to a particular message.

Stated another way, how a receiver decodes a message depends greatly on that person's own perception. How an individual comprehends a message is a key to effective communications. The fact is, everyone is biased; no two people perceive a message identically. Personal biases are nurtured by many factors, including stereotypes, symbols, semantics, peer group pressures, and—especially in today's culture—the media.

Stereotypes

Everyone lives in a world of stereotypical figures. Gen Xers, policy wonks, feminists, bankers, blue-collar workers, PR types, and thousands of other characterizations cause people to think of specific images. Public figures, for example, are typecast regularly. The dumb blond, the bigoted right-winger, the bleeding-heart liberal, the computer geek, and the snake oil salesman are the kinds of stereotypes perpetuated by our society.

Like it or not, most of us are victims of such stereotypes. For example, research indicates that a lecture delivered by a person wearing glasses will be perceived as significantly more believable than the same lecture delivered before the same audience by the same lecturer without glasses. The stereotyped impression of people with glasses is that they are more trustworthy and more believable.

Also, like it or not, such stereotypes influence communication.

Symbols

The clenched-fist salute, the swastika, and the thumbs-up sign all leave distinct impressions on most people. Marshaled properly, symbols can be used as effective persuasive elements (Figure 3-5). The Statue of Liberty, the Red Cross, the Star of David, and many other symbols have been used traditionally for positive persuasion. On the other hand, the symbols chosen by the terrorists of September 11, 2001—the World Trade Center, the Pentagon, and most likely the U.S. Capitol and the White House—were clearly chosen because of their symbolic value as American icons.

Semantics

Public relations professionals make their living largely by knowing how to use words effectively to communicate desired meanings. Occasionally, this is tricky because the same words may hold contrasting meanings for different people. Today's contentious debate about abortion is a case in point, with the debate buttressed by confusing semantic

FIGURE 3-5 What's in a symbol?
Located on Mount Lee in Griffith Park, the Hollywood sign is the most famous sign in the world. Originally built in 1923 for $21,000 as an advertising gimmick to promote home sales, the 45-foot high, 450-foot long, 480,000-pound sign was restored in 1978—Tinseltown's most enduring and instantly identifiable symbol. (Courtesy of Global Icons)

terms—*pro-life* to signify those against abortion and *pro-choice* to signify those in favor of allowing abortions.

Controversy also surrounds the semantics associated with certain forms of rap and hip-hop music. To critics, some artists preach a philosophy of violence and hate and prejudice against women. But gangsta rappers claim that they are merely "telling it like it is" or "reporting what we see in the streets." When reporters and record company executives give credence to such misguided rhetoric, they become just as responsible as the artists for the often unfortunate outcomes that result—for example, the child pornography charges against singer R. Kelly in 2003 and the sexual battery verdict against rapper Mystikal in 2002.

Because language and the meanings of words change constantly, semantics must be handled with extreme care. Good communicators always consider the consequences of the words they plan to use before using them.

Peer Groups

In one famous study, students were asked to point out, in progression, the shortest of the following three lines.

A _____

B _____

C _____

Although line B is obviously the shortest, each student in the class except one was told in advance to answer that line C was the shortest. The object of the test was to see whether the one student would agree with his peers. Results generally indicated that, to a statistically significant degree, all students, including the uncoached one, chose C.

Such an experiment is an example of how peer pressure prevails in terms of influencing personal bias. Public relations professionals, intent on framing persuasive communications messages, must understand the importance of peer group influences on attitudes and actions.

Media

The power of the media—particularly as an agenda setter—is substantial. Agenda-setting is the creation of public awareness by the media—the ability to tell us what issues are important. As early as 1922, the legendary newspaper columnist Walter Lippman was concerned that the media had the power to present biased images to the public. Indeed, two basic assumptions underlie most research on agenda-setting: (1) the press and the media do not reflect reality; they filter and shape it; (2) media concentration on a few issues and subjects leads the public to perceive those issues as more important than other issues.[8]

In the summer of 2005, for example, the media seized on the leak of information from the Bush administration identifying the CIA agent wife of a Bush critic. For months, the media "agenda" was focused on revealing the source of the illegal leak. In December of that same year, however, when another leak on page one of the *New York Times* revealed that the Bush administration had wiretapped, without a court order, American citizens suspected of al-Qaeda ties, the media ignored the leak and jumped, instead, on the wiretap story. Such are the 21st-century vagaries of agenda-setting by the media.

By the same token, in interesting the media to pursue client-oriented stories, public relations professionals also have a direct role in setting the agenda for others. The point is that people base perceptions on what they read or hear, often without bothering to dig further to elicit the facts. This is a two-edged sword: Although appearances are sometimes revealing, they are also often deceiving.

Feedback

A communicator must get feedback from a receiver to know what messages are or are not getting through and how to structure future communications.

You really aren't communicating unless someone is at the other end to hear and understand what you're saying and then react to it. This situation is analogous to the old mystery of the falling tree in the forest: Does it make a noise when it hits the ground if there's no one there to hear it? Regardless of the answer, effective communication doesn't take place if a message doesn't reach the intended receivers and exert the desired effect on those receivers.

Even if a communication is understood clearly, there is no guarantee that the motivated action will be the desired one. In fact, a message may trigger several different effects.

1. **It may change attitudes.** This result, however, is very difficult to achieve and rarely happens.

2. **It may crystallize attitudes.** This outcome is much more common. Often a message will influence receivers to take actions they might already have been thinking about taking but needed an extra push to accomplish. For example, a receiver might want to contribute to a certain charity, but seeing a child's photo on a contribution canister might crystallize his or her attitude sufficiently to trigger action.

3. **It may create a wedge of doubt.** Communication can sometimes force receivers to modify their points of view. A persuasive message on cable TV can cause viewers to question their original thinking on an issue.

4. **It may do nothing.** At times, the best laid communication plans result in no action at all. For years, the expensive communications campaigns to reduce cigarette sales, waged by government and fueled by a $246 billion industry settlement, yielded less than stellar results. More recently, the campaign has started to pay off, with the number of smokers among U.S. adults numbering 20.9 percent in 2004, down from 21.6 percent in 2003 and 22.5 percent in 2002.[9] This indicates another communication truism—changing attitudes and motivating action takes time.

Whether the objectives of a communication have been met can often be assessed by such things as the amount of sales, number of letters, or number of votes obtained. If individuals take no action after receiving a communication, feedback must still be sought. In certain cases, although receivers have taken no discernible action, they may have understood and even passed on the message to other individuals. This person-to-person relay of received messages creates a two-step flow of communications: (1) vertically from a particular source and (2) horizontally from interpersonal contact. The targeting of opinion leaders as primary receivers, for example, is based on the hope that they will distribute received messages horizontally within their own communities.

Talking Points

Whaaat?

Extra credit for anyone who can decode the following communication (in the form of one of the longest sentences in the history of the free world):

> We respectfully petition, request, and entreat that due and adequate provision be made, this day and the date herein after subscribed, for the satisfying of this petitioner's nutritional requirements and for the organizing of such methods as may be deemed necessary and proper to assure the reception by and for said petitioner of such quantities of baked products as shall, in the judgment of the aforesaid petitioner, constitute a sufficient supply thereof.

Whaaat? In other words:

> Give us this day our daily bread.

Ohhh. Perhaps this one is easier to decode:

The Lord is my external–internal integrative mechanism.

I shall not be deprived of gratifications for my visogeneric hungers or my need dispositions.

He motivates me to orient myself toward a nonsocial object with affective significance.

He positions me in a nondecisional situation.

He maximizes my adjustment.

Say again?

The Lord is my shepherd.

I shall not want.

He leadeth me beside the still waters.

He maketh me to lie down in green pastures.

He restoreth my soul.

Last Word

Knowledge of how and when and to whom to communicate is the primary skill of the public relations practitioner. Above all else, public relations professionals are professional communicators. That means they must understand the theoretical underpinnings of what constitutes a credible message and how to deliver it.

The early years of the 21st century indicate that effective communication has never been more important. With the emergence of worldwide terrorism, anti-American sentiments in the Middle East and elsewhere, the deepening cultural chasm between West and East, the puncturing of the dotcom bubble and loss of trillions of dollars of wealth in society, illegal acts on the part of corporate CEOs and the conse-

quent failure of once respected companies—the need for honest, straightforward, and credible communication is critical.

There is no trick to effective communication. In addition to some facility with techniques, it is knowledge, experience, hard work, and common sense that are the basic guiding principles. Naturally, communication must follow performance; organizations must back up what they say with action. Slick brochures, a winning Web site, engaging speeches, intelligent articles, and good press may capture the public's attention, but in the final analysis the only way to obtain continued public support is through proper performance.

Discussion Starters

1. Why is it important that public relations professionals understand communication?
2. What are some principal goals of communication, and what are some contemporary examples?
3. Why do words such as *liberal, conservative, profits,* and *consumer activist* spark semantic skyrockets?
4. What is the role of a public relations professional in the S-E-M-D-R communications process?
5. What is the difference between the symmetric and asymmetric models of communication?

6. What is meant by constructivism and coordinated management of meaning?
7. What is meant by the media as *agenda setter?*
8. Why is feedback critical to the communications process?
9. What common mistakes do people make when they communicate?
10. What are some contemporary examples of the changing meanings of words over time?

Top of the Shelf

You're Too Kind: A Brief History of Flattery

Richard Stengel, New York: Simon & Schuster, 2000.

Time.com editor Richard Stengel has blown the cover off of a little practiced but sure-fire 21st-century communication device—flattery.

Stengel points out that flattery particularly "thrives" in Fortune 500 hierarchical settings and Hollywood, where greetings of "You look good!" or "Hey, you look great!" have replaced "How are you?"

He says flattering phrases must be delivered with "real enthusiasm," lest the flatterer appear to be a "toady."

In client-oriented fields, like public relations, one technique is "preemptive conformity," in which the flatterer anticipates the client's or boss's opinion and states it before one of them does. Another technique is disagreeing with the client at first, but gradually coming around to his or her opinion.

While the author is often lukewarm to the concept about which he writes, if *stroking, sucking up, schmoozing, snowing,* and *kissing-up* are part of your communications arsenal, read this book.

Wal-Mart Wages War to Regain Its Reputation

By 2005, the world's largest private employer, serving an astounding 138 million customers per week worldwide, had had enough. Wal-Mart, with 1.2 million domestic employees—called *associates*—and annual profits of $10 billion and annual sales of $256 billion—more than $21 billion a month—accounted for about 5 percent of all U.S. retail sales. In 2003 and 2004, Wal-Mart was named Most Admired Company in America by *Fortune* magazine.

How quickly they forget.

By 2005, Wal-Mart had become a target for all variety of snipers. Like a "retail Rodney Dangerfield," the bigger Wal-Mart became, the less "respect" it received.

- The United Food and Commercial Workers (UFCW) union tried to organize Wal-Mart workers, accusing the company of providing poverty-level wages and low benefits. Meanwhile, a union-backed nonprofit group, Wal-Mart Watch, tracked the company's every move on the Web.

- Local "Save Our Community—Stop Wal-Mart" efforts attempted to block the creation of Wal-Mart stores from New York, Los Angeles, and Chicago to Rosemead, California, and Bennington, Vermont.

- A group of female employees and former employees sued Wal-Mart for "systematically underpaying and underpromoting women for nearly a decade."

- A Michael Moore–like documentary film, *Wal-Mart: The High Cost of Low Price,* kicked off its nationwide run with 7,000 house party screenings.

- Right-wing groups condemned Wal-Mart for "taking Christ out of Christmas" by emphasizing the term "happy holidays" in seasonal advertising.

- One Christmas shopper even claimed she was "trampled" by Wal-Mart shoppers in a desperate 6 a.m. stampede to secure cheap DVD players. (The woman's claim was later found to be bogus.)

Over four decades, the mammoth retailer, which emerged from the simple early Bentonville, Arkansas, salesmanship of its legendary founder Sam Walton, took the criticism stoically, silently. It traditionally ignored its critics and went about its business. By the start of the 21st century, Wal-Mart was truly one of America's most insular companies.

But by the beginning of 2005, in the face of such virulent and entrenched opposition, Sam Walton's successors in Wal-Mart management were ready to take the gloves off.

"For too long," said Wal-Mart CEO H. Lee Scott, "others have had free rein to say things about our company that just aren't true. Our associates are tired of it, and we've decided it's time to draw our own line in the sand."

CEO Scott's "line in the sand" took the form of a multi-spoked public relations initiative that covered all fronts.

Starting with Research

Properly, Wal-Mart based its public relations campaign on hardnosed research of its business practices. The company engaged management consultant McKinsey and Company to study everything from its activities in local markets to its treatment of employees. The McKinsey report outlined a long-term approach to "managing change," suggesting specific areas in which Wal-Mart should concentrate. Among them were these suggestions:

- Convincing the public that Wal-Mart's wages and benefits were better than widely perceived

- Creating initiatives to benefit workers and spreading messages that it cared about its employees

- Building better local relationships

- Increasing local philanthropy

- Taking public leadership on broad societal issues

Summarized Wal-Mart communications director Mona Williams (see Voice of Authority at chapter end),

Like any company, we want to make sure our associates, customers, and local communities feel good about us.
This research provided a benchmark to help us understand what we are doing well and where we need to improve.

Accordingly, the company's public relations initiative attempted to focus on the areas the management consultants highlighted.

Blasting Out with Ads

Wal-Mart's national "coming out announcement" took the form of a blockbuster, full-page ad in the nation's leading newspapers (Figure 3-6). The ad, acknowledged CEO Scott, was an "unusual approach" for Wal-Mart.

In the ad, CEO Scott said it was time for the public hear the

unfiltered truth about Wal-Mart and time for the company to stand up on behalf of a workforce that includes 1.2 million Americans.
We understand that, as one of the most visible corporations in the world, we will be a target for criticism. When it is valid, we try to learn from it and become a better company. But we have made a commitment to our associates, customers and suppli-

WAL-MART IS WORKING FOR <u>EVERYONE</u>.

Some of our critics are working only for themselves.

— LEE SCOTT, PRESIDENT AND CEO, WAL-MART STORES, INC.
JANUARY 13, 2005

As one of the world's most visible companies, Wal-Mart expects attention and criticism. When the criticism is warranted, we use it as a tool to improve the way we operate.

But when special-interest groups and critics spread misinformation about Wal-Mart, the public deserves to hear the truth. In other words, everyone is entitled to their own opinions about our company, but they are not entitled to make up their own facts.

The truth is Wal-Mart provides great value for customers, opportunities for our workforce, economic support for communities and a helping hand for charities across America. We work hard to make life better for <u>everyone</u>. Can our critics truly say the same?

Wal-Mart is committed to those who shop with us every day — many of whom depend on us to provide value for the products they want at the lowest prices possible. Last year, more than 90 percent of Americans — 270 million people — chose to shop at Wal-Mart.

Wal-Mart is also working for our associates. It's time to set the record straight with the real facts about Wal-Mart as a place to work, presented by the people who know — not by people who presume to know.

Wal-Mart provides good jobs with excellent advancement opportunities to our 1.2 million U.S. associates.

• This year, we plan to create more than 100,000 new jobs in the United States. It takes a lot of talent to fuel that growth, which in turn offers advancement opportunity for associates who want to run some of our 58 in-store departments or move into management.

• We promote from within. Seventy-six percent of our store management team started at Wal-Mart in hourly positions.

• Our average wage for full-time hourly store associates — such as cashiers, stockers and sales associates — is almost twice the federal minimum wage.

• Wal-Mart benefits — available to full- and part-time associates — include healthcare insurance with no lifetime maximum. Associate premiums begin at less than $40 per month for an individual and less than $155 per month for a family, no matter how large.

• Other benefits include a profit-sharing/401(k) plan, merchandise discounts, company-paid life insurance, vacation pay and pay differential for those in active military service. More than half of our associates own company stock through our associate purchase plan.

• Seventy-four percent of Wal-Mart's hourly associates in the United States work full-time. That's well above the 20 – 40 percent typically found in the retail industry.

• Our workforce is unique in its size and diversity — from full-time career professionals to students working their way through college, from senior citizens seeking a break from retirement to people with disabilities.

Given these facts, it is no surprise that more than half of the associates we surveyed said the benefits package, including healthcare, was a very important factor in their decision to accept a position at Wal-Mart.

Thank you for being open to the facts about Wal-Mart. You can learn more at a Web site we are launching today — www.walmartfacts.com.

Sincerely,
Lee Scott
President and CEO
Wal-Mart Stores, Inc.

WAL★MART *Always.*

FIGURE 3-6 Breakout ad. Wal-Mart struck back at its critics with a hard-hitting, straightforward ad and CEO follow-up interviews on national television. (Reprinted by permission of Wal-Mart, Inc.)

ers that when false allegations are made about Wal-Mart, we will actively correct the record.

The ad was presaged by an exclusive CEO Scott interview with *USA Today* and a follow up blitz of interviews on national cable and broadcast programs. Wal-Mart had officially "taken off the gloves."

To follow-up, Wal-Mart launched a noncommercial Web site, www.walmartfacts.com, to help rebut the charges against it.

At least one group was immediately pleased with Wal-Mart's new open approach. The National Newspaper Association (NNA) praised the company for placing full-page ads in 336 community newspapers. Earlier, the group had criticized Wal-Mart for "ignoring" its members by not advertising enough.

Said Williams, "If there is a significant return, we would consider incorporating the local papers into our overall ad strategy."

Reaching Out to the Community

In a further effort to "reach community leaders and understand the value" that Wal-Mart brings, the company announced a spate of sponsorships, among them:

- Becoming a sponsor on National Public Radio, underwriting the African American–oriented *The Tavis Smiley Show*. As part of the sponsorship, Wal-Mart delivered the tagline, "bringing communities job opportunities, goods, and services and support for neighborhood programs."

- Sponsoring programs on public television. Another first for Wal-Mart, the company recognized public television's strong viewership among local community leaders.

- Providing $500,000 in journalism scholarships to minority students at 10 different programs, including Howard University, University of Southern California, and Columbia University.

The company also reached out to the environmental community. It announced a program to make its trucking fleet and stores more energy efficient and committed $500 million to technology to reduce greenhouse gas emissions and to seek out products with limited packaging made in sustainable ways. Wal-Mart's announcement drew immediate praise from the Sierra Club.

Unquestionably, Wal-Mart's most meaningful community relations initiative was its response in the fall of 2005 to Hurricane Katrina, which ravaged New Orleans and surrounding communities.

The company immediately committed $2 million in cash to aid emergency efforts. It followed this contribution with $15 million to jump-start a national effort to aid Katrina victims. As part of this commitment, Wal-Mart established mini-Wal-Mart stores in areas impacted by the hurricane. Items such as clothing, diapers, baby wipes, food, formula, tootbrushes, bedding, and water were given out free of charge to those with a demonstrated need.

Wal-Mart made these contributions despite that its New Orleans stores were the subject of unrestrained looting in Katrina's aftermath.

Its efforts in response to Katrina won Wal-Mart universal praise.

Fighting Back

Most striking in the Wal-Mart public relations initiative was the company's new desire to come out swinging when it felt it had been wronged publicly. In April 2005, the company took the unprecedented step of inviting reporters to its Bentonville headquarters (Figure 3-7). CEO Scott addressed the reporters and

FIGURE 3-7 Standing tall. The world's largest retailer stood ready to aggressively confront its public relations challenges in the 21st century. (Courtesy of Wal-Mart)

confronted the criticisms. After pointing to headlines on editorial pages that said, "Wal-Mart's low prices come at too high a cost," Scott told the journlists, "I'd suggest a better headline: *Wal-Mart is great for America!*"

In light of intense criticism about the supposed unfairness of Wal-Mart's health plan, the company announced it would add a more compassionate corporate program. In addition, CEO Scott called on Congress to raise the federal minimum wage.

Not unexpectedly, even these announcements were met by Wal-Mart watchers with some skepticism. Wal-Mart Watch, for one, was unimpressed. Huffed a spokesman, "The jury's out on how much of this will amount to real and meaningful, lasting change." And then the *New York Times* published a leaked Wal-Mart internal memo suggesting ways the company might cut health care costs, including hiring "healthier, younger workers."

In the winter of 2005, documentary producer Robert Greenwald released his anti–Wal-Mart film *Wal-Mart: The High Cost of Low Price*. The Greenwald film featured whistle blowers who described Wal-Mart managers cheating workers out of overtime pay and encouraging them to seek state-sponsored health care when they couldn't afford the company's insurance.

Wal-Mart itself refused to make its executives available to Greenwald. Alternatively, it responded with a New York City news conference a few blocks from the film's premiere, pointing out the documentary's unfairness. The company also investigated the events described in the film and produced its own short video to spotlight the factual errors.

Wal-Mart's boldest move, however, was the creation of a Bentonville "war room" to monitor media commentary about the film and the company and to rebut criticism. The war room was the brainchild of two political consultants hired by Wal-Mart: Michael Deaver, who was President Ronald Reagan's communications director, and Leslie Dach, who advised President Bill Clinton during his impeachment.

One test came in the form of the internal memo leaked to the *New York Times,* which detailed strengths and weaknesses of Wal-Mart's health care plan. The *Times* reported that the company desired to recruit younger, healthier workers. Wal-Mart responded immediately to put the story into proper context. It rushed its chief benefits executive onto the 6 a.m. CNBC *Squawk Box* program and saturated the media with interviews and statements.

At year-end, Wal-Mart was taken to task by religious groups and conservative broadcasters for a "happy holidays" rather than "Merry Christmas" promotion. Once again, the company faced up to the criticism. Explained a spokesman, "The slogan 'home for the holidays' was a matter of choosing a slogan that carries through the entire season" from mid-November to early January.

The Challenge Ahead

Armed with its new, more confrontational attitude and aggressive public relations program, Wal-Mart understood that in the final half of the 21st century's first decade, it would face continuing public challenge. Unlike his more reluctant predecessors, CEO Scott seemed more than willing to shoulder the burden of defending Wal-Mart in public forums.

At the end of 2005, a Zogby International survey found the following:

- 46 percent of Americans believed Wal-Mart's public image was worse than it was a year earlier.

- Only 39 percent believed that Wal-Mart was "good for America."

- 56 percent agreed with the statement that Wal-Mart was "bad for America."

So the numbers, at least according to this study, still showed Wal-Mart trailing. The study's sponsor? Wal-Mart's arch enemy, union-backed WakeUpWalMart.com.

At the start of 2006, Maryland's governor vetoed a bill mandating organizations with 10,000 employees in the state to spend at least 8 percent of payroll on health benefits. The only company that qualified for such an onerous law? You guessed it. A subsequent poll of Maryland residents urged state lawmakers to override the governor and single out Wal-Mart. The Maryland poll was conducted by none other than the same Zogby International, working for Wal-Mart's enemies.

Clearly, Wal-Mart would have no choice but to keep up the public relations battle.*

Questions

1. What do you think of Wal-Mart's original standoffish public relations policy?

2. Did it make sense to base a new public relations intiative on a management company audit and recommendations?

3. What is your view on beginning the public relations intiative with an advertisement?

4. Does it make sense to invite reporters to meet management at headquarters?

5. What public relations options did Wal-Mart have in responding to the negative documentary?

6. What were the pros and cons of hiring high-profile political consultants to organize a "war room"?

7. If you were Wal-Mart's public relations director, what would be your overall communications philosophy for the rest of the decade?

For further information, see Michael Barbaro, "A New Weapon for Wal-Mart: A War Room," *New York Times,* November 1, 2005, D1; Robert L. Borosage and Troy Peters, "Target Wal-Mart," *TomPaine.commonsense,* November 14, 2005; Kim Chipman, "Poll: Maryland Residents Back Bill Targeting Wal-Mart," *Bloomberg News,* January 11, 2006; Anne D'Innocenzio and Marcus Kabel, "Wal-Mart Tries to Boost Image with Benefits Plan," *Lansing State Journal,* LSJ.com, October 29, 2005; Mya Frazier, "Wal-Mart Under Attack: But Should It Fight Back?" *Advertising Age,* April 18, 2005, 12; Lorrie Grant, "Wal-Mart Critics Aren't Appeased," *USA Today,* January 14, 2005, 2B; Steven Greenhouse, "Wal-Mart's Chief Calls Its Critics Unrealistic," *New York Times,* April 6, 2005, C11; Hans Johnson, "A Healthy Choice: A Movement Builds to Take on Wal-Mart," *In These Times,* January 25, 2005; Ann Joyce and Ben White, "Wal-Mart Pushes to Soften Its Image, *Washington Post,* October 29, 2005, D01; David Murray, "Wal-Mart Wages War: Operation Reputation," *Ragan Report,* August 30, 2004, 3; Katherine Reynolds-Lewis, "Wal-Mart Frantic to Polish Its Image," *New Orleans Times-Picayune,* October 29, 2005; Ann Zimmerman, "Wal-Mart Boss's Unlikely Image: Defender in Chief," *The Wall Street Journal,* July 26, 2005, pA1.

*Assistance in compiling the Wal-Mart case was kindly provided by Professor Bonnie Grossman's 2005 public relations class at the College of Charleston in South Carolina, for which the author is most grateful.

Voice of Authority

An Interview with Mona Williams

Mona Williams is vice president of corporate communications for Wal-Mart Stores, Inc., the world's largest and most visible company. Williams assumed this role in 2002 and is responsible for all national and field communications. Since then, she has helped lead Wal-Mart's aggressive PR outreach in one of the most polarizing and high-profile corporate reputation battles in the country. She has made numerous television appearances on cable and broadcast programs and is frequently quoted in *The New York Times* and *Wall Street Journal*. Williams has been profiled in both *PR Strategist* and *Fast Company* magazines and *PR Week* continues to rank her role as one of the "10 Most Daunting PR Jobs."

What is Wal-Mart's general attitude toward the media?

Sam Walton did not see the need to spend much time with the news media. His view was that as long as we took care of our customers and associates, the outside world would leave us alone. While that might have worked at the time, we are living in a different world today.

Almost 2,000 stories a day are written about Wal-Mart. We know the media can play a huge role in shaping how others see us and that we need to be very engaged in building these relationships and sharing our side of the story. Experience has taught us that if we don't take every opportunity to define ourselves, others will step into the gap and do it for us—and maybe not in a positive way.

How would you characterize Wal-Mart's approach to public relations?

First, as business counselors, we first try to drive improvement in how the business operates, especially in areas that can impact reputation. This helps ensure we have a good story to tell. Part of this is acting as an "early warning system" for the company. Where are our vulnerabilities? Are we connected with people who will shoot straight with us, such as NGOs, elected officials and industry analysts?

Second, we put a lot of energy behind developing external relationships so that audiences are receptive to our story. We have embedded field media and public affairs teams in local communities and have established a diversity communication team. We have also engaged an outside firm and centralized our initiatives in a "PR room"—called *Action Alley*—to identify and engage third parties to speak on our behalf, such as Wal-Mart suppliers, community leaders, think tank members, and consumers.

Third, developing our story is an ongoing effort to determine the facts and then decide which ones matter. We conduct both fact-based and opinion research. How do our wages and benefits compare to our competitors'? How much money do we save consumers each year? How many American jobs do we create? Once we have our facts, we focus on shaping them into compelling messages that resonate with the audiences we are trying to reach. Whenever possible, we try to shape these facts into an emotional story.

Fourth, we rely on a broad range of initiatives to reach our target audiences. Key audiences include customers, community leaders, elected officials, financial analysts, suppliers, and our most important audience—Wal-Mart associates. Mass campaigns fall flat if our associates aren't telling a positive story about their own experience.

How did you respond to the anti–Wal-Mart documentary film?

There were three components to our strategy.

1. **Highlight critical errors in the movie.** Robert Greenwald's video had several critical errors, which caused us great concern. He misrepresented several events and took sensationalism to a new level. One of the cornerstones of his video was to highlight a hardware store in Ohio, which he claimed was closed because of Wal-Mart. The truth was that the store closed months before the Wal-Mart even opened. The owner of the store specifically told Greenwald that Wal-Mart was not responsible for their closing in any way, but Greenwald chose to ignore that fact.

2. **Focus on the many positive contributions Wal-Mart makes to American working families.** We focused on the economic impact, job creation, opportunity, and the thousands of dollars we save working families every day.

3. **Help promote another movie with an entirely different point of view.** In addition, we helped promote a movie produced by Ron Galloway, titled *Why Wal-Mart Works— and Why That Drives Some People Crazy!* Unlike the Greenwald video, Galloway's movie also interviewed several economists who discussed the positive impact Wal-Mart has on the country. Much of the coverage focused on the contrasting messages in "dueling movies" rather than simply on the anti–Wal-Mart content of the Greenwald movie.

How would you characterize your group's relationship with Wal-Mart's CEO?

We are fortunate that our CEO, Lee Scott, considers corporate communications one of the most important teams in the company. We work closely with him. He has a natural feel for which messages resonate with our audiences and is a valuable asset when it comes to telling the Wal-Mart story. His primary challenge to us is to make sure any interviews or speeches we recommend are part of an overall strategic plan to advance business objectives. Within that framework, he almost always says *yes*.

Suggested Readings

Argenti, Paul A. *Corporate Communication*. Burr Ridge, IL: Irwin Professional Publishing, 2005.

Atkin, Charles, and Ronald Rice. *Public Relations Campaigns*. Thousand Oaks, CA: Sage, 2000.

Austin, James E., *The Collaboration Challenge,* San Francisco, CA: Jossey-Bass, 2000.

Caproni, Paula J. *Management Skills for Everyday Life: The Practical Coach.* Upper Saddle River, NJ: Prentice Hall, 2004. Communication skills are stressed as priorities.

Demers, David, *Communication Theory in the 21st Century.* Mahwah, NJ: Lawrence Erlbaum Associates, 2000.

Demers, David. *Mass Communication and Media Research.* Spokane, WA: Marquette Books, 2005. Up-to-date dictionary of communication and media history and terms.

Green, Andy. *Effective Communication Skills for Public Relations.* London, England: Kogan Page Ltd., 2005.

Grunig, Larissa, James Grunig, and David M. Parker. *A Study of Communications in Three Countries.* Mahwah, NJ: Lawrence Erlbaum Associates, 2002.

Heath, Robert L. *Human Communication Theory and Research: Concepts, Context, and Challenges: Lea's Communication Theory.* Mahwah, NJ: Lawrence Erlbaum Associates, 2000.

Laermer, Richard. *Full Frontal PR: Getting People Talking about You, Your Business, or Your Product.* New York: Bloomberg Press, 2004.

McPhail, Thomas L. *Global Communications: Theories, Stakeholders, and Trends,* 2nd ed. Malden, MA: Blackwell Publishing, 2006. Contemporary view of global communications innovations and challenges.

Ragan Report. Lawrence Ragan Communications, Inc., 316 N. Michigan Ave., Chicago, IL 60601. Weekly pointed commentary on current communications issues, particularly pointed columnists.

Shepherd, G. J., J. St. John, and T. Striphas (Eds.). *Communications as . . . Perspectives on Theory.* Thousand Oaks, CA: Sage Publications, Inc., 2006. Communications, the authors say, is a "process of relating," and this book explains how those relationships are built.

Thill, John V., and Courtland L. Bovee. *Excellence in Business Communication,* 5th ed. New York: McGraw-Hill, 2000.

Notes

1. Interview with Raymond Siposs, Director, Carnet Media, San Diego, CA, December 26, 2005.

2. Patrick Jackson, "The Unforgiving Era," *Currents,* October 1998.

3. Serge Moscovici, "Silent Majorities and Loud Minorities," *Communication Yearbook* 14 (1991): 298–308.

4. J. Delia, B. O'Keefe, & D. O'Keefe, "The Constructivist Approach to Communication," *Human Communication Theory.* (New York: Harper and Row, 1982) 147–91. Also see E. Griffin, *A First Look at Communication Theory,* 4th ed. (New York: McGraw-Hill, 2000) 110–120; J. T. Wood, *Communication Theories in Action: An Introduction* (Belmont, CA: Wadsworth, 1997): 182–84.

5. W. B. Pearce and V. Cronen, Communication, *Action and Meaning: The Creation of Social Realities* (New York: Praeger, 1980). Also see G. Philipsen, "The Coordinated Management of Meaning: Theory of Pearce, Cronen, and Associates," *Watershed Research Traditions in Human Communication Theory,* Donald Cust and Branislave Kovocic, Eds. (Albany, NY: State University of New York Press, 1995): 13–43.

6. James E. Grunig and Todd Hunt, *Managing Public Relations* (New York: Holt, Rinehart and Winston, 1984) 21–27. See also Anne Lane, "Working at the Interface: The Descriptive Relevance of Grunig and Hunt's Theories to Public Relations Practices in South East Queensland Schools," Available: http://praxis.massey.ac.nz/working_interface.html, 2003.

7. Richard Lederer, "The Way We Word," *AARP Magazine,* March/April 2005, 86–93.

8. M. E. McCombs, D. L. Shaw, and D. L. Weaver, *Communication and Democracy: Exploring the Intellectual Frontiers in Agenda-Setting Theory.* (Mahwah, NJ: Lawrence Erlbaum, 1997).

9. Centers for Disease Control and Prevention, "Cigarette Smoking Among Adults—United States, 2004," *Morbidity and Mortality Weekly Report 2005;* 54(44): 1121–1124.

4 Public Opinion

FIGURE 4-1 Fickle finger of public opinion. In March 2005, just five months before he failed a drug test, Baltimore Orioles' first baseman Rafael Palmiero wagged his finger at members of Congress and vowed that he "never used steroids." (AP Wide World Photos)

Public opinion is an elusive and fragile commodity. It can take an organization or individual many years to build the credibility and nurture the trust that goes into winning favorable public opinion. But it can take only a matter of minutes to destroy all that has been developed.

In the summer of 2005, one person who learned this sad lesson the hard way was this man:

Rafael Palmiero was the beloved first baseman of the Baltimore Orioles. In the spring of 2005, Palmiero appeared with other players and former players at a Capital Hill hearing on steroid use. While some, most notably home run champion Mark McGwire, gave evasive answers to inquiring congressmen, Palmiero was categorical. "I have never used steroids, period," he vowed, jabbing his finger for emphasis.

Alas for Palmiero, just five months later, he failed a test for steroids and was suspended 10 days. The positive public opinion the 40-year-old veteran had built up over a stellar 19-year career was torpedoed virtually in one afternoon. As a result of his steroids slip, most observers gave Palmiero little chance of ever realizing his dream of making the Baseball Hall of Fame.[1]

The point is, as the old public relations maxim puts it, *You can't pour perfume on a skunk*.

The best public relations campaign in the world can't build trust while reality is destroying it. If your product doesn't work, if your service stinks, if you are a liar—then no amount of "public relations" will change that. You must change the "action" before credibility or trust can be built.

Society is littered with the reputational carcasses of once respected organizations and individuals who tested the goodwill of the public once too often. For example:

- In 2005, some of the most successful and wealthiest business leaders received hard jail time for corporate actions detrimental to the public. Tyco's CEO Dennis Kozlowski and CFO Mark Swartz each got 25-year prison terms. WorldCom's CEO Bernie Ebbers drew a similar sentence. Adelphia's ailing 80-year old CEO John Rigas drew a 15-year term, and his number one son, CFO Timothy, got 20 years.

- In 2006, corporate fraud focus shifted to the top executives of one of the nation's highest-flying high-tech giants, Enron, as former Chairman Ken Lay and former CEO Jeff Skilling went on trial in Texas.

FIGURE 4-2 Terrible Terrell meets the media. With his agent at his side, talented-but-troubled Philadelphia Eagles receiver Terrell Owens tries to win back public opinion, explaining why he bad-mouthed his coach and quarterback and drew an immediate suspension from the team. (AP Wide World Photos)

- In government, 2005 witnessed scandals in the House of Representatives, where Majority Leader Tom Delay was forced to step down in a contributions scandal, and his fellow Congressman Randy Cunningham, a decorated fighter pilot, resigned in disgrace after admitting to taking bribes.[2] In 2006, with the revelations of convicted super-lobbyist Jack Abramoff, a gaggle of Washington political leaders were implicated in corruption scandals—and a lot more were worried. No wonder, according to most public opinion polls, politicians ranked near the bottom in terms of trust.

- The world of entertainment was rocked in 2005 when pop icon Michael Jackson went on trial for child molestation and actor Robert Blake was charged with murder. While both were acquitted, their credibility was crushed.

- In sports in 2005, public opinion also suffered. As the steroids scandal upset Major League Baseball, a huge fight with fans in the stands rocked the National Basketball Association (see Case Study at the end of this chapter), and a bone-headed superstar named Terrell Owens disrupted the National Football League (Figure 4-2).

Such are the vulnerabilities of public opinion in a culture driven by media and dominated by celebrity. Public opinion in the 21st century is a combustible and changing commodity.

As a general rule, it's difficult to move people toward a strong opinion on anything. It's even harder to move them away from an opinion once they reach it. Nonetheless, the heart of public relations work lies in attempting to affect the public opinion process. Most public relations programs are designed to

(1) persuade people to change their opinion on an issue, product, or organization; (2) crystallize uninformed or undeveloped opinions; or (3) reinforce existing opinions.

Public relations professionals therefore must understand how public opinion is formed, how it evolves from people's attitudes, and how it is influenced by communication. This chapter discusses attitude formation and change and public opinion creation and persuasion.

What Is Public Opinion?

Public opinion, like public relations, is not easily explained. Newspaper columnist Joseph Kraft called public opinion "the unknown god to which moderns burn incense." Edward Bernays called it "a term describing an ill-defined, mercurial, and changeable group of individual judgments."[3] Princeton professor Harwood Childs, after coming up with no fewer than 40 different yet viable definitions, concluded with a definition by Herman C. Boyle: "Public opinion is not the name of something, but the classification of a number of somethings."[4]

Splitting public opinion into its two components, *public* and *opinion,* is perhaps the best way to understand the concept. Simply defined, *public* signifies a group of people who share a common interest in a specific subject—stockholders, for example, or employees or community residents. Each group is concerned with a common issue: the price of the stock, the wages of the company, or the building of a new plant.

An *opinion* is the expression of an attitude on a particular topic. When attitudes become strong enough, they surface in the form of opinions. When opinions become strong enough, they lead to verbal or behavioral actions.

$$\textit{Attitudes} \longrightarrow \textit{Opinions} \longrightarrow \textit{Actions}$$

A forest products company executive and an environmentalist from the Sierra Club might differ dramatically in their attitudes toward the relative importance of pollution control and continued industrial production. Their respective opinions on a piece of environmental legislation might also differ radically. In turn, how their organizations respond to that legislation—by picketing, petitioning, or lobbying—might also differ.

Public opinion, then, is the aggregate of many individual opinions on a particular issue that affects a group of people. Stated another way, public opinion represents a consensus. That consensus, deriving as it does from many individual opinions, really begins with people's attitudes toward the issue in question. Trying to influence an individual's attitude—how he or she thinks on a given topic—is a primary focus of the practice of public relations.

What Are Attitudes?

If an opinion is an expression of an attitude on a particular topic, what then is an *attitude*?

Unfortunately, that also is not an easy question to answer. It was once generally assumed that attitudes are predispositions to think in a certain way about a certain topic.

But research indicates that attitudes may more likely be evaluations people make about specific problems or issues. These conclusions are not necessarily connected to any broad attitude.[5] For example, an individual might favor a company's response to one issue but disagree vehemently with its response to another. Thus, that individual's attitude may differ from issue to issue.

Attitudes are based on a number of characteristics.

1. **Personal**—the physical and emotional ingredients of an individual, including size, age, and social status.

2. **Cultural**—the environment and lifestyle of a particular country or geographic area. The cultures of Saudi Arabia and the United States, for example, differ greatly, and on a less global scale, cultural differences between rural and urban America are vast. National political candidates often tailor messages to appeal to the particular cultural complexions of specific regions.

3. **Educational**—the level and quality of a person's education. To appeal to the increased number of college graduates in the United States today, public communication has become more sophisticated.

4. **Familial**—people's roots. Children acquire their parents' tastes, biases, political partisanships, and a host of other characteristics. Some pediatricians insist that children pick up most of their knowledge in the first years of their life, and few would deny the family's strong role in helping to mold attitudes.

5. **Religious**—a system of beliefs about God or a higher power. Religion is making a comeback. In the 1960s, many young people turned away from formal religion. In the 21st century, even after several evangelical scandals, religious fervor has reemerged.

6. **Social class**—position within society. As people's social status changes, so do their attitudes. For example, college students, unconcerned with making a living, may dramatically change their attitudes about such concepts as big government, big business, wealth, prosperity, and politics after entering the job market.

7. **Race**—ethnic origin, which today increasingly helps shape people's attitudes. Minorities in our society, as a group, continue to improve their standard of living and their relative position. African Americans head major corporations, hold Cabinet positions, and sit on the Supreme Court. So, too, do Latinos and Asian Americans. And women, in many sectors—among them, college students and public relations professionals—are no longer considered a minority.

As their lot improves, African Americans, Latinos, Asians, and others have retained pride in and allegiance to their cultural heritage. These characteristics help influence the formation of attitudes. So, too, do other factors, such as experience, economic class, and political and organizational memberships. Again, research indicates that attitudes and behaviors are situational—influenced by specific issues in specific situations. Nonetheless, when others with similar attitudes reach similar opinions, a consensus, or public opinion, is born.

How Are Attitudes Influenced?

Strictly speaking, attitudes are positive, negative, or nonexistent. A person is for something, against it, or neutral. Studies show that for any one issue, most people don't care much one way or the other. A small percentage expresses strong support, and another small percentage expresses strong opposition. The vast majority is smack in the so-called "muddled middle"—passive, neutral, indifferent. Former Vice President Spiro T. Agnew called this group "the silent majority." In many instances—political campaigns being a prime example—this silent majority, or "swing vote," holds the key to success because they are the group most readily influenced by a communicator's message.

It's hard to change the mind of a person who is staunchly opposed to a particular issue or individual. Likewise, it's easy to reinforce the support of a person who is wholeheartedly in favor of an issue or individual.

Social scientist Leon Festinger discussed this concept when he talked about the *theory of cognitive dissonance*. He believed that individuals tend to avoid information that is dissonant or opposed to their own points of view and tend to seek out information that is consonant with, or in support of, their own attitudes.[6]

Similarly, *social judgment theory* suggests that people may have a range of opinions on a certain subject, anchored by a clear attitude.[7] While, again, it is seldom possible to change this anchor position, communicators can work within this range, called a person's "latitude of acceptance," to modify a person's opinion.

For example, while most people might not discriminate against eating Canadian seafood products, they might object to the clubbing of baby seals. Therefore, in attempting to pressure Canada to stop the seal hunt, the Humane Society of the United States attempts to link the hunt with Canada's seafood industry. In so doing, it attempts to sway the undecided to take action and also to influence others within an acceptable range (Figure 4-3).

Understanding the potential for influencing the silent majority is extremely important for the public relations practitioner, whose objective is to win support through clear, thoughtful, and persuasive communication. Moving a person from a latent state of attitude formation to a more aware state and finally to an active one becomes a matter of motivation.

FIGURE 4-3 Save the seals. The Humane Society's 2005 campaign to stop Canada's commercial seal hunt used graphic mailings, Web video, and photos to influence public opinion.
(Courtesy of the Humane Society of the United States)

Motivating Attitude Change

People are motivated by different factors, and no two people respond in exactly the same way to the same set of circumstances. Each of us is motivated by different drives and needs.

The most famous delineator of what motivates people was Abraham Maslow. Maslow's *hierarchy of needs theory* helps define the origins of motivation, which in turn helps explain attitude change. Maslow postulated a five-level hierarchy:

1. The lowest order is physiological needs: a person's biological demands—food and water, sleep, health, bodily needs, exercise and rest, and sex.
2. The second level is safety needs: security, protection, comfort and peace, and orderly surroundings.
3. The third level is love needs: acceptance, belonging, love and affection, and membership in a group.
4. The fourth level is esteem: recognition and prestige, confidence and leadership opportunities, competence and strength, intelligence and success.
5. The highest order is self-actualization, or simply becoming what one is capable of becoming; self-actualization involves self-fulfillment and achieving a goal for the purposes of challenge and accomplishment.[8]

According to Maslow, the needs of all five levels compose the fundamental motivating factors for any individual or public.

Another popular approach to motivating attitude change is the *elaboration likelihood model,* which posits that there are essentially two ways that people get persuaded:

1. When we are interested and focused enough on a message to take a direct "central route" to decision making, and
2. When we are not particularly engaged on a message and need to take a more "peripheral" route.

Translating this theory into action means that the best way to motivate interested people is with arguments that are strong, logical, and personally relevant. On the other hand, the way to motivate people who are less interested might be through putting them in a better mood—with a joke, for example, or demonstrating, through speech or clothes or mannerism, that you are very much "like" them. Such techniques, according to this theory, might help encourage listeners to accept your arguments.[9]

Power of Persuasion

Perhaps the most essential element in influencing public opinion is the principle of persuasion. Persuading is the goal of the vast majority of public relations programs.

Persuasion theory has myriad explanations and interpretations. Basically, persuasion means getting another person to do something through advice, reasoning, or just plain arm-twisting. Books have been written on the enormous power of advertising and public relations as persuasive tools.

According to classic persuasion theory, people may be of two minds in order to be persuaded to believe in a particular position or take a specific action.

Speaking of Ethics

Sony Spray-Paints Public Opinion

In the winter of 2005, Sony Corp came up with a brainstorm to win public opinion support of hip city-dwellers for its hand-held PlayStation Portable (PSP). Sony decided to hire graffiti artists in major urban areas to spray-paint buildings with simple, black-and-white images of cartoon characters riding the PSP like a skateboard, licking it like a lollipop, or cranking it like a jack-in-the-box (Figure 4-4).

In December, the stealth marketing campaign began popping up in San Francisco, New York, Chicago, Los Angeles, Miami, Atlanta, and Philadelphia. Nowhere did the graffiti mention the Sony sponsorship.

While the campaign may have convinced some urbanites that Sony was hip, it set off a public opinion backlash among local politicians and anti-blight advocates.

"They're breaking the law that regulates outdoor commercial advertising," said one concerned Philadelphia opinion leader. "This really flies in the face of everything we've been trying to do with our anti-blight initiative."

FIGURE 4-4 "Fony" public opinion? Sony's graffiti campaign to win urban support for its PlayStation in Philadelphia. (AP Wide World Photos)

Sony countered the criticism by noting that art is, by nature, "subjective." "With PSP being a portable product, our target is what we consider to be urban nomads, people who are on the go constantly," said a Sony spokesman. The company added that it had paid businesses and building owners for the right to graffiti their walls.

Even some of Sony's urban targets wondered about the ethics of the campaign. "I thought it was sneaky, not cool," said one local resident.

And in San Francisco, critics expressed their disapproval by adding some spray paint of their own over the Sony ads. Outside one bodega, someone wrote, "Get out of my city, Fony."

For further information, see Mary Claire Dale, "PlayStation Graffiti Ads Spark Controversy," Associated Press, December 29, 2005, and Ryan Singel, "Sony Draws Ire with PSP Graffiti," Wired News, December 7, 2005.

First is the "systematic" mode, referring to a person who has carefully considered an argument—actively, creatively, and alertly.

Second is the "heuristic" mode, referring to a person who is skimming the surface and not really focusing on the intricacies of a particular position to catch flaws, inconsistencies, or errors.[10]

That is not to say that all systematic thinkers or all heuristic thinkers think alike. They don't. Things are more complicated than that. Let's say your little brother wants a pair of sneakers and your dad accompanies him to the store to buy them. Both are systematic thinkers. But they have different questions.

Your dad asks:

1. How much do they cost?
2. How long will they last?
3. Is the store nearby so I can get back to watch the ball game?
4. Will they take a personal check?

Your brother asks:

1. Does Labron James endorse them?
2. Do all my homeboys wear them?
3. Will Wanda Sue go out with me if I buy them?

The point is that all of us are persuaded by different things, which makes the challenge of public relations persuading much more a complex art form than a science. No matter how one characterizes persuasion, the goal of most communications programs is, in fact, to influence a receiver to take a desired action.

How are people persuaded? Saul Alinsky, a legendary radical organizer, had a simple theory of persuasion: "*People only understand things in terms of their own experience. . . . If you try to get your ideas across to others without paying attention to what they have to say to you, you can forget about the whole thing.*"[11] In other words, if you wish to persuade people, you must cite evidence that coincides with their own beliefs, emotions, and expectations.

What kinds of "evidence" will persuade?

1. **Facts.** Facts are indisputable. Although it is true, as they say, that "liars figure and figures lie," empirical data are a persuasive device in hammering home a point of view. This is why any good public relations program always starts with research—the facts.

2. **Emotions.** Maslow was right. People do respond to emotional appeals—love, peace, family, patriotism. Arguably, the most riveting moment in George W. Bush's presidency came in the Oval Office on September 13, 2001, when a reporter asked about Bush's personal concerns.

   Q: About the prayer day tomorrow, Mr. President. Could you give us a sense as to what kind of prayers you are thinking and where your heart is for yourself, as you—

   The President: Well, I don't think about myself right now. I think about the families, the children. I am a loving guy, and I am also someone, however, who has got a job to do—and I intend to do it. And this is a terrible moment. But this country will not relent until we have saved ourselves and others from the terrible tragedy that came upon America.[12]

   In less than 50 words, a visibly shaken Bush had made an emotional connection with the American public that proved elusive through much of his presidency.

3. **Personalizing.** People respond to personal experience.
   - When poet Maya Angelou talks about poverty, people listen and respect a woman who emerged from the dirt-poor environs of the Deep South in a day of segregation.

- When *America's Most Wanted* TV host John Walsh crusades against criminals who prey on children, people understand that his son was abducted and killed by a crazed individual.

- When former baseball pitcher Jim Abbott talks about dealing with adversity, people marvel at a star athlete born with only one arm.
  Again, few can refute knowledge gained from personal experience.

4. **Appealing to "you."** The one word that people never tire of hearing is *you*. *What is in this for me?* is the question that everyone asks. One secret to persuading, therefore, is to constantly think in terms of what will appeal most to the audience.

As simple as these four precepts are, they are often difficult for some to grasp. Emotion, for example, is a particular challenge for business leaders, who presume, incorrectly, that showing it is a sign of weakness. This, of course, is wrong. The power to persuade—to influence public opinion—is the measure not only of a charismatic but also of an effective leader.[13]

Influencing Public Opinion

Public opinion is a lot easier to measure than it is to influence. However, a thoughtful public relations program can crystallize attitudes, reinforce beliefs, and occasionally change public opinion. First, the opinions to be changed or modified must be identified and understood. Second, target publics must be clear. Third, the public relations professional must have in sharp focus the "laws" that govern public opinion—as amorphous as they may be.

In that context, the "Laws of Public Opinion," developed many years ago by social psychologist Hadley Cantril, remain pertinent. Few recent events more strongly underscored the relevance of Cantril's laws than the unprecedented attacks on America of September 11, 2001.[14]

1. **Opinion is highly sensitive to important events.** Events of unusual magnitude are likely to swing public opinion temporarily from one extreme to another. Opinion doesn't become stabilized until the implications of events are seen in some perspective. For example, after the terrorist attacks, President Bush's popularity rose to unprecedented heights, as Americans of every age group and background rallied behind the war against terrorism.

2. **Opinion is generally determined more by events than by words—unless those words are themselves interpreted as an event.** In a speech to a joint session of Congress nine days after the terrorist attacks, the President vowed to "lift the dark threat of violence from our people and our future. We will rally the world to this cause by our efforts, by our courage. We will not tire, we will not falter, and we will not fail." Bush's words became a rallying cry for the nation and, temporarily at least, transformed his presidency.[15]

3. **At critical times, people become more sensitive to the adequacy of their leadership. If they have confidence in it, they are willing to assign more than usual responsibility to it; if they lack confidence in it, they are less tolerant than usual.** Relatively few voices rose in protest when the Bush administration, in the cause of fighting terrorism, imposed sweeping changes in privacy rights, regarding such traditional areas as library use and securing court orders before wiretapping suspected American evildoers.

4. **Once self-interest is involved, opinions are slow to change.** Even after the United States invaded Iraq to oust Saddam Hussein in March 2003, American support continued for the war effort. That support began to wane when the 2,000th American soldier was killed in October 2005.[16]

5. **People have more opinions and are able to form opinions more easily on goals than on methods to reach those goals.** For example, few questioned the need for a new U.S. Department of Homeland Security to protect the land within our borders from terrorism. However, the organization, components, and functions of that department were the subject of continued debate and criticism, particularly in the wake of hurricane disasters in 2005.

6. **By and large, if people in a democracy are provided with educational opportunities and ready access to information, public opinion reveals a hardheaded common sense.** In the weeks and months following the attacks of September 11, as Americans became more enlightened about the implications and threats of terrorism within the United States, the administration's strategy of continuous communication helped solidify public opinion.[17] In 2006, with opposition to the war mounting, President Bush launched a renewed campaign to inform the American public about what was happening in Iraq.[18]

Polishing the Corporate Image

Most organizations today and the people who manage them are extremely sensitive to the way they are perceived by their critical publics. This represents a dramatic change in corporate attitude from years past. Well into the 1980s, only the most enlightened companies dared to maintain anything but a low profile. Management, frankly, was reluctant to step out publicly, *to stand up for what it stood for.*

Today, however, organizations—particularly large ones—have little choice but to go public. The accounting and corporate scandals that continued into 2006 threatened the confidence of the American capitalistic system. In the wake of the scandals, smart companies and their leaders realized they simply couldn't "hide" any longer from public scrutiny.

- In the winter of 2005, when energy costs ascended to $60 a barrel and higher gas prices infuriated Americans, some oil companies wasted no time in getting "out in front" of the issue of conserving and creating energy (Figure 4-5).

- That same year, when the powerful chairman of the world's largest insurance company, American International Group, was ousted amid probes of improper accounting, he publicly went after his accuser, politically ambitious New York Attorney General Eliot Spitzer, and enlisted other opinion leaders in a full-court public relations blitz to win public opinion.[19]

- On the flip side, when secretive but successful hedge fund manager Edward Lampert took control of the venerable-but-troubled retailer Sears Roebuck, he refused to share his plans with Wall Street analysts. The result: a rapid falloff in the price of Sears stock.[20]

The point is that most organizations today understand, first, that corporate image is a fragile commodity, and second, to improve that image they must operate with the "implicit trust" of the public. That means that for a corporation in the 21st century,

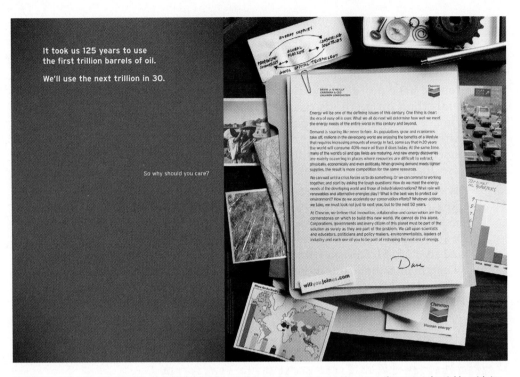

FIGURE 4-5 Setting the public opinion agenda. Chevron was one energy company that moved quickly, with its willyoujoinus.com initiative to frame the discussion on global energy issues. (Reprinted by permission of Chevron and Corbis. © Claro Cortes IV/Reuters/Corbis)

winning favorable public opinion isn't an option—it's a necessity, essential for continued long-term success.

Managing Reputation

For an organization or an individual concerned about public opinion, what it comes down to is managing reputation. Reputation is present throughout our lives. It's how we choose business partners, which dentist or mechanic to visit, the stores we frequent, the neighborhood we live in, and the friends we keep. In recent years, *reputation management* has become a buzzword in public relations and in the broader society. At the start of the century, the term was little known. Today, a Google search on "reputation management" produces upwards of 93,000 results.[21]

Many public relations firms have introduced reputation management divisions, and some have even billed themselves as being in the business of relationship management. Generally defined, relationship management aligns communications with an organization's character and action. It creates recognition, credibility, and trust among key constituents. It stays sensitive to its conduct in public with customers and in private with employees. It understands its responsibilities to the broader society and is empathetic to society's needs.

While reputation itself may be difficult to measure, its value to an organization or an individual is indisputable.[22] And it's also indisputable that "managing" reputation is a front-line responsibility of public relations.

Talking Points

Winning Reputation . . .

How do you measure reputation?

In 2004 and again in 2005, The *Wall Street Journal* combined with survey firm Harris Interactive to poll consumers on what companies they felt had the highest reputation.

The *Journal* asked respondents to rank organizations on six primary measures of reputation: (1) emotional appeal, (2) financial performance, (3) products and services, (4) vision and leadership, (5) workplace environment, and (6) social responsibility. Other characteristics, such as ethics and sincerity of corporate communications, were also probed. Not surprisingly, the companies known for candor and communications ranked best and those embroiled in scandal ranked worst.

Here are the top and bottom 10 companies for 2005, with their comparative rankings in 2004.

Top 10

1.	Johnson & Johnson	1
2.	Coca-Cola	3
3.	Google	N/A*
4.	UPS	5
5.	3M	2
6.	Sony	7
7.	Microsoft	6
8.	General Mills	9
9.	FedEx	8
10.	Intel	11

*Not included in 2004 ranking

Bottom 10

51.	Sprint	51
52.	Martha Stewart Living Omnimedia	53
53.	Exxon Mobil	44
54.	Royal Dutch Shell	N/A*
55.	Tyco International	52
56.	UAL/United Airlines	N/A*
57.	Halliburton	58
58.	Adelphia	56
59.	MCI (formerly WorldCom)	59
60.	Enron	60

*Not included in 2004 ranking

For further information, see "2005 Reputation Quotient Rankings," *Wall Street Journal,* December 6, 2005.

Talking Points

. . . Losing Reputation

On the other hand, there was everybody's favorite rapper, 50 Cent, or, as we know him and love him, "Fiddy." The rapper, aka Curtis Jackson, known for his gunshot wounds, hard time, and general thuggishness, seemed to revel in his gangsta image.

In 2006, the rapper fell under siege on two continents, in conjunction with the release of his movie, *Get Rich or Die Tryin'*. Specifically, a poster, featuring 50 holding a gun in one hand and a baby in the other was vilified in the United States and Britain as "glamorizing the use of guns" (Figure 4-6).

The rapper and his management company defended the ads as depicting the "escape from the ghetto he grew up in."

Meanwhile, not even 50's family appreciated his image. Complained his budding rapper cousin, Michael Francis, aka 25, "My relationship with him is stay on your side of the street. When you get big money . . . you get cocky."

And despite his questionable—some might say, terrible—reputation, 50 Cent did, indeed, "get big money."

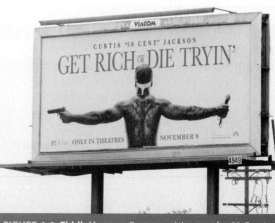

FIGURE 4-6 Fiddin' image. Controversial poster for 50 Cent's movie fit right in with the rapper's reputation. (AP Wide World Photos)

For further information, see "50 Cent's Lil' Cousin 25 Speaks Out," *Lee Bailey's Eur Web,* www.eurweb.com, January 3, 2006.

Last Word

Influencing public opinion remains at the heart of professional public relations work. Public opinion is a powerful force that can impact the earnings of corporations through such actions as product boycotts, union strikes, and the misdeeds of key executives; influence government legislation through campaign support, product recalls, and letters and e-mails from constituents; and even unify a nation through calls to action by strong and committed leaders.

In order to influence public opinion, public relations professionals must anticipate trends in our society. At the start of the 21st century, one self-styled prognosticator, John Naisbitt, predicted the new directions that would influence American lives in the near future. Among them were the following:

- Inflation and interest rates will be held in check.
- There will be a shift from welfare to workfare.
- There will be a shift from public housing to home ownership.
- There will be a shift from sports to the arts as the primary leisure preference.

- Consumers will demand more customized products.
- The media will amplify bad economic news.
- The rise of the Pacific Rim will be seen in terms of economic dominance.
- Asia will add 80 million more people.
- CEOs in a global economy will become more important and better known than political figures.[23]

With the first decade of the century half over, Nesbitt's "megatrends," while not revolutionary, nonetheless appear to be making sense. Public relations professionals need to take note of these and other trends in gauging how public opinion will impact their organizations. They also should consider what the late public relations counselor Philip Lesly once pointed out: "The real problems faced by business today are in the outside world of intangibles and public attitudes."[24]

To keep ahead of these intangibles, public attitudes, and kernels of future public opinion, managements will turn increasingly for guidance to professional public relations practitioners.

Discussion Starters

1. What is the relationship between public relations and public opinion?
2. What are attitudes, and on what characteristics are they based?
3. How are attitudes influenced?
4. What is Maslow's hierarchy of needs?
5. What is the theory of cognitive dissonance?
6. How difficult is it to change a person's behavior?
7. What are several key public opinion laws, according to Cantril?
8. What kinds of evidence persuade people?
9. What are the elements involved in managing reputation?
10. In assessing the list of best and worst companies in terms of reputation, what specific characteristics influence these rankings?

Top of the Shelf

The New York Times

New York: *The New York Times* Company, www.nytimes.com

The Wall Street Journal

Dow Jones & Company, Inc., wsj.com

Public relations can be practiced only by understanding public opinion, and two of the most prominent daily forums in which to study it are *The New York Times* and *The Wall Street Journal*. Their pages reveal the diverse views of pundits, politicians, and plain people. The *Times* is arguably the primary source of printed news in the world. The *Journal,* likewise, is the primary printed source of the world's business and investment news—an area of increasingly dominant importance.

Both papers, through their opinion pages and in-depth stories, express the attitudes of leaders in politics, business, science,

education, journalism, and the arts, on topics ranging from abortion rights to genetic engineering to race relations. Occasionally, the *Times* and the *Journal* supplement their usual coverage with public opinion polls to gauge attitudes and beliefs on particularly hot issues.

It may, indeed, be the Internet age, but if you really want to know what's going on in the world and be a lot more knowledgeable than most of those with whom you work, read *The New York Times* and *The Wall Street Journal* every day. Sure, the news is often infuriating, but it's also a joy and always worth the investment.

CASE STUDY

Dressed for Success: The NBA Cleans Up Its Image

In 2006, *Sporting News* magazine named David Stern, commissioner of the National Basketball Association, the most powerful person in sports.

Few could argue with the selection. More than any other sports figure, Stern's league was a billion-dollar enterprise, and his power as NBA commissioner was absolute and unchallenged.

Under Stern, its commissioner since 1984, the NBA had flourished. It was blessed by a continuing parade of superhuman athletes—from Larry Bird and Magic Johnson to Michael Jordan and Shaquille O'Neal. It boasted more international players than any other professional sports league. Indeed, the league's largest player, Yao Ming, stimulated the entire country of China to become NBA fans. The same was true around the world, where basketball fever became contagious, from Argentina to Australia, from Serbia to Israel.

By the start of 2006, the NBA's dominance was indisputable.

But little more than a year earlier—in one unforgettably vicious evening—the future of the NBA stood very much in doubt. The league and its commissioner faced the most significant challenge in their history: how to win back public opinion.

The Fight

On November 14, 2004, the NBA suffered one of the ugliest scenes in sports history. A beer-filled cup landed on the chest of Indiana Pacers forward Ron Artest as he lay on the scorer's table and triggered an unsightly melee between several members of the Pacers and fans of the Detroit Pistons at the Palace of Auburn Hills in Michigan.

The place was bedlam.

Players climbed into the stands to jump fans. Fans rushed the court to get at players. Security guards raced to untangle the combatants. Teams stormed into the locker room as the fans doused them with anything they could get their hands on.

The next day, televised images of the brawl ran nonstop and slow motion throughout the nation. And that was just the half of it.

- One headline read, "National Brawlers Association." Another called the melee, "basket-brawl."

- An editorial in a major newspaper described the NBA as being "long known as a halfway house for pampered, self-indulgent millionaire athletes, with minimally controlled tempers."

- Conservative talk show host Rush Limbaugh described the incident as "gang behavior on parade minus the guns. That's the culture that the NBA has become."

- Syndicated African American columnist Clarence Page commented, "The jaw-dropping footage has aired over and over again like an ad for some sort of a 'Negroes Gone Wild' video.

- *Sports Illustrated* called it "a frightening wakeup call."

NBA Commissioner Stern acknowledged that the fight had instantly turned nationwide public opinion against the league. "It became a convenient outlet for people saying 'those thugs' and 'those punks.' And that's hurtful to NBA players and undeserved."

Clearly, the NBA had a huge public relations problem (Figure 4-7).

The Aftermath

In the days that followed, players and fans were subjected to lawsuits and criminal charges. Commissioner Stern immediately recognized the severity of the public opinion problem for his league. Two days after the fight, he handed out stiff penalties and suspended nine players.

As to the fate of Artest, one of the league's premier players, Stern levied an unprecedented 73-game suspension—the remainder of the NBA season—and a $5.4 million salary loss. When reporters asked if the vote on the Artest suspension was unanimous, Stern answered, "Yes, one to nothing."

In dealing severely with those involved, Stern properly led with action rather than words. Nonetheless, the commissioner

FIGURE 4-7   Low point.   The NBA suffered its most serious public opinion setback, when the Pacers' Ron Artest had to be restrained by fans in a November 2004 game.   (AP Wide World Photos)

recognized that more would have to be done to repair the league's image.

"We certainly focused on post-Detroit as a low point as far as perception of our league," Stern said.

As to why the brawl led to a condemnation of the entire NBA, Stern was brutally candid:

I think it's fair to say that the NBA was the first sport that was widely viewed as a black sport. And whatever the numbers ultimately are for the other sports, the NBA will always be treated a certain way because of that.

Our players are so visible that if they have Afros or cornrows or tattoos—white or black—our consumers pick it up. So I think there are always some elements of race involved that affect judgments about the NBA.

Stern's challenge, then, stated simply, was to "clean up" the NBA's act.

The New Rules

Over the next several months, the NBA acted decisively to help ensure that there would never be a repeat of its worst moment.

- First, it beefed up security around the league. Some teams increased security detail by as much as 25 percent. Others repositioned guards and stopped selling seats directly behind the benches, where hecklers reigned supreme. The trade-off with such actions was that teams worried about losing the "intimacy" of the fans sitting close to the floor.

- Second, a fourth-quarter ban on beer sales was put into effect. Additionally, a Fan Code of Conduct was adopted and put on display at NBA ticket windows. While the league obviously needed to maintain its fan base, the fan ugliness in Auburn Hills couldn't be tolerated. Indeed, the Pistons banned at least one ticket holder involved in the fracas from ever returning to see a game.

- The minimum player age was raised to 19, a move away from the growing trend of high school athletes leaping into the NBA draft. The rationale? The league had been criticized for sacrificing maturity and fundamentals to a desire to gain increased "street credibility" with urban followers.

- Finally, in the winter of 2005, when hurricanes Katrina and Rita ripped though the Southeast, the NBA committed to donate $100 million, volunteer one million hours of community service, and build 100 educational and athletic facilities over five years in the devastated communities.

As the commissioner put it in characterizing the outreach initiative, dubbed NBA CARES, "You would have to be living someplace else not to realize our players are better than their reputations were described this past season."

The Dress Code

The pièce de résistance in the NBA's campaign to rewin public opinion was the imposition of a player dress code. Players were required to dress "business casual"—dress shirt or turtleneck, dress slacks or dress jeans, and dress shoes—while on team business. No longer permitted were the more likely baggy pants, sleeveless shirts, indoor sunglasses, displayed jewelry, and sandals preferred by many players.

With an average annual salary of $3.7 million, there was little question that most NBA players could afford the new dress requirements. Some, including a few of the league's brightest, and most well-behaved stars, nonetheless took offense. Said New Jersey Net all-star Vince Carter, "I just think people should be able to express themselves. I know they took out the 'do rag' stuff; I understand that. As far as guys wearing what they want to wear, I am all for that. Who really cares about what they wear from the bus to the locker room?"

Minnesota forward Wally Szczerbiak agreed, "I think they're coming on way too strict. Movie stars in L.A., they're not always in jackets and ties, and they're setting trends, and we're looked at in the same light."

Even perennial league most valuable player, San Antonio center Tim Duncan, wasn't thrilled, "I think it's a load of crap. I understand what they're trying to do. . . . But I don't understand why they would take it to this level. I think it's basically retarded."

Some players went so far as to suggest that the new dress code was discriminatory, an attack on hip-hop and black culture.

Commissioner Stern wasn't relenting: "The dress code has to do with what you do when you are on business and what uniform is appropriate on the business of the NBA. . . . Hip-hop is a style, but some of my owners, like Jay-Z, Nelly, and Usher, are hip-hop, but they dress in a different fashion. Hip-hop doesn't mean sloppy."

In the end, despite their initial squawking, the players accepted the dress code, with a few, including Indiana forward Stephen Jackson—one of those involved in the big brawl—favoring the move. Said the ever-modest Jackson, "I have no problem dressing up . . . because I know I'm a nice-looking guy."

One of the league's brightest future stars, Miami's Dwayne Wade, said, "I think it's good for us to look professional, and it's kind of fun now to see what people are wearing."

The Future

As the NBA moved further away from the Detroit meltdown, the league still was not without its critics or problems. For one thing, Artest, the instigator at Auburn Hills, was suspended permanently by the Pacers after publicly saying he wanted to be traded. Indiana, having had it with the volatile star, was only too happy to comply.

Others persisted in criticizing the league for everything from the length of its season to the failure of teams to play defense to the canned noise in arenas. But all-in-all, the changes implemented in the wake of the fight helped restore the positive public opinion that the league desperately needed. Players stopped to sign autographs, and teams became more responsive in their communities.

Detroit general manager Joe Dumars, himself a former NBA star, summarized the outcome: "Everyone is more focused on presenting the best that the league has to offer, rather than the worst."

As for the "most powerful man in sports," Stern envisioned the day that the NBA would no longer have any image problem: "All of these things are cyclical. We went through this 25 years ago, when the league was in the process of becoming predominantly African American, and people didn't think we'd survive. But here we are, we are surviving, and we're thriving, and we're doing great."

Questions

1. What other options did David Stern have in dealing with the participants in the Pacers–Pistons brawl?

2. What recommendations would you have given the commissioner in dealing with the NBA's public opinion problem?

3. Would you have instituted the dress code? How would you have handled the allegations of racism?

4. In terms of public relations initiatives, what programs and practices would you recommend the NBA adopt going forward?

For further information, see Oscar Dixon, "One Year Later: NBA on the Rebound," *USA Today,* November 17, 2005; Michael Lee, "NBA Fights to Regain Image, *Washington Post,* November 19, 2005, E01; Mark Montieth, "Time for a Change," *The Indianapolis Star,* December 2, 2005; Randy Rorrer, "NBA's Image Mandates a Makeover," *News-Journal Online,* October 29, 2005; Mark Starr, "Duds Go Out of Bounds," *Newsweek,* October 31, 2005;

Voice of Authority

An Interview with Kathleen Hessert

Kathleen Hessert (shown here with client, Indianapolis Colts' quarterback Peyton Manning) spent nearly a decade as an award-winning TV anchor, reporter, and talk show host. She is CEO of Sports Media Challenge, a nationally-renowned speaking, training, and consulting firm based in Charlotte, NC. Since 1989, she has been a media and speech coach to Olympic gold medalists and gridiron greats, NBA players, race car drivers, tennis pros, PGA golfers, and many more. In 2004, she introduced "eMonitor . . . Protecting and Enriching Sports Brands," which mines, measures, and analyzes online content for business intelligence, including traditional and Fan Generated Media™. She is the author and voice of *Winning the Media Game: A Guide for NFL Players, Power Training: How to Win the Media Game, and the Coach's Communication PlayBook.*

How important is public relations for a professional athlete, coach, team, and league?
To succeed today there are three essentials: performance, image, and exposure. For a high profile sports personality, team, or league each of the three components has to be in equal measure to maximize the enormously-powerful sports platform. If any one component is out of balance, they've placed a ceiling on their potential.

How would you assess David Stern's reaction in the aftermath of the Pistons-Pacers altercation?
Fast, strong, specific, and on target!

How has the NBA rebounded from its earlier image problems?
The league continues to work diligently on its public persona, knowing the problems didn't begin overnight, nor will they end with one pounding of the commissioner's disciplinary gavel. The NBA realizes that it has an impact on popular culture here and abroad—not just on sports fans. That kind of power brings great responsibility for the NBA and its teams, and it seems that decisions are made with that in mind.

What values do you emphasize in your work with sports figures?
Being genuine, professional, and responsible for the development and protection of their own brand and those brands they represent. I use an acronym that is better known in the financial field: *I.R.A.*

Influence. Intentionally influence the public's perception of you. Be proactive not reactive.

Responsibility. No one should be more responsible than you for your own public image.

Accountability. Be accountable for everything you say and do. Journalists rarely misquote if you have a message and clearly, succinctly, and dynamically communicate it.

What has been your experience in working with well-known athletes?

The best always want to get better. They understand the sports platform enables them to influence millions, and that with the great advantages that their physical and athletic prowess provides them come great responsibilities. Athletes and coaches understand the need and are in the habit of working consistently hard and value the benefits of practice. So when a Peyton Manning or Shaquille O'Neal are learning a speech, they don't want to read it. Rather, they want to know it and speak it so—unlike many business people who focus only on getting the content right—they practice so the content and delivery are both the best they can be.

How does a young person get into the field of sports promotion?

Network by meeting as many people in sports as possible. The value of internships is irrefutable. Without some experience, few will hire you. The experience and rapport with a professional is priceless, even when the internship is non-paying. College students should volunteer in the athletic department's sports information department, community service, or marketing departments to gain as much knowledge and know-how as possible . . . and to build relationships. The world of sports is a very small one.

Suggested Readings

Alsop, Ron J., *The 18 Immutable Laws of Corporate Reputation: Creating, Protecting, and Repairing Your Most Valuable Asset*. New York: Free Press, 2004. A *Wall Street Journal* veteran's step-by-step guide to winning a positive reputation and communicating it.

Argenti, Paul A., and Janis Forman. *The Power of Corporate Communication: Crafting the Voice and Image of Your Business*. New York: The McGraw-Hill Companies, 2002. Emphasis is on creating and communicating a consistent corporate voice.

Ferguson, Sherry Devereaux. *Researching the Public Opinion Environment, Theories & Methods*. Thousand Oaks, CA: Sage Publications, 2000.

Gladwell, Malcolm. *The Tipping Point: How Little Things Can Make a Big Difference*. New York: Little, Brown, 2000. The best seller that explains the influencers on contemporary public opinion.

Kotler, Philip, and Nancy Lee. *Corporate Social Responsibility: Doing the Most Good for Your Company and Your Cause*. Hoboken, NJ: John Wiley & Sons, 2005.

Manheim, Jarol B. *Biz-War and the Out-of-Power Elites: The Progressive-Left Attack on the Corporation*. Mahwah, NJ: Lawrence Erlbaum Associates, 2004. What certain critics in society would like public opinion to resemble.

Manheim, Jarol B. *The Death of a Thousand Cuts: Corporate Campaigns and the Attack on the Corporation*. Mahwah, NJ: Lawrence Erlbaum Associates, 2000.

Shapiro, Cynthia. *Corporate Confidential: 50 Secrets Your Company Doesn't Want You to Know—and What to Do About Them*. New York: St. Martin's Press, 2005. A human resources executive opens the curtain on the real truth about such issues as free corporate speech, age discrimination, and being too smart in a corporation.

Weissberg, Robert. *Polling, Policy and Pubic Opinion: The Case Against Heeding the "Voice of the People."* New York: St. Martin's Press, 2002.

www.mediainfo.com. *Editor & Publisher* magazine's database offers access to more than 11,000 news Web sites.

www.prnewswire.com. Public Relations Newswire. Features corporate press releases and background, with a link to Expert Contacts.

www.publicagenda.org. Public Agenda Online. "The inside source for public opinion and policy analysis."

Notes

1. "Palmiero Docked 10 Days for Steroids," Associated Press, August 2, 2005.
2. Josh Marshall, "Rep. Cunningham Scandal Just Keeps Getting Deeper," *The Hill*, July 6, 2005.
3. Cited in Edward L. Bernays, *Crystallizing Public Opinion* (New York: Liveright, 1961): 61.
4. Cited in Harwood L. Childs, *Public Opinion: Nature, Formation, and Role* (Princeton, NJ: Van Nostrand, 1965): 15.
5. James E. Grunig and Todd Hunt, *Managing Public Relations* (New York: Holt, Rinehart & Winston, 1984): 130.
6. Leon A. Festinger, *A Theory of Cognitive Dissonance* (New York: Harper & Row, 1957): 163.
7. Richard M. Perloff, *The Dynamics of Persuasion: Communication and Attitudes in the 21st Century*, 2nd ed. (Mahwah, NJ: Lawrence Erlbaum Associates, 2003). Ample discussion of social judgment theory, pioneered by Muzafer and Carolyn Sherif in 1967.
8. Abraham Maslow, *Motivation and Personality* (New York: Harper & Row, 1954).
9. R. E. Petty and J. T. Cacioppo. *The Elaboration Likelihood Model of Persuasion* (New York: Academic Press, 1986.)
10. T. C. Brock and S. Shavitt, *Persuasion: Psychological Insights and Perspectives* (Chicago: Allyn & Bacon, 1999).
11. Saul D. Alinsky, *Rules for Radicals* (New York: Vintage Books, 1971): 81.
12. "President Pledges Assistance for New York in Phone Call with Pataki, Giuliani," White House news release, September 13, 2001.
13. Robert L. Dilenschneider, *Power and Influence* (New York: Prentice Hall, 1990): 5.
14. Hadley Cantril, *Gauging Public Opinion* (Princeton, NJ: Princeton University Press, 1972): 226–230.
15. D. T. Max, "The 2,988 Words That Changed a Presidency: An Etymology," *New York Times* on the Web, October 7, 2001.

16. Saad Abedine, "U.S. Death Toll in Iraq Reaches 2000," *CNN.com,* October 26, 2005.

17. Richard Benedetto, "Business News Alters Perceptions of Bush," *USA Today,* July 10, 2002, 6A.

18. "Senate GOP Planning Iraq PR Blitz to Counter 'Frustration' with Media Coverage of War," *Bulldog Reporter's Daily' Dog,* January 4, 2006.

19. Randall Smith, "Greenberg's Pals Ship a Letter Rallying Support," *Wall Street Journal,* October 29, 2005, B1.

20. Riva D. Atlas, "For Sears Shareholders, Silence Stirs Anxiety," *New York Times,* December 7, 2005, C3.

21. "Reputation: The Significant Shadow," *Mount Vernon Report,* Vol. 3 No. 2, Spring 2005, 1–2.

22. "Doorley Is Selling CEOs on the Value of Reputation," *PR Week,* November 18, 2002.

23. John Naisbitt and Patricia Aburdene, *Megatrends 2000* (New York: Morrow, 1990).

24. Philip Lesly, "How the Future Will Shape Public Relations—and Vice Versa," *Public Relations Quarterly,* Winter 1981–82, 7.

5 Management

It has been said that the only difference between the public relations director and the CEO is that the latter gets paid more.

In many ways, that's quite true. The CEO, after all, is the firm's top manager, responsible for, in addition to setting strategy and framing policy, serving as the organization's chief spokesperson, corporate booster, and reputation defender—not at all unlike the responsibilities assigned the public relations professional.

Any CEO who questions the value of positive public relations and disputes his or her own responsibilities in defending the firm's reputation has obviously never run up against this man:

Twenty years ago, corporate nemesis Michael Moore first turned his scathing film-making sights on the then-largest automobile company in the world, General Motors. In his blockbuster *Roger and Me,* Moore set out to confront GM CEO Roger Smith for closing plants in poverty-stricken areas.[1] Later, Moore turned his cameras on the big pharmaceutical

FIGURE 5-1 CEO's worst nightmare. Filmmaker Michael Moore terrorized 21st-century corporate management whenever he chose to focus his dark cameras on their activities. (AP Wide World Photos)

industry and President Bush and spawned a whole group of documentary producers to cast a dark eye on companies from McDonald's to Wal-Mart (see Case Study at end of this chapter).

The anti-management activities of Moore and his ilk underscored the importance of effective public relations to organizational leadership and the necessity for public relations professionals to understand management. That means that public relations people must master a knowledge of such management functions as planning, budgeting, objective setting, and how top management thinks and operates. That's what this chapter discusses.

It also deals with the differences between working as a staff public relations practitioner inside a corporation, nonprofit, or other organization, where the job is to support management in achieving its objectives and working as a professional in a public relations agency, where the job is to contribute to the revenue generation of the company. Finally, it provides some feel of what to expect in terms of income in public relations.

Management Process of Public Relations

Like other management processes, professional public relations work emanates from clear strategies and bottom-line objectives that flow into specific tactics, each with its own budget, timetable, and allocation of resources. Stated another way, public relations today is much more a planned, persuasive social managerial science than a knee-jerk, damage-control reaction to sudden flare-ups.

Don't get me wrong. As we will learn later, the public relations professionals who have the most organizational clout and get paid the most are those who demonstrate the ability to perform in a crisis. Thinking "on your feet" is very much a coveted ability in the practice of public relations. But so, too, is the ability to think strategically and plan methodically to help change attitudes, crystallize opinions, and accomplish the organization's overall goals.

Managers insist on *results,* so the best public relations programs can be measured in terms of achieving results in building the key relationships on which the organization depends. The relevance of public relations people in the eyes of top management depends largely on the contribution they make to the management process of the organization.

With nearly a century under its belt, the practice of public relations has developed its own theoretical framework as a management system. According to communications professors James Grunig and Todd Hunt, public relations managers perform what organizational theorists call a *boundary* role: they function at the edge of an organization as a liaison between the organization and its external and internal publics. In other words, public relations managers have one foot inside the organization and one outside. Often this unique position is not only lonely but also precarious.

As boundary managers, public relations people support their colleagues by helping them communicate across organizational lines both within and outside the organization. In this way, public relations professionals also become systems managers, knowledgeable about and able to deal with the complex relationships inherent in the organization.[2]

Top managers are forced to think strategically about reaching their goals. So, too, should public relations professionals think in terms of the strategic process element of their own roles. Specifically, they must constantly ask, in relation to their departments, functions, and assignments:

- What are we attempting to achieve, and where are we going in that pursuit?
- What is the nature of the environment in which we must operate?
- Who are the key audiences we must convince in the process?
- How will we get to where we want to be?

It is this procedural mind-set—directed at communicating key messages to realize desired objectives to priority publics—that makes the public relations professional a key adviser to top management.

Reporting to Top Management

The public relations function, by definition, must report to top management.

If public relations, as noted in Chapter 1, is truly to be the "interpreter" for management philosophy, policy, and programs, then the public relations director should report to the CEO.

In many organizations, this reporting relationship is not the case. Public relations is often subordinated to advertising, marketing, legal, or human resources. Whereas marketing and advertising promote the product, public relations promotes the entire organization. Therefore, if the public relations chief reports to the director of marketing or advertising, the job mistakenly becomes one of promoting specific products rather than promoting the entire organization.

For the public relations function to be valuable to management, it must remain independent, credible, and objective as an honest broker. This also mandates that public relations professionals have not only communication competence but also an intimate knowledge of the organization's business. Without the latter, according to research, public relations professionals are much less effective as top-management advisers.[3]

Public relations, rightfully, should be the *corporate conscience*. An organization's public relations professionals should enjoy enough autonomy to deal openly and honestly with management. If an idea doesn't make sense, if a product is flawed, if the general institutional wisdom is wrong, it is the duty of the public relations professional to challenge the consensus. As Warren Buffet, the legendary CEO of the Berkshire Hathaway company, put it, "We can afford to lose money—even a lot of money. But we cannot afford to lose reputation—even a shred of reputation."[4]

This is not to say that advertising, marketing, and all other disciplines shouldn't enjoy a close partnership with public relations. Clearly, they must. All disciplines must work to maintain their own independence while building long-term, mutually beneficial relationships for the good of the organization. However, public relations should never shirk its overriding responsibility to enhance the organization's credibility by ensuring that corporate actions are in the public interest.

To perform that function effectively, it needs to report directly to top management.

Conceptualizing the Public Relations Plan

Strategic planning for public relations is an essential part of management. Planning is critical not only to know where a particular campaign is headed but also to win the support of top management. Indeed, one of the most frequent complaints about public relations is that it is too much a "seat-of-the-pants" activity, impossible to plan and difficult to measure. Management's perspective is, "How do we know the public relations group will deliver and fully leverage the resources they're asking for?" They must see a plan.[5] With proper planning, public relations professionals can indeed defend and account for their actions.

Speaking of Ethics

Super-Sized Duplicity?

No question that the first decade of the 21st century has seen its share of management transgressions. And Michael Moore and his fellow corporate attack dogs have helped root out corporate abuse.

But sometimes, even big-company CEOs are handed a raw deal.

In 2004, Moore disciple Morgan Spurlock set out to expose the fat-inducing initiatives of McDonald's. Spurlock's film, *Super Size Me,* was an instant multimillion dollar hit, showing McDonald's to be a company less interested in the nutrition and good health of its customers than in manipulating marketing messages to turn a profit. The film presented the company and its management as greedy, condescending, and unscrupulous (Figure 5-2).

But in reaching his cinematic conclusions, Spurlock wasn't exactly the most "fair and balanced" pursuer of the truth. Here is an excerpt of an e-mail he sent to McDonald's public relations department in order to convince management to talk to him:

> I am amazed at the work currently being done by McDonald's in conjunction with their franchisees to create and deliver healthy alternatives to their consumers. You cannot go anywhere in the country now without seeing advertisements for the new premium salads or improved Veggie Burgers. The decision to create these alternatives, as well as the road ahead, is something I would love to cover in the interview.
>
> McDonald's has always been a leader in the food service industry and the steps they are taking continue to reinforce that they will set the example and the standard as we move forward.

FIGURE 5-2 Crooked crusader? McDonald's menace, Morgan Spurlock. (AP Wide World Photos)

For some reason, even after such a flattering come-on, McDonald's management declined Spurlock's kind request. Perhaps they thought he was being just a tad disingenuous in the correspondence and might be similarly biased on the screen.

For further information, see Fraser P. Seitel, "Beware the Super-Sized Fraud," odwyerpr.com, May 24, 2004.

Before organizing for public relations work, practitioners must consider objectives and strategies, planning and budgets, and research and evaluation. The broad environment in which the organization operates must dictate overall business objectives. These, in turn, dictate specific public relations objectives and strategies. Once these have been defined, the task of organizing for a public relations program should flow naturally.

Environment
  └► Business objectives
        └► Public relations objectives and strategies
              └►Public relations programs

Setting objectives, formulating strategies, and planning are essential if the public relations function is to be considered equal in stature to other management processes. Traditionally, the public relations management process involves four steps:

1. **Defining the problem or opportunity.** This requires researching current attitudes and opinions about the issue, product, candidate, or company in question and determining the essence of the problem.
2. **Programming.** This is the formal planning stage, which addresses key constituent publics, strategies, tactics, and goals.
3. **Action.** This is the communications phase, when the program is implemented.
4. **Evaluation.** The final step in the process is the assessment of what worked, what didn't, and how to improve in the future.[6]

Each of these four process steps is important. Most essential is starting with a firm base of research and a solid foundation of planning.

All planning requires thinking. Planning a short-term public relations program to promote a new service may require less thought and time than planning a long-term campaign to win support for a public policy issue. However, in each case, the public relations plan must include clear-cut objectives to achieve organizational goals, targeted strategies to reach those objectives, specific tactics to implement the strategies, and measurement methods to determine whether the tactics worked.

Creating the Public Relations Plan

The public relations plan must be spelled out in writing. Its organization must answer management's concerns and questions about the campaign being recommended. Here's one way it might be organized and what it should answer.

1. **Executive summary**—an overview of the plan.
2. **Communication process**—how it works, for understanding and training purposes.
3. **Background**—mission statement, vision, values, events that led to the need for the plan.
4. **Situation analysis**—major issues and related facts the plan will deal with.
5. **Message statement**—the plan's major ideas and emerging themes, all of which look to the expected outcome.
6. **Audiences**—strategic constituencies related to the issues, listed in order of importance, with whom you wish to develop and maintain relationships.
7. **Key audience messages**—one- or two-sentence messages that you want to be understood by each key audience.
8. **Implementation**—issues, audiences, messages, media, timing, cost, expected outcomes, and method of evaluation—all neatly spelled out.
9. **Budget**—the plan's overall budget presented in the organization's accepted style.
10. **Monitoring and evaluation**—how the plan's results will be measured and evaluated against a previously set benchmark or desired outcome.[7]

A simpler, hypothetical five-part public relations plan for the fictional Fribbert's Frosty Frappacino might break down like this:

I. Situation.

Our world is moving faster than ever before. PDAs and cell phones have overtaken our every minute. Even leisure time activities have morphed into intensity—from power yoga to power lunch to the 20-minute workout. The coffee break has become passé. In short, the world desperately needs "to chill." And what better beverage to chill with than Fribbert's Frosty Frapp?

II. Business Objectives.

- To increase Fribbert's Frosty Frapp market share nationally by 20%.
- To increase Fribbert's Frosty Frapp market share among young adults by 30%.
- To increase product recall of Fribbert's among all cold beverages by 25%.

III. Public Relations Objectives.

- Tie coffee break time with the need to "chill" with Fribbert's Frosty Frapp.
- Generate buzz among younger workers to chill not with coffee but with Fribbert's Frosty Frapp.
- Instill the importance of "chillin'."

IV. Strategies.

- Leverage a familiar concept—the coffee break—with a new approach—the Frapp chill.
- Spread the word about the Frosty Frapp chill.
- Commission original research to underscore the importance of chillin'.
- Recruit topic-specific experts to discuss chillin' and Frosty Frapp.

V. Public Relations Program Elements.

- Fribbert's commissions survey of human resources professionals on the importance of short breaks during the day and associated increases in productivity. The survey will determine how a selection of leading companies handle the need for chillin' time among employees.
- Fribbert's launches national "Need to Chill" (NTC) program to introduce the ritual of "chillin' breaks" in workplaces across America. The NTC program will be led by a board composed of professionals in pertinent areas, such as a psychiatrist, a life coach, a relaxation expert, and a food expert.
- Fribbert's launches a viral e-mail campaign across the nation to encourage recipients to sign a "petition" to appeal to Congress to make the Chillin' Break a federally mandated activity.
- Fribbert's announces a nationwide Chillin' Day, designating a moment in time when employees around the nation will be asked to "stop and chill."
- Advertising support is leveraged with Chillin' Day promotions, particularly on local radio.
- A Chillin' Day spokesperson is appointed, representative of what it means to be "cool and chillin'." Such "cool" personalities as Labron James, Tiki Barber, Snoop Dogg, and Matthew McConaughey will be considered.
- Local news hooks in key market areas are investigated to promote Fribbert's and chillin'.

The beauty of creating a plan like this is that it clearly specifies tactics against which objectives can be measured and evaluated. In devising the public relations plan along these lines, an organization is assured that its public relations programs will reinforce and complement its overall business goals.

Activating the Public Relations Campaign

Any public relations campaign puts all of the aspects of public relations planning—objectives, strategies, research, budgeting, tactics, and evaluation—into one cohesive framework. The plan specifies a series of *what's* to be done and *how's* to get them done—whatever is necessary to reach the objectives.

Every aspect of the public relations plan should be designed to be meaningful and valuable to the organization. The four-part skeleton of a typical public relations campaign plan resembles the following:

1. **Backgrounding the problem.** This is the so-called situation analysis, background, or case statement that specifies the major aims of the campaign. It can be a general statement that refers to audiences, known research, the organization's positions, history, and the obstacles faced in reaching the desired goal. A public relations planner should divide the overriding goal into several subordinate objectives, which are the *what's* to be accomplished.

2. **Preparing the proposal.** The second stage of the campaign plan sketches broad approaches to solve the problem at hand. As in the Fribbert's hypothetical, it outlines the strategies—the *how's*—and the public relations tools to be used to fulfill the objectives. The elements of the public relations proposal may vary, depending on the subject matter, but generally include the following:

   - Situational analysis—description of the challenge as it currently exists, including background on how the situation reached its present state.

   - Scope of assignment—description of the nature of the assignment: what the public relations program will attempt to do.

   - Target audiences—specific targets identified and divided into manageable groups.

   - Research methods—specific research approach to be used.

   - Key messages—specific selected appeals: What do we want to tell our audiences? How do we want them to feel about us? What do we want them to do?

   - Communications vehicles—tactical communications devices to be used.

   - Project team—key players who will participate in the program.

   - Timing and fees—a timetable with proposed costs identified.

   The specific elements of any proposal depend on the unique nature of the program itself. When an outside supplier submits a proposal, additional elements—such as cancellation clauses, confidentiality of work, and references—should also be included.

3. **Implementing the plan.** The third stage of a campaign plan details operating tactics. It may also contain a time chart specifying when each action will take place. Specific activities are defined, people are assigned to them, and deadlines are established. This stage forms the guts of the campaign plan.

4. **Evaluating the campaign.** To find out whether the plan worked, evaluation methods should be spelled out here.

- Did we implement the activities we proposed?
- Did we receive appropriate public recognition for our efforts?
- Did attitudes change—among the community, customers, management—as a result of our programs?

Pretesting and posttesting of audience attitudes, quantitative analysis of event attendance, content analysis of media success, surveys, sales figures, staff reports, letters to management, and feedback from others—the specific method of evaluative testing is up to the practitioner. But the inclusion of a mechanism for evaluation is imperative in terms of verifying results based on shifts in public opinion or actions taken to benefit an organization and its goals.[8]

Finally, although planning the public relations campaign is important, planning must never become an end in itself. The fact is that no matter how important planning may be, public relations is still assessed principally in terms of its action, performance, and practice.

Setting Public Relations Objectives

An organization's goals must define what its public relations goals will be, and the only good goals are ones that can be measured. Public relations objectives and the strategies that flow from them must achieve results. As the baseball pitcher Johnny Sain used to say, "Nobody wants to hear about the labor pains, but everyone wants to see the baby."

So, too, must public relations people think strategically. Strategies are the most crucial decisions of a public relations campaign. They answer the general question, *How will we manage our resources to achieve our goals?* The specific answers then become the public relations tactics used to implement the strategies. Ideally, strategies and tactics should profit from pretesting.

As for objectives, good ones stand up to the following questions:

- Do they clearly describe the end result expected?
- Are they understandable to everyone in the organization?
- Do they list a firm completion date?
- Are they realistic, attainable, and measurable?
- Are they consistent with management's objectives?

Increasingly, public relations professionals are managing by objectives (MBO) and results (MBR) to help quantify the value of public relations in an organization. The two questions most frequently asked by general managers of public relations practitioners are, *How can we measure public relations results?* and *How do we know whether the public relations program is making progress?* MBO can provide public relations professionals with a powerful source of feedback. MBO and MBR tie public relations results to management's predetermined objectives in terms of audiences, messages, and media. Even though procedures for implementing MBO programs differ, most programs share four points:

1. Specification of the organization's goals, with objective measures of the organization's performance
2. Conferences between the superior and the subordinate to agree on achievable goals

3. Agreement between the superior and the subordinate on objectives consistent with the organization's goals

4. Periodic reviews by the superior and the subordinate to assess progress toward achieving the goals

Again, the key is to tie public relations goals to the goals of the organization and then to manage progress toward achieving those goals. The goals themselves should be clearly defined and specific, practical and attainable, and measurable.

The key to using MBO effectively in public relations work can be broken down into seven critical steps:

1. Defining the nature and mission of the work

2. Determining key result areas in terms of time, effort, and personnel

3. Identifying measurable factors on which objectives can be set

4. Setting objectives or determining results to be achieved

5. Preparing tactical plans to achieve specific objectives, including:

   - Programming to establish a sequence of actions to follow

   - Scheduling to set time requirements for each step

   - Budgeting to assign the resources required to reach the goals

   - Fixing individual accountability for the accomplishment of the objectives

   - Reviewing and reconciling through a testing procedure to track progress

6. Establishing rules and regulations to follow

7. Establishing procedures to handle the work[9]

Budgeting for Public Relations

Like any other business activity, public relations programs must be based on sound budgeting. After identifying objectives and strategies, the public relations professional must detail the particular tactics that will help achieve those objectives. No organization can spend indiscriminately. Without a realistic budget, no organization can succeed. Likewise, public relations activities must be disciplined by budgetary realities.

In public relations agencies responsible for producing revenue, *functional budgeting* is the rule; that is, dollars for staff, resources, activities, and so on, are linked to specific revenue-generating activities. Employees are required to turn in time sheets detailing hours worked in behalf of specific clients. In organizations where public relations is a "staff" activity and not responsible for revenue generation, *administrative budgeting* is the rule; that is, budget dollars are assigned generally against the department's allocation for staff and expenses.

The key to budgeting may lie in performing two steps: (1) estimating the extent of the resources—both personnel and purchases—needed to accomplish each activity, and (2) estimating the cost and availability of those resources. With this information in hand, the development of a budget and monthly cash flow for a public relations program becomes easier. Such data also provide the milestones necessary to audit program costs on a routine basis and to make adjustments well in advance of budget crises.

In recent years, as media outlets have expanded exponentially, public relations budgets have increased. National campaigns for national companies—including public relations writing and media placement, media monitoring, toolkits for localized grassroots programs, and special events—often exceed $1 million per year. The Defense Department's public relations work to influence attitudes in the Middle East ran into the tens of millions of dollars. In perhaps the largest public relations budget ever awarded, the American Legacy Foundation—established as a result of the Master Settlement Agreement between 46 states and the tobacco industry in 1999—named Arnold Communications of Boston and its partnering agencies to lead an antismoking public education campaign. The fee? The contract was valued at 50 percent to 85 percent of the $300 million received annually by the foundation.[10]

Whew!

Such whopping budgets are still very much the exception. Most public relations programs operate on limited budgets. In a growing number of instances, "pay-for-performance" public relations has emerged. The premise of this arrangement is that the buyer pays only for what he or she gets, meaning that fees are based on the depth of coverage and the circulation or audience rating of the venue in which coverage appears. If no coverage is achieved, no fee is paid. Most public relations agencies, however, make "no guarantees" that their efforts will be successful and therefore frown on pay-for-performance contracts.[11]

Most public relations agencies treat client costs in a manner similar to that used by legal, accounting, and management consulting firms: The client pays only for services rendered, either on a monthly or yearly retainer basis or on minimum charges based on staff time. Time records are kept by every employee—from chairperson to mail clerk—

Talking Points

Fudging the Fleishman Budget

Public relations budgeting is an art, not a science. And public relations counselors make their living defending clients who find themselves thrashing about in the midst of scandal. Such representation demands that public relations advisors themselves command pristine reputations.

But in 2005, one of the world's foremost public relations agencies found itself on the wrong end of a media onslaught because of one of the ugliest budgetary snarls in the history of public relations practice. Fleishman-Hillard, founded in St. Louis in 1946, has offices stretching from Australia to Tokyo, from Frankfurt and Atlanta. Fleishman represents some of the world's largest companies.

Late in 2004, one of those clients, the City of Los Angeles, hired a private investigator to assist in a lawsuit that charged Fleishman-Hillard with massively overbilling the city as much as $30,000 a month under a $3 million-a-year contract with several city agencies, including the Department of Water and Power, the Department of Airports, and the Convention and Visitors Bureau.

After a three month investigation, the city claimed Fleishman overbilled it by a whopping $4.2 million over six years. Fleishman management was livid, blasting the audit as representing "erroneous assertions to arrive at an inflated overall estimate of questioned costs."

Or at least that's what the company said initially.

Five months later, a more sheepish Fleishman agreed to settle the overbilling lawsuit by paying $4.5 million and waiving an additional $1.3 million in unpaid invoices for public relations services. Fleishman's Los Angeles office manager was one of two senior managers indicted on 15 counts of wire fraud and a single charge of conspiracy. Another Fleishman senior officer pleaded guilty to three counts of fraud for his role in padding the bills.

The overbilling budget scandal was a stunning embarrassment to Fleishman. Summarized the Los Angles Controller, "Fleishman-Hillard not only violated the public trust, they broke the time-honored principles of the public relations profession."

For further information, see "F-H Hits Audit Report, Admits Mistakes," *Jack O'Dwyer's Newsletter* Vol. 37, No. 46, November 24, 2004, 1; "F-H Settles L.A. Legal Squabble," *Jack O'Dwyer's Newsletter,* Vol. 38, No. 17, April 27, 2005, 1; Greg Hazley, "Political Winds Blow as F-H Takes Stand in L.A.," *O'Dwyer's PR Services Report,* January 2005, 1–13; Rick Orlov, "City Hires Private Eye in P.R. Case," *Los Angeles Daily News,* August 13, 2004.

on a daily basis to be sure that agency clients know exactly what they are paying for. Hourly charges for public relations agency employees can range from low double figures per hour to more than $350 to $500 an hour for agency superstars.

Because agency relationships are based on trust, it is important that clients understand the derivation of costs. In recent years, debate has raged over markups on expenses paid on behalf of clients by public relations firms. Out-of-pocket expenses—for meals, hotels, transportation, and the like—are generally charged back to clients at cost. But when an agency pays in advance for larger expense items—printing, photography, graphics, design—it is standard industry practice to mark up such expenses by a factor approximating 17.65 percent. This figure, which the vast majority of agencies use, was borrowed from the advertising profession and represents the multiplicative inverse of the standard 15 percent commission that ad agencies collect on advertising placement.

The guiding rule in agency budgeting is to ensure that the client is aware of how charges are being applied so that nasty surprises might be avoided when bills are received.

Implementing Public Relations Programs

The duties and responsibilities of public relations practitioners are as diverse as the publics with whom different institutions deal. Specific public relations tasks are as varied as the organizations served. Here is a partial list of public relations duties:

- **Media relations:** Coordinating relationships with the online, print, and electronic media, which includes arranging and monitoring press interviews, writing news releases and related press materials, organizing press conferences, and answering media inquiries and requests. A good deal of media relations work consists of attempting to gain favorable news coverage for the firm.

- **Internal communications:** Informing employees and principals through a variety of means, including intranet, newsletters, television, and meetings. Traditionally, this role has emphasized news-oriented communications rather than benefits-oriented ones, which are usually the province of personnel departments.

- **Government relations and public affairs:** Coordinating activities with legislators on local, state, and federal levels. This includes legislative research activities and public policy formation.

- **Community relations:** Orchestrating interaction with the community, perhaps including open houses, tours, and employee volunteer efforts designed to reflect the supportive nature of the organization to the community.

- **Investor relations:** Managing relations with the investment community, including the firm's present and potential stockholders. This task emphasizes personal contact with securities analysts, institutional investors, and private investors.

- **Consumer relations:** Supporting activities with customers and potential customers, with activities ranging from hard-sell product promotion activities to "soft" consumer advisory services.

- **Public relations research:** Conducting opinion research, which involves assisting in the public policy formation process through the coordination and interpretation of attitudinal studies of key publics.

- **Public relations writing:** Coordinating the institution's printed voice with its public through reprints of speeches, annual reports, quarterly statements, and product and company brochures.
- **Special publics relations:** Coordinating relationships with outside specialty groups, such as suppliers, educators, students, nonprofit organizations, and competitors.
- **Institutional advertising:** Managing the institutional—or nonproduct—advertising image as well as being called on increasingly to assist in the management of more traditional product advertising.
- **Graphics:** Coordinating the graphic and photographic services of the organization. To do this task well requires knowledge of desktop publishing, typography, layout, and art.
- **Web site management:** Coordinating the organization's online "face," including Web site design and ongoing counsel, updating, and even management of the site.
- **Philanthropy:** Managing the gift-giving apparatus, which ordinarily consists of screening and evaluating philanthropic proposals and allocating the organization's available resources.
- **Special events.** Coordinating special events, including travel for company management, corporate celebrations and exhibits, dinners, groundbreakings, and grand openings.
- **Management counseling.** Advising managers on alternative options and recommended choices in light of public responsibilities.

Again, this is but a partial list of the tasks ordinarily assigned to public relations professionals.

Public relations managers frequently use the visualization tools of Gantt and PERT charts to control and administer these project tasks. The Gantt chart, developed by Charles Gantt in 1917, focuses on the sequence of tasks necessary for completion of the project at hand. Each task on a Gantt chart is represented as a single horizontal bar. The length of each bar corresponds to the time necessary for completion. Arrows connecting independent tasks reflect the relationships between the tasks. PERT (program evaluation and review technique) charts were first developed in the 1950s by the Navy to help manage complex projects with a high degree of intertask dependency. The PERT chart shows the relationship between each activity. These relationships create pathways through the process. The "critical path" is a series of tasks that must be completed in a certain time period for the project to be completed on schedule (Figure 5-3).

The Public Relations Department

Public relations professionals generally work in one of two organizational structures: (1) as a staff professional in a public relations department of a corporation, university, hospital, sports franchise, political campaign, religious institution, and so on, whose task is to support the primary business of the organization, or (2) as a line professional in a public relations agency, whose primary task is to help the organization earn revenue.

Consider the public relations department. Once an organization has analyzed its environment, established its objectives, set up measurement standards, and thought about appropriate plans, programs, and budgets, it is ready to organize a public relations

Prototype Gantt Chart
Packaged Goods Product
Target Start of Ship at Start of Year, Retail Availability in March, Marketing Support in April

Category	Activity	Jan	Feb	Mar	Apr	May	Jun	Jul	Aug
Product	Exploratory Research	XXX							
	Concept Development		XXX						
	Quantitative Research			XXX	XXX				
Package	Product Development			XXX	XXX	XXX	XXX	XXX	
	Structural Package Dev			XXX	XXX	XXX	XXX	XXX	
	Graphics Development				XXX	XXX	XXX	XXX	
Financial	Pricing & Profit	XXX			XXX				
	Volume Projections	XXX			XXX	XXX			
	Budget Development								
Marketing Plan	Sales Promotion				XXX	XXX	XXX	XXX	
	Advertising				XXX	XXX	XXX	XXX	
	Publicity						XXX	XXX	
	Produce Ads/Collateral Material								XXX
Purchasing	Long Lead Supplies				XXX	XXX	XXX	XXX	XXX
	Shorter Lead Supplies						XXX	XXX	XXX
Begin Production	Inventory Build								XXX
	Ship To Field Warehouses								
Sales Meetings	Present To Sales Force								
	Present To Trade								
Start Shipping	Begin Delivery To Trade								

FIGURE 5-3 Critical path chart. Daniel Jay Morrison & Associates (www.djmconsult.com) created this prototypical chart to trace the critical path of a product coming to market. (Courtesy of Daniel Jay Morrison & Associates, Inc.)

department. Departments range from one-person operations to far-flung networks of hundreds of people, such as at the U.S. Department of Defense or ExxonMobil, with staff around the world, responsible for relations with the press, investors, civic groups, employees, and many different governments.

Today, correctly, about half of all corporate communications departments report to the chairman, president, and/or CEO. This is an improvement from the past and indicative of the higher stature that the function enjoys. About one sixth of public relations departments report to advertising or marketing, and another one sixth report to a vice president of administration.[12] Clearly, reporting to the CEO is eminently preferable to reporting to a legal, financial, or administrative executive, who may tend to "filter" top-management messages.

In government, public relations professionals (although, as we will see in Chapter 13, they're not called "public relations" professionals) typically report directly to department heads. In universities, the public relations function is frequently coupled with fund-raising and development activities. In hospitals, public relations is typically tied to the marketing function.

As for the names of the departments in which public relations is housed, organizations use a wide variety of names for the function. Ironically, the trend today seems to be away from use of the traditional term *public relations* and toward *corporate communications*.

Whatever the department is called and to whomever it reports, the pressing need today for chief communications officers and their colleagues is to demonstrate a high level of skills—from writing to counseling to understanding the critical importance of information in the wired world in which we live.

The Public Relations Agency

Now consider the public relations agency. The biggest difference between an external agency and an internal department is perspective. The former is outside looking in; the latter is inside looking out (often literally for itself). Sometimes the use of an agency is necessary to escape the tunnel-vision syndrome that afflicts some firms, in which a detached viewpoint is desperately needed. An agency unfettered by internal corporate politics might be better trusted to present management with an objective reading of the concerns of its publics.

An agency has the added advantage of not being taken for granted by a firm's management. Unfortunately, management sometimes has a greater regard for an outside specialist than for an inside one. This attitude frequently defies logic but is nonetheless often true. Generally, if management is paying (sometimes quite handsomely) for outside counsel, it tends to listen carefully to the advice.

Agencies generally organize according to industry groupings. Larger agencies are divided into such areas as health care, sports, fashion, technology, finance, and so on. Account teams are assigned specific clients. Team members bill clients on an hourly basis, with most firms intending to retain two thirds of each individual's hourly billing rate as income. In other words, if an account executive bills at a rate of $300 per hour—and many senior counselors do—the firm expects to retain $200 of that rate toward its profit. In recent years, as clients have begun to manage resources more rigorously, agencies have gotten much more systematic in measuring success and in keeping customers from migrating to a competitor. Indeed, the most difficult part of agency work is not *attracting* clients but *retaining* them.

Public relations agencies today, as noted, are huge businesses. The Council of Public Relations Firms estimates the revenue of the worldwide public relations industry at approximately \$5.4 billion.[13] Worldwide revenues of the top 50 public relations firms totaled in excess of \$3.7 billion in 2001. Over the past two decades, most of the top public relations firms have been subsumed by communications holding companies, the most prominent of which, along with the agencies they own, are the following:

- **Omnicom:** Fleishman-Hillard, Ketchum, Porter-Novelli, Brodeur Worldwide, Clark & Weinstock, Gavin Anderson & Company, and Cone
- **Interpublic Group:** Access Communications; Carmichael, Lynch, Spong; DeVries Public Relations; Golin-Harris; MWW; Tierney Public Relations; and Weber-Shandwick Worldwide
- **WPP Group:** Burson-Marsteller, Cohn & Wolfe, Hill & Knowlton, and Ogilvy Public Relations Worldwide
- **Havas:** Euro RSCG Middleberg, Magnet Communications, and Noonan Russon Presence Euro RSCG West
- **Grey:** APCO Worldwide and GCI Group
- **Publicis:** Manning, Selvage & Lee, Publicis Dialog, and Rowland Worldwide

Public relations purists bemoan the incursion of these mammoth companies because many are dominated by advertising agencies. Defenders point to the potential synergy between the two disciplines. One casualty of the takeover of the world's leading public relations firms by these holding companies is that the largest agencies no longer make public their annual revenues and earnings. Nonetheless, a compilation of the net fees of the largest independent public relations firms still shows robust annual revenues (Table 5-1). What is indisputable is the tremendous growth of the profession.

While an outsider's fresh point of view can be helpful in focusing a client on particular problems and opportunities and on how best to capitalize on them, outside agencies are still just that—"outside." As a consequence, they are often unfamiliar with details affecting the situation of particular companies and with the idiosyncrasies of company management. The good external counselor must constantly work to overcome this barrier. The best client–agency relationships are those with free-flowing communications between internal and external public relations groups so that both resources are kept informed about corporate policies, strategies, and tactics. A well-oiled, complementary department–agency relationship can result in a more positive communications approach for an organization.

Reputation Management

Many public relations agencies in recent years, particularly those purchased by the large advertising agency conglomerates, have declared special emphasis on *reputation management*.

What is reputation management? Public relations purists argue that this is precisely what they have been doing all along—helping to "manage" an organization's "reputation," that is, its brand, position, goodwill, or image.

Essentially, an organization's reputation is composed of two elements: (1) the more "rational" products and performance, and (2) more "emotional" behavioral factors, such as customer service, CEO performance, personal experience with the company, and the like.

Table 5-1

O'Dwyer's Rankings (Top 25) of Independent PR Firms with Major U.S. Operations

In 2004, more than half of the top 50 independent public relations firms enjoyed double-digit gains in fee income, testifying to the strength of the public relations counseling business.

Firm	2005 Net Fees	Empl	% Change from 2004
1. Edelman	$261,858,702	1,848	+13.6%
2. Ruder Finn	92,110,000	568	+2.7
3. Waggener Edstrom	84,871,000	594	+8.0
4. APCO Worldwide	73,300,000	405	+29.0
5. Schwartz Comms	22,134,350	173	+21.2
6. Zeno Group	19,915,941	113	+19.9
7. Dan Klores Comms	19,500,000	131	+12.1
8. Qorvis Comms	18,245,000	69	+19.1
9. Gibbs & Soell	17,245,000	105	+14.2
10. A&R Partners	14,092,229	95	+17.6
11. Clear!Blue Comms	13,375,071	66	+31.0
12. Alan Taylor Comms	13,275,000	75	+36.0
13. Access Public Relations	12,299,478	60	+38.2
14. Padilla Speer Beardsley	11,750,335	91	+13.1
15. Integrated Corporate Rels	11,580,151	43	+36.0
16. CRT/tanaka	10,433,358	56	+16.3
17. The Rogers Group	10,409,889	62	−3.0
18. RFBinder Partners	10,178,000	67	+17.5
19. The Hoffman Agency	9,500,000	41	+3.8
20. Widmeyer Comms	9,264,000	51	+11.6
21. French/ West/ Vaughan	8,697,995	66	+9.0
22. Spectrum Science Comms	8,674,064	58	+35.0
23. Levick Strategic Comms	8,280,372	29	+8.4
24. M Booth & Assocs	8,069,262	52	+32.8
25. Cooney/Waters Group	7,968,070	33	+2.6

(Courtesy of Jack O'Dwyer Company, www.odwyerpr.com. Reprinted by permission)

Reputations matter because a company with a good reputation can charge premium prices, have greater access to new markets and products, have greater access to capital, profit from greater word-of-mouth endorsement, and possess an unduplicated identity. Such distinctive organizations as Tiffany, Dell Computer, Dreamworks film studio, and the New York Yankees baseball team are all examples of entities with unique and positive reputations that translate into hard-nosed advantages.

Reputation management, then, is *the ability to link reputation to business goals to increase support and advocacy and increase organizational success through profits, contributions, attendance, and so on.*

What do reputation managers do? The behaviors they attempt to influence include (1) persuading consumers to recommend and buy their products, (2) persuading investors to invest in their organization, (3) persuading competent job seekers to enlist as employees, (4) persuading other strong organizations to joint venture with them, and (5) persuading people to support the organization when it is attacked.

Stated another way, the requisite of reputation managers is to help build, defend, and maintain an organization's reputation. Public relations purists, however, would argue that these reputation management functions have always been the province a specific group within an organization—its public relations professionals.

Thus, the bottom line on reputation management is that it is—and has been for the better part of a century—the fundamental mandate for the public relations person to promote and maintain and defend and enhance and sustain the organization's reputation, in perpetuity—in other words, forever.

Where Are the Jobs?

Like other support functions, public relations suffered when the high-tech, stock market bubble burst at the beginning of the 21st century. In recent years, however, the field has made a substantial comeback.

The future of the practice of public relations, like the future of the U.S. and world economy, promises to be steady and strong.

- In terms of industry specialization, public relations positions in health care–related fields have been particularly strong in recent years, and the area of consumer/retail has also rebounded nicely.[14]

- Meanwhile, the high-tech industry, which fell farther and faster than most others after its unprecedented buildup in the 1990s, will need skilled public relations managers to help it regain a position of prominence, trust, and respect among investors and others.

- In terms of functional areas of specialization, the function of managing a company's reputation ranks high on the public relations job scale. So, too, do the areas of investor relations and crisis management. These three specialties also pay considerably more than other areas of the field.[15]

- Worldwide corporations, faced with increased scrutiny from the media, government, and the general public to act ethically and behave responsibly, have recognized the need for talented, top communications managers.

- Public relations agencies, wiser and more experienced after the boom-bust phenomenon of the early years of the 21st century, will continue to expand in the 21st century. Just as a plethora of high-tech public relations agencies emerged in the 1990s, so, too, is it likely that the move toward public relations specialization among agencies will continue in the 21st century.

- In the nonprofit realm, public relations positions in hospitals, in particular, are likely to grow as managed care becomes the reality and health care organizations become more competitive in attracting patients and winning community approval. Other nonprofits—schools, museums, associations—all faced with fewer resources and more competition for community funding—will also require increased public relations help to attract development and membership funds.

- Finally, one other public relations skill that will be in increased demand, certainly for the remainder of this decade, is employee communications. Employees in the 21st century, burned by layoffs, pension fund losses and restructurings, and failures of management to be credible, must be convinced that their organizations deserve their allegiance. This will be a job largely for public relations practitioners—to win back employee trust.[16]

What Does It Pay?

Without question, the communications function has increased in importance and clout in the new century. Top communications professionals in many large corporations today draw compensation packages well into six figures. According to one survey, the average vice president of corporate communications earned almost $190,000 annually.[17]

The same survey indicated that although entry-level jobs for writers and editors generally fall into the $20,000 to $30,000 range, more senior writers can expect to earn in the $50,000 range. Managers of public relations units, press relations, consumer relations, and financial communications may earn anywhere from $40,000 to beyond $100,000. Agency account executives fall into a similar range. Public relations directors may earn salaries from $40,000 to more than $500,000.

According to a 2004 report of the U.S. Bureau of Labor Statistics, annual mean wages in major categories of public relations work break down as follows:

- Public relations agencies: $111,860
- Companies and other enterprises: $101,990
- Professional organizations: $ 79,820
- Philanthropic services: $ 76,870
- Colleges and universities: $ 74,780[18]

Yet another 2005 study, by *PR Week* magazine and Korn/Ferry International, of 1,864 public relations people, indicated that the average salary of public relations professionals—with an average of 12 years in the business—was once again on the upswing, rising 7 percent year-to-year to $87,461. As one executive recruiter summarized the renewed demand for public relations workers, "There is a real sense of optimism. Companies are willing to spend. There is a huge increase in demand for corporate communications."[19]

In terms of geography, the top-paying U.S. cities for public relations practitioners were the following (see also Figure 5-4):

- Boston: $132,087
- New York: $115,730
- San Francisco: $108,985
- San Jose/Silicon Valley: $106,119
- Seattle: $101,700
- Milwaukee: $100,500

As to the difference in public relations skills, the *PR Week* survey revealed that investor relations specialists earned the highest salaries, followed by specialists in reputation management and crisis management. At the top of the pile, according to the research, were chief communications officers with significant experience in the public relations field, earning an average of $327,000 annually. At the very top were 8 percent earning $1 million or more for public relations work. Not bad.

Women and Minorities

Two decades ago, the practice of public relations was overwhelmingly a bastion of white males. Today, it is women who predominate in public relations work. And minorities—African Americans, Asians, and Hispanics—while still small in total numbers in the field, have nonetheless all increased their participation in public relations.

Salary by City

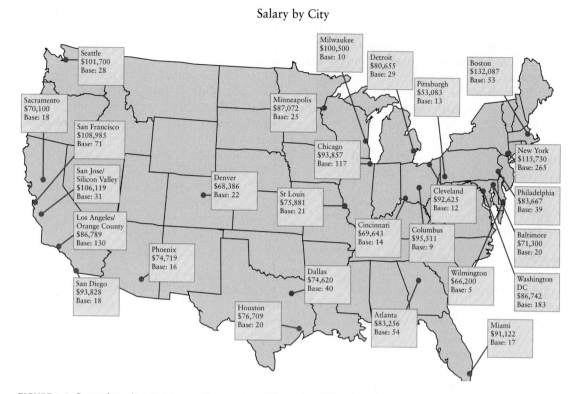

FIGURE 5-4 Coasts have it. Want to earn the most in public relations? Then head for the coast, with eastern cities like Boston and New York and western ones like Seattle and San Francisco pacing the field. (Reprinted from *PR Week* magazine, February 21, 2005.)

The issue of increased feminization of public relations—the establishment of a so-called "velvet ghetto"—is a particularly thorny one for the practice. One area of constant consternation is the traditional discrepancy between men's and women's salaries and upper-management positions—the glass ceiling for women in public relations.

Recent experience suggests that times are changing. University public relations programs across the country report a preponderance of female students, outnumbering males by as much as 80 percent. Moreover, the number of women executives in public relations has also increased in recent years. While the number of male public relations executives still greatly exceeds the number of female public relations executives, the existence of a glass ceiling seems to be a relic of the past.[20]

That's the good news.

The not-so-good news is that women and minorities are still paid less than their male counterparts. One 2005 survey reported that while a white male averaged $107,960 annually, the average woman earned $75,498. On the plus side, companies report that an increasing number of newly recruited public relations practitioners are members of diverse populations.[21]

Last Word

In the 21st century, the practice of public relations is firmly accepted as part of the management process of any well-run organization.

Public relations objectives and goals, strategies, and tactics must flow directly from the organization's overall goals. Public relations strategies must reflect organizational strategies, and tactics must be designed to realize the organization's business objectives. Stated another way, public relations programs are worth little if they fail to further management's and the organization's goals.

As media of communications have proliferated and an organization's reputation has become more essential, the practice of public relations enjoys a significant management role and challenge in this new century. Coming out of the corporate and accounting scandals of the early 2000s and the loss of confi-

dence in business and CEOs, management must depend on the able assistance of proper public relations practice to help reestablish trust in society's major institutions.

That may be one reason why *Fortune* listed PR specialists as one of the fastest-growing professional jobs between now and 2012, predicted to increase by more than 20 percent.[22] Or, in the words of one public relations recruiter, "There has never been a better time to be in the business. And that will continue for the next 10 to 20 years."[23]

Discussion Starters

1. What is the management process of public relations?
2. Why is it imperative that public relations report to top management?
3. What are the elements that make up a public relations plan?
4. What questions must be answered in establishing valid public relations objectives?
5. What elements go into framing a public relations budget?
6. What safeguards could Fleishman-Hillard impose that would protect against further budget padding problems?

7. What are the fundamental differences between working in a corporation and working in an agency as a public relations professional?
8. What are several of the primary tactical tasks assigned to the public relations function?
9. What may be the primary areas of opportunity for public relations professionals in the years ahead?
10. Why has the field of public relations been accused of being a "velvet ghetto"?

Top of the Shelf

IdeaWise: How to Transform Your Ideas into Tomorrow's Innovations

Steve Rivkin and Fraser P. Seitel, New York: John Wiley & Sons, 2002.

According to these two authors (whose names, frankly, are eerily familiar), anyone is capable of being an innovator. The book exposes as high-priced charlatans the vast majority of motivational consultants hired annually by desperate, innovation-starved managers. The authors argue that top managers of organizations, groping to be creative, waste millions on off-site retreats and misguided motivational mantras that lead them to such creative catastrophes as Crystal Clear Pepsi, Premier smokeless cigarettes, and Susan B. Anthony dollar coins.

Instead, they suggest that you "steal" to be creative. Collect ideas from your surroundings. Borrow ideas from others. Adapt existing ideas and then apply solutions to substitute, combine, magnify/minimize, exchange, eliminate, and reverse.

Then it's time to apply a six-question checklist to see if a creative suggestion makes sense. If it does, then you, too, can become *IdeaWise*.

CASE STUDY

Exxon Corporation's Bad Good Friday

In the history of public relations practice, few communications issues have been handled as questionably, received as much global notoriety, and had such far-reaching implications on the profession as those involving the Exxon Corporation in 1989.

At 8:30 a.m. on March 24, 1989—Good Friday, no less—Lawrence G. Rawl, chairman and chief executive of the Exxon Corporation, one of the world's largest companies, was in his kitchen sipping coffee when the phone rang.

"What happened? Did it lose an engine? Break a rudder?" Rawl asked the caller.

What happened was that an Exxon tanker had run aground and was dumping gummy crude oil into the frigid waters of Prince William Sound, just outside the harbor of Valdez, Alaska.

What was about to happen to Mr. Rawl and his company—and to the environment—was arguably the worst environmental disaster in the history of the United States.

The facts, painfully portrayed in media across the country, were these: The *Exxon Valdez*, a 987-foot tanker (Figure 5-5), piloted by a captain who was later revealed to have been legally drunk, ran aground on a reef 25 miles southwest of the port of Valdez. The resulting rupture caused a spill of 260,000 barrels, the largest spill ever in North America, affecting 1,300 square miles of water, damaging some 600 miles of coastline, and killing as many as 4,000 Alaskan sea otters.

The communications disaster also enshrined the name Exxon in the all-time Public Relations Hall of Shame.

To Go or Not to Go

The first problem that confronted Exxon and its top management after news of the Good Friday spill had broken was whether Chairman Rawl should fly to Prince William Sound to demonstrate the company's concern. This was what Union Carbide Chairman Warren Anderson did when his company suffered a devastating industrial explosion in Bhopal, India.

FIGURE 5-5 The Exxon Valdez. (Courtesy of O'Dwyerpr.com)

If Rawl went to Alaska, the reasoning went, he might be able to reassure the public that the people who run Exxon acknowledged their misdeed and would make amends. What could be a better show of concern than the chairman flying to the local scene of the tragedy?

On the other hand, a consensus of executives around Rawl argued that he should remain in New York. "What are you going to do?" they asked. "We've already said we've done it, we're going to pay for it, and we're responsible for it." Rawl's more effective role, said these advisers, was right there at Exxon headquarters in Manhattan.

In the end, the latter view triumphed. Rawl did not go to Alaska. He left the cleanup in "capable hands" and sent a succession of lower-ranking executives to Alaska to deal with the spill. As he summarized in an interview one year after the Prince William Sound nightmare, "We had concluded that there was simply too much for me to coordinate from New York. It wouldn't have made any difference if I showed up and made a speech in the town forum. I wasn't going to spend the summer there; I had other things to do."

Rawl's failure to fly immediately to Valdez struck some as shortsighted. Said one media consultant about Rawl's communications decision, "The chairman should have been up there walking in the oil and picking up dead birds."

Where to Establish Media Central

The second dilemma that confronted Exxon was where to establish its media center. This decision started, correctly enough, with Exxon senior managers concluding that the impact of the spill was so great that news organizations should be kept informed as events unfolded. Exxon wanted to take charge of the news flow and give the public, through the news media, a credible, concerned, and wholly committed corporate response.

It decided that the best place to do this would be in Valdez, Alaska, itself." Just about every news organization worth its salt had representatives in Valdez," said Exxon's publicity chief." But in retrospect, we should have sent live broadcasts of news conferences to several points around the country."

The problem was that Valdez was a remote Alaskan town with limited communications operations. This complicated the ability of Exxon to disseminate information quickly. As *Oil & Gas Journal* stated later: "Exxon did not update its media relations people elsewhere in the world. It told reporters it was Valdez or nothing."

Additionally, there was a four-hour time difference between Valdez and New York. The phone lines to Valdez quickly became jammed, and even Rawl couldn't find a knowledgeable official to brief him.

That left news organizations responsible for keeping the public informed cut off from Exxon information during the early part of the crisis. Because news conferences took place at unsuitable viewing hours for television networks and too late for many morning newspapers, predictable accusations of an Exxon cover-up resulted. Said one Exxon official about the decision to put the communications center in Valdez, "It didn't work."

Rapidity of Response

A cardinal rule in any crisis is: Keep ahead of the information flow—try not to let events get ahead of you. Here Exxon had a third problem.

First, it took Chairman Rawl a full week to make any public comment on the spill. When he did, it was to blame others: The U.S. Coast Guard and Alaskan officials were "holding up" his company's efforts to clean up the spill. But Rawl's words were too little, too late. The impression persisted that, in light of the delay in admitting responsibility, Exxon was not responding vigorously enough.

A full 10 days after the crisis, Exxon placed an apologetic advertisement in 166 newspapers. To some readers, the ad seemed self-serving and failed to address the many pointed questions raised about Exxon's conduct.

"It seems the company was a bit too relaxed in its capabilities," offered the president of the Public Relations Society of America. Meanwhile, one group that wasn't relaxed was the Alaska state legislature, which enacted a tax increase on oil from the North Slope fields within weeks of the Exxon spill. Congressional committees in Washington moved just as quickly to increase liability limits and potential compensation for oil-spill damage and to increase the money available through the industry-financed Offshore Oil Pollution Compensation Fund. When Exxon hesitated, its opponents seized the initiative. Concluded another public relations executive, "They lost the battle in the first 48 hours."

How High the Profile

Exxon's communications response in the face of this most challenging crisis in its history was, to put it mildly, muted.

From an operations and logistics viewpoint, Exxon did a good job. The company immediately set up animal rescue projects, launched a major cleanup effort, and agreed to pick up a substantial percentage of the cost. But it made the mistake of downplaying the crisis in public.

Exxon's public statements sometimes contradicted information from other sources. At one point, an Exxon spokesperson said that damage from the oil spill would be minimal. Others watching the industry said the damage was likely to be substantial.

Chairman Rawl, an otherwise blunt and outspoken CEO, seemed defensive and argumentative in his public comments. In one particularly disastrous personal appearance on *CBS Morning News,* Rawl glared at interviewer Kathleen Sullivan and snapped: "I can't give you details of our cleanup plan. It's thick and complicated. And I haven't had a chance to read it yet. The CEO of a major company doesn't have time to read every plan."

Exxon's attempts to calm the public also were criticized. Its ad drew fire for not expressing enough concern. It hired an outside firm to do a series of video news releases to show how the company was cleaning up the spill. At an estimated cost of more than $3 million, a 13-minute tape was shown at the corporation's annual meeting. The video, called *Progress in Alaska,* attracted intense criticism from those attending the conference as well as from the press. *USA Today* called the tape "Exxon's worst move of the day." When the consultant who devised the video wrote an article in the *New York Times* defending Exxon's approach in Alaska, the Alaskan representative to the National Wildlife Federation responded with a blistering letter to the editor, noting that the consultant omitted in his article that the spill had resulted in the death of more than 15,000 sea birds and numerous otters and eagles.

Exxon then added an environmental expert to its board of directors, but only after pension funds, which control a large chunk of its stock, demanded such a response.

Dealing with the Aftermath

Finally, Exxon was forced to deal with all the implications of what its tanker had wrought in Valdez. The company became embroiled in controversy when it sent a $30,000 contribution to the Alaska Public Radio Network, which covered the crisis on a daily basis. The network, sniffing "conflict of interest," flatly turned down Exxon's attempted largesse. Subsequently, a special appropriations bill was introduced in the Alaskan legislature to forward an identical amount to Alaska Public Radio.

The accident and the company's reaction to it also had consequences for the oil industry. Plans to expand drilling into the Alaskan National Wildlife Refuge were shelved by Congress, and members called for new laws increasing federal involvement in oil spills.

The company's employees, too, felt confused, embarrassed, and betrayed. Summarizing the prevailing mood at the company, one Exxon worker said, "Whenever I travel now, I feel like I have a target painted on my chest."

In 1996, seven years after the *Exxon Valdez* ran aground, a weary Exxon announced to the world that it was closing the books on its unforgettable disaster.

Total cost to Exxon: $2.5 billion.

But that wasn't all. In 1999, a full decade after the *Exxon Valdez* dumped 11 million gallons of oil into Prince William Sound, the Exxon Corporation—rechristened ExxonMobil—went to court in Alaska to get the courts to overturn an unusual federal restriction. The unique law barred one ship, the *Exxon Valdez,* from ever again sailing into Prince William Sound. Exxon alleged that the ship, renamed the *SeaRiver Mediterranean,* was being unfairly singled out. Specifically, the legislation barred "vessels that have spilled more than 1 million gallons of oil into the marine environment after March 22, 1989" from entering Prince William Sound.

Coincidentally, only one sailing vessel fit that description.

The Lessons

The lessons of the *Exxon Valdez*'s Good Friday oil spill would not soon be forgotten by corporate managers. The episode, predicted one, "will become a textbook example of what not to do when an unexpected crisis thrusts a company into the limelight."

Questions

1. What would you have recommended Chairman Rawl do upon learning of the Prince William Sound oil spill?

2. How would you have handled the media in this case?

3. What would have been your timing in terms of public relations responses in this case?

4. What would be your overall public relations strategy—aggressive, low key, or middle-of-the-road—if you were Exxon's public relations director?

5. Do you think this case will ever qualify as a "textbook example" of what not to do in a crisis?

6. Now that Exxon has merged with Mobil, what is the corporation doing about environmental issues? Visit the news release homepage (www.exxon.com/em_newsrelease/index.html) and follow the link to browse the oil giant's recent news releases. What is ExxonMobil doing about environmental issues? Why would the company continue to issue news releases about environmental activities so many years after the Exxon Valdez incident?

For further information about the *Exxon Valdez* case, see Richard Behar, "Exxon Strikes Back," *Time* (March 26, 1990): 62–63; Claudia H. Deutsch, "The Giant with a Black Eye," *New York Times* (April 2, 1989): B1–4; E. Bruce Harrison, with Tom Prugh, "Assessing the Damage," *Public Relations Journal* (October 1989): 40–45; John Holusha, "Exxon's Public-Relations Problem," *New York Times* (April 21, 1989): D1–4; Peter Nulty, "Exxon's Problem: Not What You Think," *Fortune* (April 23, 1990): 202–204; James Lukaszewski, "How Vulnerable Are You? The Lessons from Valdez," *Public Relations Quarterly* (Fall 1989): 5–6; Phillip M. Perry, "Exxon Falters in PR Effort Following Alaskan Oil Spill," *O'Dwyer's PR Services Report* (July 1989): 1, 16–22; Bill Richards, "Exxon Is Battling a Ban on an Infamous Tanker," *Wall Street Journal* (July 29, 1998): C1; Allanna Sullivan, "Rawl Wishes He'd Visited Valdez Sooner," *Wall Street Journal* (June 30, 1989): B7; Joseph B. Treaster, "With Insurers' Payment, Exxon Says *Valdez* Case is Ended," *New York Times* (November 1, 1996): B2; and Paul Wiseman, "Firm Finds *Valdez* Oil Fowls Image," *USA Today* (April 26, 1990): B1.

Voice of Authority

An Interview with Peter Drucker

Peter Drucker, who died in 2005 at the age of 95, was called the "greatest thinker management theory has produced" by the *London Economist.* His work influenced Winston Churchill, Bill Gates, Jack Welch, and the Japanese business establishment. His more than three dozen books, written over 66 years and translated into 30 languages, also delivered his philosophy to newly promoted managers just out of the office cubicle. Dr. Drucker counseled presidents, bishops, baseball managers, CEOs, and symphony conductors on the finer points

of management success. In his 88th year, Dr. Drucker sat with the author for this interview.

What would you say have been your greatest contributions to business and society?
One, I made management visible. People say I've discovered management—that's nonsense. I made it into a discipline.

Second, I was also the first one who said that people are a resource and not just a cost, and they have to be placed where they can make a contribution. The only ones who took me up on it were the Japanese for a long time.

The third one is knowledge—that knowledge work would be preeminent.

Four, I was the first to say that the purpose of business is to create the customer and to innovate. That I think is a major contribution. That took a long time to sink in—that management is not this mad dog of internal rules and regulations, that it's a discipline that can be learned and taught and practiced.

I think those four. The rest are secondary.

What is your view of today's public relations practice?
There is no public relations. There's publicity, promotion, advertising, but "relations" by definition is a two-way street. And the more important job and the more difficult is not to bring business and the executives to the outside but to bring the outside to these terribly insulated people. And this will be far more important in the next 20 years, when the outside is going to change beyond all recognition. I'm not only talking business CEOs but also university presidents and

even bishops—several of my charity patients are bishops—all need to know what's going on outside.

Can you elaborate?

With an example. Have you ever heard of Paul Garrett?

Paul Garrett came out of journalism. He wanted to build a proper public relations department, to bring to General Motors what the outside was like. He would have been very effective. But GM didn't let him. Alfred Sloan (GM's CEO) brought Garrett in 1930 to keep GM out of *Fortune*. *Fortune* was founded as a muckraking magazine with investigative journalism.

Why didn't Sloan, supposedly one of the greatest managers of all time, want to listen to Garrett?

Neither Sloan nor anybody else in top management of General Motors wanted to hear what Garrett would have told them. And this was still the case much later.

Paul Garrett was a professional who would have told them things they didn't want to hear and wouldn't believe. Killing the messenger is never the right policy.

And in GM's case, the employee relations people totally failed to warn the company of the horrible sit-down strike they would suffer. And then when investor relations became important, it wasn't assigned to the public relations people.

And to this day, most institutions still look upon public relations as their "trumpet" and not as their "hearing aid." It's got to be both.

What do you see as the future of the practice of public relations?

I think there is a need. It is a very complicated and complex function. The media are no longer homogenous and are much more critical. But there is a need for an intermediary to tell the truth to management. Public relations people today don't do that because they're scared, because the people they work for don't like to hear what they don't want to hear.

Let's face it. There's an old saying, "If I have you for a friend, I don't need an enemy."

Suggested Readings

Austin, Erica Weintraub, and Bruce E. Pinkleton. *Planning and Managing Effective Communication Programs*. New York: Lawrence Erlbaum Associates, 2001.

Center, Allen H., and Patrick Jackson. *Public Relations Practices, Managerial Case Studies and Problems*, 5th ed. Upper Saddle River, NJ: Prentice Hall, 1995.

Davies, G., R. Chun, and S. Roper. *Corporate Reputation and Competitiveness*. New York: Rutledge, 2003.

Dowling, G. *Creating Corporate Reputations: Identity, Image and Performance*. New York: Oxford University Press, 2002.

Fombrun, D. J., and R. VanRiel. *Fame and Fortune: How Successful Companies Build Winning Reputations*. Upper Saddle River, NJ: Financial Times Prentice Hall, 2004.

Ind, N. (Ed.). *Beyond Branding: How the New Values of Transparency and Integrity Are Changing the World of Brands*. London, England: Kogan Page Ltd., 2004.

Ledingham, John A., and Stephen D. Bruning. *A Relational Approach to the Study and Practice of Public Relations*. Mahwah, NJ: Lawrence Erlbaum Associates, 2001.

Lordan, Edward J. *Essentials of Public Relations Management*. Chicago: Branham, 2003. Introduction to organizing and managing a public relations function within an organization.

Mosten, Forrest S., *Mediation Career Guide, A Strategic Approach to Building a Successful Practice*. San Francisco, Jossey-Bass, 2001.

Pagano, B., E. Pagano, and S. Lundin. *The Transparency Edge: How Credibility Can Make or Break You in Business*. New York: McGraw-Hill, 2003.

Rayner, J. *Managing Reputational Risk: Curbing Threats, Leveraging Opportunities*. New York: John Wiley & Sons, 2003.

Rice, Ronald E., and Charles K. Atkin. *Public Communication Campaigns*. Thousand Oaks, CA: Sage, 2000.

Schultz, M., M. J. Hatch, and M. H. Larsen, *The Expressive Organization: Linking Identity, Reputation, and the Corporate Brand*. New York: Oxford University Press, 2000.

Smith, Ronald D., *Strategic Planning for Public Relations*. Mahwah, NJ: Lawrence Erlbaum Associates, 2002.

Trout, Jack, and Steve Rivkin. *Differentiate or Die*. New York: John Wiley, 2000. The future of organizations depends on their ability to separate themselves from the pack—or else, *sayonara*.

Notes

1. Spencer Rumsey, "The New York Newsday Interview with Roger Moore," *New York Newsday*, January 25, 1990.

2. James E. Grunig and Todd Hunt, *Managing Public Relations* (New York: Holt, Rinehart, & Winston, 1984): 89–97.

3. "Study Results Find Communications Competence Must Be Combined with Knowledge of the Business," Study sponsored by Deloitte & Touche and IABC Research Foundation, June 14, 2001.

4. Internal Berkshire Hathaway memo from Warren Buffet, August 12, 1998, as quoted in *Business Week*, July 5, 1999, 62.

5. Stuart Z. Goldstein, "Building Reputation through Communication," *Strategic Communication Management*, 8(6), October/November 2004, 23.

6. Scott Cutlip, Allen Center, and Douglas Broom, *Effective Public Relations*, Vol. 8 (Saddle Brook, NJ: Prentice-Hall, Inc., 2000): 340.

7. Lester R. Potter, "How to Be a Credible Strategic Counselor to Your Organization," delivered at IABC International Conference, Chicago, June 2002.

8. Stuart Z. Goldstein, "Information Preparedness," *Strategic Communication Management,* 3(1), December/January 1999.

9. Norman R. Nager and T. Harrell Allen, *Public Relations Management by Objectives* (New York: Longman Publishing Group, 1984).

10. "American Legacy Foundation Board Names Arnold Communications for Multi-Million Dollar Anti-Tobacco Account," American Legacy Foundation news release, September 15, 1999.

11. Richard Virgilio, "Pay for Placement PR—The What, Why and How of No-Risk, Pay-for-Results Media Placements," *The Journal for Business Marketing & Advertising Professionals.*

12. "O'Dwyer's Director of Corporate Communications 2005" (New York: J. R. O'Dwyer Company, 2005): A5.

13. "2002 Public Relations Industry Revenue and Performance Data Fact Sheet," Council of Public Relations Firms, New York, NY, 2005.

14. Ibid.

15. "Salary Survey 2005," *PR Week,* February 21, 2005.

16. Fraser P. Seitel, "Reputation Management," *odwyerpr.com,* July 9, 2002.

17. "Mercer Releases Corp. Comm Salary Survey," *Ragan Report,* December 10, 2001, 4.

18. "Occupational Employment and Wages, November 2004," U.S. Department of Labor Bureau of Labor Statistics, www.bls.gov, November 9, 2005.

19. Anita Chabria, "2005 Salary Survey Reveals Growth in Wages and Hiring," *PR Week,* February 21, 2005, 1.

20. Richard Bailey, "A Glass Ceiling in PR?" *PR Studies weblog* from Leeds Business School at Leeds Metropolitan University, http//prstudies.typepad.com, April 2, 2005.

21. "PR Week Salary Survey 2005," *PR Week,* February 21, 2005, 22.

22. "Hot Careers for the Next 10 Years," *Fortune,* March 21, 2005, 131.

23. "PR Week Salary Survey 2005."

6 Ethics

FIGURE 6-1 Fact or fiction? Oprah Winfrey's selection of a controversial book club pick in 2006 raised serious ethical questions. (AP Wide World Photos)

The practice of public relations is all about earning *credibility*. Credibility, in turn, begins with telling the truth. Public relations, then, must be based on "doing the right thing"—in other words, acting ethically.

In the 21st century, with scandals materializing in every sector of society—from politics to religion, from business to sports—the subject of ethics is a pervasive one.

Occasionally, society's most revered citizens find themselves embroiled in ethical conundrums. That even includes this woman:

Oprah Winfrey, a billionaire talk-show host beloved by millions, found herself defending a questionable author in 2006 when it was revealed that the man "embellished" his best-selling memoir. Oprah had hailed author James Frey's painful account about a life of drug addiction and then was forced to defend the author after he admitted making up facts for the book. "The underlying message of redemption . . . still resonates with me," said Oprah.[1]

Perhaps, but the ethical implications of Frey's disclosures were less convincing. So much so, that two weeks later in a stunning reversal, Winfrey excoriated her former pick-to-click and told her national television audience that she had "made a mistake" and that the fibbing author had "betrayed millions of people."[2]

What precisely are *ethics*?

A sociologist posed that question to businesspeople and got these answers:

- "Ethics has to do with what my feelings tell me is right or wrong."
- "Ethics has to do with my religious beliefs."
- "Being ethical is doing what the law requires."
- "Ethics consists of the standards of behavior our society accepts."
- "I don't know what the word means."

Classical ethics means different things to different people. Ethics theories range from utilitarianism (i.e., the greatest good for the greatest number) to deontology (i.e., do what is right, though the world should perish).

While the meaning of ethics may be hard to pin down, there's no secret to what constitutes unethical behavior. Unfortunately, it's all around us. Consider the following:

- In politics, ethical lapses know no party affiliation. Washington was rocked in 2006 by the revelations of multimillionaire lobbyist Jack Abramoff, who pleaded guilty to fraud, tax evasion, and conspiracy to bribe public officials. Abramoff dispensed most favors to Republicans, including former Speaker of the House Tom Delay, but he also trapped Democrats in his web of corruption.[3]

- In business, the corporate trial of the century kicked off in Houston at the start of 2006, when the two highest-ranking officials of once high-flying energy trading firm Enron Corporation former Chairman Ken Lay and former CEO Jeffrey Skilling were charged with lying about the financial health of the company, so they could dump company stock before Enron went bankrupt.[4]

- In sports, the baseball steroids scandals of 2005 and the NBA "basketbrawl" of 2004 (see Case Study in Chapter 4) renewed ethical questions about athletes as role models.

- In education, the president of American University was drummed out in 2005 after it was revealed that he spent more than $100,000 for such expenses as French wine, expensive foreign restaurants, and chauffers who ran personal errands.[5]

- Even in religion, the Catholic Church, the ostensible symbol of morality and decency in society, was rocked in the spring of 2002 by a priest pedophilia scandal in the United States. In July, Pope John Paul II called the crimes and misdeeds of some priests "a source of shame."[6] And the aftermath of the scandal continued to plague the Church under his successor, Pope Benedict XVI.

- Not even the practice of public relations could escape serious ethical lapses. Early in 2005, one of public relations' most respected firms, Ketchum, was embroiled in a "pay for publicity" scandal involving its client, the U.S. Department of Education (see Case Study at the end of this chapter).

The Ketchum calamity was particularly troubling, because the heart of public relations counsel is to *do the right thing*. The cardinal rule of public relations is to *never lie*.

Nonetheless, in one startling survey of 1,700 public relations executives, it was revealed that 25 percent of those interviewed admitted they had "lied on the job," 39 percent said they had exaggerated the truth, and another 44 percent said they had felt "uncertain" about the ethics of what they did.[7]

That was reason enough to propel the Public Relations Society of America (PRSA) to invest $100,000 in revamping its code of ethics. The code (Appendix A), underscored by six fundamental values that the PRSA believes vital to the integrity of the profession (Figure 6-2), demonstrates the significance of ethics to the practice of public relations.

PRSA Member Code of Ethics 2000

PRSA Member Statement of Professional Values

This statement presents the core values of PRSA members and, more broadly, of the public relations profession. These values provide the foundation for the Member Code of Ethics and set the industry standard for the professional practice of public relations. These values are the fundamental beliefs that guide our behaviors and decision-making process. We believe our professional values are vital to the integrity of the profession as a whole.

ADVOCACY

We serve the public interest by acting as responsible advocates for those we represent. We provide a voice in the marketplace of ideas, facts, and viewpoints to aid informed public debate.

HONESTY

We adhere to the highest standards of accuracy and truth in advancing the interests of those we represent and in communicating with the public.

EXPERTISE

We acquire and responsibly use specialized knowledge and experience. We advance the profession through continued professional development, research, and education. We build mutual understanding, credibility, and relationships among a wide array of institutions and audiences.

INDEPENDENCE

We provide objective counsel to those we represent. We are accountable for our actions.

LOYALTY

We are faithful to those we represent, while honoring our obligation to serve the public interest.

FAIRNESS

We deal fairly with clients, employers, competitors, peers, vendors, the media, and the general public. We respect all opinions and support the right of free expression.

The Public Relations Society of America, 33 Irving Place, New York, NY 10003-2376

FIGURE 6-2 PRSA's six values. The values of advocacy, honesty, expertise, independence, loyalty, and fairness form the basis of the PRSA ethical code. (Courtesy of the Public Relations Society of America)

Are We Doing the Right Thing?

What exactly are ethics? The answer isn't an easy one.

The Josephson Institute, which studies ethics, defines ethics as *standards of conduct that indicate how one should behave based on moral duties and virtues.*

In general, ethics are the values that guide a person, organization, or society—concepts such as right and wrong, fairness and unfairness, honesty and dishonesty. An individual's conduct is measured not only against his or her conscience but also against some norm of acceptability that society or an organization has determined.

Roughly translated, an individual's or organization's ethics comes down to the standards that are followed in relationships with others—the real integrity of the individual or organization. Obviously, a person's ethical construct and approach depend on numerous factors—cultural, religious, and educational, among others. Complicating the issue is that what might seem right to one person might not matter to someone else. No issue is solely black or white but is rather a shade of gray—particularly in making public relations decisions.

That is not to say that classical ethical distinctions don't exist. They do. Philosophers throughout the ages have debated the essence of ethics.

- *Utilitarianism* suggests considering the "greater good" rather than what may be best for the individual.

- To Aristotle, the *golden mean of moral virtue* could be found between two extreme points of view.

- Kant's *categorical imperative* recommended acting "on that maxim which you will to become a universal law."

- Mill's *principle of utility* recommended "seeking the greatest happiness for the greatest number."

- The traditional *Judeo-Christian ethic* prescribes "loving your neighbor as yourself." Indeed, this golden rule makes good sense as well in the practice of public relations.

Because the practice of public relations is misunderstood by so many—even including some of those for whom public relations people work—public relations people, in particular, must be ethical. They can't assume that ethics are strictly personal choices without relevance or related methodology for resolving moral quandaries. Public relations people must adhere to a high standard of professional ethics, with truth as the key determinant of their conduct.

Professional ethics, often called *applied ethics,* suggests a commonly accepted sense of professional conduct that is translated into formal codes of ethics.

The essence of the codes of conduct of both the Public Relations Society of America and the International Association of Business Communicators is that honesty and fairness lie at the heart of public relations practice. Indeed, if the ultimate goal of the public relations professional is to enhance public trust of an organization, then only the highest ethical conduct is acceptable.

Inherent in these standards of the profession is the understanding that ethics have changed and continue to change as society changes. Over time, views have changed on such issues as discrimination, the treatment of women and minorities, pollution of the environment, concern for human rights, acceptable standards of language and dress, and so on. Again, honesty and fairness are two critical components that will continue to determine the ethical behavior of public relations professionals.

Boiled down to its essence, the ethical heart of the practice of public relations lies in posing only one question to management: *Are we doing the right thing?* In posing that critical question, the public relations officer becomes the "conscience" of the organization.

Often the public relations professional will be the only member of management with the nerve to pose such a question. Sometimes this means saying no to what the boss wants to do. Public relations professionals must be driven by one purpose—to preserve, defend, sustain, and enhance the health and vitality of the organization. Simply translated, the bottom line for public relations professionals must always be to counsel and to do what is in the best long-term interests of the organization.

Ethics in Business

For many people today, regrettably, the term *business ethics* is an oxymoron. Its mere mention stimulates images of disgraced CEOs being led away in handcuffs after bilking their shareholders and employees out of millions of dollars. In one period alone, the 2002 "summer of shame," a dizzying array of corporate executives was charged with ethical violations.

- The summer began with executives of Enron being charged with massive accounting fraud, which effectively destroyed the life savings of shareholders— many of them longtime Enron employees. Even before Lay and Skilling were put on trial in 2006, other Enron executives were serving hard time.
- In Enron's wake, the bedrock accounting firm of Arthur Andersen was decimated for aiding and abetting in the Enron accounting duplicity.
- WorldCom, Global Crossing, and Qwest Communications executives, accused of massive accounting fraud, were charged soon thereafter, and several were later taken into custody by the FBI.
- The executives of Adelphia Communications, a leading cable TV company, were charged with using the corporation as their own private "piggy bank."[8] Even worse, the three chief culprits were members of the founding Rigas family. Although they were believed to be pillars of their Pennsylvania community, they were common criminals in the eyes of the law (Figure 6-3).
- Even Martha Stewart, celebrity homemaking idol, was charged with insider trading violations (see Case Study in Chapter 1).

In the first decade of the 21st century, the nation's confidence in its business leaders had reached an all-time low. In addition to corporate ethical scandals, people were outraged at executive compensation packages, such as Philip Purcell's $113 million payout to resign as Morgan Stanley's CEO and James M. Kilts's $165 million payoff for selling Gillette to Procter & Gamble. No wonder a 2005 Roper poll found that 66 percent of a representative sample of Americans felt that wrongdoing was widespread in industry. Only 2 percent found CEOs "very trustworthy."[9]

Indeed, many believed the term "crooked CEO" was redundant. One book, written by former management consultants, described CEOs thusly:

Among the more than 14,000 publicly registered companies in the U.S. and the even larger number of privately held companies there is a class of people who will lie to the public, the regulators, their employees and anyone else in order to increase personal wealth and power.[10]

FIGURE 6-3 Perp walk. Adelphia CEO John Rigas, 80, was sentenced to 15 years in jail for his role in the fraud that led to the collapse of his company. (AP Wide World Photos)

To stem the feeling that chief executives and their companies weren't acting ethically, a number of firms increased their efforts to make their activities more transparent to the public. Companies from Coca-Cola to Amazon.com to General Electric announced plans to make accounting procedures more understandable. In June 2002, CEO Henry Paulson of investment banking giant Goldman Sachs called on his fellow CEOs to reform before regulation forced them to do so. "In my lifetime, American business has never been under such scrutiny. To be blunt, much of it is deserved," said Paulson.[11]

Corporate Codes of Conduct

In the summer of 2002, in the wake of corporate accounting and executive scandals, the New York Stock Exchange (NYSE) mandated that its member companies, among other corporate governance measures, immediately implement internal corporate codes of conduct to ensure that they act ethically toward all of their key constituents.

A code of conduct is a formal statement of the values and business practices of a corporation. A code may be a short mission statement, or it may be a sophisticated document that requires compliance with articulated standards and has a complicated enforcement mechanism.

Even before the 2002 NYSE mandate, codes of ethics, standards of conduct, and similar statements of corporate policies and values proliferated. The reasons corporations have adopted such codes vary from company to company.

- **To increase public confidence.** The scandals in recent years have shaken investor confidence and have led to a decline of public trust and confidence in business. Many firms have responded with written codes of ethics.

- **To stem the tide of regulation.** As public confidence has declined, government regulation of business has increased. Some estimated the cost to society of compliance with regulations at $100 billion per year. Corporate codes of conduct, it was hoped, would help serve as a self-regulation mechanism.

- **To improve internal operations.** As companies became larger and more decentralized, management needed consistent standards of conduct to ensure that employees were meeting the business objectives of the company in a legal and ethical manner.

- **To respond to transgressions.** Frequently, when a company itself is caught in the web of unethical behavior, it responds with its own code of ethics.

Ralph Waldo Emerson once wrote, "An organization is the lengthened shadow of a man." Today, many corporate executives realize that just as an individual has certain responsibilities as a citizen, so, too, does a corporate citizen have responsibilities to the society in which it is privileged to operate.

As business becomes globalized, companies are being encouraged by interest groups, governments, educational institutions, industry associations, and others to adopt codes of conduct. Accordingly, formal ethical codes, addressing such topics as executive compensation, accounting procedures, confidentiality of corporate information, misappropriation of corporate assets, bribes and kickbacks, and political contributions, have become a corporate fact of life for every company executive, up to and including the members of the board of directors (Figure 6-4).

Corporate Social Responsibility

Closely related to the ethical conduct of an organization is its social responsibility. Simply stated, corporate social responsibility is about how companies manage the business processes to produce an overall positive impact on society. This implies that any social institution, from the smallest family unit to the largest corporation, is responsible for the behavior of its members and may be held accountable for their misdeeds.

In the late 1960s, when this idea was just emerging, initial responses were of the knee-jerk variety. A firm that was threatened by increasing legal or activist pressures and harassment would ordinarily change its policies in a hurry. Today, however, organizations and their social responsibility programs are much more sophisticated. Social responsibility is treated just like any other management discipline: Analyze the issues, evaluate performance, set priorities, allocate resources to those priorities, and implement programs that deal with issues within the constraints of the organization's resources. Many companies have created special committees to set the agenda and target the objectives.

Social responsibility touches practically every level of organizational activity, from marketing to hiring, from training to work standards. A partial list of social responsibility categories might include the following:

i'm lovin' it™

Code of Conduct for the Board of Directors of McDonald's Corporation

The members of the Board of Directors of McDonald's Corporation acknowledge and accept the scope and extent of our duties as directors. We have a responsibility to carry out our duties in an honest and businesslike manner and within the scope of our authority, as set forth in the General Corporation Laws of the State of Delaware and in the Certificate of Incorporation and By-Laws of McDonald's Corporation. We are entrusted with and responsible for the oversight of the assets and business affairs of McDonald's Corporation in an honest, fair, diligent and ethical manner. As Directors we must act within the bounds of the authority conferred upon us and with the duty to make and enact informed decisions and policies in the best interests of McDonald's and its shareholders. The Board of Directors has adopted the following Code of Conduct and our Directors are expected to adhere to the standards of loyalty, good faith, and the avoidance of conflict of interest that follow:

Board Members will:

- Act in the best interests of, and fulfill their fiduciary obligations to, McDonald's shareholders;
- Act honestly, fairly, ethically and with integrity;
- Conduct themselves in a professional, courteous and respectful manner;
- Comply with all applicable laws, rules and regulations;
- Act in good faith, responsibly, with due care, competence and diligence, without allowing their independent judgment to be subordinated;
- Act in a manner to enhance and maintain the reputation of McDonald's;
- Disclose potential conflicts of interest that they may have regarding any matters that may come before the Board, and abstain from discussion and voting on any matter in which the Director has or may have a conflict of interest;
- Make available to and share with fellow Directors information as may be appropriate to ensure proper conduct and sound operation of McDonald's and its Board of Directors;
- Respect the confidentiality of information relating to the affairs of the Company acquired in the course of their service as Directors, except when authorized or legally required to disclose such information; and
- Not use confidential information acquired in the course of their service as Directors for their personal advantage.

A Director who has concerns regarding compliance with this Code should raise those concerns with the Chairman of the Board and the Chair of the Governance Committee, who will determine what action shall be taken to deal with the concern. In the extremely unlikely event that a waiver of this Code for a Director would be in the best interest of the Company, it must be approved by the Governance Committee.

Directors will annually sign a confirmation that they have read and will comply with this Code.

Adopted by the Board of Directors
as of May 22, 2003

FIGURE 6-4 Conduct of the Board. Many companies, such as McDonald's, ensure that even the members of the board of directors live by a code of conduct. (Used with premission from McDonald's Corporation)

- **Product lines**—dangerous products, product performance and standards, packaging, and environmental impact
- **Marketing practices**—sales practices, consumer complaint policies, advertising content, and fair pricing
- **Corporate philanthropy**—contribution performance, encouragement of employee participation in social projects, and community development activities
- **Environmental activities**—pollution-control projects, adherence to federal standards, and evaluation procedures for new packages and products
- **External relations**—support of minority enterprises, investment practices, and government relations
- **Employment diversity in retaining and promoting minorities and women**—current hiring policies, advancement policies, specialized career counseling, and opportunities for special minorities such as the physically handicapped
- **Employee safety and health**—work environment policies, accident safeguards, and food and medical facilities

More often than not, organizations have incorporated social responsibility into the mainstream of their practice. Most firms recognize that social responsibility, far from being an add-on program, must be a corporate way of life. They recognize that in a skeptical world, business must be responsible to act ethically and improve the quality of life of their workforce, their families, and the broader society.

Ethics in Government

Politics has never enjoyed an unblemished reputation when it comes to ethics. In the early years of the 21st century, politicians seemed to be losing further ground in terms of trustworthiness and ethical values.

Talking Points

Ethical Rocky Road at Ben & Jerry's

Ben & Jerry's, Vermont ice-cream maker extraordinaire, prides itself as a socially responsible company with a commitment to creating "economic opportunities for those who have been denied them."

Apparently, the company's former chief financial officer decided he deserved some "economic opportunities" too.

In 2005, the U.S. Attorney of Vermont brought charges against former Ben & Jerry's CFO Stuart Wiles for charging personal expenses to his company credit card and issuing company checks for nonexistent obligations, using the funds to pay his own bills.

Wiles, uniquely positioned to commit fraud because he was the final corporate gatekeeper of expense funds, scammed the company into paying $58,000 for an addition to his home. He pleaded guilty to wire fraud.

Summarized a perplexed Ben & Jerry's spokesman, "This situation, while unfortunate, appears ... to be an isolated one that in no way reflects on the character of the outstanding people who work for Ben & Jerry's."

For further information, see Rob Garver, "Et Tu, Ben and Jerry's?" *CFO*, November 2005, 18.

Both the legislative and executive branches of the federal government took a beating in the public eye. Congress continued its downward slide with only 45 percent of the public holding at least a "somewhat favorable" view of the body, including a mere 7 percent who declared a "very" favorable opinion. Overall, the federal government scored no better: Its favorability rating fell from a high of 73 percent in 2003 to 46 percent at the beginning of 2006.[12]

The advent of 24-hour cable news and the 24/7 Internet blogosphere cast a perpetual 21st-century spotlight on the activities of the President and his allies. No administration could escape the harsh glare of prying eyes noting ethical failures. Both President George Bush and Vice President Dick Cheney were criticized for favoring past corporate energy affiliations. President Bill Clinton, of course, suffered the ultimate ethical ignominy: being impeached for his inexplicable and embarrassing behavior with a young intern in the White House.

The "sleaze factor" in government continued to poison politics.

- Republican House majority leader Tom Delay, one of the nation's most powerful politicians, was forced to step down from the leadership in 2005 and ultimately left office after being implicated in a corruption scandal and later linked to renegade lobbyist Abramoff.

- That same year, decorated Republican war hero Randy "Duke" Cunningham tearfully resigned his congressional seat after pleading guilty to taking more than $2 million in bribes.

- In 2006, another congressman, Democrat William Jefferson, was linked to a bribery scandal promoting a business deal in Africa.

- Earlier in the decade, Ohio Republican Congressman James Traficant was convicted of racketeering, using his office for political favors; and Democratic Congressman Gary Condit was defeated for reelection after becoming a national pariah for an alleged affair he conducted with an intern, who was later found to have been murdered.

After all the white-collar crime and political scandals that have marked the first few years of the 21st century, the public is less willing to tolerate such ethical violations from their elected officials. It is likely that ethics in government will become an even more important issue as voters insist on representatives who are honest, trustworthy, and ethical.

Ethics in Journalism

The Society of Professional Journalists is quite explicit on the subject of ethics (Figure 6-6).

Journalists at all times will show respect for the dignity, privacy, rights, and well-being of people encountered in the course of gathering and presenting the news.

1. The news media should not communicate unofficial charges affecting reputation or moral character without giving the accused a chance to reply.

2. The news media must guard against invading a person's right to privacy.

3. The media should not pander to morbid curiosity about details of vice and crime.

And so on.

Unfortunately, what is in the code often doesn't reflect what appears in print or on the air. More often than not, journalistic judgments run smack into ethical principles.

Speaking of Ethics

Ducking the High Hard One

New Mexico Governor Bill Richardson was an undisputed star of the Democratic Party. A former energy secretary in the Clinton administration, ambassador to the United Nations, and four-time nominee for the Nobel Peace Prize, Richardson was also quite a baseball player, good enough to have been drafted by the Kansas City A's (Figure 6-5).

Or at least that's what his official biography said.

But an investigation by the *Albuquerque Journal* found no record of Richardson's ever being drafted by a major league team. Informed by the newspaper of its findings, the red-faced governor acknowledged the inaccuracy, which had been included on his resume for four decades.

Said Richardson, "After being notified of the situation and after researching the matter," he had come "to the conclusion that I was not drafted by the A's."

He explained that he originally believed the story had been true based on an old program from an amateur team he had played for in Massachusetts. He said that he was certain his name had appeared on a "draft list of some kind" and that he had been told by specific scouts that he "would or could" be drafted.

FIGURE 6-5 Deceptive pitch. New Mexico Governor Bill Richardson was a good pitcher, but perhaps not as good as his resume suggested. (AP Wide World Photos)

As to whether the particular scouts could be reached to verify the story . . . well, slight problem: They died.*

*For further information, see "Governor Says Big Leagues Never Called Him After All," *New York Times,* November 25, 2005, A33.

The 2006 Oprah Winfrey flap, referenced at the beginning of the chapter, in which author James Frey made up portions of his supposedly accurate memoir, caused a furor about ethics among writers. Frey's lies were particularly painful to journalists trying to live down ethical challenges of their own.

- Plagiarism scandals at three of the nation's leading newspapers—*The New York Times, Washington Post,* and *Boston Globe*—resulted in the firings of high-profile journalists. The *Times* fell victim to the new century's most embarrassing instance of suspect journalistic ethics. In 2003, the "Great Gray Lady" was stunned when one of its promising young reporters, Jayson Blair, was discovered to have fabricated numerous dispatches for the paper over an extended period. The *Times* found out about Blair's fraud only when a reporter from another paper tipped it off. Blair was immediately fired, and the *Times* took a major reputation hit.

THE SOCIETY OF PROFESSIONAL JOURNALISTS, SIGMA DELTA CHI

Code OF Ethics

THE SOCIETY of Professional Journalists, Sigma Delta Chi believes the duty of journalists is to serve the truth.

WE BELIEVE the agencies of mass communication are carriers of public discussion and information, acting on their Constitutional mandate and freedom to learn and report the facts.

WE BELIEVE in public enlightenment as the forerunner of justice, and in our Constitutional role to seek the truth as part of the public's right to know the truth.

WE BELIEVE those responsibilities carry obligations that require journalists to perform with intelligence, objectivity, accuracy and fairness.

To these ends, we declare acceptance of the standards of practice here set forth:

RESPONSIBILITY:
The public's right to know of events of public importance and interest is the overriding mission of the mass media. The purpose of distributing news and enlightened opinion is to serve the general welfare. Journalists who use their professional status as representatives of the public for selfish or other unworthy motives violate a high trust.

FREEDOM OF THE PRESS:
Freedom of the press is to be guarded as an inalienable right of people in a free society. It carries with it the freedom and the responsibility to discuss, question and challenge actions and utterances of our government and of our public and private institutions. Journalists uphold the right to speak unpopular opinions and the privilege to agree with the majority.

ETHICS:
Journalists must be free of obligation to any interest other than the public's right to know the truth.
1. Gifts, favors, free travel, special treatment or privileges can compromise the integrity of journalists and their employers. Nothing of value should be accepted.
2. Secondary employment, political involvement, holding public office and service in community organizations should be avoided if it compromises the integrity of journalists and their employers. Journalists and their employers should conduct their personal lives in a manner which protects them from conflict of interest, real or apparent. Their responsibilities to the public are paramount. That is the nature of their profession.

3. So-called news communications from private sources should not be published or broadcast without substantiation of their claims to news value.
4. Journalists will seek news that serves the public interest, despite the obstacles. They will make constant efforts to assure that the public's business is conducted in public and that public records are open to public inspection.
5. Journalists acknowledge the newsman's ethic of protecting confidential sources of information.

ACCURACY AND OBJECTIVITY:
Good faith with the public is the foundation of all worthy journalism.
1. Truth is our ultimate goal.
2. Objectivity in reporting the news is another goal, which serves as the mark of an experienced professional. It is a standard of performance toward which we strive. We honor those who achieve it.
3. There is no excuse for inaccuracies or lack of thoroughness.
4. Newspaper headlines should be fully warranted by the contents of the articles they accompany. Photographs and telecasts should give an accurate picture of an event and not highlight a minor incident out of context.
5. Sound practice makes clear distinction between news reports and expressions of opinion. News reports should be free of opinion or bias and represent all sides of an issue.
6. Partisanship in editorial comment which knowingly departs from the truth violates the spirit of American journalism.
7. Journalists recognize their responsibility for offering informed analysis, comment and editorial opinion on public events and issues. They accept the obligation to present such material by individuals whose competence, experience and judgment qualify them for it.
8. Special articles or presentations devoted to advocacy or the writer's own conclusions and interpretations should be labeled as such.

FAIR PLAY:
Journalists at all times will show respect for the dignity, privacy, rights and well-being of people encountered in the course of gathering and presenting the news.
1. The news media should not communicate unofficial charges affecting reputation or moral character without giving the accused a chance to reply.
2. The news media must guard against invading a person's right to privacy.
3. The media should not pander to morbid curiosity about details of vice and crime.
4. It is the duty of news media to make prompt and complete correction of their errors.
5. Journalists should be accountable to the public for their reports and the public should be encouraged to voice its grievances against the media. Open dialogue with our readers, viewers and listeners should be fostered.

PLEDGE:
Journalists should actively censure and try to prevent violations of these standards, and they should encourage their observance by all newspeople. Adherence to this code of ethics is intended to preserve the bond of mutual trust and respect between American journalists and the American people.

FIGURE 6-6 Journalists' Code. The Society of Professional Journalists has elaborated in some detail on the ethical guidelines that should govern all journalists. (Courtesy of the Society of Professional Journalists)

- In 2005, the *Times* was shocked again after one of its star reporters, Judith Miller, served 85 days in prison for refusing to reveal confidential administration sources related to stories involving the leak of the name of a CIA operative married to a Bush administration critic. Upon her release, the *Times* criticized her for being too cozy with the White House. Miller hastily resigned after 28 years at the *Times*.

- In the new millennium, the proliferation of blogs—expanding at the rate of 70,000 sites a day—and other online media, publishing round the clock, as well as the exponential increase in TV news, cable stations, and programming on the Internet, increased the pressure on news outlets to report as scrupulously as possible lest they be caught in an inextricable ethical crisis.[13] Such was the case late in 2004, when venerable CBS anchor Dan Rather cited "exclusive documents" alleging that President George W. Bush had shirked his duties while in the Texas Air National Guard. When the documents turned out to be forgeries, CBS launched its own investigation, which resulted in the firing of several longtime staff members. Less than a year later, after 43 years with CBS, Dan Rather was gone (Figure 6-7).

- Television news itself, particularly cable TV, was rocked by the phenomenon in the 21st century of "nonstop screaming," where adversaries on either side spent most of their air time declaring a "my way or the highway" point of view. Partisanship was the order of the day. Such popular programs as Fox News Channel's *The O'Reilly Factor,* MSNBC's *Hardball with Chris Matthews,* and CNN's *Nancy Grace,* all distinguished by their voluble hosts, added plenty of heat but little light to the national dialogue.

Such was the state of journalistic ethics in the last half of the first decade of the 21st century.

FIGURE 6-7 End of an era. After 24 years as anchor of the CBS Evening News, Dan Rather stepped down in the spring of 2005, after suffering the stings of a bogus broadcast regarding President Bush's National Guard service. (AP Wide World of Photos)

Ethics in Public Relations

As noted, ethics is—or at least, should be—the great differentiator between public relations and other professions. In light of numerous misconceptions about the practice of public relations, it is imperative that practitioners emulate the highest standards of personal and professional ethics. Within an organization, public relations practitioners must be the standard bearers of corporate ethical initiatives. By the same token, public relations consultants must always counsel their clients in an ethical direction—toward accuracy and candor and away from lying and hiding the truth.

The public relations department should be the seat of corporate ethics. At least four ethical theories are relevant to the practice of public relations.

- The *attorney/adversary model,* developed by Jay Barney and Ralph Black, compares the legal profession to that of public relations in that (1) both are advocates in an adversarial climate and (2) both assume counterbalancing messages will be provided by adversaries. In this model, Barney and Black suggest practitioners have no obligation to consider the public interest or any other outside view beyond that of their client.

- The *two-way communication model,* developed by Jim Grunig, is based on collaboration, working jointly with different people, and allowing for both listening and give-and-take. In this model, Grunig suggests that the practitioner balance his or her role as a client advocate with one as social conscience for the larger public.

- The *enlightened self-interest model,* developed by Sherry Baker, is based on the principle that businesses do well by doing good. In this model, Baker suggests that companies gain a competitive edge and are more respected in the marketplace if they behave ethically.

- The *responsible advocacy model,* developed by Kathy Fitzpatrick and Candace Gauthier, is based on the ideal of professional responsibility. It postulates that practitioners' first loyalty is to their clients, but they also have a responsibility to voice the opinions of organizational stakeholders. In this model, Fitzpatrick and Gauthier suggest that the practitioner's greatest need for ethical guidance is in the reconciliation of being both a professional advocate and a social conscience.

The PRSA has been a leader in the effort to foster a strong sense of professionalism among its membership, particularly in its new code of ethics. Its six core values underpin the desired behavior of any public relations professional.

- **Advocacy.** The PRSA Code endorses the Fitzpatrick and Gauthier model in stating: "We serve the public interest by acting as responsible advocates for those we represent." For example, public relations professionals must never reveal confidential or private client information, even if a journalist demands it. The only way such information might be revealed is after a thorough discussion with the client.

- **Honesty.** For example, a client asking a public relations representative to "embellish" the performance the company expects to achieve should be told diplomatically, but firmly, no. Public relations people don't lie.

- **Expertise.** For example, a client in need of guidance as to whether to accept a sensitive interview invitation for a cable TV talk show must be carefully guided through the pros and cons by a skilled public relations practitioner.

- **Independence.** For example, when everyone in the room—lawyer, human resources, treasurer, and president—all agree with the CEO's rock-headed scheme to disguise bad news, it is the public relations professional's duty to strike an independent tone.

- **Loyalty.** For example, if a competing client offers a practitioner more money to abandon his or her original employer, the public relations professional should understand his or her loyalties must remain constant.

- **Fairness.** For example, when a rude and obnoxious journalist demands information, a practitioner's responsibility is to treat even the most obnoxious reporter with fairness.

Sadly, the practice, itself, has not always emulated these admirable tenets.

- In 2004, one of the nation's most admired public relations agencies, Fleishman-Hillard, was embroiled in a scandal for overbilling the city of Los Angeles to the tune of $4 million. The ethical breach resulted in grand jury indictments against

Talking Points

Test Your Workplace Ethics

So you want to enter the workplace? The question of ethics looms larger today than at any previous time, especially with the advent of technology and the potential abuses it brings.

To test how you might measure up as an ethical worker, answer the following questions. And don't cheat!

Questions

1. Is it wrong to use company e-mail for personal reasons?
2. Is it wrong to use office equipment to help your family and friends with homework?
3. Is it wrong to play computer games on office equipment during the workday?
4. Is it wrong to use office equipment to do Internet shopping?
5. Is it unethical to visit pornographic Web sites using office equipment?
6. What's the value at which a gift from a supplier or client becomes troubling?
7. Is a $50 gift to a boss unacceptable?
8. Is it okay to take a pair of $200 football tickets as a gift from a supplier?
9. Is it okay to take a $120 pair of theater tickets?
10. Is it okay to take a $100 holiday fruit basket?
11. Is it okay to take a $25 gift certificate?
12. Is it okay to accept a $75 prize won at a raffle at a supplier's conference?

Answers

From a cross-section of workers at nationwide companies, the answers to these questions were compiled by the Ethics Officer Association, Belmont, Massachusetts, and the Ethical Leadership Group, Wilmette, Illinois.

1. Thirty-four percent said personal e-mail on company computers is wrong.
2. Thirty-seven percent said using office equipment for schoolwork is wrong.
3. Forty-nine percent said playing computer games at work is wrong.
4. Fifty-four percent said Internet shopping at work is wrong.
5. Eighty-seven percent said it is unethical to visit pornographic sites at work.
6. Thirty-three percent said $25 is the amount at which a gift from a supplier or client becomes troubling. Another 33 percent said $50. Another 33 percent said $100.
7. Thirty-five percent said a $50 gift to the boss is unacceptable.
8. Seventy percent said it is unacceptable to take $200 football tickets.
9. Seventy percent said it is unacceptable to take $120 theater tickets.
10. Thirty-five percent said it is unacceptable to take a $100 fruit basket.
11. Forty-five percent said it is unacceptable to take a $25 gift certificate.
12. Forty percent said it is unacceptable to take the $75 raffle prize.

Fleishman L.A. executives, and the mayor of Los Angeles imposed a temporary ban on city contracts with public relations agencies.[14]

■ The next year, an even bigger ethical scandal erupted around yet another high-powered public relations agency. Ketchum Communications was found to be smack in the middle of disclosures that its client, the U.S. Department of Education, had secretly paid conservative columnist Armstrong Williams to promote its No Child Left Behind program. Ketchum, which initially tried to duck the controversy, was roundly criticized by public relations professionals. Some even suggested that its ethical lapse in the Armstrong Williams case might someday qualify as a public relations industry case study. They were right. (See Case Study at the conclusion of this chapter.)

As a consequence of such missteps, the practice of public relations still has a way to go to gain universal public respectability. The most recent Public Relations Society of America study on credibility, for example, indicated that while Supreme Court justices and teachers ranked highest on the credibility index, public relations specialists ranked near the bottom.[15] Combating this unethical mind-set poses a great challenge for the field in the 21st century.

Last Word

The scandals in government and business in the early years of the 21st century have placed a premium in every sector of society on acting ethically. More than half of the 3,000 workers who took part in a 2005 National Business Ethics Survey said they witnessed at least one type of ethical misconduct on their job.[16] That's disgraceful. As the CEO of Eaton Corporation, the manufacturing giant, put it, "There is no truer window into a corporation's soul than its approach to ethics."[17]

The same can be said for the practice of public relations.

The success of public relations in the 21st century will depend largely on how the field responds to the issue of ethical conduct. Public relations professionals must have credibility in order to practice. They must be respected by the various publics with which they interact. This is as much true overseas as it is in the United States (see Appendix B). To be credible and to achieve respect, public relations professionals must be ethical. It is that simple.

Stated another way, for public relations practice in general and individual public relations professionals in particular, credibility in the next few years will depend on how scrupulously they observe and apply the principles and practice of ethics in everything they do.

Discussion Starters

1. How would you define ethics?
2. How would you describe the state of ethics in business, government, and journalism?
3. How important is the ethical component of the practice of public relations?
4. Why have corporations adopted corporate codes of conduct?
5. What is corporate social responsibility?
6. What were the ethical implications of Governor Bill Richardson's bogus resume?
7. What are the pros and cons of the attorney/adversary public relations model compared to the enlightened self-interest model?
8. Is the public more tolerant or less tolerant of ethical violators today? Why?
9. What is the significance of the six ethical values that underscore the Public Relations Society of America Code of Ethics?
10. What are the ethical responsibilities of a public relations professional?

Top of the Shelf

The Governance Game: Restoring Boardroom Excellence and Credibility in Corporate America

Marilyn Seymann and Michael Rosenbaum, Mahwah, NJ: Aspatore, 2003.

This book explores one of corporate America's most prominent ethical vulnerabilities, the board of directors. Corporate boards are notorious for not paying attention, for looking the other way, and for being guilty of all kinds of conflict of interest with corporate management. Enron, Tyco, WorldCom, and many of the other corporate culprits of the 21st century were guilty of such inferior boards.

The authors suggest what corporate boards can do to improve their performance in terms of management of the board and the ethical behavior of directors. They stress that corporate boards must go beyond making sure their companies are simply complying with existing laws and regulations. Their focus, correctly, is on the ethics of the CEO, who, they say, should be careful about the other boards he sits on, hiring consulting firms that serve both companies, or retaining family members for consulting—all of which is good advice that the Enrons and Tycos and WorldComs of the world should have listened to.

CASE STUDY

Ketchum Captured in Pay-for-Play Ethical Lapse

Armstrong Williams, co-founder of Graham Williams Group, was one of the nation's most well-known African American commentators (Figure 6-8). His agency partner, Stedman Graham, was Oprah Winfrey's long-time boyfriend. Williams himself was a syndicated columnist, a frequent presence on cable TV, and an outspoken advocate for the George W. Bush administration.

That's why it seemed logical through 2003 and 2004, when Williams began to campaign forcefully for the U.S. Department of Education's (DOE) No Child Left Behind program, the centerpiece of its nationwide educational standards-setting offensive. Armstrong Williams was passionate on the subject. He was devoted, committed, and fired up.

He was also "bought."

Play for Pay

In January 2005, *USA Today* reported that the Department of Education had secretly paid Williams $240,000 to promote No Child Left Behind on TV and radio.

Immediately, Mr. Williams's independence and ethics were attacked. He was guilty, critics charged,

FIGURE 6-8 The semi-objective spokesman. Conservative columnist Armstrong Williams (left) with former Republican presidential candidate and publisher, Steve Forbes. (AP Wide World of Photos)

of engaging in "play for pay"—appearing to support a position independently when, in reality, his views were sponsored. The appearance of "objectivity," designed to convince the public that his views were not influenced by anything other than personal conviction, was a serious ethical breach.

Upon being confronted with the negative publicity, Williams at first tried to deflect the criticism. "I wanted to do it because it's something I believe in," A few days later, after some in Congress questioned the legality of the contract with the DOE, Williams acknowledged the ethical error of his ways. A few days after the revelation appeared, Williams offered an apology to readers on his Web site:

> In 2003, I agreed to run a paid ad on my syndicated television show, promoting the Department of Education's No Child Left Behind Act. I subsequently used my column space to support that legislation. This represents an obvious conflict of interest.
>
> I understand that I exercised bad judgment in running paid advertising for an issue that I frequently write about in my column. People need to know that my column is uncorrupted by any outside influence. I would like to take this opportunity to apologize for my bad judgment and to better explain the circumstances.

The Plot Thickens

The "circumstances" Williams went on to describe implicated others in the unethical scheme, most particularly, one of the nation's foremost public relations firms.

> In 2003, Ketchum Communications contacted a small PR firm that I own, Graham Williams Group, to buy ad space on a television show that I own and host. The ad was to promote the Department of Education's "No Child Left Behind" plan.

Williams's implication was clear: that Ketchum, working on behalf of its client, the DOE, served as the "bag man" to get him to pretend to be objective in supporting the program that Ketchum was being paid to promote. So Ketchum, an old and distinguished public relations representative founded in 1923, now owned by the formidable Omnicom Group, was now caught squarely in the crosshairs of a national ethical controversy.

The next move was Ketchum's. What would its response be to serious questions of ethical impropriety?

The answer?

Nada.

A week after the Williams story broke, the *New York Times* reported that a Ketchum spokesman "had no comment and referred inquiries to the Education Department."

Industry Backlash

The public relations industry was stunned by the Williams–DOE story and the Ketchum silence. The president of the Public Relations Society of America, while stopping short of confronting Ketchum's role, declared, "Any paid endorsement that is not fully disclosed as such and is presented as objective news coverage is a violation of the PRSA Code of Ethics."

Other industry leaders were even more categorical. Said Al Golin, founder and chairman of GolinHarris, another industry giant, "You have to be smart enough to say no to a client. You may keep the client happy by saying yes all the time. But it's very short-sighted."

Feeling the heat, ten days after the Williams story broke, Ketchum responded. In an op-ed and interview in an industry publication, Ketchum executives blamed Williams for not disclosing his status as a paid advocate for the DOE. Ketchum, according to the executives, had not acted inappropriately. Indeed, the firm's CEO played down the controversy, likening it to "sportscasters who double as product pitchmen."

Crow Time

Shortly after its public defense of its actions, Ketchum reversed course. The day after a story in the *Times* condemned it for not accepting some ethical guilt and two weeks after the start of the controversy, Ketchum finally saw the light. In a statement released to the news media, the firm's CEO acknowledged that Ketchum bore part of the guilt.

> We should have recognized the potential issues in working with a communications firm operated by a commentator. This work did not comply with the guidelines of our agency and our industry.

Summarized the president of the PRSA, "The industry needs to continue to promote ethical standards and to look at the application of ethics in a changing media world."

Amen.

Questions

1. What's your reaction to the idea of paying a commentator to promote a client's program?

2. How do you feel Ketchum handled the controversy? What would you have done differently?

3. Had your client proposed a similar idea to that which the DOE proposed to Williams, how would you have responded?

For further information on the Armstrong Williams–Ketchum case, see Stuart Elliott, "An Undisclosed Paid Endorsement Ignites a Debate in the Public Relations Industry," *New York Times,* January 12, 2005, C2; Stuart Elliott, "Strong Stands Taken as the Public Relations Industry Debates Payments Made to a Commentator," *New York Times,* January 19, 2005, C5; Stuart Elliott, "Agency Admits Errors in Deal with TV Host," *New York Times,* January 20, 2005, C10; Timothy L. O'Brien, "Spinning Frenzy: PR's Bad Press," *New York Times,* February 13, 2005, Section 3-1; Greg Toppo, "Education Dept. Paid Commentator to Promote Law," *USA Today,* January 7, 2005, A1.

Voice of Authority

An Interview with Howard J. Rubenstein

Howard J. Rubenstein, president of Rubenstein Associates since founding the firm in 1954, is one of the world's most well-known and respected public relations counselors, advising some of the world's most influential corporations, organizations, and opinion leaders. In addition to managing the day-to-day activities of his firm, Rubenstein is involved in numerous civic and philanthropic organizations. A Phi Beta Kappa graduate of the University of Pennsylvania, he finished first in his class in the night school division of St. John's University School of Law, which subsequently awarded him an honorary Doctor of Law degree. As an attorney, he served as assistant counsel to the House of Representatives Judiciary Committee.

How would you define the practice of public relations?
Public relations is the art of conveying an idea or message to a wide variety of publics utilizing multiple forms of communications. It can be broadly applied and used to advance the interests of businesses, governments, and society in general. It can achieve objectives as narrow as promoting a product or as broad as creating a movement. The communications themselves can be targeted to the general public or to very select groups of individuals, conveyed via media or person-to-person. The tools employed encompass a wide array, from press releases, news conferences, special events, speaking engagements, webinars, blogs, and grassroots organizations down to a single conversation with one influential person.

How important is communications for organizations in today's society?
Communications in its many forms creates and projects messages with the power to affect great change and achieve tremendous success, while a breakdown in communications can lead to dismal failure. Clearly, communications is critical for organizations as they seek public acceptance, support, and understanding of their activities. Communication today is a major focus for presidents, prime ministers, and legislators as well as religious leaders, as they try to shape the directions of entire societies and world events.

What are the key attributes that distinguish the best public relations professionals?
Ethics, intelligence, and willingness to put in the time and hard work are core characteristics. Good PR professionals should have the ability to write well and speak effectively. The final attribute is creativity and imagination, combined with an understanding of reality and practicality. Professionals in the field should be able to stretch the envelope as far as technique and methodology go, without forgetting what they are trying to achieve.

What is the key to interesting a journalist in a client's story?
There are many keys to piquing media interest. First, however, you must know the media outlet and understand what a news story is and what a reporter wants to see as the components of a story. You must target and reach out selectively, rather than just send out releases. Then, once you know where to go, find the human-interest angle, keep the pitch succinct, and offer what the reporter needs to cover the story. Forget the term *spinmeister*. Offer a story that is accurate, do it in an honorable and forthright way, and help the reporter do his or her job well. Above all, don't waste reporters' time with something that isn't right for the publication or the beat the reporter covers. And don't be nasty if your idea is rejected. You'll likely want to approach that reporter again some day. Instead take that rejection as a sign that you need to refine the pitch or find a better fit for it.

What inspired you, personally, to go into public relations?
I was inspired to enter public relations by my father, who was a crime reporter with the *New York Herald Tribune*. From his perspective as a journalist, he believed that PR had the untapped potential to be a great career. Not only did he get me my first account, he explained to me the importance of ethics, honesty, and integrity in dealing with the press, conducting business, and communicating with the public. He taught me the importance of good writing, finding the news value in a story, and working hard to achieve coverage in the media. He was very supportive when I began my company with that single account at my new office, which was also known as *my mother's kitchen table!* He encouraged me and always believed that public relations had a bright future. I remember his saying that public relations as a field was malleable, like clay, and could be formed to fit any idea that I had. As a result, I started out believing that if I was honest, thoughtful, and hard working, I could

be successful, earn a living, and establish a good reputation in what was then a barely recognized field. That's what happened, so I guess my father was right.

What are the greatest challenges facing the practice of public relations?

In every aspect of society, leaders seek public relations counsel. Because media scrutiny is so intense today, it takes a professional to understand and advise society's leaders as to how best to respond and engage. As a result, PR people today are professionals with as much credibility and weight as lawyers, accountants, bankers, architects, or engineers. We alone offer the ability to design communica-tions programs, judge their potential, and execute them to achieve results. That guarantees for PR professionals tremendous opportunity and a seat at the table at the highest levels.

Yet for all that progress in the evolution of the profession, there are still too many people, especially in the general public, who hold public relations in low esteem. PR professionals are still viewed in many quarters as snake-oil salesmen, ready to stoop to conquer or employ deceptive tactics. The great challenge today is changing that perception and winning for the profession the respect that it deserves. The way to meet that challenge as an industry is through superb professional performance and continued adherence to the highest ethical and business standards.

Suggested Readings

Badaracco, Jr. Joseph L. *Leading Quietly: An Unorthodox Guide to Doing the Right Thing.* Cambridge, MA: Harvard Business School Press, 2002. A Harvard professor focuses on how leadership can be both effective and ethical at the same time.

Barney, Ralph, and Jay Black. *Ethics and New Media Technology.* Mahwah, NJ: Lawrence Erlbaum Associates, 2002.

Beaucamp, Tom, and Norman E. Bowie (Eds.). *Ethical Theory and Business,* 6th ed. Upper Saddle River, NJ: Prentice Hall, 2000.

Beder, Sharon. *Selling the Work Ethic: From Puritan Pulpit to Corporate PR.* Victoria, Australia: Scribe Publications Pry Ltd., 2000. A view from Down Under on the stresses—both physical and ethical—on working people.

Boatright, John Raymond. *Ethics and the Conduct of Business,* 4th ed. Upper Saddle River, NJ: Prentice Hall, 2002.

Business Ethics, "Corporate Social Responsibility Report," Marjorie Kelly, editor. Bimonthly magazine, Mavis Publications, Minneapolis, MN.

Day, Louis A. *Ethics in Media Communications: Cases and Controversies,* 4th ed. Belmont, CA: Wadsworth, 2002.

Hartley, Robert F. *Business Ethics: Mistakes and Successes.* New York: John Wiley & Sons, 2005. This book discusses all the killer ethical cases of our time, from Ford's Explorer and Firestone tires to World-Com's accounting fraud to "Chainsaw" Al Dunlap's duplicity at Sunbeam.

Manheim, Joel. *The Death of 1000 Cuts: Corporate Campaigns and the Attack on the Corporation.* Mahwah, NJ: Lawrence Erlbaum Associates, 2000.

Snoeyenboes, Milton, Robert Almeder, and James Humber, (Eds.). *Business Ethics,* 3rd ed. Amherst, NY: Prometheus Book, 2001. A classic, comprehensive view of the ethical issues that confront business, from drug testing to Internet privacy to conflicts of interest.

Stauber, John, and Sheldon Rampton. *Trust Us, We're Experts.* New York: Penguin Putnam, 2001. The anti–public relations authors of *Toxic Sludge Is Good for You* are at it again. This time, they explain—from their unique perspective—how "corporations and public relations firms have seized upon remarkable new ways of exploiting your trust to get you to buy what they have to sell." Strap yourself in.

Toth, Elizabeth L. *Public Relations Values in the New Millennium,* Special Issue of the *Journal of Public Relations Research,* 2000.

Trevino, Linda K., and Katherine A. Nelson. *Managing Business Ethics: Straight Talk About How to Do It Right,* 3rd ed. New York: John Wiley & Sons, 2004. Discusses not only what business ethics are but also why business should care.

Notes

1. Marc Peyser, "The Ugly Truth," *Newsweek,* January 23, 2006.

2. Edward Wyatt, "Oprah Calls Defense of Author a 'Mistake,'" *New York Times,* January 27, 2006.

3. Susan Schmidt and James V. Grimaldi, "Abramoff Pleads Guilty to 3 Counts," *Washington Post,* January 4, 2006, A1.

4. Alexei Barrionuevo and Vikas Bajaj, "At Enron Trial, 2 Sides Chart Widely Different Courses," *New York Times,* January 31, 2006, D1.

5. Rob Capriccioso, "Learning from American U's Mistakes," Inside-highered.com, October 28, 2005.

6. Frank Bruni, "Pope Tells Crowd of 'Shame' Caused by Abusive Priests," *New York Times,* July 29, 2002, A1–8.

7. "In Public Relations, 25% Admit Lying," *New York Times,* May 8, 2000, C20.

8. Jonathan Alter and Howard Fineman, "A Dynasty Dilemma," *Newsweek,* July 29, 2002, 24–29.

9. Claudia Deutsch, "New Surveys Show that Big Business Has a PR Problem," *New York Times,* December 9, 2005.

10. A. Larry Elliott and Richard J. Schroth. *How Companies Lie: Why Enron Is Just the Tip of the Iceberg* (New York: Crown Publishers, 2002).

11. Henry M. Paulson, Address to the National Press Club, Washington, DC, June 5, 2002.

12. "What Was and Wasn't on the Public's Mind," The Pew Research Center for the People and the Press, December 27, 2005.

13. Tom Zeller, Jr., "For Bloggers Seeking Name Recognition, Nothing Beats a Good Scandal," *New York Times,* October 31, 2005, 6.

14. Beth Barrett, "New PR Campaign Won't Violate City's Moratorium: Educational Message About Oil Disposal Mandated," *Los Angeles Daily News,* August 30, 2005, N5.

15. Jennifer Harper, "Supreme Court Justices Rank Highest in Credibility, Index Says," *Washington Times,* July 8, 1999, 20.

16. Teresa M. McAleavy, "Survey: Ethics Abuses on Rise," *The Record,* October 13, 2005, B1.

17. James Patrick Thompson, "Enforcing the Code of Conduct," *NYSE Magazine,* January 2006, 23.

7 The Law

FIGURE 7-1 The lawyer in red. Public relations–savvy attorney Gloria Allred (right) escorts client Amber Frey (left) after she testified against former boyfriend Scott Peterson, ultimately convicted of killing his pregnant wife and unborn son. (AP Wide World of Photos)

As the practice of public relations has gained stature, a natural tension has developed between public relations practitioners and lawyers. Ideally, public relations counselors and lawyers should work together to achieve a client's desired outcomes. Indeed, this is often the case. But there is also a fundamental difference in legal versus public relations advice.

- Lawyers correctly advise clients on what they *must* do, within the letter of legal requirements, to defend themselves in a court of law.

- Public relations advisers counsel clients on not what they *must* do but what they *should* do to defend themselves in a different court—the court of public opinion.

There is a vast difference between the two.

In recent years, however, lawyers have moved increasingly to invade the publicity turf traditionally manned by public relations professionals. Some lawyers have become ubiquitous—on radio and television and in the middle of press conferences—in using public relations techniques to further their clients' and their own ends.

One of the greatest proponents of this 21st-century legal incursion into public relations activity was this woman:

California attorney Gloria Allred was typical of the new breed of public relations–savvy lawyers. A perpetual guest on cable TV, Allred, it was said, "never met a camera she didn't like." When Governor Arnold Schwarzenegger was accused of groping a former movie mate, attorney Allred called a press conference to announce a lawsuit. When a former Hooters general manager was charged with secretly taping applicants as they changed into waitress uniforms, there was attorney Allred marching with the Hooters girls. And when California fertilizer salesman Scott Peterson was accused in 2004 of murdering his wife and unborn son, there was attorney Allred escorting the defendant's secret mistress to court. Allred—usually dressed in her namesake "all red"—literally was everywhere.

In many ways, it makes sense that lawyers and public relations people should work in common. Public relations and the law both begin with the First Amendment to the Constitution that guarantees freedom of speech in our society.

But in the 21st century, ensuring freedom of speech is not as easy as it sounds. One question is, *Where does one's freedom start and another's end?* Another question is, *How much freedom of speech is appropriate—or advisable—in any given situation?*

Such are the dilemmas in the relationship between public relations principles and the law.

Public Relations and the Law: An Uneasy Alliance

The legal and public relations professions have historically shared an uneasy alliance. Public relations practitioners must always understand the legal implications of any issue with which they become involved, and a firm's legal position must always be the first consideration.

From a legal point of view, normally the less an organization says prior to its day in court, the better. That way, the opposition can't gain any new ammunition that will become part of the public record. A lawyer, the saying goes, tells you to say two things: "Say nothing, and say it slowly!"

From a public relations standpoint, though, it may often make sense to go public early on, especially if the organization's integrity or credibility is being called into public question. In the summer of 2003, for example, when NBA star Kobe Bryant was accused of raping a woman at a Colorado hotel, Bryant immediately held a press conference, with his wife at his side, to acknowledge he had erred but denied the charges. (A year later, the sexual assault charge was dismissed and the case was settled.)

The point is that legal advice and public relations advice may indeed be different. In an organization, a smart manager will carefully weigh both legal and public relations counsel before making a decision.

It also should be noted that law and ethics are interrelated. The Public Relations Society of America's Code of Professional Standards (see Appendix A) notes that many activities that are unethical are also illegal. However, there are instances in which something is perfectly legal but unethical and other instances in which things might be illegal but otherwise ethical. Thus, when a public relations professional reflects on what course to take in a particular situation, he or she must analyze not only the legal ramifications but also the ethical considerations.[1]

This chapter examines the relationship between the law and public relations and the more prominent role the law plays in public relations practice and vice versa. The discussion introduces the legal concerns of public relations professionals today: First Amendment considerations, insider trading, disclosure law, ethics law, privacy law,

Talking Points

Saving the Juice

Perhaps never has a legal trial gripped the entire nation so pervasively as the murder charges against Orenthal J. Simpson in the killings of Nicole Brown Simpson and Ron Goldman in 1994. O. J. Simpson was a revered football player, broadcaster, and actor who seemed to be leading a charmed life, until one summer evening he stunned the nation by leading it—via national TV—on a low-speed car chase through the highways and byways of Brentwood, California (Figure 7-2).

The Simpson trial shocked the nation, but the real drama lay in how Simpson's high-powered attorney team of Johnnie Cochran, F. Lee Bailey, and Robert Shapiro used publicity to forward their cause and wallop the hapless Los Angeles District Attorney's Office.

Here's how Mr. Shapiro described the winning public relations approach.

- **Lawyer as public relations person.** "When we are retained for those high-profile cases, we are instantly thrust into the role of a public relations person—a role for which the majority of us have no education, experience, or training. The lawyer's role as spokesperson may be [as] equally important to the outcome of a case as the skills of an advocate in the courtroom."

FIGURE 7-2 Free Juice. Fallen—but not convicted—O. J. Simpson. (AP Wide World Photos)

- **Power of the media.** "The importance and power of the media cannot be overemphasized. The first impression the public gets is usually the one that is most important."
- **"No comment."** "'No comment' is the least appropriate and least productive response. Coming at the end of a lengthy story, it adds absolutely nothing and leaves the public with a negative impression."
- **Lying to the media.** "It is never a good idea to lie to the press. To simply make up facts in the hope that they will later prove correct is too big a risk."
- **Media relationships.** "Initial relationships with legitimate members of the press are very important. Many times a lawyer will feel it is an intrusion to be constantly beset by seemingly meaningless questions that take up a tremendous amount of time. But the initial headlines of the arrest often make the sacred presumption of innocence a myth. In reality, we have the presumption of guilt. This is why dealing with the media is so important."
- **Responding to the press.** "The wire services depend on immediate updates. Therefore, all calls should be returned as quickly as possible. Wire service reporters can also provide a valuable source of information to you."
- **Framing answers.** "Just as you would do in trial, anticipate the questions a reporter will pose. Think out your answers carefully.... Use great care in choosing your words. Keep your statements simple and concise. Pick and choose the questions you want to answer. You do not have to be concerned with whether the answer precisely addresses the question, since only the answer will be aired."
- **The tabloids.** "My experience is that cooperating with tabloid reporters only gives them a legitimate source of information which can be misquoted or taken out of context and does little good for your client. My personal approach is not to cooperate with tabloid reporters."
- **Dealing with TV hordes.** "The television media, either consciously or unconsciously, create an atmosphere of chaos. Immediately upon arriving at the courthouse, you are surrounded by television crews. We have all seen people coming to court and trying to rush through the press with their heads down or covering them with newspapers or coats. Nothing looks worse. I always instruct my clients upon arrival at the courthouse to get out in a normal manner, to walk next to me in a slow and deliberate way, to have a look of confidence and acknowledge with a nod those who are familiar and supportive."*

Robert Shapiro's treatise is fitting testimony to how lawyers use public relations techniques and are fully cognizant of the value and power of the practice of public relations.

*Excerpted from Robert Shapiro, "Secrets of a Celebrity Lawyer," *Columbia Journalism Review* (September/October 1994): 25–29.

copyright law, and the laws concerning censorship of the Internet—issues that have become primary concerns for public relations practitioners in the 21st century.

Public Relations and the First Amendment

Any discussion of law and public relations should start with the First Amendment, which states: "Congress shall make no law . . . abridging the freedom of speech or the press." The First Amendment is the cornerstone of free speech in our society: This is what distinguishes democratic nations from many others.

Recent years have seen a blizzard of problems and challenges regarding the First Amendment.

- In 2006, when an obscure Danish newspaper published cartoons depicting the prophet Muhammad in a tasteless way, Muslims protested around the world, resulting in destruction, injuries, and deaths. While the Western world considered the cartoons—as offensive as they were—examples of "freedom of expression," much of the Muslim world was outraged (Figure 7-3).

- That same year, a former top aide to Vice President Dick Cheney told a federal grand jury that his superiors authorized him to give secret information to reporters as part of the Bush administration's defense of intelligence used to justify invading Iraq.[2]

- During President Bush's 2006 State of the Union Address in the Capitol, two individuals, one a war protester and the other the wife of a Florida congressman,

FIGURE 7-3 Freedom of speech? In 2006, Indonesian protesters burned a Danish flag in anger over a Denmark newspaper's use of scurrilous cartoons depicting the Prophet Muhammad. (AP Wide World Photos)

were removed from the visitors' gallery because of the T-shirts they wore. Both were told they were violating regulations prohibiting "protests" in those seats.[3]

- In the summer of 2002, the Bush administration was livid when a judge ruled that the Justice Department couldn't keep secret the names of more than 1,000 people picked up in connection with the September 11, 2001, attacks.[4]

As these skirmishes suggest, interpreting the First Amendment is no simple matter. One person's definition of obscenity or divulging state secrets may be someone else's definition of art or freedom of expression. Because the First Amendment lies at the heart of the communications business, defending it is a front-line responsibility of the public relations profession.

Public Relations and Defamation Law

The laws that govern a person's privacy have significant implications for journalists and other communicators, such as public relations professionals, particularly laws that touch on libel and slander—commonly known as defamation laws—by the media.

Defamation is the umbrella term used to describe libel—a printed falsehood—and slander—an oral falsehood. For defamation to be proved, a plaintiff must convince the court that four requirements have been met.

1. The falsehood was communicated through print, broadcast, or other electronic means.
2. The person who is the subject of the falsehood was identified or easily identifiable.
3. The identified person has suffered injury—in the form of monetary losses, reputational loss, or mental suffering.
4. The person making the statement was malicious or grossly negligent.[5]

Generally, the privacy of an ordinary citizen is protected under the law. A citizen in the limelight, however, has a more difficult problem, especially in proving defamation of character through libel or slander.

To prove such a charge, a public figure must show that the media acted with actual malice in their reporting. *Actual malice* in a public figure slander case, as noted, means that statements have been published with the knowledge that they were false or with reckless disregard for whether the statements were false. In a landmark case in 1964, *New York Times* v. *Sullivan,* the Supreme Court nullified a libel award of $500,000 to an Alabama police official, holding that no damages could be awarded "in actions brought by public officials against critics of their official conduct" unless there was proof of actual malice. And proving actual malice is a difficult task.

Several historic libel cases have helped pave the case law precedent.

- In 1992, *The Wall Street Journal* and its award-winning reporter Bryan Burrough were served with a $50 million libel suit by Harry L. Freeman, a former communications executive of American Express. The suit stemmed from the way Freeman was characterized in Burrough's book, *Vendetta: American Express and the Smearing of Edmund Safra.*[6]
- A decade earlier, in a landmark case, the *Washington Post* initially lost a $2 million suit after a federal jury decided that the newspaper had libeled William P. Tavoulareas when it alleged that he had used his position as president of Mobil Oil to further his son's career in a shipping business. The next year, a federal

judge overturned the verdict against the *Post* because the article in question didn't contain "knowing lies or statements made in reckless disregard of the truth." The Supreme Court later corroborated the ruling in favor of the *Post*.

■ In another celebrated case, Israeli General Ariel Sharon brought a $50 million libel suit against *Time* magazine. Once again, the jury criticized *Time* for negligent journalism in reporting Sharon's role in a massacre in a Palestinian refugee camp. However, this case, too, ended without a libel verdict.

■ In 1996, Atlanta security guard Richard A. Jewell sued both *NBC News* and the *Atlanta Journal-Constitution* for reporting that he was the lead suspect in the Atlanta Olympic bombing, which led to two deaths. The reports caused a media feeding frenzy, which disrupted Jewell's life and tarnished his name. Jewell was cleared of any involvement in the bombing and reached a settlement with his media accusers, averting a libel lawsuit.

The 21st-century proliferation of cable and radio talk shows, where hosts and guests say what they want regardless of factual accuracy or impact on a person's life, has resulted in defamation becoming more complex and devastating.

Typical of the new defamation danger was the appearance of a *Boston Herald* reporter on *The O'Reilly Factor* in 2002, who previewed a story on a Boston judge who reportedly told a 14-year-old rape victim, "Get over it." Although the judge denied ever making such an outlandish statement, the damage was done. The *O'Reilly* mention spread throughout the nation and as a result, the judge received death threats, his two daughters were threatened with rape on a *Herald*-sponsored chat room, and the man's life was ruined. The judge sued the *Herald* and four of its writers for a "malicious and relentless campaign of libel unprecedented in the history of this Commonwealth"[7] (Figure 7-4).

FIGURE 7-4 Slander factor. Cable programs, like the nightly verbal slugfest *The O'Reilly Factor,* introduced a new source of potential media defamation. (Fraser P. Seitel)

Public relations practitioners must be aware of situations involving libel and slander. Many public relations professionals create, write, and edit internal print and online newsletters. In this context, they must be careful not to defame fellow employees or others in what they write. The same caution should be the rule for public relations professionals who make statements to the media on behalf of their organizations. Care must be the watchword in such public speech.

Public Relations and Insider Trading

Every public relations professional should know the laws that govern his or her organization and industry.

1. A practitioner in a hospital should have an understanding of managed care and its ramifications.
2. A practitioner at a nonprofit organization should understand the laws that govern donors and recipients.
3. A practitioner at a college ought to understand the laws that govern privacy of student and faculty records.
4. A practitioner in a particular industry—chemicals, computers, banking, sports—should understand the laws germane to that particular area.

With 100 million Americans participating in the securities markets, either directly or through company pension plans, nowhere in public relations practice is an understanding of the law more important than in the area of securities law.

Every public company has an obligation to deal frankly, comprehensively, and immediately with any information that is considered *material*. A material announcement is one that might cause an investor to buy, hold, or sell a stock. The Securities and Exchange Commission (SEC)—through a series of court cases, consent decrees, complaints, and comments over the years—has painted a general portrait of disclosure requirements for practitioners (see Appendix C), with which all practitioners in public companies should be familiar. The SEC's mandate stems from the Securities Act of 1933 and the Securities Exchange Act of 1934, which attempted to protect the public from abuses in the issuance and sale of securities.

The SEC's overriding concern is that all investors have an opportunity to learn about material information as promptly as possible. Basically, a company is expected to release news that may affect its stock market price as quickly as possible. Through its general antifraud statute, Rule 10b-5 of the Securities and Exchange Act, the SEC strictly prohibits the dissemination of false or misleading information to investors. It also prohibits insider trading of securities on the basis of material information not disclosed to the public.

Unfortunately, the 20th century ended and the 21st century began with front-page insider trading scandals. The two most celebrated insider trading cases of the 1990s were those against Ivan Boesky and Michael Milken, two Wall Street legends, who were both slapped with nine-figure fines and jail terms. Many of their associates, equally guilty of insider trading violations, also were dispatched to the slammer.

In the first years of the 21st century, one celebrated insider trading case involved ImClone Systems CEO Sam Waksal, who, along with family members, unloaded ImClone stock after the CEO learned that the Food and Drug Administration was about to reject a key ImClone drug. The stock was subsequently crushed, as was CEO Waksal, his family, his stockbroker, and his good friend Martha Stewart (Case Study in Chapter 1)—all embroiled in an insider trading scandal.[8]

Nor did journalists escape the accusation of insider trading convictions. In the late 1990s, a columnist at *The Wall Street Journal* was convicted of illegally using his newspaper column to give favorable opinions about companies in which a couple of his stockbroker friends had already invested heavily. He went to jail. In the early 2000s, stock commentator James Cramer was accused by a former colleague of "pumping up stocks by feeding rumors" to friendly broadcasters at CNBC.[9] Cramer denied the allegations, and when no charges were brought, Cramer became a program host at CNBC.

As to public relations counselors, they, too, must be careful to act only on public information when trading securities. The investor relations director of Dallas-based Carreker Corporation and his brother were fined more than $600,000 in 2002 for netting a combined $209,000 on an insider trading transaction.[10]

No one is immune from the law, least of all the public relations professionals whose job it is to deal with the public.

Public Relations and Disclosure Law

Besides cracking down on insider trading, the SEC has challenged corporations and public relations firms on the accuracy of information they disseminate for clients. Today, in an environment of mergers, takeovers, consolidations, and the incessant rumors that circulate around them, a knowledge of disclosure law, a sensitivity to disclosure requirements, and a bias toward disclosing rather than withholding material information are important attributes of public relations officials.

In the new millennium, with securities trading extending beyond the traditional 9:30 a.m.–4 p.m. stock market trading day and with instantaneous online trading a reality for millions of investors, the responsibilities on public relations people for full and fair and immediate disclosure have intensified. The SEC, in turn, has increased its focus on private meetings between companies and analysts, which are closed to the media and therefore to individual investors who rely on the media for financial information.

To combat such selective disclosure, the SEC in 2000 adopted Regulation FD, or "fair disclosure." Basically, Regulation FD requires companies to widely disseminate any material announcement.

In the past, companies would share such material news with securities analysts or large investors, who then might act on it before the public found out. Under Regulation FD, even if a material announcement slips out to an analyst, the company is obligated to issue a news release within 24 hours "to provide broad, non-exclusionary disclosure information to the public."[11]

In 2002, Regulation FD was bolstered by the passage of the Sarbanes-Oxley Act, sponsored by U.S. Senator Paul Sarbanes and U.S. Representative Michael Oxley. Sarbanes-Oxley came as a result of the large corporate financial scandals involving Enron, WorldCom, Global Crossing, and Arthur Andersen. Among other requirements, Sarbanes-Oxley mandated all publicly traded companies to increase financial disclosure and submit an annual report of the effectiveness of their internal accounting controls to the SEC, with criminal and civil penalties for noncompliance.[12]

Although many analysts and investors complained that the combination of Regulation FD and Sarbanes-Oxley would have a costly, "chilling impact" on companies that previously were willing to communicate, Congress and the regulators were unwilling to yield.

The escalating importance of the stock market to average Americans, coupled with the corporate management and accounting scandals of the early years of the century, increased the necessity of full, fair, and immediate disclosure to all investors.

Public Relations and Ethics Law

The laws on ethical misconduct in society have gotten quite a workout over the last two decades.

- In 1996, when Swiss banks were accused of making it difficult for the heirs of Jewish Holocaust victims to recover the assets of relatives, the Swiss Bank Association hired Kekst and Company, a New York firm long associated with Jewish causes, to defend the banks. Critics accused the firm of an ethical breach, allowing its clients to exploit it.

- In a celebrated case, translated into the 1999 movie *The Insider,* the late public relations counselor John Scanlon faced a grand jury subpoena, stemming from his efforts to discredit Jeffrey Wigand, an internal critic of Scanlon's cigarette client Brown & Williamson.[13]

- In the political public relations arena, the late Lyn Nofziger, former White House political director and communications counselor, was sentenced to 90 days in prison and fined $30,000 for violating the Federal Ethics in Government Act, which forbids lobbying former contacts within one year of leaving the government. A related fate was meted out to former White House Deputy Chief of Staff Michael K. Deaver, another well-known public relations professional, who was found guilty of perjury over his lobbying activities. He also faced a jail sentence and a serious fine.

The activities of lobbyists, in particular, have been closely watched by Congress since the imposition of the Federal Regulation of Lobbying Act of 1946. In recent years, however, the practice of lobbying has expanded greatly.

In 1998, the Clinton administration drew public fire for accepting political contributions from influential representatives of Indonesia and China. New Jersey Senator Robert Torricelli was "severely admonished" in 2002 by the Senate Ethics Committee for gifts received from a wealthy Korean constituent. Subsequently, Torricelli was forced to give up his seat. In 2006, the Bush administration was rocked by the ethical violations connected to the Jack Abramoff lobbying scandal.

In recent years, Campaign Finance Reform, to limit—if not eradicate—the acceptance by legislators of favors and money from wealthy interest groups has intensified. With the reputation of politicians, particularly on the national level, at an all-time low, Congress had to focus on restoring ethics to government and winning back the public trust.[14]

Public Relations and Copyright Law

One body of law that is particularly relevant to public relations professionals is copyright law and the protections it offers writers. Copyright law provides basic, automatic protection for writers, whether a manuscript is registered with the Copyright Office or even published. Under the Copyright Act of 1976, an "original work of authorship" has copyright protection from the moment the work is in the following fixed form:

- literary works
- musical works
- dramatic works
- pantomimes and choreographic works
- pictorial, graphic, or sculptural works
- motion pictures
- sound recordings

The word *fixed* means that the work is sufficiently permanent to permit it to be perceived, reproduced, or otherwise communicated.[15]

Copyright law gives the owner of the copyright the exclusive right to reproduce and authorize others to reproduce the work, prepare derivative works based on the copyrighted material, and perform and/or display the work publicly. That's why Michael Jackson had to pay $47.5 million for the rights to the Beatles' compositions to the duly sworn representatives and heirs of John, Paul, George, and Ringo.

Copyright law is different from trademark law, which refers to a word, symbol, or slogan, used alone or in combination, that identifies a product or its sponsor—for example, the Nike swoosh.

What courts have stated again and again is that for the purposes of criticism, news reporting, teaching, scholarship, or research, use of copyrighted material is not an infringement but rather constitutes *fair use*. Although precise definitions of fair use—like everything else in the law—is subject to interpretation, such factors as "the effect on the future market" of the copyrighted work in question or the "volume of quotation used" or even whether the "heart" of the material was ripped off are often considered.[16]

Over time, the Supreme Court has strengthened the copyright status of freelance artists and writers—many of whom are independent public relations practitioners— ruling that such professionals retain the right to copyright what they create "as long as they were not in a conventional employment relationship with the organization that commissioned their work." As a result of this ruling, public relations professionals must carefully document the authorization that has been secured for using freelance material. In other words, when engaging a freelance professional, public relations people must know the law.

Public Relations and Internet Law

The Internet has introduced a new dimension to the law affecting free speech. The premise in American law is that "not all speech is created equal."[17] Rather, there is a hierarchy of speech, under Supreme Court precedents dating back many decades, that calibrate the degree of First Amendment protection with, among other tests, the particular medium of expression. For example, speech that would be perfectly acceptable if uttered in a public park could constitutionally be banned when broadcast from a sound truck.

Dealing with the Internet has introduced new ramifications to this legal principal. Indeed, cyberlaw has brought into question many of the most revered communications law principles.

Speaking of Ethics

Seizing the Prepubescent Pirates

In the summer of 2003, the Recording Industry Association of America (RIAA) announced that it would begin suing users of peer-to-peer (P2P) file-sharing systems for violating the copyright of artists, producers, and record companies.

The music industry was correctly up in arms about the theft of its product that cost it millions of dollars. Said Universal Records artist Nelly, "We really look at it as stealing, because to us, it's black and white. Either you pay for it or you don't" (Figure 7-5).

But in enforcing its new rules, the RIAA ran into a public relations buzz saw. First, it sent 700 lawyers to find alleged perpetrators. The lawyers' initial assault on 260 music file-swappers resulted in well-publicized lawsuits of 21st-century pirates, from a 12-year-old New York girl who lives in a public housing project to a septuagenarian Texas grandfather.

As one Internet swapping service president put it, the recording companies "in their infinite wisdom have decided to not only alienate their own customers but to drive them into bankruptcy through litigation."

Some suggested that rather than suing for copyright damage, the RIAA might have tried other more consumer-friendly devices, such as:

FIGURE 7-5 Bash the pirates. Rapper Nelly was among those in 2003 who screamed "foul" over copyright infringement of those who illegally downloaded music. (AP Wide World Photos)

- **Cut the cost of CDs.** Many music downloaders justified their actions by claiming that CD costs "are outrageous." In 2002, the industry settled a lawsuit with 43 states over charges the record companies conspired in the 1990s to set minimum prices for CDs. Indeed, one company, Universal Music Group, announced it would slash the wholesale price of its CDs and recommend retailers lower prices by 30 percent. In a less positive sign, the other major record companies pointedly refused to follow suit.
- **Package more individual or two-song CDs.** File-swappers claimed that since most CDs don't contain more than one or two good tunes, plunking down $22 bucks for 10 un-

wanted songs is a waste. So they illegally download the one song on the CD they find appealing.

In response, the industry might have thought about increasing production of mini-CD singles, or doubles, or triples.

- **Devise an Internet solution.** Historically, record company executives considered the Internet a threat, opting to "frustrate" its use rather than accommodate its customers' desire to use it. Sure enough, when Apple Computer launched its iTunes service, it sold more than one million songs in the first week. By the middle of 2005, iTunes had sold more than 500 million songs, and Apple's iPod was a roaring success.

Had the music industry itself been less willing to sue and more willing to refine its offerings, it, too, might have profited.

For further information, see Fraser P. Seitel, "Seizing the Prepubescent Pirates," TechCentralStation.com, September 17, 2003.

Censorship

In 1996, Congress passed the Communications Decency Act (CDA) as an amendment to a far-reaching telecommunications bill. The CDA introduced criminal penalties, including fines of as much as $250,000 and prison terms up to two years, for making "indecent" speech available to "a person under 18 years of age." A Philadelphia court a few months later struck down the law, contending that such censorship would chill all discourse on the Internet.[18]

Then, in the summer of 1997, the Supreme Court, in a sweeping endorsement of free speech, declared the CDA unconstitutional. The decision, unanimous in most respects, marked the highest court's first effort to extend the principles of the First Amendment into cyberspace and to confront the nature and the law of this new, powerful medium. In summarizing the Court's finding, Justice John Paul Stevens said the Court considered the "goal of protecting children from indecent material as legitimate and important" but concluded that "the wholly unprecedented breadth of the law threatened to suppress far too much speech among adults and even between parents and children."[19]

In 1998, Congress passed the Child Online Protection Act, which made it a federal crime to "knowingly communicate for commercial purposes material considered harmful to minors." In 2002 and again in 2004, the high court once again repelled legislation to censor child pornography on the Internet, ruling that it would be unconstitutional to criminalize protected free speech on the Internet.

In 2006, federal prosecutors preparing to defend the 1998 Act asked Google, Microsoft, Yahoo!, and America Online to hand over millions of search records. Google alone refused, claiming such a disclosure would violate the privacy of its users.[20] On the other hand, in the same year, Google agreed to censor its results in China, adhering to the country's free-speech restrictions, in return for better access in the Internet's fastest-growing market.[21]

Intellectual Property

Few cyberlaw cases have drawn more headlines than the 2001 case against Napster, the popular application that allowed users to exchange music files. Because Napster ran the file-swapping through a central server, it was an easy target for legislation.

In the end—for Napster—the protest, led by those heavy-metal defenders of the First Amendment, Metallica, and backed by the large music companies, convinced the Court that the company was infringing on copyright protections of intellectual property.[22]

Two years later, as noted, the recording industry waged all-out war on those who downloaded intellectual property without paying. On a larger level, intellectual piracy of everything from video games to music to software has become rampant, with estimates that 90 percent of virtually every form of intellectual property in China is pirated.[23]

Cybersquatting

Another complex issue is that of cybersquatting—grabbing domain names in bad faith, expressly for the purpose of tormenting or "shaking down" a rightful registrant. It costs an infiltrator about $35 to register a variation of a domain name.

Companies from Wendy's to General Motors to Wal-Mart have been beset by cybersquatters. Kmart Corporation successfully mounted a legal challenge to fight a rogue Web site, Kmartsucks.com. Ultimately, the site was forced to change its name to Themartsucks.com.

Current trademark law prohibits a company from registering a name that exactly duplicates a registered trademark, but cybersquatters frequently register names that differ only slightly. They know that Web surfers will type in a variation of a company's name when searching for its site. They then either attempt to sell the names or use the sites to disrupt the company's commerce.[24]

E-Fraud

Fraud is fraud, no matter where it is domiciled. And on the World Wide Web, where anyone who wants to can choose anonymity, fraud runs rampant.

The problem is that e-crooks are difficult to stop. Often it depends on companies policing the Internet themselves, frequently to go after former employees.

For example:

- Varian Medical Systems of Palo Alto won a $775,000 verdict against two former employees who posted 14,000 messages on 100 message boards, accusing the firm of being homophobic and of discriminating against pregnant women.
- A California court ruled against a fired Intel employee who sent e-mails to about 35,000 staffers, criticizing the company.

And then there's "click fraud," which threatens to disrupt the largest search engines. Search engines rank listings by the number of clicks they receive: the more clicks, the higher the ranking. Click fraud occurs when a concerted effort is initiated to register multiple clicks to drive specific listings higher in a search-ranking algorithm. Such fraudulent activity effects marketers, who advertise on a site and pay rates based on usage.[25]

These are but a few of the burgeoning legal issues that surround the World Wide Web.

Litigation Public Relations

In court cases, plaintiffs and defendants are often scrupulously warned by judges not to influence the ultimate verdict outside the courtroom.

Forget it.

In the 21st century, with CNN, MSNBC, Fox News Channel, CNBC, and talk radio incessantly jabbering about possible trials, upcoming trials, and current trials, there is little guarantee that any jury can be objective about any high-profile legal case.

That's why litigation public relations has become so important.

Litigation public relations can best be defined as managing the media process during the course of any legal dispute so as to affect the outcome or its impact on the client's overall reputation.

Although court proceedings have certain rules and protocols, dealing in the public arena with a matter of litigation has no such strictures. The Sixth Amendment to the Constitution guarantees accused persons "a speedy and public trial, by an impartial jury," but television commentary by knowledgeable—and in many cases, unknowledgeable—"experts" can help influence a potential jury for or against a defendant.

As a consequence, communications has become central to the management of modern litigation.[26] Smart lawyers understand that with cable TV, in particular, being so pervasive, they have little choice but to engage in litigation public relations to provide their clients with every advantage.

According to one counselor who works exclusively with litigation, there are seven keys to litigation visibility.

1. **Learn the process.** All involved should be aware of the roadmap for the case and the milestones ahead, which may lend themselves to publicity.

2. **Develop a message strategy.** Think about what should be said at each stage of a trial to keep the press and public focused on the key messages of the client.

3. **Settle fast.** Settlement is probably the most potent litigation visibility management tool. The faster the settlement, the less litigation visibility there is likely to be. This is often a positive development.

4. **Anticipate high-profile variables.** Often in public cases everybody gets into the act—judges, commentators, jury selection experts, psychologists, and so on. Always anticipate all that could be said, conjectured, and argued about the case. Always try to be prepared for every inevitality.

5. **Keep the focus positive.** Ultimately, it's a positive, productive attitude that leads to effective negotiations with the other side. So the less combative you can be—especially near settlement—the better.

6. **Try settling again.** Again, this ought to be the primary litigation visibility strategy—to end the agony and get it out of the papers.

7. **Fight nicely.** Wars are messy, expensive, and prone to producing casualties. It is much better to be positive. This will give both sides a greater chance of eventually settling.[27]

Last Word

As our society becomes more contentious, fractious, and litigious, public relations must become more concerned with the law. On the one hand, because management must rely so heavily on legal advice and legal judgments, it is imperative that public relations people understand the laws that govern their organizations and industries. Public relations people must understand that their views may differ from those of an attorney. As a defense lawyer once described his role, "You should do what a client wants, period. That's what you're paid for." By contrast, public relations people are paid to advise their clients what is "the right thing to do." And they should never shrink from that obligation.

On the other hand, public relations advisers must depend on "buy-in" from others in management. Lawyers are among the most influential of these associates. Therefore, forming an alliance with legal counselors must be a front-line objective for public relations professionals.

Beyond the working relationship between public relations people and lawyers, the practice of public relations has, itself, wrestled with legal questions in recent years. Increasingly, public relations practice is based on legal contracts: between agencies and clients, employers and employees, purchasers and vendors. All contracts—both written and oral—must be binding and enforceable.

In recent years, controversy in the field has erupted over noncompete clauses, in which former employees are prohibited, within certain time parameters, from working for a competitor or pitching a former account. Time and again, the courts have ruled in favor of public relations agencies and against former clients in noncompete cases.

Likewise, legal challenges have been made relative to the markup of expenses that public relations agencies charge clients. Standard practice in the industry is to mark up by 15 percent to 20 percent of legitimate printing and advertising bills submitted to clients.

Add to these the blurring of the lines between public relations advice on the one hand and legal advice on the other, and it becomes clear that the connection between public relations and the law will intensify dramatically in the 21st century.

Discussion Starters

1. What is the difference between a public relations professional's responsibility and a lawyer's responsibility?
2. What have been recent challenges to the First Amendment?
3. How can someone prove that he or she has been libeled or slandered?
4. What is meant by the term *insider trading*?
5. What is the SEC's overriding concern when considering disclosure?
6. How have Regulation FD and Sarbanes-Oxley changed the disclosure environment?
7. Whom does copyright law protect?
8. What are some of the dominant issues in laws affecting the Internet?
9. What are several general principles with respect to litigation public relations?
10. What general advice should a public relations professional consider in working with lawyers?

Top of the Shelf

Slander: Liberal Lies about the American Right

Ann Coulter, New York: Crown Publishers, 2002.

While her book perhaps is not technically a book on "law," Ann Coulter, the fire-breathing, liberal-bashing columnist, is a card-carrying attorney.

In this nonstop beratement of all things liberal, Coulter takes on the mainstream media and what she says is its "bias" against conservatives. And she isn't subtle about it. For starters, she declares America's liberal sweetheart *Today* co-anchor Katie Couric "the Eva Braun [Hitler's mistress] of morning television." Now that ain't subtle.

Among other historical references, Coulter documents how the mainstream media portrayed conservative antagonists in the Bill Clinton scandal, for example, as "ugly," thus exposing their editorial bias.

Coulter points out how the Internet and the sustained popularity of radio are beginning to provide balance to liberal media views. Someday, she says, the way we now think of *bias* may become an anachronism.

CASE STUDY

Winning a National Venue for Eminent Domain

The mission of the Institute for Justice (IJ), a Washington, DC, public interest law firm, is to defend small property owners. As such, the firm was deeply concerned about the legal issue of "eminent domain" through which state and local governments use their power to take away homes and small businesses not for a public use—such as a road—but for politically connected private developers who use the land for private developments that promise to create more jobs and taxes.

As IJ saw it, if jobs and taxes can justify taking someone's private property, then no home or small business, house of worship, or farm would be safe. Each could be replaced with a big-box retail store or high-end condominium that could create more jobs or taxes.

In the fall of 2005, with the incidence of eminent domain seizures growing, IJ set out to limit the government's use of eminent domain. If IJ was to be successful in its long-term efforts to restrict government's power of eminent domain, it would have to heighten the public's awareness of the issue and create an environment in which the courts could rule favorably for property owners. To achieve that end, it desperately sought to place the issue on the national agenda.

Complicated, Isolated Issue

Attracting national interest in a topic as complicated as eminent domain was difficult for a number of reasons.

- For one thing, each incident in which the government took private land for public use happened in relative isolation around the country. The media saw the issue, therefore, as a "local" one.

- For another, no statistics existed as to how often eminent domain taking had occurred nationwide. It would consequently be challenging to interest the media in a national story on the subject.

- Finally, even though the U.S. Constitution and each state constitution required that private property only be taken for a "public use," for decades the courts had blurred the definition of public use so that any use—including private development—could justify this government power.

To elevate the issue to national prominence required dealing with each of these public relations roadblocks.

Starting with the Big "R"

As with any complex public relations challenge, the issue required research. IJ undertook a first-of-its-kind study, called *Public Power, Private Gain,* that analyzed how often eminent domain abuse occurred in every state (Figure 7-6). After 2 years of research, what IJ discovered was shocking: More than 10,000 properties in 41 states were either threatened or taken by eminent domain for private use in just a 5-year time period.

Its findings encouraged IJ to launch a grassroots movement committed to saving the homes of individuals whose properties were threatened and to ending eminent domain abuse.

FIGURE 7-6 A campaign commences. First salvo in a campaign to bring national attention to the legal use of eminent domain was this 5-year research project. (Courtesy of Institute for Justice)

It also set out to attract national publicity.

As a result of the study's publication and its promotion, the issue of eminent domain was featured in nearly every major daily newspaper nationwide, as well as on the CBS news program *60 Minutes*. Within days of the *60 Minutes* feature, IJ won an important eminent domain case in Arizona. Weeks later, voters in Ohio rejected a project that would have bulldozed an entire neighborhood for an upscale private shopping mall and condominiums.

And that was only the beginning.

Earning a PhD in Media Relations

To continue to increase the visibility of the issue, IJ followed a three-pronged PhD strategy of media relations to *personalize, humanize,* and *dramatize* an otherwise dry legal issue.

■ **First, personalize.** IJ carefully targeted individual reporters, with some interest in the law or the subject, to report on eminent domain legislation. In all, it set out to reach 400 journalists nationwide, from those covering the U.S. Supreme Court to reporters in local communities where eminent domain abuse was taking place. It pitched each reporter, editor, editorial writer, and broadcaster on a personal basis, constructing arguments and issues that pertained to that specific journalist.

■ **Second, humanize.** Rather than pitching the story as a "global" one, IJ decided to make it the story of individuals whose rights were being violated by the government. IJ worked with its clients to connect them with journalists and help them tell their own stories in their own words, through interviews, op-eds, and other devices. IJ then supplemented client information with additional legal, historical, and political research to put the issue in perspective.

In one celebrated 2004 case, IJ encouraged the media to visit and interview seven families in New London, Connecticut, who were fighting to save their homes from eminent domain abuse. The families were visited by most of the major mainstream media.

■ **Third, dramatize.** Throughout its campaign, the Institute for Justice never lost sight of the human drama. It arranged for compelling photographs, client quotes, media visits to client homes, and other initiatives designed to attract publicity. IJ continually hammered at the potential tragedy of the government taking someone's home or business not for a public use but for someone else's private profit.

In another battle, one fought on behalf of small business owners in Pittsburgh, IJ dramatized the campaign by focusing on Mayor Tom Murphy, who sought to take away 60 buildings and more than 100 businesses to make way for a Chicago developer's private mall. In that campaign, IJ created huge billboards lambasting Murphy for his callousness toward small businesses (Figure 7-7).

Earning a Spot on the Agenda

As a result of IJ's campaign, the Supreme Court, in 2005, accepted the firm's *Kelo v. City of New London* case, filed on behalf of New London residents.

The Institute's pleading was an uphill battle. In the previous 50 years, the High Court had never ruled in favor of a property owner challenging government's power of eminent domain. Predictably, the Supreme Court ruled against the Institute by a 5 to 4 vote. The

FIGURE 7-7 Fighting Murphy's Law. The Institute for Justice went after Pittsburgh's mayor when he sought to tear down small businesses to build a shopping mall. (Courtesy of Institute for Justice)

justices upheld the taking of private property for private development.

But that didn't stop the Institute for Justice.

A week after the Supreme Court turn down in the *Kelo* case, IJ launched its *Hands Off My Home* campaign—an effort to shore up property rights at the local, state, and national levels (Figure 7-8). Within weeks, legislators from nearly 40 states either sought to introduce or had already passed legislation along those lines.

Today, largely as a result of IJ's efforts, the issue of eminent domain has clearly become a front-burner topic for many Americans committed to protecting what is rightfully theirs. Consequently, courts are more carefully examining eminent domain cases before them and more frequently ruling in favor of the small property owner over the government.

Questions

1. Was it wise for IJ to wait to launch its public relations campaign for two years, until its research was completed?

2. Was the eminent domain issue really worth all the time and effort expended by IJ?

3. What other options did IJ have in publicizing eminent domain?

4. Do you agree with IJ's decision to keep going even after losing its case in the Supreme Court?

5. What further public relations activities can IJ adopt in fighting eminent domain?

FIGURE 7-8 Hands on public relations. After losing in the Supreme Court, the Institute for Justice launched a more personalized campaign to spur homeowner support. (Courtesy of Institute for Justice)

Voice of Authority

An Interview with John E. Kramer

John E. Kramer is vice president for communications of the Institute for Justice in Washington, DC. For the better part of a decade, Mr. Kramer has directed the IJ's strategic media relations work in protecting homeowners and small businesses nationwide from eminent domain abuse as well as securing the right of entrepreneurs in the face of government challenge. His work has earned top honors from, among others, the Public Relations Society of America, *Bulldog Reporter,* and the International Association of Business Communicators. Mr. Kramer is a former journalism professor at the University of Nevada–Reno.

In setting strategy for the eminent domain campaign, how did your attorneys look upon the use of public relations?

As a *public interest* law firm, the attorneys at the Institute for Justice recognize that to win, we must litigate not only in court, but also in the court of public opinion. Public relations is central to the success of each of our cases. Our management and the attorneys know that when we couple cutting-edge litigation with strategic public relations, we can change the world. The public relations implications of each case and client are carefully considered from the very beginning.

How vocally "antigovernment" did you decide to be?

Recognizing how egregiously the government was acting—using its power to kick people out of their homes not for public use, such as for a courthouse or a post office, but for a Costco or Target or so richer people could build homes on that land—we decided to be

very vocal against the abuse of government power. When the government essentially rents out its power to the highest bidder, like a developer, it is the government that is most at fault. Your home should be your castle and it should be your choice whether or not to sell. Throughout our public relations campaigns fighting eminent domain abuse, we kept the focus on the government as the primary source of this problem while still criticizing companies that abuse eminent domain.

Was there difference of opinion within the organization, relative to how aggressive the media campaign should be?

Not at all. From the Institute for Justice's founding, we recognized the important role media relations plays in a public interest case. In a public interest case, our media work communicates that our litigation is not just about the specific clients we represent, but that it has a broader impact on people nationwide in similar situations.

What should the relationship be between an attorney and a public relations professional?

Mother Teresa said, "Facing the press is more difficult than bathing a leper." But, if done well, public relations offers significant opportunities that cannot be achieved through any other means. Attorneys and PR professionals should be each other's respected counselors.

How important are public relations tactics in managing a legal case?

At the Institute for Justice, legal considerations are paramount in each lawsuit, but public relations tactics are carefully considered from the inception of a case and the client selection through our announcement of our ultimate victory or loss. As each lawsuit unfolds, we work to find new PR tactics to mitigate challenges, maximize opportunities, and connect with the media and the public to help them better appreciate individual rights. This has run the gamut from renting out a movie theater and showing a free feature presentation to mounting marches on city hall. We are always looking for the next great idea!

What is the proper role of a public relations professional, as opposed to an attorney, in counseling management?

Organizations are increasingly recognizing that even the most routine decisions carry not only management and legal implications, but public relations implications as well. A trusted public relations practitioner should be part of the inner circle of an organization's leadership and be kept apprised of all areas of operation, whether it involves management, litigation, production, sales, or service. The earlier PR implications are considered and PR counsel is offered, the more likely it is that an organization can avoid a crisis and steer toward success. All of this underscores why the PR practitioner's office should be located close to the president's office.

Suggested Readings

Brinson, J. Dianne, and Mark F. Radcliffe. *Internet Law and Business Handbook*. Port Huron, MI: Ladera Press, 2004.

Fishman, Stephen. *The Copyright Handbook*. Berkeley, CA: Nolo, 2004. A comprehensive guide on what one needs to know to protect authored works.

Heins, Marjorie. *Not in Front of the Children: Indecency, Censorship and the Innocence of Youth*. New York: Hill & Wang, 2001. Exploration of all phases of censorship, from Internet filters to the V-chip.

Hiller, Janine. *Internet Law and Policy*. Upper Saddle River, NJ: Prentice-Hall, 2002.

Lessig, Lawrence. *Code and Other Laws of Cyberspace*. New York: Basic Books, 2000. Attorney Lessig issues a series of bold arguments for guiding the regulatory process concerning the Internet. He promotes a "constitution" for the Internet that accepts the inevitable regulatory authority of both government and commerce, while constraining them within values that we hold by consensus.

Moore, Roy L. *Mass Communications Law and Ethics*. Mahwah, NJ: Lawrence Erlbaum Associates, 1999.

Poindexter, J. Carl. *Cyberlaw and E-Commerce*. New York: Irwin, McGraw-Hill, 2001.

Sell, Susan K. *Private Power, Public Law: The Globalization of Intellectual Property Rights*. Cambridge, UK: Cambridge University Press, 2003. This book examines the role of private enterprise in shaping government policy.

Notes

1. Gerhart L. Klein, *Public Relations Law: The Basics* (Mt. Laurel, NJ: Anne Klein & Associates, 1990): 1–2.
2. "Libby Claims Cheney Authorized Disclosure of Classified Information," *CNN The Situation Room*, February 9, 2006.
3. James Kuhnhenn, "Sheehan Draws Apology for Ejection from Speech," *Buffalo News*, February 2, 2006, A5.
4. "Bush Administration Condemns Order to Release Detainee Names," *Associated Press*, August 5, 2002.
5. Dennis L. Wilcox and Glen T. Cameron, *Public Relations Strategies and Tactics*, 8th ed. (Boston: Allyn & Bacon, 2002.): 265.
6. Thomas K. Grose, "$50 Million Lawsuit Against WSJ and Burrough May Make Some Authors-to-Be Think Twice," *TFJR Report*, April 1992, 3.
7. Alicia Mundy, "Libel Suit Takes Aim at Print Reporter's Words on TV," *Washington Post*, December 14, 2004, A01.
8. Constance L. Hays, "Aide Was Reportedly Ordered to Warn Stewart on Stock Sales," *New York Times*, August 6, 2002, C1–2.
9. Wil Deener, "Lights, Camera, Madness: Cramer is CNBC's Best," *Dallas Morning News*, February 4, 2006.
10. Louis M. Thompson, Jr., "SEC Cites Investor Relations Officer for Insider Trading," National Investor Relations Institute release, July 2, 2002.
11. Managing Tidal Wave of Corporate Disclosure," *Business Wire Newsletter*, April 2002, 2.
12. Joseph Nocera, "For All Its Costs, Sarbanes-Oxley is Working," *New York Times*, December 3, 2005, C1.
13. Alix M. Freedman and Suein L. Hwang, "Brown & Williamson Faces Inquiry," *Wall Street Journal*, February 6, 1996, A1.
14. Kate Ackley, "McCain, Witnesses Weigh 'Indian Loophole' Fix," *Roll Call*, February 9, 2006.
15. Wilcox and Cameron, op. cit, *Public Relations Strategies and Tactics*, 271.
16. Harold W. Suckenik, "PR Pros Should Know the Four Rules of 'Fair Use,'" *O'Dwyer's PR Services Report*, September 1990, 2.
17. Linda Greenhouse, "What Level of Protection for Internet Speech?" *New York Times*, March 24, 1997, D5.
18. Steven Levy, "U.S. v. the Internet," *Newsweek*, March 31, 1997, 77.
19. Linda Greenhouse, "Decency Act Fails," *New York Times*, June 27, 1997, 1.
20. "Government Seeks Google Records in Pornography Investigation," *Associated Press*, January 19, 2006.
21. Michael Liedtke, "Google's New Chinese Search Engine to Censor Results," Associated Press, January 25, 2006.
22. Chuck Kapelke, "Cyberlaw 101," *Continental*, May 2001, 42.
23. Kristi Heim, "Inside China's Teeming World of Fake Goods," *Seattle Times*, February 12, 2006.
24. "In Pursuit of Cybersquatters," *CFO Magazine*, November 1999, 16.
25. Kevin Lee, "Click Fraud: What It Is, How to Fight It," *ClickZ Experts*, February 18, 2005.
26. Greg Hazley, "PR, Legal Need to Play on Same Team," *O'Dwyer's PR Services Report*, December 2005, 1.
27. James E. Lukaszewski, "Managing Litigation Visibility: How to Avoid Lousy Trial Publicity," *Public Relations Quarterly*, Spring 1995, 18–24.

8 Research

FIGURE 8-1 Two faces of research. Protestors hold signs of disgraced South Korean Professor Hwang Woo-suk who stunned the scientific community in 2006 when he acknowledged that his groundbreaking stem cell research was false. (AP Wide World Photos)

Research is the natural starting point for any public relations assignment—from promoting a product to designing a program to confronting a crisis. The first step in solving any public relations challenge is to conduct research.

At the same time, it should be recognized that research, particularly in an art form as intuitive as public relations, is no panacea. Research is but a foundation upon which a sensible programmatic initiative must be based. Research must always be complemented by analysis and judgment.

In extreme cases, research can be flawed. The old expression that "figures lie and liars figure" occasionally is unfortunately the case. As in the situation with this man:

South Korean scientist Hwang Woo-suk stunned the world in 2004 by announcing the creation of the first cloned human embryo. Two years later, Hwang acknowledged that his research, for which he received millions of dollars, was a fraud and that he had falsified the data.[1]

Such is the danger of blindly trusting research data.

Nonetheless, as noted, in public relations it is obligatory to begin with research.

Why?

Frankly, the answer stems from the fact that few managers understand what public relations is and how it works. Managers—particularly those guided by quantitative, empirical measurement—want "proof" that what we advise is based on logic and clear thinking.

In other words, most clients are less interested in what their public relations advisers *think* than in what they *know*. The only real way to know your advice is on the right track is by ensuring that it is grounded in hard data whenever possible. In other words, before recommending a course of action, public relations professionals must analyze audiences, assess alternatives, and generally do their homework.

In other words, do research.

Essential First Step

Every public relations program or solution should begin with research. Most don't, which is a shame.

The various approaches to public relations problem solving, discussed in Chapter 1, all start with research.

Instinct, intuition, and gut feelings all remain important in the conduct of public relations work, but management today demands more—measurement, analysis, and evaluation at every stage of the public relations process. In an era of scarce resources, management wants facts and statistics from public relations professionals to show that their efforts contribute not only to overall organizational effectiveness but also to the bottom line. Why should we introduce a new intranet publication? What should the publication say, and how much should it cost? How will we know it's working? Questions such as these must be answered through research.

In a day when organizational resources are precious and companies don't want to spend money unless it enhances results, public relations programs must contribute to meeting business objectives.[2] That means that research must be applied to help segment market targets, analyze audience preferences and dislikes, and determine which messages might be most effective with various audiences. Research then becomes essential in helping realize management's goals.

Research should be applied in public relations work both at the initial stage, prior to planning a campaign, and at the final stage to evaluate a program's effectiveness. Early research helps to determine the current situation, prevalent attitudes, and difficulties that the program faces. Later research examines the program's success, along with what else still needs to be done. Research at both points in the process is critical.

What Is Research?

Research is the systematic collection and interpretation of information to increase understanding (Figure 8-2). Most people associate public relations with conveying information; although that association is accurate, research must be the obligatory first step in any project. A firm must acquire enough accurate, relevant data about its publics, products, and programs to answer these questions:

- How can we identify and define our constituent groups?
- How does this knowledge relate to the design of our messages?
- How does it relate to the design of our programs?

FIGURE 8-2 Early research. An early research effort, albeit a futile one, was the return of the biblical scouts sent by Moses to reconnoiter the land of Canaan. They disagreed in their reports, and the Israelites believed the gloomier versions. This failure to interpret the data correctly caused them to wander another 40 years in the wilderness. (An even earlier research effort was Noah's sending the dove to search for dry ground.) (Courtesy of Trout & Partners)

- How does it relate to the media we use to convey our messages?
- How does it relate to the schedule we adopt in using our media?
- How does it relate to the ultimate implementation tactics of our program?

It is difficult to delve into the minds of others, whose backgrounds and points of view may be quite different from our own, with the purpose of understanding why they think as they do. Research skills are partly intuitive, partly an outgrowth of individual temperament and partly a function of acquired knowledge. There is nothing mystifying about them. Although we tend to think of research in terms of impersonal test scores, interviews, or questionnaires, these methods are only a small part of the process. The real challenge lies in using research—knowing when to do what, with whom, and for what purpose.

Principles of Public Relations Research

For years, public relations professionals have debated the standards of measuring public relations' effectiveness. In 1997, the Institute for Public Relations Research and Education offered seven guiding principles in setting standards for public relations research.

- Establishing clear program objectives and desired outcomes tied directly to business goals.
- Differentiating between measuring public relations "outputs," generally short-term and surface (e.g., amount of press coverage received or exposure of a par-

ticular message), and measuring public relations "outcomes," usually more far-reaching and carrying greater impact (e.g., changing awareness, attitudes, and even behavior).

- Measuring media content as a first step in the public relations evaluation process. Such a measure is limited in that it can't discern whether a target audience actually saw a message or responded to it.

- Understanding that no one technique can be expected to evaluate public relations effectiveness. Rather, this requires a combination of techniques, from media analysis to cyberspace analysis, from focus groups to polls and surveys.

- Being wary of attempts to compare public relations effectiveness with advertising effectiveness. One particularly important consideration is that while advertising placement and messages can be controlled, their equivalent on the public relations side cannot be.

- The most trustworthy measurement of public relations effectiveness is that which stems from an organization with clearly identified key messages, target audiences, and desired channels of communication. The converse of this is that the more confused an organization is about its targets, the less reliable its public relations measurement will be.

Public relations evaluation cannot be accomplished in isolation. It must be linked to overall business goals, strategies, and tactics.[3]

Types of Public Relations Research

In general, research is conducted to do three things: (1) describe a process, situation, or phenomenon; (2) explain why something is happening, what its causes are, and what effect it will have; and (3) predict what probably will happen if we do or don't take action. Primary, or original, research in public relations is either theoretical or applied. Applied research solves practical problems; theoretical research aids understanding of a public relations process.

Most public relations analysis, however, takes the more informal form called secondary research. This relies on existing material—books, articles, Internet databases, and the like—to form the research backing for public relations recommendations and programs.

Applied Research

In public relations work, applied research can be either strategic or evaluative. Both applications are designed to answer specific practical questions.

- Strategic research is used primarily in program development to determine program objectives, develop message strategies, or establish benchmarks. It often examines the tools and techniques of public relations. For example, a firm that wants to know how employees rate its candor in internal publications would first conduct strategic research to find out where it stands.

- Evaluative research, sometimes called summative research, is conducted primarily to determine whether a public relations program has accomplished its goals and objectives. For example, if changes are made in the internal communications program to increase candor, evaluative research can determine whether the goals have been met. A variant of evaluation can be applied during a program to monitor progress and indicate where modifications might make sense.

Theoretical Research

Theoretical research is more abstract and conceptual than applied research. It helps build theories in public relations work about why people communicate, how public opinion is formed, and how a public is created.

Knowledge of theoretical research is important as a framework for persuasion and as a base for understanding why people do what they do.

Some knowledge of theoretical research in public relations and mass communications is essential for enabling practitioners to understand the limitations of communication as a persuasive tool. Attitude and behavior change has been the traditional goal in public relations programs, yet theoretical research indicates that such a goal may be difficult or impossible to achieve through persuasive efforts. According to such research, other factors are always getting in the way.

Researchers have found that communication is most persuasive when it comes from multiple sources of high credibility. Credibility itself is a multidimensional concept that includes trustworthiness, expertise, and power. Others have found that a message generally is more effective when it is simple, because it is easier to understand, localize, and make personally relevant. According to still other research, the persuasiveness of a message can be increased when it arouses or is accompanied by a high level of personal involvement in the issue at hand.

The point here is that knowledge of theoretical research can help practitioners not only understand the basis of applied research findings but also temper management's expectations of attitude and behavioral change resulting from public relations programs.

Secondary Research

Secondary research is research on the cheap. Basically, secondary research allows you to examine or read about and learn from someone else's primary research, such as in a library.

Also called "desk research," secondary research uses data that have been collected for other purposes than your own. Among the typical sources of secondary research are the following:

- Industry trade journals
- Government
- Informal contacts
- Published company accounts
- Business libraries
- Professional institutes and organizations
- Omnibus surveys
- Census data
- Public records
- Online databases

The latter are particularly important for public relations researchers. Such online resources as Claritas, which supplies marketing analysis and demographic tools; surveymonkey.com, which provides the resources to create tailored online surveys; and the omnipresent Google search engine, are popular outlets to aid public relations researchers.

Because public relations budgets are limited, it always makes sense first to consider secondary sources in launching a research effort.

Methods of Public Relations Research

Observation is the foundation of modern social science. Scientists, social psychologists, and anthropologists make observations, develop theories, and, hopefully, increase understanding of human behavior. Public relations research, too, is founded on observation. Indeed, examining human behavior was pivotal to the early public relations work of Edward Bernays. Three primary forms of public relations research dominate the field.

- *Surveys* are designed to reveal attitudes and opinions—what people think about certain subjects.
- *Communications audits* often reveal disparities between real and perceived communications between management and target audiences. Management may make certain assumptions about its methods, media, materials, and messages, whereas its targets may confirm or refute those assumptions.
- *Unobtrusive measures*—such as fact-finding, content analysis, and readability studies—enable the study of a subject or object without involving the researcher or the research as an intruder.

Each method of public relations research offers specific benefits and should be understood and used by the modern practitioner.

Surveys

Survey research is one of the most frequently used research methods in public relations. Surveys can be applied to broad societal issues, such as determining public opinion about a political candidate, or to more focused issues, such as satisfaction of hospital patients or hotel guests or reporting relationships of public relations people (Figure 8-3).

Surveys come in two types.

1. *Descriptive surveys* offer a snapshot of a current situation or condition. They are the research equivalent of a balance sheet, capturing reality at a specific point in time. A typical public opinion poll is a prime example.

2. *Explanatory surveys* are concerned with cause and effect. Their purpose is to help explain why a current situation or condition exists and to offer explanations for opinions and attitudes. Frequently, such explanatory or analytical surveys are designed to answer the question, why?: Why are our philanthropic dollars not being appreciated in the community? Why don't employees believe management's messages? Why is our credibility being questioned?

Surveys generally consist of four elements: (1) sample, (2) questionnaire, (3) interview, and (4) analysis of results. (Direct-mail surveys, of course, eliminate the interview

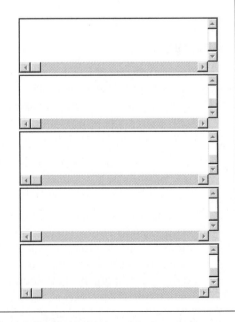

PR News/IABC Joint Survey: Getting a Taste of the C-Suite

Please take a few minutes to fill out the following survey by April 25th. Coverage of the study's results will appear in the May 4th issue of PR News as well as the May 2005 edition of IABC's CW Bulletin. We're hopeful that the results will enable senior PR pros to devise strategies that will help them reach the corporate summit—and stay there.

1. I report directly to the CEO — [Please Choose ▼]

2. I am a member of the top management team — [Please Choose ▼]

3. I regularly attend meetings of the top management team (whether or not I am a member): — [Please Choose ▼]

4. How many employees are there in your corporate affairs/PR department? — [Please Choose ▼]

5. What country are you in? — [Please Select ▼]

	Strongly Agree	Agree	Neither Agree nor Diagree	Disagree	Strongly Disagree
6. My CEO:					
a . . . understands the importance of communication, not just when there is an issue or crisis	○	○	○	○	○
b. . . . sees PR as an investment in the future not just a cost	○	○	○	○	○
c. . . . asks my opinion about PR implications of future directions of the business	○	○	○	○	○
d. . . . usually accepts my recommendations	○	○	○	○	○
e. . . . would say I understand the business	○	○	○	○	○
7. My CEO values corporate affairs / PR advice at least as much as that from:					
a. . . . Advertising	○	○	○	○	○
b. . . . Sales	○	○	○	○	○
c. . . . Marketing	○	○	○	○	○
d. . . . Legal	○	○	○	○	○
e. . . . Human Resources	○	○	○	○	○
8. My CEO makes an effort (e.g. willingly puts in time) to maintain good relations with the following stakeholders:					
a. . . . employees	○	○	○	○	○
b. . . . stockholders	○	○	○	○	○
c. . . . analysts	○	○	○	○	○
d. . . . customers/clients	○	○	○	○	○
e. . . . business or alliance partners	○	○	○	○	○
f. . . . media	○	○	○	○	○

9.
a. What do you mostly discuss at your meetings with the CEO? (e.g. high-level strategy, business reputation, communication tactics, your career path, media relations, CEO presentations, analyst relationships, publications?)

b. Has the CEO redefined your role or mandate at any stage (e.g. upgraded it, expanded it, downgraded it, etc.)? Please explain what and why.

10.
a. To what extent does your CEO expect PR results to be measured? Does he/she take PR less seriously because measurement is not easy to do? To what extent is your CEO skeptical of anything without numbers attached?

b. What demands does the CEO have of the PR function that are not currently being met?

c. What three things would you like to see improved in regard to the CEO and PR/coms function or your relationship with him/her?

FIGURE 8-3 Reaching the Corporate Summit survey. This survey, co-sponsored by *PR News* and the International Association of Business Communicators, polled reporting relationships among public relations professionals. (Reprinted with permission from the International Association of Business Communicators)

step.) Because survey research is so critical in public relations, we examine each survey element in some detail.

The Sample

The sample, or selected target group, must be representative of the total public whose views are sought. Once a survey population has been determined, a researcher must select the appropriate sample or group of respondents from which to collect information. Sampling is tricky. A researcher must be aware of the hidden pitfalls in choosing a representative sample, not the least of which is the perishable nature of most data. Survey findings are rapidly outdated because of population mobility and changes in the political and socioeconomic environment. Consequently, sampling should be completed quickly.

Two cross-sectional approaches are used in obtaining a sample: random sampling and nonrandom sampling. The former is more scientific, the latter more informal.

Random Sampling

In random sampling, two properties are essential—equality and independence. *Equality* means that no element has any greater or lesser chance of being selected. *Independence* means that selecting any one element in no way influences the selection of any other element. Random sampling is based on a mathematical criterion that allows generalizations from the sample to be made to the total population. There are four types of random or probability samples.

1. **Simple random sampling** gives all members of the population an equal chance of being selected. First, all members of the population are identified, and then as many subjects as are needed are randomly selected—usually with the help of a computer. Election polling uses a random approach; although millions of Americans vote, only a few thousand are ever polled on their election preferences. The Nielsen national television sample, for example, consists of 5,000 homes. The Census Bureau uses a sample of about one out of six households to obtain estimates of employment and other population characteristics among the 116 million households in the U.S.[4]

   How large should a random sample be? The answer depends on a number of factors, one of which is the size of the population. In addition, the more similar the population elements are in regard to the characteristics being studied, the smaller the sample required. In most random samples, the following population-to-sample ratios apply, with a 5 percent margin of error:

Population	Sample
1,000	278
2,000	322
3,000	341
5,000	355
10,000	370
50,000	381
100,000	383
500,000	383
Infinity	384

Random sampling owes its accuracy to the laws of probability, which are best explained by the example of a barrel filled with 10,000 marbles—5,000 green ones and 5,000 red ones. If a blindfolded person selects a certain number of marbles from the barrel—say, 400—the laws of probability suggest that the most frequently drawn combination will be 200 red and 200 green. These laws further suggest that with certain margins of error, a very few marbles can represent the whole barrel, which can correspond to any size—for example, that of a city, state, or nation.

2. **Systematic random sampling** is closely related to simple random sampling, but it uses a random starting point in the sample list. From then on, the researcher selects every nth person in the list. As long as every person has an equal and independent chance to be selected on the first draw, then the sample qualifies as random and is equally reliable to simple random sampling. Random telephone dialing, for example, which solves the problem of failing to consider unlisted numbers, may use this technique.

3. **Stratified random sampling** is a procedure used to survey different segments or strata of the population. For example, if an organization wants to determine the relationship between years of service and attitudes toward the company, it may stratify the sample to ensure that the breakdown of respondents accurately reflects the makeup of the population. In other words, if more than half of the employees have been with the company more than 10 years, more than half of those polled should also reflect that level of service. By stratifying the sample, the organization's objective can be achieved.

4. **Cluster sampling** involves first breaking the population down into small heterogeneous subsets, or clusters, and then selecting the potential sample from the individual clusters or groups. A cluster may often be defined as a geographic area, such as an election district.

Nonrandom Sampling

Nonrandom samples come in three types: convenience, quota, and volunteer.

1. **Convenience samples,** also known as accidental, chunk, or opportunity samples, are relatively unstructured, rather unsystematic, and designed to elicit ideas and points of view. Journalists use convenience samples when they conduct person-on-the-street interviews. The most common type of convenience sample in public relations research is the focus group. Focus groups generally consist of several people, with a moderator encouraging in-depth discussion of a specific topic. Focus groups generate concepts and ideas rather than validate hypotheses.

2. **Quota samples** permit a researcher to choose subjects on the basis of certain characteristics. For example, the attitudes of a certain number of women, men, blacks, whites, rich, or poor may be needed. Quotas are imposed in proportion to each group's percentage of the population. The advantage of quota sampling is that it increases the homogeneity of a sample population, thus enhancing the validity of a study. However, it is hard to classify interviewees by one or two discrete demographic characteristics. For example, a particular interviewee may be black, Catholic, female, under 25, and a member of a labor union all at the

same time, making the lines of demographic demarcation pretty blurry. (A derivative of quota sampling is called purposive sampling.)

3. **Volunteer samples** use willing participants who agree voluntarily to respond to concepts and hypotheses for research purposes.

The Questionnaire

Before creating a questionnaire, a researcher must consider his or her objective in doing the study. What you seek to find out should influence the specific publics you ask, the questions you raise, and the research method you choose. After determining what you're after, consider the particular questionnaire design. Specifically, researchers should observe the following in designing their questionnaire:

1. **Keep it short.** Make a concerted attempt to limit questions. It's terrific if the questionnaire can be answered in five minutes.

2. **Use structured rather than open-ended questions.** People would rather check a box or circle a number than write an essay. But leave room at the bottom for general comments or "Other." Also, start with simple, nonthreatening questions before getting to the more difficult, sensitive ones. This approach will build respondent trust as well as commitment to finishing the questionnaire.

3. **Measure intensity of feelings.** Let respondents check "very satisfied," "satisfied," "dissatisfied," or "very dissatisfied" rather than "yes" or "no." One popular approach is the semantic differential technique shown in Figure 8-4.

4. **Don't use fancy words or words that have more than one meaning.** If you must use big words, make the context clear.

5. **Don't ask loaded questions.** "Is management doing all it can to communicate with you?" is a terrible question. The answer is always no.

6. **Don't ask double-barreled questions.** "Would you like management meetings once a month, or are bimonthly meetings enough?" is another terrible question.

7. **Pretest.** Send your questionnaire to a few colleagues and listen to their suggestions.

8. **Attach a letter explaining how important the respondents' answers are, and let recipients know that they will remain anonymous.** Respondents will feel better if they think the study is significant and their identities are protected. Also, specify how and where the data will be used.

9. **Hand-stamp the envelopes, preferably with unique commemorative stamps.** Metering an envelope indicates assembly-line research, and researchers have found that the more expensive the postage, the higher the response rate. People like to feel special.

10. **Follow up your first mailing.** Send a reminder postcard three days after the original questionnaire. Then wait a few weeks and send a second questionnaire, just in case recipients have lost the first.

11. **Send out more questionnaires than you think necessary.** The major weakness of most mail surveys is the unmeasurable error introduced by

nonresponders. You're shooting for a 50 percent response rate; anything less tends to be suspect.

12. **Enclose a reward.** There's nothing like a token gift of merchandise or, better yet, money to make a recipient feel guilty for not returning a questionnaire.

FIGURE 8-4 Measuring intensity, rewarding the respondent. One common device to measure intensity of feelings is the semantic differential technique, which gives respondents a scale of choices from the worst to the best. Respondents will comply more gladly if a "crisp new bill" is included. (Courtesy of Norwood Research Group)

Northeast Research Group

103 Godwin Avenue, Suite 225, Midland Park, New Jersey 07432

Hello...

We'd like to know how you feel about the hospitals in Pittsburgh, and we'd appreciate your completing the questionnaire on the inside of this booklet.

The two-part survey is quick and easy, and should take no more than two minutes of your time.

In Part One, there is a series of attributes listed. Just circle the number that best reflects your feeling on how important a particular attribute is when choosing a hospital.

In Part Two, circle the number that best reflects your opinion of how well a particular hospital performs in that area. For example:

| __Hospital XYZ__ | Poor | | | | | | | | | Excellent |
| Advanced surgical care............... | 1 | 2 | 3 | 4 | 5 | (6) | 7 | 8 | 9 | 10 |

If you're not familiar with one of the hospitals, or have no opinion on a particular attribute, just leave it blank.

Please return the questionnaire in the enclosed envelope. It's already stamped and addressed.

And thank you for participating. Your response will be an important part of our research.

Sincerely,

Sally Williams

Sally Williams
Vice President

P.S. Please accept the enclosed token of our thanks.

Marketing and Advertising Research • Awareness and Usage Studies • Concept Testing • Survey Data Analysis

Interviews

Interviews can provide a more personal, firsthand feel for public opinion. Interview panels can range from focus groups of randomly selected average people to Delphi panels of so-called opinion leaders. Interviews can be conducted in a number of ways, including face-to-face, telephone, mail, and through the Internet.

Focus Groups

This approach is used with increasing frequency in public relations today. A traditional focus group consists of a 90- to 120-minute discussion among eight to ten individuals who have been selected based upon having predetermined common characteristics, such as buying behavior, age, income, family composition, and so on.[5]

With the focus group technique, a well-drilled moderator leads a group through a discussion of opinions on a particular product, organization, or idea. Participants represent the socioeconomic level desired by the research sponsor—from college students to office workers to millionaires. Almost always, focus group participants are paid for their efforts. Sessions are frequently videotaped and then analyzed, often in preparation for more formal and specific research questionnaires.

Focus groups should be organized with the following guidelines in mind:

1. **Define your objectives and audience.** The more tightly you define your goals and your target audience, the more likely you are to gather relevant information. In other words, don't conduct a focus group with friends and family members, hoping to get a quick and inexpensive read. Nothing of value will result.

2. **Recruit your groups.** Recruiting participants takes several weeks, depending on the difficulty of contacting the target audience. Contact is usually made by phone with a series of questions to weed out employees of competitors, members of the news media (to keep the focus group from becoming a news story), and those who don't fit target group specifications.

3. **Choose the right moderator.** Staff people who may be excellent conversationalists are not necessarily the best focus group moderators. The gift of gab is not enough. Professional moderators know how to establish rapport quickly, how and when to probe beyond the obvious, how to draw comments from reluctant participants, how to keep a group on task, and how to interpret results validly.

4. **Conduct enough focus groups.** One or two focus groups usually are not enough. Four to six are better to uncover the full range of relevant ideas and opinions. Regardless of the number of groups, however, you must resist the temptation to add up responses. That practice gives the focus group more analytical worth than it deserves.

5. **Use a discussion guide.** This is a basic outline of what you want to investigate. It will lead the moderator through the discussion and keep the group on track.

6. **Choose proper facilities.** The discussion room should be comfortable, with participants sitting around a table that gives them a good view of each other. Observers can use closed-circuit TV and one-way mirrors, but participants should always be told when they are being observed.

7. **Keep a tight rein on observers.** Observers should rarely be in the same room with participants; the two groups ordinarily should be separated. Observers should view the proceedings seriously; this is not "dinner and a show."

8. **Consider using outside help.** Setting up focus groups can be time consuming and complicated. Often the best advice is to hire a professional firm to conduct the research.

Telephone Interviews

In contrast to personal interviews, telephone interviews suffer from a high refusal rate. Many people just don't want to be bothered. Such interviews may also introduce an upper-income bias because lower-income earners may lack telephones. However, the increasing use of unlisted numbers by upper-income people may serve to mitigate this bias. Telephone interviews must be carefully scripted so that interviewers know precisely what to ask, regardless of a respondent's answer. Calls should be made at less busy times of the day, such as early morning or late afternoon.

With both telephone and face-to-face interviews, it is important to establish rapport with the interview subject. It makes good sense to begin the interview with nonthreatening questions, saving the tougher, more controversial ones—on income level or race, for example—until last.

Mail Interviews

This is the least expensive approach, but it often suffers from a low response rate. Frequently, people who return mail questionnaires are those with strong biases either in favor of or (more commonly) in opposition to the subject at hand. As noted, one way to generate a higher response from mail interviews is through the use of self-addressed, stamped envelopes or enclosed incentives such as dollar bills or free gifts.

Drop-off Interviews

This approach combines face-to-face and mail interview techniques. An interviewer personally drops off a questionnaire at a household, usually after conducting a face-to-face interview. Because the interviewer has already established some rapport with the interviewee, the rate of return with this technique is considerably higher than it is for straight mail interviews.

Intercept Interviews

This approach is popular in consumer surveys, where researchers "intercept" respondents on the street, in shopping malls, or in retail outlets. Trained interviewers typically deliver a short (5- to 20-minute) questionnaire concerning attitudes, perceptions, preferences, and behavior.

Delphi Panels

The Delphi technique is a qualitative research tool that uses opinion leaders—local influential persons as well as national experts—often to help tailor the design of a general public research survey. Designed by the Rand Corporation in the 1950s, the Delphi technique is a consensus-building approach that relies on repeated waves of questionnaires sent to the same select panel of experts. Delphi findings generate a wide range of responses and help set the agenda for more meaningful future research. Stated another way, Delphi panels offer a "research reality check."

Internet Interviews

The latest technique of interviewing constituent publics is via the Internet. Web-based surveying is becoming more widely used. In its ubiquitous availability, the Web offers significant advantages over more traditional survey techniques. However, Internet interviews also introduce problems, among them that significant numbers of people do not have access or choose not to use the Internet. Several studies have found Internet surveys have significantly lower response rates than comparable mailed surveys. Several factors have been found to increase response rates, including personalized e-mail cover letters, follow-up reminders, prenotification of the intent to survey, and simpler formats. While there is a need for caution, the use of Web-based surveying is clearly growing.[6]

Results Analysis

After selecting the sample, drawing up the questionnaire, and interviewing the respondents, the researcher must analyze the findings. Often a great deal of analysis is required to produce meaningful recommendations.

The objective of every sample is to come up with results that are valid and reliable. A margin of error explains how far off the prediction may be. A sample may be large enough to represent fairly the larger universe; yet, depending on the margin of sampling error, the results of the research may not be statistically significant. That is, the differences or distinctions detected by the survey may not be sizable enough to offset the margin of error. Thus, the margin of error must always be determined.

Popular political polls, in particular, are fraught with problems. They cannot predict outcomes scientifically. Rather, they provide a snapshot, freezing attitudes at a certain point in time—like a balance sheet for a corporation. Obviously, people's attitudes change with the passage of time, and pollsters, despite what they claim, can't categorically predict the outcome of an election. Perhaps the most notorious example of this was the political poll sponsored by the *Literary Digest* in 1936, which used a telephone polling technique to predict that Alf Landon would be the nation's next president. Landon thereupon suffered one of the worst drubbings in American electoral history at the hands of Franklin Roosevelt. It was probably of little solace to the *Literary Digest* that most of its telephone respondents, many of whom were Republicans wealthy enough to afford phones, did vote for Landon.

The point is that in analyzing results, problems of validity, reliability, and levels of statistical significance associated with margins of error must be considered before concrete recommendations are volunteered.

Talking Points

Figures and Faces—Lie

If you don't believe the old maxim that "figures lie and liars figure," consider the following: In often repeated research, randomly selected participants are shown the following two faces and asked, "Which woman is lovelier?" Invariably, the answer is split 50–50.

However, when each woman is named, one "Jennifer" and the other "Gertrude," respondents overwhelmingly—more than 80 percent—vote for Jennifer as the more beautiful woman (Figure 8-5).

Why? "Jennifer" is more hip, more happening, more, uh, "phat." (Sorry, all you Gertrudes out there!)

The point is that people can't help but introduce their own biases, including even in presumably "objective" research experiments. This factor always should be taken into account in evaluating public relations research.

FIGURE 8-5 Jennifer/Gertrude. (Fraser P. Seitel)

Communications Audits

Communications audits are an increasingly important method of research in public relations work. Such audits are used frequently by corporations, schools, hospitals, and other organizations to determine whether a communications group and the products it produces are realizing objectives and also how the institution is perceived by its core constituents. Communications audits help public relations professionals understand more clearly the relationships between management actions and objectives, on the one hand, and communications methods to promote those objectives, on the other.

Communications audits are typically used to analyze the standing of a company with its employees or community neighbors; to assess the readership of routine communication vehicles, such as annual reports and news releases; or to examine an organization's performance as a corporate citizen. Communications audits often provide benchmarks against which future public relations programs can be applied and measured. The data uncovered are frequently used by management to make informed decisions about future communications needs and goals

Audit Scope

The scope of an audit may be as broad or as narrow as the size and complexity of the organization's demands. The audit can measure the effectiveness of communications programs across the organization or the programs of a single division. It can also hone in on a specific subject—readability of written materials, understanding of an issue, or use of an internal intranet, for example. An audit can also uncover misunderstandings and information barriers and bottlenecks, as well as opportunities.

Audit Subjects

Typically, communications audits are used to provide information on issues such as the following:

- Objectives and goals—short and long term
- Existing communications programs—methods and media
- Existing communications vehicles—publications, manuals, bulletin boards, closed-circuit TV, videotape, slides, teleconferencing, memos, meetings, Internet, reports, correspondence, and so on
- Uneven communications workloads
- Employees working at cross-purposes
- Hidden information within an organization that, to the detriment of the institution, is not being used
- Bottlenecked information flows
- Conflicting notions about what the organization is and does

Audit Methodology

A communications audit is a straightforward analysis.

1. It begins with a researcher studying all pertinent literature about the organization.
2. Competitive literature is then reviewed for purposes of comparison and contrast.
3. Interviews with top management and the rank and file are then conducted to detect areas of commonality and discontinuity. In other words, what do people

agree on and where do they disagree? Interviews with key outsiders, such as the board and customers, also may be included.

4. Recommendations are then presented from the audit knowledge gleaned.

A communications audit, of course, is not an end in itself. Rather it must be part of a process of measurement and performance improvement.[7] In that context, an extensive

Speaking of Ethics

Assessing an "Unbiased" Testing Agency

In April 2000, a federal jury cleared the publisher of *Consumer Reports* magazine of liability for reporting that Isuzu Troopers were dangerous. But the damage to the research agency's testing procedures and objectivity was done.

For six decades, there was no more trusted research source of information about products and their strengths and weaknesses than *Consumer Reports*. The independent, self-proclaimed bastion of "independent testing and research" was looked upon as one of the most unbiased sources of pertinent product information in the United States. By the end of the century, however, questions emerged as to just how unbiased the vaunted research agency was.

What triggered the questions was a *Consumer Reports* attack on Isuzu Motors Limited, maker of the successful Trooper, a popular sport utility vehicle.

The drama started one August morning in 1996 when executives of Isuzu Motors in California were notified by *Consumer Reports* that "an Isuzu product would be discussed at a news conference in 30 minutes." Isuzu executives had no clue as to which product would be discussed or what would be said about it. However, their suspicion was that whatever was said, it wouldn't be very good.

Boy, were they right.

At the news conference, *Consumer Reports* played a videotape that showed an out-of-control Isuzu Trooper, unable to negotiate a turn with its right wheels more than two feet off the ground, headed for immediate disaster. The conference concluded with a warning from *Consumer Reports'* technical director that, "Consumers shouldn't buy the Isuzu Trooper, and owners of the vehicle should drive it only when necessary."

Five minutes after the news conference, Isuzu received its first call from the media. By day's end, it had received more than 100 press calls, and that night, the incriminating report was prominently featured on CBS and CNN; the next day, it was in all of the nation's most prestigious newspapers. It mattered little that the company adamantly claimed that the Trooper had never experienced any problems. The damage was done.

In the 12 months following the news conference, sales of the Isuzu Trooper declined from 23,000 to 13,000—the dramatic, but not wholly unexpected, impact from a negative piece in a magazine rated as "the most believable and objective source of information about products and services."

Deeply stung, Isuzu fired back. It sued the magazine and questioned its testing methods, claiming that *Consumer Reports* is beholden to its funders, including foundations with specific anti-business agendas. Specifically, Isuzu charged that *Consumer Reports* and its parent company, Consumers Union, nurtured a long-standing bias against SUVs.

The company alleged that *Consumer Reports'* charges were trumped up as ammunition in its parent company's battle with the federal government over regulation of SUVs. Indeed, prior to the Isuzu offensive, the magazine had run three stories in 18 months asking, *How safe are SUVs?* Consumers Union even petitioned the National Highway Traffic Safety Administration to tighten standards for SUVs.

In its suit, Isuzu alleged that the Consumers Union test driver purposely tipped the vehicle and also that the driver chose to negotiate around an object in his path rather than hitting the brakes. In other words, Isuzu claimed that *Consumer Reports* rigged the test to increase sales of its magazine.

Consumer Reports denied all charges, and the case went to court in February 2000. Although the jury ruled that nearly half of the statement Isuzu questioned in its suit was in fact false, it decided against awarding monetary damages to Isuzu. Reportedly, eight of ten jurors wanted to award the company as much as $25 million, but the entire jury couldn't be persuaded.

Nonetheless, it was curious that the *Consumer Reports* gave Isuzu only a brief warning before its press conference. In addition, Isuzu claimed it could learn nothing about how the test was conducted until after the damage had been done. If nothing else, such issues tended to cloud the reputation of the consumer research testing service as "unbiased."

For further information, see Jennifer Greenstein, "Testing Consumer Reports," *Brill's Content* (September 1999):70–77; Rhonda H. Kapartkin, "When Attacked CU Will Probably Shut Up," *Consumer Reports* (December 1999); and "Jury Clears *Consumer Reports Magazine* of Liability in Isuzu Case," *Court TV Online* (April 7, 2000).

audit should be conducted every five years or so, with "quick and dirty" studies serving in the interim to keep an organization's communications fresh and relevant.

Unobtrusive Methods

Of the various unobtrusive methods of data collection available to public relations researchers, probably the most widely used is simple fact-finding. Facts are the bricks and mortar of public relations work; no action can be taken unless the facts are known, and the fact-finding process is continuous.

Each organization must keep a fact file of the most essential data with which it is involved. For example, such items as key organization statistics, publications, management biographies and photos, press clippings, media lists, competitive literature, pending legislation, organizational charters, and bylaws should be kept on file and updated.

Another unobtrusive method is content analysis, the primary purpose of which is to describe a message or set of messages. For example, an organization with news releases that are used frequently by local newspapers can't be certain, without research, whether the image conveyed by its releases is what the organization seeks. By analyzing the news coverage, the firm can get a much clearer idea of the effectiveness of its communications. Such content analysis might be organized according to the following specific criteria:

- **Frequency of coverage.** How many releases were used?
- **Placement within the paper.** Did releases appear more frequently on page 1 or page 71?
- **People reached.** What was the circulation of the publications in which the releases appeared?
- **Messages conveyed.** Did the releases used express the goals of the organization, or were they simply informational in content?
- **Editing of releases.** How much did the newspaper edit the submitted copy? Were desired meanings materially changed?
- **Attitude conveyed.** Was the reference to the organization positive, negative, or neutral?

Copy testing, in which public targets are exposed to public relations campaign messages to be used in brochures, memos, online, and so on, in advance of their publication, is another viable method that ensures campaign messages are understandable and effective.

Finally, case study research that analyzes how other organizations handled similar challenges is a constructive, unobtrusive research method.

Clearly, there is nothing particularly mysterious or difficult about unobtrusive methods of research. Such methods are relatively simple to apply, yet they are essential for arriving at appropriate refinements for an ongoing public relations program.

Evaluation

No matter what type of public relations research is used, results of the research and the research project itself should always be analyzed for meaning and action. Evaluation is designed to determine what happened and why by measuring results against established objectives.

The key word in organizations today is *accountability*, which means taking responsibility for achieving the performance promised. With resources limited and competition fierce, managers at every level demand accountability for every activity on which they spend money. That's what evaluation is all about. Public relations professionals are obligated today to assess what they've done to determine whether the expense was worth it.

Evaluation of public relations programs depends on several things:

- **Setting measurable public relations program objectives.** Goals should specify who the target publics are, what impact the program seeks to have on those publics, and when the results are expected.

- **Securing management commitment.** Public relations people and management should always agree in advance on the program's objectives so that the results can be clearly evaluated. Without management buy-in that the program is objective and well targeted, management may not believe the results.

- **Determining the best way to gather data.** Again, raw program records and observation are a rudimentary but acceptable method of evaluative measurement. Better would be attitude pretesting and posttesting to determine if a particular program helped facilitate a shift in attitudes toward a program, company, or issue. Surveys may or may not be called for.

- **Reporting back to management.** Evaluation findings should be shared with management. This reinforces the notion that public relations is contributing to management goals for the organization.

- **Selecting the most appropriate outcomes.** Although public relations outputs are important, public relations *outcomes* are more important. Outcome evaluation may be a measurement of the press clippings a program received—that is, the number of column inches or airtime devoted to the program. A more sophisticated evaluation of program effectiveness is a content analysis of the messages conveyed as a result of the program.

  Outcome evaluation measures whether targets actually *received* the messages directed to them, *paid attention* to them, *understood* the messages, *retained* those messages, and even *acted* on them.[8]

In many respects, a measurement of public relations outcomes is the most important barometer in assessing success or failure of a program.

Measuring Public Relations Outcomes

What kinds of tools are used to measure public relations outcomes? Here are four of the most common.

Awareness and Comprehension Measurement

This measurement probes whether targets received the messages directed at them, paid attention to them, and understood them. Measuring awareness and comprehension levels requires "benchmarking," or determining preliminary knowledge about a target's understanding so that the furthering of that knowledge can be tracked. Stated another way, both "before" and "after" research should be conducted. To do this, both quantitative (e.g., surveys and polls) and qualitative (e.g., focus groups and interviews) methods should be applied.

Recall and Retention Measurement

This is a commonly used technique in advertising in which sponsors want to know if their commercials have lasting impact. Such measurement analysis may be equally important in public relations. It is one thing for a target to have seen and understood a message but quite another for someone to remember what was said. In applying such follow-up research, it is also instructive to see if targets can differentiate between public relations and advertising media. In other words, did the target audience retain the knowledge through media stories, speeches, presentations, or ads?

Attitude and Preference Measurement

Even more important than how much someone retained from a message is a measure of how the message moved an individual's attitudes, opinions, and preferences. This involves the areas of opinion research and attitude research. The former is easier because it can be realized simply by asking a few preference questions. The latter, however, is derived from more complex variables, such as predispositions, feelings, and motivational tendencies regarding the issue in question. Preference measurement is often derived by listing alternative choices and asking respondents to make decisions about their relative worth.

Behavior Measurements

This is the ultimate test of effectiveness. Did the message get people to vote for our candidate, buy our product, or agree with our ideas?

Measuring behavior in public relations is difficult, especially in "proving" that a certain program "caused" the desired outcome to occur. In other words, how do we know that it was our input in particular that caused people to contribute more to our charity, or legislators to vote for our issue, or an editor to report favorably on our organization? So although it's difficult to measure causation in public relations behavioral research, it's less difficult to show correlations of outcomes with public relations activity.[9]

Regardless of the evaluative technique, by evaluating after the fact, researchers can learn how to improve future efforts. Were the right target audiences surveyed? Were the correct research assumptions applied to those audiences? Were questions from research tools left unanswered?

Again, research results can be evaluated in a number of ways. Unfortunately, the most common method in public relations may be "seat-of-the-pants" evaluation, in which anecdotal observation and practitioner judgment are used to estimate the effectiveness of the public relations program. Such evaluation might be based on feedback from members of a key public, personal media contacts, or colleagues, but the practitioner alone evaluates the success of the program with subjective observation.

In the fiercely competitive, resource-dear 21st century, the practice of public relations will increasingly be called on to justify its activities and evaluate the results of its programs with formal research.

Research and the Web

Research techniques in evaluating the effectiveness of programs and products on the Web are still very much in their infancy.

Evaluating Web Sites

In assessing the impact of the Web, the two most frequent research terms discussed are *hits* and *eyeballs*. The former refers to the number of times a Web site is visited by an individual. The latter refers to the orbital lobes affixed to that hit. Obviously, these are but the most rudimentary of measurement tools in that they don't assess the visitors' interest in the product or service or information conveyed, the duration of their stay at the site, or whether they were driven to act on the information—buy the product, subscribe to the service, or vote for the candidate. Indeed, the first 5,000 hits to a new Web site may mean nothing more than the firm's employees checking out the latest communications tool.

In light of this inherent problem in extracting value from Web site measurement data, the best advice is to begin by identifying the key questions the Web site sponsor wants answered. For example:

- How much traffic is coming to the site?
- What pages are people looking at?
- How often do they go beyond the homepage?
- What is it they find most useful and interesting?
- What parts never get looked at?
- Where do visitors come from?
- Is the site functioning as expected—for advertisers, sales leads, requests, and so on?[10]

Value of Web Research

Like everything else associated with the Internet, measurement techniques will develop rapidly. Consider the additional contributions Web research offers:

- **Intimacy.** Site-based research can bring organizations closer to their constituents.
- **Precision.** Web-based research can provide more detailed answers about consumers than traditional research methods.
- **Timeliness.** Web-based research is eminently more timely than traditional methods.
- **Cost.** Web-based research will reduce costs considerably compared to traditional surveying methods.

Web Research Considerations

The value of Web-oriented research is indisputable. In preparing for such Internet evaluation—just as in preparing for any public relations research—an organization should take several factors into consideration first:

1. **Establish objectives.** Again, implicit in any meaningful measurement is the setting of objectives. Why are we on the Web? What is our site designed to do? What are we attempting to communicate?

2. **Determine criteria.** Define success with tangible data—for example, percentage of people likely to purchase from the site and positive interactive publication mentions that the site will receive.

3. **Determine benchmarks.** Project the hits the site will receive. Base this on competitive data to see how this site stacks up against the competition or other forms of communication.

4. **Select the right measurement tool.** Numerous software packages exist and are being developed to track site traffic. Maybe using a survey on the site is a more meaningful measurement or maybe more than one tool is called for.

5. **Compare results to objectives.** Success of online marketing and communications cannot be concluded in a vacuum. Numbers of visitors, hits, and eyeballs must be correlated with original objectives. For example, if the objective is to strengthen investor relations, then determine how many visitors made their way to the annual report and how long they stayed reading it. Combine that information with the cost to print the annual report, and this will help determine how much money the Web might save the company.

6. **Draw actionable conclusions.** Research indicates you've received 100,000 visitors to the site. So what? Interpret the significance of the numbers and do something with the data to make progress.[11]

Finally, in terms of researching the Web, there is the aspect of monitoring what is being said about the organization. With the proliferation of rogue sites, anti-business chat rooms and newsgroups, and chain letter e-mail campaigns, monitoring the Web has become a front-line public relations responsibility. The Internet has been called the "great equalizer," which means that all individuals can have their say—mean, nasty, belligerent—and organizations must constantly keep track of what is being said about them.

Using Outside Research Help

Despite its occasional rough spots, public relations research has made substantial gains in quantifying the results of public relations activities. Counseling firms have organized separate departments to conduct attitude and opinion surveys as well as other types of research projects.

Interactive public relations specialists have emerged to help monitor organizational references on the Web. Some outside agencies even volunteer to launch "whisper" campaigns in chat rooms to neutralize negative or inaccurate messages about clients.

Beyond these services, there are research tools, such as Statistical Package for the Social Sciences (SPSS) technology, which analyzes social sciences data. Such systematic approaches are beneficial in analyzing the results of public relations research.

Often, before turning to outside consultants, the best first step is to determine whether research has already been done on what you are trying to find out. Because research assistance is expensive, it makes little sense to reinvent the wheel. It is much wiser to piggyback on existing research.

Last Word

Research is a means of both defining problems and evaluating solutions. Even though intuitive judgment remains a coveted and important skill, management must see measurable results.

Nonetheless, informed managements recognize that public relations may never reach a point at which its results can be fully quantified. Management confidence is still a prerequisite for active and unencumbered programs. Indeed, the best measurement of public relations value is a strong and unequivocal endorsement from management that it supports the public relations effort. However, such confidence can only be enhanced as practitioners become more adept in using research.

Frankly, practitioners don't have a choice. With efficiency driving today's bottom line and with communications about organizations percolating at a 24/7 clip around the world through a variety of media, organizations must always know where they stand. It is the job of public relations to keep track of, record, and research changing attitudes and opinions about the organizations for which they work. Therefore, it will become increasingly incumbent on public relations people to reinforce the value of what they do and what they stand for through constantly measuring their contribution to their organization's goals.[12]

Discussion Starters

1. Why is research important in public relations work?
2. What are the differences between primary and secondary research?
3. What are the four elements of a survey?
4. What is the difference between random and stratified sampling?
5. What are the keys to designing an effective questionnaire?
6. What is a communication audit?
7. What kinds of tools are used to measure public relations outcomes?
8. Why is evaluation important in public relations research?
9. What kinds of questions are pertinent in evaluating a Web site?
10. What is the first factor that should be considered in conducting Web-based research?

Top of the Shelf

The Best of Branding

James R. Gregory, New York: McGraw-Hill, 2004.

The Best of Branding is the fourth in a series by one of corporate brandings most well-regarded experts. This book discusses how communications affect brand image. It profiles leading companies and examines the specific strategies and tactics these firms used to make—or break—their brands.

Of special relevance, however, is Gregory's allegiance to quantifying brand management. He has developed proprietary tools for measuring the power of brands and their impact on a company's financial performance. It is this reliance on measurement and quantitative analysis that makes *The Best of Branding* a different approach to corporate imaging.

CASE STUDY

Researching a Position for Alan Louis General

The administrator at Alan Louis General Hospital confronted a problem that he hoped research could help solve. Alan Louis General, although a good hospital, was smaller and less well known than most other hospitals in Bangor, Maine. In its area alone, it competed with 20 other medical facilities. Alan Louis needed a "position" that it could call unique to attract patients to fill its beds.

For a long time, the Alan Louis administrator, Sven Rapcorn, had believed in the principle that truth will win out. Build a better mousetrap, and the world will beat a path to your door. Erect a better hospital, and your beds will always be 98 percent filled. Unfortunately, Rapcorn learned, the real world seldom recognizes truth at first blush.

In the real world, more often than not, perception will triumph. Because people act on perceptions, those perceptions become reality. Successful positioning, Rapcorn learned, is based on recognizing and dealing with people's perceptions. And so, Rapcorn set out with research to build on existing perceptions about Alan Louis General.

He decided to conduct a communications audit to help form a differentiable "position" for Alan Louis General.

Interview Process

As a first step, Rapcorn talked to his own doctors and trustees to gather data about their perceptions not only of Alan Louis General but also of other hospitals in the community. He did this to get a clear and informed picture of where competing hospitals ranked in the minds of knowledgeable people.

For example, the University Health Center had something for everybody—exotic care, specialized care, and basic bread-and-butter care. Bangor General was a huge, well-respected hospital whose reputation was so good that only a major tragedy could shake its standing in the community. Mercy Hospital was known for its trauma center. And so on.

As for Alan Louis itself, doctors and trustees said that it was a great place to work, that excellent care was provided, and that the nursing staff was particularly friendly and good. The one problem, everyone agreed, was that "nobody knows about us."

Attribute Testing

The second step in Rapcorn's research project was to test attributes important in health care. He did this to learn what factors community members felt were most important in assessing hospital care.

Respondents were asked to rank eight factors in order of importance and to tell Rapcorn and his staff how each of the surveyed hospitals rated on those factors. The research instrument used a semantic differential scale of 1 to 10, with 1 the worst and 10 the best possible score. Questionnaires were sent to two groups: 1,000 area residents and 500 former Alan Louis patients.

Results Tabulation

The third step in the research was to tabulate the results in order to determine community priorities.

Among area residents who responded, the eight attributes were ranked accordingly:

1. Surgical care—9.23
2. Medical equipment—9.20
3. Cardiac care—9.16
4. Emergency services—8.96
5. Range of medical services—8.63
6. Friendly nurses—8.62
7. Moderate costs—8.59
8. Location—7.94

After the attributes were ranked, the hospitals in the survey were ranked for each attribute. On advanced surgical care, the most important feature to area residents, Bangor General ranked first, with University Health Center a close second. Alan Louis was far down

on the list. The same was true of virtually every other attribute. Indeed, on nursing care, an area in which its staff thought Alan Louis excelled, the hospital came in last in the minds of area residents. Rapcorn was not surprised. The largest hospitals in town scored well on most attributes; Alan Louis trailed the pack.

However, the ranking of hospital scores according to former Alan Louis patients revealed an entirely different story. On surgical care, for example, although Bangor General still ranked first, Alan Louis came in a close second. Its scores improved similarly on all other attributes. In fact, in nursing care, where Alan Louis came in last on the survey of area residents, among former patients its score was higher than that of any other hospital. It also ranked first in terms of convenient location and second in terms of costs, range of services, and emergency care.

Conclusions and Recommendations

The fourth step in Rapcorn's research project was to draw some conclusions to determine what the data had revealed.

He reached three conclusions:

1. Bangor General was still number one in terms of area hospitals.
2. Alan Louis ranked at or near the top on most attributes, according to those who actually experienced care there.
3. Former Alan Louis patients rated the hospital significantly better than the general public did.

In other words, thought Rapcorn, most of those who try Alan Louis like it. The great need was to convince more people to try the hospital.

But how could this be accomplished with a hospital? Other marketers generate trial by sending free samples in the mail, offering cents-off coupons, holding free demonstrations, and the like. Hospitals are more limited in this area. Rapcorn's challenge was to launch a communications campaign to convince prospects to see other area hospitals in a different, less favorable light or to give people a specific reason to think about trying Alan Louis. In other words, he needed to come up with a communications strategy that clearly differentiated Alan Louis—admittedly, among the smallest of area hospitals—from the bigger, less personal hospitals. Rapcorn was confident that the data he had gathered from the research project were all he needed to come up with a winning idea.

He then set out to propose his recommendations.

Questions

1. What kind of communications program would you launch to accomplish Rapcorn's objectives?

2. What would be the cornerstone—the theme—of your communications program?

3. What would be the specific elements of your program?

4. In launching the program, what specific steps would you follow—both inside and outside the hospital—to build support?

5. How could you use the Internet to conduct more research about area hospitals and residents' perceptions of the care at these hospitals? How could you use the Internet to research the effectiveness of the communications program you implement?

Voice of Authority

An Interview with John James Fahey

In a communications and public relations career spanning 28 years with the IBM Corporation, **Jim Fahey** has had managerial responsibilities in all areas of public relations, from employee communications and community relations to government relations and graphic arts. For 15 years after retiring from IBM, he has been served as Associate Professor of Communications at Marist College, Poughkeepsie, NY, teaching communications and public relations courses.

How important is research in Public Relations?
Research is vital to the professional PR practitioner today.

It should be the "alpha and the omega," the beginning and the end of any public relations project.

What is the state of research among most public relations professionals?
Research in public relations today is not as good as it should be. Today's management demand facts, statistics, and results. Good research can provide these things.

Is it possible to measure public relations success?
Absolutely—by establishing methods to measure *outputs* and *outcomes* against a given time frame. No PR program is complete until it has been measured against given objectives.

How do you respond to those who say public relations is based purely on intuition?
Intuition in many ways is based on experience and knowledge and can be extremely useful in PR. However, there is no substitute for sound legitimate research to solve public relations problems. The best situation is a combination of the two.

What kinds of research are valuable for public relations professionals?
Two kinds come to mind: 1) Preliminary Research, to get the best understanding of the current problem or situation and 2) Evaluative Research, which is used to determine the success or failure of a program, project or event. I'm reminded of the quote by the British physicist Lord Calvin. "When you can measure what you are talking about and express it in numbers, you know something about it. But, when you cannot measure it, when you cannot express it in numbers, your knowledge is meager and unsatisfactory."

How important is reading the daily newspaper as part of public relations "research?"
Very important. PR professionals are the eyes and the ears of the organization and should be consistently aware of what's going on in both the local and national media as well as the Internet.

How important is the Internet as a public relations research tool?
The Internet and the computer make up the new frontier in information and communications research. As a result, PR professionals *must* be proficient in the use of the computer, both as a research and a communication tool, and they *must* stay abreast of the new techniques and applications in the use of computers.

What weight should public relations students place on research?
Students must learn to have a great appreciation for the value of research. The quality of the research is of vital importance. First, management expects it. Second, it will determine the success or failure of their PR programs. Third, the ability to provide quality research directly affects their careers.

Suggested Readings

Barzun, Jacques, and Henry F. Graff. *The Modern Researcher,* 6th ed. Ft. Worth, TX: HBJ College Publications, 2002.

Broom, Glen M., and David M. Dozier. *Using Research in Public Relations: Applications to Program Management.* Upper Saddle River, NJ: Prentice Hall, 1996.

Erikson, Robert, and Kent L. Tedin, *American Public Opinion, Its Origin, Contents and Impact,* 6th ed. New York: Longman, 2000.

Fink, Arlene, and Jacqueline Kosecoff. *How to Conduct Surveys: A Step-by-Step Guide,* 2nd ed. Thousand Oaks, CA: Sage Publications, 1998.

Fowler, Floyd J., Jr. *Survey Research Methods,* 2nd ed. Newbury Park, CA: Sage Publications, 2002.

Hoover's Handbooks of American Business, Major U.S. Companies, World Business, Emerging Companies, and Private Companies. Austin, TX: Hoover's Inc. The Web site www.hoovers.com features Hoover's Online: The Business Network and profiles of more than 12,000 public and private companies.

Jensen, Klaus Bruhn (Ed.). *A Handbook of Media and Communication Research.* New York: Routledge, 2002. A practical and theoretical analysis of the history of communications research and how to apply various research concepts.

Lindlof, Thomas R., and Bryan C. Taylor. *Qualitative Communication Research Methods,* 2nd ed. Thousand Oaks, CA: Sage Publications, 2002. Exploration through the entire research project, from the hatching of an idea to the finished report.

Pavlik, John V. *Public Relations: What Research Tells Us.* Newbury Park, CA: Sage Publications, 1987. Old but a classic in the field.

Stacks, Don W. *Primer of Public Relations Research.* New York: Guilford Press, 2002. An authoritative and comprehensive guide to public relations research motives and methods, authored by one of the field's foremost research experts.

Tourangeau, Roger, Lance Rips, and Kenneth Rasinski. *The Psychology of Survey Response.* Cambridge Universisty Press, 2000.

www.odwyerpr.com. *Jack O'Dwyer's Newsletter* offers online logos, agency statements, and complete listings of 550 PR firms. There is no cost for accessing any part of the Web site, including news from the newsletter and other publications, hyperlinks to articles on PR, job listings, and more than 1,000 PR services in 58 categories.

Zumbo, Bruno D. *Advances in Quality of Life Research 2001.* Dordrecht, Netherlands: Kluwer Academic Publishers, 2002. This book reviews research in diverse areas, including business, marketing, and public policy.

Notes

1. Bo-Mi Lim, "Cloning Scandal Spotlights Korea's Obedience Culture," *Chicago Sun-Times,* January 8, 2006.

2. Jennifer Nedeff, "The Bottom Line Beckons: Quantifying Measurement in Public Relations," *Journal of Corporate Public Relations Northwestern University,* 1996–1997, 34.

3. Walter K. Lindenmann, "Setting Minimum Standards for Measuring Public Relations Effectiveness," *Public Relations Review,* Winter 1997, 394–395.

4. "Response Rate for Census 200 Matches 1990 Rate," U.S. Census Bureau News, April 19, 2000.

5. Tom Greenbaum, "The Gold Standard: Why the Focus Group Deserves to be the Most Respected of All Qualitative Research Tools," *Quirk's Marketing Research Review,* June 2003.

6. David J. Solomon, "Conducting We-Based Surveys," *Practical Assessment, Research and Evaluation,* August 23, 2001.

7. Christine Bates, "Communications Audits and the Effects of Increased Information," *Technical Communication,* May 2003.

8. "Guidelines and Standards for Measuring and Evaluating PR Effectiveness," The Institute for Public Relations Commission on PR Measurement and Evaluation, 2003.

9. Ibid.

10. Bill Zoellick, "Who, What, Why Important to Know about Web Visitors," *The Boulder County Business Reporter,* Summer 2000.

11. Katherine D. Paine and Beth Roed, "The Basics of Internet Measurement," *Ragan's Interactive PR,* March 1999, 7.

12. Jennifer Nedeff, op. cit.

9 Print Media Relations

I n the 21st century, it's no longer your mama's media.

Where once, the media were dominated by a handful of powerful, truth-minded reporters and editors at a handful of newspapers and three national TV networks, today the media are fragmented, omnipresent, busy 24 hours a day/seven days a week, and populated by a breed of reporter who is aggressive, opinionated, sharp-elbowed, and more than willing to throw himself or herself personally into the story being covered.

This latter point presents a particular difference with the reporting style of the past century. Today, more often than not, with competition from thousands of daily newspapers, talk radio stations, cable TV channels, and bloggers as far as the eye can see, reporters have few qualms about using anonymous sources, losing their historic anonymity, and becoming part of the story.

FIGURE 9-1 When the reporter becomes the story. In 2005, *New York Times* reporter Judith Miller was thrown in jail for refusing to divulge the source responsible for outing a CIA agent. (AP Wide World Photos)

Sometimes, in fact, reporters use anonymous sources and themselves become *all* of the story. That was clearly the case with this woman:

Judith Miller, a veteran *New York Times* reporter, became front-page news herself in 2005 when she faced contempt-of-court charges for failing to reveal the source of a leak that led to the outing of a CIA operative, who was married to an outspoken critic of the Bush administration. Although it is illegal to reveal the identity of an undercover CIA agent, Miller chose to serve 85 days in the slammer before a deal was reached to reveal her source, who turned out to be a high-ranking administration official.

Shortly thereafter, the *Times* and Miller parted ways, when her editors objected to her chumminess with the White House.[1]

Judy Miller's brush with journalistic infamy was par for the course in an era when journalistic competition has been magnified exponentially with the advent of 24/7 cable news, talk radio, and the never-ending blogosphere. This is the journalistic landscape in which public relations professionals must operate to earn their living. Indeed, to most people, the term public relations is synonymous with two things: dealing with the press and getting publicity.

Modern public relations practice got its start as an adjunct to journalism, with former reporters, such as Ivy Lee, hired to refine the image of well-to-do clients. In the old days (before 1990), most of the professionals who entered the practice of public relations were former journalists.

Today, of course, with public relations professionals emanating from many different fields of study and directly from college, the field is no longer dominated by former journalists. Nonetheless, the importance of the media to the practice of public relations cannot be denied.

Put simply, if you're in public relations, you must know how to deal with the press.

Therein lies the problem, because in the 21st century, the "press" has changed, often for the worst. As President Bush's first press secretary, Ari Fleischer, has said:

We've reached a point where the press, in pursuit of its devil's advocate role, would do well to ask itself, are they "informing" the public or are they being so negative about the institutions they cover, that they're not covering all the news, but only the "bad news."[2]

This "devil's advocate" role is the key to why many people don't like the press. As the circulation of daily newspapers continues to decline, polls suggest that Americans are growing increasingly disenchanted with the media. One study indicated that while 72 percent of journalists thought "the press reports information accurately," only 39 percent of Americans agreed. Fifty-three percent believed "a story using anonymous sources" shouldn't be published.[3]

Freedom of the press, of course, is a hallmark of American democracy. It is a right guaranteed by the First Amendment to the U.S. Constitution. Written in 1789, the 45 words contained in the First Amendment protect the freedom of speech, press, religion, and assembly.

Over the years, in pursuing that freedom, the media have regularly challenged authority with pointed, nasty, even hostile questions. Their proper role in a democracy, as embodied in the First Amendment, is to independently ferret out the truth. Often this means "breaking eggs" in the process. Whether it means hounding a public figure, invading the privacy of a private figure, or just plain being obnoxious, that is what journalists have become known to do.

What this means to public relations professionals is that dealing with the press has never been more challenging. When one adds the growing impact of Internet journalism, where 70 percent accuracy is considered "acceptable," dealing with the media has become a high-risk business.

This is the business of the public relations professional, who serves as the first line of defense and explanation with respect to the media. It is the public relations practitioner who meets the reporter head on. In the 21st century, this is not a job for the squeamish.

Number One Medium

Despite the growth of the Internet and electronic media, print still stands as the number one medium among public relations professionals.

Why?

The answer probably lies in the fact that many departments at newspapers and magazines use news releases and other publicity vehicles compared to the limited opportunities on network and cable TV. In addition, online databases use wire service material destined for print usage, so the Internet often serves as a residual target for print publicity.

While it is true that newspaper circulation in recent years has continued to tumble, the nation's largest newspapers are still hugely powerful. Indeed, the growth of alternative sources of information has hurt newspaper readership. Particularly hard hit are local newspapers, which must compete with national circulation dailies, such as *The New York Times, The Wall Street Journal,* and *USA Today.* These latter national papers have shown marginal increases in recent years.[4]

Despite their circulation problems, newspapers still dominate the nation's news schedule. Specifically, electronic news directors and bloggers regularly check the national dailies to determine the news of the day. Moreover, almost one third of Internet users—close to 50 million people a month—visit newspaper Web sites. In other words, while circulation might be down, newspaper "reach" is up.[5] The conclusion, then, stated simply, even in the wired 21st century, print still sets the media agenda (Table 9-1).

Table 9-1

Top 100 Daily Newspapers in the U.S. by Circulation 2004

The nation's leading circulation newspapers, according to BurrellesLuce Press Clippings.

Rank	Newspaper	Daily	Sunday
1.	USA Today[1]	2,192,098	2,635,412
2.	The Wall Street Journal[1]	2,101,017	None
3.	The New York Times*	1,119,027	1,677,003
4.	Los Angeles Times	983,727	1,392,672
5.	Washington Post*	760,034	1,025,579
6.	(New York) Daily News*	712,671	802,103
7.	New York Post*	642,844	445,094
8.	Chicago Tribune*	603,315	1,002,398
9.	Newsday (Long Island, NY)*	553,117	662,317
10.	Houston Chronicle	549,300	740,002
11.	Dallas Morning News*	528,379	755,912
12.	San Francisco Chronicle*	499,008	553,983
13.	(Phoenix) Arizona Republic	466,926	587,159
14.	Chicago Sun-Times*	453,757	378,371
15.	Boston Globe*	446,241	686,575
16.	Atlanta Journal-Constitution[2]	409,873	629,505
17.	Star-Ledger* (Newark)	395,000	610,542

(continued)

Table 9-1 (continued)

Rank	Newspaper	Daily	Sunday
18.	Detroit Free Press[2]*	379,304	705,148
19.	(Minneapolis) Star Tribune	377,058	671,275
20.	Philadelphia Inquirer*	376,454	769,257
21.	(Cleveland) Plain Dealer	367,528	480,540
22.	San Diego Union Tribune	355,771	444,527
23.	St. Petersburg Times	348,502	442,605
24.	Denver Post*	340,168	783,274
25.	(Denver) Rocky Mountain News*	340,007	783,274
26.	(Portland) Oregonian*	339,169	412,113
27.	Miami Herald	325,032	447,326
28.	Orange County (CA) Register	310,001	374,364
29.	Sacramento Bee	303,841	356,154
30.	St. Louis Post-Dispatch	281,198	454,998
31.	San Jose Mercury News	279,539	308,425
32.	Baltimore Sun*	277,947	470,453
33.	Kansas City Star	275,747	388,425
34.	Detroit News[2]*	271,465	705,148
35.	Orlando Sentinel	269,269	385,097
36.	South Florida Sun-Sentinel (Ft. Lauderdale)*	268,297	376,551
37.	New Orleans Times-Picayune	262,008	286,802
38.	Columbus Dispatch	259,127	371,551
39.	Indianapolis Star	253,778	367,995
40.	San Antonio Express-News*	246,057	359,828
41.	Pittsburgh Post-Gazette*	242,514	406,754
42.	Milwaukee Journal Sentinel*	241,605	430,755
43.	Tampa Tribune	238,877	315,811
44.	Fort Worth Star-Telegram*	237,318	332,861
45.	Boston Herald*	236,899	152,624
46.	Seattle Times*	233,497	465,830
47.	Charlotte Observer	231,369	282,215
48.	(Oklahoma City) Daily Oklahoman	223,403	297,029
49.	Louisville Courier-Journal	216,934	279,611
50.	Investor's Business Daily[1]*	215,735	None
51.	Buffalo News	201,900	290,316
52.	(Norfolk) Virginian-Pilot	201,473	234,540
53.	Cincinnati Enquirer*	196,750	309,608
54.	Hartford Courant*	196,502	283,410
55.	Omaha World-Herald*	195,964	242,018
56.	Riverside (CA) Press-Enterprise	191,802	191,290
57.	Richmond Times-Dispatch	191,732	229,818
58.	St. Paul Pioneer Press	189,458	253,368
59.	Arkansas Democrat-Gazette (Little Rock)	187,601	285,583
60.	Contra Costa (CA) Times	186,335	195,815
61.	Austin American-Statesman	184,907	234,409
62.	(Bergen County, NJ) Record*	181,962	222,701
63.	Palm Beach (FL) Post	181,727	219,656
64.	(Memphis) Commercial Appeal*	177,723	240,712
65.	(Los Angeles) Daily News*	177,046	201,101
66.	(Nashville) Tennessean	176,231	243,796
67.	Raleigh News & Observer*	174,735	211,503

Rank	Newspaper	Daily	Sunday
68.	Las Vegas Review-Journal[2]	173,439	226,923
69.	Rochester Democrat & Chronicle	169,697	228,567
70.	Florida Times-Union (Jacksonville)	169,093	230,094
71.	Fresno Bee	166,531	195,091
72.	Providence Journal	166,460	234,147
73.	Asbury Park Press (Neptune)	161,937	217,636
74.	Birmingham News*	157,225	189,087
75.	Des Moines Register	155,898	246,246
76.	Tulsa World	155,062	214,426
77.	Arlington Heights (IL) Herald	150,794	151,279
78.	Seattle Post-Intelligencer*	147,866	465,830
79.	Honolulu Advertiser	145,943	166,585
80.	Akron Beacon Journal*	144,596	187,456
81.	Journal News (White Plains, NY)	142,145	164,636
82.	Toledo Blade	139,293	184,244
83.	Grand Rapids Press	139,216	187,174
84.	Dayton Daily News*	138,045	192,003
85.	Salt Lake City Tribune	135,730	156,508
86.	Tacoma News Tribune	128,748	147,200
87.	Philadelphia Daily News*	127,162	None
88.	Knoxville News Sentinel*	123,047	156,158
89.	La Opinion (Los Angeles)*	122,598	70,370
90.	Morning Call (Allentown, PA)*	121,751	167,335
91.	Sarasota Herald-Tribune	121,272	146,652
92.	Syracuse (NY) Post-Standard	119,158	174,581
93.	Lexington (KY) Herald-Leader*	118,070	147,004
94.	Wilmington News Journal	117,859	141,283
95.	The State (Columbia, SC)	117,595	150,030
96.	Greensburg (PA) Tribune-Review	116,362	181,057
97.	Daytona Beach (FL) News-Journal	112,945	129,385
98.	East Valley Tribune (Mesa, AZ)	112,909	92,837
99.	Hoy (NYC)	109,598	34,403
100.	Tuscon (AZ) Star	109,592	176,319

This list was compiled by Burrelles*Luce* from circulation figures for the six months ending on March 31, 2004, filed with the Audit Bureau of Circulations. Rankings are by daily circulation. In some cases, Sunday newspapers have different names. The daily circulation is Monday to Saturday, except for newspapers published five days a week, indicated by[1]. USA Today's Friday circulation is listed in the Sunday column. [2]Saturday and Sunday newspapers are combined: Detroit News and Free Press, Las Vegas Review-Journal and Sun, Denver Post and Rocky Mountain News. Tulsa World is publisher's figures, not ABC. *Figures were adjusted by Burrelles*Luce* to indicate average weekday circulation. Copyright 2004, Burrelles*Luce*. Courtesy of Burrelles*Luce*.

On the other hand, as noted, many in the public have become increasingly disenchanted with the perceived bias of many in the news media.

Although the media's image improved immediately after the attacks of September 11, 2001, public confidence in the media has dissipated as time has worn on. Four years after the attacks, the numbers for the press aren't good.

- Sixty-one percent of Americans think bias exists in news coverage.
- Fifty-three percent of Americans think a news story using unnamed sources shouldn't be published.
- Forty-three percent of Americans think the press has too much freedom.[6]

So, while the public is still reading and listening and viewing the media, its faith and trust in the press are limited.

In the United States today, 1,457 daily newspapers are published, with a total circulation of 55 million, according to the Newspaper Association of America. There are upwards of 17,000 magazines published in the United States today, according to the National Directory of Magazines. After a rough stretch in the mid-1990s, magazine readership is on the increase again with specialty publications leading the way.

With so many print outlets—newspapers, magazines, and online publications—the waterfront for public relations publicity is broad and deep.

Objectivity in the Media

Whether the mass media have lost relative influence to other proliferating alternative communications vehicles or not, the fact remains that securing positive publicity through the media still lies at the heart of public relations practice.

This chapter focuses on how to coexist with the print media, with which public relations professionals deal the most. Chapter 10 addresses the electronic media. We explore here what it takes to work with the media to convey the most effective impression for an organization—that is, to attract positive publicity.

Why attract publicity?

The answer, as we will see, is that publicity is regarded as more credible than advertising. To attract positive publicity requires establishing a good working relationship with the media. This is, of course, easier said than done. In the 21st century, faced with intense competition from on-air and online journalists, print reporters are by and large more aggressive, some would argue more hostile.

They are also decidedly less "objective."

The presumed goal of a journalist is objectivity—fairness with the intention of remaining neutral in reporting a story. But total objectivity is impossible. All of us have biases and preconceived notions about many things. Likewise, in reporting, pure objectivity is unattainable; it would require complete neutrality and near-total detachment in reporting a story. Reporting, then, despite what some journalists might suggest, is subjective. Nevertheless, scholars of journalism believe that reporters and editors should strive for maximum objectivity (Figure 9-2).

By virtue of their role, the media view officials, particularly business and government spokespersons, with a degree of skepticism. Reporters shouldn't be expected to accept on faith the party line. By the same token, once a business or government official effectively substantiates the official view and demonstrates its merit, the media should be willing to report this accurately without editorial distortion.

Stated another way, the relationship between the media and the establishment— that is, public relations people—should be one of *friendly adversaries* rather than of bitter enemies. Unfortunately, this is not always the case. According to one *Washington Post* columnist, the fault may lie with the American public:

> *We are only incidentally bringing truth to the world—although don't get me wrong, from time to time we manage to do just that. But most journalists most of the time are just trying to give the public what it wants—and much of the time, the public wants trash.*[7]

That is not to say that the vast majority of journalists don't try to be fair. They do. Despite the preconceived biases that all of us have, most reporters want to get the facts

THE JOURNALIST'S Creed

I believe IN THE PROFESSION OF

JOURNALISM.

I BELIEVE THAT THE PUBLIC JOURNAL IS A PUBLIC TRUST; THAT ALL CONNECTED WITH IT ARE, TO THE FULL MEASURE OF THEIR RESPONSIBILITY, TRUSTEES FOR THE PUBLIC; THAT ACCEPTANCE OF A LESSER SERVICE THAN THE PUBLIC SERVICE IS BETRAYAL OF THIS TRUST.

I BELIEVE THAT CLEAR THINKING AND CLEAR STATEMENT, AC-CURACY, AND FAIRNESS ARE FUNDAMENTAL TO GOOD JOUR-NALISM.

I BELIEVE THAT A JOURNALIST SHOULD WRITE ONLY WHAT HE HOLDS IN HIS HEART TO BE TRUE.

I BELIEVE THAT SUPPRESSION OF THE NEWS, FOR ANY CONSIDER-ATION OTHER THAN THE WELFARE OF SOCIETY, IS INDEFENSIBLE.

I BELIEVE THAT NO ONE SHOULD WRITE AS A JOURNALIST WHAT HE WOULD NOT SAY AS A GENTLEMAN; THAT BRIBERY BY ONE'S OWN POCKETBOOK IS AS MUCH TO BE AVOIDED AS BRIBERY BY THE POCKETBOOK OF ANOTHER; THAT INDIVIDUAL RESPONSIBIL-ITY MAY NOT BE ESCAPED BY PLEADING ANOTHER'S INSTRUC-TIONS OR ANOTHER'S DIVIDENDS.

I BELIEVE THAT ADVERTISING, NEWS AND EDITORIAL COLUMNS SHOULD ALIKE SERVE THE BEST INTERESTS OF READERS; THAT A SINGLE STANDARD OF HELPFUL TRUTH AND CLEANNESS SHOULD PREVAIL FOR ALL; THAT THE SUPREME TEST OF GOOD JOURNAL-ISM IS THE MEASURE OF ITS PUBLIC SERVICE.

I BELIEVE THAT THE JOURNALISM WHICH SUCCEEDS BEST—AND BEST DESERVES SUCCESS—FEARS GOD AND HONORS MAN; IS STOUTLY INDEPENDENT, UNMOVED BY PRIDE OF OPINION OR GREED OF POWER, CONSTRUCTIVE, TOLERANT BUT NEVER CARE-LESS, SELF-CONTROLLED, PATIENT, ALWAYS RESPECTFUL OF ITS READERS BUT ALWAYS UNAFRAID, IS QUICKLY INDIGNANT AT IN-JUSTICE; IS UNSWAYED BY THE APPEAL OF PRIVILEGE OR THE CLAMOR OF THE MOB; SEEKS TO GIVE EVERY MAN A CHANCE, AND, AS FAR AS LAW AND HONEST WAGE AND RECOGNITION OF HUMAN BROTHERHOOD CAN MAKE IT SO AN EQUAL CHANCE; IS PROFOUNDLY PATRIOTIC WHILE SINCERELY PROMOTING IN-TERNATIONAL GOOD WILL AND CEMENTING WORLD-COMRADE-SHIP; IS A JOURNALISM OF HUMANITY, OF AND FOR TODAY'S WORLD.

Walter Williams

DEAN SCHOOL OF JOURNALISM, UNIVERSITY OF MISSOURI, 1908-1935

FIGURE 9-2 Code of objectivity. "The Journalist's Creed" was written after World War I by Dr. Walter Williams, dean of the School of Journalism at the University of Missouri. (Courtesy of Luce Press Clippings)

from all sides. An increasing number of journalists acknowledge and respect the public relations practitioner's role in the process. (Some don't, but there are rotten apples in any profession!) If reporters are dealt with fairly, most will reciprocate in kind.

However, some executives fail to understand the essential difference between the media and their own organizations. That is:

1. The reporter wants the "story" whether bad or good.

2. Organizations, on the other hand, want things to be presented in the best light.

Because of this difference, some executives consider journalists to be the enemy, dead set on revealing all the bad news they can about their organization. These people fear and distrust the media. As a consequence, the practice of public relations—intermediary between the executive and the journalist—gets knocked as a profession of "*stonewallers*" intent on keeping journalists out.[8]

The Internet Factor

Further complicating the relationship between journalists and executives is the Internet. To some, the Internet has ushered in a new age of journalistic reporting: immediate, freewheeling, unbridled. To others, the Internet is responsible for the collapse of journalistic standards and the ascendancy of rumor mongering.

The credit—or blame—for the rise in Internet reporting may lie with a particular journalistic creation of the late 1990s: Matt Drudge (Figure 9-3).

Drudge, a fedora-wearing, tough-talking, "new-age journalist," reported both fact and fiction parading as fact on his Web site, which regularly ranked near the top in Web traffic each day. Drudge leaped to prominence when he became the first to report that White House intern Monica Lewinsky had retained an incriminating blue dress from her liaisons with President Bill Clinton. The story quickly turned out to be the smoking gun leading to President Clinton's 1994 impeachment. Today, Drudge's Web site, *Drudge Report,* remains "must reading" for many in the national media.

Drudge opened the media door, and 100,000 new bloggers every day now pass through it. Thus was born a huge challenge for public relations professionals: to deal

FIGURE 9-3 Drudge as in sludge. Be he journalistic curse or blessing, Matt Drudge and his round-the-clock Internet *Drudge Report* have had a profound influence on how the Internet impacts journalistic coverage. (AP Wide World Photos)

with, not to mention "harness," this powerful Internet reporting medium. One study indicated that more than half of all journalists consult blogs regularly, and more than a quarter use blogs in day-to-day reporting.[9]

Indeed, Internet reporters from every political bias and ulterior motive remain busy 24 hours a day, seven days a week, churning out continuous stories—some true, others not—about corporations, government agencies, nonprofits, and prominent individuals.

What this suggests is that the media and the organizations they cover will likely remain on different philosophical wavelengths for some time to come. The challenge for public relations professionals is to foster a closer relationship between their organizations and those who present the news. The key, once again, is fairness, with each side accepting—and respecting—the other's role and responsibility.

Dealing with the Media

It falls on public relations professionals to orchestrate the relationship between their organizations and the media. To be sure, the media can't ordinarily be manipulated in our society. They can, however, be engaged in an honest and interactive way to convey the organization's point of view in a manner that may merit being reported. First, an organization must establish a formal media relations policy (Figure 9-4). Second, an organization must establish a philosophy for dealing with the media, keeping in mind the following dozen principles:

1. **A reporter is a reporter.** A reporter is never "off duty." Anything you say to a journalist is fair game to be reported. Remember that, and never let down your guard, no matter how friendly you are.

2. **You are the organization.** In the old days, reporters disdained talking to public relations representatives, who they derisively labeled "flacks" (as in "catching flak," or bad news). Public relations people, therefore, were rarely quoted and remained anonymous. Today the opposite is true. The public relations person represents the policy of an organization. He or she is quoted by name and interviewed on camera (Figure 9-5), so every word out of the public relations professional's mouth must be carefully weighed in advance.

3. **There is no standard issue reporter.** The sad fact is that many business managers want nothing to do with the press. They believe them to be villains. But that isn't necessarily true. As noted, most are simply trying to do their jobs, like anyone else, so each should be treated as an individual, until, cynics might say, "proven guilty."

4. **Treat journalists professionally.** As long as they understand that your job is different than theirs and treat you with deference, you should do likewise. A journalist's job is to get a story, whether good or bad. A public relations person's job is to present the organization in the best light. That difference understood, the relationship should be a professional one.

5. **Don't sweat the skepticism.** Journalists aren't paid to ask nice questions. They are paid to be skeptical. Some interviewees resent this. Smart interviewees realize it comes with the territory.

6. **Don't "buy" a journalist.** Never try to threaten or coerce a journalist with advertising. The line between news and advertising should be a clear one. No self-respecting journalist will tolerate someone trying to "bribe" him or her for a positive story.

FIGURE 9-4 **Media relations policy.** Every organization should have a formal policy such as the one shown here to guide its activities with the press. Public relations should have the primary responsibility of liaison with the media.

7. **Become a trusted source.** Journalists can't be "bought," but they can be persuaded by your becoming a source of information for them. A reporter's job is to report on what's going on. By definition, a public relations person knows more about the company and the industry than does a reporter. So become a source and a positive relationship will follow.

8. **Talk when not "selling."** Becoming a source means sharing information with journalists, even when it has nothing to do with your company. Reporters need

Most reporters with whom the bank deals with respect an officer's wishes to maintain anonymity. Most journalists recognize that it is as important for them to honor the wishes of their sources at the bank as it is for the bank to disseminate its comments and information to the public through the news media. Chase's policy toward the media should be one of mutual trust, understanding, and benefit.

Interviews with the Media

In order to monitor the bank's relationships with journalists, all requests for interviews with bank officers by journalists must be routed through the Public Relations Division.

As a rule, public relations officers check the credentials of the journalist and determine the specific areas of inquiry to be examined. The public relations officer will then decide whether the interview is appropriate for the bank. When the decision is affirmative, the public relations officer will discuss subject matter with the recommended interviewee and together they will decided on a course of action and Chase objectives for the interview.

A member of the public relations staff is normally present during any face-to-face interview with an officer of the bank. The purpose of the public relations staffer's attendance is to provide assistance in handling the interview situation as well as to aid the reporter with follow-up material.

When a reporter calls an officer directly to request an interview, the officer should check with the Public Relations Division before making a commitment.

Authorized Spokespersons

Vice presidents and above are normally authorized to speak for the bank on matters in their own area of responsibility.

Normally, officers below the level of vice president are not authorized to speak for attribution on behalf of the bank except where they are specialists in a particular field, such as technical directors, economists, etc.

Exceptions may be made in special situations and in concert with the Public Relations Division.

Written Material for the Media

Chase articles bylined by officers may either be written by the officer approached or by a member of the public relations staff. If an officer decides to author his or her own article, the public relations division must be consulted for editing, photographic support and policy proofing.

Occasionally, customers or suppliers may wish to include Chase in an article or advertisement they are preparing. This material too must be routed through the Public Relations Division for review.

FIGURE 9-4 (Continued)

leads and story ideas. If you supply them, once again a positive relationship will follow.

9. **Don't expect "news" agreement.** A reporter's view of "news" and an organization's view of "news" will differ. If so, the journalist wins. (It's the reporter's paper, after all!) Don't complain if a story doesn't make it into print. Sometimes there is no logical reason, so never promise an executive that a story will "definitely make the paper."

10. **Don't cop a 'tude.** Don't have an attitude with reporters. They need the information that you possess. If you're coy or standoffish or reluctant to share, they

FIGURE 9-5 Anonymous no more. Once regarded by the media as ancillary, public relations people today have become veritable "sex symbols," quoted by name and appearing on camera. (Well, at least they're "quoted by name and appear on camera!") (Courtesy of Fraser P. Seitel)

    will pay you back. Although reporters vary in look and type, they all share one trait: They remember.

11. **Never lie.** This is the cardinal rule. As one *Wall Street Journal* reporter put it, "Never lie to a reporter or that reporter will never trust you again."[10]

12. **Read the paper.** The number one criticism of public relations people by journalists is that they often don't have any idea what the journalist writes about. This is infuriating, especially when a journalist is approached on a story pitch. Lesson: Read the paper!

    Although some may deny it, reporters, are human beings, so there is no guarantee that even if these principles are followed, all reporters will be fair or objective. Most of the time, however, following these dozen rules of the road will lead to a better relationship between the journalist and the public relations professional.

Attracting Publicity

Publicity, through news releases and other methods, is eminently more powerful than advertising. Publicity is most often gained by dealing directly with the media, either by initiating the communication or by reacting to inquiries. Although most people—especially CEOs!—confuse the two, *publicity* differs dramatically from *advertising*.

    First and most important, advertising costs money—lots of it. A full-page, one-time, nonrecurring ad in the national edition of *The Wall Street Journal,* for example, costs upwards of $180,000—for one ad!

    On the other hand, the benefits of paid advertising include the following communications areas that can be "guaranteed":

- **Content:** What is said and how it is portrayed and illustrated.
- **Size:** How large a space is devoted to the organization.
- **Location:** Where in the paper the ad will appear.
- **Reach:** The audience exposed to the ad—that is, the number of papers in which the ad appears.
- **Frequency:** How many times the ad is run.

Frequency is extremely important. Today, with 500 cable and broadcast television channels, thousands of newspapers and magazines, and millions more Internet sites, people often skip over or surf by the ads or commercials. The only way to get through is to repeat the ad over and over again. In that manner, the largest advertisers—McDonald's, Microsoft, Coca-Cola, and so on—blast their way into public consciousness.

Publicity, on the other hand, offers no such guarantees or controls. Typically, publicity is subject to review by news editors who may decide to use all of a story, some of it, or none of it. Many news releases, in fact, never see the light of print.

When they story will run, who will see it, and how often it will be used are all subject to the whims of a news editor. However, even though attracting publicity is by no means a sure thing, it does offer two overriding benefits that enhance its appeal far beyond that of advertising:

- First, although not free, publicity costs only the time and effort expended by public relations personnel and management in conceiving, creating, and attempting to place the publicity effort in the media. Therefore, relatively speaking, its cost is minimal compared to advertising; rough rule of thumb is 10 percent of equivalent advertising expenditures.
- Second and more important, publicity, which appears in news rather than in advertising columns, carries the implicit *third-party* endorsement of the news source that reports it. In other words, publicity is perceived not as the sponsoring organization's self-serving view but as the view of the objective, unbiased, neutral, impartial news source. For years, for example, when surveys asked people to name their most trusted American, respondents invariably answered not the president or first lady but rather Walter Cronkite, the former news anchor at CBS. NBC's Tom Brokaw became equally trusted over the years.

That is the credibility that a news reporter or publication enjoys. When an organization's publicity is reported by such a source, it instantly becomes more credible, believable, and, therefore, valuable *news*.

That, in essence, is why publicity is more powerful than advertising.

Value of Publicity

For any organization, then, publicity makes great sense in the following areas:

- **Announcing a new product or service.** Because publicity can be regarded as news, it should be used before advertising commences. A new product or service is news only once. Once advertising appears, the product is no longer news. Therefore, one inflexible rule—that most organizations, unfortunately, don't follow—is that publicity should precede advertising (Figure 9-6).
- **Reenergizing an old product.** When a product has been around for a while, it's difficult to make people pay attention to advertising. Therefore, publicity

FIGURE 9-6 New product publicity launch. When Gillette launched its new razor in 2005, it chose formerly bearded, new New York Yankee Johnny Damon to do the honors. (Courtesy of O'Dwyer.com)

techniques—staged events, sponsorships, and so on—may pay off to rejuvenate a mature product.

- **Explaining a complicated product.** Often there isn't enough room in an advertisement to explain a complex product or service. Insurance companies, banks, and mutual funds, which offer products that demand thoughtful explanation, may find advertising space too limiting. Publicity, on the other hand, allows enough room to tell the story.

- **Little or no budget.** Often organizations don't have the budget to accommodate advertising. To make an impact, advertising requires frequency—the constant repetition of ads so that readers eventually see them and acknowledge the product. In the case of Samuel Adams Lager Beer, for example, the company lacked an advertising budget to promote its unique brew, so it used public relations techniques to spread the word about this different-tasting beer. Over time, primarily through publicity about its victories at beer-tasting competitions, Samuel Adams grew in popularity. Today its advertising budget is robust, but the company's faith in publicity endures.

- **Enhancing the organization's reputation.** Advertising is, at its base, self-serving. When a company gives to charity or does a good deed in the community, taking out an ad is the wrong way to communicate its efforts. It is much better for the recipient organization to commend its benefactor in the daily news columns.

- **Crisis response.** In a crisis, publicity techniques are the fastest and most credible means of response. Indeed, in the 21st century, it has become a cliché for celebrities to "apologize" for transgressions by seeking out a high-profile TV interviewer for instant publicity.

These are just a few of the advantages of publicity over advertising. A smart organization, therefore, will always consider publicity a vital component in its overall marketing plan.

Pitching Publicity

The activity of trying to place positive publicity in a periodical—of converting publicity to news—is called *pitching*. The following hints may help achieve placement of a written release:

1. **Know deadlines.** Time governs every newspaper. Even with the flexibility of the computer, newspapers have different deadlines for different sections of the paper. For example, *The New York Times* business section essentially closes down between 6:00 and 7:00 p.m. News events should be scheduled, whenever possible, to accommodate deadlines. An old and despised practice (at least by journalists) is to announce bad news on Friday afternoon, the premise being that newspaper journalists won't have time to follow up on the story and that few people will read Saturday's paper anyway. Although this technique may work on occasion, it leaves reporters and editors feeling hostile.

2. **Generally write, don't call.** Reporters are barraged with deadlines. They are busiest close to deadline time, which is late afternoon for morning newspapers and morning for afternoon papers. Thus, it's preferable to mail or send news releases by messenger rather than try to explain them over the telephone. Follow-up calls to reporters to "make sure you got our release" also should be avoided. If reporters are unclear on a certain point, they'll call to check.

3. **Direct the release to a specific person or editor.** Newspapers are divided into departments: business, sports, style, entertainment, and so on. The release directed to a specific person or editor has a greater chance of being read than one addressed simply to "Editor." At smaller papers, a few people may handle all news. Public relations people should know who covers their beat and target releases accordingly.

4. **Determine how the reporter wants to be contacted.** E-mail, mail, fax, paper, and so on: Treat the reporter as the client. How he or she prefers to get the news should guide how you deliver it.

5. **Don't badger.** Newspapers are generally fiercely independent about the copy they use. Even a major advertiser will usually fail to get a piece of puffery published. Badgering an editor about a certain story is bad form, as is complaining excessively about the treatment given a certain story. Worst of all, little is achieved by acting outraged when a newspaper chooses not to run a story.

6. **Use exclusives, but be careful.** Reporters get credited for getting "scoops" and citing "trends." So public relations people might promise exclusive stories to particular newspapers. The exclusive promises one publication or other news source a scoop over its competitors. Although the chances of securing a story are heightened by the promise of an exclusive, the risk of alienating the other papers exists. Thus, the exclusive should be used sparingly.

7. **When you call, do your own calling.** Reporters and editors generally don't have assistants. Most do not like to be kept waiting by a secretary calling for the boss. Public relations professionals should make their own initial and follow-up

calls. Letting a secretary handle a journalist can alienate a good news contact. Above all, be pleasant and courteous.

8. **Don't send clips of other stories about your client.** This will just suggest to the journalist that others have been there before him or her and make the story potential less attractive.

9. **Develop a relationship.** Relationships are the name of the game. The better you know a reporter, the more understanding and accommodating to your organization he or she will be.

10. **Never lie.** The cardinal rule.

Although cynics continue to predict "the end of reading as we know it," newspapers and magazines continue to endure. Magazines, as noted, are proliferating. They range from the mainstream *Time* and *Newsweek* to the trendy, not to mention just a tad egotistical, *O,* the Oprah Winfrey magazine, and *Martha Stewart Living;* from the gossipy *People* and *Vanity Fair* to one publication so exclusive, it has no name. To get a subscription, you have to hold a Centurion card offered by American Express, by invitation only to those who spend at least $200,000 a year on their credit card. In fact, "controlled circulation" magazines that "pick you" now number more than 300 in the United States.[11]

The fact remains that dealing with the print media is among the most essential technical skills of the public relations professional. Anyone who practices public relations must know how to deal with the press. Period.

Online Publicity

With online outlets increasing in numbers and use, it is important to consider how to secure online publicity. While those who predicted that the Internet would change public relations thinking forever are wrong, it's still a "relationship business"—seeking Internet outlets for publicity is an important complement to publicity in more traditional media.

Knowledge of Web hosting and Web casting and online printing and chat rooms and discussion groups and investor "threads" and all the rest are critical for modern public relations people. At the top of this list of Internet public relations tools is knowledge of online publicity.

Here, in summary, are the several vehicles that form the nucleus of online publicity.

- **News releases.** What else? The news release forms the backbone of all publicity, and that applies as well to online efforts. The release is the document that lets the media know what might merit coverage.

  On the Internet, news releases are delivered by e-mail and should be shorter than their offline counterparts. Often the Internet "release" is more an *editorial advisory* to interest a journalist in a story.

- **Announcements.** An announcement is posted to online discussion groups, including Usenet newsgroups, Internet mailing lists, forums on commercial online services, and discussion threads built into Web sites.

  Like a news release, an announcement is short—a few paragraphs—and designed to encourage readers to visit a Web site or request further information. Announcements are used to promote online events, chats, or sites.

- **Links.** Links are vehicles that transport readers to Web sites. On the surface, a link is an image or a word that, once clicked, retrieves a file for the reader. When a link is activated, a new Web site appears on screen.

    Links are important publicity vehicles in that they immediately and automatically deliver the audience to a Web site being promoted. Indeed, links are the simplest way to get potentially interested parties to visit Web sites. Links also take viewers to new pages within the current site.

- **Newsletters.** Online newsletters are used to keep audiences updated on new products, services, issues, or events. Newsletters are easy and cheap to set up online. They also provide a continuing point of contact with key publics through automatic e-mail delivery.

    As with any other vehicle written for the Internet, online newsletters should be more succinct than print counterparts. One-paragraph items are standard fare. Also, the graphic touches of print newsletters have little relevance on the Web.

- **Libraries.** The ability of the Web to cheaply store vast quantities of information online is a clear advantage over print. Online news releases or announcements can be "backed up" with a library of supporting data at a Web site—support files, product brochures and facilities statements, backgrounders, press kits, frequently asked questions (FAQ) files, newsletters, events calendars, interview transcripts, help files, audio sound bites, video clips, press clips, and more. A well-structured library of supporting data adds depth to online publicity efforts and makes responding to inquiries as easy and instantaneous as pushing a button.

- **Public Appearances.** Online chat sessions can be the equivalent of offline press conferences or public forums. Chats allow special guests to entertain questions from online audiences in a real-time format. Also possible are "dead chats," where guests (still very "live") answer questions that have been solicited in advance and posted in the form of an interview. Finally, there is the cyber-media tour, which links the spokesperson with television, radio, Web site, and print journalists via satellite, the Web, and telephone simultaneously. The cyber-media tour takes advantage of streaming video and audio, both becoming commonplace in Web usage.

- **Promotions.** Internet users are notorious giveaway fanatics. Entering a sweepstakes online is so easy that such promotions often make eminent sense. Promotions—treasure hunts, trivia contests, coupons, quizzes, surveys, and the like—are often tied to other online activities, such as the launch of a new Web site or a major Web event.

- **Events.** Staging events is another way to draw reporters and other publics online. Popular events include movie sneak previews, concerts broadcast online, candidate debates, roundtable forums, Web site grand openings, conventions, and trade shows.

    As the Internet has become a more commonplace communications vehicle, the bar for Web events has been raised. A new Web site is no longer cause for attention. Nor is an online news conference. So a Web event today, to attract publicity, must be really "big."[12]

Although establishing a relationship with online reporters may not be as easy as with print journalists because of the physical remoteness, the same principle still holds: The closer you are to reporters, the more fairly they will treat you.

Dealing with the Wires

Wire services are a compulsory vehicle for distributing news. The Associated Press, founded in 1848, is the largest and oldest news organization in the world. AP's mission is to provide news to the world, via its wire, when it happens, wherever it happens. With 240 bureaus and more than 15,000 clients worldwide, AP is the general news leader. It and the three primary financial wires—Dow Jones, Reuters, and Bloomberg—actively report news of the largest companies around the clock. However, these wires are selective in the news they choose, so public relations professionals may or may not be successful in having their announcements carried by these free wire services.

Accordingly, because the onslaught of 21st-century competition to make news is so ferocious, organizations of even moderate size should consider using one of the paid wire services to make their voices heard. These are wires that guarantee use of your material (you pay them!), and then they, in turn, distribute your material to media outlets. News rooms regularly check the paid wires for information of interest.

The three paid wire services, PR Newswire, Business Wire, and Market Wire, charge a flat fee for distributing releases. Prices vary: PR Newswire charges $635 for the first 400 words and $170 for each additional 100 words; Business Wire charges $595 and $150; and Market Wire charges $175 and $50. Market Wire, the upstart of the group, was founded as an Internet-based company that created computer technology to disseminate public relations material.

In preparing copy for paid wires, public relations professionals must consider the following:

- **Always include headlines.** This is essential. Most editors receive wire service copy over their computers, and all they initially see is the headline, so it must be eye-catching and provocative.

- **The "lead" is critical.** The lead or first paragraph generally determines whether the release will be used. Include the dateline of the release so the editor knows the place and date of release.

- **Identify the stock symbol.** One purpose of the release is to get it into as many online databases as possible. Therefore, public companies must list right after the first mention of their name the stock symbol of the release originator and the symbol of any other public entity mentioned—for example, "(Nasdaq Goog)" for Google. This is the key to database entry.

- **Include contact names and numbers at the end.** Reporters must know whom to call for accuracy and follow-up.

- **Specify timing.** The busiest times of day are 8:00 to 9:30 a.m. (prior to stock market openings) and 4:00 to 5:00 p.m. (after markets close). The best policy is to try to avoid peak hours so that organizational announcements have a better chance of being read.

- **Specify targets.** The list of targeted recipients is up to you. Part of a paid wire service's job is to feed the release to any media outlet you indicate.

- **Check for accuracy.** Wires make mistakes. In the final analysis, the wire copy is your responsibility.

Beyond the wire services, feature syndicates, such as the Washington Post Syndicate, North American Newspaper Alliance, and King Features, are another source of editorial material for newspapers and magazines. They provide subscribing newspapers with a broad spectrum of material, ranging from business commentaries to comic strips

Speaking of Ethics

Condemning the Prize-Winning Wire Photo

There's always second-guessing when the Pulitzer Prize winners are named for outstanding journalism. But when the Associated Press won the award for breaking news photography in 2005, for depicting the war in Iraq, conservative bloggers went bananas.

The bloggers were incensed that one of the AP's winning photos, which captured at close range the murder of an Iraqi election worker by an insurgent, seemed to indicate a collaboration between the murderers and the photographer (Figure 9-7).

The AP's director of photography called the charges "outrageous and implausible, given the high journalistic standards that we have." He explained that the photographer, a stringer whose identity the AP refused to divulge, had gone to the site to take pictures after receiving a tip about vehicles burning from an earlier attack. The execution that won the prize, the AP said, occurred unexpectedly.

Bloggers were outraged that the Pulitzer Prize committee didn't discuss the issues raised before bestowing the prize. Said the chairman of the committee, who acknowledged that he was unaware of the controversy, "I think it's a valid cricism to say, 'This is gruesome. This is horrible. What can we do about this?' On the other hand, it's a gruesome situation. It's a war."

FIGURE 9-7 Questionable shot? A Pulitzer Prize-winning photo, depicting a gunman killing an Iraqi election worker on a Baghdad street, drew condemnation from bloggers, who suspected collusion between the photographer and the killers. (AP Wide World Photos)

For further information, see "Blogs Incensed Over Pulitzer Photo Award," *The New York Times,* (April 11, 2005): C9.

to gossip columns. Some of their writers—such as Maureen Dowd, Dave Barry, and Jane Bryant Quinn—have built national reputations. Many such columnists are open to source material provided by public relations personnel.

Measuring Publicity

After an organization has distributed its press materials, it needs an effective way to measure the results of its publicity. A variety of outside print and online services can help.

Media Directories

A variety of directories exist that describe in detail the various media. From *Editor & Publisher* and *News Media Yellow Book,* which list media across the United States, to *Bacon's Publicity Checker,* which focuses on trade and business publications, to specialized directories such as *Hudson's Washington News Media Directory* and the *Anglo-Jewish Media List*—these resources help public relations people target their publicity efforts.

Press Monitoring Bureaus

Press clipping bureaus monitor company mentions in the press, supplying news-paper and magazine clippings on any subject and about any company. The largest, Burrelles*Luce,* an amalgam of the two foremost companies in the field, receives hun-dreds of newspapers and magazines daily and dispatches nearly 50,000 clippings to clients each day, subscribing to about 1,700 daily newspapers, 8,300 weeklies, 6,300 consumer and trade magazines, as well as providing online monitoring.

Other Web-only monitoring services include eWatch (www.ewatch.com) and Deja News (www.dejanews.com). Both track Web hits for customer names across the World Wide Web.

Broadcast Transcription Services

Specialized transcription services monitor broadcast stories. A handful of such broad-cast transcription services exist in the country, with Radio-TV Reports and the Video Monitoring Service the largest, monitoring major radio and TV stations around the clock, checking for messages on client companies, and distributing video tapes, DVDs, CDs, and transcripts.

Media Distribution Services

Public relations people often resort to outside agencies to assist in distributing releases and other press materials. Media Distribution Services' Mediamatic database contains more than 250,000 editorial contacts by name and "beat" covered. PR Newswire offers a related service, Profnet, an online service that notifies subscribers several times daily with leads about journalists working on specific topics.

Content Analysis Services

A more sophisticated analysis of media results is supplied by firms that evaluate the content of media mentions on clients. Firms such as Ketchum Public Relations, Carma In-ternational, Delahaye Medialink, and PR Data use computer analysis to find positive and negative mentions about organizations, thus helping obtain a clearer idea of their portrayal by the media.

Handling Print Interviews

Another primary task of public relations people is to coordinate interviews for their ex-ecutives with the media. Most executives are neither familiar with nor comfortable in such interview situations. For one thing, reporters ask a lot of searching questions, some of which may seem impertinent. Executives aren't used to being put on the spot. In-stinctively, they may resent it, and thus the counseling of executives for interviews has become an important and strategic task of the in-house practitioner as well as a lucra-tive profession for media consultants.

In conducting interviews with the media, the cardinal rule to remember is that such interviews are not "intellectual conversations." Neither the interviewee nor the inter-viewer seek a lasting friendship. Rather, the interviewer wants only a good story, and the interviewee wants only to convey his or her key messages.

Talking Points

One-Minute Media Relations

How well would you do if you were asked to go toe-to-toe with a reporter? Take this yes-or-no quiz and find out. Answers follow.

Questions

1. When addressing a print reporter or electronic medium moderator, should you use his or her first name?
2. Should you ever challenge a reporter in a verbal duel?
3. Are reporters correct in thinking that they can ask embarrassing questions of anyone in public office?
4. Should you answer a hypothetical question?
5. Should you ever say "No comment"?
6. When a reporter calls on the telephone, should you assume that the conversation is being taped?
7. Do audiences remember most of the content of a television interview 30 minutes after it is broadcast?
8. Should you ever admit you had professional training to handle the media?
9. If you don't know the correct answer to a reporter's question, should you try to answer it anyway?

Bonus Question

What did Henry Kissinger say at the start of his press briefings as secretary of state?

Answers

1. Yes. In most cases, using first names is the best strategy. It makes the discussion much more conversational and less formal than using Mr. or Ms.
2. No. Most people should try to gain goodwill in an interview. This is rarely achieved by getting into an acrimonious debate.
3. Yes. Journalists must be suspicious of any claim by a public person that he or she is telling not only the truth but also the whole truth. Anyone in public office must be prepared to respond to such questions.
4. No. Avoid hypothetical questions. Rarely can you win by dealing with them.
5. No. It is tantamount to taking the Fifth Amendment against self-incrimination. You appear to be hiding something.
6. Yes. Many state laws no longer require the "beep" that signals a taped call. Always assume that everything you say is being recorded and will be used.
7. No. Studies have found that audiences remember only 60 percent of the content after 30 minutes. They remember 40 percent at the end of the day and 10 percent by the end of the week.
8. Yes. By all means. You should point out that good communication with the public is a hallmark of your organization and that you're proud it has such a high priority.
9. No. Don't be afraid to say, "I don't know." Offer to find the answer and get back to the interviewer. Don't dig yourself into a hole you can't get out of.

Bonus answer: "Does anyone have any questions ... for my answers?"

Accordingly, the following 10 do's and don'ts are important in newspaper, magazine, or other print interviews:

1. **Do your homework in advance.** An interviewee must be thoroughly briefed—either verbally or in writing—before the interview. Know what the interviewer writes, for whom, and his or her opinions. Also, determine what the audience wants to know.

2. **Relax.** Remember that the interviewer is a person, too, and is just trying to do a good job. Building rapport will help the interview.

3. **Speak in personal terms.** People distrust large organizations. References to "the company" and "we believe" sound ominous. Use "I" instead. Speak as an individual, as a member of the public, rather than as a mouthpiece for an impersonal bureaucracy.

4. **Welcome the naive question.** If the question sounds simple, it should be answered anyway. It may be helpful to those who don't possess much knowledge of the organization or industry.

5. **Answer questions briefly and directly.** Don't ramble. Be brief, concise, and to the point. An interviewee shouldn't get into subject areas about which he or

she knows nothing. This situation can be dangerous and counterproductive when words are transcribed in print.

6. **Don't bluff.** If a reporter asks a question that you can't answer, admit it. If there are others in the organization more knowledgeable about a particular issue, the interviewee or the practitioner should point that out and get the answer from them.

7. **State facts and back up generalities.** Facts and examples always bolster an interview. An interviewee should come armed with specific data that support general statements. Again, the practitioner should furnish all the specifics.

8. **If the reporter is promised further information, provide it quickly.** Remember, reporters work under time pressures and need information quickly to meet deadlines. Anything promised in an interview should be granted soon. Forgetting (conveniently) to answer a request may return to haunt the organization when the interview is printed.

9. **There is no such thing as being off the record.** A person who doesn't want to see something in print shouldn't say it. It's that simple. Reporters may get confused as to what was off the record during the interview. Although most journalists will honor an off-the-record statement, some may not. It's not generally worthwhile to take the risk. Occasionally, reporters will agree not to attribute a statement to the interviewee but to use it as background. Mostly, though, interviewees should be willing to have whatever they say in the interview appear in print.

10. **Tell the truth.** It sounds like a broken record, but telling the truth is the key criterion. Journalists are generally perceptive; they can detect a fraud. So don't be evasive, don't cover up, and, most of all, don't lie. Be positive but be truthful. Occasionally, an interviewee must decline to answer specific questions but should candidly explain why. This approach always wins in the long run. Remember, in an interview, your integrity is always on the line. Once you lose your credibility, you've lost everything.[13]

Press Conferences

Press conferences, the convening of the media for a specific purpose, are generally *not* a good idea. In fact, they can often prove suicidal.

Unless an organization has real news to communicate, press conferences can flop. Reporters don't have the time for meetings that offer little news. They generally don't like to schlep across town to hear news they could have received through a release. They also don't like learning of the news at the same time as their competitors.

Before attempting a conference, ask this question: Can this information be disseminated just as easily in a news release? If the answer is yes, the conference should be scratched.

Eventually, though, every organization must face the media in a conference—in connection with an annual meeting or a major announcement or a presentation to securities analysts. The same rules and guidelines that hold true for a one-on-one interview hold true for dealing with the press in conference. Be honest, forthright, and fair. Follow these additional guidelines in a press conference:

1. **Don't play favorites.** Invite representatives from all major news outlets. Normally, it makes sense to alert wire services, which in turn may have the resources to advise their print and broadcast subscribers. For example, the AP carries daily listings, called the "Daybook," of news events in major cities.

2. **Notify the media by mail well in advance.** Ordinarily, the memo announcing the event should be straightforward and to the point, listing the subject, date, time, and place. If possible, the memo should reach the editor's desk at least a week to 10 days before the event.

3. **Follow up early and often.** Journalists are notorious "no shows." They say they'll be somewhere and they don't make it. So follow up frequently to get an accurate expected count.

4. **Schedule the conference in midmorning.** Journalists get to work late and leave work later. They are on deadline in the afternoon, so 11 a.m. to noon is about right for most press conferences.

Talking Points

Confessions of a Media Maven

Dealing with the media for fun and profit, even for an experienced public relations hand, is a constant learning experience. It is also risky business. Consider the real-life case of an up-and-coming, daring, but wet-behind-the ears public relations trainee.

In the 1980s, many of the nation's largest banks were a bit jittery about negative publicity on their loans to lesser developed countries. One of the most vociferous bank bashers was Patrick J. Buchanan, a syndicated columnist who later became President Reagan's communications director and still later ran for president (Figure 9-8).

After one particularly venomous syndicated attack on the banks, the young and impetuous bank public affairs director wrote directly to Buchanan's editor asking whether he couldn't "muzzle at least for a little while" his wild-eyed columnist. The letter's language, in retrospect, was a tad harsh.

Some weeks later, in a six-column article that ran throughout the nation, Buchanan wrote in part:

Another sign that the banks are awaking to the reality of the nightmare is a screed that lately arrived at this writer's syndicate from one Fraser P. Seitel, director of public affairs of the Chase Manhattan Bank.

Terming this writer's comments "wrong," "stupid," "inflammatory," and "the nonsensical ravings of a lunatic," Seitel nevertheless suggested that the syndicate "tone down" future writings, "at least 'til the frenetic financial markets get over the current hysteria."*

Buchanan went on to describe the fallacy in bankers' arguments and ended by suggesting that banks begin immediately to cut unnecessary frills—such as "directors of public affairs!"

FIGURE 9-8 Thumbs down for the PR man. Syndicated columnist and presidential contender Patrick Buchanan wasn't thrilled with the "media relations skills" of one bright-eyed public relations hopeful. (AP Wide World Photos)

Moral: Never get into a shouting match with somebody who buys ink by the barrel.

Secondary moral: Just because you write a textbook doesn't mean you know everything!

*Patrick J. Buchanan, "The Banks Must Face Up to Losses on Third World Loans," New York Post (July 12, 1984): 35.

5. **Hold the conference in a meeting room, not someone's office.** You want enough space but not too much space. There's nothing worse than a sparsely attended event in an oversized room.

6. **The time allotted for the conference should be stated in advance.** Reporters should be told at the beginning of the conference how much time they will have. That will help keep people from drifting out at various intervals.

7. **Keep the speaker away from the reporters before the conference.** Mingling prior to the conference will only give someone an edge. Keep all reporters on equal footing in their contact with the speaker.

8. **Prepare materials to complement the speaker's presentation.** Just because journalists are there doesn't mean they'll write the story the way you'd like it. Therefore, press kits and releases are a must.

9. **Remember television.** This means prepare your executives for the entry of the Cro-Magnon persona. Television reporters, light technicians, and sound technicians are notorious for knocking things over, disrupting organized proceedings, and generally being clumsy. Prepare for the worst if you want television coverage. (And you do!)

10. **Let the reporters know when the end has come.** Just before the stated time has elapsed, the practitioner should announce to the reporters that the next question will be the last one.

11. **Cue the reinforcements.** The worst thing that can happen to you is that 10 minutes before the press conference, there is one bored reporter sitting among 30 empty chairs. When that happens (and, alas, it will), get on the phone to the public relations department and summon every last man, woman, and child to get upstairs with pads, pens, and trench coats to save your job.[14]

Last Word

When journalists were asked at the beginning of the 21st century how much respect they had for public relations people, less than half answered in the affirmative. That's the bad news. The better news is that the scores accorded public relations professionals ranked higher in the eyes of these scribes than did the scores of lawyers, salespeople, celebrities, or politicians.[15] So there's always hope. On the other hand, it must be acknowledged that journalists still regard public relations people with suspicion and maybe even (though they won't admit it) envy.

As is true of any other specialty in public relations work, the key to productive media relations is professionalism. Because management relies principally on public relations professionals for expertise in handling the media effectively, practitioners must not only know their own organization and management

but also be conversant in and respectful of the role and practice of journalists.

Indeed, public relations professionals must understand the pressures a reporter faces daily—deadlines, spotty information, frequently uncooperative sources, and sometimes even danger.

All that has been discussed in this chapter must be practiced: sending journalists information that is newsworthy, knowing how to reach reporters most expeditiously, understanding that journalists have become more pressured to produce material that is "entertaining" and therefore potentially controversial for most organizations; and recognizing that a journalist has a job to do and should be treated with respect.

At the same time, all public relations practitioners should understand that their role in the news-gathering process has become more respected by journalists. As a former business/finance editor of the *New York Times,* once said:

> PR has gotten more professional. PR people can be a critical element for us. It makes a difference how efficiently they handle things, how complete the information is that they have at

hand. We value that and understand all the work that goes into it.[16]

Indeed, the best public relations–journalist relationship today—the only successful one over the long term—must still be based on mutual understanding, trust, and respect.

Discussion Starters

1. What is meant by the "devil's advocate" role of the media?
2. What is the current state of the newspaper industry?
3. What is the importance of objectivity to a reporter?
4. What are some of the key principles in dealing with the press?
5. What is the difference between advertising and publicity?
6. What is the value of publicity?
7. What are some of the keys in pitching publicity?
8. What are the several do's and don'ts of interviews?
9. What are several methods of online publicity?
10. Why are press conferences not advisable in most cases?

Top of the Shelf

Media Relations: From a Journalist's Perspective

David Henderson, Lincoln, NE: Universe, Inc., 2005.

David Henderson was an award-winning network news correspondent for CBS News, so he knows whereof he speaks. And just to make sure, Henderson interviewed 60 other journalists for insight on how public relations people can better work with the media. What he found was that, by and large, public relations people don't take the time either to get to know reporters or to learn what might be relevant for their readers or viewers. This, according to Henderson, is a key problem for the public relations profession.

While the author sees considerable challenge in the public relations professional–journalist relationship, he acknowledges that the former are needed by the latter. To earn better relationships, says Henderson, use the six-step model made famous by public relations pioneer Arthur Page: (1) tell the truth, (2) prove it with action, (3) listen to the audience, (4) manage for tomorrow, (5) conduct public relations as if the whole organization depends on it, and (6) remain calm, patient, and good-humored.

CASE STUDY

Bagging the Elusive Exclusive

"How can we maximize publicity on the new survey?" asked Sarah Jane Persimmon, vice president for public relations of Quagmire, Incorporated.

Quagmire, one of the nation's largest asset management firms, catering to the wealthiest Americans, had finished conducting its first survey of the "Attitudes of the Affluent." The survey had been the brain child of Quagmire President R. Ulrich Widmee.

President Widmee had been hopeful that by maximizing publicity on the survey's findings. Quagmire would be linked positively to its target audience. "What would be great," he told Sarah Jane as they discussed the survey, "would be a major piece in the *Wall Street Journal* that our clients would notice."

He left it to Sarah Jane and her public relations department to figure out how to achieve the firm's publicity goals.

"I've got it," breathlessly responded Samantha Shram, one of the department's newest associates. "Let's have a press conference and have the president preside."

Sarah Jane was loath to stage a press conference, aware of the liabilities that press conferences always evoked. But this time, in light of the company's new survey data, she was intrigued.

The survey had revealed that despite terrorist attacks and stock market declines, affluent Americans were still optimistic about the economy and the market.

"This should be big news," Sarah Jane said. "The entire business press will be interested, and I'm certain we can get R. U. on the cable channels too. So we need a splash, and a press conference may just be the ticket. Samantha, you take charge."

"Gladly," answered Samantha.

The Media Plan

Samantha's first step was to devise the media plan, including targets and literature. She decided to invite all the leading business dailies and periodicals, as well as CNN, CNBC, Fox News, MSNBC, and the local Chicago affiliates. She planned to notify the media with a "media advisory" on Tuesday, alerting them to a "news conference of major significance next Monday."

She recommended and Sarah Jane agreed that President R. U. Widmee would host the conference and reveal the findings of the survey. It would be held in the wood-paneled Quagmire boardroom. Canapes, finger sandwiches, and assorted cookies would be available. (Samantha knew the press had a "nose for news" and a "stomach for food.")

Samantha carefully worded the advisory, so as not to give away the primary findings. She wrote:

> The results of Quagmire, Inc.'s first survey of the most affluent Americans will be revealed by President R. Ulrich Widmee at 11 a.m. Monday in Quagmire's boardroom.
>
> Among the findings that will be reported [are]:
> 1. Affluent attitudes post terrorist attacks and stock market losses
> 2. Affluent confidence or lack thereof in the economy and the administration
> 3. Affluent investment strategy in an uncertain time
> 4. Affluent primary concerns for their children and themselves
>
> We know this will be a much-discussed survey, and we hope you can be with us.

In light of the subject matter, the prestige of Quagmire, and the fact that the company's president would preside, Samantha felt con-

fident she would draw a full house on Monday. She messengered the advisories to every top journalist in town.

The Exuberant Response

By Thursday, Quagmire had already received 10 acceptances to the press conference, including the *New York Times,* CNN, *Chicago Tribune,* and *Chicago Sun Times,* among others.

"This is going to be great," Sarah Jane exulted to Samantha. "You're doing a great job."

And Samantha, in all humility, agreed with her superior officer's assessment, particularly when she got the encouraging voice mail from Max Womflash, the *Wall Street Journal's* asset management editor.

"I got your note about the new survey. It sounds intriguing. Please call me."

"Bingo," shouted Samantha. "The *Journal* is hot to trot."

She dialed back immediately to reel in the big fish.

The Fly in the Punch Bowl

"Max, hi, Samantha Shram returning your call."

"Hey Samantha. Listen, this survey of yours sounds fascinating. We're very interested and would like to take a look at it."

"Great, Max. But I'm afraid you'll have to wait until Monday for that. But I know R. U. would love to speak with you personally about it, maybe just after the press conference."

"Samantha, you don't understand. We really need to see the survey *before* the press conference. If we like it and can have it exclusively before the press conference, then we'll run a piece in the *Journal* on Monday morning."

"But, Max, that's the day of our press conference. If you run the story in advance of the press conference, I'm going to have 20 very upset journalists on my hands."

"I guess that's why they pay you the big bucks, Samantha. Anyway, the only way we'll use the story is if we run it in advance. If we can't get it early, then we won't be at the press conference. Sorry. But them's the rules."

"Max, you're putting me in an impossible box."

"Sorry about that. I don't need a decision on it right now, but I will need one in an hour. Let me know."

Questions

1. What are Samantha's options in deciding on a response?

2. What are the pros and cons of each option?

3. What are the key questions that must be asked in seeking to determine an appropriate response?

4. What would you do if you were Samantha?

Voice of Authority

An Interview with John Stauber

John Stauber is typically described as an "investigative journalist and left-wing advocate." As executive director of the Center for Media & Democracy, http://www.prwatch.org, Mr. Stauber is a prolific author. He and partner Sheldon Rampton are co-authors of *Toxic Sludge Is Good for You!, Mad Cow U.S.A.,* and *Trust Us, We're Experts!* Mr. Stauber is as "outspoken" a critic of the public relations industry as there is (as you will detect from his answers to the following questions). But despite that, he's still a real good guy. So read on — if you've got the guts.

How would you describe the practice of public relations?
In a single word, and quoting the father of "spin" Edward Bernays, public relations is propaganda. PR is a multi-billion dollar business conducted by professionals trained in communications and politics and employed primarily by businesses and governments to strategically manage public perceptions, opinions, information, and policy.

How is public relations looked at by journalists?
Most media professionals seem to flatter and fool themselves that they are immune to PR manipulations, while using public relations professionals to further their journalistic goals.

How much influence does public relations exert on the media?
PR professionals have tremendous influence with the media although media professionals generally fail to admit or recognize this fact. Of course, it is in the interest of PR professionals to also downplay their influence with the media to preserve the public myths of vetted journalism and courageous, independent news reporting. Academic studies attempting to measure how much of the news results from PR have typically found that 40% or more of what is read, seen, and heard in mainstream media is the result of, or heavily influenced by, public relations. For example, most Americans get most of their news from television, yet every year thousands of Video News Releases (VNRs) are aired by TV news producers as if they were their own independent reporting, constituting the largest ongoing plagiarism scandal in U.S. history.

What is the proper relationship between a reporter and a public relations professional?
From the standpoint of the reporter, the relationship must be viewed as adversarial, although of course the PR professional generally strives to position him or herself as a helpful facilitator or gatekeeper for the reporter.

Were you a reporter, how would you approach your dealings with public relations professionals?
I *am* a reporter and I view my relationship with any PR professional as adversarial.

Do you think public relations professionals serve any purpose?
PR professionals make life much easier for lazy and compliant journalists, and they generally strive to protect their clients in government and business from scrutiny, criticism, and reform.

If you could "fix" the practice of public relations, what steps would you take?
Propaganda will always exist within a democracy, but it's a nemesis. I strive to fix and strengthen news reporting by educating and informing journalists, researchers, citizens, and policy-makers about the realities of PR and propaganda. PR works best when it is an invisible manipulator of public perceptions; my job is to spray paint that Invisible Man with a bright safety orange. Democracies function best without hidden persuaders.

Suggested Readings

Beckwith, Sandra. *Complete Publicity Plans: How to Create Publicity that Will Spark Media Excitement and Exposure*. Avon, MA: Adams Media, 2003.

Crilley, Jeff. *Free Publicity: A TV Reporter Shares Secrets for Getting Covered on the News*. Dallas, TX: Charisma Press, 2003. Crilley, an Emmy Award–winning journalist from Dallas with more than two decades of TV news experience, tells readers that journalists want fun, interesting, newsworthy stories with good visuals.

D'Vari, Marisa. *Building Buzz: How to Reach and Impress Your Target Audience*. Franklin Lakes, NJ: Career Press, 2006. A primer, from soup to nuts, on securing publicity, including news release and interview tips, media training, and branding advice.

Goldberg, Bernard. *Bias*. Washington, DC: Regnery Publishing, 2001. The tell-all memoir of a conservative, former CBS News reporter, who argues that political correctness in network news rooms puts "sensitivity ahead of facts."

Howard, Carole M., and Wilma K. Matthews. *On Deadline: Managing Media Relations*, 3rd ed. Prospect Heights, IL: Waveland Press, 2000. This new, expanded edition includes the latest on Internet and e-mail media relations. The first chapter sets the new tone: "Technology and Tabloids: How the New Media Is Changing Your Job."

Levinson, Jay Conrad, Rick Frishman, and Jill Lublin. *Guerrilla Publicity*. Avon, MA: Adams Media, 2002. The latest in the Guerrilla series of books created by co-author Jay Conrad Levinson takes an aspiring public relations pro from grassroots efforts among friends to gain recognition for a product or service to the post-arrival stages of crisis management, cozying up to reporters and seeking outside counsel.

Marthis, Mark. *Feeding the Media Beast*. West Lafayette, IN: Purdue University Press, 2002. A 12-step guide to securing publicity, emphasizing such elements as difference, timing, simplicity, and emotion.

Mundy, Alicia. *Dispensing with the Truth*. New York: St. Martin's Press, 2001. A novel about corporate greed, government incompetence, and public relations agencies unfamiliar with the concept of "ethics."

O'Dwyer, Jack (Ed.). *O'Dwyer's Directory of Corporation Communications*. New York: J. R. O'Dwyer, annually. This guide provides a full listing of the public relations departments of thousands of public companies and shows how the largest companies define public relations and staff and budget for it.

O'Dwyer, Jack (Ed.). *O'Dwyer's Directory of PR Firms*. New York: J. R. O'Dwyer, annually. This directory lists thousands of public relations firms. In addition to providing information on executives, accounts, types of agencies, and branch office locations, the guide provides a geographical index to firms and cross-indexes more than 8,000 clients.

Parkhurst, William. *How to Get Publicity (And Make the Most of It Once You've Got It)*. New York: HarperBusiness, 2000.

Press, Bill. *Spin This*. New York: Pocket Books, 2001. The liberal, former CNN host suggests, surprisingly, that "all spin isn't bad" because "without it, the harsh truths of our time might be too tough to swallow."

Rampton, Sheldon, and John Stauber. *Weapons of Mass Deception: The Uses of Propaganda in Bush's War on Iraq*. New York: Tarcher/Penguin Press, 2003. The two irrepressible anti-Bush zealots are at it again with the aggressive publicity campaign that led to the invasion of Iraq. Right-wing conservatives beware.

Salzman, Jason. *Making the News: A Guide for Activists and Nonprofits*. London, UK: Westview Press, 2003. This former official with Greenpeace provides a provocative look at manufacturing publicity when you don't have much money. Such techniques as "wheatpasting," "wildposting," and "swimming in the cold New York harbor" are all discussed.

Schenkler, Irv, and Tony Herrling. *Guide to Media Relations*. Upper Saddle River, NJ: Prentice Hall, 2004. The book offers guidelines on all areas of media relations, including how to identify media contacts, establish relationships with reporters, prepare for media interviews, write news releases, and communicate with the financial media, among many other areas.

Stewart, Sally. *Media Training 101: A Guide to Meeting the Press*. New York: John Wiley & Sons, 2003. Written by a former *USA Today* journalist, this book gives insight into how reporters think, what appeals to them, and what doesn't.

Trump, Donald, and Robert Slater. *No Such Thing as Over-Exposure*. Upper Saddle River, NJ. Pearson Prentice-Hall, 2005. And, of course, there isn't, particularly if you're a self-inflated megalomaniac who can afford to hire a competent business writer willing to sacrifice his pride to extol the virtues of a somewhat questionable man of wealth and privilege. (And that's the good part.)

Warren, Lissa. *The Savvy Author's Guide to Book Publicity*. New York: Caroll & Graf Publishers, 2004. Lots of people are authors, and precious few sell books. That's why book publicity is a special art that requires special expertise. This is as good an explanation as any.

Yale, David R., and Andrew J. Carothers. *The Publicity Handbook*. Lincolnwood, IL: NTC Business Books, 2001. Inside tips from more than 100 journalists and public relations professionals.

Notes

1. Lynne Duke, "The Reporter's Last Take: In an Era of Anonymous Sources, Judy Miller is a Cautionary Tale of the Times," *Washington Post*, November 10, 2005, C01.
2. Interview with Ari Fleischer, for *The Practice of Public Relations*, 9th ed., August 7, 2002.
3. Jennifer Harper, "Journalists, Public Know Little About Press Freedom," *Washington Times*, May 16, 2005, A3.
4. Eric Dash, "Newspapers' Circulation Still Going Down," *New York Times*, May 3, 2005, C2.
5. Katharine Q. Seelye, "Newspaper Daily Circulation Down 2.6%," *New York Times*, November 8, 2005, C6.
6. Jennifer Harper.
7. David T. Z. Mindichi, "The New Journalism," *Wall Street Journal*, July 15, 1999, A18.
8. Sathnam Sanghera, "How Corporate PR Has Turned into the Art of Stonewalling, *Financial Times*, February 10, 2006.
9. "Survey: Half of Reporters Use Blogs," *Jack O'Dwyer's Newsletter*, June 29, 2005, 3.
10. Lee Berton, "Avoiding Media Land Mines," *Public Relations Strategist*, Summer 1997, 16.
11. Michael Hastings and Yepoka Yeebo, "Luxurious Reading," *Newsweek*, October 17, 2005, E24.
12. Steve O'Keefe, *Publicity on the Internet*, New York: John Wiley & Sons, 1997.
13. Fraser P. Seitel, "Preparing the CEO for a Print Interview," odwyerpr.com, July 11, 2001.
14. Fraser P. Seitel, "Press Conferences," odwyerpr.com, April 17, 2001.
15. Adam Leyland, "Journalists Grudging Respect for PR Execs," *PR Week*, September 20, 1999, 1.
16. "Getting into the Times: How Andrews Views PR," *Across the Board*, August 1989, 21.

10 Electronic Media Relations

In the 21st century—with apologies to all the bloggers and talk radio ditto heads and distinguished newspaper editors and reporters—television is still the "800-pound gorilla."

Most Americans still spend more hours in front of a television set than occupied by any other communications medium. According to one study that tracked the media consumption habits of 400 people from morning to night, television dominated. According to the 5,000 hours of observations recorded by project researchers, overall minutes per user per day broke down as follows:[1]

Television:	241 minutes
Computer use:	136 minutes
Internet:	93 minutes
Music:	65 minutes
Telephone:	42 minutes
Print media:	33 minutes
VCR/DVD	33 minutes
Newspapers:	12 minutes
Game console:	12 minutes

While television has retained its power, the medium itself has changed dramatically, particularly the delivery of television news, thanks, principally, to this man:

FIGURE 10-1 **Fake newsman.** Jon Stewart's *The Daily Show*, even though it spoofed the real news, nonetheless revolutionized television newscasts. (AP Wide Eorld Photos)

Comedian Jon Stewart was probably the last person anyone would have expected to revolutionize television news, but revolutionize it he did. Stewart's nightly *The Daily Show* on Comedy Central spoofed the news of the day in an irreverent, implausible, irrepressible manner and attracted 1.4 million viewers for its efforts. Stewart, some media analysts contended, was "as important in shaping political opinions as Walter Cronkite," the CBS dean of television news readers.[2] No wonder Stewart's show was a sought-after destination of every politician and newsmaker. The news Jon Stewart delivered may have been "fake," but lots of people believed him anyway.

The number of Americans turning to cable shows like *The Daily Show* was one of the most notable developments of the early years of the 21st century.*

By 2005, the overall audience for cable television news exceeded that for network television news by a narrow margin; 38 percent said they regularly watched cable news channels compared with 34 percent who regularly watched the nightly news on one of the three major broadcast networks.[3]

Such is the power in society of television—and right behind it, radio—as communications media. Television and radio are everywhere, which is both good and bad for society.

- Once, as noted, three television news networks dominated the airwaves. Today, in addition to NBC, CBS, and ABC, CNN, Fox News Channel, and MSNBC all hum along 24/7, keeping the nation and the world posted on the breaking news of the day.

- The effect is that Americans are provided with a continuous loop of unrelated national events that seem to all run together in perpetual images, from terrorism and kidnapped children to insider trading scandals and pending murder verdicts. One outgrowth of this is that by the time the average child graduates from elementary school, he or she will have witnessed at least 8,000 murders and more than 100,000 other assorted acts of violence on television.[4]

- Specialized cable networks, offering everything from food and fashion to weather and history, beam nonstop across the land. In the financial area alone, CNBC, Bloomberg Television, PBS Nightly Business Report, and other similar efforts have become enormously popular barometers of the nation's stock market appetite.

- Meanwhile, talk radio has become an enormous political and social force. Each week, mostly conservative talk show hosts lead call-in discussions of the issues of the day. The dean of this ilk, Rush Limbaugh, reaches a gargantuan 14.5 million listeners (known as "ditto heads" because they *always* agree with the host!). Liberals and progressives, starved for equal time, started their own radio network, Air America Radio, in 2004 to combat Limbaugh and his conservative armada.[5]

What makes the electronic media's news dominance so disconcerting—some would say scary—is that the average 30-minute television newscast would fill, in terms of words, only one-half of one page of the average daily newspaper! That means that if you're getting most of your news from television, you're *missing* most of the news.

*Jon Stewart may have been loosey-goosey, but the people he worked for sure weren't. In the winter of 2006, after Stewart took a disastrous turn hosting the Academy Awards in Hollywood, a hypersensitive Comedy Central responded to a kindly, public relations textbook author's simple request for an official Stewart photo with a terse, "We will be unable to license an image of Jon Stewart to you for use in this project." So there.

The electronic media undoubtedly will remain a force in the new millennium. Given the extent to which the electronic media dominate society, public relations people must become more resourceful in understanding how to deal with television and radio.

24/7 Television News

Video news, in particular, has overwhelmed society. In the 21st century, no situation comedy, ensemble drama, miniseries, movie, or documentary—not even programs about becoming a 30-second celebrity or marrying a millionaire!—dominate American television the way news and talk shows do.

After the terrorist attacks on America in 2001, according to the Pew Internet and American Life Project, more than 80 percent of Americans relied primarily on television for coverage of the unfolding drama. Indeed, on Tuesday, September 11, 2001, 77 million viewers turned to television news to find out what was happening in New York, Washington, and Pennsylvania.

In the daytime, it's wall-to-wall stock market coverage on CNBC and Bloomberg television and sports coverage on ESPN, ESPN 1, 2, 3, and so on. In the evening, it's the nightly network news on ABC, CBS, and NBC; the higher brow, more relaxed *News Hour with Jim Lehrer* on PBS; the perpetual news cycle on CNN, MSNBC, and Fox News; the news-oriented gabfests of *Crossfire, Hardball, The O'Reilly Factor, Larry King Live,* ad nauseum; the news magazines of *60 Minutes, 20/20,* and *NBC Dateline;* not to mention the local news. Even the weekends are loaded with news/talk shows, such as *Meet the Press, Face the Nation,* and ABC's *This Week*. Moreover, in times of national crisis—for example, a kidnapping, a car chase, a terrorist attack, an airplane crash—television news is there immediately and nonstop.

The credit for the rise of television news around the world has been the growth of the Cable News Network (CNN), the brainchild of controversial entrepreneur Ted Turner. CNN—which competitors mocked as "Chicken Noodle Network" when it began nearly 30 years ago—today reaches hundreds of millions of people around the world and is part of AOL Time Warner, the world's largest media empire.

The growth of cable television has created enormous new publicity placement possibilities for public relations professionals. Cable networks offer so-called "narrowcasting" opportunities for everyone—on the Food Channel, History Channel, Game Show Channel, Black Entertainment Television, MTV, VHI, National Empowerment Television, and others.

On the other hand, the push toward breathless investigatory reporting, nonstop issues discussion, and inflammatory commentary on television has created additional problems for public relations professionals assigned to ensure their organizations are treated with fairness.

■ News magazine programs have been attacked in recent years for occasional bias and distortion. The most celebrated news magazine dissembling came in 2004, when legendary anchorman Dan Rather used the CBS *60 Minutes II* forum to reveal internal Texas National Guard memos that indicated President George W. Bush was given preferential treatment to get into the Guard in the first place and then to miss numerous meetings. The report, secretly delivered by a Bush enemy, turned out to be bogus. Rather's producer and several associates were fired. In March 2005, Dan Rather stepped down as anchor and managing editor of the CBS Evening News.

- Talk shows, hosted by such personalities as Oprah Winfrey, Tony Danza, Bill O'Reilly, Chris Matthews, Paula Zahn, Rita Cosby, Geraldo Rivera, and Larry King, have become standard stomping grounds for politicians, authors, and anyone else seeking to sell a product or an issue.

- Finally, vying for the bottom of the television barrel was the gaggle of reality-based shows, pushing the boundaries of taste and tolerance, from *Unsolved Mysteries* and *Cops,* which staged reenactments of real-life events; to *Fear Factor, Dog Eat Dog,* and *Survivor,* which pit would-be actors against each other in cut-throat competition for million-dollar payoffs; to *The Surreal Life, Growing Up Gotti, The Anna Nicole Show,* and *My Big Fat Obnoxious Fiancé,* which. . . . well, never mind.

Speaking of Ethics

Judging the Judge at *American Idol*

In the early years of the 21st century, no television program was more powerful than Fox's *American Idol,* the talent contest that offered amateur entertainers a chance for riches and stardom—all for the price of a little humiliation before 30 million fixated viewers.

Idol judge Simon Cowell, an arrogant British music industry veteran, was especially noted for his venomous, unrelenting attacks on talent-challenged television wanna-be's. Much more understanding were Cowell's judging cohorts, record producer Randy Jackson and singer Paula Abdul (Figure 10-2).

The question of how "understanding" Abdul was came to national attention in the spring of 2005, when a former *Idol* contestant, Corey Clark, told ABC News *Primetime Live* that Abdul had provided him with off-camera tips and assistance while they engaged in an off-camera sexual relationship. He said she begged him not to talk about their relationship.

When the man was disqualified from the show after a previous criminal arrest was disclosed, he went public with his charges against *American Idol* and its judge. Fox said it would investigate the charges and responded sternly, "We recommend that the public carefully examine Mr. Clark's motives, given his apparent desire to exploit his prior involvement with *American Idol* for profit and publicity."

Said a stunned Abdul, "I will not dignify the false statements made by Corey Clark with a response." But Abdul's nondenial denial failed to quell the firestorm. To stifle the crisis completely, Abdul chose the time-tested method of self-deprecation, agreeing to poke fun at her own compromising situation on NBC's *Saturday Night Live.* Reportedly, after participating in a few awkward rehearsals, Abdul balked at appearing in the *SNL* skits about her. Instead, she sheepishly emerged after the skit was over to show that at least she was willing to appear.

FIGURE 10-2 Generous judge? *American Idol* judge Paula Abdul, flanked by co-judges Simon Cowell (left) and Randy Jackson, found herself in public relations crisis mode when a former contestant claimed a "special relationship" with her. (AP Wide World Photos)

In the end, Fox's investigation found insufficient evidence to hold Abdul responsible for breaking the network's code of conduct. However, the network also issued an enhanced "nonfraternization policy" between contestants, judges, and other *Idol* employees.

As for Corey Clark, he wound up as a "secret houseguest" on VH1's *The Surreal Life,* sharing the limelight with such notables as Flavor Flav and Brigitte Nielsen.

For further information, see "An Illicit Affair on 'American Idol,'" *abcnews.go.com,* May 3, 2005; and Fraser P. Seitel, "21st Century Crisis Management," *odwyerpr.com,* May 23, 2005.

As new *CBS News* anchor Katie Couric put it, "Some news coverage has become more salacious, more sensationalistic, less intelligent, more giving people what they want to hear or what you think they want to hear, rather than what you think they need to or should ideally hear."[6] Organizations have gone to great lengths to protect themselves from "ambush interviews" and unfair exposure on national television. The most famous case in public relations history occurred in 1979, when Illinois Power Company followed *60 Minutes* reporter Harry Reasoner with its own camera and produced a video that clearly indicated the CBS program's one-sided presentation.

Today, the "dumbing down" of television news has put added pressure on public relations people to deal cautiously when contemplating coverage of the organizations they represent.

Handling Television Interviews

Although appearing on television may indeed be dangerous for one's health, it nonetheless can also be most persuasive. Accordingly, as television has become a more potent channel of news, executives from all fields are being called on to air their views on news and interview programs. For the uninitiated and the unprepared, a television interview can be a harrowing experience—more pleasant than root canal, perhaps, but only slightly so.

To be effective on television takes practice. Executives must accept guidance from public relations professionals on how to act appropriately in front of a camera that never blinks. The following do's and don'ts may help:

1. **Do prepare.** Preparation is the key to a successful broadcast appearance. Executives should know the main points they wish to make before the interview begins. They should know the audience. They should know who the reporter is and something about the reporter's beliefs. They should also rehearse answering tough hypothetical questions before entering the studio. (Figure 10-3)

2. **Do be yourself.** Interviewees should appear relaxed. Smiles are appropriate. Nonverbal signs of tension (clenching fists, gripping the arms of a chair, or tightly holding one hand with the other) should be avoided. Gesturing with the palms opened, on the other hand, suggests relaxation and an eagerness to discuss issues. Giggling, smoking, or chewing gum should be avoided. Proper posture also is important.

3. **Do be open and honest.** Television magnifies everything, especially phoniness. If facts are twisted, it will show. On Television, a half-truth becomes a half-lie. Credibility must be established early.

4. **Do be brief.** Television and radio have no time for beating around the bush. Main points must be summarized at the beginning of sentences. Language must be understandable. Neither the reporter nor the public is familiar with technical jargon, so avoid it.

5. **Do play it straight.** An interviewee can't be giddy, vacuous, or irreverent. Attempts to be a comic may be interpreted as foolishness. Natural and relaxed use of appropriate humor may be a big plus in getting a point across. If humor doesn't come naturally, interviewees should play it straight. That way, they won't look stupid.

6. **Do dress for the occasion.** Bold patterns, checks, or pinstripes should be avoided; so should jewelry that shines or glitters. Skirts should fall easily below a woman's

FIGURE 10-3 Just chatting. Or at least that's the way it ought to seem in a Television interview, even though the key for an interviewee is to be prepared. (Courtesy of Fraser P. Seitel)

knees. Men's socks should be high enough to prevent a gap between socks and pants. Colors of shirts, socks, suits, and accessories generally should be muted.

7. **Don't assume the interviewer is out to get you.** Arguments and hostility come through clearly on Television, and the guest frequently comes out looking like the villain. Therefore, all questions, even naive ones, should be treated with respect and deference.

8. **Don't think everything you say will be aired.** Television is a quick and imperfect medium—very imperfect. A guest might be interviewed for 45 minutes and appear as a 10-second segment on a newscast. That's why an interviewee must constantly hammer home his or her main points.

9. **Don't let the interviewer dominate.** Interviewees can control the interview by varying the length and content of their responses. If a question requires a complicated answer, the interviewee should acknowledge that before getting trapped in an incomplete and misleading response. If interviewees make mistakes, they should correct them and go on. If they don't understand the question, they should ask for clarification.

10. **Don't say "No comment."** "No comment" sounds evasive, and most Americans assume it means "guilty." If interviewees can't answer certain questions, they should clearly explain why. Begging off for competitive or proprietary reasons is perfectly all right as long as some explanation is offered.

11. **Do stop.** One common broadcast technique is to leave cameras running and microphones on even after an interviewee has responded to a question. Often the

most revealing, misleading, and damaging statements are made by interviewees embarrassed by the silence. Don't fall for the bait. Silence can always be edited out later. Interviewers know this and interviewees should, too, especially before getting trapped.

These are just a few hints in dealing with what often becomes a difficult situation for the uninitiated. Most important, recognize that an interview is not an "intellectual conversation." You—or your client—are submitting to the interview for a purpose: to deliver your key messages to the public.[7] The best advice, then, for a television interviewee is to be natural, straightforward, and most of all, ready for battle.

Video News Releases

If it is true that most Americans get most of their news from television—and it is—then public relations people must try to get their organizations covered on the tube.

News releases in video form, known as video news releases (VNRs), have become standard tools in the practice of public relations. The best VNRs are those that cover "breaking" news—a press conference or news announcement that broadcasters would cover themselves if they had the resources. Such breaking-news VNRs are delivered by satellite directly to television newsrooms (Figure 10-4).

Satellite feeds of unedited footage, called B-roll, include a written preamble—story summary—and sound bites from appropriate spokespersons. The television stations then assemble the stories themselves, using as much or as little of the VNR footage as they see fit.

The second method of VNR delivery is for stories without a breaking news angle. These "evergreen" VNRs are usually delivered by cassette to broadcasters and are more timeless in terms of content.

Before a VNR is attempted, the following questions must be considered:

1. **What is a reasonable expectation of a VNR?** A well-done, timely VNR should receive 40 to 50 station airings with an audience of 2.5 to 3 million viewers. Some may reach more; others may not be used by stations at all.

2. **How should a VNR be distributed?** The answer is the same as with a print news release: any way the reporters want it. If a station prefers satellite or hard-copy cassette, give them what they want.

FIGURE 10-4 The real deal. Once a VNR makes it into a newsroom like CNN's and over the airwaves, few viewers question the story's authenticity or origination. (Courtesy of Mark Hill, CNN Image Source)

3. **Are you out of luck if a VNR doesn't get picked up?** Not necessarily. It can be lightly edited, removing the breaking-news aspect, and redistributed as an evergreen.

4. **How important is it to localize a VNR?** Localization—tailoring for local interest—is quite important. Anything that can be done to include local personalities, contacts, or statistics will help potential usage.

5. **Do all stations use VNRs?** Some say they don't. But virtually every Television station nationwide will use a VNR, at least in part. Much depends on the subject matter.

6. **What makes a good VNR?** It has to tell a story and tell it in television format: effective sound bites, graphics, and a short, punchy style. In other words, it has to look and feel just like the evening news.

7. **What kinds of subjects should a VNR treat?** The short answer is anything newsworthy and visual—a legitimate medical, scientific, or industrial breakthrough that the video clarifies or for which it provides a new perspective and helps a news department create a better story.

8. **When is a VNR not appropriate?** If a story has no visuals to complement it, save your money. Television is a visual medium. Without the pictures, you have little chance for making the airwaves. Also, you need a wide enough audience and a large enough budget.

9. **How much should a VNR cost?** They're not cheap. A nationally distributed VNR should cost $20,000 at a minimum, so the point is that it must be worth the expense.[8]

VNR Caveats

As noted, VNRs are not without risks. For one thing, they are expensive. They must be created, produced, packaged, and distributed professionally. Before a VNR is created—and because a good one is expensive—the following questions must be asked:

- Is the VNR needed?
- How much time do we have?
- How much do we have to spend to make the VNR effective?
- What obstacles must be considered, including bad weather, unavailability of key people, and so on?
- Is video really the best way to communicate this story?

Then, too, there is the controversy surrounding VNRs in general. In 1992, *TV Guide*, angered primarily by the Kuwaiti VNR distributed by Hill and Knowlton to build support for the Desert Storm offensive, labeled VNRs "fake news—all the PR that news can use." *TV Guide*'s researchers reported that although broadcasters used elements from VNRs, rarely were they labeled so that viewers could know their sponsor's identity.

A decade later, the "fake news" issue reappeared with a vengeance.

In 2005, the U.S. Department of Health and Human Services was excoriated for producing a VNR that praised the Bush administration's controversial new Medicare bill. The VNR featured a former television journalist-turned-public relations professional, posing as a reporter. One professor called the VNR an example of "PR's 'just fake it' mentality,"

Talking Points

When Is a Television Spokesman Not a Spokesman?

Answer? When he's an imposter.

At least that's what the vaunted British Broadcasting Company found out in the winter of 2004 when it did a story on the 20th anniversary of one of the world's worst industrial disasters at Bhopal, India. In 1984, escaping gas from a Union Carbide chemical plant killed 3,600 people.

To commemorate the event, *BBC World* interviewed a Paris spokesman for the company that bought Union Carbide in 2001, Dow Chemical. Or at least they *thought* the man was a Dow Chemical spokesman.

The "spokesman," identified as Jude Finisterra, stunned his interviewers by announcing that Dow Chemical "accepted responsibility" for the Bhopal disaster and had set up a multibillion-dollar compensation package to aid victims.

The BBC rushed the interview out to the wires. Reuters picked it up and ran with it. And BBC's international channel repeated the interview in a later broadcast.

The problem was that "Finisterra" was actually notorious hoaxer Andy Bichlbaum, a member of The Yes Men, a group based in Europe which initiates elaborate hoaxes on businesses and governments.

Bichlbaum aka Finisterra (which means "end of the earth") explained to an interviewer that his group had set up a Web site "that looked a lot like the real Dow Chemical Web site." Bichlbaum said the site fooled a lot of people.

Including, as it turned out, a particularly red-faced BBC.

For further information, see Jeffrey Goldfarb, "BBC Apologizes After Bhopal Hoax by Dow Imposter," *Reuters,* December 3, 2004, and "Yes Men Hoax on BBC Reminds World of Dow Chemical's Refusal to Take Responsibility for Bhopal Disaster," *democracynow.org,* December 6, 2004.

and one U.S. senator called the VNR "covert propaganda."[9] The next year, the Senate Commerce Committee approved a bill requiring so-called "prepackaged news," funded by the government, to reveal their origins.[10]

Despite their problems, the fact remains that if an organization has a dramatic and visual story, using VNRs—properly labeled—may be a most effective and compelling way to convey its message to millions of people.

Satellite Media Tours

The 21st-century equivalent to the sit-down, in-studio interview is the satellite media tour (SMT), which is a series of preset, direct, live interviews, conducted via satellite, between an organization's spokesperson and television station personalities across the nation or around the world.

An SMT originates with a subject speaking from one location, who is then whisked electronically from station to station where he or she enjoys on-air, one-on-one discussions. A derivative of the in-studio SMT is a remote SMT, which originates on location from a site outside the studio.

Corporate executives, celebrities, and "experts" of every stripe have taken advantage of the privatization of satellites and downlink dishes at local television stations by conducting these rapid-fire "personalized" television interviews. Television stations, too, can benefit from SMTs, gaining unprecedented local access to major celebrities (Figure 10-5).

With or without a celebrity, a successful SMT relies on the immediate relevance of an organization's issue and message. In addition, several steps must be taken to ensure the viability of an SMT:

FIGURE 10-5 Celebrity SMTs. When Samsung honored sports and entertainment legends for their work with children, it offered local television stations the SMT opportunity to interview the likes of Magic Johnson, Arnold Palmer, Jon Bon Jovi (bordered by two Samsung execs), Wayne Gretzky, and Joe Torre. (Courtesy of HWH Public Relations)

1. **Defining objectives.** As in any public relations program, the organization's objectives must first be considered. What is the "news hook" required to interest stations? Who is the target audience? In which markets do we want interviews? What stations do we prefer? Within which programs on these stations will our interviews play best?

2. **Pitching the SMT.** Television producers must be contacted, first by letter and then by phone, about the availability of the organization's spokesperson. The key issue that must be stressed is news value. Press kits and background material should be sent to the stations at least two weeks in advance of the interview.

3. **Last-minute juggling.** Stations often request time changes. Maintain contact with station personnel, even when placed on a waiting list, so that any scheduling holes can be filled if a station cancels an interview close to the SMT date.

4. **Satellite time.** Satellite time needs to be contracted for well in advance to ensure that the SMT is aired when the organization wants it to be aired.

5. **B-roll: background footage.** B-roll video should be available to further illustrate the topic and enhance the interest of stations.

6. **Availability of dedicated phone lines.** Several dedicated phone lines to communicate with stations should be available, especially in case of interrupted feedback audio—in other words, static.

7. **Spokespersons briefing.** It is essential to brief spokespersons to avoid potential confusion on the names and locations of interviewers during an SMT. All

names should be written out on a studio TelePrompTer or on large cue cards, which the spokesperson should refer to before the interview. In addition, the spokesperson should become accustomed to the earpiece because the director's voice can be distracting initially.

8. **Consider controversy.** Don't worry about stirring up a storm; it often makes news.

9. **Avoid becoming too commercial.** Of course, the spokesperson is there to "plug" the organization or product, but don't overdo it or you won't be invited back. SMTs can save time and streamline logistics for any organization. But they are expensive—costing upwards of $20,000 for a 3-hour studio-produced tour reaching 12 to 20 outlets.[11]

The latest wrinkle in SMTs is video podcasting, which make the SMT available as a Web posting on an MP3 player.

Public Service Announcements

The public service announcement (PSA) is a television or radio commercial, usually 10 to 60 seconds long, that is broadcast at no cost to the sponsor. Nonprofit organizations are active users of PSAs. Commercial organizations, too, may take advantage of PSAs for their nonprofit activities, such as blood drives, voter registration drives, health testing, and the like. The spread of local cable television stations has expanded the opportunity for placing PSAs on the air.

In the United States, radio and television stations allot a limited amount of airtime to PSAs and other service-oriented programming. In other countries, there may be opportunities for nonprofit organizations to purchase media time and space at a reduced cost.

Because broadcast and cable stations survive on advertising and PSAs are free, precious little time is devoted to them. The top four broadcast networks donate an average of 17 seconds an hour (five seconds in prime time) to PSAs. Cable networks donate an average of seven seconds an hour in prime time. Univision, the dominant Spanish-language network, donates 48 seconds per hour to PSAs. A significant portion of all PSAs—43 percent—are aired during the late-night hours between midnight and 6 a.m.[12]

PSAs can be grouped loosely into three categories:

1. **Public affairs:** information about environmental or public policy issues, such as voter registration campaigns.

2. **Public relations:** information about free-of-charge government, association, or corporate services, such as blood drives.

3. **Marketing communications:** information about safety, health, or lifestyle issues within a context that allows brand identification and even promotion of products and services in a generic way, such as in the areas of food, fitness, and nutrition.

Unlike news releases, PSAs are generally written in advertising-copy style: punchy and pointed. The essential challenge in writing PSAs is to select the small amount of information to be used, discard extraneous information, and persuade the listener to take the desired action. The following is a typical 20-second PSA:

President Bush asked all Americas to volunteer their time for the service of others. By giving of yourself, you are helping to improve yourself, your community, and doing your part to make a difference in the world.

The Volunteers of America need your help. Sign up today, and make someone's life a lot more fulfilling—yours.

This message is brought to you by the Advertising Council.

According to survey research, broadcasters use three primary criteria in determining which PSAs make the air: (1) sponsorship, (2) relevance of the message to the community, and (3) message design. In terms of sponsorship, the reputation of the sponsor for honesty and integrity is critical.

As to the relevance of the message, urgent social problems, such as health and safety issues and education and training concerns, all rank high with broadcasters. In message design, the more imaginative, original, and exciting the message, the better the chance of its getting free play on the air.

Growth of Talk Radio

Each week, 15 million people listen to radio, and talk radio listeners tune in about 21 percent more than all others. Talk radio has become an influential communications medium in contemporary America. Today, 17 percent of American adults regularly listen to ncws/talk radio. The talk radio audience is mostly male, middle-aged, well-educated, and conservative. Among those who regularly listen to talk radio, 41 percent are Republican and 28 percent are Democrats. By contrast, of the 16 percent of Americans who regularly listen to National Public Radio, 41 percent are Democrats and 24 percent are Republicans.[13]

With many downsized and outsized Americans working from home and many others on the road, the radio has returned as a primary communications medium. All-news, all-sports, and talk have become a steady communications diet for many Americans. According to journalist Mark Sommer, "Talk radio is the town meeting of our time. . . . Potentially the most democratic and interactive medium we have."[14]

Talk radio really emerged as a result of the 1987 repeal of the Fairness Doctrine, which opened the door to uninhibited discussion of controversial issues on the radio. Prior to that, opposing views had to be given equal time out of "fairness." The next year, Rush Limbaugh entered national syndication, and talk radio was off and running.

Part of the appeal of talk radio is that it offers almost every shade of opinion. And it's unfiltered; that is, talk radio cuts out the middleman. There is no reporter interceding between the listener and the speaker. Communication on talk radio, then, can be considered "purer" than other methods.

Talk radio is also among the only media in which the voices of "everyday people" can be heard immediately. No wonder: Talk radio must fill 24 hours of airtime each day, 168 hours a week, 8,736 hours a year. That's a lot of talk!

With FM radio dominated by music, talk radio has resurrected AM radio. Talk radio is still dominated by conservative viewpoints; it's estimated that 70 percent of talk radio hosts nationally are conservatives.[15] Indeed, the list of top talk radio hosts is overwhelmingly to the right of the aisle (Figure 10-6). Beyond commercial talk radio, there is the growth of satellite radio. In 2006, radio bad boy Howard Stern joined Sirius Satel-

---

The Top Talk Radio Audiences, Fall 2005

1. Rush Limbaugh
2. Sean Hannity
3. Michael Savage
4. Dr. Laura Schlessinger; Howard Stern
5. Laura Ingraham
6. Neal Boortz; Mike Gallagher
7. Jim Bohannon; Clark Howard; Bill O'Reilly; Doug Stephan
8. Glenn Beck; Dr. Joy Browne; Don Imus; George Noory
9. Jerry Doyle; Kim Komando; Michael Medved; Dave Ramsey
10. Bill Bennett; Jim Rome
11. Bob Brinker; Ed Schultz
12. Tom Leykis; G. Gordon Liddy
13. Jim Cramer; Al Franken; Tony Snow
14. Alan Colmes; Dr. Dean Edell; Phil Hendrie; Rusty Humphries; Stephanie Miller

---

FIGURE 10-6 Big talkers. According to *TALKERS* magazine, most of the leading talk show hosts are conservative, led by Rush Limbaugh, Sean Hannity, and Michael Savage, who cumulatively reach nearly 35 million people a week. (*TALKERS* magazine)

lite Radio, which together with XM Satellite—which signed Oprah Winfrey—boasts approximately 10 million subscribers. The expected growth of satellite radio will add to the increasing power of radio as a communications medium.

Securing Radio Publicity

What makes radio especially effective for public relations people is the sheer number of radio outlets in the United States. There are more than 13,000 radio stations but only 1,740 television broadcast stations, according to the *The World Factbook 2005*.

All-news radio stations—"You give us 20 minutes, we'll give you the world"—are regularly consulted for quick updates by people on the go. After the terrorist attacks on September 11, 2001, 11 percent of the public got most of their information from radio.[16]

Since 1990, the number of talk radio stations has almost tripled, from 405 to 1,130. Nonetheless, talk radio is still virgin territory for most public relations practitioners. Indeed, talk radio is one of the best-kept public relations secrets.[17]

Four aspects must be considered paramount in penetrating the radio market.

1. **Strong, focused message.** Stations must be given valuable information that will enhance the lives of listeners.

2. **Localization.** The local angle is key. The message must be tailored to suit the needs of targeted listeners.

3. **Positive spokespersons.** Spokespersons must radiate enthusiasm and goodwill. Since there are no visuals in radio, the vocal exuberance of the spokesperson is key. In fact, the voice becomes the vehicle through which key words and phrases must be delivered.

4. **Timeliness.** Finally, the message must be timely and topical. If not, a radio station won't be interested.

As with television, audio news releases (ANRs) and radio media tours (RMTs) are available as part of the public relations arsenal. ANRs, prepackaged interviews and sound bites—called *actualities*—sent to radio stations often have a difficult time making the air. One study reported that 80 percent of radio respondents said they never or rarely used ANRs. In most cases, radio stations said they would rather interview news sources directly.[18]

RMTs, on the other hand, are a cost-effective way to maximize a spokesperson's time by scheduling back-to-back telephone interviews with radio news directors and talk show hosts. Authors, for example, find RMTs a good way to promote a book around the country. The cost of RMTs is considerably less than their SMT equivalent. A typical RMT of 25 interviews would cost approximately $10,000.

Although radio, broadcasting 24 hours a day, is difficult to monitor, the growth in listenership makes the medium a prime choice for public relations professionals.

Last Word

The pervasiveness of television and radio in society has made it even more important for public relations professionals to be knowledgeable about the electronic media. Adding to the challenge is the trend of softer news and heightened sensationalism. If much of journalism today has become "entertainment," television and radio are the most guilty of the media.

As generations weaned on television enter the public relations field, familiarity with broadcast methods will increase. Indeed, one significant broadcast challenge is to attract younger viewers to the traditional broadcast networks' nightly news. A majority (56 percent) of those age 65 and older say they regularly watch nightly network news; only a quarter of those age 30 to 49 are regular viewers; and less than a third as many Americans under age 30 (18 percent) regularly watch these news programs.[19]

As cable television stations in particular proliferate and cable news continues to gain ground on the networks, the need for additional programming—for more material to fill news and interview holes—also will expand. Finally, as the Internet becomes more dominant as an electronic carrier—with streaming audio and video, video blogs, podcasting, and who knows what else—this will only add to the necessity that public relations professionals master the electronic media.

Advances in communications technology open the door to a new breed of public relations professional, comfortable with and proficient in the art of writing for, dealing with, and mastering the art of electronic communication.

Discussion Starters

1. Why has video become more important for public relations professionals?
2. How has the definition of news changed because of video?
3. What has happened over the years to the impact of network television news?
4. What are several keys to handling a television interview?
5. Is it a good idea for an executive to be spontaneous in a television interview?
6. Should an interviewee always try to be humorous?
7. When should an organization consider using a video news release?
8. What are the benefits of a public service announcement?
9. What is a satellite media tour, and when does it make sense?
10. How important to a public relations initiative is talk radio?

Top of the Shelf

60 Minutes

CBS Television News Magazine program

Still relevant after all these years—for decades, the most widely watched television program in the nation has been a Sunday night news magazine program that is the subject of fear and loathing for politicians, presidents, and corporate potentates.

60 Minutes, as the saying goes, has been often imitated, never duplicated—although weekdays, *60 Minutes II* now appears. The brainchild of news producer Don Hewitt, the show and its correspondents—Mike Wallace, Morley Safer, Dan Rather, Diane Sawyer, Lesley Stahl, Steve Kroft, the late Harry Reasoner, Ed Bradley, and others—have become synonymous with investigative television journalism.

In its first decade, *60 Minutes* was despised and avoided by most business organizations. They feared the consequences of a national television skewering, and most refused to be interviewed. Invariably, this cost them, because *60 Minutes* correspondents ordinarily don't accept "not available" or "no comment" for an answer.

In recent years, smart organizations have realized that, in some cases, it makes sense to cooperate with *60 Minutes.* Adolph Coors Company and Johnson & Johnson, for example, found that the program treated them fairly in the midst of terrible crisis.

Although Hewitt is gone and Wallace, Safer, and Bradley are on the way out, *60 Minutes,* miraculously, has retained its place at the top of electronic investigative journalism.

CASE STUDY

They're Heeere!

Suppose you gave a party and *60 Minutes* showed up at the door. Would you let them in? Would you evict them? Would you commit hara-kiri?

Those were the choices that confronted the Chase Bank at the American Bankers Association convention, when *60 Minutes* came to Honolulu to "get the bankers."

The banking industry was taking its lumps. Profits were lagging. Loans to foreign governments weren't being repaid. Financings to bankrupt corporations were being questioned. And it was getting difficult for poor people to open bank accounts.

Understandably, few bankers at the Honolulu convention cared to share their thoughts on camera with *60 Minutes.* Some headed for cover when the cameras approached. Others barred the unwanted visitors from their receptions. In at least one case, a *60 Minutes* cameraman was physically removed from the hall. By the convention's third day, the *60 Minutes* team was decrying its treatment at the hands of the bankers as the "most vicious" it had ever been accorded.

By the third night, correspondent Morley Safer and his *60 Minutes* crew were steaming and itching for a confrontation.

That's when *60 Minutes* showed up at our party.

For 10 years, with your intrepid author as its public affairs director, Chase Manhattan had sponsored a private convention reception for the media. It combined an informal cocktail party, where journalists and bankers could chat and munch hors d'oeuvres, with a more formal, 30-minute press conference with the bank's president. The press conference was on the record, no-holds-barred, and frequently generated news coverage by the wire services, newspapers, and magazines that regularly sent representatives. No television cameras were permitted.

But when we arrived at Honolulu's scenic Pacific Club, there to greet us—unannounced and uninvited—were Morley and the men from *60 Minutes,* ready to do battle.

The ball was in our court. We faced five questions that demanded immediate answers.

- **First, should we let them in?** What they wanted, said Safer, was to interview our president about "critical banking issues." He said they had been "hassled" all week and were "entitled" to attend our media reception. But we hadn't invited them. And they hadn't had the courtesy to let us know they were coming. It was true that they were members of the working press. It was also true that our reception was intended to generate news. So we had a dilemma.

- **Second, should we let them film the press conference?** Chase's annual convention press conference had never before been filmed. Television cameras are bulky, noisy, and intrusive. They threatened to sabotage the normally convivial atmosphere of our party. Equally disconcerting would be the glaring camera lights that would have to be set up. The *60*

Minutes crew countered that their coverage was worthless without film. Theirs, after all, was a medium of pictures, and without pictures, there could be no story. As appetizing as this proposition sounded to us, we were worried that if we refused their cameras, what they might film instead would be us blocking the door at an otherwise open news conference. So we had another problem.

- **Third, should we let them film the cocktail party?** Like labor leader Samuel Gompers, television people are interested in only one thing:"More!" In the case of our reception, we weren't eager to have CBS film the cocktails and hors d'oeuvres part of our party. We were certain the journalists on hand would agree with us. After all, who wants to see themselves getting sloshed on national television when they're supposed to be working?

- **Fourth, should we let them film a separate interview with our president?** Because few top people at the convention were willing to speak to CBS, *60 Minutes* was eager to question our president in as extensive and uninterrupted a format as possible. Safer wanted a separate interview before the formal press conference started. So we also had to deal with the question of whether to expose our president to a lengthy, one-on-one, side-room interview with the most powerful—and potentially negative—television news program in the land.

- **Fifth, should we change our format?** The annual media reception/press conference had always been an informal affair. Our executives joked with the journalists, shared self-deprecating asides, and generally relaxed. Thus, in light of the possible presence of *60 Minutes,* we wondered if we should alter this laid-back approach and adopt a more on-guard stance.

We had 10 minutes to make our decisions. We also had splitting headaches.

Questions

1. Would you let *60 Minutes* in?
2. Would you let them film the press conference?
3. Would you let them film the cocktail party?
4. Would you let them film a separate interview with the president?
5. Would you change the format of the party?
6. How does the American Bankers Association (ABA) deal with the media today? Visit its online press room (www.aba.com/aba/PressRoom/PR_mainmenu.asp). What resources can members of the press access on this site? How does ABA make it easy for reporters to make contact?

Voice of Authority

An Interview with Rita Cosby

Rita Cosby is the host of MSNBC's *Rita Cosby Live & Direct,* a one-hour primetime program, broadcast Monday–Thursday across the nation. She also serves as MSNBC's special correspondent. She formerly served as an anchor and reporter at Fox News. Ms. Cosby has covered all of the major global stories of contemporary times and interviewed many of the world's newsmakers, from former Yugoslav President Slobodan Milosevic and Pakistani President Pervez Musharraf to former U.S. Presidents Reagan, Ford, Clinton, and George H.W. Bush. Among her most famous exclusives were back-to-back interviews with Palestinian leader Yasser Arafat and Israeli Prime Minister Ariel Sharon, and an exclusive interview with Arafat when his compound was under siege in April 2002. She also was granted a rare, private meeting with the Pope after receiving an exclusive letter from Timothy McVeigh, explaining why he carried out the Oklahoma City bombing.

How would you characterize the state of the relationship between public relations people and journalists?

It's a co-dependency, almost like Siamese twins. A relationship of mutual necessity—one cannot live without the other, although many in journalism would never admit to that! It is also a love/hate relationship. There are days PR people make you so angry, and other days where you want to kiss and embrace them.

What do you believe constitutes the ideal public relations person?

Someone who knows when to call and when not to call. I appreciate a PR person who understands me and my specific show and doesn't waste my or their time with pitches that we would never consider. There are some PR people who will send a dozen pitches a week, and none is appropriate for my show, given the news environment. I'd rather have one good, clear pitch every few weeks, than many bad ones from the same person every month. Some PR people overload me and my staff.

What, in general, do journalists think of public relations people—helpers, obstacles, or necessary nuisances?

It depends on the PR person. Some are tremendous helpers, to whom I am grateful for their assistance in getting access to their client. Some are necessary; others are a nuisance. Overall, my experience has been quite good with most PR people. I feel the majority get what we need and don't need.

How can a public relations person build a relationship of trust with a journalist?

They must be honest and make an effort to be forthcoming in good *and* bad times. There are some PR people who will call you constantly during their client's positive times, but won't return your calls when it's bad news. Even worse, they will mislead you. A news person never forgets someone who does that one time. You will never trust that person again or whatever he or she tells you. It's always better, as President Clinton learned first hand, not to mislead, especially publicly. It will come back to haunt you in the long run.

How important is speaking "off the record" to a reporter?

I think you should feel comfortable to go "off the record" with any reputable journalist. I think it is helpful to give journalists leads to follow, and point them in the right direction, so they can dig up the correct facts. This is especially true when you don't want to be quoted "on the record," but want to make sure the story that comes out publicly is the true story, with all sides included.

What's the worst thing a public relations person ever did/said to you?

They said, "Trust me!" That person then broke their promise. I never spoke to that person again. I'm a big believer in your word is your bond, and that applies to journalists, public relations people, and everybody else.

Had you one recommendation to make to public relations people, what would it be?

Know when we're on deadline and be respectful of our schedule and time. I have had some PR people call me minutes before my live show and ask to talk about a segment they are pitching for next month! Meanwhile, I'm busy working on the next hour!

To that end, I also believe they need to craft their pitches so they are crisp and clear. I often get these long multi-page story/guest pitches, where the news hook is buried several pages in. It's a waste of my time and their time. News people have crazy, demanding schedules and if you want to make a successful pitch, it must be brief and to the point. Any pitch that's too cumbersome or unclear often gets deleted midway out of frustration. A pointed, powerful pitch gets my attention and shows they respect my time and helps me see the relevance to the news of the day and my specific show.

Study a journalist's work before you make that pitch, see *what* they like to cover and *how* they cover it, then make the pitch accordingly and briefly. Don't waste their time or your time when the pitch is so different than what they cover or have done in the past. It's easy with broadcasters to review their bio and watch their program before you decide whether to contact them.

It's like sports . . . get to know the *receiver*, then make the right *pitch*.

Suggested Readings

Block, Bruce. *The Visual Story*. Woburn, MA: Focal Press, 2001. This book focuses on the images presented by visual media and breaks them down into building blocks.

Clements, Steve. *Show Runner*. Beverly Hills: Silman-James Press, 2004. A veteran television producer provides an inside glimpse of what it takes to produce a television show.

Cronkite, Walter. *A Reporter's Life*. New York: Knopf, 1996. Reminiscences of the "most trusted man in America."

Dotson, Bob. *Make It Memorable*. Chicago: Bonus Books, 2000. A veteran NBC reporter talks about what it takes to sharpen television copy.

Deweese, Scott. Radio Syndication. Bellevue, WA: Elfin Cove Press, 2001. A step-by-step guide to creating a radio program that will merit syndication. Any budding Rush Limbaugh should read.

Howard, Carol, and Wilma K. Mathews. *On Deadline: Managing Media Relations*. Prospect Heights, IL: Waveland Press, 2000.

Kerbel, Matthew R. *If It Bleeds, It Leads*. Boulder, CO: Westview Press, 2001. Fascinating anatomy of a two-hour period in the life of television news.

Lewis, Jeff, and Dick Jones. *How to Get Noticed by the National Media*. Duluth, MN: Trellis Publishing, 2001. Soup to nuts discussion of attracting publicity, including discussion of electronic media.

Mathis, Mark. *Feeding the Media Beast, An Easy Recipe for Great Publicity*. West Lafayette, IN Purdue U. Press, 2002.

Newcomb, Horace. *Television: The Critical View*, 6th ed. New York: Oxford University Press, 2000. A book of essays that discuss the most contemporary issues in television, from late-night programming to prime-time news.

Walker, T. J. *Media Training: A Complete Guide to Controlling Your Image, Message and Sound Bites*. New York: Media Training Worldwide, 2005. A veteran media trainer recommends walking into an interview with three main points and sticking to them. Good advice.

Notes

1. "TV Still Dominates Media Space," *O'Dwyer's PR Services Report,* November 2005, 42.
2. Jacques Steinberg, "A First-Time Oscar Host in Search of That Fine Line," *New York Times,* February 20, 2006, E1.
3. *Where Americans Go for News,* Pew Research Center for the People and the Press, Washington, DC, 2005.
4. William F. Baker, "The Lost Promise of American Television," *Vital Speeches of the Day,* June 5, 1998, 684.
5. Robert J. Samuelson, "Picking Sides for the News," *Newsweek,* June 28, 2004, 37.
6. Peter Johnson, "NBC's Couric Reflects on the State of TV News," *USA Today,* February 19, 1997, D3.
7. Fraser P. Seitel, "Media Training," *odwyerpr.com,* March 26, 2002.
8. "Answers to the Most Frequently Asked VNR Questions," *PR Tactics,* June 1999, 21.
9. Jay Rosen, "Why Karen Ryan Deserved What She Got," *PressThink,* March 31, 2004.
10. "Commerce Okays Weaker VNR Measure," *Jack O'Dwyer's Newsletter,* October 26, 2005, 6.
11. "Satellite Media Tours: Gaining Exposure with Proper Disclosure," *PR Week,* October 3, 2005, 18.
12. "Most PSAs Run After Midnight," *O'Dwyer's PR Services Report,* March 2002, 39.
13. *Where Americans Go for News.*
14. Fraser P. Seitel, "Talk Radio," *odwyerpr.com,* February 12, 2002.
15. Terrence Smith, "Cable News Wars," *NewsHour with Jim Lehrer,* March 5, 2002.
16. "Nation Turns to TV for News," *Jack O'Dwyer's Newsletter,* September 26, 2001, 3.
17. Jerry Walker, "Publicists Get Clients Tuned into Talk Radio," *O'Dwyer's PR Services Report,* August 2003, 32.
18. Debra Zimmerman Murphey, "New Study by Tobin Communications Shows 80% of Radio Stations Are Not Using Audio News Releases," Tobin Communications, December 3, 2003.
19. *Where Americans Go for News,* op. cit.

11 Employee Relations

FIGURE 11-1 Mass layoffs. Employees exit the Wixom Assembly Plant in Michigan in 2006, part of Ford Motor Company's decision to cut as many as 30,000 jobs and idle 14 facilities. (AP Wide World Photos.)

The headline in the summer of 2002 said it all: "Unhappy Campers Growing in Number."[1] The story, which ran coast to coast, described the increasing disenchantment of the nation's workers with what they do for a living and with their employers. In fact, only 51 percent were satisfied with their jobs. Only about one worker in five was satisfied with his or her company's promotion policy and bonus plans.

- In one prominent study, when asked whether they believed their organizations as a whole were "well-managed," just 40 percent of workers said yes. One third (33 percent) said no, and the remainder (27 percent) gave a neutral response. Even among senior managers, only 66 percent agreed that their organization was well-managed.

- Even worse, only 42 percent of employees said they could "trust management to communicate honestly." And 26 percent said "management doesn't care about employee well-being."[2]

The clear conclusion from employee satisfaction research was that workers were less content, more suspicious, and less trusting than at any time in recent history.

The reasons for employee dissatisfaction weren't difficult to fathom. One need have only considered these individuals:

Workers in manufacturing industries, in particular, were hit by a wave of layoffs by the spring of 2006. In January of that year alone, employers took more than 1,100 mass layoff actions, involving more than 108,000 workers.[3] The corporate push toward productivity, resulting from increased computerization and more rigorous control of resources, meant that more workers than ever before faced an uncertain future. Household names in traditionally solid industries, like General Motors and Ford, no longer promised "cradle-to-grave" employment prospects.

As a consequence, workers in the early years of the 21st century became more vulnerable, more brittle, and more suspicious of management. Modern-day managers are challenged—particularly in the wake of the corporate scandals of the decade's early years—to build "employee trust."[4]

All of this underscores the notion that there is no job in public relations today that is more important than employee communications.

Strong Employee Relations Equals Solid Organizations

In the 21st century, employee relations matters—a lot. Approximately 60 percent of corporate CEOs, according to one well-regarded survey, reported spending more of their time communicating with employees.[5]

The reason is obvious, when one considers the fortunes of employees in recent years and the growing importance of internal communications.

- First, the wave of downsizings and layoffs that dominated business and industry both in the United States and worldwide after the high-tech bubble burst in the early years of the 21st century has taken its toll on employee loyalty. Although employees once implicitly trusted their organizations and superiors, today they are more hardened to the realities of a job market dominated by technological change that reduces human labor. Today, when companies lay off workers, they are often rewarded by the stock market for becoming more productive and efficient. This phenomenon has caused employees to understand that in today's business climate, every employee is expendable and there is no such thing as "lifetime employment." Consequently, companies must work harder at honestly communicating with their workers.

- The widening gulf between the pay of senior officers and common workers is another reason organizations must be sensitive to employee communications. The heads of America's 500 biggest companies received an aggregate 54 percent pay raise in 2004. As a group, their total compensation amounted to $5.1 billion—a whopping $11 million a man or, in infrequent cases, woman—versus $3.3 billion a year earlier.[6] Meanwhile, the gap between CEO pay and worker pay keeps increasing. According to one study, the ratio of this average CEO pay to worker pay ($27,460) spiked up from 301-to-1 in 2003 to 431-to-1 in 2004.[7]

- The move toward globalization, including the merger of geographically dispersed organizations, is another reason for increased focus on internal communications. Technology has hastened the integration of business and markets around the world. Customers on far-away continents are today but a mouse-click away. Alliances, affiliations, and mergers among far-flung companies have proliferated. Organizations have become much more cognizant of the importance of communicating the opportunities and benefits that will enhance support and loyalty among worldwide staffs.

■ Finally, research indicates that companies that communicate effectively with their workers financially outperform those that don't. One study found that companies with the most effective internal communications programs returned 57 percent more to their shareholders than companies with the least effective programs.[8]

These phenomena suggest that the value of "intellectual capital" has increased in importance. In the new information economy, business managers have realized that their most important assets are their employees. Employee communications, then, has become a key way to nurture and sustain that intellectual capital.

This was not always the case. For years, employee communications was considered less important than the more glamorous and presumably more critical functions of media, government, and investor relations.

Today, with fewer employees expected to do more work, staff members are calling for empowerment—for more of a voice in decision making. Just about every researcher who keeps tabs on employee opinion finds evidence of a "trust gap" that exists between

Speaking of Ethics

Scripting the Trust Gap

The "trust gap" that may exist between subordinates and superiors may not have been helped much by one attempt at employee communications by the White House in October 2005.

Ahead of the first vote on the new Iraqi constitution, the Bush administration arranged a videoconference for the president with members of the Army's 42nd Infantry Division, on the ground in Tikrit, Iraq. The White House said the exchange was a chance for Bush to thank the troops for their service and ask them about the situation in Iraq.

A noble intent indeed. But then, the wheels fell off....

Before the event started, a Defense Department official put the soldiers through their paces rehearsing the order and substance of the questions. Even worse, this dress rehearsal was witnessed by reporters viewing the satellite feed while waiting for the president to arrive.

Predictably, the videoconference was benign with upbeat soldiers "volunteering" as to how the "partnership with Iraqis" was improving daily (Figure 11-2). Equally predictably, Democrats and reporters alike criticized the proceedings as little more than a well-rehearsed publicity stunt to win public favor for the Iraq war.

Administration observers and employee communications experts scratched their heads in unison, wondering why the White House didn't simply let the soldiers say whatever was on their minds, unscripted, unprompted, and unrehearsed.

FIGURE 11-2 Candid communicator or puppet master? President Bush's proposed extemporaneous videoconference with soldiers in Iraq was criticized for being a well-rehearsed propaganda vehicle. (AP Wide World Photos)

For further information, see Julie Mason, "White House Watch," *Houston Chronicle,* October 16, 2005, A16, and Warren Vieth and Mark Mazzetti, "Chat with Troops Draws Flak," *Los Angeles Times,* October 14, 2005, A14.

management and workers. To narrow that gap demands that more effective employee communications play a pivotal role.

Dealing with the Employee Public

Just as there is no such thing as the "general public," there is also no single "employee public."

The employee public is made up of numerous subgroups: senior managers, first-line supervisors, staff and line employees, union laborers, per diem employees, contract workers, and others. Each group has different interests and concerns. A smart organization will try to differentiate messages and communications to reach these segments.

Indeed, in a general sense, today the staff is younger, increasingly female, more ambitious and career oriented, less complacent, and less loyal to the company than in the past. Today's more hard-nosed employee demands candor in communications. Internal communications, like external messages, must be targeted to reach specific subgroups of the employee public.

Grounding in effective employee communications requires management to ask three hard questions about the way it conveys knowledge to the staff.

- Is management able to communicate effectively with employees?
- Is communication trusted, and does it relay appropriate information to employees?
- Has management communicated its commitment to its employees and to fostering a rewarding work environment?

In many instances, the biggest problem is that employees don't know where they stand in the eyes of management. In addition, they often don't understand how compensation programs work or what they need to do to move ahead. This lack of understanding leads to discontent, frustration, miscommunication, problems, and eventually to the feeling that the grass is greener elsewhere.[9]

Clearly, organizing effective, believable, and persuasive internal communications in the midst of organizational change is a core critical public relations responsibility in the 21st century.

Communicating Effectively in a Sea of Doubt

An organization truly concerned about "getting through" to its employees in an era of downsizing, displacement, and dubious communications must reinforce five specific principles:

- **Respect.** Employees must be respected for their worth as individuals and their value as workers. They must be treated with respect and not as interchangeable commodities.
- **Honest feedback.** By talking to workers about their strengths and weaknesses, employers help employees know where they stand. Some managers incorrectly assume that avoiding negative feedback will be helpful. Wrong. Employees need

to know where they stand at any given time. Candid communications will help them in this pursuit.

- **Recognition.** Employees feel successful when management recognizes their contributions. It is the duty of the public relations professional to suggest mechanisms by which deserving employees will be honored.

- **A voice.** In the era of talk radio and television talk shows and blogs, almost everyone wants their ideas to be heard and to have a voice in decision making. This growing "activist communications" phenomenon must be considered by public relations professionals seeking to win internal goodwill for management.

- **Encouragement.** Study after study reveals that money and benefits motivate employees up to a point, but that "something else" is generally necessary. That something else is encouragement. Workers need to be encouraged. Communications programs that provide encouragement generally produce results. What distinguishes the communication effort at a "better place to work"?

According to Milton Moskowitz, coauthor of the *100 Best Companies to Work For in America,* six criteria, in particular, have stood the test of time:

1. **Willingness to express dissent.** Employees, according to Moskowitz, want to be able to "feed back" to management their opinions and even dissent. They want access to management. They want critical letters to appear in internal publications. They want management to pay attention.

2. **Visibility and proximity of upper management.** Enlightened companies try to level rank distinctions, eliminating such status reminders as executive cafeterias and executive gymnasiums. They act against hierarchical separation, says Moskowitz. He adds that smart CEOs practice MBWA—"management by walking around."

3. **Priority of internal to external communication.** The worst thing to happen to any organization is for employees to learn critical information about the company on the 10 o'clock news. Smart organizations always release pertinent information to employees first and consider internal communication primary.

4. **Attention to clarity.** How many employees regularly read benefits booklets? The answer should be "many" because of the importance of benefit programs to the entire staff, but most employees never do so. Good companies write such booklets with clarity—to be readable for a general audience rather than for human resources specialists.

5. **Friendly tone.** According to Moskowitz, the best companies "give a sense of family" in all that they communicate. One high-tech company makes everyone wear a name tag with the first name in big block letters. These little things are most important, declares Moskowitz.

6. **Sense of humor.** People are worried principally about keeping their jobs. Corporate life for many is grim. Moskowitz says this is disastrous. "It puts people in straitjackets, so they can't wait to get out at the end of the day."[10]

What internal communications comes down to—just like external communications—is, in a word, *credibility.* The task for management is to convince employees that it not only desires to communicate with them but also wishes to do so in a truthful, frank, and direct manner. That is the overriding challenge that confronts today's internal communicator.

Credibility: The Key

The employee public is a savvy one. Employees can't be conned because they live with the organization every day. They generally know what's going on and whether management is being honest with them. That's why management must be truthful.

Employees want managers to level with them. They want facts, not wishful thinking. The days when management could say, "Trust us, this is for your own good" are over. Employees like hearing the truth, especially in person. Indeed, survey after survey suggests that face-to-face communications—preferably between a supervisor and subordinate—is the hands-down most effective method of employee communications.

Employees also want to know, candidly, how they're doing. Research indicates that trust in organizations would increase if management (1) communicated earlier and more frequently, (2) demonstrated trust in employees by sharing bad news as well as good, and (3) involved employees in the process by asking for their ideas and opinions. Effective employee communication means that an organization's leaders have taken the time to clearly and succinctly articulate the vision of the business, show how employees can contribute to it, and demonstrate how it can be "lived" in the daily jobs.[11]

Today, smart companies realize that well-informed employees are the organization's best goodwill ambassadors. Managements have become more candid in their communications with the staff. Gone are the days when all the news coming from management is all good. In today's environment, being candid means treating people with dignity, addressing their concerns, and giving them the opportunity to understand the realities of the marketplace (Figure 11-3).

One reason that organizations such as Hewlett-Packard, which cut out its magazine for employees in 2001 after 58 years, opt out of print publications is the tremendous growth of e-mail and intranets. These instant, direct devices provide greater opportunity today to increase the frequency and candor of communications. A major part of the challenge that confronts internal communicators is to reflect credibility in communicating that underscores the level of respect with which employees should be held by management.

Most employees desperately want to be treated as important parts of an organization; they should not be taken for granted, nor should they be shielded from the truth. Thus, the most important ingredient of any internal communications program must be credibility.

S-H-O-C the Troops

Enhancing credibility, being candid, and winning trust must be the primary employee communications objectives in the new century. Earning employee trust may result in more committed and productive employees. But scraping away the scar tissue of distrust that exists in many organizations requires a strategic approach.

The question is: How does management build trust when employee morale is so brittle?

Part of the answer lies in an approach to management communication built around the acronym S-H-O-C. That is, management should consider a four-step communications

AN UPDATE ON THE "BRIDGE TO EXCELLENCE" PROGRAM

THE BRIDGE REPORT
VOLUME 1 NUMBER 10
MAY 21, 2004

United Health Services

Chenango Memorial Hospital

A number of important developments have occurred recently in our *Bridge to Excellence* initiative that I wanted to bring to your attention, before announcing to the general community.

First, we have reached agreement with Crothall Services Group to assume all environmental services, effective June 21.

Crothall, based in Wayne, Pennsylvania, has extensive experience in managing and operating environmental services for 300 healthcare institutions in the U.S. and Canada.
Our agreement calls for Crothall to provide leadership, training and capital equipment, to enhance the professionalism and improve the delivery of environmental services at Chenango Memorial Hospital.
The Crothall Chenango management team will arrive here in early June. All current CMH environmental services employees will become employees of Crothall, effective June 21.

Similarly, we have reached agreement with Morrison Healthcare Food Services to assume Chenango Memorial's food services, also effective June 21. Morrison, which has served the healthcare food and nutrition business for nearly a century, has been providing us with management and dietician services for some time.

Under this new agreement, all food services personnel will become Morrison employees, effective June 21. This will not only provide continuity of food services management at CMH but also, like the environmental services change, introduce a new level of professionalism

and quality to our food services operation.

In a related move, we have retained Canteen Corp. to replace our current vending machine supplier.

Canteen, which like Crothall and Morrison is an operating unit of the $6 billion Compass Group North America, has been charged with the task of upgrading our vending machine equipment and expanding available offerings.

All three of these moves, which affect about 10% of our workforce, will not only benefit the hospital financially but will also allow us to focus on our primary mission – delivering the highest quality patient care to the people of Chenango County.

With the encouragement and support of United Health Services we are also moving forward the business relationship with Bassett Healthcare that I announced in the last *Bridge Report*.

By July 1, we hope to have credentialed Bassett physicians in the areas of orthopedics, gastroenterology, urology and general surgery. The Bassett physicians will be utilizing our operating rooms to perform procedures on their patients. This change will make it more convenient for Bassett patients in our community, who currently travel to Oneonta and Cooperstown for treatment, and will also enable us to take advantage of underutilized CMH capacity, while increasing our volumes and improving our financial situation. The arrangement will not affect our referral patterns to United Health

Executive Leadership Team

Frank W. Mirabito
President & CEO
Ext. 4113

Jay Alfirevic
Project Director/CTO
Ext. 4169

Julie Briggs, RN
VP Patient Care/CNO
Ext. 4243

Shirley Caezza, RN
Dir. of Performance
Improvement
Ext. 4033

Ronald Cerow
Administrator, RHCF
Ext. 4715

Mark Kishel, MD
Interim CMO
Ext. 4239

Robert McCarthy
VP Finance/CFO
Ext. 4221

Peter Mike
Interim Materials Mgr.
Ext. 4106

Richard Park
Dir. of Human Resources
Ext. 4508

Garry Root
Director Comm. Relations
Ext. 4028

Gary Van House
Interim Clinic Admin.
Ext. 4260

Employee Hotline
Ext. 4578

Employee Hotline
Drop Box Locations
Hops Yard Bistro
2nd Floor RHCF
4th Floor Ambulatory Dept.
Main Lobby

FIGURE 11-3 Credible communication. The best communication is direct communication, which is what Chenango Memorial Hospital in Norwich, New York, did in 2004 when questions of layoffs pervaded the staff. The CEO answered the questions directly and in print. (Courtesy of Chenango Memorial Hospital)

THE BRIDGE REPORT   **Page 2**

Services and United Medical Associates, which will remain our clinical partners. CMH patients will continue to be referred within our system.

In terms of orthopedics, Dr. Jose Lopez will leave Chenango Memorial at the end of this month. As a result, we have accordingly downsized and restructured the Orthopedic Institute staff. Efforts are underway to establish additional relationships with Bassett and United Medical Associates (UMA) to help serve the patients of Dr. Lopez.

Finally, I am pleased to report that we have received the $500,000 grant from the New York State Healthcare Reform Act, which I mentioned in a prior *Bridge Report.* The proceeds of this will go toward completing the Wellspring consultant engagement. Most important, this grant triggers an equivalent amount in the form of a 0% interest loan from the New York State Dormitory Authority. We expect to receive the proceeds of this loan, which will be used for general hospital purposes, by the end of the month.

As you can tell, much has been happening around our hospital, as we continue to make progress in restoring our financial strength and rebuilding our reputation in the community.

We continue to receive questions and suggestions on the x4578 Hotline and in the Hotline Drop Boxes. Here are some of the most recent:

Is it true all nurses receive a bonus?
No. We have no bonus plan in effect at this time for any Chenango Memorial employee, from the CEO on down.

How about pay increases for long term employees?
Our general procedure with respect to pay increases is to evaluate each employee on an annual basis. Once an employee has maxed out due to length of service, he or she is awarded a $1,000 annual longevity increase. I might add that despite our current financial challenges, pay policies have remained constant.

Shouldn't we have a sign posted on the 4th Floor near the elevators, so that patients know where Dr. Converse is located?
Yes we should. It's in the works. Thanks for the good suggestion.

I have heard various talk about PTO policy. What is the situation?
The whole area of PTO is currently under review. Once we have clarified our intentions, I will discuss this issue in depth in a future *Bridge Report*.

As always, thank you for your questions and comments and your continuing best efforts in our *Bridge to Excellence* initiative.

Juanl W Mialb

FIGURE 11-3 (Continued)

approach—built on communications that are **strategic, honest, open,** and **consistent**—to begin to rebuild employee trust.

- **First, all communications must be strategic.** What strategic communication essentially boils down to is this: Most employees want you to answer only two basic questions for them:

    1. Where is this organization going?

    2. What is my role in helping us get there?

    That's it. Once you level with the staff as to the organization's direction and goals and their role in the process, even the most ardent bellyachers will grudgingly acknowledge your attempt to "keep them in the loop."

- **Second, all communications must be honest.** The sad fact is that while most executives may pay lip service to candor and honesty, in the end, too many turn out like the management at Enron, WorldCom, Adelphia, Tyco, and all the other companies caught in the early years of the 21st century, dissembling, obfuscating, and pulling their punches.

    They seem to fear, as Jack Nicholson raged in *A Few Good Men,* that the staff "can't handle the truth."

    Such trepidation is foolish. For one thing, the staff already may discount anything management tells them. For another, you can't hope to build credibility through prevaricating or sugar-coating.

- **Third, all communications must be open.** This is another way of saying that there must be feedback. The best communications are two-way communications. That means that no matter how large the organization, employee views must be solicited, listened to, and most important, acted upon.

    That latter aspect is most important. Often, managers stage elaborate forums and feedback sessions, listen to employee gripes and suggestions, and yet do nothing. The key must be *action*.

- **Fourth, all communications must be consistent.** Once you've begun to communicate, you must keep it up. Maintain a regular, on time, and predictable program of internal newsletters, employee forums, leadership meetings, and reward celebrations.

    On again, off again communications or programs that start with bold promises only to peter out question management's commitment to keeping the staff informed. Generally, employee information, education, and morale-boosting programs start with great pomp and promise. The CEO blusters his way through a rousing speech, literature pours out from on high, task forces plunge into quick-fix assignments, and then, over time, nada.

    Wrong. Communications, if they are to work, must be steadily, sometimes painfully, consistent.[12]

Employee Communications Tactics

Once objectives are set, a variety of techniques can be adopted to reach the staff. The initial tool again is research. Before any communications program can be implemented, communicators must have a good sense of staff attitudes.

Internal Communications Audits

Both a strategy and a tactic, the internal communications audit is the most beneficial form of research on which to lay the groundwork for effective employee communications. Ideally, this starts with old-fashioned, personal, in-depth interviews with both top management and communicators. It is important to find out from top management what it "wants" from the communications team. It is also important to find out what communicators "think" management wants. Often the discontinuities are startling. The three critical audit questions to probe are:

1. How do internal communications support the mission of the organization?

2. Do internal communications have management's support?

3. How responsive to employee needs and concerns are internal communications?[13]

Audits help determine staff attitudes about their jobs, the organization, and its mission, coupled with an analysis of existing communications techniques. The findings of such audits are often revealing, always informative, and never easily ignored.

Internal audits can be conducted by organizational personnel or consultants. Sometimes consultants provide a more objective analysis of the situation and what is required to improve it. (But, then, as a consultant, I'm biased!)

Once internal communications research is completed, the public relations practitioner has a clearer idea of the kinds of communications vehicles that make sense for the organization.

Online Communications

The age of online communications has ushered in a whole new set of employee communications vehicles—from e-mail to voice mail to tailored organizational intranets to individual blogs. Such vehicles are more immediate than earlier print versions. They reach employees at their desks and are more likely to be read, listened to, and acted on. Indeed, employees without computer access are increasingly losing their "voice" and ability to be heard, especially the ability to submit ideas for improvement or to access a company intranet remotely.

Online communications also have the capability of reaching virtual employees at their desks in their homes, on their Blackberrys or Palm Pilots, in their cars, or wherever they remotely may be.

As print publications become steadily fewer, tailored online newsletters have begun to replace them.

Many organizations, from traditional companies such as Xerox, Exxon, and Ford to the new high-tech giants such as Cisco Systems, Intel, and Oracle, increasingly rely on intranets to exchange information quickly and effectively. Miller Brewing Company's intranet, "Miller Time," sponsors an interactive forum through which employees offer suggestions to and ask questions of management. Everyone who offers an idea through the Miller intranet is guaranteed a response (not a beer!). Such feedback is critical to corporate credibility.[14]

The newest online tools, such as blogs and wikis, are still relatively unfamiliar as internal communications vehicles.

- *Blogs*—or technically, Web logs—are a type of frequently updated online journal. Blogs provide an easy way for employees to post opinions and views of the company on the Internet. Blogging by senior management, a potentially useful device to reach the staff, is still quite uncommon.

- *Wikis,* a dynamic Web site to which any user can add pages, modify content, and comment on existing content, is even less widespread than blogs internally. Wikis may be better suited than a blog for a smaller group, and their ability to provide instant interactive capabilities are unmatched.[15]

The Intranet

In 1997, the people at Forrester Research predicted that within the first few years of the 21st century, the vast majority of American companies would have intranet capability.[16] They were right. Today, in many organizations, the intranet has overtaken and even emulsified print communications. Intranet investments remain strong as companies continue to convert sites to portal technology and add streaming video capability. At IBM, for example, where just about everyone is computer savvy, the company has eliminated every other internal communications medium but the corporate intranet to reach IBM's 300,000 employees.[17]

Unfortunately, having an intranet site doesn't mean employees will necessarily go there for information. Sites high in visual appeal but low in usefulness will likely be ignored. To prevent that, intranet creators should keep in mind several important considerations:

1. **Consider the culture.** If the organization is generally collaborative and collegial, it will have no trouble getting people to contribute information and materials to the intranet. But, if the organization is not one that ordinarily shares, a larger central staff may be necessary to ensure that the intranet works.

2. **Set clear objectives and then let it evolve.** Just as in setting up a corporate Web site, intranets must be designed with clear goals in mind: to streamline business processes, to communicate management messages, and so on. Once goals are established, however, site creators ought to allow for growth and evolution as new intranet needs become apparent.

3. **Treat it as a journalistic enterprise.** Company news gets read by company workers. That's a truism throughout all organizations. Employees must know what's going on in the company and complain bitterly if they are not given advance notice of important developments. In this way, the intranet can serve as a critical journalistic communications tool within the organization.

4. **Market, market, market.** The intranet needs to be "sold" within the company. Publicize new features or changes in content. Weekly e-mails can be used to highlight noteworthy additions and updates. Just as with any other internal communications vehicle, the more exposure the site gets, the more frequently it will be used.

5. **Link to outside lives.** Some CEOs may not recognize it, but employees have lives outside the corporation. An intranet site that recognizes that simple fact can become quite popular. Links to classified ads, restaurant and movie reviews, and information on local concerts are ways to reinforce both the intranet's value and the organization's concern for its staff.

6. **Senior management must commit.** Just like anything else in an organization, if the top executive is neither interested nor supportive, the idea will fail. Therefore, the perceived value of an organization's intranet will increase dramatically if management actively supports and uses it.[18]

Print Publications

The advent of online internal communications has been hard on print publications. It's happening all over corporate America: Print editors are being told to either kill their publication entirely or move it onto the company's intranet.[19]

- At Tennessee's Eastman Chemical Company, for example, the CEO's drive to convert the firm to a Web-based organization tolled the death knell for the *Inside Eastman* newsletter after 50 years of publication.

- At another Eastman, New York's Eastman Kodak Company, the internal publication was not used when the company announced that it would lay off 16,600 workers and save $1 billion. Supervisors were briefed by special e-mails and then directed to personally relay the bad news to their subordinates.

- When Michigan's Fel-Pro Incorporated agreed to be acquired by Federal-Mogul Corporation, it "cascaded" the information down from departmental managers to supervisors to staff.

To print critics, these instances are exemplary of the trend across corporate internal communications departments to move from print to Internet-oriented employee information.

Print defenders, on the other hand, argue that print still must play a role, particularly in helping create a "climate" that bears the stamp of management (Figure 11-4). Writing and editing employee newsletters, for example, are typical entry-level public relations responsibilities.

One innovation that enhanced the role of internal editors was the advent of desktop publishing, which allows a user to control the typesetting process in-house, provides faster turnaround for clients, and saves money on outside design. The desktop operation allows scanning photos and drawings, incorporating those images into page layouts, using the computer to assign color in design elements, and producing entire color-separated pages of film from which a printer can create plates for printing.

Whether using conventional print or desktop publishing, an internal newsletter editor must consider the following steps in approaching the task:

1. **Assigning stories.** Article assignments must focus on organizational strategies and management objectives. Job information—organizational changes, mergers, reasons behind decisions, and so on—should be stressed.

2. **Enforcing deadlines.** Employees respect a newsletter that comes out at a specific time. An editor, therefore, must assign and enforce rigid copy deadlines on contributors. Deadline slippage can't be tolerated if the newsletter is to be respected.

3. **Assigning photos.** People like photographs. Because internal publications compete with glossy, high-tech newspapers and magazines and the Internet, organizational photos can't be dull (Figure 11-5).

4. **Editing copy.** An editor must be just that: a critic of sloppy writing, a student of forceful prose, a motivator to improve copy style. This is especially true now that the computer does at least part of the job for you. However, spell check isn't foolproof, especially when it comes to context.

5. **Formatting copy.** An editor, particularly a desktop editor, must also make the final decisions on the format of the newsletter: how long articles should run, where to put photos, how to crop artwork, what headlines should say, and so on.

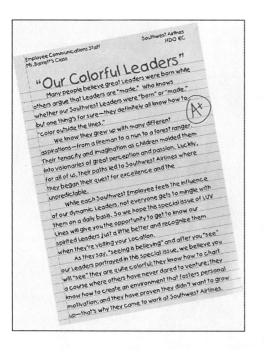

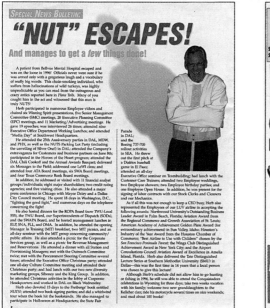

FIGURE 11-4 Prince of print. Southwest Airlines is a one-of-a-kind company, thanks principally to its founder and former CEO Herb Kelleher. Kelleher helped build a climate of creativity, productivity, and fun at Southwest by sponsoring some of the most far-out internal print publications ever seen on this planet (and perhaps any other!). (Courtesy of Southwest Airlines)

FIGURE 11-5 Alien crowd. Publicity photos for internal and external use don't have to be mundane. At least that's the view of Sue Bohle Public Relations and Infogames Entertainment, which decked out these Southwest Airlines passengers in out-of-this-world masks on the way to the E3 Entertainment Trade Show. (Courtesy of the Bohle Company)

6. **Ensuring on-time publication.** In publishing, timeliness is next to godliness. It is the editor's responsibility to ensure that no last-minute glitches interfere with on-time publication.

7. **Critiquing.** After the fact, the editor's job must continue. He or she must scrupulously review copy, photos, placement, content, philosophy, and all the other elements to ensure that the next edition will be even better.

One organization devoted originally to internal communications, the International Association of Business Communicators, founded in 1970, has come to rival the older Public Relations Society of America. With more than 13,000 members throughout the United States and in 60 countries, the IABC helps set journalistic standards for internal communicators of both print and online publications.

Employee Annual Reports

It often makes sense to print a separate annual report just for employees. Frequently, the lure of this report—published in addition to the regular corporate shareholder annual report—is that it is written for, about, and by the employees.

Most employees do care about how their organization functions and what its management is thinking. The annual report to the staff is a good place to discuss such issues informally yet candidly. The report can be both factual, explaining the performance of the organization during the year, and informational, reviewing organizational changes and significant milestones during the year. It can also be motivational in its implicit appeal to team spirit and pride.

Staff reports observe few hard-and-fast rules about concept and format. Staff annuals can be as complex as the shareholder annual report itself or as simple as a brief outline of the company's highlights of the year. Typical features of the employee annual report include the following:

1. **Chief executive's letter:** a special report to the staff that reviews the performance and highlights of the year and thanks employees for their help.

2. **Use-of-funds statement:** often a graphic chart that describes how the organization used each dollar it took in.

3. **Financial condition:** frequently a chart that describes the assets and liabilities of the corporation and the stockholders' equity.

4. **Description of the company:** simple, graphic explanation of what the organization is and where its facilities are located.

5. **Social responsibility highlights:** discussion of the organization's role in aiding society through monetary assistance and employee participation during the year.

6. **Staff financial highlights:** general description, usually in chart form, of salaries, benefits, and other staff-related expense items.

7. **Organizational policy:** discussion of current issues about which management feels strongly and for which it seeks employee support.

8. **Emphasis on people:** in-depth profiles of people on the job, comments from people about their jobs, and pictorial essays on people at work to demonstrate, throughout the report, the importance of the people who make up the organization.

Employees appreciate recognition. The special annual report is a measure of recognition that does not go unnoticed—or unread—by a firm's workers.

Bulletin Boards

Bulletin boards, among the most ancient of employee communications vehicles, have made a comeback in recent years.

For years, bulletin boards were considered second-string information channels, generally relegated to the display of federally required information and policy data for such activities as fire drills and emergency procedures. Most employees rarely consulted them. But the bulletin board has experienced a renaissance and is now being used to improve productivity, cut waste, and reduce accidents on the job. Best of all, employees are taking notice.

How come?

For one thing, yesterday's bulletin board has become today's news center. It has been repackaged into a more lively visual and graphically arresting medium. Using enlarged news pictures and texts, motivational messages, and other company announcements—all illustrated with a flair—the bulletin board has become an important source of employee communications (Figure 11-6). Hospitals, in particular, have found that a strategically situated bulletin board outside a cafeteria is a good way to promote employee understanding and cooperation.

One key to stimulating readership is to keep boards current. One person in the public relations unit should be assigned to this weekly task.

LOCKHEED MARTIN
Setting the Standard

ETHICS

QUESTIONS OR CONCERNS

For help...

STEP 1

Contact your supervisor. If necessary, take it up the chain of command at your location.

STEP 2

Contact your Company Ethics Officer in person, by phone, or by mail.

LMASC Ethics Director:	**Tom Salvaggio**
Location:	**B-2, 2nd Floor, Col. 28**
Phone:	**Helpline Coordinator, (770) 494-3999**
Mailing Address:	**LMASC Ethics Office** **P O Box 1771** **Marietta, GA 30061**

STEP 3

If the first two steps do not resolve the matter, contact the Corporate Office of Ethics and Business Conduct for confidential assistance:

Helpline:	**800 LM ETHIC (800 563-8442)**
Fax:	**(818) 876-2082**
Or Write:	**Corporate Office of Ethics and Business Conduct** **Lockheed Martin Corporation** **P O Box 34143** **Bethesda, MD 20827-0143**

STEP 4

Contact the Department of Defense Hotline to report fraud, waste and abuse, and/or security violations.

Hotline:	**800 424-9098**
Or Write:	**Defense Hotline** **The Pentagon** **Washington, DC 20301-1900**

IDENTITIES OF WRITERS AND CALLERS ARE FULLY PROTECTED.

LOCKHEED MARTIN

FIGURE 11-6 Comeback kid. Among important announcements included on organizational bulletin boards are updates on key corporate issues such as ethical questions and concerns.

Suggestion Box and Town Hall Meetings

Two other traditional staples of employee communication are the suggestion box and the town hall meeting.

In the old days, suggestion boxes were mounted on each floor, and employees, often anonymously, deposited their thoughts on how to improve the company and its processes and products. Often rewards were awarded for the most productive or profitable suggestions.

Today, the only necessity in implementing a successful suggestion box program is to ensure that there is "feedback"—that is, management action that deals with valid suggestions.

Town hall meetings are large gatherings of employees with top management, where no subject is off limits and management–staff dialogue is the goal. That was the conclusion of one study of 200 employees, some of whom labeled these vehicles "charades, phony, management games, and a joke."[20]

Town hall meetings must encourage unfettered two-way communication. Too often, questions from the floor are screened by public relations people, thus causing suspicion from the crowd. The more open the format, the greater management and the organization will be trusted. The Bush administration, not particularly trusting of how the media would treat its messages, favored internal and external town hall meetings as a principal mode of communications (Figure 11-7).

Internal Video

As important as broadcast and cable television are as communications media in society today, video has had an up-and-down history as an internal communications medium. On the one hand, internal television, including streaming video, can be demonstrably effective. A 10-minute videotape of an executive announcing a new corporate policy imparts hundreds of times more information than an audiotape of that same message, which in turn contains hundreds of times more information than a printed text of the same message.

A number of organizations work skillfully with internal video:

- Burger King produced a video in an in-house studio and soundstage to train workers in its 5,000 restaurants.

- Miller Brewing Company produced a 20-minute video magazine and distributed it to all company locations. It featured new company commercials, brand promotions, happenings at Miller plants, and employee human interest stories.

FIGURE 11-7 Live and direct.
Defense Secretary Donald H. Rumsfeld preferred to answer internal questions at town hall meetings, such as this one at the Pentagon, to discuss the war in Iraq. (AP Wide World Photos)

- The Ford Motor Company took the unprecedented step of stopping work on assembly lines to show videotapes to workers.
- The most unique internal video ever produced was the legendary "Southwest Shuffle," in which the employees of Southwest Airlines—from maintenance crews to pilots—chimed in on a rap video extolling the virtues of their innovative carrier. Deejay for the rap extravaganza was—who else?—former Southwest CEO Herb Kelleher!

On the downside, internal video is a medium that must be approached with caution. Unless video is of broadcast quality, few will tolerate it—especially an audience of employees weaned on television. So there are always risks in producing an internal video.

The keys to any internal video production are first to examine internal needs; next to plan thoughtfully before using the medium; and finally to reach target publics through the highest-quality programming possible. Broadcast quality is a tough standard to meet. If an organization can't afford high-quality video, it shouldn't get involved.

Face-to-Face Communications

First and foremost, employees want information face-to-face from the individual for whom they work. Supervisors, in fact, are the preferred source for 90 percent of employees, making them the top choice by far. The reason is obvious. You report to your supervisor, who awards your raise, promotes you, and is your primary source of corporate information.

That's the good news.

The bad news is that despite paying attention to enhanced supervisory communications, most companies are still inconsistent when it comes to supervisors relaying important information. Thus, even though most employees vastly prefer information from their supervisor over what they learn through rumors, many still rely on the grapevine as a primary source of information.

What can public relations departments do to combat this trend?

Some departments formalize the meeting process by mixing management and staff in a variety of formats, from gripe sessions to marketing or planning meetings. Many organizations embrace the concept of skip-level meetings in which top-level managers meet periodically with employees at levels several notches below them in the organizational hierarchy. As with any other form of communication, the value of meetings lies in their substance, their regularity, and the candor managers bring to face-to-face sessions.

The Grapevine

In far too many organizations, it's neither print nor the Internet that dominates communications but rather the company grapevine. The rumor mill can be treacherous. As one employee publication described the grapevine:

> *"Once they pick up steam, rumors can be devastating. Because employees tend to distort future events to conform to a rumor, an organization must work to correct rumors as soon as possible.*

Talking Points

Preempting *Sicko*

In the old days, it was the CBS exposé program *60 Minutes* that CEOs most dreaded. Today, more often than not, it's relentless movie producer and social crusader Michael Moore.

In 2006, when Moore went after the healthcare industry in a film titled *Sicko,* Europe's biggest drug maker, GlaxoSmithKline (GSK), fought back by mobilizing its "internal army."

Largely to preempt Moore's efforts, GSK launched a Value of Medicine campaign, which turned its 8,000 U.S. workers into public relations ambassadors. Employees were armed with speeches and talking points and encouraged to meet with local community groups to tell its story in a more direct manner.

Said one pharmaceutical trade group executive of the GSK effort, "It's not enough for salespeople to be marketers of products. They need to be ambassadors of the industry as well. We have a great industry and shouldn't be ashamed of defending it."

No word whether any of this employee communications mobilization gave the intrepid Moore second thoughts about sacking *Sicko.*

For further information, see Danny Fortson, "GSK in PR Blitz Ahead of Moore's 'Sicko' Blast at Drugs Companies," *The Independent Online,* March 5, 2006.

Identifying the source of a rumor is often difficult, if not impossible, and it's usually not worth the time. However, dispelling the rumor quickly and frankly is another story. Often a bad-news rumor—about layoffs, closings, and so on—can be dealt with most effectively through forthright communication. Generally, an organization makes a difficult decision after a thorough review of many alternatives. The final decision is often a compromise, reflecting the needs of the firm and its various publics, including, importantly, the workforce.

In presenting a final decision to employees, management often overlooks the value of explaining how it reached its decision. By comparing alternative solutions so that employees can understand more clearly the rationale behind management decisions, an organization may make bad news more palatable.

As diabolical as the grapevine can become, it shouldn't necessarily be treated as the enemy of effective communications with employees. Management might even consider ways to use it to its advantage. A company grapevine can be as much a communications vehicle as internal publications or employee meetings. It may even be more valuable because it is believed, and everyone seems to tap into it.

Last Word

The best defense against damaging grapevine rumors is a strong and candid internal communications system. Employee communications, for years the most neglected communications opportunity in corporate America, is today much more appreciated for its strategic importance. Organizations that build massive marketing plans to sell products have begun today to apply that same knowledge and energy to communicating with their own employees.

A continuing employee relations challenge for public relations communicators is to work hand in hand with human resources officials. In the 1950s, personnel departments began to change their name to "human resources" to more accurately reflect the personal focus of their responsibilities. Over the past half century, human resources functions have concentrated on such areas as organization, staffing, benefits, and recruitment rather than communications.

The responsibility for communicating to employees has largely fallen on the public relations function, which must coordinate its initiatives with human resources priorities to create a culture of professionalism, accountability, and candor.

In the 21st century, organizations have no choice but to build rapport with and morale among employees. The shattering of morale and distrust of top management prevalent in the early years of the century will take time to repair. Building back internal credibility is a long-term process that depends on several factors—among them, listening to employees, developing information exchanges to educate employees about changing technologies, empowering them with new skills and knowledge through strategic business information they require, and adapting to the new culture of job "mobility" that is replacing job "stability."

Most of all in this new century, effective employee communications requires openness and honesty on the part of senior management. As legendary Berkshire Hathaway CEO Warren Buffet has said, "We can afford to lose money—even a lot of money. We cannot afford to lose reputation—even a shred of reputation."[21]

Public relations professionals must seize this initiative to foster the open climate that employees want and the two-way communications that organizations need.

Discussion Starters

1. What societal factors have caused internal communications to become more important today than in the past?
2. What is the general mood of the employee public today?
3. What are the key elements to effective employee relations?
4. What are some important employee communications strategies today?
5. What are the key questions of an employee communications audit?
6. What is the status of internal print communications?
7. What are the key considerations in communicating through an intranet?
8. What are the primary tasks of an employee newsletter's editor?
9. What are the primary considerations in adopting internal video?
10. What is the best way to combat the grapevine?

Top of the Shelf

Corporate Conversations: A Guide to Crafting Effective and Appropriate Internal Communications

Shel Holtz, New York, NY: ANACOM, 2004.

Shel Holtz knows more about communicating via the Internet than anybody in public relations. In his book, *Corporate Conversations*, he expands that knowledge by presenting a guidebook to managing all aspects of internal communications and managing it to aid in business success. The book treats the most effective methods of internally communicating, encompassing print, the Internet, and everything in between.

Holtz fills the book with practical examples of how the best organizations motivate and nurture their people by providing constant, consistent, and candid "conversations."

CASE STUDY

The Chairman's E-Mail

From: Solomon Doophis, Chairman

To: All Doophis Corp. Headquarters Managers

Re: Work Standards

I have had it. I have been making this point to most of you for the better part of a year, and I'll take it no longer.

We are getting less than 40 hours of work from a large number of headquarters employees.

The parking lot is sparsely used at 8 a.m., when I arrive, and likewise at 7 p.m., when I depart. At 4:30 p.m. each day, it starts to empty out.

My point is that as managers, you either don't know what YOUR employees are doing or YOU simply don't care. You have created expectations of the work effort, which allowed this to happen inside Doophis, creating a very unhealthy environment.

In either case, you have a problem, and you will fix it or you will be replaced.

NEVER in my career have I allowed a team which worked for me to think they had a 40-hour job. I, personally, work 12 hours a day, everyday. I don't expect YOUR employees to work as hard as I do, but I will permit this no longer.

At the end of next week, I will implement the following:

1. Closing of the cafeteria to employees between the hours of 9 and 12 and 2 and 5 each day.
2. Implementing a hiring freeze on all headquarters positions. Exceptions must be granted by one person, ME.
3. Implementing a time clock system, requiring ALL EMPLOYEES to "punch in" and "punch out" of work. Any unapproved absences will be charged to the EMPLOYEE'S vacation.
4. Last month, the Board passed a Stock Purchase Program, allowing for employees to purchase Doophis stock at a 15% discount. HELL WILL FREEZE OVER before this CEO allows another employee benefit in this culture.
5. Implement a 5% reduction of staff at headquarters.
6. I am deferring all promotions and raises currently scheduled, until such time as I am convinced that the ones being promoted are the solution, not the problem. (If YOU are the problem, pack your bags!)

Believe me, I think this parental type action SUCKS. Ordinarily, I am a good and kind boss. But what you are doing as managers with this company makes me SICK. It makes me sick to have to write this directive.

We have a big vision. It will take a big effort. Too many at headquarters are not making this effort.

I STRONGLY suggest that you call some 7 AM, 6 PM, AND SATURDAY AM team meetings with the employees who work directly for you. Discuss this serious issue with them, and if they balk or complain, don't be reluctant to fire their butts. I suggest that you call your first Meeting TONIGHT. I suggest that STRONGLY.

I will give you two weeks to fix this. My measurement will be the parking lot; it should be substantially full at 7:30 a.m. and 6:30 p.m. The pizza girl should show up at 7:30 p.m. to feed the starving peasants working late. The lot should be half full on Saturday mornings.

Folks, this is a MANAGEMENT problem not an EMPLOYEE problem.

Congratulations, you are management. And you aren't working HARD enough. You have the responsibility for our EMPLOYEES. I will hold you accountable. You have allowed this to get to this state. You have two weeks.

Tick tock.

Sol

Solomon Doophis
Chairman and Chief Executive
Doophis Corporation
"We Treat You Right"

Questions

1. How would you rate this letter as an employee communication?
2. How would you rate the CEO's language, grammar, punctuation?
3. What would you imagine would be the reaction to this e-mail from those who receive it?
4. How would you "improve" this correspondence?
5. Do you think a "real" CEO could ever send such an e-mail?

Voice of Authority

An Interview with Shaunée L. Wallace

Shaunée L. Wallace, an experienced public relations teacher and practitioner, is pursuing a Ph.D. in mass communication and media studies at Howard University. In addition to serving as an adjunct professor at Iona College, she has worked with a variety of clients, including Def Jam Recordings, *Essence* magazine, the government of Hong Kong, Kmart, Sally Hansen Beauty Products, Royal Caribbean Cruise Lines, and United States Postal Service.

How important is employee communications today?
Employee communications is extremely important. No corporation can succeed with poor communication skills among management and their employees. In order for most organizations to accomplish their internal and external goals, communication on several levels is essential. Whether it is verbal, nonverbal, via e-mail, or through listening, employee communications is significant.

How would you assess the level of trust between management and employees?
The level of trust between managers and employees solely depends on the individual organization. Every corporation is different. Ideally,

trust is an important element within the workplace that is needed to strengthen these professional relationships.

Are print publications still effective in dealing with employees?
Print publications will always be effective, because although technology has provided that many publications can be electronic, there are still those who rely on print. As a result, you must cater to all employees.

How has the Internet effected employee communications?
The Internet has effected employee communications in a major way. Technology has made great strides in our society in general. Whether it is being used as a research tool or for e-mail, the Internet is a necessity for most corporations. Some critics say that e-mail has cut down on face-to-face communication time between employees and management. From an organizational communication perspective, this can have negative effects. However, overall the Internet has contributed to corporations being able to communicate more effectively and efficiently.

What can management do to improve the climate of trust within an organization?
Management can reach out to employees by showing its appreciation in several ways. These include having events such as employee appreciation days, company banquets, summer barbeques, and holiday gatherings. Additionally, providing workshops for the betterment of employees, discounts on gym memberships, and summer or relaxed Fridays (where employees in the summertime can either work half days or wear casual attire on Fridays) may ensure a comfortable work environment.

What communications advice would you give any CEO?
The advice that I would give a CEO is to have an open door policy. This states that at any time he or she is willing to listen to any issues that employees may have within the organization. I would also remind him or her that making a commitment to the success of the organization also means making a commitment to the well-being of the employees.

What can students do to prepare for internal communications work?
Students' preparation for work in internal communications can start right now. While in college, students can apply for work-study positions on campus in the communications department. I also recommend joining the student division of professional organizations such as Public Relations Society of America. Additionally, they can intern at communications firms during the summer months. This will provide a foundation for the students as they begin to build their careers in communications.

Suggested Readings

Aud, Jody Buffington. "What Internal Communicators Can Learn from Enron," *Public Relations Strategist,* Spring 2002, 11–12.

Cohen, Allan. *Effective Behavior in Organizations,* 7th ed. New York: McGraw-Hill, 2001.

Grossman, Jack, and Robert Parkinson. *Becoming a Successful Manager: How to Make a Smooth Transition from Managing Others to Managing Yourself.* New York: Contemporary Books, 2001.

Kreitner, Robert, and Angelo Kinicki. *Organizational Behavior,* 5th ed. New York: McGraw Hill College Division, 2001.

Leat, Mike, *Exploring Employee Relations.* Woburn, MA: Butterworth-Heinemann, 2001. Used in colleges, this text is an excellent introduction to the art of dealing with employees.

Miller, Debra A. "Measuring the Effectiveness of Your Intranet" *Public Relations Strategist,* Summer 2001, 35–39.

Mogel, Leonard. *An Insider's Guide to Career Opportunities,* 2nd ed. Lawrence Erlbaum, 2002.

Ragan Report. Chicago: Ragan Communications. Weekly newsletter, written in an irreverent tone, that captures the very best and worst in internal communications.

Taylor, Winnifred. *The Dragon Complex, Identifying and Conquering Workplace Abuse.* Leawood, KS: Cypress Publishing, 2002.

Ward, Peter, and Rae Andre. *The 59-Second Employee: How to Stay One Second Ahead of Your One-Minute Manager.* Lincoln, NE: iUniverse.com, 2000.

Notes

1. Robert O'Neill, "Unhappy Campers Growing in Number," *The Record,* August 22, 2002, B1–5.
2. "Employee Opinion Surveys—US Workers Feel Pride in Jobs, Organizations, but Don't Trust Managers," Mercer Human Resources Consulting news release, August 29, 2002.
3. "Mass Layoffs in January 2006," U.S. Bureau of Labor Statistics news release, February 23, 2006.
4. Remarks by Fraser P. Seitel, *Ragan Communications International Leadership Summit,* Toronto, Canada, September 30, 2005.
5. "CEOs Rely Most on Public Relations Professionals for Reputation Management," Burson-Marsteller news release, November 12, 2004.
6. Scott DeCarlo, "Special Report on CEO Compensation," *Forbes,* April 21, 2005.
7. "CEO: Worker Pay Ratio Shoots Up to 431:1," United for a Fair Economy news release, August 30, 2005.
8. "Effective Employee Communication Linked to Stronger Financial Performance," Watson Wyatt news release, November 8, 2005.
9. Paul Dorf, "Is Turnover Back in Vogue?" *Ezinearticles.com,* November 2005.
10. "An Employee's Eye View of Business," *Ragan Report,* November 25, 1991, 1, 2.
11. "Management Failing to Connect with Employees at Almost Half of Companies," Right Management Consultants, October 11, 2005.
12. Fraser P. Seitel, "Rebuilding Employee Trust Through S-H-O-C," *odwyerpr.com,* July 11, 2005.
13. Jerry Stevenson, "How to Conduct a Self-Intranet Audit," *Ragan Report,* August 19, 2002, 7.
14. "Two Ways to Pull People to the Intranet," *Ragan Report,* October 18, 1999, 6.
15. "New Frontiers in Employee Communications: Current Practices and Future Trends," survey of Edelman Public Relations, 2004.
16. Scott Rodrick, "Use Intranets to Connect Employee Owners," *Interactive Investor Relations,* January 1997, 3.
17. "All Intranet, All the Time," *Ragan Report,* May 14, 2001, 6.
18. John R. Kessling, "Maintaining a Successful Intranet: The KGN Experience," *PR Tactics,* November 1999, 20.
19. "Kissing Off Your Print Publication," *Ragan Report,* October 11, 1999, 6.
20. John Guiniven, "Suggestion Boxes and Town Hall Meetings: Fix 'Em or Forget 'Em," *Tactics,* February 2000, 22.
21. "Talking to the Troops," *Business Week,* July 5, 1999, 62.

12 Multicultural Community Relations

FIGURE 12-1 Hail to the chief . . . of global social responsibility, that is. Bono, the lead singer of U2 fame, crisscrossed the globe meeting with world leaders, such as President Bush, to spread the gospel of helping the world's impoverished. (Eric Draper/Corbis/All Rights Reserved)

In the old days—1960s, 1970s, and 1980s—corporations prided themselves on their "social responsibility." Their premise was that with the great opportunities they were afforded, companies needed to "give back" to society through participation in and contributions to not-for-profit organizations committed to confront society's most pressing problems—from poverty to education to cultural enrichment.

Then came the 1990s, and corporate social responsibility took a back seat to making money—as much money as possible. The go-go 1990s and early years of the 21st century ended, of course, in the bursting of the stock market bubble, top executives from leading companies being escorted away in handcuffs, and a general reevaluation of the obligations companies have to their communities and the larger society.

In the final years of the first decade of the 21st century, social responsibility is back with a vengeance. And no one is more responsible than this unlikely hero:

Paul David Hewson, also known as Bono, lead singer of the Irish rock band U2, became an iconic symbol of global social responsibility as he met with world leaders and spoke before world bodies to convince governments and institutions to help the world's poor. His efforts were rewarded in countries around the world: Many government and institutions responded by reducing the debt owed them by third-world nations. Meanwhile, in 2005 alone, U2 performed before four million people in 130 sold-out shows and grossed more than $300 million.[1]

The lesson?

In the 21st century, serving one's community once again makes good business sense. The importance of being responsible to diverse, multicultural communities has, in fact, become a front-burner business mandate.

Today's society is increasingly multicultural. America has always been a melting pot, attracting freedom-seeking immigrants from countries throughout the world. Never has this been more true than today, as America's face continues to change. Consider the following:

- In 2000, the U.S. population of 281 million was approximately 75 percent Anglo. Latinos and African Americans represented about 70 million people. By the year 2050, Latinos alone are projected to represent 25 percent of the population; African Americans, about 15 percent, and Asians, 2 percent.[2] Today ethnic minorities spend upwards of $600 billion a year out of a total U.S. economy of $4.4 trillion. This amount is certain to increase substantially.

- In 1940, 70 percent of U.S. immigrants came from Europe; today the vast majority of immigrants arrive from Asia, Latin America, and the Caribbean.

- In 1976, there were 67 Spanish-language radio stations in the United States; today that number has increased fivefold. There are also 100 Spanish-language television stations, 350 Spanish-language newspapers, and a potential audience of 30 million.

- In New York City alone, 12 percent of the population under 18 is foreign-born, and that percentage continues to increase.

- The Internet, a broad canvas of interactive communities uniting the world, has spawned numerous micro-community sites, such as iVillage for women, Africana.com and BlackPlanet.com for blacks, SeniorNet for senior citizens, and Myspace.com for Generation Xers.

Such is the multicultural diversity enjoyed today by America and the world. The implications for organizations are profound. Almost two thirds of the new entrants into the workforce now are women. People of color make up nearly 30 percent of these new entrants. Meanwhile, the Hispanic population has spread out across the nation faster and farther than any previous wave of immigrants.[3]

As the arbiters of communications in their organizations, public relations people must be sensitive to society's new multicultural realities. This is a particular challenge with respect to an increasingly disenfranchised Muslim community in the wake of September 11, 2001, and the war with Iraq. Dealing in an enlightened manner with multicultural diversity and being sensitive to nuances in language and differences in style are logical extensions of the social responsibility that has been an accepted part of American organizational life since the 1960s.

Community Social Responsibility

In light of the increasing diversity of U.S. society, both profit and nonprofit organizations must become more diverse as well and must learn to deal and communicate with those who differ in work background, education, age, gender, race, ethnic origin, physical abilities, religious beliefs, sexual orientation, and other perceived differences. The corporate scandals of the early 21st century underscored the importance of organizations building a reservoir of goodwill among all residents within their host communities.

More and more, organizations acknowledge their responsibilities to the community: helping to maintain clean air and water, providing jobs for minorities, enforcing policies in the interests of all employees, and, in general, enhancing everyone's quality of life. This concept of social responsibility has become widely accepted among enlightened organizations.

For example, most companies today donate a percentage of their profits to nonprofit organizations—schools, hospitals, social welfare institutions, and others. The best companies donate as much as 2 percent or more of pretax profits. In 2004, according to the Conference Board, which polled 189 companies and corporate foundations, the philanthropic numbers were striking:

- $12 billion total estimated corporate charitable contributions in the world
- $7.8 billion corporate giving in the U.S. and abroad
- 54 percent proportion of U.S. giving to health and human services
- 22 percent rise in U.S. giving from 2003 to 2004[4]

Until recent years, corporate philanthropy and social responsibility were uniquely American concepts. U.S. firms feel an obligation to support thousands of community-based groups working to expand affordable housing, create economic opportunity, improve public schools, and protect the environment.

Increasingly, corporate leaders—long absent from the public dialogue on community issues—have begun again to take an active stance in confronting societal challenges, such as protecting the environment. General Electric CEO Jeffrey Immelt, for example, has led his company's effort to reduce its greenhouse gas emission by 1 percent by 2012, which is really a 40 percent reduction when factoring in GE's presumed growth. Ford Motor Company CEO Bill Ford has worked to shift his company's energy use to renewable sources, which today account for 3 percent of Ford's energy use.[5] Tiger Management founder and legendary Wall Street investor Julian Robertson has also devoted significant foundation money to curbing greenhouse gasses.

Corporate contributions like these very much depend on profits. If a company earns little, it can't give much to the community. Lucent Technologies, for example, whose foundation annually contributed more than $50 million, is among many firms that scaled back considerably after hitting hard times (Figure 12-2).

Another element of "giving back to the community" is voluntarism. Many firms, which have given generously to their communities, have become more directly involved by actively encouraging executives and employees to roll up their sleeves and volunteer to help out in their communities. At the Walt Disney Company, for example, Disney VoluntEARS spent more than 800,000 hours in volunteer services over a two-year span. At Volvo, hundreds of car dealers join forces to raise funds for pediatric cancer research at local hospitals (Figure 12-3 and Figure 12-4).

Such initiatives reject the oft-quoted notion of University of Chicago economics professor Milton Friedman that a corporation's only responsibility is to make money and sell products so that people can be hired and paid. It is the job of the individual, not the company, Friedman argued, to serve society through philanthropy. Most companies today flatly reject the Friedman argument. They understand that in the 21st century an organization must be a *citizen* of the community in every respect and accept its role as an agent for social change in the community.

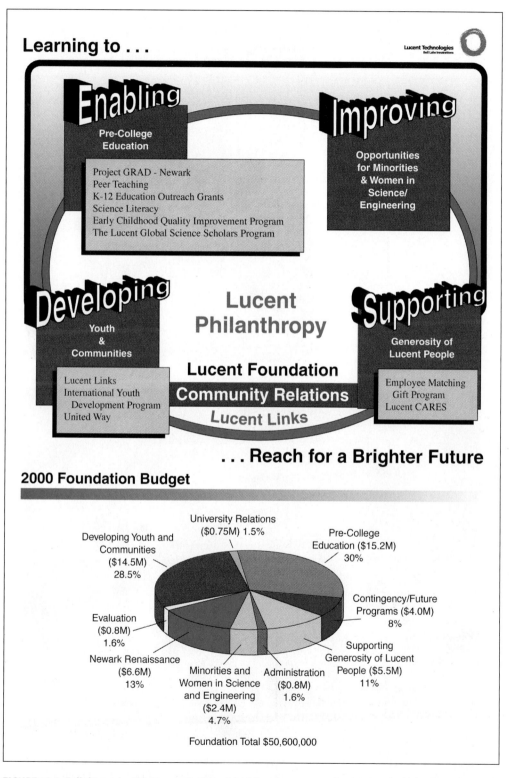

FIGURE 12-2   **Enlightened self-interest.**   Until the fall of the telecom sector in 2000, Lucent Technologies was one of the most "enlightened" of corporations, annually donating more than $50 million to a wide variety of worthwhile charitable endeavors in education and youth development.

FIGURE 12-3 From this ...

FIGURE 12-4 ... to this In 2004, *Volvo for Life Days* celebrated the memory of Alexandra Scott, a young Philadelphia cancer patient, who earned a *Volvo for Life* award by selling lemonade to raise money for pediatric cancer in 2003. A year later, Alex died, and the car company sponsored Alex's Lemonade Stands throughout the country, such as this one in Minneapolis, to raise funds for pediatric cancer research. (Courtesy of Alex's Lemonade Stand Foundation)

Community Relations Expectations

For an organization to coexist peacefully in its community, three skills in particular are required: (1) determining what the community knows and thinks about the organization, (2) informing the community of the organization's point of view, and (3) negotiating or mediating between the organization and the community and its constituents should there be a significant discrepancy.

Basically, every organization wants to foster positive reactions in its community. This becomes increasingly difficult in the face of protests from and disagreements with community activists. Community relations, therefore—to analyze the community, help understand its makeup and expectations, and communicate the organization's story in an understandable and uninterrupted way—are critical.

The community of an organization can vary widely, depending on the size and nature of the business. The 7-Eleven convenience store may have a community of only a few city blocks, the community of a Buick assembly plant may be the city where the plant is located, and the community of a multinational corporation may embrace much of the world.

What the Community Expects

Communities expect from resident organizations such tangible commodities as wages, employment, and taxes. But communities have come to expect intangible contributions, too:

■ **Appearance.** The community hopes that the firm will contribute positively to life in the area. It expects facilities to be attractive, with care spent on the grounds and structures. Increasingly, community neighbors object to plants that belch smoke and pollute water and air. Occasionally, neighbors organize to oppose the entrance of factories, coal mines, oil wells, drug treatment centers, and other facilities suspected of being harmful to the community's environment. NIMBY, "not in my back yard," is their rallying cry.

■ **Participation.** As a citizen of the community, an organization is expected to participate responsibly in community affairs, such as civic functions, park and recreational activities, education, welfare, and support of religious institutions.

■ **Stability.** A business that fluctuates sharply in volume of business, number of employees, and taxes paid can adversely affect the community through its impact on municipal services, school loads, public facilities, and tax revenues. Communities prefer stable organizations that will grow with the area. Conversely, they want to keep out short-term operations that could create temporary boom conditions and leave ghost towns in their wake.

■ **Pride.** Any organization that can help put the community on the map simply by being there is usually a valuable addition. Communities want firms that are proud to be residents. For instance, to most Americans, Battle Creek, Michigan, means cereal; Armonk, New York, means IBM; and Hershey, Pennsylvania, means chocolate. That's why the residents of Hershey were fearful when, in 2002, Nestlé USA offered to buy the pride of Hershey for $11.5 billion. Organizations that help build the town generally become revered symbols of pride.

What the Organization Expects

Organizations, in turn, expect to be provided with adequate municipal services, fair taxation, good living conditions for employees, a good labor supply, and a reasonable degree of support for the business and its products. When some of these requirements are missing, organizations may move to communities where such benefits are more readily available.

The great inner-city exodus of the 1970s is a case in point. New York City experienced a substantial exodus of corporations when firms fled to neighboring Connecticut and New Jersey, as well as to the Sun Belt states of the Southeast and Southwest. New York's state and city legislators responded to the challenge by working more closely with business residents on such issues as corporate taxation. By the new century, not only had the corporate flight to the Sun Belt been arrested, but with business-oriented billionaire Michael Bloomberg as mayor, many firms reconsidered the Big Apple and returned to the now more business-friendly city and state.

The issue for most urban areas faced with steadily eroding tax bases is to find a formula that meets the concerns of business corporations while accommodating the needs of other members of the community.

Community Relations Objectives

Research into community relations indicates that winning community support for an organization is no easy matter. Studies indicate difficulty in achieving rapport with community neighbors, who expect support from the company but object to any dominance on its part in community affairs.

One device that is helpful is a written community relations policy that clearly defines the philosophy of management as it views its obligation to the community. Employees, in particular, must understand and exemplify their firm's community relations policy; to many in the community, the workers are the company.

Typical community relations objectives may include the following:

1. To tell the community about the operations of the firm: its products, number of employees, size of the payroll, tax payments, employee benefits, growth, and support of community projects.
2. To correct misunderstandings, reply to criticism, and remove any disaffection that may exist among community neighbors.
3. To gain the favorable opinion of the community, particularly during strikes and periods of labor unrest, by stating the company's position on the issues involved.
4. To inform employees and their families about company activities and developments so that they can tell their friends and neighbors about the company and favorably influence opinions of the organization.
5. To inform people in local government about the firm's contributions to community welfare and to obtain support for legislation that will favorably affect the business climate of the community.
6. To find out what residents think about the organization, why they like or dislike its policies and practices, and how much they know of its policy, operations, and problems.

7. To establish a personal relationship between management and community leaders by inviting leaders to visit the plant and offices, meet management, and see employees at work.

8. To support health programs through contributions of both funds and employee services to local campaigns.

9. To contribute to culture by providing funds for art exhibits, concerts, and drama festivals and by promoting attendance at such affairs.

10. To aid youth and adult education by cooperating with administrators and teachers in providing student vocational guidance, plant tours, speakers, films, and teaching aids and by giving financial and other support to schools.

11. To encourage sports and recreational activities by providing athletic fields, swimming pools, golf courses, or tennis courts for use by community residents and by sponsoring teams and sports events.

12. To promote better local and county government by encouraging employees to run for public office or to volunteer to serve on administrative boards; by lending company executives to community agencies or to local government to give specialized advice and assistance on municipal problems; and by making company facilities and equipment available to the community in times of emergency.

13. To assist the economy of the community by purchasing operating supplies and equipment from local merchants and manufacturers whenever possible.

14. To operate a profitable business in order to provide jobs and to pay competitive wages that increase the community's purchasing power and strengthen its economy.

15. To cooperate with other local businesses in advancing economic and social welfare through joint community relations programs (Figure 12-5).

Community Relations on the Internet

At the heart of the Internet is a sense of community. Indeed, the Internet links people of like-minded interests in a virtual community, although "community members" may live continents away.

From this concept of community has emerged an effort to use the Internet for social good, to expand educational and commercial opportunities for minority communities as well as provide a philanthropic forum for the less fortunate. For example:

- Black Entertainment Television created BET.com to bring "connectivity, content, and commerce" to African Americans, a community relatively underrepresented in cyberspace. Although 80 percent of non-Hispanic white children use a computer at home, only 48 percent each of African American and Hispanic children use a computer at home.[6] So, armed with $35 million, the largest online investment ever aimed at African Americans, BET.com hoped to help African Americans become more computer savvy. Although some black-oriented sites, among them the NetNoir.com pop culture portal and the hip, urban Volume.com portal, suffered layoffs when the Internet bubble burst, such sites still showed great potential. In 2000, for example, Time Warner paid $10 million for Africana.com in an effort to attract more African American users to AOL.[7]

FIGURE 12-5 Community favorite. The Lowell Spinners baseball team in Lowell, Massachusetts, is an example of a beloved member of the community. The Spinners' innovative public relations director Jon Goode (center) created a host of fan-sponsored events to raise money for local cerebral palsy and cystic fibrosis causes. Here, he brought back two blasts from the past, two-time Super Bowl champion Mark Bavaro (left) and Average Joe 2: Hawaii finalist Brian Worth. (Courtesy of Lowell Spinners)

- In a more global community effort, AOL teamed up with the world's greatest musicians in July 2005 to present LIVE 8, a simultaneous concert in Philadelphia, London, Paris, Berlin, and Rome, designed to turn the world's attention to ending poverty. AOL streamed the broadcast, featuring artists from Alicia Keys and Linkin Park in Philadelphia to Paul McCartney and UB40 in London to Green Day and Roxy Music in Berlin. Five days after the concerts, the G8 leaders of the world's most industrialized nations met and promised to contribute $50 billion more in aid per year by 2010 and to cancel debts owed by 18 of the world's poorest countries.[8]

- Perhaps the most ambitious socially responsible undertaking on the Internet was GreaterGood.com, one of a number of Internet firms that introduced a cause orientation to e-commerce. GreaterGood.com was aimed at America's 650,000 registered not-for-profit charities—from Big Brothers/Big Sisters to Special Olympics to Elizabeth Glaser Pediatric AIDS Foundation. It helped fund these charities by arranging the sale of name-brand retail items on not-for-profit Web sites and then donating part of the purchase price back to the charity.[9]

Although the Internet may be characterized by some as anonymous, acrimonious, and heartless, efforts such as these underscore the Internet's immense potential in furthering human relations and progress—across common communities and for the larger society.

Serving Diverse Communities

What were once referred to as minorities are rapidly becoming the majority. Today, 35 million Americans are foreign born.[10] The U.S. Census Bureau reports that more than two thirds of current U.S. and future population growth is and will be the result of immigration. The 11.2 million immigrants who indicated they arrived in the United States between 1990 and 2000, plus the 6.4 million children born to immigrants in the United States during the 1990s, are equal to almost 70 percent of the U.S. population growth over the last 10 years.[11]

According to the Census Bureau, Latinos, who along with African Americans represent just under 13 percent of the U.S. population, will soon overtake African Americans as the largest minority group. The fastest-growing segment of minorities will be Asians and Pacific Islanders, who now represent a little over 4 percent of the U.S. population.[12]

For many years, women were considered a minority by public relations professionals. This is no longer the case; women now dominate not only the public relations field but also many service industries. Women, African Americans, Latinos, Asians, gays, seniors, persons with disabilities, and a variety of other groups have become not only important members of the labor force but also important sources of discretionary income.

Public relations professionals must be sensitive to the demands of all for equal pay, promotional opportunities, equal rights in the workplace, and so on. Communicating effectively in light of the multicultural diversity of society has become an important public relations challenge.

Women

In the 21st century, women have made great strides in leveling the playing field between their roles and compensation schedules and those of their male counterparts. The days of "mommy tracks" and "mommy wars," glass ceilings, and pink-collar ghettos are rapidly falling by the wayside.

Women today head large corporations, especially in the high-tech area, where Meg Whitman is given great credit as eBay's dynamic CEO and Anne Mulcahy is credited with helping Xerox Corporation come back from the brink of disaster. Other high-profile women executives, most notably Carly Fiorina, who floundered as Hewlett-Packard's CEO before being dumped in 2005, have fared less well.

In public relations, women have steadily climbed into middle- and upper-management positions, both at corporations and public relations agencies. Indeed, with women comprising upwards of 80 percent of public relations practitioners, the field is among the strongest for opportunities for women.

African Americans

Today, 25 of the nation's largest cities—including Chicago, Detroit, and Los Angeles—have a majority population of African Americans, Latinos, and Asians. In addition, foreign-born blacks have increased materially in numbers. In Miami, the West Indian population makes up 48 percent of the black population. In New York, nearly a third of the black population is foreign-born.

The socioeconomic status of African Americans has improved markedly, with disposable income increasing fivefold over the past decade. Despite their continuing evolution in the white-dominated workplace, the nation's 29 million African Americans can still be reached effectively through special media:

- Black Entertainment Television is a popular network that has done well.
- Local African American radio stations have prospered.
- Pioneering Internet sites, such as BlackFamilies.com, Blackvoices.com, Net-Noir.com, and the Black World Today (www.tbwt.com) have created a culture of acceptance and desirability for Web access among African Americans.
- Magazines such as *Black Enterprise* and *Essence* are national vehicles. *Ebony*, the largest African American–oriented publication in the world, has a circulation of 1.5 million.[13]
- Newspapers, such as the *Amsterdam News* in New York City and the *Daily Defender* in Chicago, also are targeted to African Americans. Such newspapers are controlled by active owners whose personal viewpoints dominate editorial policy.

All should be included in the normal media relations functions of any organization. In recent years, companies have made a concerted effort to understand the family structure, traditions, and social mores of the black community through sponsorship of programs targeted to pressing community needs.

One area of frustration in improving the livelihood of African Americans is the practice of public relations. The field has failed to attract sufficient numbers of African American practitioners to its ranks. In recent years, the Public Relations Society of America has increased outreach efforts to attract and retain African Americans. It established the D. Parke Gibson Pioneer Award in 1994 to recognize a practitioner who increases awareness of public relations within multicultural communities. Parke Gibson was a pioneer in multicultural relations and author of two books on African American consumerism.

The National Black Public Relations Society was created to increase the participation of and resources available to black public relations professionals. It has seven chapters and sponsors an annual conference.

Attracting African Americans to the field remains a great challenge to public relations leaders in the new century.

Latinos

There is little question that companies need to reach Latinos. Currently 35 million strong, the group is growing three times faster than the rest of the country. The Census Bureau predicts that the Latin population will jump to 14 percent of the U.S. population in the next five years. At the same time, the African American population is expected to level off at approximately 12.5 percent. Thus, Latinos will soon be the nation's most prominent minority group, and by 2050, Latinos will comprise one third of the population, nearly 100 million people.[14]

The U.S. Hispanic population already ranks as the fifth largest in the world, behind Mexico, Spain, Colombia, and Argentina. In the United States, 77 percent of Hispanics reside mainly in seven states—California, Texas, New York, Florida, Arizona, New Jersey, and Illinois.

New York City has the largest Latin population with 2 million residents. Los Angeles rates second with 1.7 million. The majority of U.S. Latinos—59 percent—are of Mexican origin. About 10 percent are of Puerto Rican origin, and 4 percent are of Cuban origin. In Los Angeles, Latino kindergarten enrollment is 66 percent and rising. The Anglo enrollment is 15 percent and falling.[15]

Accordingly, Latinos comprise a potent political and economic force. Between 1994 and 1998, Latino voting in nationwide midterm elections jumped 27 percent, even as overall voter turnout dropped. In terms of commerce, U.S. Latinos pump $400 billion a year into the economy.[16]

FIGURE 12-6 Todas las Noticias. Television is a key medium for reaching Latinos. News anchors Eduardo Quezada and Andrea Kutyas delivered *Noticias 34* for KMEX-TV. (Courtesy KMEX-TV Univision Los Angeles)

Latinos are voracious media consumers, relying heavily on television and radio to stay informed (Figure 12-6). Two large Spanish-programming networks, Univision and Telemundo, dominate the airwaves, with Univision drawing 83 percent of the country's adult, prime-time, Spanish-language viewing audience. CNN also offers a daily program in Spanish for its Latin American viewers.

Magazines also are a great source of entertainment to the Latino community, with more than 200 Hispanic publications hitting the market in the last 10 years, including *Latin CEO* for top executives to *Latina* magazine for teenage girls to *Healthy Kids en Español* for parents to the general-interest Latina and *People en Español*.[17]

In addition, radio stations and newspapers that communicate in Spanish, such as *El Mundo, El Tiempo, El Diario,* and *La Prensa,* are all prominent voices in reaching this increasingly important community.

Other Ethnic Groups

Beyond Latinos, other ethnic groups—particularly Asians—have increased their importance in the American marketplace.

Japanese, Chinese, Koreans, Vietnamese, and others have gained new prominence as consumers and constituents. Asians and Pacific Islanders account for 4 percent of the U.S. population. At about 7 million today, that number is expected to nearly quintuple—to 32 million by 2050.

The formation of the Asian American Advertising and Public Relations Alliance in California underscored the increasing prominence of Asian Americans in the public relations profession.

Finally, there is perhaps the most misunderstood and put-upon public in this post-9/11 world: Muslims, particularly those living in the United States. Since the attacks on America in 2001, life has become more difficult for many of the estimated 2 to 9 million Muslims living in the United States. Traditionally, many of these people received most of their information from Arabic television stations like Al Jazeera or PTV, the state-run Pakistan Television. In 2004, however, Bridges TV, an English-language network with programming aimed at American Muslims, made its debut. The primary purpose of

Speaking of Ethics

Losing Support for Supporting Gay Rights

Ford Motor Company, besieged by declining sales and worker cutbacks, couldn't get a break in 2005, even when it chose to do the right thing. The company, led by Henry Ford descendant William Clay Ford, found its rebuilding efforts stymied by recurring side issues, including a controversy surrounding advertisements in gay publications (Figure 12-7).

Caught in an ideological divide between a Christian conservative group and gay rights advocates over its advertising plans, Ford announced its Jaguar and Land Rover luxury brands would pull all advertising from gay publications after facing a boycott threat from the American Family Association (AFA), a Christian conservative group, which criticized the automaker for being gay-friendly and

FIGURE 12-7 Rebuilding amidst controversy. Ford CEO William Clay Ford found himself between Christian conservatives and gay advocates in advertising—then not advertising—then advertising again in gay publications. (Courtesy of Ford Archives)

rebuilding

This plan focuses on three key elements: products, cost reduction and aligning our manufacturing capacity with worldwide demand. It lets us get back to the basics of building great products, and doing so profitably.

A legitimate question to ask is whether our intense focus on the economic side of our business will distract us from our environmental corporate citizenship. But that doesn't mean we will abandon our goals or change our direction.

Our revitalization plan is working. Although it includes many short-term actions, the plan gains momentum over the next several years as we launch new products. By mid-decade, we will generate billions of dollars of improved profitability.

And we are proceeding on schedule with the development of the Ford Rouge Center, which will transform our historic Rouge manufacturing complex in Dearborn, Michigan, into a global model of lean and sustainable manufacturing.

Socially, we continue to have a major impact as a large company with a worldwide presence. In 2001, for example, our total charitable giving reached an all-time high of $139 million for projects focused on education, the environment and community development.

Unfortunately, our efforts to strengthen our business economically will have an adverse effect on some employees and communities. We expect to reduce our workforce by 35,000 people worldwide, on a base of 350,000, when all our actions are completed—including closing five plants in North America by mid-decade. We will make every effort to make the changes as non-disruptive and mutually beneficial as possible.

> *Difficult business conditions make it harder to achieve the goals we set for ourselves in many areas, including corporate citizenship. But that doesn't mean we will abandon our goals or change our direction.*

and social efforts. As we said in last year's report, corporate citizenship can only be achieved in the context of a strong and profitable business. But it's also true that businesses can only be as successful as the communities, and the world, that they exist in. That makes ongoing corporate citizenship efforts essential.

Difficult business conditions make it harder to achieve the goals we set for ourselves in many areas, including

Our environmental efforts also build momentum as we introduce new products. In the United States, we are committed to continuous improvement in the fuel economy of all of our vehicles. In Europe, we have agreed, along with others, to reduce the average CO_2 emissions of the vehicles we sell there.

The Company also has set a global target to reduce energy use at its facilities on a production-normalized basis.

We realize that some of the things that must be done will be painful and will impact people's lives in difficult ways. But I sincerely believe that these actions will do the most good for the most people in the long term.

2001 Corporate Citizenship Report — Our Learning Journey   3

FIGURE 12-7 (Continued)

sent out 2 million emails urging supporters not to buy Ford cars and trucks.

Ford said the reason for pulling the ads was "cost-cutting."

"Nonsense," screamed gay advocates, who met with Ford to seek a reversal of the decision.

And that's precisely what Ford did. The company announced that in light of the "misconception about our intent," it would not only reinstitute advertising in publications like *The Advocate* and *Out* but would increase its spending in these publications. "This really proves that at Ford Motor Company, fairness and equality win out," said the president of the Human Rights Campaign, a gay advocacy group.

Predictably, in the spring of 2006, it was the American Family Association's turn to cry foul. The group was furious with Ford's turnaround and reinstituted its boycott. Said AFA chairman the Rev. Donald E. Wildmon, "Ford reneged on the agreement to stop funding homosexual organizations and activities and advertising in homosexual media."

Observers wondered, after the AFA boycott reimposition, if Ford would again change its mind.

For further information, see Jeremy W. Peters, "Still Advertising to Gays, Ford Under Boycott Again," *New York Times,* March 15, 2006.

Bridges TV, said its founder, was to "build bridges of understanding between American Muslims and mainstream America."[18]

Gays, Seniors, and Others

In the 21st century, a diverse assortment of special communities has gravitated into the mainstream of American commerce. One such group is the gay market. To some, homosexuality may remain a target of opprobrium, but in the new century, the gay market, estimated at 12 to 20 million Americans, comprises a major target of opportunity.

An increasing number of marketers, including IBM, United Airlines, and Anheuser-Busch, run advertisements with gay themes. Generally, marketers confine such advertising to the gay press. However, in 2000, Gfn.com devoted $6 million to advertise its Gay Financial Network Internet Web site in the mainstream media. This groundbreaking campaign indicated that gay advertising was ready to cross over into the more widely read and seen media.[19]

Attitudes toward gay people, too, are changing. The number of Americans who think gays should have access to equal rights in employment and public accommodations rose from 56 percent in 1977 to 83 percent in 2000.[20] And gay marriage has become a prominent issue in state and federal elections.

The clear conclusion is that the gay market—average age 36, household income six times higher than the national average and with more discretionary income than average, three times more likely to be college graduates than the national average, and 86 percent of whom saying they would purchase products specifically marketed to them—has become extremely attractive to all kinds of marketers.

Senior citizens also have become an important community for public relations professionals and the organizations they represent. The baby boomer generation has passed 50 years of age. Together, the over-50 crowd controls more than 50 percent of America's discretionary income. The AARP, founded in 1958 for women and men over 50, has a membership of more than 35 million, about half of whom still work for a living.

As the American population grows older, the importance of senior citizens—as consumers, voters, and opinion leaders—will increase. Public relations professionals must be sensitive to that reality and to the fact that other special communities in society will increasingly demand specialized treatment and targeted communications.

At no time was this fact more apparent than when actor Christopher Reeve was paralyzed in 1996 after falling off a horse. Mr. Reeve, who gained fame as the movie hero Superman, became an effective and outspoken advocate for people with disabilities and raised millions of dollars for medical research before his death in 2004.

Nonprofit Public Relations

Among the most important champions of multiculturalism in any community are not-for-profit or just plain *nonprofit* organizations. Nonprofit organizations serve the social, educational, religious, and cultural needs of the community around them. So important is the role of public relations in nonprofit organizations that this sector is a primary source of employment for public relations graduates.

The nonprofit sector is characterized by panoply of institutions: hospitals, schools, trade associations, labor unions, chambers of commerce, social welfare agencies, religious institutions, cultural organizations, and the like. The general goals of nonprofit agencies are not dissimilar to those of corporations. Nonprofits seek to win public support of their mission and programs through active and open communications.

Unlike corporations, though, nonprofits also seek to broaden volunteer participation in their efforts, often through the use of controversial communications tactics to raise public awareness through *media advocacy*. Media advocacy, simply defined, is public relations without resources. Protests, marches, stealth Internet campaigns, and the like are all fair game in media advocacy (Figure 12-8).

Do you feel ripped off having to pay over $100 for a pair of sneakers?

How do you think the men and women who made your sneakers feel?

Most of NIKE's sneakers are made in Indonesia, Vietnam, and China. They make up to 100 shoes and get paid between $2 and $4 per day.

How do you think Philip Knight feels? He's the Chief Executive Officer of NIKE and the 6th richest man in America worth over $5 billion dollars!

Join the SNEAKER GIVE-BACK and protest.

SATURDAY, SEPTEMBER 27, 11:00 A.M.
at
NIKE TOWN, USA
6 East 57th Street off 5th Ave.

Join Youth from community centers in NYC as they turn in sneakers and speak out to protest NIKE business practices here and overseas.

Tell Philip Knight (NIKE's CEO) to pay a decent "LIVING WAGE" to employees in southeast Asia and to stop overcharging and misleading youth here. Reinvest profits in our communities and youth.

Participating Organizations (list in formation, call to participate):
Citizen's Advice Bureau
Edenwald Gun Hill Neighborhood Center
Goddard Riverside Community Center
James Weldon Johnson Comm. Center
School Settlement
United Neighborhood Houses Of NYC
East Side House
Forrest Hills Community House
Hartley House
Kingsbridge Heights Community Center
United Community Center

For additional information:
Edenwald GunHill Neighborhood Center
1150 East 229th Street, Bronx, N.Y. 10466
Phone: (718) 652-2232

Goddard Riverside Community Center
593 Columbus Ave, N.Y., N.Y. 10024
Phone: (212) 873-6600 ext. 204

Labor donated

FIGURE 12-8 Power to the people. Huge corporations, such as Nike, are sensitive when their policies and public image are questioned by protests and placards organized by grassroots community nonprofits.

Talking Points

13 Rules for Radicals

Want to know how to organize a winning protest on campus with no money?

No problem.

Here are the time-honored suggestions of labor leader Saul Alinsky, from his 1971 classic, *Rules for Radicals* (See "Top of the Shelf," this chapter). They are just as relevant now as they were nearly four decades ago. (Just don't tell anybody where you learned 'em!)

1. Power is not only what you have but what the enemy thinks you have.
2. Never go outside the experience of your people.
3. Whenever possible, go outside the experience of the enemy.
4. Make the enemy live up to its own book of rules.
5. Ridicule is a person's most potent weapon.
6. A good tactic is one that your people enjoy.
7. A tactic that drags on too long becomes a drag.
8. Keep the pressure on.
9. The threat is usually more terrifying than the thing itself.
10. The major premise for tactics is the development of operations that will maintain a constant pressure on the opposition.
11. If you push a negative hard and deep enough, it will break through to its counter side.
12. The price of a successful attack is a constructive alternative.
13. Pick the target, freeze it, personalize it, and polarize it.

Master of Many Trades

Also unlike corporations, nonprofits generally don't have much money for key activities. That's why public relations professionals in nonprofits must be masters of many functions, key among them are positioning the organization, developing a marketing or promotional plan, orchestrating media relations, and supporting fund-raising.

Positioning the Organization

With thousands of competitors vying for support dollars, a nonprofit must stand out from the rest. This positioning initiative, to differentiate itself, depends largely on the public relations function. To successfully position the organization, a practitioner must ask:

1. What position do we own; that is, who are we?
2. What position do we want?
3. Who else is out there, and what is their position?
4. Do we have the funds to get us where we wish to go?
5. Can we stick it out over time?
6. Do all our communications line up with each other?

No organization, particularly a resource-challenged nonprofit, can afford to be all things to all people. The best nonprofits, like the best corporations, stand for something. And they are unafraid to "break a few eggs" in order to achieve a clear and differentiable identity (Figure 12-9).

Developing a Marketing/Promotional Plan

Often in nonprofits, the public relations director is the marketing director is the advertising director is the promotion director. The job, simply, is marketing the organization to raise its profile, respect, and levels of support. This requires planning in terms of audiences, messages, and vehicles to deliver those messages to those audiences. Crucial in

FIGURE 12-9 **Communications hardball.** Nonprofits must make every communications dollar count: When the American Cancer Society, American Heart Association, American Lung Association, and Campaign for Tobacco-Free Kids got together against big tobacco, they pulled no punches.

framing these messages is to recognize the *cause-related* quotient—that is, what the organization stands for—around which the marketing campaign is based.

Nonprofit public relations campaigns must depend on clear and coherent messages that articulate well-formulated strategies. Therefore, the nonprofit public relations professional must (1) plan, (2) define issues, (3) build strategies, (4) frame issues, (5) develop talking points, (6) choose appropriate spokespersons, (7) develop communications materials, and (8) target messages.

Media Relations

Because most nonprofits lack sufficient resources for advertising or formal marketing, the use of "free" media is a critical public relations function. As National Public Radio broadcaster Daniel Schorr once put it, "If you don't exist in the media, for all practical purposes you don't exist." Nonprofits desperately need media advocates who champion their cause and mission. Advocacy strategy can take the form of a variety of initiatives:

- **Talk radio.** The extensive audience of this medium is a natural way to spread the nonprofit gospel.
- **Cable Television.** So, too, is the nonstop menu of nightly cable talk television programs, all hungry for outspoken, opinionated, articulate guests.
- **Op eds.** Opinion editorials drafted by nonprofit executives are another prominent—and cheap!—way of getting points of view aired to an influential audience.
- **Cable access.** Community channels are generally willing repositories for nonprofit programming and talent.
- **Internet access.** The Internet has opened up a limitless vista for nonprofits to spread their messages, not only throughout the community but around the world.

Supporting Fund-Raising

Nonprofits depend on donors for support. Fund-raising, therefore, is a key nonprofit challenge that must engage the attention of the organization's key executives. Public relations professionals must be intimately involved in fund-raising communications and appeals so that messages can be targeted and consistent with the organization's general position.

Clearly, there are many other duties of the nonprofit public relations professional. Nonprofit public relations and marketing are described by some as "performing, pleading, petitioning, and praying."

Nonetheless, because America is a nation of joiners and belongers, nonprofit organizations in our society will most certainly continue to proliferate. And the need for competent public relations help will continue to be central to their existence and vitality.

Fund-raising—the need to raise money to support operations—lies at the heart of every nonprofit institution. Schools, hospitals, churches, and organizations—from the mighty United Way to the smallest block association—can't exist without a constant source of private funds. Frequently, the fund-raising assignment becomes the province of public relations professionals. Like other aspects of public relations work, fund-raising must be accomplished in a planned and programmatic way.

A successful fund-raising campaign should include the following basic steps:

1. **Identify campaign plans and objectives.** Broad financial targets should be set. A goal should be announced. Specific sectors of the community from which funds might be extracted should be targeted in advance.
2. **Organize fact-finding.** Relevant trends that might affect giving should be noted. Relations with various elements of the community should be defined. The national and local economies should be considered, as should current attitudes toward charitable contributions.
3. **Recruit leaders.** The best fund-raising campaigns are those with strong leadership. A hallmark of local United Way campaigns, for example, is the recruitment of strong business leaders to spearhead contribution efforts. It is the responsibility of the nonprofit itself to direct its leaders, particularly outside directors, so that their efforts can be targeted in the best interests of the organization.

4. **Plan and implement strong communications activities.** The best fund-raising campaigns are also the most visible. Publicity and promotion must be stressed. Special events should be organized, particularly featuring national and local celebrities to support the drive. Updates on fund-raising progress should be communicated, particularly to volunteers and contributors.

5. **Periodically review and evaluate.** Review the fund-raising program as it progresses. Make midcourse corrections when activities succeed or fail beyond expectations. Evaluate program achievements against program targets. Revise strategies constantly as the goal becomes nearer.[21]

Because many public relations graduates enter the nonprofit realm, knowledge of fund-raising strategies and techniques is especially important. Beginning practitioners, once hired in the public relations office of a college, hospital, religious group, charitable organization, or other nonprofit organization, are soon confronted with questions about how public relations can help raise money for the organization.

Last Word

The increasing cultural diversity of society in the 21st century has spawned a wave of "political correctness," particularly in the United States. Predictably, many have questioned whether sensitivity to women, people of color, the physically challenged, gays, seniors, and other groups has gone too far. One thing, however, is certain. The makeup of society—of consumers, employees, political constituents, and so on—has been altered inexorably. The number of discrete communities with which organizations must be concerned will continue to increase.

Intelligent organizations in our society must be responsive to the needs and desires of their communities. Positive community relations must begin with a clear understanding of community concerns, an open door for community leaders, an open and honest flow of information from the organization, and an ongoing sense of continuous involvement and interaction with community publics.

The public relations profession, responsible as it is for managing the communications of an organization, must take the lead in dealing with diversity. Indeed, in 2004, the Public Relations Society of America initiated Advancing Diversity, a national initiative uniting various elements to promote multiculturism in both the public relations industry and the business community.[22]

Community relations is only as effective as the support it receives from top management. Once that support is clear, it becomes the responsibility of the public relations professional to ensure that the relationship between the organization and all of its multicultural communities is one of mutual trust, understanding, and support.

Discussion Starters

1. How is the atmosphere for community relations different today than it was even at the turn of the century?
2. What is meant by the term *multicultural diversity?*
3. In general terms, what does a community expect from a resident organization?
4. What are typical community relations objectives for an organization?
5. What was the philosophy of corporate responsibility espoused by economist Milton Friedman?
6. What is meant by the term *media advocacy?*
7. Why do companies need to reach the Latino community?
8. What are the primary responsibilities of a nonprofit public relations professional?
9. What is meant by the term *corporate social responsibility?*
10. What are the basic steps of a fund-raising campaign?

Top of the Shelf

Rules for Radicals: A Practical Primer for Realistic Radicals

Saul D. Alinsky, New York: Vintage Books, 1989.

As ancient as it is, Alinsky's *Rules for Radicals,* originally published in 1971, is still the classic handbook for those bent on organizing communities, rattling the status quo, and effecting social and political change as well as for those who wish to learn from a legendary master.

Alinsky, a veteran community activist who fought on behalf of the poor from New York to California, provides strategies for building coalitions and for using communication, conflict, and confrontation advantageously.

In "Of Means and Ends," Alinsky lists his 13 tactics of engagement and 11 rules of ethics that define the uses of radical power.

Alinsky supports his principles with numerous examples, the most colorful of which occurred when he wanted to draw attention to a particular cause in Rochester, New York. Alinsky and his group attended a Rochester Symphony Orchestra performance—after a meal of nothing but beans. The results were predictable—and very funny.

Alinsky died in 1972, but his lessons endure in this offbeat guide to seizing power. Whether your goal is to fluster the establishment or defend it, *Rules for Radicals* is the organizer's bible.

CASE STUDY

The Summers of Harvard's Diversity Discontent

As any self-respecting professor knows all too well, the halls of academia are loaded with sharks. And few are more vulnerable than university presidents who choose to rock the boat. When the presidential boat-rocking concerns the issue of diversity—look out.

An Ideal President

When Lawrence Summers became the president of Harvard University in 2001, it seemed like the perfect choice. His career as a college professor and government official had culminated in his service as U.S. Secretary of the Treasury under President Clinton. A distinguished academic in his earlier days at Harvard, Summers seemed ideal to lead his alma mater, arguably the nation's most prominent institution of higher learning.

Summers, known for his candor and outspokenness, dedicated his presidency to refining Harvard's approach to enhance student learning. He called for a new emphasis on undergraduates and argued that their curriculum should focus more on actual knowledge and quantitative disciplines and less on ways of thinking. And he took bold steps to make a Harvard education more accessible to low-income families. While these objectives were all laudable, the approach Summers took to realize them was most controversial—particularly in an environment like Harvard's, where professors were used to calling their own shots.

Rapping the Rapper

Summers's first public brouhaha occurred when he called in well-known black studies professor Cornel West for a private chat. The president was concerned that West was falling down in one particular area: scholarly activities. Summers wanted West to produce more scholarly articles and do more scholarly research. While West wrote prolifically, the caliber of that writing, according to some, left something to be desired. The *New Republic,* for example, labeled West's books as "almost completely worthless."

Not that Cornel West wasn't busy. He was a frequent talking head on cable television talk shows, an outspoken political activist, and an active entertainer, writing and performing rap music. As a teacher, West was renowned for giving out lots of A's. The students loved him.

When Summers, in West's opinion, pushed too hard, the professor loudly went public to protest. The dispute quickly took on overtones of racism, and when the dust cleared and Summers had apologized, West had flown the coop to take up residence at Harvard rival Princeton University.

Summers also stirred up the campus by belittling a campaign that urged divestment of Harvard investments in Israeli companies, suggesting that such an approach was a form of subtle anti-Semitism. This bold stance, too, angered some in the faculty.

Women and Science

Summers's diversity dilemma deteriorated further in the spring of 2001 when, at a closed-door, off-the-record conference of economists, he raised the subject of why there were so few women in the sciences and engineering profession. The leaked transcript revealed that Summers wondered about the "intrinsic aptitude" of women, the career pressures they face, and discrimination within universities.

The Harvard president went on to compare the relatively low number of women in the sciences to the numbers of Catholics in investment banking, whites in the National Basketball Association, and Jews in farming.

As soon as the remarks hit the press—in the form of a front page story in the *New York Times*—the Harvard campus went ballistic. Irate faculty members called for the president's scalp. Charges of sexism were added to the earlier charges of racism.

Lost in the hysteria were other remarks Summers made at the same conference, that racial and sex discrimination needed to be "absolutely, vigorously" combated. It didn't seem to matter. It was open season on the president. As one "authority" quoted by the *Times,* Princeton Professor Cornel West, charitably put it, "It was good to see the faculty wake up. The chickens have come home to roost."

Once again, faced with growing hostility, Summers went public and apologized, offering to redouble resources for women in science. But his apology wasn't in time to stop a "no confidence" vote of the faculty of Arts and Sciences (Figure 12-10).

The Final Straw

The end for Larry Summers at Harvard came a year after the women in science flap, ignominiously enough, with the president away on a skiing vacation in the first months of 2006.

Summers's detractors among Harvard's faculty were circling to unseat him. While Summers was vacationing, a former Arts and Sciences dean went public with the two-word reason for his departure a year earlier: "Larry Summers."

The former dean gave the *Boston Globe,* Harvard's hometown newspaper, a searing account of Summers's autocratic management style, accusing the president of declaring that those in the field of economics (Summers's field) were "smarter than political scientists and sociologists." The interview ended with the former dean calling for the resignation of his former boss.

The groundswell of faculty opprobrium could not be stopped. Calls came for Summers's firing. Even supporters in the faculty expressed frustration that Summers was forever apologizing for

FIGURE 12-10 Blinding 'em with science. Embattled Harvard President Larry Summers met the press in 2005 after receiving a no confidence vote for remarks he made about women and science. (Steven Senne/AP Wide World Photos)

FIGURE 12-11 Sayonara, Mr. President. At an outdoor news conference attended by the students who wanted him to stay, Larry Summers announced his resignation in 2006 as Harvard president. (Michael Dwyer/AP Wide World Photos)

his remarks. An emergency meeting of the Harvard Board was discussed.

And Summers, the experienced Washington political hand hunkered down in his mountaintop vacation retreat, knew the party was over.

On February 21, Larry Summers returned to Harvard, called a news conference on the quadrangle, and announced his resignation (Figure 12-11).

In a poll of the Harvard student body, only 19 percent thought the president should resign. It was too late.

Questions

1. Do you think Larry Summers was too outspoken?

2. How would you characterize Summers's remarks about diversity?

3. Was it wise for the president to apologize after his public spats with the faculty?

4. If you were Larry Summers's public relations advisor, what would you have counseled him to do in presiding over such a tumultuous situation?

5. If you were the Harvard Board's public relations advisor, what would you have advised it to do about the Summers situation?

For further information, see Dean Barnett, "The End of Summers," *Weekly Standard,* February 22, 2006; Peter Beinart, "Harvard: Coup of the Selfish," *New York Post,* February 25, 2006; Sara Rimer and Patrick D. Healy, "Furor Lingers as Harvard Chief Gives Details of Talk on Women," *New York Times,* February 18, 2005, A1, 20; Thomas Sowell, "Another Victim of Academe Run Amok," *The Record,* February 26, 2006; James Traub, "Lawrence Summers, Provocateur," *New York Times,* January 23, 2005.

Voice of Authority

An Interview with Mike Paul

Mike Paul is an 18-year veteran of strategic public relations, corporate communications, and reputation management. He is president and senior counselor of MGP and Associates PR (MGP). MGP was founded by Paul in 1994 and is a leading boutique public relations and reputation management firm based in New York, providing senior counseling services to top corporate, government, nonprofit, sports, and entertainment clients. In 2004, *PRWeek Magazine* named Paul one of the top crisis communications and reputation management counselors in the world.

How important is an organization's or individual's reputation?
Reputations of all types are so important, I made it our firm's tag line: "Because Your Reputation Is Everything!"™ A reputation is the greatest asset we have, for both a public company and an individual. It must be built, maintained, and repaired to thrive for a lifetime. Sadly, many corporations, organizations, and individuals talk the talk of the importance of reputation, but don't walk the walk.

How can reputation be managed?
The big "bricks" of managing an excellent reputation include truth, humility, transparency, accountability, consistency. Honesty and humility are the most important tools in a reputation management tool belt. Like any disease, a reputation in crisis is a disease that can be cured or can grow out of control and cause severe damage in other areas. Admitting mistakes, lies, and deceit is the first step in reputation management.

What is the state of community relations among organizations today?
Community relations among U.S. organizations are becoming much better, but there is still much work to be done and further commitment and accountability from senior management is necessary to achieve excellence. For example, many community organizations are not teaming up with similar organizations in their arena to achieve community goals. Many are islands among themselves and believe partnering with other community organizations is not part of their mission. One goal of any community relations campaign should be to mirror the population in which you serve.

What is the state of social responsibility among corporations?
Corporate social responsibility has become a key communications and business tool for most corporations today. However, corporations must realize social responsibility has both a community responsibility and a business obligation. For example, a successful social responsibility campaign—local, national, or global—cannot be just a pet project of a CEO or senior management. It must include social and community responsibility interests important to many key audiences, including employees, investors, customers, and the communities in which the corporation operates.

How important is it for an organization to focus on dealing with minorities?
Minorities have become the majority in many communities across the U.S. and around the world. As a result, minority is not an accurate word to use any more for communities or people of color. People, employees, or executives of color are now the appropriate terms to use because of the huge demographic shift in the world. As a result, corporate America and other organizations have begun to truly embrace diversity, but there is much more work to be done. However, the executive ranks are still void of many people of color, and sadly, racism is still alive in many corporations, organizations, and communities in the U.S. and around the world.

What is the state of African Americans in the public relations business?
Two words: in crisis. There are still few African Americans in public relations overall and even fewer executives of color in leadership positions. Most work for community organizations and in government. There has still not been an African American CEO within any of the top 10 global PR firms and very few top global corporate communications executives. Until the CEOs of PR firms and corporate America embrace the problem with the same intensity from both the bottom and the top levels, diversity in PR will continue to be in crisis. Accountability and transparency are both necessary to develop lasting change.

What advice would you give young minority members interested in a public relations career?

First, for young people of color, there are not many executives of color in our business. As a result, seeking a career in our business is a tougher road. The numbers don't lie. Second, seek employment at a top global PR firm to best learn the business and work in as many different divisions as possible. The training programs at these firms are superior to others, and the type of clients you will work with are top notch and best for building skills and an excellent resume. Third, seek out an excellent mentor, and the mentor does not have to be an executive of color. For example, I have the best mentor in our business, Harold Burson of Burson-Marsteller. He gave me excellent advice years ago when I was at B-M, and he still gives me excellent advice today. Many young professionals of color make the mistake of only seeking executives of color. This is a big mistake.

Suggested Readings

Adams, Mauriane, and John H. Bracey. *Strangers & Neighbors: Relations Between Blacks and Jews in the United States.* Boston, MA: University of Massachusetts Press, 2000. A book that moves beyond stereotypes to explore a complex historical relationship.

Banks, James A., and Cherry Banks. *Multicultural Education: Characteristics and Goals.* Hoboken, NJ: John Wiley & Sons, 2005. A compilation of leading academic scholars and researchers about multiculturalism.

Dresser, Norine. *Multicultural Manners: Essential Rules of Etiquette for the 21st Century.* Hoboken, NJ: John Wiley & Sons, 2005. The do's and don'ts of dealing in business with peoples of different backgrounds.

Fineglass, Art. *The Public Relations Handbook for Nonprofits.* San Francisco: Josey-Bass, 2005. All a nonprofit organization needs to organize and implement an effective public relations program.

Fiore, Douglas J. *School Community Relations.* Larchmont, NY: Eye on Education, 2002. This book provides education-related professionals with an introduction to effective community relations.

Gibson, Dirk C. (Ed.). *American Hispanic Public Relations* (Spring 2002). Special issue of Public Relations Quarterly featuring six articles on the subject.

Grunig, Larissa, Elizabeth Toth, and Linda Hon. *Women in Public Relations: How Gender Influences Practice.* New York: Guilford, 2001. Three leaders in the quest for gender equality in public relations share the results of their five-year research of men and women in the field.

Kotler, Philip, and Nancy Lee. *Corporate Social Responsibility: Doing the Most Good for Your Company and Your Cause.* Hoboken, NJ: John Wiley & Sons, 2005. Real-world advice from noted marketing professor Kotler and a respected colleague.

McLaughlin, Shane. "Communicating Across the Gender Gap in Corporate Leadership." *Public Relations Strategist,* Spring 2002, 20–24.

McLaughlin, Shane. "Diversity Drives Dollars for Corporate Communications." *Public Relations Strategist,* Summer 2002, 25–29.

Miller, Patrick. *Sport and the Color Line: Black Athletes and Race Relations in Twentieth Century America.* London, England: Routledge, 2004. A historical look at how race relations has influenced sports in America.

Newsom, Doug A., and Bob J. Carrell. *Silent Voices.* Lanham, MD: University Press of America, 1995. A collection of articles examining issues concerning the status of women worldwide.

Rao, C. P. *Marketing and Multicultural Diversity.* Westport, CT: Quorum Books, 2002.

Rubenstein, Doris. *The Good Corporate Citizen: A Practical Guide.* Hoboken, NJ: John Wiley & Sons, 2004. A primer for CEOs, COOs, and public relations professionals on how to maintain responsible corporate citizenship.

Schreiber, Alfred L. *Multicultural Marketing.* New York: Contemporary Books, 2000.

Tharp, Mary C. *Marketing and Consumer Identity in Multicultural America.* Thousand Oaks, CA: Sage Publications, 2001.

Vogel, David. *The Market for Virtue: The Potential and Limits of Corporate Social Responsibility.* Washington, DC: The Brookings Institution, 2005. A candid look at the constant business battle of "doing what's right" versus "doing what makes the most money."

Weinstein, Stanley. *The Complete Guide to Fund-Raising Management.* Hoboken, NJ: John Wiley & Sons, 2002. From running capital and endowment campaigns to structuring grantsmanship programs, this book tells it all.

Notes

1. David Carr, "Media Age Business Tips from U2," *New York Times,* November 28, 2005, C1.
2. "Profiles of General Demographic Characteristics," 2000 Census of Population and Housing, U.S. Department of Commerce, May 2001.
3. Lynette Clemetson, "Latino Population Growth Is Widespread, Study Says," *New York Times,* July 31, 2002, A14.
4. "The Numbers," *Barron's,* January 16, 2006, 11.
5. "CEO Forum: Environmental Impact," *NYSE Magazine,* January/February 2006, 13.
6. "Computer and Internet Use in the United States: 2003," U.S. Census Bureau, October 2005.
7. Daniel Golden, "Time Warner to Buy Henry Gates's Africana.com," *Wall Street Journal,* September 7, 2000, B1–4.
8. Emmanuel Legrand, "Live 8 Yields a Windfall," *Billboard,* November 5, 2005, Upfront News.
9. Peter Santucci, "Giving a Heart to E-Commerce," *Washington CEO,* October 1999.
10. Anna Quindlen, "Open to All: The Big Job," *Newsweek,* January 9, 2006.
11. Steven A. Camarota, "Immigrants in the United States—2000," Center for Immigration Studies, January 2001.
12. "We the People: Asians in the United States," United States Census 2000, U.S. Census Bureau, December 2004.
13. Jeremy Mullman, "*Ebony* Falls Short of Circulation Promise," *Crain's Chicago Business,* February 23, 2006.
14. "Reaching the Hispanic Audience," *fastforward,* Fall 1999, 1.
15. "The Hispanic Population," United States Census 2000, U.S. Census Bureau, May 2001.
16. "2002 U.S. Hispanic Market," Strategy Resource Corporation, June 2002.
17. "Hispanic Pubs Surge," *Jack O'Dwyer's Newsletter,* January 25, 2006, 3.
18. Laurie Goodstein, "Start-Up Television Venture Is Aiming Its Programming at American Muslims," *New York Times,* November 29, 2004, C7.
19. Ronald Alsop, "Web Site Sets Gay-Themed Ads for Big, National Publications," *Wall Street Journal,* February 17, 2000, B4.
20. "What's So Important about Diversity?" *Ragan Report,* August 9, 2004, 3.
21. Nicole Lewis, "Multiple Missions and a Thousand Ideas," *Chronicle of Philanthropy,* December 8, 2005, 37.
22. "Public Relations Society of America Launches National Diversity Initiative," Public Relations Society of America news release, September 14, 2004.

13 Government Relations

It is ironic that the practice of "public relations"—so defined—has been barred from the federal government since 1913. Congress at the time was worried that those who inhabited the corridors of power might be tempted to use the privileges granted and the attention paid to them by the American people for the advancement of their own agendas or, heaven forefend, the promotion of themselves.

One wonders, therefore, how the legislators of that day would think of their 21st-century publicity-seeking successors, like this individual:

Maryland Democrat Joseph Biden, a perpetual presidential wannabe was typical of the new breed of senators and representatives from both sides of the aisle who seemed to think publicity first and policy second.

Every day, the Washington, D.C. seat of the federal government is a public relations free-for-all, with 435 congressmen, 100 sena-

FIGURE 13-1 Publicity-seeking missile. Maryland Senator Joseph Biden bids for the spotlight at the 2006 confirmation hearings of Supreme Court Justice Joseph Alito by donning a cap from the nominee's Princeton University alma mater. (Susan Walsh/AP Wide World Photos)

tors, 15 cabinet secretaries, and thousands of federal employees supporting them, all jockeying to make the morning newspapers and evening talk shows. One U.S. senator, Democrat Charles Schumer of New York, was legendary for holding press conferences every Sunday—some (most?) of dubious value—simply because Sunday was a notoriously slow news day. On the state and local levels, where the situation is just slightly less blatant, politicians similarly jockey for attention in the media.

Legislators in the 21st century, it seems, have come a far distance from days of President Dwight D. Eisenhower, a former general, who once famously remarked, "If the Army is good, the story will be good, and the public relations will be good. If the Army is bad, the story will be bad, and the public relations will be bad."[1]

Today, by contrast—good, bad, or indifferent; story or no story—politicians crave publicity. Indeed, in the aftermath of September 11, the practice of public relations—and how the government communicates both in the United States and around the world—has probably never been as pivotal.

The war on terrorism depended on candid, frank, and informative communications with the American people and the world. Said President Bush's first press secretary, Ari Fleischer, "The American people are appreciative of the forthrightness of the government. I think the government has an obligation to be forthright."[2]

"Why do they hate us?" the president asked rhetorically about the Muslim attackers and their sympathizers in his historic speech before Congress the week after the terrorist attacks.[3] To combat such hate and to reassure the American people about the goodness of the war effort, the government's public relations initiatives took center stage, particularly in the initial stages of the conflict. Among those initiatives were the following:

- The White House created a permanent Office of Global Communications to coordinate the administration's foreign policy message and supervise America's image abroad.[4]

- Bush mounted the "bully pulpit" of the American presidency often in the first days of the war to win public support. In a riveting speech before Congress and the nation, Bush vowed: "I will not yield. I will not rest. I will not relent in waging this struggle. We will not tire. We will not falter, and we will not fail."[5] As the war in Iraq drifted into its third year, casualties climbed, and support waned, Bush became more reluctant to man the pulpit.

- Also, early on in the war, the Bush cabinet, particularly Defense Secretary Donald Rumsfeld, Attorney General John Ashcroft, and Secretary of State Colin Powell, regularly conducted press conferences of their own to keep the country apprised of developments in their spheres and to cut off critics suspicious of secrecy. Here again, once Ashcroft and Powell departed in Bush's second term and Rumsfeld's popularity diminished, so did the frequency of press conferences.

- The position of Undersecretary for Public Diplomacy and Public Affairs was created in the State Department, immediately after the 2001 attacks, to work to convince the Muslim world of the true values and ethics of America. In 2005, to spearhead this effort, President Bush named his long-time, close public relations advisor, Karen Hughes, to be Undersecretary of State for Public Diplomacy and Public Affairs. (See Case Study, Chapter 15.)

Although the war magnified the role of strategic communications, the fact remains that the smartest politicians recognize the importance of the practice of public relations to their own success in getting themselves elected, their programs supported, and their policies adopted.

As such, the practice of public relations is represented throughout government—in each government branch, in all government agencies, on the state and local levels, and also in lobbying the government to maintain or change legislation. All of these functions are part of the multiple levels of public relations communications in and around government.

Public Relations in Government

The growth of public relations work both with and in the government has exploded in recent years. Although it is difficult to say exactly how many public relations professionals are employed at the federal level, it's safe to assume that thousands of public relations–related jobs exist in the federal government and countless others in government at state and local levels. Thus, the field of government relations is a fertile one for public relations graduates.

Since the 1970s, more than 20 new federal regulatory agencies have sprung up—including the Office of Homeland Security, the Environmental Protection Agency, the Consumer Product Safety Commission, the Department of Energy, the Department of Education, and the Drug Enforcement Administration. Moreover, according to the Government Accounting Office (GAO), more than 120 government agencies and programs now regulate business.

It is little wonder that American business spends more time calling on, talking with, and lobbying government representatives on such subjects as trade, interest rates, taxes, budget deficits, and all the other issues that concern individual industries and companies. It is also little wonder that political interest groups of every stripe—from Wall Street bankers to American Indian tribes to friends of the Earth—contribute more to political coffers than ever before. Thus, today's organizations continue to emphasize and expand their own government relations functions.

Beyond this, the nation's defense establishment offers some 7,000 public relations jobs, although, again, none are labeled "public relations," in Department of Defense military and civilian positions. Indeed, with military service now purely voluntary and an increasingly difficult war in the daily headlines, the nation's defense machine must rely on its public information, education, and recruiting efforts to maintain a sufficient military force. Thus, public relations opportunities in this realm of government work should continue to expand.

As noted, the public relations function has traditionally been something of a "poor relation" in the government. In 1913, Congress enacted the Gillette Amendment, which almost barred the practice of public relations in government. The amendment stemmed from efforts by President Theodore Roosevelt to win public support for his programs through the use of a network of publicity experts. The law was a specific response to a Civil Service Commission help wanted advertisement for a "publicity man" for the Bureau of Public Roads. Congress, worried about the potential of this unlimited presidential persuasive power, passed an amendment stating: "Appropriated funds may not be used to pay a publicity expert unless specifically appropriated for that purpose."

Several years later, still leery of the president's power to influence legislation through communication, Congress passed the gag law, which prohibited "using any part of an appropriation for services, messages, or publications designed to influence any member of Congress in his attitude toward legislation or appropriations." Even today, no government worker may be employed in the "practice of public relations." Public affairs, yes. But public relations, no. Indeed, the government is flooded with "public affairs experts," "information officers," "press secretaries," and "communications specialists."

Government Practitioners

Most practitioners in government communicate the activities of the various agencies, commissions, and bureaus to the public. As consumer activist and recurring presidential candidate Ralph Nader has said, "In this nation, where the ultimate power is said to rest with the people, it is clear that a free and prompt flow of information from government to the people is essential."

It wasn't always as essential to form informational links between government officials and the public. In 1888, when there were 39 states in the Union and 330 members in the House of Representatives, the entire official Washington press corps consisted of 127 reporters. Today, even with the cutbacks in the ranks of newspaper reporters, there are close to 4,000 full-time journalists covering the capital.

In 1990, the U.S. Office of Personnel Management reported nearly 15,000 public relations–related jobs in the federal government. Other estimates are much higher. The National Association of Government Communicators is a national not-for-profit professional network of federal, state, and local government employees who disseminate information within and outside government. Its members are editors, writers, graphics artists, video professionals, broadcasters, photographers, information specialists, and agency spokespersons.

The closest thing to an audit of government public relations functions came in 1986 when former Senator William Proxmire, a notorious gadfly, asked the GAO to tell him "how much federal executive agencies spend on public relations."

At the time, the GAO reported that the 13 cabinet departments and 18 independent agencies spent about $337 million for public affairs activities during fiscal 1985, with almost 5,600 full-time employees assigned to public affairs duties. In addition, about $100 million was spent for congressional affairs activities, with almost 2,000 full-time employees assigned.

Now fast-forward to 2005, where a similar GAO revealed that the Bush administration paid $1.6 billion—that's $1.6 *billion*—on advertising and public relations contracts over a two-and-a half-year period, with $88 million spent in 2004 alone. The Department of Defense spent $1.1 billion of that for recruitment campaigns and public relations efforts. A total of 54 public relations firms were contracted as part of this effort.[6]

Two Prominent Departments

Even before the war on terrorism, the most potent public relations voices in the federal government, exclusive of the president, were the U.S. departments of State, first, and Defense, second. After September 11, 2001, the communications importance of both increased, but their relative positions were reversed.

The State Department

The State Department, like other government agencies, has an extensive public affairs staff, responsible for press briefings, maintaining secretary of state homepage content, operating foreign press centers in Washington, New York, and Los Angeles, as well as managing public diplomacy operations abroad.

In October 1999, as part of the Foreign Affairs Reform and Restructuring Act of 1998, the State Department inherited the United States Information Agency (USIA), for many years the most far-reaching of the federal government's public relations arms. USIA had been an independent foreign affairs agency within the executive branch created in 1953 by President Dwight Eisenhower. Its job was to explain and support American foreign policy and promote U.S. national interests through a wide range of overseas information programs and educational and cultural activities.

The State Department consolidated USIA's 6,352 employees, of whom 904 are Foreign Service personnel and 2,521 are locally hired Foreign Service nationals overseas. There are 2,927 civil service employees based in the United States, of whom 1,822 work in international broadcasting and 1,105 are engaged in USIA's educational and informational programs.

The director of the USIA had reported directly to the president and received policy guidance from the secretary of state. Under the 1999 integration plan, an undersecretary for public diplomacy and public affairs within the State Department was chosen to head the operation. The USIA's annual appropriation has exceeded $1 billion since the late 1980s.

In the 21st century, with America's motives for the war on terrorism challenged around the world, the former USIA's mission—"to support the national interest by conveying an understanding abroad of what the United States stands for"—has been modified to include new challenges:

- Build the intellectual and institutional foundations of democracy in societies around the globe.

- Support the war on drugs in producer and consumer countries.

- Develop worldwide information programs to address environmental challenges.

- Bring the truth to any society that fails to exercise free and open communication.

In its 46-year history, the USIA was a high-level public relations operation and not without controversy. Under the direction of such well-known media personalities as Edward R. Murrow, Carl Rowan, Frank Shakespeare, and Charles Z. Wick, the agency prospered. In 2002, the Voice of America (VOA), the State Department's leading voice overseas, named veteran *Time* magazine correspondent David Jackson as director.

The communications initiatives of the State Department to spread the "gospel of America" are far-reaching. Among them are the following:

1. **Radio.** VOA, which first went on the air in 1942, broadcasts more than 1,000 hours of programming weekly in 44 languages, including English, to an international audience of more than 100 million listeners. In 2006, the U.S. Congress appropriated $166 million for VOA. In addition to VOA, the USIA in 1985 began Radio Marti, in honor of José Marti, father of Cuban independence. Radio Marti's purpose is to broadcast 24 hours a day to Cuba in Spanish and "tell the truth to the Cuban people" about ruler Fidel Castro and communism.

2. **Film and television.** The agency annually produces and acquires an extensive number of films and videocassettes for distribution in 125 countries. VOA produces more than 30 hours of television per week in 24 languages, from Albanian to Urdu. TV Marti in Cuba, for example, telecasts four-and-a-half hours daily.

3. **Internet.** VOA uses a distributed network, including more than 14,000 servers in 65 countries, to deliver Internet content. News is also available via e-mail subscription service in English and an increasing number of broadcast languages. Electronic journals were created to communicate with audiences overseas on economic issues, political security and values, democracy and human rights, terrorism, the environment, and transnational information flow.[7]

4. **Media.** About 25,000 words a day are transmitted to 214 overseas posts for placement in the media.

5. **Publications.** Overseas regional service centers publish 16 magazines in 18 languages and distribute pamphlets, leaflets, and posters to more than 100 countries.

6. **Exhibitions.** Approximately 35 major exhibits are USIA-designed annually for worldwide display, including in Eastern European countries and the former Soviet Union.

7. **Libraries and books.** The agency maintains or supports libraries in more than 200 information centers and binational centers in more than 90 countries and assists publishers in distributing books overseas.

8. **Education.** The agency is also active overseas in sponsoring educational programs through 111 binational centers where English is taught and in 11 language centers. Classes draw about 350,000 students annually.

The Defense Department

The importance of Department of Defense (DOD) communications has been intensified in wartime. The DOD's public affairs network is massive—3,727 communicators in the Army, 1,250 in the Navy, 1,200 in the Air Force, 450 in the Marines, and 200 at headquarters. The DOD public affairs department is headed by an assistant secretary of defense for public affairs, one of six direct reports to the deputy secretary of defense (Figure 13-2).

With the DOD consisting of more than 3 million active duty forces, reserves, and civilian employees, information is the strategic center of gravity. Communications must be organized, secure, and rapid to fulfill the department's mission.

Although each service has its own public affairs organization and mission, DOD's American Forces Information Service (AFIS) promotes cooperation among the various branches. AFIS is responsible for maintaining the Armed Forces Radio and Television Service, *Stars and Stripes* newspaper, communications training at the Defense Information School, and a variety of other functions (Figure 13-3).

Postwar public relations efforts of the Department of Defense have run the gamut from drawing universal praise to generating opprobrium. When the United States invaded Iraq in 2003, the department was lauded for "embedding" reporters with the troops in the field in order for Americans to get first-hand information about the battle.

Two years later, the department generated harsh criticism for elaborate psychological operations, or "psy-ops," which included using information as a tool of war by such means as planting information—often for pay—with sources used by Arabic television and newspapers to help influence the portrayal of the United States in Muslim media. One mysterious Washington-based "public relations firm," the Lincoln Group, received a $20 million, 2-month DOD contract to plant such stories in Iraq. This set off a battle within the Pentagon as to the proper use of information and public relations methods in wartime.[8]

Other Government Agencies

Beyond the State and Defense departments, other government departments also have stepped up their public relations efforts. The Department of Health and Human Services has a public affairs staff of 700 people. The departments of Agriculture, State, and Treasury each have communications staffs in excess of 400 people, and each spends more than $20 million per year in public relations–related activities. Even the U.S. Central Intelligence Agency has three spokespersons. Out of how many CIA public relations people, you ask? Sorry, that's classified.

The President

Despite early congressional efforts to limit the persuasive power of the nation's chief executive, the president today wields unprecedented public relations clout. The president travels with his own media entourage, controls the "bully pulpit," and with it, a large part of the nation's agenda. Almost anything the president does or says makes news.

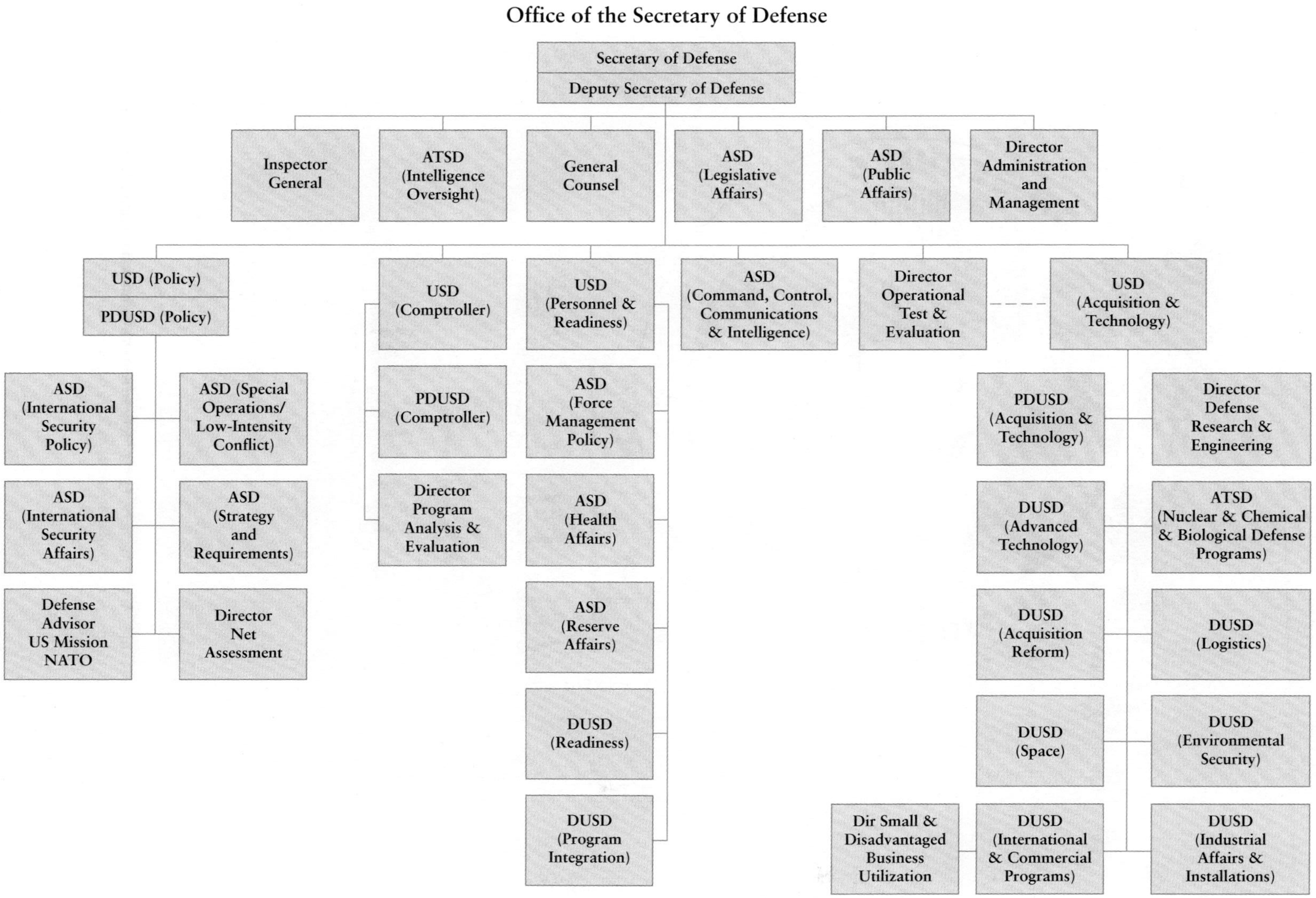

Office of the Secretary of Defense

FIGURE 13-2 DOD public relations organization. The Assistant Secretary of Defense for Public Affairs was one of six who reported to the Defense Secretary's chief deputy. (Courtesy of Department of Defense)

FIGURE 13-3 AFIS. The primary mission of the American Forces Information Service is to integrate the vast communications resources of the various military branches under one communications umbrella. (Courtesy of Department of Defense)

About AFIS

Mission

Provide high-quality news, information, and entertainment to U.S. Forces worldwide in order to promote and sustain unit and individual readiness, quality of life and morale.

AFIS trains public affairs, broadcast and visual information professionals, and provides communications services to support the informational needs of commanders and combat forces through the entire range of military operations and contingencies.

Vision

Keep America's Armed Forces the best informed Armed Forces in the world.

Initiatives

- Take a leadership role in promoting cooperation among the Military Services in all aspects of internal communications.

- Ensure that access to AFIS products by internal audiences is free (or lowest possible cost) and consistent among all commands/Services.

- Identify and promote AFIS products to all audiences.

- Develop integrated AFIS website for DefenseLINK.

FIGURE 13-3 (Continued)

The broadcast networks, daily newspapers, and national magazines follow his every move. His press secretary provides the White House press corps (a group of national reporters assigned to cover the president) with a constant flow of announcements supplemented by daily press briefings. Unlike many organizational press releases that seldom make it into print, many White House releases achieve national exposure.

Ronald Reagan and Bill Clinton were perhaps the most masterful presidential communicators in history. Reagan gained experience in the movies and on television, and even his most ardent critics agreed that he possessed a compelling stage presence. As America's president, he was truly the "Great Communicator." Mr. Reagan and his communications advisers followed seven principles in helping to "manage the news":

1. Plan ahead.
2. Stay on the offensive.
3. Control the flow of information.
4. Limit reporters' access to the president.
5. Talk about the issues you want to talk about.
6. Speak in one voice.
7. Repeat the same message many times.[9]

So coordinated was Reagan's effort to "get the right story out" that even in his greatest public relations test—the accusation at the end of his presidency that he and his aides shipped arms to Iran and funneled the payments to support Contra rebels in Nicaragua, in defiance of the Congress—the president's "Teflon" image remained largely intact. The smears simply washed away.

George H. W. Bush was not as masterful as his predecessor in communicating with the American public. Indeed, Bush met his communications match in 1992 when Bill Clinton beat him soundly in the presidential race.

The press had a love–hate relationship with President Clinton. On the one hand, Clinton's easygoing, "just folks" demeanor, combined with an unquestioned intelligence and grasp of the issues, was praised by the media. On the other hand, the president's legendary "slickness," accentuated by his false statements and downright lying to the American people during the Monica Lewinsky affair caused many journalists to treat him warily.[10]

President Clinton's accessibility to the media—except during the Lewinsky saga—and his commonsense approach to dealing with media were greatly responsible for his popularity, despite a series of embarrassing scandals afflicting his administration during both terms of his presidency. (Of course, a booming economy helped too!)

George W. Bush, like his father, wasn't particularly comfortable with the press and public speaking. However, the second President Bush came of age as a communicator with the events of September 11, 2001. After the terrorist attacks, Bush delivered a historic speech before Congress, addressed workers at the World Trade Center site through a bullhorn, and conducted frequent press conferences in Washington and at his ranch in Crawford, Texas. The terrorist challenge of Bush's first term had awakened his communications instincts (Figure 13-4).

In his second term, however, particularly as reports from the war in Iraq became increasingly pessimistic, Bush's relationship with the media soured significantly. In 2006, as his popularity plummeted to around the 35 percent level, Bush was charged with being "too isolated."[11] To combat this feeling, the president's advisors answered with a full-fledged public relations program centered around lengthy question-and-answer sessions around the country with editors, students, and community leaders.

FIGURE 13-4 Hail to the publicity chief. As a wartime president, George W. Bush, here with first-term press secretary Ari Fleischer, met the media challenge immediately after 9/11 with strength and confidence. (Courtesy of the White House Photo Office)

Talking Points

The First Public Relations Lady

Beginning with the presidency of Lyndon Baines Johnson, the president's wife—the first lady—also has borrowed the bully pulpit of public relations to promote pet causes.

In Lady Bird Johnson's case, it was national beautification. President Gerald Ford's wife, Betty, promoted mental health; Nancy Reagan fought drug abuse; and Barbara Bush and her daughter-in-law, Laura, both spoke against illiteracy. The latter became more publicity-oriented in her husband's second term to help boost his sagging popularity.

But by far the most outspoken public relations–oriented first lady was President Bill Clinton's wife, Hillary. As first lady, Hillary Clinton took an active role in education and health care policy, and then later parlayed that involvement by becoming the junior senator from New York (Figure 13-5).

All eyes turned to 2008 and the next run for the roses, when some suspected Hillary Clinton might be the first first lady to run for president.

FIGURE 13-5 Looking presidential. Senator Hillary Clinton, the nation's most visible first lady, seemed poised to take a shot at making her husband the nation's first "first man." (Stuart Ramson/AP Wide World Photos)

The President's Press Secretary

Some have called the job of presidential press secretary the second-most difficult position in any administration. The press secretary is the chief public relations spokesperson for the administration. Like practitioners in private industry, the press secretary must communicate the policies and practices of the management (the president) to the public. Often it is an impossible job.

In 1974, Jerald terHorst, President Ford's press secretary, quit after disagreeing with Ford's pardon of former President Richard Nixon. Said terHorst, "A spokesman should feel in his heart and mind that the chief's decision is the right one so that he can speak with a persuasiveness that stems from conviction."[12]

A contrasting view of the press secretary's role was expressed by terHorst's replacement in the job, former NBC reporter Ron Nessen, who said, "A press secretary does not always have to agree with the president. His first loyalty is to the public, and he should not knowingly lie or mislead the press."[13] A third view of the proper role of the press secretary was offered by a former public relations professional and Nixon speechwriter who became a *New York Times* political columnist, William Safire:

> *A good press secretary speaks up for the press to the president and speaks out for the president to the press. He makes his home in the pitted no-man's land of an adversary relationship and is primarily an advocate, interpreter, and amplifier. He must be more the president's man than the press's. But he can be his own man as well.*[14]

In recent years, the position of press secretary to the president has taken on increased responsibility and has attained a higher public profile. Jimmy Carter's press secretary, Jody Powell, for example, was among Carter's closest confidants and frequently advised the president on policy matters. He went on to found his own Washington public relations agency. James Brady, the next press secretary, who was permanently paralyzed in 1981 by a bullet aimed at President Reagan, later joined his wife, Sarah, to lobby hard for what would become known as the Brady Bill, establishing new procedures for licensing handguns.

Over time, the position of press secretary has been awarded more to career public relations people than to career journalists. Larry Speakes, who followed Brady, was a former Hill and Knowlton executive and was universally hailed by the media for his professionalism. During Reagan's second term, Speakes apparently was purposely kept in the dark by Reagan's military advisers planning an invasion of the island of Grenada. The upset press secretary later apologized to reporters for misleading them on the Grenada invasion.

The next press secretary was a low-key, trusted, and respected lifetime government public relations professional, Marlin Fitzwater. His successor was another career political public relations professional, Dee Dee Myers, who was respected by the media and brought a refreshing perspective to her role as President Clinton's press secretary. She went on to become a cable talk show host and magazine editor.

The trend toward retaining experienced communications people continued in the second Clinton White House, with the president hiring political public relations veteran Mike McCurry. When McCurry left in 1998 to help form a new Washington public affairs agency, he was replaced by another public relations veteran, Joe Lockhart.

President George W. Bush appointed another government communications veteran, Ari Fleischer, as his press secretary. Upon taking over, Fleischer looked at the challenge optimistically, "I may be crazy, but I like working with reporters."[15] In his second term, Bush appointed his longtime Texas press aide Scott McClellan as press secretary.

McClellan, a member of a prominent Texas political family, had his hands full as White House reporters grew increasingly more testy when Bush's second term ran into problems.[16] McClellan's ineffectual performance as press secretary made him an easy target for the press and only added to Bush's public relations problems in his second term. (See "non-Interview" at the end of this chapter.) In April 2006, McClellan was dumped and replaced by Fox News host Tony Snow.

Over the years, the number of reporters hounding the presidential press secretary—dubbed by some "the imperial press corps"—has grown from fewer than 300 reporters during President Kennedy's term to around 3,000 today. Salaries approaching six figures, rare in most media offices in prior years, are today common in Washington bureaus. Television network White House correspondents command higher incomes, with each

Speaking of Ethics

Shooting V.P. "Ducks" the Media

By far the most bizarre incident of the George W. Bush administration was the shooting accident in February 2006 involving Vice President Dick Cheney. Cheney, a former congressman, secretary of defense, and aide to former presidents, was considered the most secretive and shadowy of all the George W. Bush advisors. He was also considered smart and mistake-free. That's why the news emanating from Texas one winter weekend that Cheney "had shot a fellow hunter" while quail hunting seemed so preposterous.

What complicated the situation even further was the unusual way the information was communicated to the public. Rather than a Cheney public relations person disseminating the news to the White House press, the story was communicated by the owner of the ranch on which the hunting accident took place. The recipient of the communication was the local newspaper in Corpus Christi, which didn't put the information on the news wires until 24 hours later.

FIGURE 13-6 **"Duck!"** (Courtesy of O'Dwyer.com)

Particularly incensed was the White House press corps, which vented its anger on a harassed Presidential Press Secretary Scott McClellan. McClellan gamely explained that the woman who communicated the news of the shooting had been an eyewitness and that she delivered the news immediately to the newspaper, which in turn was expected to get it to the Associated Press for dissemination around the country. As to the vice president's unavailability to speak to the media about the incident until several days later, McClellan explained that Cheney was primarily concerned about the condition of the man he shot (Figure 13-6).

The media weren't buying it. Said one outraged NBC correspondent, "This is a false debate, stoked by a president and vice president who have made no bones about the fact that they don't have much respect for the press corps as an institution."

For further information, see Katherine Q. Seelye, "Another White House Briefing, Another Day of Mutual Mistrust," *New York Times,* February 27, 2006, C1, and Fraser P. Seitel, "The Final Word on Dangerous Dick Cheney," odwyerpr.com, February 21, 2006.

major network assigning two or three correspondents to cover the White House simultaneously.

Dealing with such a host of characters is no easy task, and the role of press secretary is neither easy nor totally satisfactory. As former press secretary McCurry, who began the practice of televising the daily White House press secretary press briefing, put it, "Having a single person standing at a podium and answering questions and trying to explain a complicated world is not a very efficient way to drive home the idea that government can make a difference."[17] Perhaps President Johnson, the first chief executive to be labeled an "imperial president" by the Washington press corps, said it best when asked by a Television reporter what force or influence he thought had done the most to shape the nature of Washington policy. "You bastards," Johnson snapped.[18]

Lobbying the Government

The business community, foundations, and philanthropic organizations have a common problem: dealing with government, particularly the mammoth federal bureaucracy. Because government has become so pervasive in organizational and personal life, the number of corporations and trade associations with government relations units has grown steadily in recent years.

The occupation of lobbyist is one of the nation's greatest growth industries. The number of registered lobbyists in Washington has more than doubled since 2000 to more than 34,750—a 66 percent increase. Why? Three factors, according to experts:

1. Rapid growth in government
2. Republican control of both the White House and Congress
3. Wide acceptance among corporations that they need to hire professional lobbyists to secure their share of the federal budget[19]

In terms of spending, lobbying is such big business that approximately $2 billion a year—$6 million a day—is spent lobbying the federal government.[20] And that's just federal. State government lobbying is only slightly less active. In New Jersey alone, lobbyists spent $28.5 million in 2005, moving or stopping particular legislation.[21]

Government relations people are primarily concerned with weighing the impact of impending legislation on the company, industry group, or client organization. Generally, a head office government relations staff complements staff members who represent the organization in Washington, D.C., and state capitals. These representatives have several objectives:

1. To improve communications with government personnel and agencies
2. To monitor legislators and regulatory agencies in areas affecting constituent operations
3. To encourage constituent participation at all levels of government
4. To influence legislation affecting the economy of the constituent's area, as well as its operations
5. To advance awareness and understanding among lawmakers of the activities and operations of constituent organizations

Carrying out these objectives requires knowing your way around the federal government and acquiring connections. A full-time Washington representative is often employed for these tasks.

To the uninitiated, Washington (or almost any state capital) can seem an incomprehensible maze. Consequently, organizations with an interest in government relations usually employ a professional representative, who may or may not be a registered lobbyist, whose responsibility, among other things, is to influence legislation. Lobbyists are required to comply with the federal Lobbying Act of 1946, which imposed certain reporting requirements on individuals or organizations that spend a significant amount of time or money attempting to influence members of Congress on legislation.

In 1995, the Lobbying Disclosure Act took effect, reforming the earlier law. The new act broadened the activities that constitute lobbying and mandated government registration of lobbyists. Under the new law, a lobbyist is an individual who is paid by a third party to make more than one "lobbying contact," defined as an oral or written communication to a vast range of specific individuals in the executive and legislative branches of the federal government.

In fact, one need not register as a lobbyist in order to speak to a senator, congressional representative, or staff member about legislation. But a good lobbyist can earn the respect and trust of a legislator. Because of the need to analyze legislative proposals and to deal with members of Congress, many lobbyists are lawyers with a strong Washington background. Lobbying ranks are loaded with former administration officials and congressional members, who often turn immediately to lobbying when they move out of office. In 2006, even the former attorney general of the United States, John Ashcroft, announced that he, too, would hang up his shingle as a lobbyist.[22]

Lobbyists, at times, have been labeled everything from influence peddlers to fixers to downright crooks. In 2005, with the admissions of super-lobbyist Jack Abramoff about luring congressmen on golf outings and in the process ripping off American Indian tribe clients for millions of dollars, the practice of lobbying reached a new low.

Despite the slings and arrows, the fact is that today's lobbyist is likely to be a person who is well informed in his or her field and who furnishes Congress with facts and information necessary to make an intelligent decision on a particular issue. This task—the lobbyist's primary function—is rooted in nothing less than the First Amendment right of all citizens to petition government.

What Do Lobbyists Do?

The number of lobbyists registered with the U.S. Senate has increased from just over 3,000 in 1976 to just under 35,000 today. Lobbying has become big business.

But what exactly do lobbyists do?

The essence of a lobbyist's job is to inform and persuade. The contacts of lobbyists are important, but they must also have the right information available for the right legislator. The time to plant ideas with legislators is well before a bill is drawn up, and skillful lobbyists recognize that timing is critical in influencing legislation. The specific activities performed by individual lobbyists vary with the nature of the industry or group represented. Most take part in these activities:

1. **Fact-finding.** The government is an incredible storehouse of facts, statistics, economic data, opinions, and decisions that generally are available for the asking.

2. **Interpretation of government actions.** A key function of the lobbyist is to interpret for management the significance of government events and the potential implications of pending legislation. Often a lobbyist predicts what can be expected to happen legislatively and recommends actions to deal with the expected outcome.

3. **Interpretation of company actions.** Through almost daily contact with congressional members and staff assistants, a lobbyist conveys how a specific group feels about legislation. The lobbyist must be completely versed in the business of the client and the attitude of the organization toward governmental actions.

4. **Advocacy of a position.** Beyond the presentation of facts, a lobbyist advocates positions on behalf of clients, both pro and con. Hitting a congressional representative early with a stand on pending legislation can often mean getting a fair hearing for the client's position. Indeed, few congressional representatives have the time to study—or even read—every piece of legislation on which they are asked to vote. Therefore, they depend on lobbyists for information, especially on how the proposed legislation may affect their constituents.

5. **Publicity springboard.** More news comes out of Washington than from any other city in the world. It is the base for thousands of press, television, radio, and magazine correspondents. This multiplicity of media makes it the ideal springboard for launching organizational publicity. The same holds true, to a lesser degree, in state capitals.

6. **Support of company sales.** The government is one of the nation's largest purchasers of products. Lobbyists often serve as conduits through which sales are made. A lobbyist who is friendly with government personnel can serve as a valuable link for leads to company business.[23]

Do-It-Yourself Lobbying

Even though, in recent years, the activity of lobbying has been associated with the largest corporations, individuals and smaller groups can also benefit through legislative contact. The following are the principles that any citizen can use in lobbying a legislator:

■ **Know the subject and status of the legislation.** Like any other practitioner of public relations, lobbyists must demonstrate a comprehensive knowledge of the legislation on which they seek action. That means first—before even considering calling on a legislator—you must review thoroughly the history of the bill in question, its supporters and detractors over time, and the detours it has experienced as it has meandered its way through the legislative process.

■ **Know the position of the legislator and the staff.** Just as you would never approach a journalist about a story without first reviewing how he or she has treated similar subject matter, so, too, would you never approach a legislator about a piece of legislation without first considering the person's background and biases.

- **Represent a key constituency.** Obviously, you can't dictate the importance of your employer to the legislator. The hard reality is that regardless of the cogency or urgency of your arguments, legislators will be a lot more interested in your views if you represent a group that means *votes.* After all, politicians are, by definition, well, *politicians.*

- **Be available and eager to please.** A good lobbyist must be an eager supplicant to the distinguished legislator. That means making himself or herself available whenever the legislator needs to talk. It also means delivering requested information immediately and in a form readily understandable.

- **Have influential backup at the ready.** It is also obligatory for a lobbyist to prepare influential backup support in the legislator's home state, district, or community. Part of a lobbyist's homework—well before confronting the legislator—is to identify important local opinion leaders, speak with them, determine where they stand on the issue in question, and attempt to prevail upon them to support your view.

- **Keep your word.** The cardinal rule in the practice of public relations is, *Never lie.* That goes double for lobbyists.

- **Know how the system functions.** Common sense: If you're a state house lobbyist, know all you can about the real workings of the state legislative body and its members. If you're a federal lobbyist, you simply must understand the real-world workings of the Congress and the Executive Branch.[24]

Just as in any other part of public relations practice, the success of a lobbyist depends largely on one thing: preparation.

Emergence of E-Lobbying

As it has in every other area of society and public relations work, the Internet has influenced the practice of lobbying as well. In terms of political campaigning and grassroots lobbying, the presidential campaign of 2000 established the role of the Web in political campaigning. The Bush–Gore campaign was politics at cyberspeed. Gore's camp, in particular, regularly barraged 1,200 reporters and news editors on their e-mail list with positive references to Gore positions and negative critiques of their opponents' proposals. Ironically, the more e-mail grew as a direct communications electioneering mechanism, the more voters used the new technology—voice mail, caller ID, satellite dishes, remote controls, and digital programming—to shut out political messages.[25]

By the time the 2004 Bush–Kerry campaign rolled around, candidates at every level were creating sophisticated Web sites to discuss issues, provide biographies, offer campaign schedules, solicit funds, and recruit volunteers and support.

Beyond these measures, the Internet has become a pivotal tool, used by both parties, to inform voters about election issues (Figure 13-7). One Democrat Web site, in particular, MoveOn.org, financed by the billionaire George Soros, was credited as "one of the most influential . . . organizations in U.S. politics."[26] Founded in 1998 by Clinton sympathizers opposed to impeachment and eager for the Congress to "move on," the site has become a rallying point for liberal issues. On the other side, a host of conservative sites—from GOP Cyber Volunteers to Log Cabin Republicans to GOPAC—lead the charge from the right of the aisle.

Not the Face of American Values

Dear ROSEMARY SEITEL,

Every day, it becomes more apparent that we need a president who knows how to lead in a way that reflects America's values—a president who trusts the people with the truth.

Click here now!

It's as simple as this. We can't let George Bush, Dick Cheney, John Ashcroft and Donald Rumsfeld be the face of American values any longer.

We've seen enough. And that's why your immediate financial support is absolutely critical. John Kerry and other candidates committed to moving America in a new, more promising direction need your help now.

Click here to make a donation that
will let American be America again.

We've seen enough:

- Enough of the **damage that can be done to democracy's cause** around the world.
- Enough of the **hardship and pain inflicted on America's families** by George W. Bush's gross mismanagement of the economy.
- Enough of the fear and heartache that result when we find our future in the hands of a president who is **constantly scheming to undermine Medicare and Social Security.**
- Enough of a president who has **tried every trick in the book to stack our courts** with right-wing judges and put our most fundamental freedoms in jeopardy.

Here's the bottom line. This election is a test of our deepest-held values—and of our willingness to put it all on the line in defense of those values.

If you're tired of Bush, Cheney, Ashcroft, and Rumsfeld being the face of American values, now is the time to act. Please respond right now—and remember everything we believe in, everything we stand for—is at stake in this election.

Click here to donate.

Sincerely,

Terry McAuliffe

Terry McAuliffe
Chairman
P.S.: Make sure to forward this message on to your friends!

FIGURE 13-7 E-lobbying. In the 21st century, political parties used the Web as a primary source of fund-raising and lobbying. (Courtesy of the Democratic National Committee)

Political Action Committees

The rise of political action committees (PACs) has been among the most controversial political developments in recent years. In the mid-1970s, there were about 600 PACs. Today, the number of registered PACs is slightly less than 4,000, representing labor unions, business groups, corporations, nonprofit organizations, and so on.

Each PAC can give a maximum of $5,000 to a federal candidate in a primary election and another $5,000 for the general election. The top 50 PACs contribute in excess of $60 million annually. Among the nation's largest PACs are those controlled by U.S. realtors; trial lawyers; state, county, and municipal employees; and the American Medical Association. An organization with many individual PACs, then, can have a tremendous monetary influence on an election.

The increased influence of such groups on candidates is one reason why Senators John McCain and Russ Feingold led the Congress in 2002 to pass new strictures on campaign financing and particularly advertising for or against a candidate just prior to an election. Some would like to go further to see PACs severely curtailed or even banned. Indeed, over the years, Congress has limited what its members could accept in the form of trips and other niceties from the sponsors of PACs.

Critics of campaign finance reform argue that the First Amendment allows the freedom to speak out for or against any candidate. The tobacco industry, they note, was one of the most prominent PAC contributors to Congress, but the industry still got hammered. Although the number and size of PACs have increased, evidence of PAC-inspired indiscretions or illegalities has been minimal.

Dealing with Local Government

In 1980, Ronald Reagan rode to power on a platform of New Federalism, calling for a shift of political debate and public policy decisions to state and local levels. Presidents Clinton and Bush picked up the same initiative when they assumed power.

Dealing with local entities, of course, differs considerably from dealing with the federal government. For example, opinion leaders in communities (those constituents with whom an organization might want to affiliate to influence public policy decisions) might include such sectors as local labor unions, teachers, civil service workers, and the like. Building a consensus among such diverse constituents is pure grassroots public relations. The very nature of state and local issues makes it impossible to give one all-encompassing blueprint for successful government relations strategies.

Although the federal government's role in wielding power and employing public relations professionals is significant, state and local governments also are extremely important. Indeed, one viable route for entry-level public relations practitioners is through the local offices of city, county, regional, and state government officials.

Local agencies deal directly—much more so than their counterparts in Washington—with individuals. State, county, and local officials must make themselves available for local media interviews, community forums and debates, and even door-to-door campaigning. In recent years, local and state officials have found that direct contact with constituents—often through call-in radio programs—is invaluable not only in projecting an image but also in keeping in touch with the voters.

The public information function at state and local levels—to keep constituents apprised of legislative and regulatory changes, various government procedures, and notices—is a front-line public relations responsibility on the local level.

Local government officials, assigned to ensure the quality of local schools, the efficiency of local agencies, and the reliability of local fire and police departments, increasingly require smart and experienced public relations counsel. State and local information officer positions, therefore, have become valued and important posts for public relations graduates.

Last Word

The pervasive growth of government at all levels of society may not be welcome news for many people. However, government's growth has stimulated the need for increased public relations support and counsel. Indeed, in recent years, the once overwhelming power of television advertising on political campaigns has declined, and the importance of individuals has increased.[27] The importance of communicating directly with individual voters therefore has become paramount for politicians.

The massive federal government bureaucracy, organized through individual agencies that seek to communicate with the public, is a vast repository for public relations jobs. The most powerful position in the land—that of president of the United States—has come to rely on public relations counsel to help maintain a positive public opinion of the office and the incumbent's handling of it.

On state and local levels, public relations expertise also has become a valued commodity. Local officials, too, attempt to describe their programs in the most effective manner. In profit-making and nonprofit organizations alike, the need to communicate with various layers of government also is imperative.

Like it or not, the growth of government in our society appears unstoppable, particularly now that the United States is engaged in a long-term war on terror. As a result, the need for public relations support in government relations will clearly continue to grow in the 21st century.

Discussion Starters

1. Why is the public relations function regarded as something of a stepchild in government?
2. What is the current status of the Voice of America, and what are its responsibilities?
3. What is meant by the term *embedded reporter?*
4. Why was Ronald Reagan called the Great Communicator?
5. What is the function of the White House press secretary?
6. What are the objectives of government relations officers?
7. What are the primary functions of lobbyists?
8. What impact has the Internet had on lobbying?
9. What are the pros and cons of PACs?
10. What are the key considerations in individually lobbying a legislator?

Top of the Shelf

Lipstick on a Pig

Torie Clarke, New York: Free Press, 2006.

The individual credited with creating the concept of embedded reporters, public relations veteran Torie Clarke, served as Donald Rumsfeld's Assistant Secretary of Defense for Public Affairs.

Clarke praises her former boss. She says that Donald Rumsfeld felt strongly about the embedding program and believed that American citizens deserved to know as much about the military as possible. And Clarke states that her group did everything possible to make the military accessible to them.

Her premise is that spin is out and transparency is in. She says that corporations and governments must be open with the public because eventually their audiences will discover anything they are trying to hide.

Clarke herself is honest enough to admit that President Bush's premature declaration of "Mission Accomplished" in the Iraq War was a major public relations blunder. "You can put a lot of lipstick on a pig," she warns, "but it's still a pig."

CASE STUDY

The Katrina Kalamity

In August 2005, with the nation transfixed on the third year of war in Iraq and its mounting casualties, few could contemplate that a potentially greater threat might lie within American's own borders.

That's why no one—most pointedly, the government—was ready when one of the most ferocious storms in the nation's history, Hurricane Katrina, pounded ashore on August 28. Hurricane Katrina would become as destructive a domestic force as the nation had ever seen. And in its wake, the public relations fallout was severe.

Here is a timeline of what took place over eight excruciating days.

Friday, August 26

Governor Kathleen Blanco declares a state of emergency in Louisiana.
    Gulf coast states request troop assistance from the Pentagon.

Saturday, August 27

Governor Haley Barbour declares a state of emergency in Mississippi.
    Katrina is upgraded to a category 3 hurricane.
    Governor Blanco asks President Bush to declare a federal state of emergency in Louisiana.
    A federal emergency is declared, with the Department of Homeland Security (DHS) and the Federal Emergency Management Administration (FEMA) given full authority to respond to Katrina.

Sunday, August 28

Katrina is upgraded to a category 4 hurricane and an hour later is upgraded to a category 5.

New Orleans newspapers report that, "Forecasters Fear Levees Won't Hold Katrina."

Mayor Ray Nagin issues the first ever mandatory evacuation of New Orleans, saying, "We're facing the storm most of us have feared. This is going to be an unprecedented event."

The National Weather Service issues a special hurricane warning: In the event of a category 4 or 5 hit, "most of the area will be uninhabitable for weeks, perhaps longer.... At least one half of well-constructed homes will have roof and wall failure. All gabled roofs will fail, leaving those homes severely damaged or destroyed.... Power outages will last for weeks.... Water shortages will make human suffering incredible by modern standards."

With water toppling over levees, approximately 30,000 evacuees gather at the New Orleans Superdome, with roughly 36 hours worth of food.

Louisiana National Guard requests 700 buses from FEMA for evacuations. FEMA sends only 100 buses.

Monday, August 29

Katrina makes landfall as a category 4 hurricane.
    The Bush administration finds out that a levee in New Orleans was breached.
    Mayor Nagin reports on the *Today Show* that, "I've gotten reports this morning that there is already water coming over some of the levee systems. In the lower ninth ward, we've had one of our pumping stations to stop operating, so we will have significant flooding; it is just a matter of how much."

In a briefing, FEMA Director Mike Brown warns Bush, "This is, to put it mildly, the big one, I think." He also voices concerns that the government may not have the capacity to "respond to a catastrophe within a catastrophe" and that the Superdome is ill-equipped to be a refuge of last resort.

Bush shares birthday cake photo-op with Senator John McCain.

Michael Brown requests, via memo, that DHS dispatch 1,000 employees to the region and gives them two days to arrive. The memo politely ends, "Thank you for your consideration in helping us to meet our responsibilities."

A large section of the vital 17th Street Canal levee gives way, unleashing a torrent of water into New Orleans.

Bush visits an Arizona resort to promote a medicare drug benefit. Later, the president travels to a California senior center to discuss the Medicare program. Meanwhile, Secretary of Defense Donald Rumsfeld is attending a San Diego Padres baseball game as a guest of the team's president.

Governor Blanco again requests Washington assistance. "Mr. President, we need your help. We need everything you've got."

Tuesday, August 30

DHS Secretary Michael Chertoff says he is aware that the levee has failed.

Pentagon spokesperson Lawrence Di Rita says the states have adequate National Guard units to handle the hurricane needs.

Reports from New Orleans indicate that "the looting is out of control. The French Quarter has been attacked. We're using exhausted, scarce police to control looting when they should be used for search and rescue while we still have people on rooftops." Television photos confirm the looting.

President Bush plays guitar with country singer Mark Willis and returns to his ranch in Crawford for the last night of his vacation.

Wednesday, August 31

National Guard troops arrive in Lousiana, Mississippi, Alabama, and Florida, two days after they are requested. Evacuation efforts of stranded residents continue around the clock (Figure 13-8).

President Bush organizes a task force to coordinate federal response. Bush says he will "fly to Washington to begin work … with a task force that will coordinate the work of 14 federal agencies involved in the relief effort."

With 3,000 or more evacuees stranded at the Convention Center, dire reports begin to emerge. Police Superintendent Edwin Compass reports, "The tourists are walking around there, and as soon as these individuals see them, they're being preyed upon." Newspapers and television news rush to print and air with reports of unspeakable violence in the impossible conditions. Later, most of these accounts were proven not to have happened.

A public health emergency is declared for the entire Gulf Coast, with fears of diseases like cholera, typhoid, hepatitis, and mosquito-borne illnesses.

DHS Secretary Chertoff declares, "We are extremely pleased with the response that every element of the federal government, all of our federal partners, have made to this terrible tragedy."

Bush gives his first major address on Katrina.

FIGURE 13-8 Watery nightmare. Residents stranded by Katrina floodwaters waited on roofs to be rescued. (David J. Phillip/AP Wide World Photos)

Thursday, September 1

Bush reports, "I don't think anybody anticipated the breach of the levees."

Terry Ebbert, New Orleans Homeland Security Director declares, "This is a national emergency. This is a national disgrace. FEMA has been here three days, yet there is no command and control. We can send massive amounts of aid to tsunami victims, but we can't bail out the city of New Orleans."

Mayor Nagin issues a desperate SOS. "Right now we are out of resources at the Convention Center and don't anticipate enough buses. We need buses." Later it is revealed that hundreds of unused school buses were stationed at a nearby New Orleans holding area.

FEMA Director Brown reports, "I've had no reports of unrest, if the connotation of the word unrest means that people are beginning to riot, or you know, they're banging on walls and screaming and hollering or burning tires or whatever. I've had no reports of that."

Friday, September 2

White House aides are quoted as saying that the president was slow to grasp the enormity of the situation. The reality, say several aides, did not really sink in until Thursday night. Some White House staffers were watching the evening news and thought the president needed to see the horrific reports coming out of New Orleans. White House Communications Counselor Dan Bartlett made a DVD of the newscasts so Bush could see them in their entirety as he flew down to the Gulf Coast the next morning on Air Force One.

On the ground in New Orleans, President Bush says, "I am satisfied with the response. I am not satisfied with all the results."

With his FEMA director at his side, the president praises Michael Brown, "Brownie, you're doing a heck of a job" (Figure 13–9).

Ten days later, Michael Brown resigned, and the Bush administration was left with its most serious disaster—not to mention public relations problem—since the tragedy of 9/11.

Questions

1. How would you assess the federal response to Hurricane Katrina? The state and local response?

2. What should President Bush have done first in response to Hurricane Katrina?

3. How would you assess his public statements relative to Michael Brown?

4. How would you assess the role of the media in reporting on Hurricane Katrina?

5. Had you been the president's public relations advisor, what would your counsel have been relative to Katrina?

FIGURE 13-9 Heckuva job. The president's faith in FEMA Director Michael Brown was short-lived, as Brown was quickly replaced after fumbling the response to Katrina. (Susan Walsh/AP Wide World Photos)

Voice of Authority

An Interview with Scott McClellan (Not)

No-show Press Secretary Scott McClellan (Not).

Scott McClellan replaced Ari Fleischer as President George W. Bush's White House Press Secretary in July 2003. When asked to be interviewed for this book, Mr. McClellan first accepted, then changed his mind, then re-changed his mind and accepted again, and finally, at deadline, decided not to participate.

In so doing, he became the first White House Press Secretary in 17 years—after Marlin Fitzwater, Dee Dee Myers, Mike McCurry, Joe Lockhart, and predecessor Ari Fleischer—to decline an invitation to be interviewed for the book.

While unfortunate, Mr. McClellan's declination to participate in this project wasn't entirely unexpected.

In truth, his on again/off again, "yes I will/no I won't" dithering was symptomatic of the uncertain and rudderless public relations philosophy and policy that plagued the second term of the Bush Administration. (*Hey, I voted for the guy!*)

In the second Bush term, an increasingly-unpopular war in Iraq, botched federal response to Hurricane Katrina, charges of selective leaks of confidential government information by high officials, and a general sense of aloofness and secrecy, helped mire McClellan as a spokesman who some uncharitably described as "hapless, inept, an unanswer man" and worse.

Scott McClellan's futility as the most visible administration spokesperson suggested several lessons for students of public relations.

Lesson #1—"Loyalty," while important, should not be blind.

Scott McClellan was the most loyal of Bush employees. After spending post-college days working in support of his mother's campaigns for Texas Comptroller, McClellan joined then Texas Governor Bush and remained with him for the duration. So besides his mother, Bush was McClellan's only boss.

While no one, therefore, questioned his loyalty, many wondered if such a "good soldier" could ever "challenge" his boss on policy or performance. A good public relations advisor, of course, as Ivy Lee first counseled, must always ensure first that policy and performance are appropriate, before going out to promote them. A strong public relations advisor, in other words, will occasionally challenge the boss.

Lesson #2—Don't be a robot.

Every spokesman must rely on "standby statements" and agreed-upon answers from which he or she must not waver. Lawyers describe this hewing to the party line as "staying within the box." The challenge for a spokesman is to stay "within the box," while appearing to remain flexible.

This was McClellan's problem. His responses to journalists' questions on controversial issues were so robotic—repeating over and over again the same mantra—that they and he were often dismissed as worthless.

This was in sharp contrast to his predecessor who, although sticking to the administration line, would alter his language and appear responsive. Summarized one observer, "What came so easily to Fleischer utterly eludes McClellan. If the two of them ever sat down at a poker table, Fleischer would probably walk away will all of McClellan's money and the shirt off his back."

Lesson #3—Don't get chummy with the vipers.

Reporters, as noted in this text, should be considered "friendly adversaries"—as opposed to "friends."

Fleischer understood this well, responding this way to a question about the media in the prior edition of this book:

> We've reached a point where the press, in pursuit of this devil's advocate role, would do well to ask itself if they are "informing" the public or are they being so negative about the institutions they cover that they're not covering all the news but only the "bad news."

Accordingly, reporters knew where the press secretary was coming from, treated him warily but with respect.

McClellan, by contrast, seemed to consider reporters his friends, went to dinner with them, and was well-liked by the very people who daily treated him as a human piñata. Said one such friend, "He seems to have the right temperament to be a punching bag."

Lesson #4—Stand for something.

No accomplished public relations professional would ever accept a function that rendered him or her a "second class citizen." Good public relations people must "stand for something."

There was little question where Ari Fleischer stood on the media. Nor was there doubt about the savvy and independence of Clinton press secretary Mike McCurry, even in the midst of an impossible presidential intern crisis. In an earlier day, Press Secretary Larry Speakes even threatened to quit the Reagan administration after he was lied to about the invasion of Grenada.

These individuals and other White House press secretaries had the courage to stand up for what they stood for.

Scott McClellan, alas, to his own and his administration's detriment, seemed to lack this key quality—even when it came to answering a few softball questions in a college text book.* **

---

*For further information, see Jonathan Chait, "Scott McClellan, Bad Liar, Honest Mistake," *The New Republic,* March 29, 2004; Mark Leibovich, "After Cheney's Shooting Incident, Time to Unload," *Washington Post,* February 14, 2006, C01; Mark Leibovich, "Unanswer Man," *Washington Post,* December 22, 2005, C01.

** Scott McClellan was replaced as White House press secretary in April 2006 by Fox News host Tony Snow.

Suggested Readings

Avner, Marcia. *The Lobbying and Advocacy Handbook for Nonprofit Organizations,* St. Paul, MN: Amherst H. Wilder Foundation, 2002. A first-class guide to lobbying for anyone, not just not-for-profits.

Crawford, Alan Pell. "D.C. Clients: A Capital Challenge." *Public Relations Strategist,* Summer 2002, 18–21.

Fitzwater, Marlin. *Call the Briefing.* New York: Xlibris, 2000. President Reagan's press secretary weighs in with life with the press during the years of the Great Communicator.

Fleischer, Ari. *Taking Heat: The President, the Press and My Years in the White House.* New York: HarperCollins, 2005. First-hand account from President Bush's first press secretary, who answered the media mob during wartime.

Francia, Peter L., John C. Green, Paul S. Herrnson, Lynda W. Powell, and Clyde Wilcox. *The Financiers of Congressional Elections.* New York: Columbia University Press, 2003. The real story behind who pays for the "best Congress money can buy."

Howard, Elizabeth, moderator, "Capital Gains," *Public Relations Strategist,* Summer 2002, 6–13.

Hughes, Karen. *Ten Minutes from Normal.* New York: Penguin Books, 2004. A personal account of tumultuous days in the White House and a return to civilian life by the closest public relations advisor to the president.

Klein, Joe. *The Natural: The Misunderstood Presidency of Bill Clinton.* New York: Random House, 2002. A critical view of the man "born to be president" from a journalist who got in trouble for writing a thinly disguised novel about Clinton and then wouldn't admit he wrote it.

Stateman, Alison. "Life at the Pentagon." *Public Relations Strategist,* Summer 2002, 22–24.

Notes

1. David Murray, "PR is Not the Problem—or the Solution," *Ragan Report,* November 24, 2003, 1.
2. Fraser P. Seitel, *The Practice of Public Relations,* 9th ed. Upper Saddle River, NJ: Prentice-Hall, 2004, 341.
3. Karen De Young, "Bush to Create Formal Office to Shape U.S. Image Abroad," *Washington Post,* July 30, 2002, A1.
4. Sonya Ross, "White House Opens Office to Put a Better Face on U.S. Policy and Messages Abroad," Associated Press, July 30, 2002.
5. Fraser P. Seitel, "Words of Speech = Weapons of War," *odwyerpr.com,* October 15, 2001.
6. "GAO: Bush Administration Paid $200M for PR," *Jack O'Dwyer's Newsletter,* February 22, 2006, 2.
7. "About VOA," Voice of America, Office of Public Affairs, 330 Independence Avenue, S.W., Washington, D.C. 20237.
8. Mark Mazzetti and Kevin Sack, "The Challenges in Iraq: Planted PR Stories Not News to Military: PR Meets Psy-Ops in War on Terror," *Los Angeles Times,* December 18, 2005, A1.
9. Mark Hertsgaard, "Journalists Played Dead for Reagan—Will They Roll Over Again for Bush?" *Washington Journalism Review,* January–February 1989, 31.
10. "Give Him an 'F,'" *The Scudder Media Report,* October 1998, 1, 6.
11. "Bush to Engage Media, Public More Aggressively," Bulletin News Network, March 13, 2006.
12. Robert U. Brown, "Role of Press Secretary," *Editor & Publisher,* October 19, 1974, 40.
13. William Hill, "Nessen Lists Ways He Has Improved Press Relations," *Editor & Publisher,* April 10, 1975, 40.
14. William Safire, "One of Our Own," *New York Times,* September 19, 1974, 43.
15. Laurence McQuillan, "Ari Fleischer Warms Up for Grillings," *USA Today,* January 23, 2001, 6A.
16. Richard W. Stevenson, "Press Secretary on Trial in the Briefing Room," *New York Times,* November 3, 2005, A25.
17. Remarks by Mike McCurry, "A View from the Podium," New York, May 5, 1999.
18. Michael J. Bennett, "The 'Imperial' Press Corps," *Public Relations Journal,* June 1982, 13.
19. Jeffrey H. Birnbaum, "The Road to Riches is Called K Street," *Washington Post,* June 22, 2005, A01.
20. Hubert B. Herring, "$6 Million a Day to Whisper in Lawmakers' Ears," *New York Times,* January 9, 2005.
21. "Spending for Lobbyists Hits Record High in N.J.," *The Record,* February 26, 2006, A4.
22. Leslie Wayne, "John Ashcroft Sets Up Shop as a Well-Connected Lobbyist," *New York Times,* March 17, 2006, 1.
23. Fraser P. Seitel, "Lobbying Do's and Don'ts," *O'Dwyer's PR Services Report,* December 2005, 31.
24. Fraser P. Seitel, "Lobbying Part II: Making the Sale," *O'Dwyer's PR Services Report,* January 2006, 92.
25. Bob Davis and Jeanne Cummings, "A Barrage of E-Mail Helps Candidates Hit Media Fast and Often," *Wall Street Journal,* September 21, 2000, A1,16.
26. Robert Stacy McCain, "MoveOn.org: Don't Believe the Hype," *Ripon Forum,* Fall 2004, 16.
27. Adam Nagourney, "TV's Tight Grip on Campaigns Is Weakening," *New York Times,* September 5, 2002, A1–19.

14 Consumer Relations

FIGURE 14-1 Global pitchman. NBA all star Yao Ming shakes with fellow company spokesman Ronald McDonald (the little guy, left), as McDonald's celebrates the signing of Yao as its global spokesman. (AP Wide World Photos)

While those who worry about global warming may not like it, the fact is that the world has become one large territory of consumers. Approximately 1.7 billion people worldwide now belong to the "consumer class"—the group of people characterized by diets of highly processed food, desire for bigger houses, more and bigger cars, higher levels of debt, and lifestyles devoted to the accumulation of nonessential goods.[1] Rising consumption has helped meet basic needs and create jobs around the world. Today nearly half of global consumers reside in developing countries, including 240 million in China and 120 million in India—markets with the most potential for expansion.

Brand name companies know no national borders, as products and the public relations representatives who promote them are ubiquitous around the globe. As proof, rare is the citizen, regardless of location, who is unaware of the identity of these two public relations representatives:

Basketball giant Yao Ming teamed with Ronald McDonald in 2004 to promote the fast food products of McDonald's Restaurant chain over the far corners of the globe. McDonald's, in fact, became an international symbol of the new consumption, for better or worse.

Companies like McDonald's work constantly to improve their image with consumers around the world. Globalization and the spread of the Internet introduce new pressures on corporations to walk a

fine line between behaving "responsibly" and promoting their products. Complicating this task are the
hundreds of thousands of products and services from
which consumers may choose (Figure 14-2).

More often than not, meeting this challenge
means differentiating one's product from all the rest.
Often it is public relations techniques and sensitiv-
ities that help distinguish a company and its products
from the competition.

FIGURE 14-2 So many products. So important to use
public relations to help differentiate. (Mehau Kulyk & Victor de
Schwanberg/Photo Researchers, Inc.)

- In 2000, the California Prune Board petitioned
  the Food and Drug Administration for permission to use the term *dried plums* as an alternative to prunes on packages of the fruit.
  Prunes, it was felt, hurt the more youthful
  image of the prune—uh, plum—people
  wished to convey to attract younger consumers.[2]

- In 2001, Yahoo! announced it would remove adult-oriented products from its shopping, auc-
  tions, and classified sections because many of its users complained about the raunchy nature
  of the merchandise. Said Yahoo!'s president, "We value the strong relationships we have with
  our members and have consistently listened to them."[3]

- In 2005, McDonald's announced it would add facts on nutrition to its packaging so that customers can tell how many calories, grams of fat, protein, carbohydrates, and so on, they were
  consuming. While McDonald's had always made this information available on the Web and in
  brochures, the company was sensitive to criticism about disclosing nutritional information.[4]

Such were the public relations initiatives companies used to enhance consumer relations.

As Bruce Springsteen has put it, with "57 channels and nothin' on," all offering commercial after
commercial, it has become increasingly difficult for consumers to penetrate the advertising clutter to
identify winning products and services.

In an era overwrought with advertising "noise"—tens of thousands of blaring messages beamed in
the direction of a single consumer—public relations solutions can help cut through the clutter and
distinguish one company from the next, enhancing the sale of a firm's products. This chapter examines
how public relations helps attract, win, and keep consumers.

Consumer Relations Objectives

Building sales is the primary consumer relations objective. A satisfied customer may return; an unhappy customer may not. Here are some typical goals:

- **Keeping old customers.** Most sales are made to established customers. Consumer relations efforts should be made to keep these customers happy. Pains
  should be taken to respond to customers' concerns. For example, telephone companies typically suspend normal charges in areas hit by natural disasters so that
  residents can make calls to loved ones.

- **Attracting new customers.** Every business must work constantly to develop new customers. In many industries, the prices and quality of competing products are similar. In choosing among brands, customers may base decisions on how they have been treated.

- **Marketing new items or services.** Customer relations techniques can influence the sale of new products. Thousands of new products flood the market each year, and the vast array of information about these products can confuse the consumer. When General Electric's research revealed that consumers want personalized service and more information on new products, it established the GE Answer Center, a national toll-free, 24-hour service that informs consumers about new GE products and services. Building such company and product loyalty lies at the heart of a solid consumer relations effort.

- **Expediting complaint handling.** Few companies are free of complaints. Customers protest when appliances don't work, errors are made in billing, or deliveries aren't made on time. Many large firms have established response procedures. Often a company ombudsperson can salvage a customer relationship with a speedy and satisfactory answer to a complaint.

- **Reducing costs.** To most companies, an educated consumer is the best consumer. Uninformed buyers cost a company time and money—when goods are returned, service calls are made, and instructions are misunderstood. Many firms have adopted programs to educate customers about use of their products.

Consumer-Generated Media

For decades, publicity to consumers about products and services revolved around the mass media. While the traditional media are still important avenues through which to promote organizational offerings, there is a new voice in town: The Internet, far more than any other medium, has given consumers a voice, a publishing platform, and a forum where their collective voices can be heard, shared, and researched.

Consumer-generated media (CGM) encompasses the millions of consumer-generated comments, opinions, and personal experiences posted in publicly available online sources on a wide range of issues, topics, products, and brands. CGM is also referred to as "online consumer word-of-mouth," originated from a variety of sources:

- blogs
- message boards and forums
- public discussions (Usenet newsgroups)
- discussions and forums on large e-mail portals (Yahoo!, AOL, MSN)
- online opinion/review sites and services
- online feedback/complaint sites

Consumers seem to place trust in their fellow consumers. For any marketer trying to be heard or to break through the clutter, understanding and managing CGM may be critical. Then too, CGM is increasingly easy and inexpensive to create. Online discussion forms, membership groups, boards, blogs, and Usenet newsgroups are all easy to access.[5]

One ethical consideration for companies is how aggressive—and visible—they should be in directly accessing CGM. The best policy, always, is to disclose one's identity in Internet locales to avoid subsequent criticism.

Office of the Ombudsperson

Research indicates that only a handful of dissatisfied customers—4 percent—will ever complain. But that means that there are many others with the same complaint who never say anything. And the vast majority of dissatisfied customers won't repurchase from the offending company.

In the old days, a frequent response to complaint letters was to dust off the so-called "bedbug letter"—a term that stemmed from occasional letters to the railroads complaining about bedbugs in the sleeper cars. To save time, railroad consumer relations personnel simply dispatched a prewritten bedbug letter in response. Today, with the volume of mail, e-mail, and faxes at a mountainous level, 21st-century versions of the bedbug letter still appear from time to time (Figure 14-3).

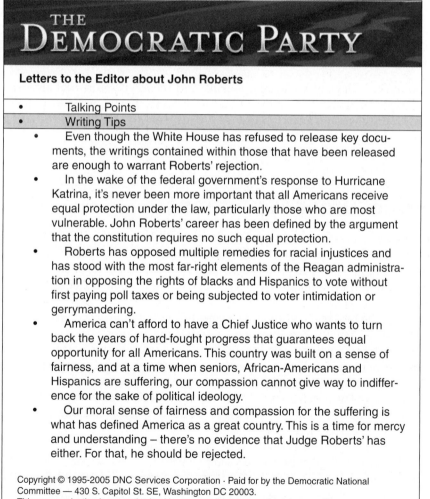

FIGURE 14-3 21st-century bed bug. In the days of e-commerce, "form letters" have taken on a more contemporary complexion, such as this from the Democratic National Committee promoting letters urging the rejection of John Roberts as Supreme Court Justice. (He made it.) (Courtesy of The Democratic National Committee)

At many companies, the most immediate response to complaints has been the establishment of ombudsperson offices. The term *ombudsman* originally described a government official—in Sweden and New Zealand, for example—appointed to investigate complaints about abuses committed by public officials. In most firms, the office of the ombudsperson investigates complaints made against the company and its managers. Such an office generally provides a central location that customers can call to seek redress of grievances.

Typically, the ombudsperson monitors the difficulties customers are having with products. Often he or she can anticipate product or performance deficiencies. Ombudspersons are in business to inspire customer confidence and to influence an organization's behavior toward improved service. They accomplish this by responding, more often than not, in the following manner:

- "We'll take care of that for you."
- "We'll take full responsibility for that defect."
- "We want your business."
- "Thank you for thinking of us."
- "Consider it done."

Alas, in these days of voice mail, e-mail, and recorded sequential answering systems, such personalized "magic words" seem to be in short supply. Pity. The companies that express such understanding and courtesy will be the ones that keep the business.

The Consumer Movement

Although consumerism is considered to be a late-20th-century concept, legislation to protect consumers first emerged in the United States in 1872, when Congress enacted the Criminal Fraud Statute to protect consumers against corporate abuses. In 1887, Congress established the Interstate Commerce Commission to curb freewheeling railroad tycoons.

However, the first real consumer movement came right after the turn of the century when journalistic muckrakers encouraged legislation to protect the consumer. Upton Sinclair's novel *The Jungle* revealed scandalous conditions in the meatpacking industry and helped usher in federal meat inspection standards as Congress passed the Food and Drug Act and the Trade Commission Act. In the second wave of the movement, from 1927 to 1938, consumers were safeguarded from the abuses of manufacturers, advertisers, and retailers of well-known brands of commercial products. During this time, Congress passed the Food, Drug, and Cosmetic Act.

Later, the movement was boosted by the activities of a lone consumer crusader, Ralph Nader, who brought the world's most powerful auto company, General Motors, to its knees. Nader's thin 1965 book, *Unsafe at Any Speed,* pointed out how the GM Corvair was literally a "death trap." After trying to stop Nader at every turn—including assigning private detectives to trail his every move—GM relented and stopped production of the Corvair. Consumerism had won its most significant battle.

By the early 1960s, the movement had become stronger and more unified. President John F. Kennedy, in fact, proposed that consumers have their own bill of rights, containing four basic principles:

1. **The right to safety:** to be protected against the marketing of goods hazardous to health or life.

2. **The right to be informed:** to be protected against fraudulent, deceitful, or grossly misleading information, advertising, labeling, or other practices and to be given the facts needed to make an informed choice.

3. **The right to choose:** to be assured access, whenever possible, to a variety of products and services at competitive prices.

4. **The right to be heard:** to be assured that consumer interests will receive full and sympathetic consideration in the formulation of government policy.

Subsequent American presidents have continued to emphasize consumer rights and protection. Labeling, packaging, product safety, and a variety of other issues continue to concern government overseers of consumer interests.

Federal Consumer Agencies

Today a massive government bureaucracy attempts to protect the consumer against abuse: more than 900 different programs administered by more than 400 federal entities. Key agencies include the Justice Department, Federal Trade Commission, Food

Speaking of Ethics

So You Want to Be an Ombudsperson

The mantra of consumer relations officers, like that of public relations officers, is not necessarily that "the customer is always right" but rather "do the right thing."

With that in mind, consider the following random selection of complaints received by the consumer affairs division of a local bank. How would you handle each?

1. A businesswoman carrying an attaché case made a deposit at a midtown branch before going to her office. Inadvertently, she left her case on the main banking floor. By the time she discovered that it was missing, the police bomb squad had smashed the innocent case and cordoned off the area. The owner asked the bank for a replacement. Would you have given it to her?

2. After making a deposit and leaving the bank, a woman reported that a huge icicle fell from the bank's roof and nearly hit her. She complained bitterly to consumer affairs. How would you appease her?

3. A young installment loan customer claimed that his car had been taken because of delinquent loan payments. He claimed that he had paid the loan on time and objected to the illegal

seizure. On checking, it was determined that several loan payments were, in fact, delinquent. The car was returned but in a damaged condition. The young man sought reimbursement for the repairs. What would you recommend?

4. A customer complained that she had received no response to her numerous letters concerning the hostile treatment accorded her at her local branch. After investigation, it was learned that the woman was a nuisance to branch officers, yet she kept a very healthy balance in her savings account. Furthermore, all the correspondence to which she referred was written on the backs of checks she submitted in loan payments. How would you handle this problem?

5. A new depositor complained that he was not given a promised toaster for making his deposit. After checking, it was learned his deposit was made the day after the premium offer ended. What would you do?

6. The executor of an estate complained that his deceased brother, who had been a bank customer, received a card reading, "Best wishes in your new residence." What remedial action would you suggest?

and Drug Administration, Consumer Product Safety Commission, and Office of Consumer Affairs.

- **Justice Department.** The Justice Department has had a consumer affairs section in its antitrust division since 1970. Its responsibilities include the enforcement of such consumer protection measures as the Truth in Lending Act and the Product Safety Act. The Justice Department is particularly concerned with antitrust and monopolistic activities. This was the root of the initiative against the world's largest computer company, Microsoft, in the early years of the George W. Bush administration.

- **Federal Trade Commission.** The FTC, perhaps more than any other agency, has vigorously enforced consumer protection. Its national advertising division covers television and radio advertising, with special emphasis on foods, drugs, and cosmetics. Its general litigation division covers areas not included by national advertising, such as magazine subscription agencies, door-to-door sales, and income tax services. Its consumer credit and special programs division deals with such areas as fair credit reporting and truth in packaging.

- **Securities and Exchange Commission.** The SEC is the government agency that supervises disclosure among public companies. This is the province of investor relations, which was born in the mid-1930s, shortly after the passage of the Securities Act of 1933 and the Securities Exchange Act of 1934, which attempted to protect the public from abuses in the issuance and sale of securities. In recent years, with the corporate fraud of Enron, WorldCom, Tyco, Adelphia, and too many others, the SEC has been busy.

- **Food and Drug Administration.** The FDA is responsible for protecting consumers from hazardous items: foods, drugs, cosmetics, therapeutic and radiological devices, food additives, and serums and vaccines. Under Dr. David Kessler, during the Clinton administration, the FDA waged an all-out war against cigarette advertising to children, in particular. After years of fighting, the industry finally capitulated and removed its teenager-targeted Joe Camel symbol from its ads (Figure 14-4).

- **Consumer Product Safety Commission.** This bureau is responsible for overseeing product safety and standards and has been particularly aggressive in recent years in the area of seat belt restraints, strollers, blankets, and other products for small children.

- **Office of Consumer Affairs.** This agency, the central point of consumer activities in the government, publishes literature to inform the public of recent developments in consumer affairs.

In the 21st century, clearly the best policy for any public company is to communicate directly and frequently with regulators in Washington, ultimately to win their understanding and support.

Consumer Activists on the Internet

The consumerist movement has attracted a host of activists in recent years. Although private testing organizations that evaluate products and inform consumers about potential dangers have proliferated, the most significant activity to keep companies honest has occurred on the Internet.

Does RJR Nabisco Lie About Marketing To Kids?

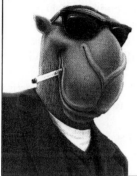

In public they say:

"I do not want to sell tobacco to children. I'd fire anyone on the spot if I found they were doing it." (Steven Goldstone, CEO, RJR Nabisco Holdings Corp., 12/6/96).

But a 1976 RJR internal memo stated:

"Evidence is now available to indicate that the 14-to-18-year-old group is an increasing segment of the smoking population. RJR-T must soon establish a successful new brand in this market if our position in the industry is to be maintained over the long term."

You Decide.

In 1988, RJR introduced Joe Camel. Subsequently, Camel's share of the kids' market quadrupled. Camel is now the second most popular cigarette among children, and kids were found to be as familiar with Joe Camel as Mickey Mouse.

Tell your elected officials to support restrictions on tobacco marketing to children, including the Food and Drug Administration rule.

Tobacco vs. Kids. Where America draws the line.

CAMPAIGN for TOBACCO-FREE Kids

To learn more, call 1-800-284-KIDS.

This ad supported by: American Cancer Society; American Lung Association; American Heart Association; Center for Women Policy Studies; National Federation of State High School Associations; Committee for Children; Intercultural Cancer Council; Interreligious Coalition on Smoking OR Health; Youth Service America; American College of Preventive Medicine; Girl Scouts USA; Child Welfare League of America; National Association of Secondary School Principals; National Association of Elementary School Principals; American Federation of Teachers; Women's Legal Defense Fund; Association of State and Territorial Health Officials.

The National Center for Tobacco-Free Kids, 1707 L Street NW, Suite 800, Washington, DC 20036

FIGURE 14-4   Good-bye, Joe. For years, Joe Camel was the too-cool symbol that helped lure teenage smokers. Ultimately, the industry, at the government's insistence, killed old Joe. (Courtesy of Tobacco-Free Kids)

Perhaps the best-known testing group, Consumers Union was formed in 1936 to test products across a wide spectrum of industries. It publishes the results in a monthly magazine, *Consumer Reports,* which reaches about 3.5 million readers. Often an evaluation in *Consumer Reports,* either pro or con, greatly affects how customers view particular products. Consumers Union also produces books, a travel newsletter, a column for 450 newspapers, and monthly features for network television. It has an annual budget of $70 million.

The Consumer Federation of America was formed in 1968 to unify lobbying efforts for pro-consumer legislation. Today the federation consists of 200 national, state, and local consumer groups, labor unions, electric cooperatives, and other organizations with consumer interests.

With 70 million American households owning computers and more than half of these having Internet access, the Internet poses a hotbed of consumer activism.[6] Internet activism uses Internet communications technologies to enable faster communications and coordination by citizen movements. From the Yahoo! Boycott Board, which lists actions being taken against organizations, to so-called rogue Web sites, which air the gripes of dissatisfied consumers, to wildfire e-mail campaigns and discussion groups directed at product abuse—the Internet has become a prime source of consumer activism.

The most stirring example of anticorporate Internet activism took place in 1999, when opponents of corporate-led globalization used the Internet effectively to coordinate protests against the World Trade Organization, an effort that came to be known as the Battle in Seattle.

Internet activism has been criticized on grounds that it gives disproportionate access to affluent activists because poor people, minorities, and elderly citizens either lack access or are inexperienced in the new technologies.

Nonetheless, smart companies take Internet challenges seriously and act on them immediately. They have found that word-of-mouth criticism, aided and abetted by the Internet, must be dealt with—quickly.

Although companies often find such activists' criticism annoying, the emergence of the consumer watchdog movement has generally been a positive development for consumers. Ralph Nader, still going strong into the 21st century, and others have forced organizations to consider, even more than usual, the downside of the products and services they offer. Smart companies have come to take seriously the pronouncements of consumer activists.

Business Gets the Message

Obviously, few organizations can afford to shirk their responsibilities to consumers. Consumer relations divisions have sprung up, either as separate entities or as part of public relations departments. The title of vice president for consumer relations is showing up with more frequency on corporate organization charts.

In many companies, consumer relations began strictly as a way to handle complaints, an area to which all unanswerable complaints were sent. Such units have frequently provided an alert to management. More recently, companies have broadened the consumer relations function to encompass such activities as developing guidelines to evaluate services and products for management, developing consumer programs that meet consumer needs and increase sales, developing field-training programs, evaluating service approaches, and evaluating company effectiveness in demonstrating concern for customers.

The investment in consumer service apparently pays off. Marketers of consumer products say that most customer criticism can be mollified with a prompt, personalized reply. Throw in a couple of free samples and consumers feel even better. In any case, consumers are impressed when a company takes the time to drop them a line for whatever reason.

On the other hand, failing to answer a question, satisfy a complaint, or solve a problem can result in a blitz of bad word-of-mouth advertising.

In adopting a more activist consumerist philosophy, firms have found that consumer relations need not take a defensive posture. Consumer relations professionals must themselves be activists to make certain that consumers understand the benefits and realities of using their products.

The consumer philosophy of the DaimlerChrysler Corporation is typical of the more enlightened attitude of most companies today. Its Car Buyer's Bill of Rights states:

1. Every car buyer has the right to quality.
2. Every buyer has the right to long-term protection.
3. Every buyer has the right to friendly treatment, honest service, and competent repairs.
4. Every buyer has the right to a safe vehicle.
5. Every buyer has the right to address grievances.
6. Every buyer has the right to satisfaction.

Talking Points

Promoting an Unapologetic Monster

Even in the days of consumer activism and food company nutrition-mindedness, one has to admire an organization committed to the blissful piling on of calories.

So it was, with the help of Weber Shandwick public relations, that Hardee's announced with great fanfare, in the spring of 2005, the Monster Thickburger, a mammoth 1,420-calorie hamburger with 104 grams of fat (Figure 14-5).

Launch of the Monster Thickburger generated publicity across the globe, including a skit about a new "Killer Kamikaze Burger" on *The Tonight Show* with Jay Leno. The publicity took on an "anti-political correctness" tone, with critics citing the dangers of obesity and fad diets in the United States. The *London Telegraph* quipped, "America's appetite for junk food has taken on terrifying new proportions."

Hardee's not only took it in stride but, as sales went up, ran with the criticism. Said Hardee's marketing director, "We're unapologetic about the product and getting out the word that the Thickburger may not be for everyone."

Besides, you could always wash it down with a Diet Coke.

FIGURE 14-5 The monster. Hardee's hit the publicity jackpot with its very un-politically correct new offering. (Courtesy of O'Dwyer.com)

For further information, see Kevin McCauley, "Monster Thickburger Gives Hardee's PR Lift," *O'Dwyer's PR Services Report,* March 2005, 8.

Last Word

Without consumers, there would be no companies. Despite periodic legislative setbacks and shifting consumerist leadership, the cause of consumerism seems destined to remain strong. The increasing use of seat belts and air bags, increased environmental concerns about packaging and pollution, rising outrage about second-hand smoke and all smoking in general, and numerous other causes indicate that the push for product safety and quality will likely increase in the years ahead.

Indeed, the smartest companies are those that tie their products and services to larger societal causes, thus establishing a link in the minds of consumers that represents "loftier" goals than merely making money (Figure 14-6).

That is not to say there is anything wrong with making money. Companies depend on their profits to exist. Without profitability, corporations can't contribute to bettering society.

Safeguarding the relationship with consumers of products and services is fundamental to continuing to earn profits. That's why the efforts of public relations professionals, assigned to maintaining, sustaining, and enhancing a company's standing with its customers, is a core communications challenge in the 21st century.

Discussion Starters

1. Why is dealing with consumers so important for public relations?
2. What are typical consumer relations objectives?
3. What is the office of the ombudsperson?
4. What is consumer-generated marketing?
5. What key federal agencies are involved in consumerism?
6. What is the purpose of the SEC?
7. What is a consumer bill of rights?
8. What is the impact of the Internet on a company's consumer relations?
9. Who is Ralph Nader, and what is his significance to consumerism?
10. What constitutes a quality consumer-oriented company?

FIGURE 14-6 Loftier goals. Smart companies take advantage of the efforts to link products to health and safety, typified by this "Esuvee Safety Campaign," publicized by former *Today Show* host Katie Couric and Connecticut Attorney General Richard Blumenthal. (Courtesy of O'Dwyer.com)

Top of the Shelf

New Product Launch: 10 Proven Strategies

Joan Schneider with Jeanne Yocum, Deerfield, IL: Stagnito Communications, 2004.

This book provides a roadmap for companies ready to launch a new product. And companies evidently need it. According to the authors, of the 33,000 products introduced every year, 75 percent fail.

Launch timing is critical, say the authors. Planning and executing timing can mean the difference between a success and a bust. The best innovators, according to the two experienced product pub-

licity professionals, are those that regularly innovate and introduce new products.

Public relations looms large in the advice these authors proffer. A strong public relations effort, out-of-the-gate, can also be pivotal for a company. Public relations builds awareness for a new product that advertising cannot equal.

CASE STUDY

Tobacco Wars

The manufacturers of cigarettes, among the most powerful corporations in the world, learned a valuable lesson in the first years of the 21st century:

If you violate the faith of consumers, you will lose—big time.

The case of the rise and fall of the tobacco industry is one of the most significant in the history of the practice of public relations.

In the final years of the 20th century and the first years of the 21st, cigarette companies have seen their products and advertising restricted, their executives denigrated before national panels, and their reputations tarnished with accusations of lying and worse.

The enemies of smoking have recast the pastime as nothing short of sin. Today, smokers can no longer light up on airplanes or in restaurants, offices, or stadiums. They have been branded as outcasts, forced to vacate the premises if they wish to light up.

As recently as the 1980s, congressional and business deals were still made in smoke-filled rooms. Even the first Americans, as Christopher Columbus wrote, carried a "fire brand in the hand, and herbs to drink the smoke thereof, as they are accustomed."

Smoking had always been politically sacrosanct, like guns. Tobacco companies produced jobs for workers and profits for shareholders and, not coincidentally, also financed political campaigns. Tobacco was untouchable, right up until 1994.

And then the roof caved in.

Permanent Political Shift

As more activist politicians spoke out against the dangers of smoking, particularly to young people, the political landscape began to shift. Some believe the shift is irreversible.

- President Clinton proposed steep excise taxes on cigarettes as part of health care reform efforts.

- The Environmental Protection Agency classified second-hand smoke as a serious health risk. The House approved legislation barring smoking from most public places. The Department of Defense prohibited smoking in its workplaces worldwide.

- FDA Commissioner Dr. David A. Kessler, considered public enemy number one by tobacco companies, proposed treating tobacco products as drugs, based on "accumulating evidence" that the industry was using unnecessarily high levels of nicotine to create and maintain smokers' addiction.

- Lawsuits began to be filed around the country, including one by Mississippi's attorney general, seeking reimbursement for the estimated tens of millions of dollars that the state spent on medical care for tobacco-related illness. Other states, like Florida, initiated similar efforts.

The major manufacturers of tobacco products increasingly found themselves under pressure and under the spotlight.

Fatal Congressional Testimony

In February 1994, tobacco makers appeared before Congress, denying that nicotine is addictive and that cigarettes have been proved to cause disease and more than 400,000 deaths a year. It was the first of many bitter confrontations.

As part of the hearing process, internal company documents were made public that shed light on the approach of cigarette companies in selling their product. Among the documents was one detailing minutes of a meeting of Brown & Williamson executives held just before tobacco advertising was banned from radio and television in 1971. Code-named Project Truth, the text of the presentation made at the meeting read in part:

Doubt is our product, since it is the best means of competing with the "body of fact" that exists in the minds of the general public. With the general public, the consensus is that cigarettes are in some way harmful to their health.

Unfortunately, we cannot take a position directly opposing the anti-cigarette forces and say that cigarettes are a contributor to good health. No information that we have supports this claim.

The objective of Project Truth was to "lift the cigarette from the cancer identification as quickly as possible and restore it to its proper place of dignity and acceptance in the minds of men and women in the marketplace of American free enterprise."

By the mid-1980s, according to the documents revealed at the hearing, the companies had forsaken attempts to exonerate smoking as a health hazard and seemed to shift to a legal concern "about what would happen if the years of studies on biological hazards of cigarettes were to become available to plaintiffs in court cases."

In later testimony, Commissioner Kessler revealed information that Brown & Williamson developed a genetically engineered tobacco that would more than double the amount of nicotine delivered in some cigarettes. The company responded by calling Dr. Kessler's testimony "exaggerated."

Public Perception Grows Negative

The confusion and disputes resulting from the cigarette manufacturers' testimonies before Congress began to build up. The American Heart Association, American Cancer Society, American Lung Association, and American Medical Association began to work together to win smoking bans. Activists began to get access to caches of internal tobacco industry documents through lawsuits, such as the one filed by the family of Rose Cipollone, who died in 1984 at age 58. Her family won initially but dropped its suit in 1992 after years of costly litigation. The cigarette companies refused to acquiesce.

Perhaps the most damning report was the EPA document on second-hand smoke, which said that environmental tobacco smoke causes 3,000 lung cancer deaths each year. When incoming Clinton administration EPA Administrator Carol Browner was apprised of the findings, she said, "Let that thing rip," and she began promoting the report heavily.

In the latter years of the 1990s, tobacco manufacturers slid further into the public abyss:

- In February 1997, the FDA implemented regulations that forbade merchants from selling tobacco to minors.

- Cigarette advertising was the next to be attacked, with critics vowing to rid such advertising from the airwaves, where minors are exposed to it. The primary target was R. J. Reynolds's Joe Camel advertising campaign. Joe Camel, it was charged, represented a seductive appeal to young people.

- The Campaign for Tobacco-Free Kids was begun with a vigorous public relations and advertising barrage that mobilized children in the pursuit against big tobacco (Figure 14-7).

FIGURE 14-7 Kids against cancer. The Campaign for Tobacco-Free Kids was relentless in its attacks on smoking. (Courtesy Campaign for Tobacco-Free Kids)

- Cigarette package labeling became more restrictive. U.S. legislators looked toward Great Britain, where cigarette advertising is more tightly regulated and packs are labeled with dire warnings (Figure 14-8).

- In 1997, the Liggett Group tobacco company agreed that its tests had indicated that cigarette smoking was in fact harmful to health and agreed to label its products accordingly. Liggett also acknowledged that it had consciously marketed its products to children.

FIGURE 14-8 Smoking Kills. Warnings posted on cigarettes sold in Great Britain left nothing to the imagination in terms of the relative danger.

Company Capitulation

For their part, the cigarette companies themselves remained adamant in their fight—at least at first. Said the Philip Morris public affairs director, "There are risk factors in smoking. But 50 million adults have chosen to smoke, and they have the right to make that decision."

In the wake of the Liggett bombshell, however, the industry was on shaky ground. In 1998, the tobacco industry settled a battery of legal cases with 46 individual states' attorneys general. The settlement was expected to total $246 billion over 25 years. As part of the settlement with the states, $1 billion was devoted to a multiyear public relations program to fight tobacco use. Nonetheless, more suits loomed, and the Justice Department readied further litigation as the drumbeat against tobacco increased (Figure 14-9).

In 1999, Philip Morris, the largest tobacco company, announced plans to repair its tarnished image. Centerpiece was a $100 million Philip Morris Youth Smoking Prevention Initiative public relations

FIGURE 14-9 **Pitched battle.** The wave of antismoking advertising continued, even after huge industry class-action settlements. (Courtesy of Campaign for Tobacco-Free Kids)

program. By 2000, the Philip Morris stock, once one of the bluest of all blue chips, had plunged by more than half.

Faced with an unprecedented loss of public opinion and a tide against cigarettes that now swept around the world, the companies could have but one overriding objective as they faced the new century: to restore their public image.

Road to Resurrection

By the new century, most cigarette companies had gotten the message. Although still vigilantly fighting antismoking lawsuits in court, tobacco manufacturers were no longer equally vigorous in promoting their primary products. Those with food-oriented sub-

No matter how often a snake sheds its skin...
It's still a snake.

Altria *is* **Philip Morris.**

Why is Philip Morris changing its name? After decades of marketing to kids, deceiving the public and manipulating its products, Philip Morris now wants to hide from its past. But it can't hide this: More kids still smoke "Altria's" Marlboros than all other brands combined. 2,000 kids still get hooked on tobacco every day. 1 in 3 will die prematurely. Philip Morris may be changing its name, but it's not changing its ways.

New Name. Same Deadly Habits.
www.PhilipMorrisCantHide.org

FIGURE 14-10 Still a snake. Even after humongous settlement payments, cigarette companies could not escape the wrath of the Campaign for Tobacco-Free Kids. (Courtesy of Campaign for Tobacco-Free-Kids)

sidiaries, such as Philip Morris, became much more eager to promote that side of the business than the cigarette side. Philip Morris, in fact, wound up spinning out its Kraft food division to separate it from the tarnished tobacco name.

By 2002, while the Campaign for Tobacco-Free Kids still attacked aggressively and states' attorneys general still occasionally railed against tobacco companies, the pressure had died down considerably (Figure 14-10).

Ironically, many states used their 2002 tobacco settlement payments of $8.9 billion to balance their sagging budgets. This was in direct contradiction to the states' promise to use settlement funds for tobacco prevention.

Nonetheless, the cigarette manufacturers themselves had learned their lesson. As proof, in 2002, the world's largest tobacco company, Philip Morris, changed its name to Altria (meaning "higher" in Latin), once and for all shedding the stigma that had cost it so much with consumers.

Questions

1. How would you assess the credibility of the cigarette industry today?

2. If you were hired as public relations counsel to the tobacco industry, what would you advise it to do?

3. What do you think of Philip Morris changing the name of its company?

4. Visit the Philip Morris tobacco Web site (www.philipmorris.com/tobacco_bus/index.html). Read the home page and then follow the link to "Tobacco Issues." How is Philip Morris using this Web site to boost its credibility?

For further information on the Tobacco Wars, see "Defending an Embattled Industry," *Public Relations Strategist* (Summer 1999): 7; Stuart Elliott, "When the Smoke Clears, It's Still Reynolds," *New York Times* (September 13, 1995): D1; Suein L. Hwang, "Philip Morris Plans to Take Steps to Mend Its Image," *Wall Street Journal* (June 29, 1999): B9; Youssef M. Ibrahim, "Cigarette Makers Cope with British Ad Restrictions," *New York Times* (April 18, 1997): D5; Mary Kuntz and Joseph Weber, "The New Hucksterism," *Business Week* (July 1, 1996); Otto Lerbinger, "Branding vs. Identity," *PR Reporter* (June 24, 2002): 1; William D. Novelli, "Waging War on Tobacco," *Public Relations Strategist* (Fall 1999): 15; Tara Parker-Pope, "Danger: Warning Labels May Backfire," *Wall Street Journal* (April 28, 1997): B1; "Philip Morris Launches $100M Anti-Smoking Pitch," *O'Dwyer's PR Services Report* (January 1999): 1, 20; Eben Shapiro, "RJR Nabisco's Tobacco Unit Escapes Fight with FTC Over Joe Camel Ads," *Wall Street Journal* (June 2, 1994); John Schwartz, "Double Blow for Tobacco Industry: Waxman Assails Research Council, Justice Dept. Probe Sought," *Washington Post* (May 27, 1994): A1.

Voice of Authority

An Interview with Amy Binder

Amy Binder is CEO of the New York City–based RF|Binder Partners, Inc., one of the companies of the Ruder Finn Group. In addition to overseeing the business direction and growth of the agency, Binder is focused on ensuring that every client receives consistent, high-quality service and has continual access to the agency's best creative and strategic thinking. She is a veteran of two-and-a half decades in public relations, developing corporate reputations and branding programs for some of the world's largest organizations. For the five years leading to the formation of RF|Binder Partners, she was president/Ruder Finn Americas.

Did you study public relations in college?

No, I went to Brown University and majored in history. While at Brown, I also studied photography, which had been a passion of mine since I was a teenager. I actually combined both interests in my thesis, which was about using photographs taken by 19th-century British photographers to gain a better and different understanding of society in Victorian England. Photographers at that time, in many ways, were photojournalists documenting their time. Through my thesis, I began to be interested in how outside third parties could shape public opinion.

Did your family influence you to seek a career in public relations?

When I grew up, very few people understood what public relations was. In the 1960s, it was still a relatively young field. As a child, people would ask me what my father did and when I said public relations, they would stare at me blankly. Saying your father was a doctor, lawyer, banker, or businessman would have been much easier. It finally got to a point where I would say, one, do you know what the public is; two, do you understand what relationships are all about, three, public relations is about building relationships among different publics. That they got. Given how people reacted, public relations was not a career that came to mind first.

What qualities are most important for a client's benefit?
The following five qualities are the most important:

- **Learning how to listen:** All consultants need to understand the problem and the challenge that a client is facing. We need to listen to our clients to better understand their culture as well as their specific business challenges.

- **Being strategic:** Public relations is perceived to be a soft discipline, and many ideas for programs come out of creative sessions. An idea needs to emerge from logical thinking and research that can demonstrate the rationale for choosing a specific creative platform. One needs the discipline to be able to demonstrate the framework for why an idea is right for addressing a specific business challenge. And one needs the research or data, which will help you understand the dynamics in the marketplace.

- **Being creative:** We live in a world where there is a lot of clutter. Consumer and business people are being bombarded with messages from a variety of brands, businesses, institutions, et cetera. Creativity enables you to find a new way of looking at something or enabling other people to hear the message that you want to convey. That is more important than ever.

- **Being interested in how opinion is shaped:** While it is still critical for someone going into this profession to read, listen, and watch the media, that is no longer enough. With the fragmentation of the media, there are so many ways that consumers and customers get information and are influenced. There are think tanks which issue reports, individuals who write blogs on the Internet, seminars held every day both offline and online through webcasts. It is important that a consultant is very aware and interested in learning about the new ways that are emerging to influence opinions.

- **Being curious:** You have to be interested in learning about a lot of different industries and business issues. One day you might find yourself dealing with skincare issues and the next day a crisis with an oil company. As a consultant, you need to be curious about learning new areas.

What is most compelling about the public relations consulting business?

There are pros and cons. On the one hand, we can never truly understand our clients' business because we are outsiders. Until you sit inside a corporation, you cannot understand as fully the culture and challenges that the company faces every day. On the other hand, being an outsider can be a real advantage. We are willing to take risks that insiders might be more hesitant to take. We also bring the objectivity of an outsider. One of the most compelling aspects of the consulting business is bringing new points of view and different types of insights to solving a problem. The task of changing opinions and closing communications gaps is

not easy. Sometimes you need to do something bold to accomplish this task.

Why should an organization seek outside public relations counsel?

There are four important reasons to bring in an outside agency.

1. The most important is to support the launch of a new strategic, proactive initiative. An internal public relations group, unless it is very large, most often is driven by addressing the reactive needs of a company and servicing their internal business partners. An outside agency can be very helpful in taking an objective point of view about an issue and investing the time to develop a program which addresses all of the challenges facing either the brand or the company. The outside agency can also devote staff that will not be distracted by another internal issue or crisis of the day, ensuring that the program is well executed.

2. A second important role is when there is a crisis. The outside agency can offer an objective or outsider's point of view, which is critical because during a crisis, one can become mired in the details and the pressures of the moment. In addition, there is always a need for seasoned professionals who have been through a crisis before.

3. Third, an agency can bring relationships with key opinion leaders and the media that are important. The agency may have developed programs for clients who have faced similar challenges and will bring knowledge about what will work and what won't.

4. And finally, more often than not, consultants can bring a different—if not broader—perspective on an issue because of the range of his or her experiences. This perspective is useful in helping a company take a fresh view on an issue.

How would you assess the state of the public relations business today?

This may be one of the strongest times in the history of this profession. The media from the *Economist* to *The Wall Street Journal* have written articles recently about the growing recognition for the field and what it can offer. The public relations field is all about building credibility. In a time when so many organizations have had their reputations called into question, there is an important opportunity for the field.

Suggested Readings

Careers in Advertising and Public Relations: The WetFeet Insider Guide. San Francisco: WetFeet, Inc., 2004. Soup-to-nuts primer on getting a job in one of these creative fields.

Dyche, Jill. *The CRM Handbook: A Business Guide to Customer Relationship Management*. Boston: Addison Wesley, 2001.

Greenberg, Paul. *CRM At the Speed of Light, Capturing and Keeping Customers in Internet Real Time*. New York: McGraw-Hill, 2001.

Hawkins, Del I., and Kenneth A. Coney. *Consumer Behavior: Building Marketing Strategy*. New York: McGraw-Hill Irwin, 2004. This book tells you everything you need to know about consumer behavior— what it is and why it's worthy of study.

Jones, Don, Mark Scott, and Rick Villars. *E-Commerce for Dummies*. New York: Hungry Media, 2001. Real-life analysis of what sells and what doesn't on the Internet. And you don't have to be a genius to understand!

Kush, Christopher. *The One Hour Activist*. San Francisco: Josey-Boss, 2004. Packed with advice on getting your message across.

Locke, Christopher, Rick Levine, Doc Searls, and David Weinberger. *The Cluetrain Manifesto*. Cambridge, MA: Perseus Books, 2001. This book began as a Web site, www.cluetrain.com, when the Silicon Valley authors posted 95 theses that proclaimed what they felt was the new reality of the marketplace, among them, "forget advertising."

Peppers, Don, and Martha Rogers. *The One to One Future: Building Relationships One Customer at a Time*. New York: Bantam Doubleday Dell, 1997.

Ries, Laura, and Al Ries. *The Fall of Advertising and the Rise of PR*. New York: Harper Business, 2002. Legendary positioning guru and his talented daughter declare that their former business has had it. Long live public relations!

Notes

1. Hillary Mayell, "As Consumption Spreads, Earth Suffers, Study Says," *National Geographic News*, January 12, 2004.
2. Richard Peterson, "Rejuvenating the Humble Prune," *New York Times*, August 13, 2000, D2.
3. "Yahoo! Removing Adult Products," *Thestreet.com*, April 13, 2001.
4. Melanie Warner, "McDonald's to Add Facts on Nutrition to Packaging," *New York Times*, October 26, 2005, C1.
5. "Consumer-Generated Media Exceeds Traditional Advertising for Influencing Purchasing Behavior," *PR Newswire-Intelliseek*, September 26, 2005.
6. "Computer and Internet Use in the United States: 2003," U.S. Census Bureau, October 2005.

15 International Relations

FIGURE 15-1 Global defiance. Pakistani rape victim Mukhtar Mai, right, accompanied by a woman police officer, departs Islamabad to inform the world about the plight of women in her country. (Khalid Tanveer/AP Wide World Photos)

Nearly a half century ago, the late Canadian communications professor Marshall McLuhan wrote that "the world is a global village." Today, of course, there is no question but that that is the case. As a consequence, the practice of public relations is very much an international phenomenon.

As Professor Daniel Awodiya has written, "The opportunities for public relations are increasing in the face of phenomenal growth in information technology and the pace-setting trend of corporate mergers and acquisitions."[1]

As the world has become a smaller place and the power of communications has expanded exponentially, the public relations challenge for nations and governments used to operating in secrecy has also increased. This change in approach was brought home most graphically in 2006 as a result of the international campaign spearheaded by this courageous woman:

Mukhtar Mai was a Pakistani teacher whose defiant response to being gang-raped by order of a tribal court brought her worldwide attention. In January 2006, she set off worldwide alarm bells when the United Nations refused to allow her to speak after Pakistan protested that it would embarrass the country's prime minister, who was visiting the United States at the same time. Ms. Mai's cause received even more publicity, as the United Nations and Pakistan Kabuki-danced around the issue.[2]

As trade and information flows have become borderless, so, too, has public relations. Indeed, the International Public Relations Association, founded in 1955, has members in 95 countries.

Although the reality of peoples and nations of the world becoming more closely connected is largely positive for society, there is also a dark side. The images beamed by satellite signals and the Internet have, in some quarters, fomented misunderstandings and jealousies, as the chasm between rich and poor, haves and have-nots, comes more sharply into focus.

The attacks on America of September 11, 2001, exacerbated these problems, particularly with respect to understanding the practice of Islam and relations with people of Middle Eastern descent. Repairing these rifts will take time as well as thoughtful action and communication from all sectors of society. This is a key international public relations challenge in the 21st century. (See Case Study at the conclusion of this chapter.)

In this chapter, we briefly explore the state of public relations practice around the world and the opportunities available for international public relations practice.

Operating Around the Globe

The actions of individuals and organizations in one part of the world are felt instantly and irrevocably by people around the globe. As a consequence, multinational corporations, in particular, must be sensitive to how their actions might affect people of different cultures in different geographies.

Companies, in fact, have become the most prominent standard bearers of their countries. American companies, with eight of the 10 most powerful brands in the world (see Talking Points), are the most prominent of the prominent.

Consider the challenges multinational companies face.

- In 2006, when French students rioted to protest proposed changes in France's employment policies, one of the most prominent targets was McDonald's. Why? Because it was American, it represented "evil capitalism," and it was there. Earlier in Paris, demonstrators protested working conditions at McDonald's restaurants.[3]

- In 2001, when Muslim restaurant owners took to the streets of Bombay, India, to demonstrate against America's military action in Afghanistan, they didn't burn the Stars and Stripes—they vented their anger by pouring bottles of Coke and Pepsi out into the road. Worse, a Coca-Cola bottling plant in Buntur, India, was bombed.[4]

- Around the world, other symbols of American capitalism, from Nike to Citibank to Microsoft, remain on guard to local conflagration.

All foreign companies operating internationally must constantly reinforce the notion that they are responsible and concerned residents of local communities. Most resort to the public relations philosophy of leading with proper action and then communicating it. KFC, for one, has 158 franchises in Indonesia, most of which are locally owned and operated. McDonald's, for another, has a poster in the window of the Jakarta McDonald's that reads:

> *In the name of Allah, the merciful and the gracious, McDonald's Indonesia is owned by an indigenous Muslim Indonesian.*

Smart multinationals also support local causes and incorporate international audiences and celebrities in their philanthropic efforts. Among intelligent multinational concerns, the overriding mantra must be "thinking global, acting local" in order to win lasting friendship and support in other countries.

Talking Points

Global Brand Leaders

According to Interbrand, which annually publishes a ranking of the 100 most valuable global brands, more than half are U.S.-based. American companies account for eight of the 10 most powerful brands in the world. Here's the Interbrand 2005 top 10 (Figure 15-2).

1. Coca-Cola
2. Microsoft
3. IBM

4. General Electric
5. Intel
6. Nokia—Finland
7. Disney
8. McDonald's
9. Toyota—Japan
10. Marlboro

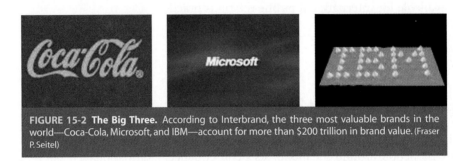

FIGURE 15-2 The Big Three. According to Interbrand, the three most valuable brands in the world—Coca-Cola, Microsoft, and IBM—account for more than $200 trillion in brand value. (Fraser P. Seitel)

For further information, see "Business Week/Interbrand Annual Ranking of the 100 Top Global Brands," www.businessweek.com, July 21, 2005.

Hopscotching the World for Public Relations

In the 21st century, public relations has become a global phenomenon. Major political shifts toward democracy throughout the world, coupled with the rapidity of worldwide communications and the move to form trading alliances of regional nations, have focused new attention on public relations. The collapse of communism, the coming together of European economies, wars against totalitarianism in Afghanistan and Iraq, and the growth of democracy everywhere from Eastern Europe to South Africa have brought the global role of public relations into a new spotlight.

In 2000, the Global Alliance for Public Relations and Communications Management was formally established at a meeting in Bled, Slovenia, linking 63 member countries and representing more than 75,000 practitioners around the world. The purpose of the alliance was to provide a forum to share ideas and best public relations practices, seek common standards, and provide a better understanding of each culture in which practitioners operate.[5]

Here, in globe-trotting summary, are developments depicting the state of public relations beyond the borders of the United States.

Canada

Canadian public relations is the rival of American practice in terms of its level of acceptance, respect, sophistication, and maturity. The Canadian Public Relations Society (CPRS), formed in 1948, is extremely active, representing more than 1,600 public relations professionals in 16 member societies throughout the country.

Like its American counterparts, the CPRS maintains a code of professional standards that revolves around "dealing fairly and honestly with the communications media and the public." A professional accreditation program, job registry, and affiliations with Canadian university public relations programs are included in CPRS offerings.

Canadian public relations professionals must be conversant not only in the English-speaking parts of their country but also in the French-speaking markets, such as Quebec. Also, Canada in recent years, like America, has become a nation of nations, with great multicultural diversity. Dealing with diverse ethnicity also becomes a public relations challenge. Beyond Canada, America's other neighbors to the north also have become active in public relations efforts (Figure 15-3).

Europe

The emergence of a more unified Europe through the formation of the European Community (EC) in 1992, has major implications on the practice of public relations in Europe. As in Canada, public relations developed more or less simultaneously in Europe and the United States during the 20th century. In Germany, in particular, public relations writings appeared in the early 1900s.

In the new century, privatization and the synthesis of the European Community into a more unified bloc have spurred increased public relations action in many European countries. Public relations has experienced tremendous growth in Great Britain, employing 30,000 practitioners and growing at a rate of 20 percent annually.[6]

The Institute of Public Relations, headquartered in London and in its fifth decade, is the largest professional organization in Europe, with 8,000 public relations practitioner members. It encompasses 13 regional groups, has a Web site at www.ipr.org.uk, and produces a monthly magazine. It also issues a CIPR Diploma for practitioners who demonstrate the requisite knowledge of theory and practice of public relations.

The stature of the field in Europe was underscored in 2006, when British Prime Minister Tony Blair's oldest son, Euan, interned at a leading financial public relations firm. Said the *Financial Times,* "Skillful, well-judged PR advice can make or break a situation."[7] Such journalistic praise for public relations was unheard of even a decade earlier.

Europe is the domicile of some of the world's mightiest companies, from BMW and Volkswagen in Germany to HSBC and British Petroleum in Britain to Nestlé and Rolex in Switzerland. As European organizations pay increased attention to their reputations and how they are perceived, public relations is certain to be at the forefront of European commercial concern in the years ahead.

Latin America

Latin America is expanding at a faster rate than virtually any other region in the world. In terms of public relations development in Latin America, the scene is more chaotic than in the United States, Canada, or Europe.

The field is most highly developed in Mexico, where public relations practice began in the 1930s. Mexican corporations all have communications and public relations departments, and many employ local or U.S. public relations agencies. Mexican schools of higher learning also teach public relations. The passage of NAFTA under President Clinton and the reinforcement of generally solid relations with Mexico under President Bush signal increasing opportunities for U.S–Mexican trade and therefore for public relations growth.

FIGURE 15-3 Natural public relations. The Icelandic Tourist Board called on Salo Productions to introduce the country's many wonders to its southern neighbors. (Courtesy of Salo Productions)

In the other countries of Latin America, public relations is an important growing phenomenon. Argentina, Brazil, and Chile all have developed practices. Chile, with its robust economy and approach to capitalism, is a particularly prominent candidate for increased public relations activity. In 2004, one of Chile's most prominent public relations educational institutions, Universidad De Vina Del Mar, staged an international public relations summit, Congreso Internacional de Relaciones Publicas, attracting prominent professionals from across the country and the world.

Further indication of potential Latin American public relations expansion is the fact that *The Wall Street Journal Americas* edition, nestled amidst the pages of 20 Latin American newspapers, reaches more than 2.5 million readers.

Japan

Public relations in Asia has experienced sharp growth in recent years. In Japan, the practice of public relations, by definition, is contrary to the nation's cultural heritage. Japanese culture values modesty and promotes silence over eloquence. Public relations, mistakenly equated with self-publicity, has therefore not traditionally been valued in Japanese society.

Speaking of Ethics

Socialist's Social Responsibility One-Ups Big Oil

Venezuelan President Hugo Chavez was not the world's most "stable" leader. An avowed socialist, amigo of Fidel Castro, and enemy of President Bush and his administration, Chavez was the least liked head of state this side of his buddy in Cuba (Figure 15-4).

But in the winter of 2005, with the price of oil hovering at sky-high rates, Chavez pulled a public relations coup that had rock-ribbed capitalists shaking their heads in admiration.

Using his country's oil wealth to strike back at the American government he loathed, Chavez made a deal to supply cheap fuel to thousands of poor residents in Boston and New York.

To the anger of many in Washington—most undoubtedly including the U.S. president Chavez once labeled a "genocidal madman"—Citgo Petroleum Corporation, a company controlled by the Venezuelan government, agreed to supply more than 12 million gallons of oil to poor people at a rate 40 percent below market prices.

Citgo and its populist proprietor trumpeted their unprecedented generosity with full-page ads in U.S. newspapers, tweaking their neighbors to the north—particularly those in the oil business. Indeed, many American pundits wondered why Exxon-Mobil and Shell and their energy brethren weren't willing to make similar offers.

"Why are we doing this?" asked the ad.

"It's about offering humanitarian aid to those who need it. What could be more American than that?"

Touché.

FIGURE 15-4 Beneficent enemy oil baron. Venezuelan President Hugo Chavez dons his state oil company helmet to extol a deal to help the poor in U.S. cities. (HO-Miraflores Palace/AP Wide World Photos)

For further information, see Alec Russell, "Chavez's Cheap Oil for US Poor Angers Washington," *Sydney Morning Herald,* November 25, 2005.

The public relations profession in Japan was established after World War II. Although the Japanese take a low-key approach to public relations work—especially self-advocacy—the field is growing, particularly as the six major national newspapers and four national networks become more aggressive in investigating a proliferation of national scandals. By far the most important aspect of Japanese public relations is dealing with the media.

The mass media in Japan are extremely powerful—much more so than their equivalents in the United States. Newspapers like the *Yomiuri Shimbun* and the *Asahi Shimbun* are among the world's most dominant. The *Yomiuri* alone sells 14 million copies a day—compared to *The New York Times,* which sells one million. The combined circulation of Japan's 120 newspapers is a mind-boggling 70 million copies. Moreover, more than 58 million people—about one-half the Japanese population—can access Web-delivered media sources via their mobile phones. In recent years, television in general and talk shows in particular have become increasingly popular in Japan. The average Japanese person watches just under 4 hours of television each day.

As a consequence of the nation's media and communications literacy, the practice of hiring a public relations agency to assist in navigating journalistic waters has grown. The three largest Japanese indigenous firms, Dentsu, Kyoto, and Prap Japan, employ about 200 people each and share the business with several American and European firms with Japanese offices.

Japanese public relations differs markedly from that of the West. For example, the need for maintaining an outward display of harmony that influences much of Japanese business has ramifications for public relations. The majority of Japanese companies shun the kind of aggressive public relations favored by American companies. They prefer, instead, to disseminate only the most positive news, taking care not to boast or appear to triumph through the failures of others.[8]

Unlike in the West, where organizations arrange their own press coverage, in Japan, *Keiretsu* business associations, or press clubs, which bring together individual firms, operate with enormous influence as intermediaries in arranging press events.

In sum, the need for effective public relations in Japan is indisputable.

China

After a number of false starts, China holds great potential for public relations expansion. By 2020, some predict, 70 percent of the world will speak Mandarin as their principal language. China is the world's fastest-growing economy, second only to the United States, which it should pass soon. As the nation with the largest consumer population, China ranks eleventh in world trade and holds magnificent promise.

Western-style public relations is a recent phenomenon in China, having been introduced only in 1980 by way of a foreign joint venture. Today, there are 1,500 public relations firms in China, employing more than 30,000 people, including more than 15,000 professionals. China's public relations industry accounts for upwards of $400 million in annual revenue.

With media competition in China consisting of 8,000 magazines, 2,000 newspapers, and 3,000 television stations, the numbers of public relations professionals are certain to skyrocket.[9]

In 2004, the Shanghai International Public Relations Summit, co-sponsored by the Shanghai Public Relations Association, the China International Public Relations Association, and the Institute of Public Relations of Singapore, attracted more than 200 practitioners from the region. Public relations courses are offered at leading universities, such as China's Institute of International Relations in Beijing, Nankai University in Tianjin, and Zhongshan University in Guangzhou.

As China modernizes its way into the 21st century, one of the greatest challenges for indigenous business enterprises will be increased foreign and domestic competition in everything from soap products to household appliances and from cars to banking to telecommunications.[10] Public relations will be called on to help differentiate these enterprises from the competition. Already, major U.S. public relations agencies have moved into the country through solely funded enterprises or joint ventures (Figure 15-5).

All of these developments suggest that the public relations business in China has only just begun and will enjoy a bright future in the 21st century.

Asia

Elsewhere in Asia, public relations also has begun to take root. It is important to remember that every Asian country is different, and public relations practice differs considerably from that in the United States. For example, in certain Asian nations, news releases are printed verbatim—a practice not followed in the United States.

In India, the antecedents of modern public relations practice have been traced to around 300 B.C., when the Indian Emperor Asoka used rock and pillar edicts as effective communications tools. Modern-day Indian public relations emerged during World War II, as public opinion became more important and mass-circulation newspapers proliferated. It was at this time that the powerful Tata industrial conglomerate formed the first public relations department in India.[11]

In 1958, eight years after India became a republic, the Public Relations Society of India was formed. Today, public relations practice in India is largely a subordinate of the marketing function. This is not uncommon throughout Asia and around the world.

FIGURE 15-5 Entry celebration. Edelman Worldwide's entry into China was celebrated at a gala Beijing banquet honoring the Chicago-based firm. (Courtesy of Fraser P. Seitel)

In recent years, American firms have continued their march through Asia and into India. In 2005, Burson-Marsteller acquired Genesis, India's leading public relations company, with close to 200 employees in five cities. As India continues to progress as a high tech nation and a fertile source of knowledge workers, its public relations industry will expand greatly.

In Malaysia, with more than 50 colleges and universities offering public relations as a professional course and degree program, the nation has created a pool of talent, vying to become a hub in the field.[12] The Institute of Public Relations Malaysia (IPRM) was formed in the early 1960s and trains 2,000 professionals annually. Like its counterpart in the United States, IPRM has launched an accreditation program and received government funds to increase its role and leadership in the practice of public relations.

In Singapore, a bastion of private enterprise, public relations was boosted in the late 1990s by new companies raising funds through a booming stock market and active economy. Technology, financial services, and real estate development also are burgeoning areas of public relations growth. The Institute for Public Relations Singapore, begun in 1970, today boasts 500 members and offers training courses in the field.

In the other Asian capitals, Korea has an active public relations community, as do Indonesia and Taiwan. In Vietnam, too, opportunities for public relations work promise to emerge as the country increases its financial might and entrepreneurial class.

Perhaps the truest test of the public relations boom in Asia was seen in the Philippines in 2006, when President Gloria Arroyo faced increasing disenchantment at home. In a speech before the Third Public Relations Summit in the country, the president's press secretary appealed to the Philippines public relations community to balance a negative media and use their offices "to support and assist the president instead of wishing her downfall."[13] Yes, in Asia, the practice of public relations had most certainly taken hold.

Eastern Europe

In the new democracies of Eastern Europe, there are 370 million consumers, and so the prospects for public relations expansion are enticing.

- More than 80 percent of all Eastern Europeans watch television daily. Nearly all watch several times a week.
- In Hungary, about 20 percent of the population have television sets connected to satellite dishes.
- In Poland, 13 percent of the population report owning VCRs.
- In Hungary, Serbia, and Croatia, about two thirds of the population read newspapers daily.

Since public relations practice follows the development of a strong business sector, the nations of Eastern Europe, which claimed their first PRSA-accredited practioner in 2001, are certain to see quantum leaps in the indigenous public relations business in the years immediately ahead.

Russia

Although "capitalist Russia" (how strange that sounds!) has suffered fits and starts—not to mention scandals and bloody internal conflicts during its initial capitalistic years—the practice of public relations has been steadily developing.

AT&T, Intel, Coca-Cola, and many other companies are already ensconced in Russia. Large American public relations firms have also set up bases. PR Newswire, in combination with the news agency TASS, distributes news releases from U.S. companies to locations in the Commonwealth of Independent States. Releases are translated into Russian and reach 40 newspapers in Moscow alone.

Even Russian President Vladimir Putin has gotten into the public relations act. When Putin's image tumbled in 2006—as a result of government crackdowns, violations of press freedoms and human rights, attempts to cut gas supplies, strong-arm tactics with enemies, and a host of other similar "imperfections"—the president enlisted media advisors to embark on an emergency propaganda campaign to bolster Russia's image among its citizens.

Based on the comments of Putin's media advisor, the practice of public relations still has a ways to go in Russia. Summarized the genius Kremlin adviser: "The Russians have become the Jews of the 21st century. They are regarded as the pariahs of Europe."[14] Ivy Lee, he wasn't.

Australia and New Zealand

Public relations in the land down under is also alive and thriving. The Public Relations Institute of Australia is an extremely active organization, and the practice is widespread, particularly in the country's two commercial centers, Melbourne and Sydney. Australian public relations practice, like Australians themselves, is more low key and less flashy than American practice but no less competent and sophisticated.

In New Zealand, too, public relations is practiced through local and international public relations agencies and communications practitioners at major companies and nonprofits. In fact, one New Zealand nonprofit, Queensland Health, was accused in 2006 of being "more interested in public relations than in health care." The organization caused a furor when it was reported that it had increased its public relations staff by 45 percent while increasing its medical workforce by just 14 percent. The public affairs director's salary? One hundred thousand dollars. Not bad for New Zealand.[15]

Africa

In Africa, too, the practice of public relations is growing. In 1990, the largest public relations meeting in the history of the continent was held in Abuja, Nigeria, with 1,000 attendees from 25 countries. In 1994, as a result of an extensive worldwide communications and public relations campaign, Nelson Mandela became the first democratically elected president of the nation of South Africa.

As the most developed country in sub-Saharan Africa, South Africa led the continent in sophisticated public relations. It boasted more than 30 public relations–related companies and a professional association, the Institute for Public Relations and Communication Management.

In several African countries, public relations practitioners are not allowed to practice their craft unless they are registered members of designated national public relations associations, which adhere to strict standards and ethics.

Middle East

Despite the misunderstandings, hostilities, and frayed feelings that exist between the Middle East and the West, the practice of public relations, in parts of the Middle East at least, has grown nicely. The practice itself is far different than that practiced in the United States.

In Egypt, according to one native consultant, "Public relations is an old-fashioned thing. It's the guy who goes to the airport; it's the flower arrangement in a hotel; it's things like this."[16] However, it is also true that in Egypt's intense business environment, where rumors spread like wildfire, public relations is essential to giving the public a clearer image of the truth.

In the United Arab Emirates, another capital of trade and commerce, one positive sign of the last decade was the admission of women students into the public relations major program at the United Arab Emirates University in Al-Ain.

Other Middle Eastern nations, from Saudi Arabia to Libya, have spent millions of dollars in recent years on public relations support to help improve their image.

What is indisputable in the Middle East is that even terrorists have adapted the techniques of public relations. Al-Qaeda terrorist leaders regularly use the Internet and Arab-language television—most typically, Al Jazeera in Qatar—to spew out their mes-

Talking Points

Think Multilingual—or Else

Steve Rivkin is America's foremost "nameologist," having written extensively on what organizations and products must consider before they choose a name (Figure 15-6). When it comes to organizations dealing overseas, the nameologist warns, you'd better think multilingual—or else.

Or else what? Or else this:

- A food company named its giant burrito a *Burrada*. Big mistake. The colloquial meaning of that word in Spanish is "big mistake."
- Estée Lauder was set to export its Country Mist makeup when German managers pointed out that *mist* is German slang for, uh, well, to put it gently, "manure." (The name became Country Moist in Germany.)
- When General Motors introduced the Chevrolet Nova in South America, it was shocked to learn that *no va* is Spanish for "does not go." After GM realized it wouldn't sell many of the "go-less" cars, it renamed the vehicle Caribe in Spanish markets.
- Ford had a similar problem in Brazil when it introduced the Pinto. The name turned out to be Brazilian slang for "tiny male genitals." Red-faced Ford pried off all the nameplates and renamed the car Corcel, which means "horse."
- Colgate introduced a toothpaste in France called Cue, the name of a notorious French porno magazine.
- The name Coca-Cola in China was first rendered as *ke-kou-ke-la*. Unfortunately, Coke did not discover until after thousands of signs had been printed that the phrase means "bite the wax tadpole." Coke then researched 40,000 Chinese characters and found a close phonetic equivalent, *ko-kou-ko-le*,

FIGURE 15-6 Namemeister extraordinaire, Steve Rivkin. (Courtesy of Rivkin & Associates, Inc.)

which loosely translates as "happiness in the mouth." Much better.

- A leading brand of car de-icer in Finland will never make it to America. The brand's name: Super Piss.
- Ditto for Japan's leading brand of coffee creamer. Its name: Creap.

Talking Points

Straighten Out Your English—or Else

On the other hand, it might be equally beneficial for our friends in foreign lands to make sure of their own English.

Consider these actual signs posted in various establishments around the world.

- In a Copenhagen airline ticket office: "We take your bags and send them in all directions."
- In a Norwegian cocktail lounge: "Ladies are requested not to have children in the bar."
- At a Budapest zoo: "Please do not feed the animals. If you have any suitable food, give it to the guard on duty."
- In a doctor's office in Italy: "Specialist in women and other diseases."

- In a Paris hotel elevator: "Please leave your values at the front desk."
- From the brochure of a Tokyo car rental firm: "When passenger of foot heave in sight, tootle the horn. Trumpet him melodiously at first, but if he still obstacles your passage then tootle him with vigor."
- In an advertisement by a Hong Kong dentist: "Teeth extracted by the latest Methodists."
- In an Acapulco hotel: "The manager has personally passed all the water served here."
- In a Bucharest hotel lobby: "The lift is being fixed for the next day. During that time we regret that you will be unbearable."

---

sages of fear and hate. Even Osama bin Laden, the orchestrator of the attacks on America, is a savvy student of public relations.

Communicating to the Global Village

Communications media around the world have truly converted the globe into one large "village," united by satellite and Internet technology. What happens in one corner of the globe is instantly transmitted to another.

The world relearned this lesson in brutal fashion in the spring of 2006, when a Danish newspaper published cartoons that depicted the prophet Muhammad in an unflattering light. The cartoons, instantly transmitted around the globe, set off a firestorm in the Arab world. It triggered demonstrations, boycotts of Danish goods, and a wave of violence resulting in at least 50 deaths.[17] Such is the danger of communications in an increasingly interconnected—not to mention, sensitive—world.

One of the most active global communications factors—especially on the Internet—are the tens of thousands of nongovernmental organizations (NGOs), from Greenpeace to Friends of the Earth, from Africa Action to the World Rainforest Movement. For minimal expense, such organizations can spread their views—often criticisms of multinationals—across the globe (Figure 15-7).

As globalization and international trade impact societies, such NGOs have become increasingly influential in world affairs. They are consulted by governments as well as international organizations, such as the United Nations, which have created associative status for them. These organizations are not directly affiliated with any national government but often have a significant impact on the social, economic, and political activity of the country or region involved.

In the 21st century, as the world continues to get "smaller" in a communications sense, public relations professionals, knowledgeable about foreign customs and cultures and skilled in the practice of communication, will be in great demand.

FIGURE 15-7 Worldview. NGOs, such as True Majority, started by the founders of Ben & Jerry's Ice Cream, are united in generally seeking "a better world." (Courtesy of True Majority)

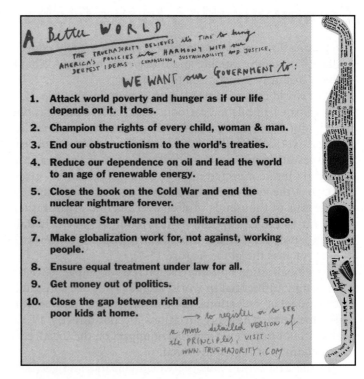

Last Word

The "brave new world" that emerged after September 11, 2001, promises to remain the reality well into the 21st century. At the same time, the world is getting "smaller," with phenomena such as MTV, CNN, basketball, baseball, hip-hop, and Britney Spears knowing no geographic boundaries.

The conflicts around the globe—between democracy and totalitarianism, Arabs and Israelis in the Middle East, Catholics and Protestants in Ireland, warring factions in Africa, and discontent in various other geographies—make it even more imperative that companies, governments, and individuals reach out to communicate with each other.

Stated another way, organizations desperately need professional communicators to navigate through this brave new world of instantaneous communication. As the world's companies continue to expand across borders, they must be sensitive to local customs and people. As global competition intensifies, so will global communications, making it easier to communicate around the world but much more difficult to be heard.

Faced with such a formidable global reality, smart organizations will deal honestly, forthrightly, and frequently with world media and work diligently to build harmonious relationships with others around the world.

Discussion Starters

1. What evidence can you point to that indicates the increased stature of public relations practice around the world?
2. What factors have necessitated the need for increased international public relations?
3. What is meant by the term *global village?*
4. What kinds of public relations practices should be observed by multinationals operating in a foreign country?
5. What is the state of public relations in the Western hemisphere?
6. What is the state of public relations in Europe?
7. What is the state of public relations in Asia?
8. What is the state of public relations in Latin America?
9. What is the significance of NGOs to public relations practice?
10. What public relations initiatives has the socialist government of Venezuela engaged in to win support in the United States?

Top of the Shelf

Global Communication: Theories, Stakeholders and Trends, Second Edition

Thomas L. McPhail. Malden, MA: Blackwell Publishing, 2006.

This tour of how the world's communications have changed over the years encompasses every corner of the globe. From the communications prevalent after the Second World War to the current complications of dealing with al-Qaeda, Osama bin Laden, Islamic Jihad, suicide bombers, and terror cells, the author discusses how these phenomena have effected government communications and the media coverage of that communication.

In addition to tracking the elements that impact global communication, the author also provides a primer on the latest global theories of communication, from electronic colonialism theory to world-system theory. A most comprehensive tome, indeed.

CASE STUDY

CASE STUDY

Karen Hughes Stumbles Selling Uncle Sam

Karen Hughes came out of retirement for this? President Bush's closest public relations advisor, who counseled him throughout his first two years in the White House, didn't exactly find her new job a bed of roses. Thorns, maybe, but roses—no way.

Hughes, who left the Bush White House to return to her family in Texas, was wooed back by the president and Secretary of State Condoleezza Rice in the spring of 2005 to become Undersecretary of State for Public Diplomacy and Public Affairs. Hughes's assignment, simply stated: *Convert the negative image of America around the world.*

Too Much Gas

Almost immediately, Hughes realized that the task of aiding America's global image was as tough as any in government. She immediately set out to visit the Muslim world to reach out to the people to demonstrate the best intentions of America (Figure 15-8).

On a trip to Indonesia a little more than six months into her tenure, Hughes defended the U.S. invasion of Iraq to a group of animated students by incorrectly claiming that Saddam Hussein had "gassed hundreds of thousands of his own people."

"The consensus of the world intelligence community was that Saddam was a very dangerous threat," she said. "After all, he used weapons of mass destruction against his own people. He had murdered hundreds of thousands of his own people using poison gas."

While it was true that at least 300,000 Iraqis were reported to have died during Saddam's bloody 24-year reign, his government's use of chemical weapons against Iraqi Kurds during a 1988 military campaign cost the lives of an estimated 5,000 people.

Hours later, Hughes was asked twice for the basis of her numbers during a meeting with journalists from foreign news organizations.

"It's something that our U.S. government has said a number of times in the past. It's information that was used very widely after his attack on the Kurds. I believe it was close to 300,000," Hughes said when questioned the first time. When asked again several minutes later, she said: "I think it was almost 300,000. It's my recollection. They were put in mass graves."

FIGURE 15-8 Best intentions. Public relations veteran Karen Hughes, shown here with the children of Turkey, found some elements of her new job more pleasant than others. (Osman Orsal/AP Wide World Photos)

At the end of the day, the State Department acknowledged that the numbers cited by its Undersecretary were incorrect.

It was a flabbergasting faux pas for the formerly-invincible presidential counselor. Thus was an experienced government public relations professional introduced to the treacherous fishbowl of international public diplomacy.

Advertising Approach

With two billion Muslims in the world, and the religion being the globe's fastest growing, the backlash among Muslims to tougher post-9/11 U.S. policies and attitudes was a source of great concern to the United States.

Hughes's predecessors in the job failed to make much impact. Both Margaret Tutweiler, a long-time Republican bureaucrat, and Charlotte Beers, a veteran of the advertising industry, were only marginally effective in countering America's image as "the Great Satan" in the Muslim world.

Beers, for example, took a traditional advertising approach to the problem, creating first a 24-page booklet, in print and on the Internet, in 14 languages, which featured graphic pictures of the September 11 attacks. The booklet used bin Laden's own words to accuse him of masterminding the murderous attacks.

A poster was also created and plastered around the Arab world, offering $25 million for information leading to the arrest of the Most Wanted Terrorists, including bin Laden and his key aides (Figure 15-9).

Public Relations Approach

Notwithstanding her difficult baptism of fire in Indonesia, Hughes's approach was much more a traditional public relations initiative. Hughes adopted a "four E" strategy of public relations—engagement, exchanges, education, and empowerment. As she described it, "One of my goals is to put a human face on America and American policy. I want to challenge the notion that public diplomacy is somehow about public relations or polls. It's about policy."

To add teeth to the effort, the Bush administration devoted $670 million to to change worldviews. Hughes set about immediately to engage in face-to-face dialogue, personally traveling around the world as a listener first and a doer second. She made a point of emphasizing that her visits were "listening tours," designed to hear, in a sincere and friendly way, the views and concerns of the people.

Hers was a noble effort but not an easy one. Opinion polls across the Muslim world suggested that U.S. favorability ratings had dropped into the single digits after the Iraq war, even in friendly countries like Egypt and Jordan, where the United States spends millions in aid.

Making Hughes's job even tougher were the often conflicting messages sent out from the home front. In 2006, for example, the country—both liberals and conservatives—rebelled when it was reported that a company, owned by U.S. friend and supporter the United Arab Emirates, would have a hand in running U.S. ports. The deal was scuttled, much to the chagrin of the administration. And Karen Hughes's job just got that much tougher.

Said the president of the Arab American Institute of Washington, D.C., "We're stepping on ourselves every day. The domestic message ends up trumping the public diplomacy message every time."

Questions

1. What would you have advised relative to Karen Hughes's unfortunate statements in Indonesia?

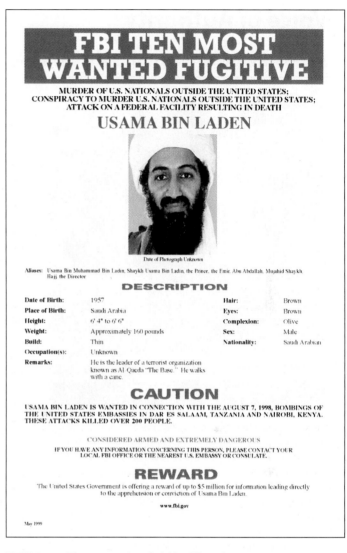

FIGURE 15-9 **The enemy.** America's Most Wanted. (AP Wide World Photos)

2. How would you compare Hughes's approach to public diplomacy with that of her predecessor?

3. If you were public relations advisor to the Undersecretary for Public Diplomacy, what other programmatic elements would you recommend be instituted?

4. If you were the Undersecretary herself, how would you go about changing the image of the United States overseas?

For further information, see Chris Brummitt, "U.S. Diplomat Defends Iraq War," Associated Press, October 21, 2005; Stephen Johnson, "Public Diplomacy Needs a Commander, Not a Spokesman," The Heritage Foundation, September 30, 2005; Glen Kessler and Robin Wright, "Report: U.S. Image in Bad Shape," *Washington Post,* September 24, 2005, A16; "Karen Hughes: Under Secretary for Public Diplomacy," *Newsweek,* October 24, 2005; Alan Sipress, "U.S. Envoy Makes Big Iraq Blunder," *Washington Post,* October 22, 2005; Robin Wright, "Hughes Launches 9/11 Anniversary Image Campaign," *Washington Post,* September 1, 2005.

Voice of Authority

An Interview with Shashi Tharoor

Shashi Tharoor is Undersecretary General for Communications and Public Information of the United Nations. He was named the first director of communications and special projects of the United Nations in 1998. He later served as interim director of the U.N.'s 735-person Department of Public Information. He is the author of five books, the most recent of which, *India: From Midnight to the Millennium,* was selected as a *New York Times* Notable Book of the Year and cited by former President Clinton in his address to the Indian Parliament in 2000. One of his novels, *Show Business,* was filmed as the motion picture *Hollywood.*

What did Secretary General Annan want you to do as the U.N.'s first communications director?

Principally two things. First, he felt we needed to coordinate the external message of the organization. He felt that the U.N. message was being slightly lost in the routine, in the shuffle. Second, he also felt—and this was recommended by a task force that he had appointed in 1997—that he should have somebody on his immediate team, directly reporting to him, who would be concerned about the way in which the world saw the U.N. and would help put the secretary general's own point of view across to those conveying the message of the organization.

How do you answer the criticism that the U.N. is little more than a glorified debating society?

We need to let Americans know that the U.N. is not merely this "talking shop." It is a talking shop part of the time, when there is the General Assembly meeting every year. As Churchill put it, "Isn't jaw boning better than world war?" I mean, wouldn't you rather have these countries boring each other to death, if necessary, in the General Assembly chamber than boring holes into each other on the battlefield?

How have you organized the U.N.'s media relations policy?

We have made more systematic use of op-eds. We've had more press conferences. One of the first things I was able to do—but really, it wasn't me but the secretary general—was the issuance for the first time in the 55 years of the United Nations of media guidelines, which authorize every single U.N. official to speak to the press, on the record within his or her area of competence. [Such guidelines] never existed before.

What was the prior policy?

The prior practice, frankly, was that bureaucrats were not supposed to speak to the press. And if they sometimes did, they did so very quietly and anonymously, on background or off the record, and they were just reluctant to tell the story. People felt that if they saw their name in the paper, it was actually bad news. There's been a 180-degree change.

How important is the communications function at the U.N.?

I see communications as integrally linked to the substantive work. It's not just a question of people doing what they want, and we then have to sell it to the world. It's that needing to be accountable to the world should help determine that we do the right thing. We must ask, in shaping our conferences, "What do we expect the world public to get out of this meeting? What is the story we have to tell them? Why do we expect them to care?" Our job is to help shape such conferences more constructively.

What does the term public relations mean to you?

Public relations is telling the truth, often to people who don't have the time to hear it. It's also about using the public to help shape what you really are doing, because the fact is that the public ultimately is why you're doing it. I've told my colleagues in the U.N. that communications and information is not an end in itself. It exists to make your substantive work successful. Therefore, our communications philosophy has to be to tell the world what we're doing, truthfully and transparently, and use communications to be accountable for the faith the world's peoples have placed in us as an institution.

Suggested Readings

Drobis, David R. "The New Global Imperative for Public Relations." *Public Relations Strategist,* Spring 2002, 36–37.

Franks, Tommy. *American Soldier.* New York: HarperCollins, 2004. The American general in charge of the first stages of the war on terrorism offers, among other things, a fascinating perspective on the use of embedded reporters.

Hackley, Carol Ann, and Qingwen Dong. "American Public Relations Networking Encounters China's *Guanxi.*" *Public Relations Quarterly,* Summer 2001, 16–19.

Howard, Carole M. "Ten Strategies to Avoid Global Gaffes in Media Relations." *Public Relations Strategist,* Fall 2001, 34–37.

Howard, Elizabeth. "A 'World' of PR Opportunities." *Public Relations Strategist,* Winter 2002, 38–39.

Hughes, Karen. *Ten Minutes from Normal.* New York: Viking Penguin, 2004. A post-9/11 memoir about returning to private life before venturing back onto a bigger, more global, more difficult stage.

Ihator, Augustine. "Understanding Cultural Patterns of the World—An Imperative in Implementing Strategic International PR Programs." *Public Relations Quarterly,* Winter 2000, 33–37.

McKinney, Bruce C. "Public Relations in the Land of the Ascending Dragon: Implications in Light of the U.S./Vietnam Bilateral Trade Agreement." *Public Relations Quarterly,* Winter 2000, 23–26.

Ritchey, David. "The Changing Face of Public Relations in China and Hong Kong." *Public Relations Quarterly,* Winter 2000, 27–32.

Wu, Xu. "Doing PR in China—Concepts, Practices and Some Misconceptions." *Public Relations Quarterly,* Summer 2002, 10–18.

Notes

1. Daniel O. Awodiya, "In International Public Relations, What Is Good for the Goose Is Good for the Gander," Suffolk County Community College, Brentwood, NY, March 11, 2000.

2. Warren Hogue, "Heeding Pakistani Protest, U.N. Blocks Talk by Rape Victim," *New York Times,* January 21, 2006, A4.

3. Sarika Gupte, "McDonald's Averts a Crisis," *Ad Age Global,* July 2001, 4.

4. Connor Digman, "Brand Builders vs. Flag Burners," *Ad Age Global,* December 2001, 4–5.

5. "Global Alliance for Public Relations Announces 2003 Executive Board," news release of the Global Alliance, July 16, 2002.

6. "Champions of Accountability Seek to Reclaim Their Crown," *London Sunday Herald,* June 5, 2002.

7. Lina Saigol and Jane Croft, "Blair's Son Puts a Different Spin on Image of the PR Business," *Financial Times,* January 16, 2006.

8. *Communicating: A Guide to PR in Japan,* Dentsu Public Relations, 2005.

9. Carole Gorney, "China's Economic Boom Brings a PR Explosion," *The Strategist,* Spring 2005, 36.

10. Carole Gorney, "Why China Is Ripe for 'Professional' Public Relations," *International Review,* May 2000.

11. Krishnamurthy Sriramesh, "The Models of Public Relations in India," *Journal of Communication Management,* Vol. 4, No. 3, 2000, 229.

12. M. Krishnamoorthy, "PR Consultants Ready to Spread Wings Overseas," *The Star Online,* February 12, 2006.

13. Paolo Romero, "Palace Turns to PR Gurus to Improve GMA's Image," *Philippine Star,* January 24, 2006.

14. "Russia Spends Big to Polish Its Image," *Sydney Herald,* January 9, 2006.

15. Malcolm Cole, "Spin Doctor Numbers Surge," *Courier Mail,* January 9, 2006.

16. "PR Industry Growing, But Still Learning," *Zawya Business Monthly,* January 2006.

17. "Muslim Scholars in Cartoon Talks," BBC News, March 23, 2006.

16 Public Relations Writing

FIGURE 16-1 Up your bucket. Deposed Guns N' Roses guitarist Buckethead (right, with, ahem, a bucket on his head) shown with Bootsy Collins of Parliament/Funkadelic, in happier days. (Mark J. Terrill/AP Wide World Photos)

E ven in the age of the computer, writing remains the key to public relations: Public relations practitioners are professional communicators. And communications means writing.

All of us know how to write and speak. But public relations professionals should write and speak better than their colleagues. Communication—that is, effective writing and speaking—is the essence of the practice of public relations.

There is no substitute for clear and precise language in informing, motivating, and persuading. The ability to write and speak with clarity is a valuable and coveted skill in any organization. Stated another way, the pen is, indeed, mightier than the sword. That, alas, was brought brutally home in the spring of 2004 to this distinguished citizen:

Guns N' Roses guitarist Buckethead learned how devestating writing can be when he was unceremoniously dismissed from the group, with the following news release from group leader Axl Rose:

> *During his tenure with the band Buckethead has been inconsistent and erratic in both his behavior and commitment—despite being under contract—creating uncertainty and confusion and making it virtually impossible to move forward with recording, rehearsals and live plans with confidence.*[1]

Ooofa! Not much love lost there.

The Rose release is exemplary of the power of writing.

The ability to write easily, coherently, and quickly distinguishes the public relations professional from others in an organization. It's not that the skills of counseling and marketing and judgment aren't just as important; some experts argue that these skills are often *more* important than knowing how to write. Perhaps. But not knowing how to write—how to express ideas on paper—may reduce the opportunities to ascend the public relations success ladder.

Senior managers usually have finance, legal, engineering, or sales backgrounds, where writing is not stressed. But when they reach the top, they are expected to write articles, speeches, memos, and testimony. They then need advisers, who are often their trusted public relations professionals. That's why it's imperative that public relations students know how to write—even before they apply public relations techniques to marketing or cyberspace.

Stated bluntly, beginning public relations professionals are expected to have mastery over the written word. So this chapter, properly preceding discussions of integrated marketing and the Internet, focuses on public relations writing.

Writing for the Eye and the Ear

The sad fact is that public relations people, by and large, are horrible writers. This is the unfortunate conclusion of public relations teachers, supervisors, and executive recruiters assigned to find jobs for public relations applicants.[2] That, of course, is unacceptable in a field the fundamental skill of which must be the ability to write.

What does it take to be a public relations writer?

For one thing, it takes a good knowledge of the basics. Although practitioners probably write for a wider range of purposes and use a greater number of communications methods than do other writers, the principles remain the same whether writing for the Internet, an annual report or a case history, an employee newsletter, or a public speech. This chapter explores the fundamentals of writing: (1) discussing public relations writing in general and news releases in particular, (2) reviewing writing for reading, and (3) discussing writing for listening.

Writing for a reader differs dramatically from writing for a listener. A reader has certain luxuries a listener does not have. For example, a reader can scan material, study printed words, dart ahead, and then review certain passages for better understanding. A reader can check up on a writer; if the facts are wrong, for instance, a reader can find out pretty easily. To be effective, writing for the eye must be able to withstand the most rigorous scrutiny.

On the other hand, a listener gets only one opportunity to hear and comprehend a message. If the message is missed the first time, there's usually no second chance. This situation poses a special challenge for the writer—to grab the listener quickly. A listener who tunes out early in a speech or a broadcast is difficult to draw back into the listening fold.

Public relations practitioners—and public relations students—should understand the differences between writing for the eye and the ear. Although it's unlikely that any beginning public relations professional would start by writing speeches, it's important to understand what constitutes a speech and how it's prepared and then be ready for the assignment when opportunity strikes. Because writing lies at the heart of the public relations equation, the more beginners know about writing, the better they will do.

Any practitioner who doesn't know the basics of writing and doesn't know how to write—even in the age of the Internet—is vulnerable and expendable.

Fundamentals of Writing

Few people are born writers. Like any other discipline, writing takes patience and hard work. The more you write, the better you should become, provided you have mastered the basics. Writing fundamentals do not change significantly from one form to another.

What are the basics? Here is a foolproof, four-part formula for writers, from the novice to the novelist:

1. **The idea must precede the expression.** Think before writing. Few people can observe an event, immediately grasp its meaning, and sit down to compose several pages of sharp, incisive prose. Writing requires ideas, and ideas require thought. Ideas must satisfy four criteria:

   - They must relate to the reader.
   - They must engage the reader's attention.
   - They must concern the reader.
   - They must be in the reader's interest.

   Sometimes ideas come quickly. Other times, they don't come at all. But each new writing situation doesn't require a new idea. The trick in coming up with clever ideas lies more in borrowing old ones than in creating new ones. What's that, you say? Is your author encouraging "theft"? You bet! The old cliché "Don't reinvent the wheel," is absolutely true when it comes to good writing. Never underestimate the importance of maintaining good files.

2. **Don't be afraid of the draft.** After deciding on an idea and establishing the purpose of a communication, the writer should prepare a rough draft. This is a necessary and foolproof method for avoiding a mediocre, half-baked product. Writing, no matter how good, can usually be improved with a second look. The draft helps you organize ideas and plot their development before you commit them to a written test. Writing clarity is often enhanced if you know where you will stop before you start. Organization should be logical; it should lead a reader in a systematic way through the body of the text. Sometimes, especially on longer pieces, an outline should precede the draft.

3. **Simplify, clarify.** In writing, the simpler the better. Today, with more and more consumers reading from computer screens, simplicity is imperative. The more people who understand what you're trying to say, the better your chances for stimulating action. Shop talk, jargon, and "in" words should be avoided. Standard English is all that's required to get an idea across. In practically every case, what makes sense is the simple rather than the complex, the familiar rather than the unconventional, and the concrete rather than the abstract. Clarity is another essential in writing. The key to clarity is tightness; that is, each word, each passage, each paragraph must belong. If a word is unnecessary, a passage redundant, a paragraph vague—get rid of it. Writing requires judicious editing; copy must always be reviewed with an eye toward cutting.

4. **Finally, writing must be aimed at a particular audience.** The writer must have the target group in mind and tailor the message to reach that audience. To win the minds and hearts of a specific audience, one must be willing to sacrifice the understanding of certain others. Writers, like companies, can't expect to be all things to all people. Television journalist Bill Moyers offered this advice for good writing:

> *Strike in the active voice. Aim straight for the enemy: imprecision, ambiguity, and those high words that bear semblance of worth, not substance. Offer no quarter to the tired phrase or overworn idiom. Empty your knapsack of all adjectives, adverbs, and clauses that slow your stride and weaken your pace. Travel light. Remember the most memorable sentences in the English language are also the shortest: "The King is dead" and "Jesus wept."*[3]

Flesch Readability Formula

Through a variety of writings, the late Rudolf Flesch staged a one-man battle against pomposity and murkiness in writing. According to Flesch, anyone can become a writer. He suggested that people who write the way they talk will be able to write better. In other words, if people were less inclined to obfuscate their writing with 25-cent words and more inclined to substitute simple words, then not only would communicators communicate better but also receivers would receive more clearly.

In responding to a letter, Flesch's approach in action would work as follows: "Thanks for your suggestion, Tom. I'll mull it over and get back to you as soon as I can." The opposite of the Flesch approach would read like this: "Your suggestion has been received; and after careful consideration, we shall report our findings to you." See the difference? In writing for the Internet, such straightforward writing is the only approach.

There are countless examples of how Flesch's simple dictum works.

■ Few would remember William Shakespeare if he had written sentences such as "Should I act upon the urgings that I feel or remain passive and thus cease to exist?" Shakespeare's writing has stood the test of centuries because of sentences such as "To be or not to be?"

■ A scientist, prone to scientific jargon, might be tempted to write, "The biota exhibited a 100 percent mortality response." But, oh, how much easier and infinitely more understandable to write, "All the fish died."

■ One of President Franklin D. Roosevelt's speechwriters once wrote, "We are endeavoring to construct a more inclusive society." FDR changed it to "We're going to make a country in which no one is left out."

■ Even the most famous book of all, the Bible, opens with a simple sentence that could have been written by a 12-year-old: "In the beginning, God created the heaven and the earth."

Flesch gave seven suggestions for making writing more readable.

1. Use contractions such as *it's* and *doesn't*.

2. Leave out the word *that* whenever possible.

3. Use pronouns such as *I, we, they,* and *you.*

4. When referring back to a noun, repeat the noun or use a pronoun. Don't create eloquent substitutions.

5. Use brief, clear sentences.

6. Cover only one item per paragraph.

7. Use language the reader understands.

To Flesch, the key to all good writing was getting to the point. Stated another way, public relations writers, in writing for the Internet or any other medium, should remember their A's and B's:

- Avoid big words.
- Avoid extra words.
- Avoid clichés.
- Avoid Latin.
- Be specific.
- Be active.
- Be simple.
- Be short.
- Be organized.
- Be convincing.
- Be understandable.

The Beauty of the Inverted Pyramid

Newspaper writing style is the Flesch formula in action. Reporters learn that words are precious and are not to be wasted. In their stories every word counts. If readers lose interest early, they're not likely to be around at the end of the story. That's where

Talking Points

Nonreadability

Although Rudolf Flesch stressed the "readability" of writing, every day we see numerous examples of writing that seeks to be anything but readable. To wit, the following, "Accident Report."

The party of the first part hereinafter known as Jack and the party of the second part hereinafter known as Jill ascended or caused to be ascended elevation of undetermined height and degree of slope, hereinafter referred as "hill." Whose purpose it was to obtain, attain, procure, secure, or otherwise gain acquisition to, by any and/or all means available to them a receptacle or container, hereinafter known as "pail," suitable for the transport of a liquid whose chemical properties shall be limited to hydrogen and oxygen, the proportions of which shall not be

less than or exceed two parts for the first mentioned element and one part for the latter. Such a combination will hereinafter be called "water."

On the occasion stated above, it has been established beyond a reasonable doubt that Jack did plunge, tumble, topple, or otherwise be caused to lose his footing in a manner that caused his body to be thrust in a downward direction. As a direct result of these combined circumstances, Jack suffered fractures and contusions of his cranial regions. Jill, whether due to Jack's misfortune or not, was known to also tumble in a similar fashion after Jack. (Whether the term "after" shall be interpreted in a spatial or time passage sense has not been determined.)

the inverted pyramid comes in. Newspaper story form is the opposite of that for a novel or short story. Whereas the climax of a novel comes at the end, the climax of a newspaper story comes at the beginning. A novel's important facts are rolled out as the plot thickens, but the critical facts in a newspaper story appear at the start. In this way, if readers decide to leave a news article early, they have already gained the basic ideas.

Generally, the first tier, or lead, of the story is the first one or two paragraphs, which include the most important facts. From there, paragraphs are written in descending order of importance, with progressively less important facts presented as the article continues—thus, the term *inverted pyramid*.

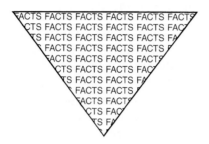

The lead is the most critical element, usually answering the questions concerning who, what, why, when, where, and occasionally how. For example, the following lead effectively answers most of the initial questions a reader might have about the subject of the news story.

> *Columbia Pictures announced today it had signed Britney Spears and Matthew McConaghey to a three-film deal for $60 million each.*

That sentence tells it all; it answers the critical questions and highlights the pertinent facts. It gets to the point quickly without a lot of extra words. In just about 20 words it captures and communicates the essence of what the reader needs to know.

After the lead, the writer must select the next most important facts and array them in descending order with the most important facts earlier in the story. In this way, the inverted pyramid style is more the *selection and organization* of facts than it is an exercise in creative *writing*.

This is the style of straightforward writing that forms the basis for the most fundamental, practical, ubiquitous, and easiest of all public relations tools: the news release.

The News Release

A valuable but much-maligned device, the news release is the granddaddy of public relations writing vehicles. Most public relations professionals swear by it. Some newspaper editors swear about it. Indeed, PR Newswire, a paid wire service used by public relations people to distribute releases, issues about 1,500 news releases every day.[4]

The reason is that everyone uses the release as the basic interpretive mechanism to let people know what an organization is doing. There is no better, clearer, more persuasive way to announce news about an organization, its products, and their applications than by issuing a news release.

A news release may be written as the document of record to state an organization's official position—for example, in a court case or in announcing a price or rate increase. More frequently, however, releases have one overriding purpose: to influence a publication to write favorably about the material discussed. Each day, in fact, professionals e-mail and mail releases to editors in the hope of stimulating favorable stories about their organizations.

Most news releases are not used verbatim, although there are occasional exceptions. Rather, they may stimulate editors to consider covering a story. In other words, the release becomes the point of departure for a newspaper, magazine, radio, or television story. Why, then, do some editors and others describe news releases as "worthless drivel"? The answer, according to researcher Linda Morton of the University of Oklahoma's Herbert School of Journalism, is threefold:

1. **Releases are poorly written.** Professor Morton found that most news releases are written in a more complicated and difficult-to-read style than are most newspaper stories. "This could be the result of pressure from administrators as they review and critique press releases," she reasoned.

2. **Releases are rarely localized.** Newspapers focus largely on hometown or regional developments. The more localized a news release, the greater the chance it has of being used. However, according to Professor Morton, "Practitioners may not want to do the additional work that localization requires." This is a bad decision because research indicates that a news release is 10 times more likely to be used if it is localized.

3. **Releases are not newsworthy.** This is the grand dilemma. An editor will use a public relations release only if he or she considers it news. If it's not newsworthy, it won't be used. What determines whether something is news?

    Professor Morton suggests five requisites:

    - *Impact:* a major announcement that affects an organization, its community, or even society.

    - *Oddity:* an unusual occurrence or milestone, such as the one-millionth customer being signed on.

    - *Conflict:* a significant dispute or controversy, such as a labor disagreement or rejection of a popular proposal.

    - *Known principal:* the greater the title of the individual making the announcement—president versus vice president—the greater the chance of the release being used.

    - *Proximity:* how localized the release is or how timely it is, relative to the news of the day.[5]

Beyond these characteristics, *human interest* stories, which touch on an emotional experience, are regularly considered newsworthy.

With this as a backdrop, it is not surprising that research indicates that in terms of the popular press, most news releases never see the light of print. Early studies, in fact, even before the exponential growth of releases, indicated that less than 10 percent of all news releases were published.[6] Nonetheless, each day's *Wall Street Journal, New York Times, USA Today,* CNN, CNBC, Associated Press wire, Google News, and other daily media around the nation and world are filled with stories generated from news releases issued by public relations professionals.

So the fact is that the news release—despite the harsh reviews of some—remains the single most important public relations vehicle.

Talking Points

Just the Facts

Writing in news release style is easy. It is less a matter of formal writing than it is of selecting, organizing, and arranging facts in descending sequence.

Here are 10 facts:

Fact 1: Supreme Court Chief Justice John Roberts will speak in Madison, Wisconsin, tomorrow.

Fact 2: He will be keynote speaker at the annual convention of the American Bar Association.

Fact 3: He will speak at 8 p.m. at the Kohl Center.

Fact 4: His speech will be a major one.

Fact 5: His topic will be capital punishment.

Fact 6: He will also address university law classes while in Madison.

Fact 7: He will meet with the university's chancellor while in Madison.

Fact 8: He became the 17th Chief Justice, replacing the late William Rehnquist in 2005.

Fact 9: He is a former practicing attorney.

Fact 10: He has, in the past, steadfastly avoided addressing the subject of capital punishment.

Organize these facts into an American Bar Association news release for tomorrow morning's Lansing newspaper. One right answer appears later in this chapter. Just don't peek.

News Release News Value

The key challenge for public relations writers is to ensure that their news releases reflect news. What is *news?* That's an age-old question in journalism. Traditionally, journalists said that when "dog bites man, it's not news, but when man bites dog, that's news." The best way to learn what constitutes news value is to scrutinize the daily press and broadcast news reports and see what they call news. In a general sense, news releases ought to include the following elements:

- Have a well-defined reason for sending the release.
- Focus on one central subject in each release.
- Make certain the subject is newsworthy in the context of the organization, industry, and community.
- Include facts about the product, service, or issue being discussed.
- Provide the facts "factually"—with no puff, no bluff, no hyperbole.
- Rid the release of unnecessary jargon.
- Include appropriate quotes from principals but avoid inflated superlatives that do little more than boost management egos.
- Include product specifications, shipping dates, availability, price, and all pertinent information for telling the story.
- Include a brief description of the company (also called a "boilerplate") at the end of the release—what it is, and what it does.
- Write clearly, concisely, forcefully.

News Release Content

Again, the cardinal rule in release content is that the end product must be newsworthy. The release must be of interest to an editor and readers. Issuing a release that has little chance of being used by a publication serves only to crush the credibility of the writer.

When a release is newsworthy and of potential interest to an editor, it must be written clearly and concisely in proper newspaper style. It must get to the facts early and answer the six key questions. From there it must follow the inverted pyramid structure to its conclusion. For example, consider the following lead for the John Roberts news release posed earlier in this chapter.

MADISON, WISCONSIN—*Supreme Court Chief Justice John Roberts will deliver a major address on capital punishment at 8 p.m. tomorrow in the Kohl Field House before the annual convention of the American Bar Association.*

This lead answers all the pertinent questions:

1. Who? Chief Justice John Roberts
2. What? a major address on capital punishment
3. Where? Kohl Field House
4. When? tomorrow at 8 p.m.
5. Why? American Bar Association is holding a convention

In this case, *how* is less important. Whether or not the reader chooses to delve further into the release, the gist of the story has been successfully communicated in the lead.

To be newsworthy, news releases must be objective. All comments and editorial remarks must be attributed to organization officials. The news release can't be used as the private soapbox of the release writer. Rather, it must appear as a fair and accurate representation of the news that the organization wishes to be conveyed.

News releases can be written about almost anything. Three frequent subjects are product and institutional announcements, management changes, and management speeches.

The Product Announcement

Frequently, practitioners want to announce a new product or institutional development, such as earnings, joint ventures, acquisitions, or company celebrations (Figure 16-2).

Typically, in an announcement release, after the lead identifies the significant aspects of the product or development, a spokesperson is quoted for additional product information. Editors appreciate the quotes because they then do not have to interview a company official. For example:

The new, lightweight plastic bottle for Coca-Cola began its national rollout today in Spartanburg, S.C. This two-liter package is the nation's first metric plastic bottle for soft drinks. "We are very excited about this new package," said John H. Ogden, president, Coca-Cola U.S.A. "Our two-liter plastic bottle represents an important advancement. Its light weight, toughness, and environmental advantages offer a new standard of consumer benefits in soft drink packaging."

The subtle product "plug" is typical of such announcements. Clearly, the organization gains if the product's benefits are described in a news story. But editors are sensitive to product puffery, and the line between legitimate information and puffery is thin.

The Management Change

Newspapers are often interested in management changes, but editors frequently reject releases that have no local angle. For example, the editor of the Valdosta, Georgia, *Citizen* has little reason to use this announcement:

SIRIUS SATELLITE RADIO AND THE NBA ANNOUNCE
MULTI-YEAR BROADCAST AND MARKETING AGREEMENT

- SIRIUS becomes The Official Satellite Radio Partner of the NBA –

- SIRIUS delivers more than 1000 live games per season -

- SIRIUS Launches NBA Radio on SIRIUS, the first 24/7 year-round NBA radio channel -

NEW YORK – Dec. 13, 2005 – The National Basketball Association and SIRIUS Satellite Radio (NASDAQ: SIRI) announced today a multi-year agreement which expands upon their current broadcast arrangement and makes SIRIUS an official NBA marketing partner.

The partnership makes SIRIUS the broadcaster of more live NBA games than any other radio outlet. As part of their original agreement, in February 2003, the NBA became the first major professional sports league to provide live games on SIRIUS.

SIRIUS and the NBA have launched *NBA Radio on SIRIUS,* the first 24/7, year-round radio channel devoted to the NBA. Airing on SIRIUS' channel 127, *NBA Radio on SIRIUS* features content from NBA TV—including news, highlights and features on the league, its teams and players—and will showcase specialized programming that will be heard exclusively on SIRIUS.

###

About SIRIUS

SIRIUS delivers more than 120 channels of the best commercial-free music, compelling talk shows, news and information, and the most extensive sports programming to listeners across the country in digital quality sound. SIRIUS offers 65 channels of 100% commercial-free music, and features over 55 channels of sports, news, talk, entertainment, traffic and weather for a monthly subscription fee of only $12.95. SIRIUS is the Official Satellite Radio Partner of the NFL, NBA and NHL, broadcasting live play-by-play games of the NFL, NBA and NHL, plus college football and basketball, including the entire NCAA® Division I Men's Basketball Championship (March 14–April 3, 2006).

About the NBA

The NBA, founded in 1946, features 30 teams in the United States and Canada. The league distributes more than 800 NBA games and 44,000 hours of programming to 215 countries and territories in 43 languages. The 2005-06 NBA season features 142 games on network television— ABC, TNT, ESPN and ESPN2. ABC's schedule, which tips off with the Christmas Day doubleheader of San Antonio-Detroit and LA Lakers-Miami, expands this season to 20 regular season game windows and will feature flexible scheduling throughout the regular season in order to provide the most compelling matchups to a national audience. NBA telecasts on all national and local networks in 2005-06 are expected to reach nearly 700 million viewers domestically. The NBA is on pace to eclipse the league's all-time attendance record for the third consecutive season.

Media Contacts:
Andrew FitzPatrick, SIRIUS, 212.901.6693, afitzpatrick@siriusradio.com
Matt Bourne, NBA, 212-407-8093, mbourne@nba.com

FIGURE 16-2 The announcement release. News releases typically announce major events, such as joint ventures, including boilerplate about the two partners. (© 2006 Sirius Satellite Radio Inc. "SIRIUS" and the SIRIUS dog logo are registered trademarks of Sirius Satellite Radio Inc. © 2005 NBA Properties, Inc.)

NEW YORK, NY, April 5, 2007—Ronald O. Schram has been named manager of the hosiery department at Bloomingdale's Paramus, NJ, store.

On the other hand, the same release, amended for local appeal, would almost certainly be used by the *Citizen.*

NEW YORK, NY, April 5, 2007—Ronald O. Schram, son of Mr. and Mrs. Siegfried Schram of 221 Starting Lane, Valdosta, has been named manager of the hosiery department at Bloomingdale's Paramus, NJ, store.

Sometimes one must dig for the local angle. For example, suppose Mr. Schram was born in Valdosta but went to school in Americus, Georgia. With this knowledge, the writer might prepare the following release, which would have appeal in the newspapers of both Georgia cities.

NEW YORK, NY, April 5, 2007—Ronald O. Schram, son of Mr. and Mrs. Siegfried Schram of 221 Starting Lane, Valdosta, and a 1986 graduate of Americus High School, was named manager of the hosiery department of Bloomingdale's Paramus, NJ, store.

Penetrating local publications with the management change release is relatively easy once the local angle has been identified, but achieving publication in a national newspaper or magazine is much harder. For national consumption, it is the importance or uniqueness of the individual or company that should be emphasized. For example, an editor might not realize that the following management change is unique:

WASHINGTON, D.C., June 6, 2007—Howie "Ducky" Barmad of Jersey City, NJ, today was promoted to the rank of admiral in the United States Navy.

However, the same release stands out clearly for its news value when the unique angle is played up.

WASHINGTON, D.C., June 6, 2004—Howie "Ducky" Barmad, born in Yugoslavia, today was named the first naturalized citizen to become an admiral in the history of the United States Navy.

Any local or unique angle to help sell the story to an editor should always be investigated.

The Management Speech

Management speeches are another recurring source of news releases. The key to a speech news release is selecting the most significant portion of the talk for the lead. A good speech generally has a clear thesis from which a lead naturally flows. Once the thesis is identified, the remainder of the release simply embellishes it.

BOONEVILLE, MO, Oct. 18, 2007—Booneville Mining Company is "on the verge of having several very profitable years," Booneville Mining President J. Kenneth Kelinson said today.

Normally, if the speechmaker is not a famous person, the release should not begin with the speaker's name but rather with the substance of the remarks. If the speaker is a well-known individual, leading with the name is perfectly legitimate. For example:

Federal Reserve Chairman Ben Bernanke called today for a "new attitude toward business investment and capital formation."

The body copy of a speech release should follow directly from the lead. Often the major points of the speech must be paraphrased and consolidated to conform to a two-page release. In any event, it is frequently a significant challenge to convert the essence of a management speech to news release form.

News Release Style

The style of writing, particularly news release writing, is almost as critical as content. Alas, many in the public relations profession overlook the importance of proper writing style. Sloppy style can break the back of any release and ruin its chances for publication. Style must also be flexible and evolve as language changes.

Most public relations operations follow the style practiced by major newspapers and magazines rather than that of book publishers. This news style is detailed in various guides published by such authorities as the Associated Press and *The New York Times*.

Because the press must constantly update its style to conform to changing societal concepts, news release style is subjective and ever changing. However, a particular firm's style must be consistent from one release to the next. The following are examples of typical style rules:

- **Capitalization.** Most leading publications use capital letters sparingly; so should you. Editors call this a down style because only the most important words begin with capital letters.

- **Abbreviations.** Abbreviations present a many-faceted problem. For example, months, when used with dates, should be abbreviated, such as Sept. 11, 2007. But when the day of the month is not used, the month should be spelled out, such as September 2007. Days of the week, on the other hand, should never be abbreviated. In addition, first mention of organizations and agencies should be spelled out, with the abbreviation in parentheses after the name, such as Securities and Exchange Commission (SEC).

- **Numbers.** There are many guidelines for the spelling out of numbers, but a general rule is to spell out numbers zero through nine and use figures for 10 and up. Yet numerals are perfectly acceptable for such things as election returns, speeds and distances, percentages, temperatures, heights, ages, ratios, and sports scores.

- **Punctuation.** The primary purpose of punctuation is to clarify the writer's thoughts, ensure exact interpretation, and make reading and understanding quicker and easier. Less punctuation rather than more should be the goal. The following are just some of the punctuation marks a public relations practitioner must use appropriately.

    1. The colon introduces listings, tabulations, and statements and takes the place of an implied "for instance."

2. The comma is used in a variety of circumstances, including before connecting words, between two words or figures that might otherwise be misunderstood, and before and after nonrestrictive clauses.

3. In general, exclamation points should be resisted in releases. They tend to be overkill!

4. The hyphen is often abused and should be used carefully. A single hyphen can change the meaning of a sentence completely. For example, *The six-foot man eating tuna was killed* means the man was eating tuna; it should be punctuated *The six-foot, man-eating tuna was killed.*

5. Quoted matter is enclosed in double or single quotation marks. The double marks enclose the original quotation, whereas the single marks enclose a quotation within a quotation.

- **Spelling.** Many words, from *adviser* to *zucchini,* are commonly misspelled. The best way to avoid misspellings is to have a dictionary always within reach. When two spellings are given in a dictionary, the first spelling is always preferred.

These are just a few of the stylistic stumbling blocks that writers must consider. In the news release, style should never be taken lightly. The style, as much as any other part of the release, lets an editor know the kind of organization that issued the release and the competence of the professional who wrote it.

News Release Essentials

Beyond the necessity of being newsworthy, news releases must include several time-honored essentials that will help get them considered for inclusion in print.

- **Rationale.** There must be a well-defined reasons for sending the release. Releases should answer the two critical questions. *What's new?* and *So what?* Stated another way, the subject matter of the release must be relevant to the readers or viewers of the target media. Lack of relevance should be enough to scuttle the release.

- **Focus.** Each release should speak about only one central subject. Lack of focus—that is, discussing many different things—is a guaranteed non-starter for a journalist.

- **Facts.** To a journalist, the *facts* about the product or service subject of the release are most important: the who, what, where, when, why, and how of the announcement. These should take precedent over the often gratuitous quotes that mark many releases.

- **No Puffery.** Releases, to paraphrase Fox commentator Bill O'Reilly, should be "puffery-free zones." Even mediocre reporters can sniff out hyperbole and puffiness, which may make them suspicious of the entire product. At all costs, avoid the taboo terms listed in the next Talking Points box.

- **Nourishing Quotes.** Include quotes, but make them count. "We think this is the best product of its type," doesn't add much. But, "This product will add 20 percent to our annual revenue growth," advances the story by providing important projections that will help put the announcement in corporate context. The rule on quotes, then, is to avoid inflated superlatives that do little more than boost management egos.

Talking Points

News Release Taboo Terms

Back in the old days of 1978, comedian George Carlin found himself in deep turbulence for uttering seven "dirty words" that the Supreme Court found to be "patently offensive" to radio listeners. (Because this is a "family textbook," we will leave the seven words to your imagination or your next visit to the *Howard Stern Show* on satellite radio.)

In the 21st century, there is nothing more patently offensive to a reporter than a news release that contains the following taboo terms.

Leading. For example, "Goniff & Co., a *leading* public relations agency, today named 16 new vice chairpersons."

The problem is that everyone considers themselves "leading." Unless the agency is bigger, more profitable, or more highly recognized than others, the term is meaningless and, worse, embarrassing.

Going Forward. For example, "Gazbak said that *going forward* the company would rely more on generally accepted accounting principles in deriving earnings."

Can you ever go any other direction but "forward"? Answer: yes, but. . . . So "going forward," like "in the future," is one of those redundancies that means nothing and takes up space. Lose it.

Unique. For example, "Dr. Delaruprup's *unique* laser technology allows a patient to discard his eyeglasses."

C'mon. That ain't "unique." Lots of others may perform the same technological accomplishment. And that's the point. For something to be labeled as unique, you must be ready to demonstrate its individuality and distinctiveness. If you can't, don't use the word.

Breakthrough. For example, "Professor Kleinswort's *breakthrough* research proves conclusively that we are not alone."

Like "unique," it must be a demonstrable "breakthrough" to be labeled as such. Anybody can call his or her research or invention or product or process a breakthrough, but few can prove it. The overused word has become the worst of clichés.

Revolutionary. For example, "Sol Seymour's *revolutionary* hair-restoral method can grow a luxurious mane on a pomegranate."

Well, perhaps if it can do that, it *is* revolutionary. But like "unique" and "breakthrough," most new products or services or methods or models may in fact be "evolutionary" advancements of what came before, but they can't be fairly construed as revolutionary.

Cutting-edge. For example, "Bilgebracket's *cutting-edge* radiology department keeps the hospital ahead of the curve in delivering health care services."

This one has really gotten out of hand in the press release business. Everything, it seems, is "cutting edge." But is what you're pitching really precedent-setting or original? If not, then it can't be considered cutting edge. Forget it.

State-of-the-art. For example, "Poobah's *state-of-the-art* measurement system allows you to empirically evaluate the benefits of the publicity you attain."

See "Cutting-edge."

World-class. For example, "Ms. Lung Lung, a *world-class* yodeler of immense proportions, has performed in concert with Shaggy and the Smyrna Philharmonic Orchestra."

Like "world-renowned" and "world-famous," this self-serving superlative should be reserved only for the most unique, revolutionary, and cutting edge of our society.

In writing a news release, then, forget these terms. Use some originality. Be more creative. Don't succumb to cheap and easy—and, as it turns out, journalistically suicidal—superlatives.

- **Limit Jargon.** Every industry, from banking to baking to rocket propulsion, has its own jargon. Reporters who cover the industry may well understand the meaning of such jargon, but maybe they won't. And certainly, readers may not know the meaning of certain jargon-laden terms. Therefore, it is always a good idea to define, to the lowest sensible denominator, the terms you choose to use.

- **Company Description.** Many reporters may not be familiar with a particular organization and what it does. Therefore, a succinct organizational description, commonly called boilerplate, is eminently appropriate to conclude a release by "positioning" the firm the way it wants to be recognized.

- **Spelling, Grammar, Punctuation.** Ask a journalist to describe the *quality* of the public relations releases he or she receives, and they'll invariably roll their eyes. If the most rudimentary writing principles of spelling, grammar, and punctuation aren't observed, how important can the release be? And how important can the reporter recipient be if the public relations writer doesn't even take the time to proofread?

Speaking of Ethics

Bad Taste News Release

In the winter of 2001, the *Washington Post Magazine* took public relations firm Porter Novelli International to task for what the paper called a tasteless news release for client Chef America's Hot Pockets sandwiches.

In the aftermath of the September 11, 2001, attacks, the release said:

Although the last few weeks have been a challenging time for everyone both personally and professionally, I know that we are all striving to return to "normal."

In the coming weeks as you begin to return to your regular areas of focus, I want you to be familiar with Chef America, makers of HOT POCKETS brand sandwiches.

The *Post* ripped Porter Novelli for the release. Said columnist Gene Weingarten, sarcastically, "This release cannot possibly be tasteless because it issues from no less distinguished a source than Porter Novelli International, a company that is, to quote its website, 'a world leader in the field of brand building and reputation management.'"

Weingarten reasoned, "People don't buy HOT POCKETS because they are grateful to the manufacturers for their humanitarian gestures. They buy HOT POCKETS because they're scared of Osama."

Porter Novelli defended itself to Weingarten, contending it was not trying to capitalize on the terrorist attacks but rather "trying to introduce the product to different people, and after September 11 less people are eating out."

- **Brevity.** A news release is not a book. It must be written as articles in *USA Today* are written: short and concise. Paragraphs should be short and varied; one-sentence paragraphs are encouraged. Words and sentences should be kept short. As to length of the entire release, the average news release runs about 500 words—no more than two and a half pages.

- **Headlines.** Headlines summarize quickly to busy reporters what the release that follows is all about. Often, a reporter will make a snap judgment, based solely on the headline, as to whether the release merits being read further and ultimately used.

- **Clarity, conciseness, commitment.** The best release from the best organizations are straightforward, understated, confident. Just like any other communications vehicle, a public relations news release can reveal much about the company that produces it.[7]

Internet News Releases

The Internet has revolutionized news releases and news release writing. Before the Internet, public companies would issue news releases only when they had newsworthy announcements to make. Today, companies regularly issue releases merely to be included on online databases. Why? This indicates to the consumers and investors who access the Web directly that the company is progressing.

The vast majority of journalists today prefer to receive news releases via e-mail. In one survey of 400 journalists, seven of 10 reporters said they read every e-mail release they received.[8]

In terms of news release writing for the Internet, brevity and succinctness are paramount. Reading from a computer screen is more difficult and tedious than extracting from paper. Therefore, Internet news release writing must conform to the following requisites:

- **One reporter per "To" line.** Nobody—least of all, reporters—likes to be lumped in with everybody else. That's why journalists despise press conferences. They want to be considered "special." So don't group journalists together on the "To" line of an e-mail release. Listing one reporter per "To" line (online

Talking Points

The Sassy Style of the Internet

The Internet, of course, has a writing style all its own. In chat rooms, a correctly spelled word may be a sign of the inarticulate. Consider, for example, this conversation:

Wuzup?
n2m
well g/g c ya

Literal translation by anyone who spends 8 to 10 hours a day in chat rooms: Not too much is up with the respondent, and so the writer has got to go and will see his friend later.

Indeed, in terms of e-mail vocabulary, the following shortened vernacular can be adjudged as "chat ready":

- pls   please
- flfre   feel free
- btw   by the way
- brb   be right back
- irl   in real life
- IMHO   in my humble opinion
- lol   laughing out loud
- rotfl   rolling on the floor laughing
- u r   you are
- info   information
- doc   document
- convo   conversation
- latr   later

Latr.

software programs exist to help accomplish this) will deliver the personalization that journalists prefer.

- **Limit subject line headers.** Most reporters are cursed with a daily e-mail box that runneth over. They're swamped with e-mail releases, just as their latter-day counterparts were swamped with print releases. Therefore, enticing them with a provocative subject line is a necessity if you want your release to be considered. You should limit subject headers to four to six words, no more.

- **Boldface "FOR IMMEDIATE RELEASE."** With this advisory on the first line of the release, right above the date and dateline, reporters will know instantly that this is news that can be used right away. As is true with print releases, "embargoing" news for later publication is rarely honored in a day of 24/7 breaking news and round-the-clock Internet publicity.

- **Hammer home the headline.** E-mail release headlines are as important as print headlines to attract immediate interest and subsequent coverage. E-mail headlines should be written in boldface upper- and lowercase and, as in all e-mail writing, should be limited in length—to 10 words or less.

- **Limit length.** E-mail news releases should be shorter than print versions. PR Newswire reports that the average print release is 500 words. E-mail releases should generally be shorter than that.

- **Observe 5W format.** E-mail news releases should observe traditional news release style, leading with the 5W format, to answer the key questions of who, what, why, when, where, and even how. The limited length of the email—to say nothing of the attention span of the e-mail reader—mandates that the writer get to the point immediately, right in the first paragraph.

- **No attachments.** Never. Never. Never. Journalists wish neither to face the risk of a virus nor take the time to download. So don't attach anything. Rather . . .

- **Link to the URL.** Accompanying information, such as photos, bios, backgrounders, and the like, should be linked in the e-mail to the organization's URL. This negates the inconvenience of downloading and allows reporters the opportunity to link at their leisure.

- **Remember readability.** E-mail releases must balance information with readability. That means short paragraphs, varied paragraph length, bullets, numbers, lists—devices that make the release more eye-friendly and scannable.[9]

The Media Kit

Beyond the news release, the most ubiquitous written vehicle in public relations work is the media or press kit. In effect, the media kit serves as a "calling card" to introduce the organization to the media.

Press kits—in print or online format—incorporate several communications vehicles for potential use by newspapers and magazines. A bare-bones media kit consists of the following items, in addition to a news release:

- **The Biography.** Next to the news release, the most popular tool is the biography, often called the biographical summary or just plain bio. The bio recounts pertinent facts about a particular individual. Bios can be written two ways:

    1. The straight bio lists factual information in a straightforward fashion in descending order of importance, with company-oriented facts preceding more personal details. For example, the straight biography of New York Yankees Manager Joe Torre might begin this way:

        On November 2, 1995, Joe Torre was named manager of the New York Yankees. In becoming the 31st manager in team history, he joined Casey Stengel, Yogi Berra, and Dallas Green as the fourth skipper to wear both Yankees and New York Mets uniforms.

        During his 17-year playing career, Torre compiled a .297 batting average, 2,342 hits, 252 home runs, and 1,185 RBI's while playing for Milwaukee, Atlanta, St. Louis, and the Mets. He hit over .300 five times in his career and was a nine-time All-Star.

        As a manager, Torre led the 1996 Yankees to their first World Series title since 1978. He was named Sportsman of the Year by The Sporting News and Co-American League Manager of the Year by the Baseball Writers Association of America.

        This biography is written straightforwardly, a chronology of the subject's work history and accomplishments, with little editorializing.

    2. The narrative bio, on the other hand, is written in a breezier, more informal way. This style gives spark and vitality to the biography to make the individual come alive. For example, in the case of Joe Torre, the narrative bio might read thusly:

        Joe Torre, a nine-time All-Star player, has become one of baseball's all-time great managers.

        In piloting the New York Yankees to six World Series appearances, Torre has earned a reputation as a savvy strategist, wise counselor, and emotional leader. He is living proof that "nice guys" do, indeed, finish first.

        The narrative bio, in addition to bringing the individual to life, doubles as a speech of introduction when that individual serves as a featured speaker. In effect, the narrative bio becomes a speech.

DODGER STADIUM FOOD FACTS

What does it take to feed the suites, private clubs and club level seating at Dodger Stadium for the 2000 baseball season?

Here's a taste:

Sushi	75,000 pieces
Chinois Chicken Salad	6,100 pounds
Jumbo Crab	2,500 pounds
Seasoned Beef Tenderloin	10,000 pounds
Spago Pizzas/Flatbread	4,200 each
Jumbo Shrimp	6,500 pounds
Chinois Rack of Lamb	1,650 pounds
Smoked Salmon	500 pounds
Giant Taffy Apples	3,000 apples
Beer	97,200 bottles
Wine	9,500 bottles

Slammin' Salads
Whether its Spago Caesar Salad or Chinois Chicken Salad, more than 12,000 pounds of salad will be provided to guests of Dodger Stadium throughout the year.

Wolfgang's MVP – Most Valuable Pizzas
Guests of the Stadium Club will enjoy more than 4,200 gourmet pizzas and flatbreads created Spago-style in the brick-oven. Featured pizzas include Smoked Salmon with dill cream fraiche, red onions and salmon caviar and Prosciutto with leeks, roasted tomatoes, thyme and goat cheese.

An Apple A Day . . .
How about an apple a day for the next 8 years! Guests will enjoy more than 3,000 Jumbo Taffy Apples over the course of the season, courtesy of the Levy Restaurants trademarked Dessert Cart.

No Wining Allowed
The competition may be tough, but the Dodgers can be sure that their fans are enjoying themselves. More than 9,500 bottles of the finest wines will be poured in the private clubs and suites at Dodger Stadium.

We Want a Pitcher...of Beer
Dodger fans know that a baseball game isn't complete without a cold beer. Premium fans will enjoy more than 97,200 bottles of beer, which also equates to approximately 21,000 pitchers.

Levy Restaurants
Sports & Entertainment
www.levyrestaurants.com

FIGURE 16-3 Just the facts. Fact sheets allow reporters to extract pertinent morsels to include in stories or complementary boxes. (Courtesy of Levy Restaurants)

■ **The Backgrounder.** Background pieces, or backgrounders, provide additional information generally to complement the news release. Backgrounders can embellish the announcement, or they can discuss the institution making the announcement, the system behind the announcement, or any other appropriate topic that will assist a journalist in writing the story. In devising a backgrounder, a writer enjoys unlimited latitude. As long as the piece catches the interest of the reader/editor, any style is permissible.

- **Fact Sheets, Q&As, Photos, and So On.** Beyond bios and backgrounders, media kits may contain any other information that will help a journalist tell a story. Increasingly today, journalists are accessing organizational media kits online. They want information in a hurry, without being delayed by voice mail or foot-dragging. Therefore, the following make great sense to include in media kits:

  - *Fact sheets,* which compile the most relevant facts concerning the product, issue, organization, or candidate discussed in quick and easily accessible fashion (Figure 16-3).

  - *Q&As,* which present the most probable questions posed about the subject matter at hand and then the answers to those questions. Again, this preempts a reporter having to ask questions of a live—and often unavailable—public relations person.

  - *Photos,* which illustrate the subject. With photo editors now downloading from the Web, online color media kit photos are a necessity (Figure 16-4). Although a detailed discussion of photographic terms and techniques is beyond the scope of this book, public relations practitioners should be relatively conversant with photographic terminology and able to recognize the attributes of good photos.

- **Etc., etc., etc.** What other material should be included in media kits? Additional pertinent photos, advertising schedules and slicks, CD-ROMs, speeches—there is no hard-and-fast rule. However, journalists have little patience for being overwhelmed with extraneous material. Therefore, as with news releases, in media kits, less is more (Figure 16-5).

FIGURE 16-4 Killer photos. Provocative photos ready for print, such as this of Shamu the killer whale, should always be included in print and online media kits. (Courtesy of Sea World of California)

PEANUT BUTTER & JELLY CUPS

Contact: Felicia Roff
Vorhaus & Company Inc.
212.554.7438 – telephone
888.639.9857 – pager
froff@vorhaus.com

**Peanut Butter and Jelly
Fun Facts**

Everybody Loves Peanut Butter and Jelly
- **Jack Nicholson** told *Marie Claire Magazine* that peanut butter and jel[...] he needs in the bedroom.*
- During the Senate Impeachment hearings, **Senator Mike DeWine** (R-[...] brown bag containing a peanut butter and jelly sandwich.
- While on the campaign trail for re-election, **Governor George Bush** [...] butter and jelly sandwich.

A Longtime Favorite
- Peanut butter and jelly sandwiches are the 3rd most frequently eaten m[...]
- Peanut butter and jelly sandwiches ranked 5th out of 100 favorite Ame[...]
- In a six month period, it is estimated that 131 million adults will eat je[...]

Restaurants Are Catching On...
- A restaurant in New York City, called Peanut Butter and Company, is [...] dishes only made with peanut butter, including the favorite peanut but[...]
- East of Chicago Pizza Company boasts a popular pizza topped with pe[...]

A Nutritional Choice
- A peanut butter and jelly sandwich provides 18 percent of the daily va[...] useful in the prevention of birth defects.***

* *Marie Claire Magazine*, February 1999
** *March of Dimes and Southeastern Peanut Farmers Brochure*
*** NET, 52 weeks ending 11/22/97

* * *

Gushing with Flavo[...]

Russell Stover Candies, 4900 Oak Street, Kansas City, Missouri[...]

PEANUT BUTTER & JELLY CUPS

Contact: Felicia Roff
Vorhaus & Company Inc.
212.554.7438 – telephone
888.639.9857 – pager
froff@vorhaus.com

What Do Bill Clinton and Marilyn Monroe Have In Common?

New York, September 7, 1999 – According to a nationwide survey, Americans most want to eat peanut butter and jelly with President Clinton and Marilyn Monroe. The nationwide survey was conducted by Yankelovich Partners[1] for Russell Stover Candies to announce their new candy, *Peanut Butter and Jelly Cups*. Other favorites include Jimi Hendrix, Sophia Loren and Albert Einstein.

Some highlights of the Peanut Butter and Jelly Survey include:

What television show reminds you of peanut butter and jelly?
- Americans are torn between the 50's classic, *Leave it to Beaver* and the 70's favorite, *The Brady Bunch.*

Baby Boomers want to hold onto their youth...with food:
- Three in four adults believe that the world would be a better place if everyone took time out of their day to remember their childhood.
- Seven out of ten Americans say peanut butter and jelly was among their favorite foods as a child.
- 75% of Americans ate their first peanut butter and jelly sandwich before age 7 and two out of three Americans still savor peanut butter and jelly today.

Peanut butter and jelly is...
- 46% said "an American tradition"
- 36% said "fun"
- 26% said "nostalgic"
- 7% said "sexy" (including Jack Nicholson)

In addition to being the nation's largest manufacturer of boxed chocolates, Russell Stover produces America's favorite candy bars including The Pecan Delight Bar and The Mint Dream Bar with plans to introduce more candy bars and other exciting products in the coming months. The third largest chocolate manufacturer in the country, Russell Stover has been producing *only the finest* candy for over 75 years. The company is headquartered in Kansas City, Missouri and remains a family owned business, run by co-presidents, Scott and Tom Ward.

[...]y, Missouri, 64112-2702, 1-800-777-4004

FIGURE 16-5 Filling in the blanks. When Russell Stover announced its Peanut Butter & Jelly Cups, it offered this fact sheet and survey report to complement media kit information. (Courtesy of Russell Stover and Vorhaus Public Relations)

The Pitch Letter

The written device used to interest journalists in a story is the pitch letter. The pitch letter is a sales letter, pure and simple. Although letter styles run the gamut, the best are direct and to the point, while being catchy and evocative.

Pitch letters, like sales letters, may contain elements that seek to entice a reader's active participation in attending an event or covering a story. Pitch letters that sell generally contain several key elements. First, they open with a grabber, an interesting statement that impels the reader to continue reading. Next, they explain why the editor and/or publication should be interested in the pitch, or invitation, and why it is rel-

---

MEDIA ALERT

****MAGIC JOHNSON AVAILABLE FOR
INTERVIEWS MAY 1****

BASKETBALL SUPERSTAR IN TRENTON
FOR ONCE-IN-LIFETIME COACHING
OF LOCAL SCHOOL TEAM

WHO: **Hall of Fame Basketball Legend Magic Johnson** will be in Trenton to host a very special event and will be available for interviews along with Top Executives from Samsung, Best Buy, and local NJ dignitaries

WHAT: Magic is bringing a once in a lifetime event to the grade school students at L.M. Rivera School in Trenton when he gives the basketball team a one-on-one coaching session and addresses all students at a special assembly. The event is the Grand Prize of a unique national "One On One With Magic" promotion sponsored by Samsung's Four Season's of Hope charity and Best Buy, which raised more than $140,000 for the Magic Johnson Foundation to help AIDS prevention and education.

WHEN: **Thursday, May 1**
10:00 am — School Assembly
10:30 am — Media Q&A with Magic
11:00 am — Coaching Session
One-On-One interviews available afterwards (by appointment)

WHERE: **L.M. Rivera Elementary School (Grades K-8)**
400 N Montgomery Street
Trenton, NJ

WHY: The "One On One With Magic" promotion is one leg of Samsung's Four Seasons of Hope, a year-round national goodwill program that brings together four of the world's greatest sports legends — golf's Arnold Palmer, football's Boomer Esiason, baseball's Joe Torre and basketball's Magic Johnson — for a unique, retail program that aims to improve the quality of life for children and their families who face major challenges.

RSVP: **Lois Whitman, HWH PR, 212-355-5049, X105**

FIGURE 16-6 **Media alert.** This derivative of the pitch letter lists all a reporter needs to know about an upcoming event.

evant to their readership. That means it must allude to the scope and importance of the story. Finally, they are personally written to specific people rather than addressed to "editor" (which is the journalistic equivalent of "occupant").[10]

Related to the pitch letter is the media advisory, a more straightforward list of facts meant to interest an editor or news director enough to attend an event (Figure 16-6).

Other Print Vehicles

The public relations professional possesses a variety of additional print vehicles in his or her arsenal, the four most prominent of which are:

- **The Case History:** Frequently used to tell about a customer's favorable use of a company's product or service. Case histories generally follow a five-part formula:

    1. They present a problem experienced by one company but applicable to many other firms.
    2. They indicate how the dimensions of the problem were defined by the company using the product.
    3. They indicate the solution adopted.
    4. They explain the advantages of the adopted solution.
    5. They detail the user company's experience after adopting the solution.

    Trade book editors, in particular, are often willing to share a case that can be generalized—and is therefore relevant—to the broader readership.

- **The Byliner:** A story signed and ostensibly authored by an officer of a particular firm—but often ghostwritten by a public relations professional. Perhaps the major advantage of a byliner is that it positions executives as experts. The fact that an organization's officer has authored an informed article on a subject means that not only are the officer and the organization credible sources but also, by inference, they are perhaps more highly regarded on the issues at hand than are their competitors.

- **The Op-Ed:** An editorial written by an organizational executive and then submitted for publication to a leading newspaper or magazine. The good ones contain the following elements:

    Grabber, which starts off the piece and "grabs" attention

    Point, which hammers home the thesis of the article

    Chain of evidence, which gives the facts that support the argument

    Summation, which summarizes the argument

    Good-bye zinger, which leaves the reader with something to think about[11]

    A successfully placed op-ed offers a prestigious forum for any executive.

- **The Roundup Article:** Reporters get rewarded for two things in particular: scoops and trends. A scoop refers to breaking a story before anyone else. A trend concerns breaking a story that speaks of an emerging trend in an industry or the broader society. Although many publications discourage publicity about a single company, they encourage articles that summarize, or "round up," the experiences of several companies within an industry. Thoroughly researching and drafting roundup articles is a good way for a public relations professional to secure stories that mention the practitioner's firm in favorable association with top competitors.

Writing for the Ear

In terms of writing for the ear, the most important public relations vehicle is the external or internal speech. Speechwriting has become one of the most coveted public relations skills. Increasingly, speechwriters have used their access to management to move up the organizational ladder. The prominence they enjoy is due largely to the importance government and business executives place on making speeches. Today's executives are called on to defend their policies, justify their prices, and explain their practices to a much greater degree than ever before. In this environment, a good speechwriter becomes a valuable—and often highly paid—asset.

One key to writing a speech is to understand that every spoken presentation possesses five main characteristics:

1. **It is designed to be heard, not read.** The mistake of writing for the eye instead of the ear is the most common trap of bad speeches. Speeches needn't be literary gems, but they ought to sound good.
2. **It uses concrete language.** The ear dislikes generalities. It responds to clear images. Ideas must be expressed sharply for the audience to get the point.
3. **It demands a positive response.** Every word, every passage, every phrase should evoke a response from the audience. The speech should possess special vitality—and so, for that matter, should the speaker.
4. **It must have clear-cut objectives.** The speech and the speaker must have a point—a thesis. If there's no point, then it's not worth the speaker's or the audience's time.
5. **It must be tailored to a specific audience.** An audience needs to feel that it is hearing something special. The most frequent complaint about organizational speeches is that they all seem interchangeable—they lack uniqueness. That's why speeches must be targeted to fit the needs of a specific audience.

Beyond adhering to these five principles and before putting words on paper, a speechwriter must have a clear idea of the process—the route—to follow in developing the speech. The best speeches break down into four organizational sections:

First, the introduction, which introduces the subject and gradually eases the audience into the talk.

Second, the thesis, which states clearly the central idea that the speaker will reinforce throughout.

Third, the body of supporting facts, statistics, illustrations, and examples that reinforce the thesis.

Fourth, the conclusion that hammers home the thesis one last time.[12]

The key to any oral presentation is having a clear and concise thesis to serve as the heart and objective of the remarks and to express it simply yet eloquently (Figure 16-7).

The Importance of Editing

Editing is the all-important final touch for the public relations writer. You must edit your work. One misspelling can sink a perfectly worthwhile release.

An editor must be judicious. Each word, phrase, sentence, and paragraph should be weighed carefully. Good editing will punch up dull passages and make them sparkle. For instance, *The satellite flies across the sky* is dead, but *The satellite roars across the sky* is alive.

My fellow Americans,

This day has brought terrible news and great sadness to our country. At 9 o'clock this morning, Mission Control in Houston lost contact with our space shuttle Columbia. A short time later, debris was seen falling from the skies above Texas.

The Columbia's lost. There are no survivors.

Onboard was a crew of seven—Colonel Rick Husband, Lieutenant Colonel Michael Anderson, Commander Laurel Clark, Captain David Brown, Commander William McCool, Dr. Kalpana Chawla, and Ilan Ramon, a colonel in the Israeli air force.

These men and women assumed great risk in this service to all humanity. In an age when space flight has come to seem almost routine, it is easy to overlook the dangers of travel by rocket and the difficulties of navigating the fierce outer atmosphere of the earth.

These astronauts knew the dangers, and they faced them willingly, knowing they had a high and noble purpose in life. Because of their courage and daring and idealism, we will miss them all the more.

All Americans today are thinking, as well, of the families of these men and women who have been given this sudden shock and grief. You're not alone. Our entire nation grieves with you. And those you loved will always have the respect and gratitude of this country.

The cause in which they died will continue. Mankind is led into the darkness beyond our world by the inspiration of discovery and the longing to understand. Our journey into space will go on.

In the skies today, we saw destruction and tragedy. Yet farther than we can see, there is comfort and hope.

In the words of the prophet Isaiah, "Lift your eyes and look to the heavens. Who created all these? He who brings out the starry hosts one by one and calls them each by name. Because of his great power and mighty strength, not one of them is missing."

The same creator who names the stars also knows the names of the seven souls we mourn today. The crew of the shuttle Columbia did not return safely to Earth, yet we can pray that all are safely home.

May God bless the grieving families, and may God continue to bless America.

FIGURE 16-7   Simple and eloquent. President George W. Bush was not a particularly gifted speaker, but these remarks, delivered when the space shuttle *Columbia* was lost in February 2003, offered just the right touch of hope and inspiration in the midst of tragedy.

In the same context, good editing will get rid of passive verbs, invariably, producing shorter sentences. For example, *George Washington chopped down the cherry tree* is shorter and better than *The cherry tree was chopped down by George Washington.*

A good editor must also be gutsy enough to use bold strokes—to chop, slice, and cut through verbiage, bad grammar, misspellings, incorrect punctuation, poorly constructed sentences, misused words, mixed metaphors, non sequiturs, clichés, redundancies, circumlocutions, and jargon. Sentences such as *She is the widow of the late Marco Picardo* and *The present incumbent is running for reelection* are intolerable to a good editor.

A good unabridged dictionary and a thesaurus provide the practitioner with significant writing and editing support. To these might be added *Bartlett's Familiar Quotations,* the *World Almanac,* and an encyclopedia. Editing should also concentrate on organizing copy. One release paragraph should flow naturally into the next.

Writing, like fine wine, should flow smoothly and stand up under the toughest scrutiny. Careful editing is a must.

Last Word

Writing is the essence of public relations practice, whether involved with print or online work. The public relations professional, if not the best writer in his or her organization, must at least be one of the best. Writing is the communications skill that sets public relations professionals apart from others.

Or should.

The fact is that the most frequent complaint of employers is that "public relations people can't write." That's why any public relations student who "can write" is often ahead of the competition.

Some writers are born. But most are not.

Writing can be learned by understanding the fundamentals of what makes interesting writing; by practicing different written forms; and by working constantly to improve, edit, and refine the written product. When an executive needs something written well, one organizational resource should pop immediately into his or her mind: public relations.

Discussion Starters

1. What is the difference between writing for the ear and for the eye?
2. What are several of the writing fundamentals one must consider?
3. What is the essence of the Flesch method of writing?
4. What is the inverted pyramid, and why does it work?
5. What is the essential written communications vehicle used by public relations professionals?
6. What are common purposes of news releases?
7. Should a news release writer try to work his or her own editorial opinion into the release?
8. What are the keys in writing releases for the Internet?
9. What are the essential qualities of an effecitve oral presentation?

Top of the Shelf

The Business Style Handbook

Helen Cunningham and Brenda Greene, New York; McGraw-Hill, Inc. 2002.

The Business Style Handbook is subtitled *An A-to-Z Guide for Writing on the Job with Tips from Communications Experts at the Fortune 500.* It was authored by two public relations professionals, who created a 33-question survey for corporate communications departments at the Fortune 500 to gauge how major corporations approach writing.

Among the 21st-century standards that the new PR style book declares are the following random rules:

1. **Dot-com.** Use a hyphen, which is what most U.S. business publications use, instead of *dot.com* or *dotcom*.

2. **FAQ.** Frequently asked questions.

3. **Internet.** Capitalize and use in the first reference. Use the *Net* interchangeably afterward. On the other hand, *intranet* is lowercased.

4. **JPEG.** Use JPEG in all references. It stands for Joint Photographic Experts Group and is a file format for Web-based images, particularly photos.

CASE STUDY

The Raina, Inc., News Release

Background: The Raina carborundum plant in Blackrock, Iowa, has been under pressure in recent months to remedy its pollution problem. Raina's plant is the largest in Blackrock, and even though the company has spent $5.3 million on improving its pollution-control equipment, black smoke still spews from the plant's smokestacks, and waste products are still allowed to filter into neighboring streams. Lately, the pressure on Raina has been intense.

- On April 7, J. K. Krafchik, a private citizen, called to complain about the "noxious smoke" fouling the environment.

- On April 8, Janet Greenberg of the Blackrock Garden Club called to protest the "smoke problem" that was destroying the zinnias and other flowers in the area.

- On April 9, Clarence "Smoky" Salmon, president of the Blackrock Rod and Gun Club, called to report that 700 people had signed a petition against the Raina plant's pollution of Zeus Creek.

- On April 10, WERS Radio editorialized that "the time has come to force area plants to act on solving pollution problems."

- On April 11, the Blackrock City Council announced plans to enact an air and water pollution ordinance for the city. The council invited as its first witness before the public hearing Leslie Sludge, manager of the Raina carborundum plant.

News Release Data

1. Leslie Sludge, manager of Raina's carborundum plant in Blackrock appeared at the Blackrock City Council hearing on April 11.
2. Sludge said Raina had already spent $5.3 million on a program to clean up pollution at its Blackrock plant.
3. Raina received 500 complaint calls in the past three months protesting its pollution conditions.
4. Sludge said Raina was "concerned about environmental problems, but profits are still what keeps our company running."
5. Sludge announced that the company had decided to commit another $2 million for pollution-abatement facilities over the next three months.
6. Raina is the oldest plant in Blackrock and was built in 1900.
7. Raina's Blackrock plant employs 10,000 people, the largest single employer in Blackrock.
8. Raina originally planned to delay its pollution-abatement program but speeded it up because of public pressure in recent months.
9. Sludge said that the new pollution-abatement program would begin in October and that the company projected "real progress in terms of clean water and clean air" as early as two years from today.

10. Five years ago, Raina received a Presidential Award from the Environmental Protection Agency for its "concern for pollution abatement."
11. An internal Raina study indicated that Blackrock was the "most pollutant laden" of all Raina's plants nationwide.
12. Sludge formerly served as manager of Raina's Fetid Reservoir plant in Fetid Reservoir, New Hampshire. In two years as manager of Fetid Reservoir, Sludge was able to convert it from one of the most pollutant-laden plants in the system to the cleanest, as judged by the Environmental Protection Agency.
13. Sludge has been manager of Blackrock for two months.
14. Raina's new program will cost the company $2 million.
15. Raina will hire 100 extra workers especially for the pollution-abatement program.
16. Sludge, 35, is married to the former Polly Yurathane of Wheeling, West Virginia.
17. Sludge is author of the book *Fly Fishing Made Easy*.
18. The bulk of the money budgeted for the new pollution-abatement program will be spent on two globe refractors, which purify waste destined to be deposited in surrounding waterways, and four hyperventilation systems, which remove noxious particles dispersed into the air from smokestacks.
19. Sludge said, "Raina, Inc., has decided to move ahead with this program at this time because of its long-standing responsibility for keeping the Blackrock environment clean and in response to growing community concern over achieving the objective."
20. Former Blackrock plant manager Fowler Aire was fired by the company in July for his "flagrant disregard for the environment."
21. Aire also was found to be diverting Raina funds from company projects to his own pockets. In all, Aire took close to $10,000, for which the company was not reimbursed. At least part of the money was to be used for pollution control.
22. Aire, whose whereabouts are presently not known, is the brother of J. Derry Aire, Raina's vice president for finance.
23. Raina's Blackrock plant has also recently installed ramps and other special apparatus to assist employees with disabilities. Presently, 100 workers with disabilities are employed in the Raina Blackrock plant.
24. Raina's Blackrock plant started as a converted garage, manufacturing plate glass. Only 13 people worked in the plant at that time.
25. Today the Blackrock plant employs 10,000 people, covers 14 acres of land, and is the largest supplier of plate glass and commercial panes in the country.
26. The Blackrock plant was slated to be the subject of a critical report from the Private Environmental Stabilization Taskforce

(PEST), a private environmental group. PEST's report, "The Foulers," was to discuss "the 10 largest manufacturing polluters in the nation."

27. Raina management has been aware of the PEST report for several months.

Questions

1. If you were assigned to draft a news release to accompany Sludge to the Blackrock City Council meeting on April 11, which items would you use in your lead (i.e., who, what, why, where, when, how)?

2. Which items would you avoid using in the news release?

3. If a reporter from the *Blackrock Bugle* called and wanted to know what happened to former Blackrock manager Fowler Aire, what would you tell the reporter?

4. How could Raina use the Internet to research public opinion of the pollution problem? How could the company use the Internet to communicate its position in advance of the Blackrock City Council meeting?

Voice of Authority

An Interview with Bonnie Grossman

Bonnie Grossman is an instructor in the School of Business, Department of Management and Entrepreneurship, at the College of Charleston in South Carolina. She has taught public relations for 12 years and has contributed student-written case studies to this and a previous edition of *The Practice of Public Relations*. Prior to joining the faculty at the College of Charleston, Grossman worked 15 years in corporate public relations, including stints as manager of employee communications for medical manufacturer Hill-Rom Company and as public relations director for a community hospital.

How important is writing in public relations?

Writing skills are a career sifter in most fields—good writers move up and poor writers get passed up. But in public relations, good writing skills are absolutely crucial. A PR professional is expected to be the *best* writer in the organization. Knowing how to write for the media is only the first expectation.

PR people write, write, write. In the end, your ability to write is your key to access within your organization. When you can write well, you are trusted with information. Externally, the people you're writing *to*—the media—are all professional writers. If you send them bad writing, it shows. You lose credibility.

What's the caliber of public relations writing today?

There was a time when PR people came from the ranks of journalism and journalism schools. Their education and experience valued and practiced good writing skills. Sadly, that basic respect for language seems to be missing in much of today's PR writing. I see too many buzzwords devoid of meaning and too much rhetoric that is not reader friendly.

Are public relations writers "born," or can they be taught?

I wouldn't be a teacher if I thought I had no impact. I've taught journalism, business writing, and PR writing. Students who work to improve the mechanical aspects of their writing and then adapt their messages to particular audiences and styles develop the confidence they need to produce professionally acceptable written work.

Would we accept the idea that athletes are born and not taught? Skill is necessary for either writers or athletes, but coaching, training, and practice make the difference between good and great. I believe some writers are born with special talent, and for them, writing is an art. Words flow from their souls. But we don't each have to be able to produce a masterpiece of American literature. Just learn to write in plain English and be readable.

Are news releases still worthwhile?

Yes. Ask yourself this: What has replaced the news release? Nothing, because nothing else is better at announcing news about the products, policies, and practices of an organization. We may change the delivery system, more often now by e-mail or by paid wire services, but the news release is still the foundation of PR writing.

What's the secret to effective public relations writing?
Have something to say. Be newsworthy, be timely, and remember there are really *six* W's: *Who? What? When? Where? Why?* and *Who cares?* Just because your CEO has declared your newest initiative "news," doesn't mean it is. You must be prepared to show your reader why he or she should care about your news item.

Understand that you don't have control of the story. If you want control, buy an ad. The secret to *all* effective communications is to stop thinking about yourself as a writer and focus on your reader.

How important is writing in one's public relations career?
There is *no* time in one's PR career that writing becomes any less vital. Public relations practitioners understand the power of words. Occasionally, students enter my class with the perception that public relations is about event planning and taking people to lunch. They leave with a greater awareness of how pervasive, varied, and exciting our career field really is.

Suggested Readings

LaRocque, Paula. *Championship Writing: 50 Ways to Improve Your Writing.* Oak Park, IL: Marion Street Press, 2000. Writing coach Paula LaRoque's book on grammar and composition is directed mainly to journalists, but anyone who writes for a living will find this interesting and entertaining.

Newsom, Doug, and Jim Haynes. *Public Relations Writing,* 7th ed. Belmont, CA: Wadsworth, 2005.

Nunberg, Gregory. *The Way We Talk Now: Commentaries on Language and Culture from NPR's "Fresh-Air."* Boston: Houghton Mifflin, 2001.

Pacelli, Lonnie. *The Truth About Getting Your Point Across . . . and Nothing but the Truth.* Saddle River, NJ: Prentice-Hall, 2006. This is a guide to communicating in all settings—at meetings, presentations, interviews, and more.

Shapiro, Roger A. *Write Right.* Bloomington, IN: AuthorHouse, 2005. This paperback guide offers 26 tips that get down to the nitty, such as avoiding prepositions and being bold. Good primer.

Simon, Raymond, and Joseph Zappala. *Public Relations Workbook: Writing and Techniques.* Lincolnwood, IL: NTC Publishing Group, 2001.

Smith, Ronald D. *Becoming a Public Relations Writer: A Writing Process Workbook for the Profession,* 2nd ed. Mahwah, NJ: Lawrence Erlbaum Associates, 2003.

Strunk, W., and E. B. White. *Elements of Style.* New York: Allyn & Bacon, 1999.

Thompson, Terri (Ed.). *Writing about Business.* New York: Columbia University, 2001. A product of Columbia's Bagehot Fellowships program, key inclusions for public relations professionals are chapters on "How to Read Financial Statements" and "Sales and Marketing."

Weinbroer, Diana Roberts, Elaine Hughes, and Jay Silverman. *Rules of Thumb for Business Writers,* 2nd ed. New York: McGraw-Hill, 2005. The answers to every writing or grammar question a business writer might have.

Wilcox, Dennis L., and Lawrence W. Nolte. *Public Relations Writing and Media Techniques,* 4th ed. New York: Longman, 2000.

Zweifel, Thomas D. *Communicate or Die.* New York: SelectBooks, 2003. Examples of how people can learn to listen and communicate more powerfully in order to be more successful in business and in life.

Notes

1. Chris Nelson, "Why Keith Richards Always Uses a Speechwriter," *New York Times,* April 5, 2004, C8.
2. Fraser P. Seitel, "PR Pros are Horrible Writers," odwyerpr.com, March 5, 2001.
3. Bill Moyers, "Watch Your Language," *The Professional Communicator,* August–September 1985, 6.
4. Fraser P. Seitel, "Newsworthy News Releases," odwyerpr.com, March 13, 2001.
5. "How to Get Editors to Use Press Releases," *Jack O'Dwyer's Newsletter,* May 26, 1993, 3.
6. Linda P. Morton, "Producing Publishable Press Releases," *Public Relations Quarterly,* Winter 1992–1993, 9–11.
7. Fraser P. Seitel, "News Release Essentials," odwyerpr.com, July 18, 2001.
8. "Journalists Prefer E-Mail: Survey," *Jack O'Dwyer's Newsletter,* August 24, 2004, 3.
9. Fraser P. Seitel, "E-mail News Releases," odwyerpr.com, February 23, 2004.
10. Fraser P. Seitel, "How to Pitch a Reporter," odwyerpr.com, April 30, 2002.
11. Jeffrey D. Porro, Porro Associates, 1120 Connecticut Ave., Suite 270, Washington D.C. 20036.
12. Fraser P. Seitel, "Speechwriting," odwyerpr.com, April 18, 2005.

17 Integrated Marketing Communications

FIGURE 17-1 In with the new, out with the old. Pepsi-Cola named Destiny's Child singer Beyoncé Knowles (left) as its spokeswoman to replace Britney Spears, who after being caught on camera drinking Coke, was canned as Pepsi spokeswoman. (Fraser P. Seitel)

Using celebrities as spokespersons, inserting product placements in movies, sponsoring concerts, and a host of other publicity-seeking techniques are examples of *integrated marketing communications*—the intersection of public relations and publicity, advertising, sales promotion, and marketing to promote organizations, products, and services.

In the 21st century, when the right spokesperson can help add up to hundreds of millions of dollars for corporations, integrated marketing campaigns are high-stakes battles with winners and losers. Like these two ladies:

Destiny's Child lead singer and aspiring actress Beyoncé Knowles replaced fellow pop icon Britney Spears as Pepsi-Cola spokeswoman in 2003, after the latter was caught on camera guzzling a rival can of Coca-Cola—a no-no that meant instant Pepsi expulsion.[1]

The Beyoncé–Britney Pepsi sweepstakes was typical of organizations integratin___ ties with their products to forge a unique promotional identity.

- Payless Shoe Source signed occasionally larger-than-life television personalit___ claimed to have 550 pairs of shoes, to be its "director of consumer style" and

- Wireless phone company T-Mobile International signed actress Catherine Z___ spokeswoman because of her "fiery character, hard work, and dedication."[3]

- Actor Michael J. Fox became a national spokesman for Parkinson's disease, with which he had been diagnosed.

Those who decry the fall of advertising and the rise of PR are a bit overzealous.[4] Advertising ain't dead yet. Neither is marketing. But it is true that public relations and publicity integrated with these other disciplines are very much the rule in many organizations today.

Therefore, the need for *communications cross-training*—to learn the different skills of marketing, advertising, sales promotion, and public relations—becomes a requirement for all communicators.

Public Relations vs. Marketing vs. Advertising

What is the difference between marketing, advertising, and public relations?

Marketing, literally defined, is the selling of a service or product through pricing, distribution, and promotion. Marketing ranges from concepts such as free samples in the hands of consumers to buzz campaigns

Advertising, literally defined, is a subset of marketing that involves paying to place your message in more traditional media formats, from newspapers and magazines to radio and television to the Internet and outdoors.

Public relations, liberally defined, is the marketing of an organization and the use of unbiased, objective, third-party endorsement to relay information about that organization's products and practices.[5]

With so many media outlets bombarding consumers daily, most organizations realize that public relations can play an expanded role in marketing. In some organizations, particularly service companies, hospitals, and nonprofit institutions, the selling of both individual products and the organization itself are inextricably intertwined.

Stated another way, although the practices of marketing and advertising create a market for products and services and the practice of public relations creates a hospitable environment in which the organization may operate, marketing and advertising success can be nullified by the social and political forces public relations is designed to confront—and, thus, the interrelationship of the three disciplines.

In the past, marketers treated public relations as an ancillary part of the marketing mix. They were concerned primarily with making sure that their products met the needs and desires of customers and were priced competitively, distributed widely, and promoted heavily through advertising and merchandising. Gradually, however, these traditional notions among marketers began to change for several reasons.

- Consumer protests about both product value and safety and government scrutiny of the truth behind product claims began to shake historical views of marketing.
- Product recalls—from automobiles to tuna fish—generated recurring headlines.
- Ingredient scares began to occur regularly.
- Advertisers were asked how their products answered social needs and civic responsibilities.
- Rumors about particular companies—from fast-food firms to pop-rock manufacturers—spread in brushfire manner.
- General image problems of certain companies and industries—from oil to banking—were fanned by a continuous blaze of media criticism.

The net impact of these challenges was that even though a company's products were still important, customers began to consider a firm's policies and practices on everything from air and water pollution to minority hiring. Beyond these social concerns, the effectiveness of advertising itself began to be questioned.

The increased number of advertisements in newspapers and on the airwaves caused clutter and placed a significant burden on advertisers who were trying to make the public aware of their products. In the 1980s, the trend toward shorter television advertising spots contributed to three times as many products being advertised on television as there were in the 1970s. In the 1990s, the spread of cable television added yet another multi-channeled outlet for product advertising. In the 2000s, the proliferation of Internet advertising intensified the noise and clutter.

Against this backdrop, the potential of public relations as an added ingredient in the marketing mix has become an imperative. Indeed, marketing guru Philip Kotler was among the first to suggest more than a decade ago that to the traditional four Ps of marketing—product, price, place, and promotion—a fifth P, *public relations,* should be added.[6]

In the 21st century, Kotler's suggestion has increasingly become reality.

Product Publicity

To many, product publicity is the essence of the value of integrating public relations and marketing. In light of how difficult it now is to raise advertising awareness above the noise of so many competitive messages, marketers are turning increasingly to product publicity as an important adjunct to advertising. Although the public is generally unaware of it, a great deal of what it knows and believes about a wide variety of products comes through press coverage.

In certain circumstances, product publicity can be the most effective element in the marketing mix. For example:

- **Introducing a revolutionary new product.** Product publicity can start introductory sales at a much higher level of demand by creating more awareness of the product.
- **Eliminating distribution problems with retail outlets.** Often the way to get shelf space is to have consumers demand the product. Product publicity can be extremely effective in creating consumer demand.
- **Small budgets and strong competition.** Advertising is expensive. Product publicity is cheap. Often publicity is the best way to tell the story. Samuel Adams Boston Lager beer, for example, became a household word almost solely through publicity opportunities.

■ **Explaining a complicated product.** The use and benefits of many products are difficult to explain to mass audiences in a brief ad. Product publicity, through extended news columns, can be invaluable.

■ **Generating new consumer excitement for an old product.** Repackaging an old product for the media can serve as a primary marketing impetus.

■ **Tying the product to a unique representative.** Try as it might, the advertising industry can't escape the staying power of unique mascots who become tied inextricably to products. Consider the following:

  • *Morris the Cat* was one answer to consumer disinterest in cat food for the 9 Lives Cat Food Company in 1968 and still appears today, well into middle age.

  • The *Jolly Green Giant* has *"ho ho ho'ed"* so long at General Mills that he now has his own Green Giant Food Company and Web site.

  • Burger King's *King* is back with a vengeance in the new century, cavorting on football fields and in other venues for a whole new generation.[7]

  • But the real "king" is McDonald's standard bearer, *Ronald McDonald,* who first appeared in 1963 and has since starred on national television, at Academy Awards ceremonies, and around the world. No other iconic figure in history has become more synonymous with any company (Figure 17-2).

■ **Creating an identity.** Many organizations can't afford to blast out expensive advertising but must be "heard" above the din of thousands of competitors. And no organization has proven better at it than the irrepressible home of the annoying chihuaha, Taco Bell (see Talking Points).

FIGURE 17-2   The king. Maybe not of "burgers" but certainly of corporate icons. Ronald McDonald, here with Olympic gold medalists Carl Lewis and Jackie-Joyner Kersee to celebrate "Go Active Day" in Athens, Greece. (Courtesy of O'Dwyer.com)

Talking Points

TACO BELL Free Tacos Publicity Bull's-Eye

Few companies rival the creative Taco Bell Corp. (Taco Bell) when it comes to conjuring up ideas for product publicity. The fast-food outlet, known for "thinking outside the bun," really outdid itself in the spring of 2001, when the Russian space station Mir was scheduled to land after 15 years in space.

Shortly before Mir was scheduled to touch down in the South Pacific, Taco Bell used a barge to tow a 40-foot by 40-foot Taco Bell® logo target out to sea off the eastern coast of Australia with the message "Free Taco Here" (Figure 17-3).

The company promised to give one free taco to each of America's 280 million citizens if any section of the space station hit the target.

According to Laurie Gannon, Taco Bell's public relations director, "buzz marketing" (i.e., creating a "buzz" around a publicity event) was the objective of the Mir bull's-eye promotion.

"For any Buzz Marketing initiative to be successful, it must first be highly topical . . . for maximum exposure and impact," Gannon said. Tying a free taco to the Mir splashdown fit the bill perfectly, although Taco Bell took out an insurance policy worth "several million dollars" to cover itself in case Mir hit the target.

FOR IMMEDIATE RELEASE

FREE TACOS FOR U.S. IF MIR HITS FLOATING *TACO BELL*® OCEAN TARGET

Taco Bell sets 40 by 40 foot target in South Pacific for Mir's Re-entry

IRVINE, CA, March 20, 2001 -- Taco Bell is offering a free taco to everyone in the U.S. if the core of the Mir space station hits a floating Taco Bell target placed in the South Pacific. Later this week, all eyes will be fixed on the sky in anticipation of the 150-ton space station's return to earth.

Taco Bell has created a 40 by 40-foot target, painted with a *Bell* bull's-eye and bold purple letters stating: "Free Taco Here." The floating target will be placed in the South Pacific Ocean off the coast of Australia in advance of Mir's descent.

"Taco Bell is capturing the imagination of millions of people as they eagerly await Mir's return to earth," said Chris Becker, vice president of brand communications, Taco Bell Corp. "If Mir rings our bell, we will offer a free taco to everyone in the U.S.," added Becker.

If the core of Mir hits the designated Taco Bell target upon its re-entry, every person in the U.S. will have an opportunity to obtain a coupon for a free taco, valid at participating Taco Bell restaurants. Coupon distribution, redemption and offer details will be made available to consumers on the Taco Bell website and in press materials should this event occur. Taco Bell has purchased an insurance policy to cover the anticipated cost of the free taco redemption should the core of Mir hit the target.

- more -

FIGURE 17-3 Inside the target, outside the bun. Taco's Bell's South Pacific inducement for product publicity. (The Taco Bell name and logo are trademarks of Taco Bell Corp. and are used with permission.)

What immediately "hit the target" was the Taco Bell announcement of the potential payoff for every American—headlines, news reports, radio commentary—all "free" and all product publicity.

In the end, Taco Bell reported:

- Approximately 127,400,000 TV viewers
- 1,650 uses of Taco Bell video news releases by TV stations
- 188 U.S. markets
- 3 network news feeds

Also (luckily for Taco Bell), the Mir came up thousands of miles short of its target (Figure 17-4), so nobody won a free taco. But somebody got lots of free product publicity.

FOR IMMEDIATE RELEASE

SPACE STATION MIR-LY MISSES THE *TACO BELL®* TARGET

IRVINE, CA, March 23, 2001 – Even with millions of Americans chanting "TA-CO, TA-CO" as Mir plummeted to earth, it wasn't enough for the space station to hit the Taco Bell bull's-eye and deliver free tacos to America.

Since the Company announced the free taco offer on Monday, thousands of television, radio and print news reports have circled the globe. The Company's phone lines have rung off the hook and millions flocked to its Web site at www.tacobell.com to find more information.

"We captured the imagination and interest of millions of people around the globe and put a smile on their faces," said Chris Becker, vice president of brand communications, Taco Bell Corp. "We're disappointed that the space station Mir-ly missed our target, but we're happy people enjoyed the challenge and the fun personality that the Taco Bell brand is known for," added Becker.

Taco Bell Corp., a division of Tricon Global Restaurants Inc. (NYSE: YUM), is the nation's leading Mexican-style quick service restaurant chain serving tacos, burritos, signature Chalupas and Gorditas, nachos and other specialty items. Taco Bell serves nearly 40 million consumers each week in over 7,200 restaurants nationwide, generating $5.2 billion in system-wide sales.

# # #

FIGURE 17-4   The "bad" news. (Thank goodness for Taco Bell!) (The Taco Bell name and logo are trademarks of Taco Bell Corp. and are used with permission.)

Third-Party Endorsement

Perhaps more than anything else, the lure of third-party endorsement is the primary reason smart organizations value product publicity as much as they do advertising. Third-party endorsement, as noted, refers to the tacit support given a product by a newspaper, magazine, or broadcaster who mentions the product as news. Advertising often is perceived as self-serving. People know that the advertiser not only created the message but also paid for it. Publicity, on the other hand, which appears in news columns, carries no such stigma. Editors, after all, are considered objective, impartial, indifferent, neutral. Therefore, publicity appears to be news and is more trustworthy than advertising that is paid for by a clearly nonobjective sponsor.

Editors have become sensitive to mentioning product names in print. Some, in fact, have a policy of deleting brand or company identifications in news columns. Public relations counselors argue that discriminating against using product names does a

FIGURE 17-5 Third-party endorsers. The New England Confectionary Company kicked off Valentine's Day 2005 with the unveiling of 10 new Sweethearts Conversation Hearts sayings, modeled by fans. (Courtesy of O'Dwyer.com)

disservice to readers or viewers, many of whom are influenced by what they read or see and may desire the particular products discussed. Counselors further argue that journalists who accept and print public relations material for its intrinsic value and then remove the source of the information give the reader or viewer the false impression that the journalist generated the facts, ideas, or photography.

In recent years, one practice that has drawn journalistic scorn is that of organizations using well-known spokespeople to promote products without identifying that they are being paid for the endorsement. Journalists argue that such presentations are patently unethical paid endorsements designed to appear objective.[8] CNN, for one, imposed a strict policy on paid spokespersons after suffering an embarrassing incident with actress Kathleen Turner, who promoted drug company products without disclosing her financial relationship with the company.[9]

Understandably, editors and producers don't soon forgive firms that sponsor such devious spokespeople. One solution to achieve product recognition through the "endorsement" of objective authorities is to create events that are certain to attract publicity (Figure 17-5).

Building a Brand

The watchword in business today is branding, creating a differentiable identity or position for a company or product.

In more traditional times, it took years for brands like Pepsi, Coke, McDonald's, Hertz, FedEx, and Wal-Mart to establish themselves. Today, with the advent of the World Wide Web, thriving Internet companies like Google, Yahoo!, Amazon.com, eBay, and AOL have become household words in a historical nanosecond. Using integrated marketing communications to establish a unique brand requires adherence to the following principles.

■ **Be early.** It is better to be first than to be best. Don't believe it? Then who was the "second" person to fly solo across the Atlantic? No, it wasn't Charles Lindbergh flying back! (Actually, it was an Australian chap named Bert Hinkler, but nobody remembers him!) We remember the "first" in a category because of the *law of primacy,* which posits that people are more likely to remember you if you were the first in their minds in a particular category. Whether yours is really the "first" brand is less important than establishing primacy in the minds of consumers.

- **Be memorable.** Equally important is to fight through the clutter by creating a memorable brand. With hundreds of participants in categories from bottled water to bathing suits, a brand needs to stand out by distinguishing itself in some way—through uniqueness or advertising slogan or social responsibility or whatever. Creating brand awareness requires boldness.

- **Be aggressive.** A successful brand also requires a constant drumbeat of publicity to keep the company's name before the public. Potential customers need to become familiar with the brand. Potential investors need to become confident that the brand is an active one. Indeed, more and more, marketers are "taking to the streets" to spread their messages (Figure 17-6). The new competitive economy leaves little room for demure integrated marketing communications.

- **Use heritage.** Baby boomers are old. Gen Xers are getting older. And *heritage* is very much in vogue. This means citing the traditions and history of a product or organization as part of building the brand. As consumers live longer, an increasing number of citizens long for "the good old days." As society longs for nostalgia, heritage works—to the point where the old reliables become "collector's items" (Figure 17-7).

FIGURE 17-6 Street cred. Friendly Ice Cream Corporation took to the streets with free samples in an effort to reinforce brand recognition. (Courtesy of O'Dwyer.com)

FIGURE 17-7 Sentimental value. Baby boomers, weaned on a heritage of Cabbage Patch Dolls and Beanie Babies, made them collectibles in the 21st century. (Fraser P. Seitel)

■ **Create a personality.** The best organizations are those that create "personalities" for themselves. Who is number one in rental cars? Hertz. What company stands for overnight delivery? FedEx. What's the East Coast university that boasts the best and the brightest? Harvard. Or at least that's what most people think. The firm's personality should be reflected in all communications materials the organization produces.

As more and more companies each year attempt to bust through the advertising and marketing clutter by resorting to such marketing devices as banner ads, proprietary Web sites, free classified advertising, e-zines and e-mail marketing, the challenge to create a differentiable brand becomes that much more difficult.

Integrating Marketing with Public Relations

Among the more traditional public relations activities used to market products are article reprints, trade show participation, use of spokespersons, cause-related marketing, and in-kind promotions.

Article Reprints

Once an organization has received product publicity in a newspaper or magazine, it should market the publicity further to achieve maximum sales punch. Marketing can be done through article reprints aimed at that part of a target audience—wholesalers, retailers, or consumers—that might not have seen the original article. Reprints also help reinforce the reactions of those who read the original article.

As in any other public relations activity, use of reprints should be approached systematically, with the following ground rules in mind:

1. Plan ahead, especially if an article has major significance to the organization and you believe it might be positive. Ideally, reprints should be ordered before the periodical goes to press so that customers can receive them shortly after the article hits the newsstands.

2. Select target publics and address the recipients by name and title. This strategy ensures that the reprint reaches the most important audience.

3. Pinpoint the reprint's significance either by underlining pertinent information in the article, making marginal notes, or attaching a cover letter. In this way, the target audience readily understands your purpose.

4. Integrate the reprint with similar articles and information on the same or related subjects. Often several reprints can be combined into a single mailing. Also, reprints can be integrated into press kits and displays.

Trade Show Participation

Trade show participation enables an organization to display its products before important target audiences. The decision to participate should be considered with the following factors in mind:

1. **Analyze the show carefully.** Make sure the audience is one that can't be reached effectively through other promotional materials, such as article reprints or local publicity. Also, be sure the audience is essential to the sale of the product.

2. **Select a common theme.** Integrate public relations, publicity, advertising, and sales promotion. Unify all elements for the trade show and avoid, at all costs, any hint of interdepartmental rivalries.

3. **Make sure the products displayed are the right ones.** Decide well in advance exactly which products should be shown.

4. **Consider the trade books.** Often trade magazines run special features in conjunction with trade shows, and editors need photos and publicity material. Always know what special editions are coming up as well as their deadline schedules.

5. **Emphasize what's new.** Talk about the new model that's being displayed. Discuss the additional features, new uses, or recent performance data of the products displayed. Trade show exhibitions should reveal innovation, breakthrough, and newness.

6. **Consider local promotional efforts.** While in town during a trade show, an organization can enhance both the recognition of its product and the traffic at its booth by doing local promotions. This strategy involves visiting trade magazine editors and local media people to stir up publicity for the product during the show.

7. **Evaluate the worth.** Always evaluate whether the whole exercise was worth it. This involves counting, qualifying, and following up on leads generated as well as looking at other intangibles to see if marketing objectives were met.[10]

Use of Spokespersons

In recent years, the use of spokespersons to promote products has increased. As noted, spokespersons shouldn't disguise the fact that they are advocates for a particular product. Their purpose is to air their sponsor's viewpoint, which often means going to bat for a controversial product.

Spokespersons must be articulate, fast on their feet, and thoroughly knowledgeable about the subject. When these criteria are met, the use of spokespersons as an integrated marketing tool can be most effective.

In recent years, the use of spokespersons to promote products has become so crazed that in 2003, Coca-Cola signed basketball phenom LeBron James to a six-year, $12 million contract to promote Sprite while James was still in high school and hadn't stepped foot onto an NBA court. Of course, at the time Coke signed him, the Ohio high schooler already had signed a shoe deal with Nike for a cool $100 million. And also, of course, James has become one of the NBA's premier players. So maybe Coke and Nike knew what they were doing, after all.[11]

Beyond question, however, the greatest pitchman of all time was also the most unlikely. Former boxing champ George Foreman sold his name and image to Salton, the maker of George Foreman's Lean Mean Fat-Reducing Grilling Machine (Figure 17-8). The price to Salton and payday for Foreman was $137.5 million.[12] Who says boxers are punchy?

Cause-Related Marketing

Public relations sponsorships tied to philanthropy are another effective integrated marketing device. With the cost of print and broadcast advertising going up each year, companies increasingly are turning to sponsorship of the arts, education, music, festivals, anniversaries, sports, and charitable causes for promotional and public relations purposes.

Cause-related marketing brings together the fund-raising needs of nonprofit groups with the business objectives of sponsoring companies. Toy company Zany Brainy sponsored contests to turn in "violent toys" and donated money to charity. Financial company Capital One's Mascot of the Year contest was billed as a "scholarship competition in which the

FIGURE 17-8 The champ. George Foreman, celebrity spokesman without equal—for 137.5 million reasons! (Courtesy of Richard Drew/AP Wide World Photos)

best mascot (judged on good sporstmanship, community service, etc.)—Penn State's Nittany Lion, Wisconsin's Bucky Badger, Georgia Tech's Yellow Jacket, and other distinguished citizens—vied to see which mascot would emerge victorious at the Capital One Bowl.[13]

Cause-related marketing will continue to grow in the 21st century. Middle-aged baby boomers, in particular, are more concerned about issues that affect their lives, like protecting the environment and aiding the less fortunate. This change in itself will drive the creation of events and decision making by corporate sponsors.

In-Kind Promotions

When a service, product, or other consideration in exchange for publicity exposure is offered, it is called an *in-kind promotion*. Examples of in-kind promotions include:

1. Providing services or products as prizes offered by a newspaper or charity in exchange for being listed as a cosponsor in promotional materials.

2. Providing services or products to a local business in exchange for having fliers inserted in shopping bags or as statement stuffers.

3. Providing services or products to doctors' offices, auto repair shops, or other businesses in exchange for having brochures prominently displayed.

4. Providing samples and gifts of products and services, along with sales literature.

5. Providing point-of-purchase displays, literature, events, demonstrations, and samples at the point where the customer decides on purchasing the product or service.

6. Providing posters of the product or service at well-trafficked locations.

Speaking of Ethics

Taking a Chance on Controversial Kate

Companies live or die with the character of the spokespeople they hire to affiliate with their products. When super model Kate Moss was photographed apparently using cocaine in a London recording studio in 2005, it looked as though her annual endorsement earnings of $9 million might be snuffed out (Figure 17-9).

But then along came British iconoclast Sir Richard Branson, owner of Virgin Mobile, who signed the wayward model for a self-deprecating commercial. In the 40-second spot, Moss was called by her agent with the news of a "perfect contract"—for a cell phone, not a modeling job.

Sir Richard was willing to hire Moss, even as other sponsors, among them Burberry, Chanel, and H&M clothing, were dropping her from their spokesperson roster.

Some questioned Virgin Mobile's wisdom in promoting the image of a hard-partying, cocaine-snorting model. But others were less troubled. Said one marketing professor, "Nobody signed on Kate Moss as a character spokesman. . . . Her brand is built on celebrity and image and glamour and night life."

FIGURE 17-9 Stupor model. British supermodel Kate Moss departs London police station in 2006 after being interviewed about alleged cocaine use. (Matt Dunham/AP Wide World Photos)

The point of in-kind promotions is to leverage the name and use of products and services, so that more potential buyers are exposed to the organization.

Public Relations Advertising

Traditionally, organizations used advertising to sell products. In 1936, though, a company named Warner & Swasey initiated an ad campaign that stressed the power of America as a nation and the importance of American business in the nation's future. Warner & Swasey continued its ads after World War II and thus was born a unique type of advertising—the marketing of an image rather than a product. This technique became known variously as institutional advertising, image advertising, public service advertising, issues advertising, and ultimately public relations—or nonproduct—advertising.

In the 1980s, the logical extension of image advertising was issues advertising, which advocated positions from the sponsor's viewpoint. Often these concerned matters of some controversy. Organizations, led by the outspoken Mobil Corporation—now, Exxon-Mobil—continued the practice of issue ads into the 2000s. Indeed, Mobil's practice of placing an issues ad on the op-ed page of the *New York Times* and other leading newspapers each Thursday, begun in the 1960s, is still going strong—although not every Thursday—in the new century.

Purposes of Public Relations Advertising

Traditional public relations advertising—as opposed to image or issue positioning—is still widely used. Such advertising can be appropriate for a number of activities:

1. **Mergers and diversifications.** When one company merges with another, the public needs to be told about the new business lines and divisions. Advertising provides a quick and effective way to convey this message.

2. **Personnel changes.** A firm's greatest asset is usually its managers, its salespeople, and its employees. Presenting staff members in advertising not only impresses a reader with the firm's pride in its workers but also helps build confidence among employees themselves.

3. **Organizational resources.** A firm's investment in research and development implies that the organization is concerned about meeting the future intelligently, an asset that should be advertised. The scope of a company's services also says something positive about the organization.

4. **Manufacturing and service capabilities.** The ability to deliver quality goods on time is something customers cherish. A firm that can deliver should advertise this capability. Likewise, a firm with a qualified and attentive servicing capability should let clients and potential clients know about it.

5. **Growth history.** A growing firm, one that has developed steadily over time and has taken advantage of its environment, is the kind of company with which people want to deal. It is also the kind of firm for which people will want to work. Growth history, therefore, is a worthwhile subject for nonproduct advertising.

6. **Financial strength and stability.** A picture of economic strength and stability is one that all companies like to project. Advertisements that highlight the company's financial position earn confidence and attract customers and investors.

7. **Company customers.** Customers can serve as a marketing tool, too. Well-known personalities who use a certain product may be enough to win additional customers. This strategy may be especially viable in advertising for higher-priced products such as expensive automobiles or sports equipment.

8. **Organization name change.** With firms in industries from banking to consumer products to communications now either merging with each other or streamlining their operations, company names change—from AOL, Time, and Warner Brothers to AOLTime Warner and back to Time Warner; from Federal Express to FedEx; from Kentucky Fried Chicken to KFC. To burnish the new name in people's minds, a name change must be well promoted and well advertised. Only through constant repetition will people become familiar with the new identity.

9. **Trademark protection.** Companies such as Xerox, Kleenex, and Coca-Cola, whose products are household names, are legitimately concerned about the improper generic use of their trademarks in the public domain. Such companies run periodic ads to remind people of the proper status of their marks. In one such ad, a perplexed secretary reminds the boss, "If you had ordered 40 photocopies instead of 40 Xeroxes, we wouldn't have been stuck with all these machines!" (Figure 17-10). Ironically, Xerox, so worried about its name, lost its direction in the aftermath of the bubble economy and nearly lost its franchise.

10. **Corporate emergencies.** Occasionally, an emergency situation erupts—a labor strike, plant disaster, or service interruption. One quick way to explain the firm's position and procedures without fear of distortion or misinterpretation by editors or reporters is to buy advertising space. This tactic permits a full explanation of the reasons behind the problem and the steps the company plans to take to resolve the dilemma.

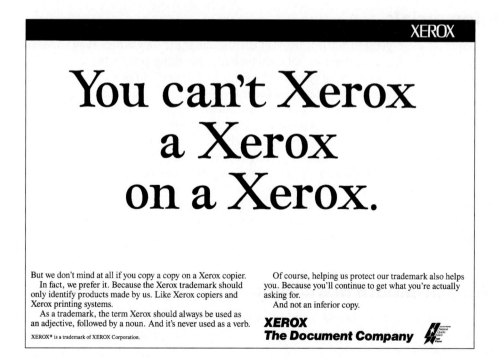

FIGURE 17-10   Still a household name?   Xerox was one company with the rare problem of a brand name that became so well known, it became a generic name for "copying"—until the firm almost lost its franchise. (Courtesy of Xerox)

Twenty-First-Century Integrated Marketing

Beyond advertising, marketing, and public relations techniques, integrated marketing, too, must keep pace with the ever-changing world of promotional innovations to help sell products and services. Among them are television brand integration, infomercials, word-of-mouth marketing, television and movie product placement, and more.

Television Brand Integration

The latest phenomenon in television is to integrate products into the fabric of what is being presented on the screen. When one of ABC's *Desperate Housewives* found herself hard up for cash, she donned an evening gown and extolled the virtues of a Buick Lacrosse at a car show. One of the stars of Warner Brothers' *What I Like About You* raved about Fruity Pebbles and competed to win a role in an Herbal Essences commercial. Fox's *Bernie Mac* referred to his need for Rolaids throughout an episode.

Such product emphases were not just coincidence.

As technology and clutter blunt the effectiveness and reach of traditional 30-second commercials, more advertisers are paying to integrate their products directly into the action of a show or film.

The process of brand integration owed its start to CBS's *Survivor,* which financed itself largely through product tie-ins with advertisers whose products were mentioned in the course of the show. This was a far cry from serendipitous—that is, unpaid—product mentions, like Junior Mints and Pez on *Seinfeld.*[14]

Infomercials

Infomercials were greeted with universal catcalls in the 1980s when they were introduced as program-length commercials, shamelessly hawking products.

Even today, the infomercial remains the Rodney Dangerfield of marketing, accorded no respect for many reasons—state and federal investigations of infomercial producers, complaints about product performance, and most important, the belief, still, that a lengthy commercial disguised as a conventional program—like a talk show, complete with theme song and studio audience—unfairly masks an advertisement.

Nonetheless, infomercials remain strong for one reason: They work. Indeed, George Foreman's success with his grills is just one example. Between $1 billion and $2 billion worth of merchandise is sold each year—from dicing and slicing kitchen utensils to exercise paraphernalia to psychic hot lines—despite condemnation and even lawsuits. Celebrities from Chuck Norris to Suzanne Somers to Donald Trump have joined the growing parade of shameless infomercial hawkers.

Word-of-Mouth Marketing

Also known as *buzz marketing,* word-of-mouth is another alternative to traditional advertising that enlists "influencers" or "trend setters" to spread the word about a particular product.

The practice began with teenagers, who appeared to be popular. Today, marketers have graduated to reaching out for "evangelists" who are already diehard fans of a particular product and persuading them to "spread the gospel." Its proponents hail word-

FIGURE 17-11 The grandaddy. This lovable alien professed his predilection for Reese's Pieces, and a new integrated marketing discipline was born. (Courtesy of Hershey Foods)

of-mouth as the most honest and ethical of advertising media. "People don't want to hurt their friends and family and colleagues with bad information," is the way one believer put it.[15]

Television and Movie Product Placements

Product placements in films also are proliferating at a rapid rate. The turning point in product plugs occurred three decades ago when M&M/Mars turned down filmmaker Steven Spielberg when he offered to link M&Ms to the hero of his new movie, *E.T.* Reese's Pieces, however, took up the movie producer's offer, and the rest is history (Figure 17-11).

In the 21st century, product placements—also known as *embedded advertisements*—have become a more integral part of movies and television shows. Among the stars in 2004 alone:

- The AFLAC duck made its film debut in Jim Carrey's *Lemony Snickets: A Series of Unfortunate Events.*

- Clorox bleach received star billing in Clint Eastwood's Academy Award winning *Million Dollar Baby.*

- Hai Karat, a men's fragrance, was featured prominently in Steven Spielberg's *The Incredibles.*

- The Kleenex tissue brand was Leonardo DiCaprio's tissue of choice in *The Aviator.*[16]

Talking Points

The Top 10

According to *Forbes* magazine, the most powerful celebrities of 2005, available for product endorsements to the highest bidder, were:

1. Oprah Winfrey, TV personality
2. Tiger Woods, golf professional
3. Mel Gibson, actor
4. George Lucas, Hollywood mogul

5. Shaquille O'Neal, basketball player
6. Steven Spielberg, Hollywood mogul
7. Johnny Depp, actor
8. Madonna, singer
9. Elton John, singer
10. Tom Cruise, actor

Peter Kafka, "The Celebrity 100," *Forbes,* June 15, 2005.

Today, many companies consider movie product placements an integral part of their integrated marketing mix.

You Name It

What other 21st-century integrated marketing venues exist? How fertile is your imagination? Consider the following:

- **Song placements:** Marketers now compete to get brands mentioned in best-selling records. Thanks primarily to hip-hop luminaries like Jay-Z and Ludacris, brands such as Nike, Mercedes-Benz, Hennessy, Louis Vuitton, and Lamborghini all benefit from the "street cred" embodied in popular music. In 2005 alone, Nike was mentioned in 63 hip-hop songs.[17]

- **Sports teams:** It used to be that stadiums were named for the highest bidder. Today, the team itself takes on the name of the sponsor who pays for it. Venues like the St. Louis Cardinals' Busch Stadium and the Washington Redskins' FedEx Field have given way to teams like the New York Red Bulls, the Major League Soccer franchise named after the sports energy drink, which paid more than $100 million for the integrated marketing privilege.[18]

- **Blogs:** The spread of blogs on the Internet has also attracted integrated marketing efforts. In 2005, companies like Budget rental cars turned to blogs to promote marketing initiatives. In Budget's case, the company used a variety of blogs to promote a contest with a scavenger hunt motif. Budget bought ads on 177 blogs to, in the words of its marketing executive, "actively engage the consumer compared with passive TV spots."[19]

- **Whaaaa?** Hands down, the most bizarre 21st-century integrated marketing technique was the use of a person's forehead for marketing purposes. In 2005, a Web-page designer in Omaha auctioned off his forehead on eBay for advertising space. Sure enough, snoring remedy SnoreStop paid the Omaha entrepreneur $37,375 for one month's use of his cranium. Summarized SnoreStop's CEO, "People will always comment on something out of the ordinary. People like weird."[20]
  Amen, brother.

Last Word

The key marketing question in the 21st century is, *How do we generate buzz?* How do we distinguish ourselves and get our voice heard in the midst of hundreds of thousands of competing voices?

To marketing expert Al Ries, who cut his teeth in the advertising industry, the answer is obvious. "In the past, it may have been true that a beefy advertising budget was the key ingredient in the brand-building process. . . . Today brands are born, not made. A new brand must be capable of generating favorable publicity in the media or it won't have a chance in the marketplace."[21]

In other words, says Ries, it is public relations and its attendant communications forms—not advertising alone—that differentiate an organization, product, or issue.

Perhaps more precisely stated, what is needed now is an integrated approach to communications, combining the best of marketing, advertising, sales promotion, and public relations.

The clear marketing need for organizations and those who serve them is to build lasting client relationships. A successful communications professional must be knowledgeable about all aspects of the communications mix. Integrated marketing communications, then, becomes paramount in preparing public relations professionals for the challenges of the 21st century.

Discussion Starters

1. What is meant by *integrated marketing communications?*
2. Describe the differences among advertising, marketing, and public relations.
3. What is meant by *third-party endorsement?*
4. In what situations is product publicity most effective?
5. Describe the pros and cons of using a well-known individual as a spokesperson.
6. What is *cause-related marketing?*
7. How can integrated marketing help build a brand?
8. What are the purposes of public relations advertising?
9. What is the significance of Warner & Swasey and Mobil Oil in terms of public relations advertising?
10. What are several 21st-century techniques of integrated marketing communications?

Top of the Shelf

The Fall of Advertising and the Rise of PR

Al Ries and Laura Ries, New York: HarperCollins, 2002.

The cover of this book features a deflated sock puppet, symbolic of the failure of Pet.com's sock puppet ads, which in turn is symbolic of the limitations of advertising, especially compared with the fact that skillful public relations is what sells—at least according to these authors, father and daughter and advertising veterans.

The Ries and Ries writing team argues that public relations should be used instead of advertising to launch new brands. Once a brand is established, advertising may then be used to maintain the brand in the consumer's mind. They cite a number of brands—Palm, Starbucks, the Body Shop, Wal-Mart, and Red Bull—that have been built with virtually no advertising.

In fairness, it's probably way premature to declare the death of advertising, but the Ries book is a provocative one that deserves consideration.

CASE STUDY

Reviving the Bryant Brand

The story of basketball superstar Kobe Bryant as an integrated marketing phenomenon is one for the history books (or at least public relations books). Bryant, the Los Angeles Lakers' star attraction and arguably the best in the NBA, was a basketball and marketing golden boy. His image was everywhere. His persona—as a good-looking, hardworking, devout family man—was an integrated marketer's dream.

Until it suddenly became a nightmare in 2003.

In June of that year, Bryant, one of the NBA's most popular athletes, signed a four-year, $45 million endorsement contract with Nike. The deal called for the company to create a line of signature sneakers and apparel for Bryant, who would receive royalties on sales. This, added to similar lucrative deals with McDonald's, Russell Corporation's Spalding basketball division, Coca-Cola, and Nutella Confections, made Bryant one of America's most marketable commodities.

Until the problem in Colorado.

A Charge of Sexual Assault

Just weeks after he signed the deal with Nike, Kobe Bryant was accused by a woman in Colorado of sexual assault. The woman claimed that the married Bryant had checked into a resort hotel where she worked, ordered room service which she delivered, and then assaulted her violently in his room.

The sports world was stunned by the revelations. Kobe Bryant, son of a respected upscale NBA family and the very picture of propriety, had been charged with a vicious crime.

Coca-Cola stopped running the Bryant ads immediately. McDonald's, Spalding, and Nutella followed suit. Nike, with a fresh four-year deal, hung back silently, waiting to see how the Bryant camp might extricate itself from a horrible story.

Bryant was subsequently charged by the Eagle County, Colorado, district attorney with one count of felony sexual assault against a 19-year-old woman. If convicted, the charges would carry a four-year prison term.

"I'm Innocent"

Within hours of being charged, Kobe Bryant struck back with a most unusual public relations strategy. With his wife of two years, Vanessa, at his side, Bryant walked into a packed press conference at Staples Center, his home court with the Los Angeles Lakers, and proclaimed that he wasn't guilty (Figure 17-12).

Bryant broke into tears, clutching his wife's hand, and said, "I'm innocent. You know I didn't force her to do anything against her will. I'm innocent."

Bryant went on to acknowledge, "You know I sit here in front of you guys furious at myself. Disgusted at myself for making a mistake of adultery. I love my wife with all my heart. She's my backbone."

Throughout his excruciatingly emotional press conference, Bryant never released his wife's hand. Most of his remarks, in fact, were addressed to her, personally.

"I'm a human being," Bryant said, as tears rolled down his cheeks. "I'm a man just like everybody else. I mourn. I cry like everybody else. And I sit here before you guys embarrassed and ashamed for committing adultery. . . . And together, my wife and our family, we're going to fight these false accusations."

With that, Kobe Bryant walked out as the throng of reporters, stunned that the reclusive star would have even shown up at the press conference, looked on silently.

FIGURE 17-12 Painful press conference. Kobe Bryant and wife Vanessa hold hands and face the press in July 2003. (Jerome T. Nakagawa/AP Wide World Photos)

Ending with a Whimper

From that moment on, Kobe Bryant stepped out of the limelight, reappearing only to perform on the basketball court. His lawyers, meanwhile, worked to have the case settled without a trial.

Over the next two years, while his lawyers worked, Bryant said little about the court proceedings, even when he was forced to appear in Colorado for hearings.

Meanwhile, anonymous charges and counter charges spread through the media about Bryant's accuser, her possible motives, and character. Again, while his attorneys jumped to file motions to expose the accuser, Bryant stayed out of the sordid drama commencing in the press, and he refused to respond to the derogatory comments and catcalls as he toured the league's arenas.

Shortly after jury selection in the criminal case, Bryant's accuser decided she couldn't take part in a trial, and prosecutors in Eagle County dropped the case.

In March 2005, a civil lawsuit filed against Bryant was similarly dropped.

With a terse news release and an even terser court filing, the sordid sexual assault case against Kobe Bryant that gripped the nation for two years abruptly ended.

81 and Out

In 2006, Kobe Bryant, the man that many "experts" said would never again regain the marketing appeal he had stupidly let slip away, came back with ferocity. He was unstoppable on the court, the overachieving leader of a mediocre team playing way beyond its capacity. His No. 8 Lakers' jersey, which had slipped ignominiously from being a top seller to the 90th position, was once again a hot item. He was an overwhelming fan favorite for the all-star game.

And then one night in January, Bryant lit up the hapless Toronto Raptors for 81 points, the second-highest scoring performance in league history. Almost instantly, the "Kobe 81 DVD" became a best seller, and the Kobe Bryant bandwagon was officially back.

So much so that Nike, carefully surveying the situation for a couple of quiet years, was ready to relaunch Bryant's career as a product endorser. The central part of the effort was a new shoe, the Zoom Kobe 1. After the 81-point performance, commercials starring Bryant appeared with increasing frequency.

And while the star himself still suffered from an image of aloofness and his redeemed potential as a marketer remained in question, there was no doubt but that within three years of confronting instant endorsement termination, Kobe Bryant had made a miraculous recovery.

Questions

1. What do you think of Kobe Bryant's public relations strategy in light of the Colorado charges?

2. What do you think of the way he handled his press conference after the allegations?

3. What public relations options were available to him as the court cases proceeded?

4. What is Kobe Bryant's current marketing potential? Upon what does this depend?

For further information, see Stephanie Kang, "Nike Relaunches Kobe Bryant After Two Years of Prep Work," *Wall Street Journal,* November 11, 2005, B1; Richard Sandomir, "Like Him or Not, Bryant the Brand is Scoring," *New York Times,* January 27, 2006, D3; Fraser P. Seitel, "Grading the Big 3 PR Transgressors," odwyerpr.com, October 27, 2003; "Suit Settlement Ends Bryant Saga," Associated Press, March 3, 2005.

Voice of Authority

An Interview with Marina Maher

Widely recognized as one of the nation's leading experts in marketing to women, **Marina Maher** is the principal of Marina Maher Communications, a New York public relations firm that she founded over 20 years ago. The agency specializes in building brand relationships for blue chip clients in the consumer products and health care categories. An early proponent of integrated communications programs, Maher has been instrumental in the creation of many award-winning campaigns that reflect her marketing mantra of "One Sight, One Sound, One Sell." She was named one of the 50 Most Influential Women in Public Relations by *PRWeek Magazine*.

How helpful can public relations be for a marketer?
PR is more than helpful—it's essential. In today's world of marketing, where consumers are bombarded with messages, hard to reach, and are skeptical, it's critical to create ways where consumers bond with a product. More than any other discipline in the marketing mix, public relations can build and nurture the relationship of a brand with its target by creating an emotional connection. Consumers who are emotionally linked become brand ambassadors, engaging other consumers in that brand.

How can public relations help build a brand?
Authenticity is an important word today, especially among younger consumers, when building and marketing a brand. By working through third parties (media, advocacy groups), public relations can facilitate endorsements. PR also excels at creating word-of-mouth, which is another important brand-building tool in today's marketplace of cynical consumers.

Is public relations more important than advertising in selling products?
The classic consumer marketing model is creating awareness, then interest, and finally, commitment. With a large enough media buy (both offline and online), advertising can quickly build awareness. Public relations builds a dialogue and endorsement, which generates interest and awareness.

What are you most proud of in the work your agency has done?
I can't pick one campaign—there are too many great ones over 23 years! However, they all have a common denominator of which I am very proud: *We have no formulas.* Each campaign is based on fresh thinking grounded in solid strategy that is unique to the brand's marketing challenges. We challenge ourselves to create new and big ideas for each brand's needs.

What qualities do you look for in an employee?
I look for the passion gene—people who have a passion for their work, their clients, and MMC. I also place a premium on people who demonstrate a sense of ethics, have a team spirit, and have a sense of fun.

What employment path would you recommend to ascend to public relations management?
One, start as young as you can with internships—in media, at ad agencies, with online media and PR agencies. Nothing beats hands-on experience.

Two, start early developing the right side and the left side of the brain. Creativity is prized, and you also need to understand business.

Three, during your first five years in the public relations business, you'll get training on writing, media pitching, client management. Almost no one trains you on people management. Do whatever necessary to learn management from the day you start—find a mentor, take management classes on the outside. Learn conflict resolution, negotiation; take assertiveness training if necessary. These skills will prepare you for management and may even get you promoted earlier. And if nothing else, they are life skills as well!

Suggested Readings

Belch, George, and Michael Belch. *Advertising and Promotion, An Integrated Marketing and Communications Perspective,* 5th ed. New York: McGraw-Hill, 2000.

Cody, Steven, and Richard Harte. *What's Keeping Your Customers Up at Night?* New York: McGraw-Hill, 2003. Two consultants explain how to "feel the clients' pain and help them succeed."

Cone, Steve. *Steal These Ideas.* New York: Bloomberg Press, 2005. An experienced brand manager offers his version of the marketing concepts that are most compelling and memorable.

D'Vari, Marissa. *Building Buzz.* Franklin Lakes, NJ: Career Press, 2005. Concepts such as visualization and getting your name in the media are reviewed.

Johnson, Winslow. *Powerhouse Marketing Plans.* New York: AMACOM, 2004. This book identifies characteristics of 14 different real-life marketing plans that can result in a profitable company.

Keller, Ed, and Jon Berry. *The Influentials.* New York: Simon & Schuster, 2003. The most influential Americans—the ones who tell their neighbors what to buy, which politicians to support, and where to vacation—are not necessarily the people you'd expect, according to these authors.

Marconi, Joe. *Reputation Marketing.* New York: NTC Business Books, 2001.

Ogilvy, David. *Confessions of an Advertising Man.* New York: Macmillan, 1963. The granddaddy of advertising texts.

Rein, Irving, and Philip Kotler, *High Visibility.* New York: McGraw-Hill, 2006. What do Oprah Winfrey, Donald Trump, and Bill Gates have in common? The answer: high visibility, which the authors claim is necessary to succeed today.

Reis, Al, and Laura Ries. *The Origin of Brands.* New York: HarperBusiness, 2004. The focus here is on diverging from established categories and creating brand new brands.

Schmitt, Bernd H., David L. Rogers, and Karen Vrotsos. *There's No Business That's Not Show Business.* Upper Saddle River, NJ: Financial Times/Prentice Hall, 2003. This book shows how show business techniques can be applied to business for appealing results.

Silverman, George. *The Secrets of Word-of-Mouth Marketing.* New York: AMACOM, 2001. The author has created "WOM" campaigns for many companies and knows whereof he speaks.

Solomon, Michael R. *Conquering Consumerspace.* New York: AMACOM, 2003. The author contends that before people buy products, they want to know more about the companies from whom they are buying.

Thompson, Harvey. *Who Stole My Customer?* Upper Saddle River, NJ: Prentice Hall, 2004. The main objective here is to help firms keep old customers and attract new ones.

Notes

1. Theresa Howard, "Beat Is on for Pepsi," *USA Today,* August 28, 2002, 3B.
2. Stuart Elliott, "New Kind of Celebrity Promoter Says the Words and Has Her Say," *New York Times,* November 25, 2002, C1–11.
3. A Good Fit," *Ragan's PR Intelligence Report,* September 2002, 1–4.
4. Al Ries and Laura Ries, *The Fall of Advertising and the Rise of PR,* New York: Harper Business, 2002, 251.
5. Darren Press, "Getting Word Out Involves 3 Strategies," *Poughkeepsie Journal,* October 16, 2005.
6. Tom Harris, "Kotler's Total Marketing Embraces MPR," *MPR Update,* December 1992, 4.
7. Daniel Gross, "Ho Ho Ho Classic," *US Airways Magazine,* February 2006, 26.
8. James Bandler, "How Companies Pay TV Experts For On-Air Product Mentions," *Wall Street Journal,* April 19, 2005, A1.
9. "CNN Clamps Down on 'Stealth' Guests," *Jack O'Dwyer's Newsletter,* September 4, 2002, 3.
10. Kathy Burnham, "Trade Shows: Make Them Worth the Investment," *Tactics,* September 1999, 11.
11. Chad Terhune and Brian Steinberg, "Coca-Cola Signs NBA Wunderkind," *Wall Street Journal,* August 22, 2003, B5.
12. Richard Sandomir, "A Pitchman with Punch," *New York Times,* January 21, 2000, C1, 4.
13. "Mascots Is Lion King?" *Newsweek,* November 25, 2002, 11.
14. Lorne Manly, "On Television, Brands Go from Props to Stars," *New York Times,* October 2, 2005, B1.
15. Julie Bosman, "Advertising is Obsolete: Everyone Says So." *New York Times,* January 23, 2006, C7.
16. Stuart Elliott, "Never Mind the Best Picture Nominees," *New York Times,* January 31, 2005, C10.
17. "The Age of Nikes, Cars and Guns—Not Roses," *Barron's,* January 16, 2006, 14.
18. Julie Bosman, "First Stadiums, Now Teams Take a Corporate Identity," *New York Times,* March 22, 2006, C9.
19. Stuart Elliott, "Placing Ads in Some Surprising Spaces," *New York Times,* November 25, 2005, C2.
20. "$37,375 Payday: That's Using Your Head," MSNBC.com, January 25, 2005.
21. Al Ries and Laura Ries, *The Fall of Advertising & The Rise of PR.* New York: HarperBusiness, 2002.

18 Public Relations and the Internet

FIGURE 18-1 The podfather. Former MTV video jockey Adam Curry became a podcasting pioneer, although his broadcasting technique with soldiers in Iraq was decidedly less "high tech." (Bullit Marquez/AP Wide World Photos)

I n the 21st century, the world is wired. From Berlin to Brooklyn, Baghdad to Boise, the Internet has become the world's dominant mode of communication. In warp speed, new Internet communications vehicles are being born, and new believers are being converted. Like this man:

Adam Curry, for seven years one of the most well-known MTV video jockeys, rediscovered himself as an Internet entrepreneur in the mid-1990s upon moving to Holland. Curry became one of the first celebrities to create and administer his own Web site and then became a key player—he would argue, "the first"—in the development of podcasting, a home-brewed radio program that can be downloaded by MP3 players around the world.[1]

And podcasting was just the half of it. Blogs, wikis, RSS feeds (see p. 393), and a host of otherworldly innovations flooded Internet communications technology, bearing great impact on the world in general and the world of public relations in particular.

So it is irrefutable that the Internet has changed communications forever with its immediacy and pervasiveness. But on the other hand, the Internet hasn't replaced human relationships as the essence of societal communications. Nor has it replaced human relationships as the essence of the practice of public relations.

Although some at the turn of the 21st century predicted that the Internet would one day dominate public relations work, that has not turned out to be the case. The Internet and communicating via the

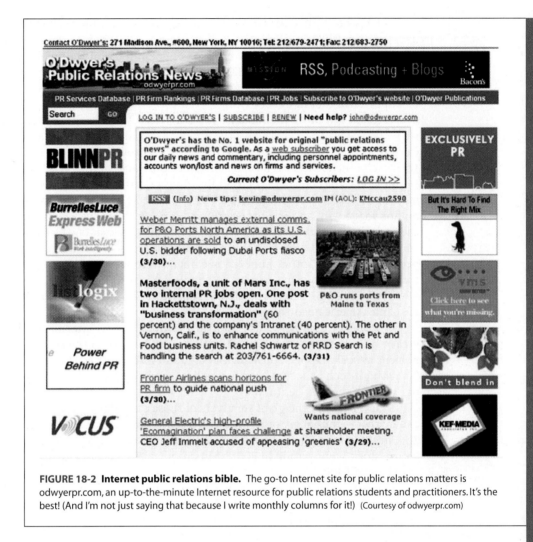

FIGURE 18-2 Internet public relations bible. The go-to Internet site for public relations matters is odwyerpr.com, an up-to-the-minute Internet resource for public relations students and practitioners. It's the best! (And I'm not just saying that because I write monthly columns for it!) (Courtesy of odwyerpr.com)

computer is but another tool in the public relations arsenal. An important tool, but a tool nonetheless (Figure 18-2).

Defining the Internet

What is the Internet? We all use it, but few of us know from whence it derived.

The Internet, technically, is a cooperatively run, globally distributed collection of computer networks that exchange information via a common set of rules. The Internet began as the ARPANET during the Cold War in 1969, developed by the Department of Defense and consultants who were interested in creating a communications network that could survive a nuclear attack.[2] It survived—even though there was, thankfully, no nuclear attack!—as a convenient way to communicate.

The World Wide Web, the most exciting and revolutionary part of the Internet, was developed in 1989 by physicist Tim Berners-Lee to enlarge the Internet for multiple uses. The Web is a collection of millions of computers on the Internet that contain information in a single format: HTML, or Hypertext Markup Language. By combining multimedia—sound, graphics, video, animation, and more—the Web has become the most powerful tool in cyberspace.

Without question, the Internet and the World Wide Web have transformed the way we work, the way we buy things, the way we entertain ourselves, the way business is conducted, and, most important to public relations professionals, the way we communicate with each other. The Internet phenomenon, pure and simple, has been a revolution.

By 2005, the Internet was used by 15 percent of the world's people, more than 972 million. Nearly 70 percent of North America used the Internet. In Asia, more than 332 million logged on, and in Europe, 285 million.[3] Perhaps even more important, by 2006, the so-called "digital divide" between haves and have nots was closing rapidly. In the United States, while the sharpest growth in Internet access and use was among young people, blacks and other minority members were rapidly merging onto the digital information highway. One survey of people 18 and older indicated that 74 percent of whites go online, 61 percent of African Americans do, and 80 percent of English-speaking Hispanic Americans do as well.[4]

In terms of commerce, the first incarnation of the Internet in the 1990s carried great—and as it turned out, unattainable—promise, with the rise and fall of such phenomena as sock puppets, push technology, and B2B (business-to-business). Most of these "great high-tech concepts" crashed and burned along with the stock market in the initial years of the 21st century.

Today, not only the giant survivors of those early days—eBay, Yahoo!, Amazon.com, among them—but many other Internet-oriented ventures have gotten their second wind and are thriving.[5] The dominator today, of course, is latter-day search engine Google, whose stock went public in 2005 at just under $90 a share and a year later was priced in excess of $400.

The new Internet explosion has taken new forms: blogs, podcasts, wiki sites, RSS feeds, social networks, and others. This time, unlike the first time around, the Internet as a communications and commercial vehicle is here to stay.

The Internet as Communications Medium

The Internet has transformed the way that people communicate and make contact with each other. Virtually all organizations, from the largest corporation to the smallest nonprofit, today has a Web site. Most of the time today, it is the Web site that serves as an organization's "first face" to the public. Public relations departments now have interactive specialists and groups responsible for communicating via the Internet. Likewise, public relations agencies boast online departments that help clients access the Internet. Although the expansive number of Internet-oriented agencies that flourished in the late 1990s has been decimated, a handful of firms still specialize in Internet-related communications.

Journalists, meanwhile—still the primary customers for most in public relations—have also embraced the Internet as their primary source for research and reporting. Most reporters today are online and prefer e-mail as their primary source of public relations correspondence. Nonetheless, personal contact with a journalist (i.e., building a relationship) is still the best way to ensure that your message will be heard.

For individual public relations practitioners then, familiarity with the Internet, mastery of it, and knowledge of its effective use have become front-line requisites of the practice.

Public Relations Internet Challenge

Use of the Internet by public relations practitioners inevitably will grow as the century proceeds, for three reasons in particular.

- **The demand to be educated rather than sold.** Today's consumers are smarter, better educated, and more media savvy. They know when they are being hustled by self-promoters and con artists. Communications programs therefore must be grounded in education-based information rather than blatant self-promotion. The Internet is perhaps the world's greatest potential repository of such information.

- **The need for real-time performance.** The wired world is moving quickly. Everything happens instantaneously and in real time. When insurgents in Iraq free an American captive held for months, her release is beamed immediately on the Internet around the world.[6] Public relations professionals can use this ability to their advantage to structure their information to respond instantly to emerging issues and market changes.

- **The need for customization.** There used to be three primary television networks. Today there are hundreds of television channels. Today's consumers expect more focused, targeted, one-on-one communications relationships. Increasingly, organizations must broadcast their thoughts to ever-narrower population segments. The Internet offers such narrowcasting to reporters, shareholders, analysts, opinion leaders, consumers, and myriad other publics.

Such is the promise of the Internet to the practice of public relations. Beyond its role as an integral component in the Internet marketing mix, public relations has become prominent in several other cyber areas:

- **E-mail.** E-mail has become the most pervasive internal communications vehicle. In companies, schools, media institutions, and homes, e-mail, delivered online and immediately, has replaced traditional print and fax technology as a rapid-delivery information vehicle.

- **Web sites.** Another rapidly expanding use of the Internet by public relations professionals is the creation and maintenance of Web sites to profile companies, promote products, or position issues. A Web site gives an individual or institution the flexibility and freedom of getting news out without having it filtered by an intermediary. There are literally millions of Web sites, all of them open for visitors. Many public relations agencies specialize in creating Web sites. Intranets, or internal Web sites, are another growing phenomenon.

- **Blogs.** Blogs, or formally Weblogs, are updated regularly by anybody with a computer and a compelling interest to offer information to the masses—in other words, made-to-order for public relations communicators.[7]

- **Online media relations.** Journalists today use the Web as a primary source of organizational information. Most journalists communicate with public relations sources via e-mail. Finally, the growth of online spin-offs of major print publications and the development of magazines on the Web—e-zines—like *Slate* and *Salon.com,* present a new, enlarged field of potential publicity play for public relations practitioners.

- **Online monitoring.** The Web's easy accessibility has also ushered in a whole new challenge to public relations professionals to monitor online media for negative comments and even threats against their organizations. The preponderance of rogue Web sites and antagonistic chat rooms that condemn organizations makes it a necessity that public relations professionals regularly monitor such Web sites, chat rooms, and discussion groups.

- **Product promotion.** The ability to reach customers and potential customers directly is another benefit created by the Web. In this area, public relations supports integrated marketing efforts on the Web.

- **Investor relations.** Speaking directly to investors and potential investors is yet another Web challenge to public relations people. The Web allows investors to check the activities of their holdings on a daily basis, enabling companies to increase their communications efforts relative to their shareholders. Investor chat rooms—or "threads"—also demand constant monitoring by public relations people to assess the latest shareholder undercurrent about the company.

- **Webcasts.** Webcasts are real-time audio or video transmissions on the Web to specific interest groups. Quarterly Webcasts have become a staple of public company management, used to explain earnings results to analysts and shareholders.

In a general sense, what television and cable television were to the advertising industry, the Internet is to public relations. Organizations, like never before, can "go direct" to build reputations with the public, investors, consumers, and the media. Using the Internet, organizations face no interruption of their message by some third-party filter, such as the press.

Directly delivering messages to key constituent publics is the true challenge and opportunity of the Internet to public relations.

E-Mail: The Dominator

E-mail has become far and away the most pervasive organizational communications vehicle. In most organizations, e-mail is the internal medium of choice for newsletters, bulletins, and internal announcements.

Although many managers are reluctant to confront employees face to face, e-mail tends to produce more honest and immediate feedback than traditionally had been the case. Because e-mail is quick and almost effortless, a manager can deliver praise or concern without leaving the office. Thus, e-mail has, by and large, improved organizational communications. That is not to say that face-to-face communication isn't always best. It is. But the ease and effectiveness of e-mail make it a viable alternative.

E-mail has also unseated the traditional employee print newsletter. Online newsletters are both more immediate and more interactive than print counterparts. Employees can "feed back" to what they've read or heard instantaneously. The organization, in turn, can apprise itself quickly of relevant employee attitudes and opinions. Such online vehicles also lend an element of timeliness that print magazines and newspapers often have a hard time offering.

E-mail newsletters for external use—to customers, investors, or the media—are equally popular and valuable. These differ from their print brethren in several important areas:

1. **No more than one page.** People won't read lengthy newsletters on the computer, so e-mail newsletter writers must write short.

2. **Link content.** Copy should be peppered with links to other material, such as teasers to full-length articles and product offers.

3. **Regular dissemination.** It is also important to send e-mail newsletters at regular intervals so that recipients expect them.

E-mail newsletters and notices can be used to sell products and services. Advertising giant J. Walter Thompson marketed the Ford Taurus automobile with a comprehensive e-mail campaign, including online brochures, fliers, and chat room for prearranged cyber-conferences. The chat room was set up much as a call-in radio show, with designers answering consumer questions about the new car.

Developing a Winning Web Site

In many ways, the organization's Web site is its most important interface with the public. Today, journalists and others turn to the Web site first for an introduction to the organization (Figure 18-3).

FIGURE 18-3 First face. More often than not in these days of Internet dominance, a Web site is the initial introduction to an organization. (Courtesy of Rivkin & Associates)

The aim of any Web site is to provide information that visitors are looking for. The more you achieve that objective, the more "sticky" your site becomes. Stickiness is often measured by the amount of time visitors spend at a site and how many pages they view. For example, if visitors spend 10 minutes at the Web site and view five or more pages, you've achieved stickiness.[8]

How should you create a winning Web site? By first asking and answering several strategic questions.

1. **What is our goal?** To extend the business? Sell more products? Make more money? Win support for our position? Turn around public opinion? Introduce our company? Without the answers to these fundamental questions, the what and how of a Web site are inconsequential. Just as in any other pursuit in public relations, the overriding goal must be established first.

2. **What content will we include?** The reason some Web sites are tedious and boring—and they are!—is because little forethought has gone into determining the content of a site. Simply cramming chronological news releases onto a Web site won't advance an organization's standing with its publics. Rather, content must be carefully considered, in substance and organization, before proceeding with a site.

3. **How often will we edit?** Often the answer to this question is, Not often enough. Stale news and the lack of updating are common Web site problems. Sites must regularly be updated. Another problem is overwriting. People seem to feel that because the Web is "free," they can write endlessly. Of course, they can. But no one will read it. So an editorial process to cull information down to its most essential parts is a necessity for a good Web site.

4. **How will we enhance design?** Like it or not, the style of the site is most important. If an organization's home page isn't attractive, it won't get many hits. Good design makes complicated things understandable, and this is essential in a Web site. The Web is a largely visual medium, so great care should be taken to professionally design a site.

5. **How interactive will it be?** Traditional communication is unidirectional, one way. You read or view it, and that's where the process stops. The great attraction of the Web, on the other hand, is that it can be bidirectional. Communication can be translated into an interactive vehicle, a game, an application, or an e-mail chat vehicle. This is what distinguishes good sites from mediocre ones.

6. **How will we track use?** As in any other communications project, the use of a Web site must be measured. The most basic form of cyberspace measurement is the rough yardstick of hits to the site. But like measuring press clippings, this doesn't tell you whether your information is being appreciated, acted on, or even read. Measuring site performance, therefore, should be a multifaceted exercise that includes such analysis as volume during specific times of day, kind of access, specific locations on the site to which visitors are clicking first, and the sequencing through the site that visitors are following.

7. **Who will be responsible?** Managing a Web site, if it is done correctly, must be someone's full-time job. Companies may subordinate the responsibility to someone—occasionally in the public relations department—who has many other "more important" responsibilities. Wrong. Or, as noted, the function may be a shared one. Also, wrong.

    Much better is to treat the Web site as a first line of communication to the public, which requires full-time attention.[9]

Blogs: The Latest Phenomenon

They're everywhere. They're everywhere. Blogs, that is.

Blogs, Weblogs that communicate personal views on any topic imaginable, are proliferating at the rate of 70,000 a day. Follow me? I said 70,000 *a day!*

There's nothing like 'em on the Internet. Every day, 700,000 to 1.3 million blog entries are posted, encouraging others to engage in unfiltered communications across cyberspace.[10]

As a consequence, blogs are starting to feel their oats, in terms of communications power (Figure 18-4).

In 2004, CBS newscaster Dan Rather was brought down by the blogosphere when it was revealed that the sources the network used for an exposé on President George W. Bush were bogus. The allegations spread across the Internet, and CBS and Rather both ultimately caved. That same year, Ana Marie Cox, the Internet blogger Wonkette, who focused on Washington gossip, signed a $300,000 contract for a novel based on her blog.[11] In 2003, venture capitalists invested $8 million in blog development. A year later, the figure had jumped 400 percent.[12]

There are two categories of blogs. One is the traditional Weblog in which a Web surfer shares his online discoveries. The second is the Web diary in which a person shares his or her thoughts of the day. Often, blogs of one style have elements of the other. A diarist might discuss a link, while traditional Webloggers commonly ramble on about something that happened to them that day.

In terms of public relations use of blogs, organizations can use them to deliver information—product uses, sales data, consumer tips, and so on—in a more personal way. Organization blogs, like direct mail, might also serve to interest potential customers in a firm's blogged expertise. Readership can be expanded through registering on the growing number of blog search engines.

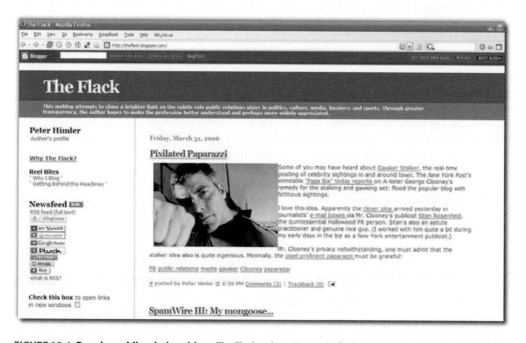

FIGURE 18-4   Premier public relations blog.   The Flack, at http://www.theflack.blogspot.com/, the brainchild of public relations impresario Peter Himler, provides a running commentary on all matters of pertinence to the field. (Courtesy of The Flack)

Public relations people should also monitor any blogs in a company or industry sense that are deemed influential. Often these are negative blogs. In the case of Wal-Mart, for example, public relations professionals need to regularly monitor anti-company blogs, such as alwayslowprices.net and laborblog, to find out the latest hot issues among the company's critics.

Blogs also can be useful as an internal communications vehicle. Among possibilities for internal blogs are the following:

- **Projects:** Project leaders can maintain blogs to announce project status and developments.

- **Departments:** Departments can maintain blogs to inform the rest of the organization about offerings and achievements.

- **Brainstorming:** Employees in a department or on a team can brainstorm about strategy, process, and ideas on their own blog.

- **Customers:** Employees can share with others internally the substance of customer visits or phone calls.

Predictably, another outgrowth of the spread of blogs is the existence of spam blogs, or just plain "splogs," or phony blogs designed to promote everything from gambling Web sites to pornography. By some estimates, as many as 8 percent of blogs created daily are fake. A typical splog contains gibberish and is full of links to other Web sites it is trying to promote. Because search engines, like Google and Yahoo!, base their rankings on how many other Web sites link to a particular site, the splogs can help artificially inflate a site's popularity.[13]

Although only in their infancy, there is no question that blogs are being woven into the culture and fabric of public relations as a method of building consumer loyalty, as a target of pitches, and even as a sardonic watchdog for the public relations industry. With companies from Microsoft to General Electric to Cingular Wireless adopting blogs to promote products and services, the use of blogs as a communications vehicle will only increase.[14]

Dealing with the Media Online

In the 21st century, the Internet has become the favored tool of reporters for discovering organizational information.[15] When asked how they prefer to work with organizations in news gathering, journalists reported the following:

- E-mail, 61 percent
- Telephone, 51 percent
- In person, 23 percent
- Fax, 4 percent

Research also indicates that journalists now overwhelmingly rank corporate Web sites as their most important source of financial information, so reaching reporters online has become a front-line responsibility for public relations professionals.

The downside of the new technology is reminiscent of the downside of media relations generally. Specifically, many reporters complain that their e-mail has become as crowded as their voice mail, which became as crowded as the little pink telephone reminder slips on their desks.

Speaking of Ethics

Wal-Mart Unleashes the Bloggers

As the world's largest retailer, Wal-Mart gets blamed for a lot of things, and it has had to fight back with a more aggressive public relations program (see Case Study, Chapter 3).

In the spring of 2006, Wal-Mart was implicated in a blog scandal for which it bore no guilt whatsoever. The story emerged when the *New York Times* revealed that bloggers were increasingly defending Wal-Mart against vocal critics. The *Times* pointed out one pro-Wal-Mart blog comment that, it said, "the giant retailer might write itself. And, in fact, it did."

The blogger received his information—and the wording—directly from the company's public relations agency, which suggested topics for posting and verbiage that might be used.

Wal-Mart acknowledged to the *Times* that it was, indeed, the source of the information and that it and its agency were forthright with bloggers about their identity and point of view. It also said it didn't compensate bloggers for shouldering its messages.

In its messages to bloggers, Wal-Mart promoted both positive news about itself, such as the high number of job applications it received, and negative news about competitors, such as highlighting rival Target's decision to ban Salvation Army red-kettle collectors from its stores.

While Wal-Mart may have been up front about its blogging information, the performance of the bloggers themselves came under ethical attack from others in the blogosphere. Said one objecting blogger, "If I reprint something, I say where it came from. A blog is about your voice, it seems to me, not somebody else's."

For its part, Wal-Mart was eager to develop ties to bloggers, inviting them to a media conference at its Arkansas headquarters, and was unapologetic about its reaching out to the blogosphere.

Said Wal-Mart Communications Director Mona Williams (see Voice of Authority, Chapter 3), "As more and more Americans go to the Internet to get information from varied, credible, trusted sources, Wal-Mart is committed to participating in that online conversation."

For more information, see Michael Barbaro, "Wal-Mart Enlists Bloggers in P.R. Campaign," *The New York Times*, March 7, 2006.

The basics of online media relations include the following:

- **Web site newsroom.** The best organizations create extranets, devoted exclusively to serving the media, as derivatives of their Web sites. These corporate newsrooms include all the traditional press materials that the media require.

- **News releases:** Every Web site begins with news releases, most often organized chronologically. However, journalists complain that they don't know precisely when an organization raised its prices or announced its earnings or promoted its president. Therefore, the best Web newsrooms organize releases both chronologically and by subject, with a search engine capable of pointing readers toward specific subjects.

- **Executive speeches:** All major speeches delivered by management should be included at the corporate newsroom site. The best sites offer an interactive speech feature through which speeches are automatically e-mailed to journalists or others who request them.

- **Annual/quarterly reports:** Every public company is obligated to report earnings to shareholders four times a year and typically issue three quarterly reports and one annual report. Quarterlies and annuals should appear on the corporate newsroom site.

- **Annual meetings:** Companies in remote locations, in particular, have begun to Webcast their annual gathering of shareholders so that those unable to attend in person may do so electronically.

- **FAQs:** The most frequently asked questions posed by reporters ought to be part of the newsroom site. Also, FAQs ought to contain the most basic corporate information, from number of offices and employees to headquarters location and stock symbol.

- **Interviews:** Online press conferences and Webcasts have also become standard fare, with a company notifying journalists of the time and password necessary to access a particular executive presiding as an online interviewee.

- **Digital press kits:** All the material included in a corporate press kit—releases, photos, backgrounders—are duplicated on the Internet for downloading purposes to journalists.

- **Photographs, profiles, ad copy, and so on:** Online executive photographs and other relevant photographs are standard at corporate newsroom sites. So, too, are executive biographical profiles. Corporate newsrooms might even offer video versions of corporate advertising. Finally, reporters appreciate ease of access to locate the pressroom and its elements, after-hours contact numbers clearly listed, and downloadable logos for ready use.[16]

- **News release via newswires.** It has become essential for public companies to issue news releases over newswires. Why? Newswire copy gets picked up by online databases, such as AOL and Yahoo! If a company wants its shareholders and potential investors to know of its activities, in order to notify them online, its releases must be included on newswires. Newswires are of three types:

  1. *General wires:* The Associated Press (AP) is the granddaddy of all general wire services, reporting on general news of interest to the broad society. United Press International (UPI), which used to compete directly with AP, has fallen into financial ill health in recent years and has diminished as a news factor.

  2. *Financial wires:* Dow Jones, the wire service of *The Wall Street Journal,* the nation's business newspaper, is perhaps the most well-known financial wire. Reuters is known as the international financial wire. Bloomberg, the creation of a former Wall Street broker turned New York City mayor, has emerged as another powerful financial wire service force in both print and broadcast.

  3. *Paid wires:* As opposed to general and financial wires, other wire services—the most prominent being PR Newswire, Business Wire, and Market Wire—are paid services that reproduce organizational news announcements verbatim, for a fee.

  All of these wire services report online, which means that releases are automatically filed on online stock databases. This allows online users to track specific company announcements and is one reason why most publicly held companies today release via wire.

- **Online publicity.** During the high-tech bubble of the 1990s, the proliferation of online versions of major periodicals, from *The New York Times* to *Business Week* to *U.S. News & World Report,* opened new publicity channels to public relations professionals. The puncturing of the bubble at the start of this century doused the ardor of media companies to invest in their online properties. Indeed some of the most venerable publications of the Internet era—from *The Industry Standard* to *Mutual Funds* magazine to *Upside* to *Forbes ASAP*—have all bitten the dust.

  Nonetheless, online publications—e-zines—such as *Salon* and *Slate,* and online special-interest sites, such as oxygen.com and ivillage.com designed for women, mentor for African Americans, senior net for senior citizens, and so on, offer opportunities for publicity. Financial news services, such as fool.com, TheStreet.com, and CBSMarketWatch.com, are also ready outlets for online publicity.

Monitor the Internet ... or Else!

Whether an organization uses the Internet for publicity, uses e-mail extensively, or even has a Web site, the one necessity for any organization today is to monitor the Internet. In the 21st century, monitoring the Internet is another front-line public relations responsibility. The World Wide Web is riddled with unhappy consumers spilling their guts, disgruntled stockholders badmouthing management in chat rooms, and rogue Web sites condemning this or that organization.

Face it. The Internet is free, wide open, international, and anonymous—the perfect place to start a movement and ruin an organization's reputation. And so it is imperative that public relations people monitor the Internet in consideration of the following.

- *Discussion groups* and *chat rooms* are hotbeds for discontented shareholders, unscrupulous stock manipulators, and disgruntled consumers. Any local or service provider message board that solicits public input about an organization is ripe for messaging contrary to the official position.[17] The Yahoo! finance boards, for example, are the source of continuing commentary about public companies from anonymous commentators, all using mysterious pseudonyms. One will start with a cryptic message. Then another will add to it. And a third will chime in. This continuous commentary—called "the thread" on Wall Street—is the bane of many a company. The thread has become such a source of corporate discontent that monitoring firms have emerged to keep track of what is being said about companies in chat rooms and even lead "whisper campaigns" to incorporate positive information.

  Small companies, in particular, must be constantly vigilant of what is being said about them in online forums. That also means monitoring newsgroups, which can act as rumor mills. Monitoring such groups can serve as public relations "radar" to help an organization anticipate problems.

- *Rogue Web sites* must also be monitored by the organizations they attack. Rogue Web sites seek to confront an organization by:

  - Presenting negative information
  - Satirizing policy and management
  - Soliciting employees, current and former, to vent publicly
  - Serving as a gateway for complaints to regulators and media
  - Confusing the public regarding which Web site represents the real organization[18]

  For instance:

  www.untied.com targets United Airlines

  www.walmartsucks.com targets Wal-Mart (Figure 18-5)

  www.mcspotlight.org targets McDonald's

  A corporation's knee-jerk reaction—to call in the lawyers—hasn't resulted in great victory in battling the rogues. In perhaps the most celebrated case, Kmart sued www.kmartsucks.com, a Web site hosted by a disgruntled employee.

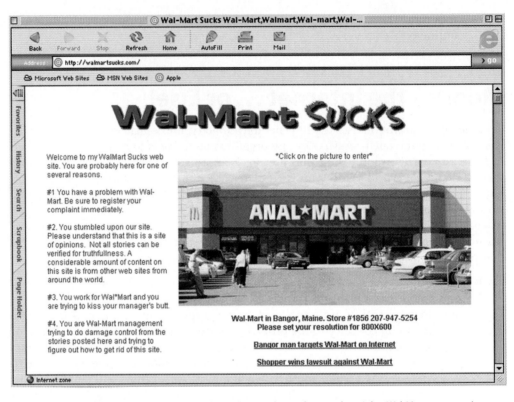

FIGURE 18-5 Wal-Mart sucks. This rogue Web site, designed to embarrass the mighty Wal-Mart company, is typical of anti-corporate sites on the Internet, all of which must be monitored.

The copyright infringement suit did succeed in forcing the site to change its name—to www.martsucks.com—but the considerable national media attention the suit received helped put the rogue Web site on the map. Eventually, the embattled Kmart launched its own "good news only" site, called Kmartforever.com to combat the bashers.[19]

Many organizations are now registering multiple URLs (domain names) to preclude access to them by others. Typically, what they register to preempt the troublemakers are names like:

www.organizationsucks.com

www.ihateorganization.com

www.organisation.com (narrow spelling change)

No technique is foolproof in the battle against rogue sites. The best response, therefore, is to keep such sites under close scrutiny as a regular public relations monitoring function (Figure 18-6).

■ *Urban legends* are yet another requisite for online monitoring. There is a growing body of corporate horror stories from bogus Internet rumors that have taken on legendary proportions. Most are spread by e-mail at lightning speed across the country and the world. For example:

• Upscale retailer Neiman Marcus was accused by an anonymous e-mailer of charging a $200 fee for its special cookie recipe. "Outrageous," cried the thousands who received the e-mail. Also completely untrue. Neiman Marcus doesn't have a cookie recipe.

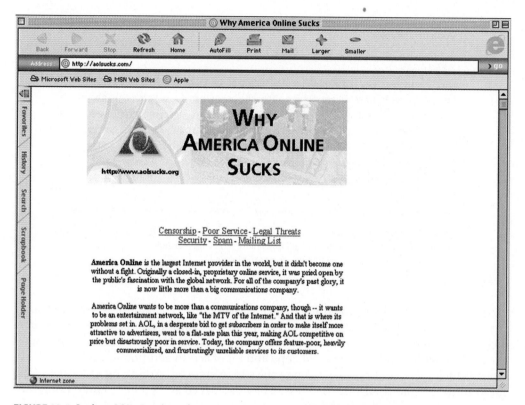

FIGURE 18-6 So does AOL. Freedom of speech is what the World Wide Web is all about, and that's why rogue Web sites such as this one are regularly monitored.

- Mrs. Fields also outraged the populace when an e-mail dispatch reported that she had sent a batch of her famous cookies to O. J. Simpson after he won his infamous murder trial. Also totally false.

- In perhaps the most pervasive and pernicious urban legend of all, retailer Tommy Hilfiger was, according to the official-sounding e-mail, evicted from *The Oprah Winfrey Show* by the lady herself when the clothes manufacturer admitted his garments weren't made for "African Americans, Hispanics, and Asians" (Figure 18-7). The reality was that Tommy Hilfiger never met Oprah Winfrey, was never on her show, and certainly didn't design his clothing solely for white people.

The lesson: Public relations professionals must constantly monitor the Web.

Product Promotion on the Internet

The Internet provides a virtual laboratory to mesh public relations, advertising, and marketing techniques to promote products. The shift from a "bricks" to a "clicks" economy was launched in full force during the nation's high-tech bubble economy of the last years of the 20th century.

On the positive side, buyers and potential buyers can access your information directly, without interference. On the negative side, you are competing with hundreds of thousands of other information providers for a visitor's attention. So promotional messages must be evocative, eye-catching, and brief.

Subject: Tommy Hilfiger

MESSAGE:

I'm sure many of you watched the recent taping of the Oprah Winfrey Show where her guest was Tommy Hilfiger. On the show she asked him if the statements about race he was accused of saying were true. Statements like if he'd known African-Americans, Hispanics and Asians would buy his clothes he would not have made them so nice. He wished these people would *not* buy his clothes, as they are made for upper class white people. His answer to Oprah was a simple "yes". Where after she immediately asked him to leave her show.

FIGURE 18-7 Stuff of legends. Urban legends like this e-mail, discussing a bogus appearance by Tommy Hilfiger on *The Oprah Winfrey Show*, have become increasingly frequent as more people, some with questionable motives, access the Internet.

One popular product promotion device is the *adlink*. The adlink is a small display advertisement that promotes another site or page. The adlink may be less than a square inch or may stretch across the screen in a rectangular block. Usually, the adlink promotes another site with a tantalizing line of copy and bit of art. In addition, the adlink will automatically hyperlink, or connect you to the site referenced. Adlink hits are easily measured to determine their effectiveness. They can serve as excellent entry points for production promotional messages.

Online discussion groups provide another potential source of product promotion. As noted, the Internet is flooded with newsgroups. Smart organizations research newsgroups to see if their company's name, product's name, or specialty area is being mentioned. If it is, they respond by e-mailing participants with product information, thus increasing awareness and, hopefully, sales.

Web-based integrated marketing can create a new relationship with customers. Not only do good sites sell products but they also offer information and education about those products. This is where public relations can play a great role.

Investor Relations on the Internet

The Internet also plays a significant role in investor relations, the public relations activity that deals with a company's stockholders and the communities—brokers and analysts—serving them.

Public companies increasingly use the Internet as a more controlled communications mechanism to reach potential investors. For the small investor, who has seen the flow of corporate information increasingly directed toward analysts, brokers, or larger institutions, the Internet is an informational blessing. Investors can keep track of their investments and the markets in real time, without depending on intermediaries to inform them.

The government that watches over securities markets is less convinced that the Internet is such a blessing for investors. Securities regulators worry about the anonymous nature of online information. Despite such concerns, with the Internet now the number-one source of information for investors, the Web has opened up enormous new avenues of investor contact for public relations people.

Accordingly, companies have invested more heavily in the investor relations Internet space. Annual reports, earnings releases, and formal regulatory filings (called Edgar filings) all are included on corporate Web sites. Although the printed document remains the most prominent communications vehicle for most companies, online financial reporting, such as annual reports, is becoming more important for several reasons:

- Electronic versions are more easily integrated with other communications. Analysts can pull out financial data and spreadsheets in electronic reports, which don't depend on stapled pages. The electronic medium can reshape and update the report at the touch of a key, making analysis and study much easier.

- Electronic reports are less static than print reports. Electronic reports can help companies "come to life" before a stockholder or prospect. Graphics can be enhanced and sound and motion added. Not only might this provide a clearer portrait of a company but it also might help "sell" it to the viewer.

- Electronic versions last longer. No longer are investors forced to keep dog-eared copies of printed reports in their files. Access to last year's report can be attained through the push of a button. Inevitably, in the 21st century, printed annual reports will be subordinated to electronic versions.

In its purest form, using the Internet for investor relations can assure all stockholders, and not just large ones, an equal opportunity for access to corporate news and information.

Of Intranets/Extranets, Wikis, Podcasts, and RSS Feeds

Any discussion of communications vehicles available on the Internet is, by definition, obsolete as soon as it hits the page. Nonetheless, public relations practitioners should at least be conversant in the following Internet vehicles:

- *Intranets* are a pervasive internal communications phenomenon among U.S. companies. Generally defined, an intranet is an internal vehicle that integrates communication with workflow, process management, infrastructure, and all other aspects of completing a job. Intranets allow communicators, management, and employees to exchange information quickly and effectively, much more quickly and effectively than any similar vehicle. Intranets, in other words, are Internets for specific organizations, designed to provide the necessary proprietary information to improve productivity.

- *Extranets,* on the other hand, allow a company to use the Internet to communicate information to finely segmented external groups, such as the media, investors, vendors, key customers, Hispanic rap artists, left-handed female *Good Morning America* producers, or upper East Side apartment-dwelling soccer players, for example. In segmenting the information in such a focused fashion—and protecting its dissemination through a complex series of firewalls—the targeted audience is assured that the data will remain confidential. Only approved individuals can access the information by using an assigned ID and password, restricted to extranet users exclusively.

- *Wikis,* which derive from the Hawaiian word for "quick," are collaborative Web sites that combine the work of many authors. Similar to a blog in structure and logic, a wiki allows anyone to edit, delete, or modify content that has been placed on the Web site, including the work of previous authors. In contrast, a blog, typically authored by an individual, does not allow visitors to change the original posted material but only to add comments to the original content. The most prominent wiki derivative is Wikipedia, the free encyclopedia on the Web, to which anyone can contribute—occasionally at a person's peril (see Talking Points).

■ *Podcasting,* which gained its name and fame after Apple's iPod burst onto the scene in 2001, refers to the act of making audio programs available for download to any MP3 player (although Apple still controls about 80 percent of the market). Listeners already have an enormous selection of podcasts from which to choose—from amateur deejays hosting alternative radio programs to authors recording their own audio books to corporate public relations professionals promoting products. The "pod revolution" will be limited only by the supply of and demand for content.[20]

■ *RSS,* which literally stands for *real simple syndication,* is an easy way to distribute content on the Internet, similar to a newsgroup. RSS feeds are widely used by the blog community, for example, to share headlines or full text. Major news organizations, including Reuters, CNN, PR Newswire, and the BBC, use RSS feeds to allow other sites to incorporate their "syndicated" news services. Companies also have begun to use RSS for delivery of news, replacing e-mail and threatening the continued existence of that time-honored but rapidly obsolescent staple of the last century, the fax.

The important thing for public relations people is to stay aware of the changing nature of Internet communications vehicles. The Internet menu changes at lightning speed, and it's the responsibility of the communications professional to change right along with it.

Talking Points

Confronting a Sticky Wiki

The advent of Wikipedia is a godsend to those seeking quick information on the Internet. But allowing anonymous users to edit material can also lead to problems. Just ask John Siegenthaler, former editor of *USA Today.*

Siegenthaler was the subject of a prankster in 2005, who "contributed" to his Wikipedia biography by linking the editor with the assassinations of President John F. Kennedy and Senator Robert F. Kennedy.

The prankster was eventually found and issued an apology. But the damage was done.

■ Wikipedia was declared "off limits" to reporters by editors at the *New York Times.*

■ A sensitive group of lawyers organized a class action suit, available to those "who believe that they have been defamed or who have been the subject of anonymous and malicious postings to the popular online encyclopedia Wikipedia."

■ And Wikipedia's founder vowed he would make changes to the system.

Sure enough, just weeks after the Siegenthaler incident, Wikipedia announced a new policy, which included barring unregistered users from creating new pages.

Katherine Q. Seelye, "A Little Sleuthing Unmasks Writer of Wikipedia Prank," *New York Times,* December 11, 2005.

Last Word

The Internet has now been around for two decades. In that short time, it has evolved into an indispensable marketing tool for organizations and a favored weapon for angry customers, disaffected employees, and consumer activists bent on attacking those same organizations.[21] As a consequence, mastering and monitoring the Internet have become a front-burner priority for public relations professionals.

As the number of the world's citizens who use the Internet expands exponentially, it is urgent that public relations professionals understand the new technology and its capabilities and increase their competence in employing and monitoring it. Those who can blend the traditional skills of writing and media and communications knowledge with the online skills of the Internet will find a rewarding calling in the practice of public relations in the 21st century.

Discussion Starters

1. What is the status of the Internet and World Wide Web in public relations today?
2. How has the Internet impacted journalism? Commerce? Internal communications?
3. How has e-mail changed the ways people and organizations communicate?
4. What are the characteristics that make up a winning Web site?
5. How has the Internet influenced preferences of the media?
6. What elements might be included in a corporate newsroom site?
7. What is the impact of the *thread* on public companies?
8. What is a *blog?* A *wiki?* An *RSS feed?*
9. Why should public relations people monitor the Web?
10. What is the difference between an intranet and an extranet?

Top of the Shelf

Buzz Marketing with Blogs for Dummies

Susannah Gardner, Hoboken, NJ: John Wiley & Sons, 2005.

This is *the* blog book. Everything you could ever wish to know about blogs, from getting started with a blog to choosing proper software to providing content and structure, is all explained by an instructor in online journalism. Blog etiquette and culture are explored, as is positioning your blog to break through the clutter. Why, the author even discusses making money with your blog.

As with the other books in this series, this "dummy" book is written in plain English, with concepts explained quickly and straightforwardly.

CASE STUDY

Wassup at the Wassup Chat Room?

"Hip-hop geniuses."

That's what most people labeled the young founders of Wassup Jeans!, the nation's fastest-growing manufacturer of casual clothing.

Founded by young college graduates Serge "the Surger" Cornblatt and Hassan "Sheik" Jabuti, the idea for Wassup Jeans! was hatched in a West Islip, Long Island, garage. Friends since junior high school, Cornblatt and Jabuti envisioned a company built on being hip and edgy, in the Nike mold.

The two partners made an unlikely pair. Cornblatt, the son of a wealthy Long Island investment banker, and Jabuti, the son of Lebanese immigrants who ran a vegetable market, had big plans for their enterprise.

Using the contacts of Cornblatt's father, the pair raised start-up capital of $5 million and opened a retail store in Manhattan's hip Soho district. By importing inexpensive garments from India and Bangladesh, Cornblatt and Jabuti kept their costs down. Meanwhile, the sword and dagger Wassup Jeans! logo was advertised on billboards and busses all over town.

Within three years, Wassup Jeans! was the hottest, hippest company around.

1. New York celebrities, from Jay-Z to Robert DeNiro to David Letterman to P. Diddy Combs, were all spotted in Wassup Jeans!.
2. Jennifer Lopez—JLo—sported Wassup Jeans! in her new movie, costarring her latest love interest, Rob Schneider.
3. "Sheik" Jabuti was frequently mentioned in gossip columns as a denizen of all the hottest night spots.
4. The two founders were splashed on the front pages of leading business magazines, and the fame of the two "hip moguls" spread far and wide.

As a result of all this positive buzz, the company's initial public offering was oversubscribed, and Wassup Jeans! became a thriving public company with thousands of shareholders and two very wealthy cofounders.

Trouble in Chatville

Upon becoming a public company, the scrutiny of Wassup Jeans! increased, particularly as consumers cut back spending and casual clothes companies began to do less well financially.

Not only did financial analysts and reporters begin to focus more closely on the company, but also greater numbers of nervous stockholders participated in online chats about the firm, its founders, and its fortunes in round-the-clock dialogue.

Although no one at Wassup Jeans! paid much attention to the chat rooms, the company began to receive some disturbing calls that rumors about it had begun to percolate online.

One morning Co-CEO Cornblatt paid a visit to the Yahoo! business chat room to gaze at the discussion surrounding Wassup Jeans!

stock. He punched up the company's stock symbol, WSP, and his jaw dropped as he read the thread.

From: Dissedman
Message-id: <20021216180717.26394. @gonzo1.aol.com>
I first bought WSP two years ago. The company is a dog, and the founders are crooks. Two spoiled brats, who've squandered their rich fathers' money. I think they're crooks.

From: Tomtomakout
Message-id: <20021214215913.12567. @mbs.aol.com>
YOU'RE RIGHT. I WOULDN'T BUY THIS WITH YOUR SISTER'S DOWRY AND A HALF DEAD MULE. CORNBLATT IS A CROOK.

From: GALPAL7348
Message-id: <20021212164502.01901.00003412@B08.aol.com>
Tom,
The real "crook" is Jabuti. His family has ties to Osama bin Laden and Al Queda. His parents hail from Riyadh. His father is still there, I believe as a biological chemist. If you catch my drift.

From: AdGitOrangeman
Message-id: <20021130090617. @mbs-rdcey.aol.com>
I knew it. Jabuti traveled to Kenya, supposedly on "safari," just two years before the embassy bombings there. I had a feeling he and Cornblatt were shady characters. (Didn't Cornblatt hang around with the Goo Goo Dolls?!) I'm not buying those stinking jeans.

From: carlabonhoff
Message-id: <200211271223453142. @mb-meroeol.com>
Even worse, they employ 11-year-old girls in sweatshops in Bangladesh to make their jeans, which they then sell here for 100 times the cost! They are sweatshop landords!

From: GeeterMon3
Message-id: <20021127122142. @mb-meieaol.com>
Boycott the jeans. Sell the stock. These guys are terrorist sympathizers. They're anti-American and should be investigated.

From: Schrambam
Message-id: <20021120225328. @mbs-m333333347.aol.com>
FBI is all over these guys. 60 Minutes on CBS is doing an exposé on them. Company should be closed down within the year. They're fronts for Osama. Jabuti is a known Queda sympathizer, and Cornblatt is his money man. They'll be out of business soon, and if you hold the stock . . .

From: Gezundheit8
Message-id:<20021129222057.00017924@df.aol.com>
. . . GOOD LUCK!

What Now?

Cornblatt was stunned.

The steady thread of accusations and innuendo was false.

1. "Sheik" Jabuti was American born. His parents came from Long Island, not Saudi Arabia.
2. Jabuti's father was a shop owner, not a chemist. He despised Osama bin Laden and al-Qaeda as much as anyone else. And, certainly, the family had no sympathy for the terrorists.
3. The company didn't employ sweatshop laborers. True, the clothes were made overseas, but by licensed, moderately paid employees.
4. He was unaware that *60 Minutes* or any other television program was doing an exposé on the company.
5. Finally, Cornblatt himself was no crook. He and his partner had earned their money legitimately, through sweat equity. And he'd never even met the Goo Goo Dolls!

"We've got a real problem here," Cornblatt sadly explained to his partner. "If this spreads, it could kill Wassup Jeans!"

"What now?"

Questions

1. What's the first action the firm's founders should take in response to these online rumors?
2. How should they handle the discussion on the thread? Should they enter the online chat room? If your answer is yes, should they do it anonymously or by name?
3. How should they handle the rumors of sweatshop labor?
4. How should they handle the rumors about a *60 Minutes* inquiry?
5. In general, what kind of public relations program would you recommend the company initiate?

Voice of Authority

An Interview with Shel Holtz

Shel Holtz, is president of Holtz Communication + Technology and one of the preeminent public relations authorities on all matters Internet. He helps organizations apply online communication capabilities to their strategic organizational communications. Clients have included Sears, Bank of America, Aetna, Hewitt

Associates, Allstate Insurance Company, Suncor, Motorola, Barclays Global Investors, Alcan, Scholastic, Novo Nordisk (Denmark and Greece), eBay, the World Bank, IBM Global Services, the International Monetary Fund, Borealis (Denmark) Motorola SPS, and PeopleSoft.

What is the role of the Internet in public relations today?
The Internet is a full-fledged medium, just like television or newspapers. In some ways, that elevates the Internet to the same level of importance as other media. In other ways, it's more important. PR practitioners need to understand the transition of the World Wide Web from a collection of static, isolated Web sites to a computing platform that delivers functionality, much of which will replace traditional desktop applications. The Web is a critical channel for delivering your messages, the audience controls those messages, and you'll be using the Web increasingly as a platform for developing and managing your communication efforts instead of software that resides on your computer.

What is the best way for a company to use the Internet in its communications?
That depends on the company, its goals, its agenda, and its messages. The Internet is a remarkably powerful tool, but in the end, it's still just that: a tool. Tools are identified at the end of the communication planning process, after goals, strategies, and objectives are put in place. The best way for one company to use the Internet may be to establish a corporate blog; another may need to improve its online

technical support; still another may need to begin a serious monitoring effort.

How accomplished are organizations in using the Internet for public relations purposes?

Sadly, not very. There are, of course, exceptions, along with examples of brilliant PR uses of the Net. But most organizations still are delivering content over the Net—and often not doing *that* well—while ignoring the massive shift toward what is known as "Web 2.0," which is defined, in part, as "a social phenomenon referring to an approach to creating and distributing Web content itself, characterized by open communication, decentralization of authority, freedom to share and reuse, and 'the market as a conversation.' "

How can organizations benefit from blogs?

Organizations can benefit from blogs in a variety of ways, again depending on the communication issues the organization faces and the goals it is trying to achieve. At the most fundamental level, blogs allow an organization to engage directly with customers and other audiences in an authentic, human conversation. That is, a blog can humanize an organization and address an increasing demand from customers that the company deal with them directly instead of using traditional corporate speak.

How does writing for e-mail differ from writing for print?

People choose what they're going to read in print from a limited set of options (e.g., headlines in a newspaper). E-mail inboxes, on the other hand, are flooded. People scan their e-mail subject lines far more than they scan print material, and they scan the contents far more than they scan print documents. In general, e-mail needs to have exceptional subject lines that convey the gist of the message contents and get right to the point. The shorter the better.

Should companies become involved in chat rooms that disparage them?

Let's change "chat rooms" to "communities," since chat rooms aren't too relevant any longer. ("Chat" refers to live, real-time online exchanges; most of the conversation these days is taking place on blogs, wikis, and traditional message boards, along with e-mail and e-mail mailing lists, all of which are asynchronous in nature.)

In general, the answer will depend on the nature of the disparagement. Each case should be assessed. But when an organization determines that a complaint or attack is genuine and threatens its reputation, then yes, the organization should consider engagement in that community.

What lies on the horizon for public relations use of the Internet?

More of the same. The tools will continue to evolve and new ones will be introduced, but they will all center around social communication. The PR agencies that succeed will be those that understand this evolution and learn how to tap into it in order to wield influence through conversation rather than traditional linear delivery of messages.

Suggested Readings

Bly, Robert, and Stephen Roberts. *Internet Direct Mail*. New York: Contemporary Books, 2000.

Bonnett, Kendra. *An IBM Guide for Doing Business on the Internet*. New York: McGraw-Hill, 2000.

Chase, Larry. *Larry Chase's Need-to-Know Marketing Sites: Web Digest for Marketers* (www.wdfm.com), 2002. Carefully selected and annotated directory of 400 marketing Web sites divided into 33 categories.

Fidler, Roger. *Mediamorphosis: Understanding New Media*. Thousand Oaks, CA: Pine Forge Press, 1997.

Gralla, Preston. *How the Internet Works*, 6th ed. Indianapolis: Que, 2001.

Levine, John R., Margaret Levine Young, and Carol Baroudi. *The Internet for Dummies*. Hoboken, NJ: John Wiley & Sons, 2005. For anyone feeling left behind, this is your introduction to the Internet.

Sweeney, Susan, Andy MacLellan, and Ed Dorey. *3G Marketing on the Internet*. Gulf Breeze, FL: Maximum Press, 2006. It's third-generation time for the Internet, and this book provides business strategies for using the internet today.

Vivian, John. *The Media of Mass Communications*, 4th ed. Boston: Allyn & Bacon, 2003.

Wong, Thomas. *101 Ways to Boost Your Web Traffic*. Intesync Web Professional Services, 2002. On the Internet, if you build it, they won't necessarily come. This book explains how to entice them.

Zyman, Sergio, and Scott Miller. *Building Brandwidth: Closing the Sale Online*. New York: HarperBusiness, 2000.

Notes

1. Xeni Jardin, "Audience with the Podfather," *Wired Magazine,* May 14, 2005.
2. "Facts and Figures," www.internetindicators.com.
3. "Internet Usage Statistics—The Big Picture," www.internetworldstats .com, November 21, 2005.
4. Michael Marriott, "Blacks Turn to Internet Highway and Digital Divide Starts to Close," *New York Times,* March 31, 2006, A1.
5. Dan Fost, "Festival Organizers Say Internet Bouncing Back with a Vengeance," *The Record,* March 11, 2006, A7.
6. Kirk Semple and Dexter Filkins, "Reporter Freed in Iraq, 3 Months After Abduction," *New York Times,* March 31, 2006, A1.
7. Fraser P. Seitel, "Blog-Communications Weapon," *O'Dwyer's PR Services Report,* November 2005, 39.
8. Sticky Sites," Cybersavvy UK, www.webpr.co.uk/practical/sticky.asp.
9. "Corporate Websites Still Coming Up Short," *The Holmes Report,* February 18, 2002, 1–2.
10. David Kesmodel, " 'Splogs' Roil Web, and Some Blame Google," *Wall Street Journal,* October 19, 2005, B1.
11. Jeffrey Rosen, "Your Blog or Mine?" *New York Times,* December 19, 2004.
12. David Kirkpatrick and Daniel Roth, "Why There's No Escaping the Blog," *Fortune,* January 10, 2005, 44.
13. David Kesmodel, op. cit.
14. Greg Hazley, "With Cautious Embrace, PR Builds Up Weblogs," *O'Dwyer's PR Services Report,"* November 2005, 1.
15. Don Middleberg and Steven S. Ross, "The Middleberg/Ross Media Survey: Change and Its Impact on Communications," (New York, NY: Columbia University) 2002.
16. Charles Pizzo, "Is Your Online Pressroom Stuck in the '90s?" *Ragan's Media Relations Report,* December 2004, 7.
17. Charles Pizzo, "Shield Your Company's Reputation from the Dark Side of Cyberspace," P.R. PR, Inc., New Orleans, LA, P.O. Box 172846, Arlington, TX 76003-2846.
18. Charles Pizzo, op. cit.
19. "Where Do You Draw The line?" *Ragan Report,* September 30, 2002, 1.
20. Angelo Fernando, "Podcasting, Anyone?" *Communication World,* September–October 2005, 10.
21. Amelia Kassel, "Guide to Internet Monitoring and Clipping: Strategies for Public Relations, Marketing and Competitive Intelligence," www.cyberalert.com/whitepaper.html.

19 Crisis Management

FIGURE 19-1 **Juiced?** In happier times, before accusations of steroids clouded his record, Barry Bonds and son Nikolai celebrated his 73rd home run of the 2001 season. (AP Wide World Photos)

I n recent years, the practice of public relations has become most known perhaps for its assistance in dealing with crisis. And in the 21st century, if there's one certainty in a most uncertain world, it's that inevitably, invariably, indubitably, people and organizations will get into real trouble and require savvy counsel. Just ask this man:

San Francisco Giant slugger Barry Bonds faced a severe credibility crisis in 2006 as accusations of steroid use threatened the legacy of his baseball home run records. As negative publicity mounted and Bonds denied the allegations, Major League Baseball Commissioner Bud Selig launched an investigation to determine Bonds's fate.[1]

Crisis, which public relations counselor James Lukaszewski once described as "unplanned visibility," can strike anyone at any time.[2] Barry Bonds's 2006 blues was but one recent example of sudden, unexpected, yet potentially fatal crisis.

Indeed, in the new century, among the most well-regarded and highest-paid professionals in public relations are those who have achieved this status through their efforts in attempting to "manage" crises.

In a world of instantaneous Internet communications, round-the-clock cable news commentary, talk radio, tabloid news journalism, and exploding communications challenges, the number and depth of crises affecting business, government, labor, nonprofits, and even private individuals have expanded exponentially.

No sector of society is immune from crisis.

- In *government,* the September 11, 2001, attacks on America opened the door to a whole new level of violence aimed at defenseless civilians, putting government officials at all levels on constant alert. Hurricane Katrina lack-of-preparedness in 2005 introduced yet another level of government crisis. And the Jack Abramoff lobbying scandals of 2006 exacerbated the credibility problems of legislators.

- The *business* scandals affecting some of the most prominent corporate names from Enron to Worldcom to Tyco, from Martha Stewart to Merrill Lynch to George Soros, introduced the notion that every corporation must be crisis ready.

- In *education,* a scandal at Duke University in 2006, involving accusations of rape and racism among the college's lacrosse players, rocked the respected university.[3]

- In the *health care* sector, the CEO of giant HealthSouth, Richard Scrushy, was indicted in a government corruption case in 2006, after being ousted from the company he allegedly bilked for a personal fortune.[4]

- In the area of *religion,* the pedophile priest scandals of 2002 brought shame and suspicion to the Catholic Church.

- Even in the world of *charitable institutions,* the American Red Cross was rocked by crisis, first after a special fund established for September 11 victims went instead for other purposes, and then for theft of relief funds among staff members after Hurricane Katrina.[5]

- In *journalism,* a story created out of whole cloth by *Newsweek* in 2005, alleging that guards at the U.S. detention center at Guantanamo Bay flushed a copy of the Koran down a toilet, left as many as 17 dead and scores injured in Afghanistan.[6]

- In *public relations,* the scandals in 2005 involving Ketchum Public Relations in pay-for-play commentators (Case Study, Chapter 6) and Fleishman-Hillard in padding bills brought crisis to the crisis counselors themselves.

These are but the tip of the iceberg—a very few of the hundreds of small and large crises that afflict elements of society today in ever-expanding magnitude (Figure 19-2).

No wonder when public relations professionals are asked what subject they want covered in mid-career seminars, crisis communications invariably heads the list. Helping to manage crisis is the ultimate assignment for a public relations professional. Smart managements value public relations advice in developing an organization's response not only to crises but also to public relations issues in general.

The list of such issues—and of the crises they often evoke—is unending. In the 21st century, society is flooded with front-burner issues that affect individuals and organizations. From war to peace, poverty to abortion, discrimination to downsizing, environmentalism to energy conservation, the domain of "issues management" has become increasingly important for public relations professionals.

If you can't do a thing about the way you look, call us.

Beauty is only skin deep. But if you're a battered woman, your bruises go straight to the heart. And you can make up, but it never lasts. You're not alone. One out of every two women in America will be abused by a man who says he loves her. You deserve our help. So do your kids. Call Rose Brooks' 24-hour crisis line at **861-6100**. Because you can't keep turning the other cheek.

Rose Brooks
For Battered Women and Their Children

FIGURE 19-2 Societal issues. In a day of managed care and more competitive hospitals, health care institutions have accelerated communications appeals to the public to deal with individual crises. (Courtesy of Rose Brooks for Battered Women and Their Children)

Issues Management

The term *issues management* was coined in 1976 by public relations counselor W. Howard Chase, who defined it this way:

> *Issues management is the capacity to understand, mobilize, coordinate, and direct all strategic and policy planning functions, and all public affairs/public relations skills, toward achievement of one objective: meaningful participation in creation of public policy that affects personal and institutional destiny.*[7]

Issues management is a five-step process that:

1. Identifies issues with which the organization must be concerned,
2. Analyzes and delimits each issue with respect to its impact on constituent publics,
3. Displays the various strategic options available to the organization,
4. Implements an action program to communicate the organization's views and to influence perception on the issue,
5. Evaluates its program in terms of reaching organizational goals.

Many suggest that the term issues management is another way of saying that the most important public relations skill is counseling management. Others suggest that issues management is another way of saying reputation management—orchestrating the process whose goal is to help preserve markets, reduce risk, create opportunities, and manage image as an organizational asset for the benefit of both an organization and its primary shareholders.

In specific terms, issues management encompasses the following elements:

- **Anticipate emerging issues.** Normally, the issues management process anticipates issues one to three years away. Therefore, it is neither crisis planning nor postcrisis planning but rather precrisis planning. In other words, issues management deals with an issue that will hit the organization a year later, thus distinguishing the practice from the normal crisis planning aspects of public relations.

- **Identify issues selectively.** An organization can influence only a few issues at a time. Therefore, a good issues management process will select several—perhaps five to 10—specific priority issues with which to deal. In this way, issues management can focus on the most important issues affecting the organization.

- **Deal with opportunities and vulnerabilities.** Most issues, anticipated well in advance, offer both opportunities and vulnerabilities for organizations. For example, in assessing higher oil prices, an insurance company might anticipate that will mean fewer people driving and therefore fewer accident claims. This would mark an opportunity. On the other hand, higher gas prices might mean that more people are strapped to pay their premiums. This would be a vulnerability that a sharp company should anticipate well in advance.

- **Plan from the outside in.** The external environment—not internal strategies—dictates the selection of priority issues. This differs from the normal strategic planning approach, which, to a large degree, is driven by internal strengths and objectives. Issues management is very much driven by external factors.

- **Bottom-line orientation.** Although many people tend to look at issues management as anticipating crises, its real purpose should be to defend the organization in light of external factors as well as to enhance the firm's business by seizing imminent opportunities.

- **Action timetable.** Just as the issues management process must identify emerging issues and set them in order, it must propose policy, programs, and an implementation timetable to deal with those issues. Action is the key to an effective issues management process.

- **Dealing from the top.** Just as a public relations department is powerless without the confidence and respect of top management, the issues management process must operate with the support of the chief executive. The chief executive's imprimatur is critical to the acceptance and conduct of issues management within a firm.

Emergence of Risk Communication

The 1990s saw the emergence of *risk communication* as an outgrowth of issues management. Risk communication began as a process of taking scientific data related to health and environmental hazards and presenting them to a lay audience in a manner that is both understandable and meaningful.

Models of risk communication have been developed based on the position that *perception is reality*—a concept that has been part of public relations for years. Indeed, the disciplines of risk communication and public relations have much in common. Risk communication deals with a high level of emotion. Fear, confusion, frustration, and anger are common feelings in dealing with crises.

Occasionally—even often—intense emotion flows from a lack of knowledge and understanding about the science that underlies societal risk. Therefore, frequent and forceful communication is necessary to inform, educate, and even dampen emotion. The first rule in responding to a perceived public risk is to take the matter seriously. After this, seven steps are helpful in planning a risk communication program:

1. Recognize risk communication as part of a larger risk management program and understand that the whole program is based on politics, power, and controversial issues.

2. Encourage management to join the "communications loop" and help train them to deal effectively with the news media.

3. Develop credible outside experts to act as news sources for journalists.

4. Become an in-house expert in your own area of risk to enhance your credibility with journalists.

5. Approach the news media with solid facts and figures before they approach you. Verify the veracity of your data.

6. Research perceptions of your organization by the media and other publics to gauge credibility and help determine if your messages will be believable.

7. Understand your target audiences and how the news media can help you communicate effectively.[8]

Like any other area of public relations, risk communication depends basically on an organization's actions. In the long run, deeds, not words, are what count in communicating risk.

Managing in a Crisis

The most significant test for any organization comes when it is hit by a major accident or disaster—that is, a *crisis.*

What is a crisis? According to the *Harvard Business Review,* "A crisis is a situation that has reached a critical phase for which dramatic and extraordinary intervention is necessary to avoid or repair major damage."[9]

How an organization handles itself in the midst of a crisis may influence how it is perceived for years to come. Poor handling of events with the magnitude of Exxon's *Valdez* oil spill, the Challenger disaster, Major League Baseball's steroids scandal, Dow Corning's silicone breast implant controversy, Denny's racial bias accusations, or Tylenol's capsule poisoning not only can cripple an organization's reputation but also can cause it enormous monetary loss or even cause its demise. It is essential, therefore, that such emergencies be managed intelligently and forthrightly with the news media, employees, and the community at large.

As any organization unfortunate enough to experience a crisis recognizes, when the crisis strikes, seven instant warning signs invariably appear:

1. **Surprise.** When a crisis breaks out, it's usually unexpected. Often it's a natural disaster—a tornado or hurricane, for example. Sometimes, it's a human-made disaster—robbery, embezzlement, or large loss. Frequently, a public relations professional first learns of such an event when the media calls and demands to know what immediate action will be taken.

2. **Insufficient information.** Many things happen at once. Rumors fly. Blogs come alive with wild stories. Wire services want to know why the company's stock is falling. It's difficult to get a grip on everything that's happening.

3. **Escalating events.** The crisis expands. The stock exchange wants to know what's going on. Will the organization issue a statement? Are the rumors true? While rumors run rampant, truthful information is difficult to obtain. You want to respond in an orderly manner, but events are unfolding too quickly.

4. **Loss of control.** The unfortunate natural outgrowth of escalating events is that too many things are happening simultaneously. Erroneous stories hit the wires, the newsstands, and the airwaves. As in the case of the mouse in the Coors can, rampant rumors can't easily be controlled.

5. **Increased outside scrutiny.** The media, stockbrokers, talk-show hosts, and the public in general feed on rumors. "Helpful" politicians and observers of all stripes comment to cable television on what's going on. Talk radio is abuzz with innuendo. The media want responses. Investors demand answers. Customers must know what's going on.

6. **Siege mentality.** The organization understandably feels surrounded. Lawyers counsel, "Anything we say will be held against us." The easiest thing to do is to say nothing. So, "No comment" is urged by the attorneys. But does that make sense?

7. **Panic.** With the walls caving in and with leaks too numerous to plug, a sense of panic pervades. In such an environment, it is difficult to convince management to take immediate action and to communicate what's going on.[10]

Planning in a Crisis

The key to crisis management is being prepared. If there is one certainty in dealing with crisis, it is that all manner of accidents or disruptions make for spectacular headlines and sensational reporting. Reporters march to a different drummer. They consider themselves the guardians of the public trust and therefore may be quick to point fingers and ascribe blame in a crisis.

Thus, heightened preparedness is always in order, with four planning issues paramount.

- **First, for each potentially impacted audience, define the risk.** "The poison in the pill will make you sick." "The plant shutdown will keep you out of work." "The recall will cost the stockholders $100 million." The risk must be understood—or at least contemplated—before framing crisis communications.

- **Second, for each risk defined, describe the actions that mitigate the risk.** "Don't take the pill." "We are recalling the product." "We are studying the possibility of closing the plant." If you do a credible job in defining the risk, the public will more closely believe in your solutions. In 2006, for example, when a bird flu pandemic threatened the world, the parent of Kentucky Fried Chicken readied a consumer education and advertising program to reassure consumers that eating cooked chicken is perfectly safe.[11]

- **Third, identify the cause of the risk.** If the public believes you know what went wrong, it is more likely to accept that you will quickly remedy the problem. That's why people get back on airplanes after crashes. Moreover, if the organization helps identify the cause of the problem, the coverage of the crisis is likely to be more balanced.

- **Fourth, demonstrate responsible management action.** Most essential to the planning phase is to move toward fixing the problem—in other words, take proper action. Some public relations people make the mistake of thinking that crises are solved through "technique" and "intuition." Hogwash. Much more important is acting to correct the issue that got you in the soup in the first place.[12]

Letting people know that the organization has a plan and is implementing it helps convince them that you are in control. Defining the issues means both having a clear sense internally of what the focus of action should be and communicating that action into the marketplace to reach key constituents.

Simple but appropriate watchwords for any crisis plan are the following:

- Be prepared.
- Be available.
- Be credible.
- Act appropriately.

Communicating in a Crisis

The key communications principle in dealing with a crisis is not to clam up when disaster strikes. Lawyers traditionally have advised clients to either (1) say nothing, (2) say as little as possible and release it as quietly as possible, (3) say as little as possible, citing privacy laws, company policy, or sensitivity, (4) deny guilt and act indignant that such charges could possibly have been made, or (5) shift or, if necessary, share the blame

Speaking of Ethics

The Times Strikes Macy's with Hot Air

Most organizations are surprised when crisis hits. But rarely is a crisis previewed by the prior day's newspaper.

But that's exactly what happened to Macy's in the winter of 2005.

The day before the annual Macy's Thanksgiving Day Parade in New York City, *The New York Times* ran a front-page Metro Section article, accusing the company of giving its balloon handlers "little training." It pointed out that in 1997, a handler lost control of a balloon that nearly killed a woman.

Macy's defended its training methods, explaining that it made sure to combine "a mixture of veteran handlers and new handlers" for every one of its massive 70- by 40-foot balloons. The *Times* wasn't convinced. "With forecasters calling for rain and heavy winds," the paper warned of great risks.

The next day, one of the Thanksgiving Day Parade's 14 balloons hit a light pole in Times Square and injured two Albany sisters, one in a wheelchair, who sustained a cut that required nine stitches. Her sister sustained a bruised forehead (Figure 19-3).

The next day, the *Times* plastered the story and a picture on its front page, alluding to its prior day's warning and castigating Macy's, which dispatched Santa Claus to visit the girls in the hospital, expressed due concern about the incident, but again defended its training methods and preparation. A day later, Macy's announced

FIGURE 19-3 What goes up. The M&M balloon sways into a lamppost and gets snagged during the 2005 Macy's Thanksgiving Day parade, triggering a corporate crisis for the New York City retailer. (AP Wide World Photos)

that the girls and their family would sit in the VIP section of the 2006 parade.

Macy's also gladly agreed to join a city task force to find out what, if anything, about the accident was preventable.

While the crisis could have been more serious, and reconsidered safety precautions were a good idea, some wondered about the ethics of the *Times* holding its story until one day before the parade and eight years after the last balloon handler accident.

For further information, see Michael Brick, "Many Balloon Handlers Get Little Training," *New York Times,* November 23, 2005, B1; Sewell Chan, "Parade Balloon Hits Light Pole; Two Are Injured," *New York Times,* November 25, 2005, A1; Sewell Chan and Richard Perez-Pena, "Panel Created to Examine How Balloon Went Awry," *New York Times,* November 26, 2005, B1; Larry McShane, "Sisters Hit by Parade Streetlight Now VIPs," Associated Press, November 30, 2005.

with others. A lawyer, correctly, is focused on defense in a court of law, although in recent years, some lawyers have begun to see the disclosure light (Figure 19-4).

Public relations advice, on the other hand, is concerned about a different court—the court of public opinion—and therefore takes a different tack.

The most effective crisis communicators are those who provide prompt, frank, and full information to the media in the eye of the storm. Invariably, the first inclination of executives is to say, "Let's wait until all the facts are in." But as President Carter's press secretary, Jody Powell, used to say, "Bad news is a lot like fish. It doesn't get better with age."

In saying nothing, an organization is perceived as already having made a decision. Indeed, research sponsored by public relations agency Porter Novelli suggests that when most people—upwards of 65 percent—hear the words "no comment," they perceive the no-commenter as guilty. Silence angers the media and compounds the problem. On the other hand, inexperienced spokespersons, speculating nervously or using emotionally charged language, are even worse.

FIGURE 19-4 **If you can't beat 'em.** Washington Legal Foundation was among the enlightened cadre of attorneys, recognizing the power and value of public relations. (Courtesy of Washington Legal Foundation)

Most public relations professionals consider the cardinal rule for communications during a crisis to be *Tell it all and tell it fast!*

As a general rule, when information gets out quickly, rumors are stopped and nerves are calmed. There is nothing complicated about the goals of crisis management. They are (1) terminate the crisis quickly, (2) limit the damage, and (3) restore credibility.

The quickest way to end the agony and begin to build back credibility is to communicate through the media.

Engaging the Media

Handling the media is the most critical element in crisis. Normally, treating the press as friendly adversaries makes great sense. But when crisis strikes, media attention quickly turns to "feeding frenzy." So dealing with the media in crisis demands certain "battlefield rules," among them:

- **Set up media headquarters.** In a crisis, the media will seek out the organizational soft spots where the firm is most vulnerable to being penetrated. To try to prevent this, organizations in crisis must immediately establish a media headquarters through which all authorized communication must flow.

Talking Points

The Lessons of *Valdez*

Remember the Exxon *Valdez* case discussed in Chapter 5? Because you've probably already dissected it thoroughly, it won't matter if we divulge here, courtesy of crisis expert Tim Wallace, how Exxon should have handled the situation.

1. **Develop a clear, straightforward position.** In a crisis, you can't appear to waffle. You must remain flexible enough to respond to changing developments, but you must also stick to your underlying position. Exxon's position seemed to waver.

2. **Involve top management.** Management must not only be involved, but it must also appear to be involved. In Exxon's case, from all reports, Chairman Lawrence Rawl was involved with the Gulf of Valdez solutions every step of the way. But that's not how it appeared in public. Rather, he was perceived as distant from the crisis. And Exxon suffered.

3. **Activate third-party support.** This support may come from Wall Street analysts, independent engineers, technology experts, or legal authorities. Any objective party with credentials can help your case.

4. **Establish an on-site presence.** This is what airline CEOs do when there is a plane crash. It's also what the CEO of Union Carbide did when a Carbide plant explosion killed thousands in Bhopal, India. His trip at least showed corporate concern. When Chairman Rawl explained that he "had better things to do" than fly to Valdez, Exxon effectively lost the public relations battle.

5. **Centralize communications.** In any crisis, a communications point person should be appointed and a support team estab-

lished. It is the point person's job—and his or hers alone—to state the organization's position.

6. **Cooperate with the media.** In a crisis, journalists are repugnant; they're obnoxious; they'll stoop to any level to get the story. But don't take it personally. Treat the media as friendly adversaries and explain your side of the crisis. Making them enemies will only exacerbate tensions.

7. **Don't ignore employees.** Keeping employees informed helps ensure that the organization's business proceeds as normally as possible. Employees are your greatest ally. Don't keep them in the dark.

8. **Keep the crisis in perspective.** Often management underreacts at the start of a crisis and overreacts when it builds. The prevailing wisdom seems to be, "Just because we're paranoid doesn't mean they're not out to get us!" Avoid hunkering down. Exxon executives made this mistake, and it cost them dearly.

9. **Position the organization for the time when the crisis is over.** Concentrate on communicating the steps that the organization will take to deal with the crisis. Admit blame if it's due. Then quickly focus on what you are doing now rather than on what went wrong.

10. **Continuously monitor and evaluate the process.** Survey, survey, survey. Take the pulse of your employees, customers, suppliers, distributors, investors, and, if appropriate, the general public. Determine whether your messages are getting through. Constantly check to see which aspects of the program are working and which are not. Adjust accordingly.

Tim Wallace, "Crisis Management: Practical Tips on Restoring Trust," *The Journal of Private Sector Policy,* November 1991, 14.

- **Establish media rules.** In a crisis, the media are sneaky. Their goal is to unearth any salient or salacious element that will advance the story line of the crisis. In this respect, they are operating very much at cross-purposes with the organization, which is desperately trying to put the crisis behind it.

   It is imperative, therefore, that the organization in the crucible set firm rules—which parts of the operation are off limits, which executives won't be available, and so on—for the media to follow.

- **Media live for the "box score."** Crisis specifics make news—the grislier, the better.

  - How many were fired?
  - How many were displaced?
  - What was the cost of the damage?
  - How much was extorted?
  - How many perished?

Stated another way, crisis is about numbers. And an organization in crisis must be ready to provide enough numbers to keep the media at bay.

- **Don't speculate.** If you don't know the numbers or the reasons or the extent of the damage, don't pretend you do. Speculation is suicidal in crisis.

- **Feed the beast.** The media in crisis are insatiable. The Internet, cable news, the wire services all must be fed 24/7. In the 21st century, the media never sleep. "Nature abhors a vacuum," goes the old saying. And in crisis, any vacuum will be filled by your enemies.

  So a smart organization in crisis will strive to keep the media occupied—even distracted—with new information that advances the story.

- **Speed triumphs.** In crisis, the media mantra is speed first, accuracy second. This sad but true fact holds major implications for public relations people, who must monitor what is being wrongly reported so that it can be nipped quickly before others run with the same misinformation.

- **Cable Rules.** Cable television is a 21st-century phenomenon—CNN, MSNBC, Fox News Channel, CNBC, and others. They compete vigorously with each other all the time—one of the last bastions of American reportorial competition. Which is good. What's not so good is that in a crisis, the drumbeat of incessant hammering is relentless.

  Once a crisis "victim" gets caught in the cable or talk radio spotlight, it is close to impossible to be extricated. Round the clock the skewering continues, on talk show after talk show, "expert" after "expert." So cable television, like talk radio, like the Internet, must be monitored scrupulously in crisis.[13]

Talking Points

When "No Comment" and "Comment" Are Equally Catastrophic

Normally, public relations crisis counselors advise avoiding "no comment" at all costs. White House press secretaries, working for administrations generally disdainful of the media's prying eyes, constantly have to parry reporters' questions with the dreaded phrase.

President George W. Bush's press secretary, Scott McClellan, for example, had to invoke the phrase repeatedly in the summer of 2005 when White House senior advisor Karl Rove was alleged to have identified Valerie Plame, the wife of an administration critic, as an undercover CIA officer.

McClellan's denials recalled the days of President Clinton's press secretary, Mike McCurry, who had to invoke a similar strategy when his boss got mixed up with a certain White House intern.

On the other hand, sometimes a comment is even worse than no comment. This turned out to be the case in early 2006, when 12 miners were caught in a West Virginia mine explosion. After 41 hours underground, the miners, according to a statement by the mine's owner, were "found alive." The media communicated the news, and the nation rejoiced.

A day later, the earlier report was found to be mistaken—wishful thinking based on misunderstood communications. The CEO of the mine company apologized immediately and profusely, but the damage perpetrated by the false report had been done.

Talking Points

Twenty-First Century Public Relations Hero

And the winner is …

… the Budweiser Clydesdales, communications symbol of Anheuser-Busch for more than 70 years.

August Busch Jr. originally presented Clydesdales to his father to celebrate the end of prohibition in 1933. And today, the majestic horses make hundreds of appearances each year in parades and special events and are the subject of everything from Budweiser press releases to ads and merchandising items.

At the 2006 Super Bowl, far and away the most popular commercial featured a starry-eyed colt dreaming of pulling the world-famous Budweiser beer wagon (Figure 19-5).

Anheuser-Busch's public relations savvy even extends to the controversial area of underage drinking. Together with its network of more than 600 independent wholesalers, the maker of Budweiser implements advertising campaigns and community-based programs that fight drunk driving and underage drinking and promote responsible drinking among adults who choose to drink (Figure 19-6). Now that's positive *public relations*.

FIGURE 19-5 **Most popular.** Budweiser's baby Clydesdale dominated the 2006 Super Bowl commercial parade, generating enormous public relations appeal. (Courtesy of © Anheuser-Busch, Inc. Used with permission of Anheuser-Busch, Inc. All rights reserved.)

In your kid's eyes, you still have all the answers.

In fact, a recent Roper study found that 74 percent* of children, ages 8 through 17, say they are most influenced by their parents about important decisions, such as whether or not to drink. So, just talk to your kids. They'll listen. For a free parent guide about preventing underage drinking, call 1-800-359-TALK or visit familytalkonline.com.

FIGURE 19-6 **Responsibility matters.** Anheuser-Busch's effort to combat underage drinking and promote responsible drinking was an example of handling crisis issues with positive public relations. (Copyright © 2005 by Anheuser-Busch, Incorporated. All rights reserved.)

As to what is said to the media, the following 10 general principles apply:

1. Speak first and often.
2. Don't speculate.
3. Go off the record at your own peril.
4. Stay with the facts.
5. Be open and concerned, not defensive.
6. Make your point and repeat it.
7. Don't wage war with the media.
8. Establish yourself as the most authoritative source.
9. Stay calm and be truthful and cooperative.
10. Never lie.

Last Word

Although prevention remains the best insurance for any organization, crisis management has become one of the most revered skills in the practice of public relations. Organizations of every variety are faced, sooner or later, with a crisis. The issues that confront society—from energy and the environment, to health and nutrition, to corporate accountability and minority rights—will not soon abate.

All of this suggests that experienced and knowledgeable crisis managers who can skillfully navigate and effectively communicate, turning crisis into opportunity, will be valuable resources for organizations in the 21st century.

In the final analysis, communicating in a crisis depends on a rigorous analysis of the risks versus the benefits of going public. Communicating effectively also depends on the judgment and experience of the public relations professional. Every call is a close one, and there is no guarantee that the organization will benefit, no matter what course is chosen. One thing is clear: Helping to navigate the organization through the shoals of a crisis is the ultimate test of a public relations professional. And crisis managers are very much in demand. Indeed, that's why, in April 2006, Wal-Mart cast its employment net for two public relations executives—one to handle "opposition research" and the other to "mobilize resources during crisis situations."[14]

In the years ahead, as the world continues to present new and more complex challenges, crisis management promises to be a *growth* area in the *growth* profession that is the practice of public relations.

Discussion Starters

1. What is meant by the term *issues management?*
2. How can an organization influence the development of an issue in society?
3. What are the general steps in implementing an issues management program?
4. What is meant by the term *risk communications?*
5. What are the usual stages that an organization experiences in a crisis?
6. What are the principles in planning for crisis?
7. What are important rules in dealing with the media in crisis?
8. What is the cardinal rule for communicating in a crisis?
9. What are the keys to successful crisis communication?
10. What are likely to be the flashpoint crisis issues in the new century?

Top of the Shelf

Tough Calls

Dick Martin, New York: AMACOM, 2005.

Dick Martin ran public relations for AT&T during its final tumultuous years as an independent company, before it merged with and morphed into other companies.

Known affectionately as "Ma Bell," AT&T was once one of America's most revered corporate names, only to lose the distinction through shoddy strategies and inept leaders. Martin describes, with sensitivity and precision, why AT&T went wrong. He details the angst surrounding the layoff of 40,000 workers by harassed CEO Bob Allen and the pie-in-the-sky—and ultimately unattainable—vision of Allen's successor—an equally-disgraced Michael Armstrong.

Tough Calls offers a front row seat at the communications wars surrounding the death of a once-great company.

CASE STUDY

Wendy's Fingers a Hoaxer

Just as airlines must be prepared for the dreaded day when crisis arrives in the form of a crash or hijacking, so, too, the public relations professionals at fast-food restaurants must be prepared for crises involving robberies or tainted food. Little, however, could have prepared the executives at Wendy's restaurants, one of the nation's leading fast-food purveyors, for the shocking report they received in March 2005.

A woman named Anna Ayala, dining at a Wendy's in San Jose, California, reportedly discovered a portion of a human finger in a bowl of beef chili. Ayala went public immediately, threatening suit, and Wendy's became embroiled in a five-alarm crisis, face-to-face with the nation's and the world's media.

No Public Relations Finger-Pointing

After the San Jose franchise owner notified management, Wendy's corporate executives leapt into action with a multipronged public relations initiative.

- Wendy's President Tom Mueller quickly stepped into the public spotlight, responding initially to the media.

- The company offered a $50,000 reward to the first person providing verifiable information leading to the identification or origin of the finger.

- A toll-free number was established to receive leads.

- A comprehensive internal investigation was undertaken to ensure that the finger didn't come from an employee.

- The company and its president made themselves available to the media to reaffirm that "Nothing is more important to us than the quality of food we serve."

The results of the internal investigation indicated that no Wendy's personnel seemed to be involved. No restaurant employees or chili suppliers had suffered hand injuries. The employee who prepared the chili was a 10-year veteran of the San Jose restaurant. Wendy's personnel appeared clean.

Nonetheless, the company was careful not to blame anyone, most of all Ayala. The company was circumspect in its public statements about the alleged victim. It never even suggested the possibility that Ayala might be involved in the crime. Even after Ayala's lawyer quit and she mysteriously dropped her threat to sue, Wendy's kept its distance from pointing fingers.

The Finger Lingers

Over the next month, the police investigation proceeded and Wendy's continued to make itself available to the media. A month to the day after the finger fracas began, Wendy's public relations director allowed the *New York Times* to follow him through damage control duties, meeting with the reporter at the restaurant scene of the crisis.

A nearly full-page, generally sympathetic story resulted, analyzing all aspects of Wendy's public relations dilemma. The story even speculated as to where the found finger may have originated, including a woman who recently lost a finger in a leopard attack. Among other things, the public relations chief acknowledged that the picture of the finger in the chili "was a gruesome image . . . and it spread across the country in no time."

Meanwhile, late-night comedians were having a field day. Jay Leno on the *Tonight Show* admitted he hadn't been aware that "Wendy's sold finger food." Leno then referred to the company's late founder: "I guess we know what Wendy's did with their founder, Dave Thomas."

FIGURE 19-7   Finger to the slammer.   Wendy's hoaxer Anna Ayala is escorted into Santa Clara County Superior Court to face the music for her fast-food finger fraud.   (AP Wide World Photos)

Also busy on the airwaves was Ayala, who willingly told ABC's *Good Morning America,* "Suddenly I chew something that's kind of hard, crunchy ... I spit it out."

As the month wore on, the Wendy's finger incident refused to go away. Sadly summarized the company's public relations director to the *New York Times,* "We can't put this behind us until we get a third party to exonerate us, if that's possible. And it may never be possible."

Fingering the Finagler

A little more than a month after Wendy's nightmare began, it ended. Just like that.

Police in Las Vegas arrested Anna Ayala at her home and charged her with attempted larceny in perpetrating a hoax against Wendy's. According to police, Ayala had been involved in other legal disputes, lots of them. She filed at least 13 civil actions in California and Nevada involving her and her children, most of the time settling for cash rather than going to trial.

When asked if police had suspected Ayala of committing a hoax, the head San Jose's police department's investigations unit answered yes.

In January 2006, Ayala and her husband pleaded guilty to the scheme to extort money from Wendy's. Ayala's husband had purchased the mysterious finger from a coworker, who lost it in an industrial accident. Ayala was sentenced to nine years in jail and her husband to 12 years. They were ordered to pay $21 million (Figure 19–7).

As for Wendy's, President Mueller said, "We're thrilled the arrest has been made."

Less thrilling was the fact that the hoax forced Wendy's to lay off dozens of workers and cost the company $2.5 million in lost sales.

Questions

1. How would you assess Wendy's handling of the crisis?

2. How would you assess its treatment of Ayala in a public relations sense?

3. Was the public relations director's interview with the *New York Times* helpful or harmful to Wendy's?

4. Had you been Wendy's public relations chief, what other options might you have pursued relative to this crisis?

For further information, see Kim Curtis, "Finger-In-The-Chili Case Ends with Prison Terms," *San Diego Union Tribune,* January 19, 2006; Dan Reed, "Copycats' Telltale Fingerprints Turn Up at Wendy's," *The Record,* April 24, 2005, A16; Matt Richtel and Alexei Barronuevo, "CSI Wendy's Restaurants," *New York Times,* April 22, 2005, C1; Matt Richtel and Alexei Barronuevo, "Finger in Chili is Called Hoax; Las Vegas Woman Is Charged," *New York Times,* April 23, 2005, A9.

Special thanks to the Spring 2005 students of Prof. Bonnie Grossman at the College of Charleston for outstanding scholarship and contributions in pursuit of the Wendy's case.

Voice of Authority

A Final Word to the Wise (Student)

Bill Heyman, founder, president, and CEO of Heyman Associates, has been the dean of public relations recruiters for more than two decades. He manages senior-level searches for blue-chip and emerging companies, leading public relations firms, nonprofit organizations, and government agencies. He is a board member of the Lagrant Foundation, which awards scholarships to minority students planning public relations careers. He is also an inaugural member of the advisory board for the Plank Center for Public Relations Studies in the College of Communication and Information Sciences at the University of Alabama. For additional information about Heyman Associates, log onto www.heymanassociates.com.

What is the employment outlook for public relations graduates today?

Public relations has become an essential business tool, not something that could be eliminated. On the whole, companies want to do a better job telling their stories. But, job seekers need to be realistic: the employment market is tied to the performance of capital markets. Those seeking jobs must recognize that salaries and perks will not match those of only a few years ago, when "new economy" companies ruled and that more will be expected from them for lower initial salaries. It also is likely to take longer for most to earn their stripes—[that is, job seekers can expect to] rise more slowly within an organization, because organizations are smaller and leaner.

Where are the most attractive public relations employment skill areas?

The most employment opportunities today are in media relations, internal communications, issues management, financial public relations, branding and image development, and social responsibility.

Each one of these specialties tends to target an audience that was underserved prior to corporations' rebuilding their images. Companies are no longer taking any audience for granted. Transparency is critical.

What are the most attractive industries for public relations employment?

The health care industry consistently looks at communications as an important way to deliver its message. Pharmaceutical and biotechnology companies lead the public relations job market. Almost on a level field is the financial services industry. Also, an increased number of the largest corporations are in the process of remaking their images, especially those whose reputations have been challenged. With communications, they can demonstrate they are broad thinkers, technologically advanced, and contemporary.

What's the best preparation for public relations employment?

Become a strong writer. There is no greater need than having a strong writing ability. Key areas of employment today are in media relations and speechwriting, and both require strong writing skills.

Students must take as many writing classes as possible and intern (for pay or not) in places where they can get real-world experience (local newspapers, public relations agencies, companies, or philanthropic organizations).

And, because they must be increasingly well rounded in their knowledge, they need to take a wide range of liberal arts classes (especially ethics) and meld that with exploring cultural experiences in the community (opera, theater, museums, etc.) and read, read, read newspapers, magazines, corporate Web sites, and books.

The most successful practitioners will be those that the CEO will want as a seatmate flying across the country or at a dinner table with the organization's most important client.

What is the ideal starting point for public relations beginners?

Often, an agency is the best training ground because of the diverse experiences. The broader the experience, the better it is. Corporate jobs, especially entry-level, tend to be more narrowly focused. Starting at a news organization enables people to learn up close what a reporter goes through and needs every day. Another area where people can consider working in the early stages of their career is a political campaign.

What are the public relations prospects in the nonprofit sector?

Public relations is becoming a valued commodity in the nonprofit sector, especially after 9/11. These jobs tend to have lower salaries, but the experience can be similar to that of a public relations agency and therefore a good training ground. Also, corporate foundations are doing more to articulate their specific business message and are looking for strong public relations executives.

What are the essential characteristics that public relations employers look for in potential employees?

There are five nontechnical characteristics that are most important: one, integrity; two, self-confidence; three, likeability (including respect for others); four, energy (including noticeable enthusiasm); and five, intellect (including business knowledge and judgment).

Added to that are two technical characteristics: the ability to write and to present well. These seven criteria transcend communications posts and organizations.

What's the best way to find a public relations job?

There is no greater way to find a position than to develop a network from the earliest stages of your career.

- Contacting people, joining professional organizations, and being involved in volunteer work are all critical ways to meet other people.

- Conducting research and learning more about the companies you want to work for is key, as is finding a specific contact within each company.

- Learn about the alumni association at your college or university and who might be working within the field and can help you start your career.

- During internships, reach out to anyone you meet.

- Always follow up with people, writing courteous notes asking for help. Two key characteristics in finding a job are to be courteous and tenacious. Always let people know how appreciative you are of any time they spend with you.

Suggested Reading

Augustine, Norman et. al. *Harvard Business Review on Crisis*. Boston: Harvard Business School Publishing, 2000. A collection of eight essays by business leaders and others, including former General Electric CEO Jack Welch's wife.

Caponigro, Jeffrey R. *A Step-by-Step Guide to Managing a Business Crisis*. New York: McGraw Hill, 2000.

Center, Allen H., and Patrick Jackson. *Public Relations Practices: Managerial Case Studies and Problems*, 6th ed. Upper Saddle River, NJ: Prentice Hall, 2000.

Cohn, Robin. *The PR Crisis Bible: How to Take Charge of the Media When All Hell Breaks Loose*. New York: St. Martin's Press, 2000.

Fearn-Banks, Kathleen. *Crisis Communications: A Casebook Approach*, 2nd ed. Mahwah, NJ: Lawrence Erlbaum Associates, 2002. Recommends a plan for preventing and dealing with crises based on communication theories.

Fink, Steven. *Planning for the Inevitable*. iUniverse.com, 2000.

Harvard Business Review on Crisis Management. Cambridge, MA: Harvard Business School Press, 2000.

Friedman, Mark L. *Everyday Crisis Management*. Naperville, IL: First Decision Press, 2002. This book teaches thinking strategically, acting quickly, and responding decisively. (Sounds like the right approach.)

Giuliani, Rudolph W. *Leadership*. New York: Hyperion, 2002. Lessons from the man who took charge immediately of the greatest crisis contemporary America has known, the attacks of 9/11.

Glaesser, Dirk. *Crisis Management in the Tourism Industry*. Burlington, MA: Butterworth-Heinemann, 2003. With people falling overboard and other crises popping up in the tourism industry, this book is particularly timely.

Jones, Clarence. *Winning with the News Media: A Self-Defense Manual When You're the Story*, 7th ed. Tampa, FL: Video Consultants, 2001. Before he wrote this book, the author was a well-regarded investigative reporter. He explains the inner workings of the news business.

McCusker, Gerry. *Tailspin*. Sterling, VA: Kogan Page, 2005. This book covers some of the biggest public relations disasters in recent years, from 9/11 to Martha Stewart.

Mickey, Thomas J. *Public Relations Criticism*. Mahwah, NJ: Lawrence Erlbaum Associates, 2002.

O'Dwyer, Jack (Ed.). *Jack O'Dwyer's Newsletter* (271 Madison Ave., New York, NY 10016).

Simon, Raymond, and Frank W. Wylie. *Cases in Public Relations Management*. Lincolnwood, IL: NTC Publishing Group, 2001. Two eminent professionals discuss some of the most famous crisis management cases, including Hill & Knowlton and Kuwait and Procter & Gamble and news leaks.

Stanton, Peter V. "Ten Communications Mistakes You Can Avoid When Managing a Crisis." *Public Relations Quarterly*, Summer 2002, 19–24.

Notes

1. Murray Chass, "Mitchell and His Investigators Have Some Noteworthy Ties," *New York Times*, April 1, 2006, D5.
2. Helio Fred Garcia, *Crisis Communications*, vol. 1, New York: American Association of Advertising Agencies, 1999, 9.
3. Ed Wiley, III, "Duke Lacrosse Suspended Amid Rape Charges," BET.com, March 29, 2006.
4. Philip Rawls, "Magistrate Rejects Scrushy's Arguments of Prosecutor Misconduct," Associated Press, March 27, 2006.
5. Jacqueline Solomon, "Red Cross Hands Over Katrina Relief Investigation to FBI," *Washington Post*, March 31, 2006.
6. Richard Lacayo, "When a Story Goes Terribly Wrong," *Time*, May 22, 2005.
7. "Issues Management Conference—A Special Report," *Corporate Public Issues 7*, no. 23, December 1, 1982, 1–2.

8. William C. Adams, "Strategic Advice in Handling Risk," presented during the Business, Environmental Issues, and Risk Conference, Washington, DC, November 12, 1992.
9. Richard K. Long, "Seven Needless Sins of Crisis (Mis)management," *PR Tactics*, August 2001, 14.
10. Fraser P. Seitel, "Spotting a Crisis," odwyerpr.com, March 20, 2001.
11. Kate MacArthur, "KFC Preps Bird-Glue Fear Plan," *Advertising Age*, November 7, 2005, 1.
12. Fraser P. Seitel, "Avoiding Crisis Mis-Steps," odwyerpr.com, September 13, 2005.
13. Fraser P. Seitel, "Crisis Media Battlefield Principles," odwyerpr.com, December 16, 2002.
14. Michael Barbaro, "Wal-Mart Begins Quest For Generals In P.R. War," *New York Times*, March 30, 2006, C3.

Appendix A

PRSA Member Code of Ethics
2000

Approved by the PRSA Assembly
October, 2000

Letter from the PRSA Board of Directors

It is with enormous professional pleasure and personal pride that we, the Public Relations Society of America Board of Directors put before you a new Public Relations Member Code of Ethics for our Society. It is the result of two years of concentrated effort led by the Board of Ethics and Professional Standards. Comments of literally hundreds and hundreds of members were considered. There were focus groups at our 1999 national meeting in Anaheim, California. We sought and received intensive advice and counsel from the Ethics Resource Center, our outside consultants on the project. Additional recommendations were received from your Board of Directors, PRSA staff, outside reviewers, as well as District and Section officers. Extensive research involving analysis of numerous codes of conduct, ethics statements, and standards and practices approaches was also carried out.

In fact, this Member Code of Ethics has been developed to serve as a foundation for discussion of an emerging global Code of Ethics and Conduct for the practice of Public Relations.

This approach is dramatically different from that which we have relied upon in the past. You'll find it different in three powerfully important ways:
1. Emphasis on enforcement of the Code has been eliminated. But, the PRSA Board of Directors retains the right to bar from membership or expel from the Society any individual who has been or is sanctioned by a government agency or convicted in a court of law of an action that is in violation of this Code.
2. The new focus is on universal values that inspire ethical behavior and performance.
3. Desired behavior is clearly illustrated by providing language, experience, and examples to help the individual practitioner better achieve important ethical and principled business objectives. This approach should help everyone better understand what the expected standards of conduct truly are.

Perhaps most important of all, the mission of the Board of Ethics and Professional Standards has now been substantially altered to focus primarily on education and training, on collaboration with similar efforts in other major professional societies, and to serve an advisory role to the Board on ethical matters of major importance.

The foundation of our value to our companies, clients and those we serve is their ability to rely on our ethical and morally acceptable behavior. Please review this new Member Code of Ethics in this context:

- Its Values are designed to inspire and motivate each of us every day to the highest levels of ethical practice.
- Its Code Provisions are designed to help each of us clearly understand the limits and specific performance required to be an ethical practitioner.
- Its Commitment mechanism is designed to ensure that every Society member understands fully the obligations of membership and the expectation of ethical behavior that are an integral part of membership in the PRSA.

This approach is stronger than anything we have ever had because:

- It will have a daily impact on the practice of Public Relations.
- There are far fewer gray areas and issues that require interpretation.
- It will grow stronger and be more successful than what we have had in the past through education, through training, and through analysis of behaviors.

The strength of the Code will grow because of the addition of precedent and the ethical experiences of other major professional organizations around the world.

Our new Code elevates our ethics, our values, and our commitment to the level they belong, at the very top of our daily practice of Public Relations.

PRSA Board of Directors

A Message from the PRSA Board of Ethics and Professional Standards

Our Primary Obligation

The primary obligation of membership in the Public Relations Society of America is the ethical practice of Public Relations.

The PRSA Member Code of Ethics is the way each member of our Society can daily reaffirm a commitment to ethical professional activities and decisions.
- The Code sets forth the principles and standards that guide our decisions and actions.
- The Code solidly connects our values and our ideals to the work each of us does every day.
- The Code is about what we should do, and why we should do it.

The Code is also meant to be a living, growing body of knowledge, precedent, and experience. It should stimulate our thinking and encourage us to seek guidance and clarification when we have questions about principles, practices, and standards of conduct.

Every member's involvement in preserving and enhancing ethical standards is essential to building and maintaining the respect and credibility of our profession. Using our values, principles, standards of conduct, and commitment as a foundation, and continuing to work together on ethical issues, we ensure that the Public Relations Society of America fulfills its obligation to build and maintain the framework for public dialogue that deserves the public's trust and support.

The Members of the 2000 Board of Ethics and Professional Standards

Robert D. Frause, APR,
Fellow PRSA
Chairman BEPS
Seattle, Washington

Kathy R. Fitzpatrick,
APR
Gainesville, Florida

Linda Welter Cohen,
APR
Tucson, Arizona

James R. Frankowiak,
APR
Tampa, Florida

James E. Lukaszewski,
APR, Fellow PRSA
White Plains, New York

Roger D. Buehrer, APR
Fellow PRSA
Las Vegas, Nevada

Jeffrey P. Julin, APR
Denver, Colorado

David M. Bicofsky,
APR, Fellow PRSA
Teaneck, New Jersey

James W. Wyckoff, APR
New York, New York

Preamble

Public Relations Society of America
Member Code of Ethics 2000

- Professional Values
- Principles of Conduct
- Commitment and Compliance

This Code applies to PRSA members. The Code is designed to be a useful guide for PRSA members as they carry out their ethical responsibilities. This document is designed to anticipate and accommodate, by precedent, ethical challenges that may arise. The scenarios outlined in the Code provision are actual examples of misconduct. More will be added as experience with the Code occurs.

The Public Relations Society of America (PRSA) is committed to ethical practices. The level of public trust PRSA members seek, as we serve the public good, means we have taken on a special obligation to operate ethically.

The value of member reputation depends upon the ethical conduct of everyone affiliated with the Public Relations Society of America. Each of us sets an example for each other—as well as other professionals—by our pursuit of excellence with powerful standards of performance, professionalism, and ethical conduct.

Emphasis on enforcement of the Code has been eliminated. But, the PRSA Board of Directors retains the right to bar from membership or expel from the Society any individual who has been or is sanctioned by a government agency or convicted in a court of law of an action that is in violation of this Code.

Ethical practice is the most important obligation of a PRSA member. We view the Member Code of Ethics as a model for other professions, organizations, and professionals.

PRSA Member Statement
of Professional Values

This statement presents the core values of PRSA members and, more broadly, of the public relations profession. These values provide the foundation for the Member Code of Ethics and set the industry standard for the professional practice of public relations. These values are the fundamental beliefs that guide our behaviors and decision-making process. We believe our professional values are vital to the integrity of the profession as a whole.

Advocacy
- We serve the public interest by acting as responsible advocates for those we represent.
- We provide a voice in the marketplace of ideas, facts, and view-points to aid informed public debate.

Honesty
- We adhere to the highest standards of accuracy and truth in advancing the interests of those we represent and in communicating with the public.

Expertise
- We acquire and responsibly use specialized knowledge and experience.
- We advance the profession through continued professional development, research, and education.
- We build mutual understanding, credibility, and relationships among a wide array of institutions and audiences.

Independence
- We provide objective counsel to those we represent.
- We are accountable for our actions.

Loyalty
- We are faithful to those we represent, while honoring our obligation to serve the public interest.

Fairness
- We deal fairly with clients, employers, competitors, peers, vendors, the media, and the general public.
- We respect all opinions and support the right of free expression.

PRSA Code Provisions

FREE FLOW OF INFORMATION

Core Principle

Protecting and advancing the free flow of accurate and truthful information is essential to serving the public interest and contributing to informed decision making in a democratic society.

Intent

- To maintain the integrity of relationships with the media, government officials, and the public.
- To aid informed decision-making.

Guidelines

A member shall:

- Preserve the integrity of the process of communication.
- Be honest and accurate in all communications.
- Act promptly to correct erroneous communications for which the practitioner is responsible.
- Preserve the free flow of unprejudiced information when giving or receiving gifts by ensuring that gifts are nominal, legal, and infrequent.

Examples of Improper Conduct Under this Provision

- A member representing a ski manufacturer gives a pair of expensive racing skis to a sports magazine columnist, to influence the columnist to write favorable articles about the product.
- A member entertains a government official beyond legal limits and/or in violation of government reporting requirements.

COMPETITION

Core Principle

Promoting healthy and fair competition among professionals preserves an ethical climate while fostering a robust business environment.

Intent

- To promote respect and fair competition among public relations professionals.
- To serve the public interest by providing the widest choice of practitioner options.

Guidelines

A member shall:

- Follow ethical hiring practices designed to respect free and open competition without deliberately undermining a competitor.
- Preserve intellectual property rights in the marketplace.

Examples of Improper Conduct Under This Provision

- A member employed by a "client organization" shares helpful information with a counseling firm that is competing with others for the organization's business.
- A member spreads malicious and unfounded rumors about a competitor in order to alienate the competitor's clients and employees in a ploy to recruit people and business.

DISCLOSURE OF INFORMATION

Core Principle
Open communication fosters informed decision making in a democratic society.

Intent
- To build trust with the public by revealing all information needed for responsible decision making.

Guidelines
A member shall:
- Be honest and accurate in all communications.
- Act promptly to correct erroneous communications for which the member is responsible.
- Investigate the truthfulness and accuracy of information released on behalf of those represented.
- Reveal the sponsors for causes and interests represented.
- Disclose financial interest (such as stock ownership) in a client's organization.
- Avoid deceptive practices.

Examples of Improper Conduct Under this Provision
- Front groups: A member implements "grass roots" campaigns or letter-writing campaigns to legislators on behalf of undisclosed interest groups.
- Lying by omission: A practitioner for a corporation knowingly fails to release financial information, giving a misleading impression of the corporation's performance.
- A member discovers inaccurate information disseminated via a Web site or media kit and does not correct the information.
- A member deceives the public by employing people to pose as volunteers to speak at public hearings and participate in "grass roots" campaigns.

SAFEGUARDING CONFIDENCES

Core Principle
Client trust requires appropriate protection of confidential and private information.

Intent
- To protect the privacy rights of clients, organizations, and individuals by safeguarding confidential information.

Guidelines
A member shall:
- Safeguard the confidences and privacy rights of present, former, and prospective clients and employees.
- Protect privileged, confidential, or insider information gained from a client or organization.
- Immediately advise an appropriate authority if a member discovers that confidential information is being divulged by an employee of a client company or organization.

Examples of Improper Conduct Under This Provision
- A member changes jobs, takes confidential information, and uses that information in the new position to the detriment of the former employer.

- A member intentionally leaks proprietary information to the detriment of some other party.

CONFLICTS OF INTEREST

Core Principle
Avoiding real, potential or perceived conflicts of interest builds the trust of clients, employers, and the publics.

Intent
- To earn trust and mutual respect with clients or employers.
- To build trust with the public by avoiding or ending situations that put one's personal or professional interests in conflict with society's interests.

Guidelines
A member shall:
- Act in the best interests of the client or employer, even subordinating the member's personal interests.
- Avoid actions and circumstances that may appear to compromise good business judgment or create a conflict between personal and professional interests.
- Disclose promptly any existing or potential conflict of interest to affected clients or organizations.
- Encourage clients and customers to determine if a conflict exists after notifying all affected parties.

Examples of Improper Conduct Under This Provision
- The member fails to disclose that he or she has a strong financial interest in a client's chief competitor.
- The member represents a "competitor company" or a "conflicting interest" without informing a prospective client.

ENHANCING THE PROFESSION

Core Principle
Public relations professionals work constantly to strengthen the public's trust in the profession.

Intent
- To build respect and credibility with the public for the profession of public relations.
- To improve, adapt and expand professional practices.

Guidelines
A member shall:
- Acknowledge that there is an obligation to protect and enhance the profession.
- Keep informed and educated about practices in the profession to ensure ethical conduct.
- Actively pursue personal professional development.
- Decline representation of clients or organizations that urge or require actions contrary to this Code.
- Accurately define what public relations activities can accomplish.
- Counsel subordinates in proper ethical decision making.

- Require that subordinates adhere to the ethical requirements of the Code.
- Report ethical violations, whether committed by PRSA members or not, to the appropriate authority.

Examples of Improper Conduct Under This Provision
- A PRSA member declares publicly that a product the client sells is safe, without disclosing evidence to the contrary.
- A member initially assigns some questionable client work to a non-member practitioner to avoid the ethical obligation of PRSA membership.

RESOURCES

Rules and Guidelines
The following PRSA documents, available in The Blue Book, provide detailed rules and guidelines to help guide your professional behavior:
- PRSA Bylaws
- PRSA Administrative Rules
- Member Code of Ethics

If, after reviewing them, you still have a question or issue, contact PRSA headquarters as noted below.

QUESTIONS

The PRSA is here to help. Whether you have a serious concern or simply need clarification, contact Judy Voss at judy.voss@prsa.org.

PRSA Member Code of Ethics
Pledge

I pledge:

To conduct myself professionally, with truth, accuracy,
fairness, and responsibility to the public;
to improve my individual competence and advance the
knowledge and proficiency of the profession through
continuing research and education;
and to adhere to the articles of the Member Code
of Ethics 2000 for the practice of public relations as adopted
by the governing Assembly of the
Public Relations Society of America.

I understand and accept that there is a consequence for
misconduct, up to and including membership revocation.

And, I understand that those who have been or are sanctioned by
a government agency or convicted in a court of law of an action that is in
violation of this Code may be barred from membership or
expelled from the Society.

_____

Signature

_____

Date

Public Relations Society of America
33 Irving Place
New York, NY 10003
www.prsa.org

Appendix B

PRIA Code of Ethics

The Public Relations Institute of Australia is a professional body serving the interests of its members. In doing so, the Institute is mindful of the responsibility which public relations professionals owe to the community as well as to their clients and employers. The Institute requires members to adhere to the highest standards of ethical practice and professional competence. All members are duty-bound to act responsibly and to be accountable for their actions.

The following Code of Ethics binds all members of the Public Relations Institute of Australia.

1. Members shall deal fairly and honestly with their employers, clients and prospective clients, with their fellow workers including superiors and subordinates, with public officials, the communications media, the general public and with fellow members of PRIA.
2. Members shall avoid conduct or practices likely to bring discredit upon themselves, the Institute, their employers or clients.
3. Members shall not knowingly disseminate false or misleading information and shall take care to avoid doing so inadvertently.
4. Members shall safeguard the confidences of both present and former employers and clients, including confidential information about employers' or clients' business affairs, technical methods or processes, except upon the order of a court of competent jurisdiction.
5. No member shall represent conflicting interests nor, without the consent of the parties concerned, represent competing interests.
6. Members shall refrain from proposing or agreeing that their consultancy fees or other remuneration be contingent entirely on the achievement of specified results.
7. Members shall inform their employers or clients if circumstances arise in which their judgment or the disinterested character of their services may be questioned by reason of personal relationships or business or financial interests.
8. Members practising as consultants shall seek payment only for services specifically commissioned.
9. Members shall be prepared to identify the source of funding of any public communication they initiate or for which they act as a conduit.
10. Members shall, in advertising and marketing their skills and services and in soliciting professional assignments, avoid false, misleading or exaggerated claims and shall refrain from comment or action that may injure the professional reputation, practice or services of a fellow member.
11. Members shall inform the Board of the Institute and/or the relevant State/Territory Council(s) of the Institute of evidence purporting to show that a member has been guilty of, or could be charged with, conduct constituting a breach of this Code.
12. No member shall intentionally injure the professional reputation or practice of another member.
13. Members shall help to improve the general body of knowledge of the profession by exchanging information and experience with fellow members.

14. Members shall act in accord with the aims of the institute, its regulations and policies.
15. Members shall not misrepresent their status through misuse of title, grading, or the designation FPRIA, MPRIA or APRIA.

Adopted by the Board of the Institute on November 5, 2001, this Code of Ethics supersedes all previous versions.

Credits

Index